Hands-On Software Engineering with Python

Second Edition

Move beyond basic programming to design, maintain, and deploy extensible Python systems

Brian Allbee

Hands-On Software Engineering with Python
Second Edition

Portfolio Director: Kunal Chaudhary

Relationship Lead: Samriddhi Murarka

Project Manager: K. Loganathan

Content Engineer: Deepayan Bhattacharjee

Technical Editor: Aditya Bharadwaj

Copy Editor: Safis Editing

Indexer: Tejal Soni

Proofreader: Deepayan Bhattacharjee

Production Designer: Shankar Kalbhor

Growth Lead: Vinishka Kalra

First Published: October 2018

Second Edition: December 2025

Production reference: 1091225

Published by Packt Publishing Ltd.

Grosvenor House

11 St Paul's Square

Birmingham

B3 1RB, UK.

ISBN 978-1-83588-800-1

www.packtpub.com

There are more people deserving of my thanks than I have room to thank. It's 99% certain, if you've ever worked with me, I learned something about this craft from you.

Thank you!

Special thanks to Bridger, Stephan, William, Dave, Bradley and the rest of the ADS&AI folks, and Dawn, for being there, always.

#GNU Charlie Allbee and Sir Terry Pratchett — Mind how you go...

— Brian Allbee

Contributors

About the author

Brian Allbee has been writing programs since the mid-1970s, and started a career in software just as the World Wide Web was starting to take off. He has worked in areas as varied as organization membership management, content/asset management, and process and workflow automation in industries as varied as advertising, consumer health advisement, technical publication, cloud-computing automation, ML integration, and health insurance processes. He has focused exclusively on Python solutions for over a decade.

About the reviewers

Chad Greer is an energizing and motivating coach and mentor who focuses on transformation using Lean, Agile, and DevOps principles and practices. His primary focus is on helping individuals achieve delivery excellence in order to meet customers' current and future business needs.

Chad has been involved in several industries including accounting, banking, residential and commercial construction, education, financial, government, health care, law enforcement, manufacturing, oil & gas, real estate, and utilities. His diverse background and broad talent range enables him to learn new business models quickly and hit the ground running.

Chad started Lucentary Academy to help bridge the gap between education and employment for software developers early in their careers. Through Lucentary Academy, he and his apprentices offer high quality consulting services in the software development space.

Nimesh Kiran Verma is a technology leader and entrepreneur with a five-year integrated degree in Mathematics and Computing from the Indian Institute of Technology, Delhi. He co-founded Upwards Fintech (acquired by Lendingkart Finance) and serves as its Chief Technology Officer, where he builds data-driven underwriting systems and scalable fintech platforms. Earlier in his career he worked in software development and data science roles at companies including LinkedIn, Paytm, and ICICI, and he is fluent in Python, Django/Flask, cloud architectures, and both SQL and NoSQL systems.

Nimesh's professional interests span across software architecture, scalable backend design, AI-driven platforms, and intelligent data systems. He is deeply passionate about Python and its ecosystem — particularly frameworks like Django and Flask — and regularly employs design patterns, AWS infrastructure, and SQL/NoSQL databases to build reliable, performant, and maintainable software systems.

He has reviewed and contributed to several technical publications and enjoys mentoring engineers and data scientists on topics related to system design, applied machine learning, and product architecture.

I am deeply grateful to my wife, Shikha, and son, Ayan and my family for their constant support and patience, and to my colleagues and friends whose ideas and feedback helped shape my thinking and this work.

Table of Contents

Chapter 14: Testing the Business Objects 387

Chapter 15: CI/CD Options 425

Chapter 17: Assembling the API   491

Chapter 18: The Final API, Deployed to AWS   537

Preface

Writing a book about software engineering, in my experience, isn't all that different from the discipline itself. Both can be frustrating — approaches don't always work the way you expect. Both offer chances to experiment and explore, though often within constraints that force compromises. And both require anticipating problems, questioning assumptions, and revisiting your goals as the work unfolds. A conscientious author — which I've tried to be — looks for the questions readers might ask and tries to answer them before they're asked.

That's what I set out to do in this edition: re-evaluate the material from the first edition through the lens of everything I've learned since. The shift from server-based to cloud-native, serverless systems fundamentally changed how I think about software. So did the experience of mentoring other engineers — teaching revealed blind spots in my own thinking. These, among other experiences, pushed me to reexamine not just how we build systems, but why we make the decisions we do.

If there's one idea I hope readers take away from this book, it's that good engineering depends on deliberate, thoughtful decisions, not automatic ones. While *The Zen of Python* says "there should be one — and preferably only one — obvious way to do it," system design rarely offers that kind of clarity. When faced with multiple viable paths, it's usually more important to choose based on real needs and constraints than to default to whatever looks simplest.

That's the lens I've tried to apply throughout the book: to present options, examine trade-offs, and explain the reasoning behind the choices made in the story behind the code. Some of the code in these pages may solve a problem you're working on — and I hope that's true. But more importantly, I hope you'll engage with it critically: adapt it, extend it, or even discard it if it doesn't suit your needs.

This book isn't a cookbook. It's a guidebook, meant to help you navigate, not hand you a recipe.

Writing this book has made me a better engineer, I feel. I hope reading it will do the same for you — not because you'll follow every pattern or agree with every choice, but because you'll ask better questions along the way.

Who this book is for

This book is written for developers who already know their way around Python but want to deepen their understanding of *software engineering as a discipline*. If you're comfortable with Python fundamentals — working with functions, modules, and packages, and navigating project structures — you're ready for what's ahead. If you're somewhere on the path from mid-level to senior engineer, or trying to build the habits and perspective that get you there, this book is for you.

To get the most out of this book

This book assumes that you're already familiar with Python and ready to go a level deeper — from simply writing code to understanding how and why software systems are built the way they are. You don't need to be an expert, but you should be comfortable with the basics of Python and the development environment around it. Specifically, you should know how to:

- Download and install Python (the examples were written using Python 3.11, but they should work with later versions as well)

- Write and use Python functions

- Define and work with basic classes

- Install packages using pip, and import functionality from installed modules

- Organize code using modules and packages across files and folders

The examples in this book are operating system-agnostic, and no specific IDE or editor is required — you can work in whatever environment you're comfortable with. You won't need an AWS account to get started, but the later chapters that cover cloud deployment and infrastructure-as-code will guide you through what's needed when you get there, and are designed to be applied in an AWS account, even if it is a temporary one.

Download the example code files

The code bundle for the book is hosted on GitHub at `https://github.com/PacktPublishing/Hands-On-Software-Engineering-with-Python-Second-Edition`. We also have other code bundles from our rich catalog of books and videos available at `https://github.com/PacktPublishing`. Check them out!

Download the color images

We also provide a PDF file that has color images of the screenshots/diagrams used in this book. You can download it here: `https://packt.link/gbp/9781835888001`.

Conventions used

There are a number of text conventions used throughout this book.

CodeInText: Indicates code words in text, database table names, folder names, filenames, file extensions, pathnames, dummy URLs, user input, and X/Twitter handles. For example: "Execute the pipenv graph command."

A block of code is set as follows:

```
@query.field("get_artisans")
def resolve_get_artisans(_, info):
    artisans = Artisan.get(db_source_name='Artisan')
    return [artisan_to_dict(a) for a in artisans]
```

When we wish to draw your attention to a particular part of a code block, the relevant lines or items are set in bold:

```
@app.route('/api/v1/artisans/', methods=['GET'])
def get_artisans_root():
    ...
```

Any command-line input or output is written as follows:

```
pipenv --python 3.11
```

Bold: Indicates a new term, an important word, or words that you see on the screen. For instance, words in menus or dialog boxes appear in the text like this. For example: "Select **System info** from the **Administration** panel."

> Warnings or important notes appear like this.

> Tips and tricks appear like this.

> *Quotes appear like this.*

Get in touch

Feedback from our readers is always welcome.

General feedback: If you have questions about any aspect of this book or have any general feedback, please email us at `customercare@packt.com` and mention the book's title in the subject of your message.

Errata: Although we have taken every care to ensure the accuracy of our content, mistakes do happen. If you have found a mistake in this book, we would be grateful if you reported this to us. Please visit `http://www.packt.com/submit-errata`, click **Submit Errata**, and fill in the form.

Piracy: If you come across any illegal copies of our works in any form on the internet, we would be grateful if you would provide us with the location address or website name. Please contact us at `copyright@packt.com` with a link to the material.

If you are interested in becoming an author: If there is a topic that you have expertise in and you are interested in either writing or contributing to a book, please visit `http://authors.packt.com/`.

Share your thoughts

Once you've read *Hands-On Software Engineering with Python*, we'd love to hear your thoughts! Scan the QR code below to go straight to the Amazon review page for this book and share your feedback.

`https://packt.link/r-1835888011`

Your review is important to us and the tech community and will help us make sure we're delivering excellent quality content.

Free Benefits with Your Book

This book comes with free benefits to support your learning. Activate them now for instant access (see the "*How to Unlock*" section for instructions).

Here's a quick overview of what you can instantly unlock with your purchase:

<table>
<tr><td align="center">PDF and ePub Copies</td><td align="center">Next-Gen Web-Based Reader</td></tr>
</table>

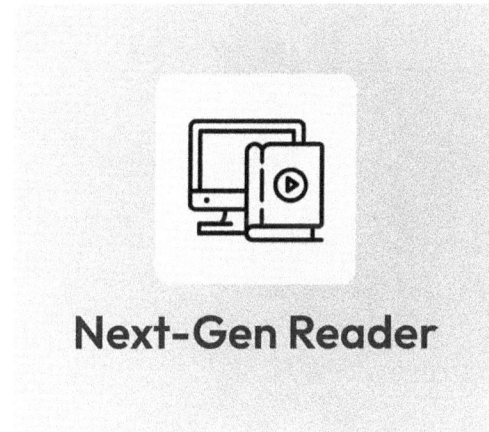

Free PDF and ePub versions

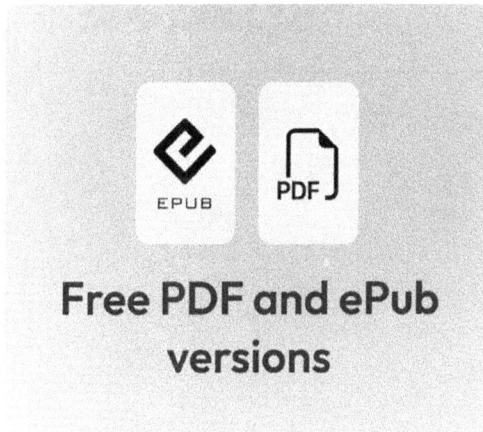

Next-Gen Reader

Access a DRM-free PDF copy of this book to read anywhere, on any device.

Use a DRM-free ePub version with your favorite e-reader.

Multi-device progress sync: Pick up where you left off, on any device.

Highlighting and notetaking: Capture ideas and turn reading into lasting knowledge.

Bookmarking: Save and revisit key sections whenever you need them.

Dark mode: Reduce eye strain by switching to dark or sepia themes.

How to Unlock

Scan the QR code (or go to packtpub.com/unlock). Search for this book by name, confirm the edition, and then follow the steps on the page.

Note: Keep your invoice handy. Purchases made directly from Packt don't require one.

1

Introduction

Pursuing a career in software engineering implies, at a minimum, a certain tolerance for change, if not an active pursuit or embrace of change. Processes and best practices evolve over time, as do the tools and even the languages themselves. While there are not a lot of truly new languages that have been released in the seven years since the first edition of this book was published, several languages have become more popular, including Go, Kotlin, Rust, and TypeScript. Ideas that appear in one language may surface in another, when the authors or maintainers of the language decide that the ideas are worth incorporating. Possible examples of that sort of cross-pollination, with capabilities being implemented in Python that may have originated in other languages, include the property decorator (.NET Framework had recognizably similar capabilities a year earlier) and the ability to annotate or type-hint functions and callables (a key capability of TypeScript, version 1.0 of which was released a year prior to Python's support for the idea).

Even the titles have the potential for change. The previous edition of this book started with a breakdown of the various levels, grades, or ranks that organizations often use to indicate degrees of experience, expertise, and wisdom expected of their development personnel.

Those categories have not changed significantly in the intervening years:

- At a **junior** or **associate** level, the aspiring software engineer is typically someone who does not have much experience. They probably know the basics of writing code, but are not expected to know much more than that.

- The level between junior and senior is typically where the first real exposure to and experience with software engineering starts to happen: Understanding how different pieces of code interact and come together as a system, and the principles involved in the *design of systems* rather than just writing code, are a major portion of the growth or knowledge expected.

- A **senior**-level practitioner has enough experience, even if it is focused on a very specific set of products, projects, or systems, to firmly grasp all of the technical skills involved in typical software development efforts. There is also, typically, a solid handle on the non-technical or semi-technical skills involved as well. Key among those are policies, procedures, strategies, and tactics that encourage or enforce business values like stability of a final product and predictability of development efforts. Seniors may not be *experts* in those areas, but are expected to recognize and call out risks, and provide options and suggestions for mitigating those risks before they become actual issues.

Typical title breakdowns for these levels include junior/associate developer/software developer/software engineer; developer and software engineer, sometimes with organization-specific suffixes; and senior developer/software developer/software engineer. In the past several years, a new category has become common enough that it bears mention and discussion: **staff engineer**. Staff engineers are senior-level technical leaders who can provide guidance on complex problems and systems, architecture, system and design strategies, and perhaps more in the context of the organizations they work for.

Staff engineering references

Staff engineer as a position or job title is new enough that it may still be in flux. Many of the basic concepts that drove the idea in the first place are described in detail in *Staff Engineer: Leadership Beyond the Management Track* by Will Larson, and *The Staff Engineer's Path: A Guide For Individual Contributors Navigating Growth and Change*, by Tanya Reilly.

The dividing line between programming and software engineering falls somewhere within the differences between the mid- and senior-level titles, as far as technical capabilities and expertise are concerned. At a junior level, and to a lesser extent at the mid-level titles, efforts are often centered around nothing more than writing code to meet whatever requirements apply, and conforming to whatever standards are in play. Software engineering, at a senior developer level, has a *bigger picture* view of the same end results.

The bigger picture involves awareness of, and attention paid to, the following things:

- Standards, both technical/developmental and otherwise, including best practices
- The goals that code is written to accomplish, including the business values that are attached to them
- The shape and scope of the entire system that the code is a part of

---

Free Benefits with Your Book

Your purchase includes a free PDF copy of this book along with other exclusive benefits. Check the *Free Benefits with Your Book* section in the Preface to unlock them instantly and maximize your learning experience.

The bigger picture

So, what does this bigger picture look like? There are three easily identifiable areas of focus, with a fourth (call it user interaction) that either weaves through the other three or is broken down into its own groups.

Software engineering must pay heed to standards, especially non-technical (business) ones, as well as to best practices. These may or may not be *followed* but, since they *are* standards or best practices for a reason, not following them is something that should always be a *conscious* (and *defensible*) decision. It's not unusual for business process standards and practices to span multiple software components, which can make them difficult to track if a certain degree of discipline and planning isn't factored into the development process to make them more visible. On the purely development-related side, standards and best practices can drastically impact the creation and upkeep of code, its ongoing usefulness, and even just the ability to find a given chunk of code, when necessary.

It's rare for code to be written simply for the sake of writing code. There's almost always some other value associated with it, especially if there's business value or actual revenue associated with a product that the code is a part of. In those cases, understandably, the people who are paying for the developmental effort will be very interested in ensuring that everything works as expected (code quality) and can be deployed when expected (process predictability).

The remaining policy and procedure-related concerns are generally managed by setting up and following various standards, processes, and best practices during the startup of a project (or perhaps a development team). Those items — things such as setting up source control, having standard coding conventions, and planning for repeatable, automated testing — will be examined in some detail in later chapters. Ideally, once these kinds of development processes are in place, the ongoing activities that keep them running and reliable will just become habits, a part of the day-to-day process, almost fading into the background.

Finally, with more of a focus on the code side, software engineering must, by necessity, pay heed to entire systems, keeping a universal view of the system in mind. Software is composed of a lot of elements that might be classified as atomic: they are indivisible units in and of themselves, under normal circumstances. Just like their real-world counterparts, when they start to interact, things get interesting, and hopefully useful. Unfortunately, that's also when unexpected (or even dangerous) behaviors — bugs — usually start to appear.

This awareness is, perhaps, one of the more difficult items to cultivate. It relies on knowledge that may not be obvious, documented, or readily available. In large or complex systems, it may not even be obvious where to start looking, or what kinds of questions to ask to try to find the information needed to acquire that knowledge.

Asking questions

There can be as many distinct questions that can be asked about any given chunk of code as there are chunks of code to ask about — even very simple code, living in a complex system, can raise questions in response to questions, and more questions in response to those questions.

If there isn't an obvious starting point, starting with the following really basic questions is a good first step:

1. Who will be using the functionality?
2. What will they be doing with it?
3. When, and where, will they have access to it?
4. What problem is it trying to solve? For example, why do they need it?
5. How does it have to work? If detail is lacking, breaking this one down into two separate questions is useful:

   - What should happen if it executes successfully?
   - What should happen if the execution fails?

Teasing out more information about the whole system usually starts with something as basic as the following questions:

- What other parts of the system does this code interact with?
- How does it interact with them?

Having identified all of the moving parts, thinking about "What happens if…" scenarios is a good way to identify potential points where things will break, risks, and dangerous interactions. You can ask questions like these to start discovering these points in the code:

- What happens if this argument, which expects a number, is handed a string?
- What happens if that property isn't the object that's expected?
- What happens if some other object tries to change this object while it's already being changed?

Whenever one question has been answered, simply ask, *What else?* This can be useful for verifying whether the current answer is reasonably complete.

Picking a Python version for a project

When the work on this book started, Python 3.11 was selected as the language version that code would be written in. There were several reasons for that selection, but the primary one was that it had been available for long enough to be in a security maintenance cycle, and with no expectation of significant changes other than for security issues. That was early in 2024, and support for the version is, as the book is being finished, going to continue for another two years, ending in October of 2027. Hand in hand with that was the fact that the bulk of the work I was doing was writing and maintaining AWS Lambda Functions written in Python, and although the 3.12 version was available for those purposes, it was new enough that I didn't have a lot of hands-on experience with it in that context.

The Python Software Foundation, the maintainers of the language, have historically been very good about publishing comprehensive documentation of the changes to the language as each new minor version is released. Their documentation for any given version can be found online at https://www.python.org/doc/versions/, and is updated as each new version is released, including the patch versions.

Python versioning follows Semantic Versioning (SEMVER)

Semantic versioning defines a version naming standard that identifies major, minor, and patch versions. In formal SEMVER, major version changes, like the change from Python 2.x to 3.x, indicate significant, incompatible changes with the previous major version. Minor version changes, for example, from 3.11 to 3.12, indicate the addition of functionality in a backward-compatible manner, and patch version changes — 3.11.12 to 3.11.13 — indicate bug fixes that are implemented in a backward-compatible manner. Python releases *may not* strictly follow SEMVER standards, though I cannot point to an example where that has not been the case. Typically, as features and functionality in Python are slated for removal, they are flagged as **deprecated** — no longer recommended for use, and planned for removal — and will raise warnings as code that uses them is executed.

Python's release schedule and support processes are well documented online (see `https://devguide.python.org/versions/`), with a cadence of approximately five years between the initial release of a minor version and its official end of life. In more recent versions, the first two years or so of a given version's life include a *bugfix* support phase, and the remaining three years are limited to *security* support. Online providers will frequently follow the life cycle of any given Python version with respect to *their* support of that version, though they may allow continued use of a version that has officially reached its end of life. By way of example, **Amazon Web Services'** (**AWS'**) Python version support, as of the end of 2025, included Python 3.9, with an official end of life in October of 2025, was a supported version, with its deprecation planned in December 2025, and limitations on the ability to create or update Lambda Functions using that version starting early in 2026.

So, taking all of these factors into consideration, the determination of what Python version to use for any given project is a decision that needs to be made based on a number of factors:

- As a general rule, the most recent version available may be preferable, simply because it will provide the most current capabilities that the language provides, and will have the longest lifespan.

- Restrictions or constraints by a provider may limit those options: Using AWS as an example again, they appear to start supporting a given version of Python about a month after it is released, but that may not always be the case. Other providers may have different limitations, or it may be that the OS where development work is being done imposes its own limitation (not uncommon for Linux systems that use Python for key applications or tools).

- Even if a just-released new version is supported, there is some risk assessment that should be undertaken: The *bugfix* phase of the version will last for two years, and there is some risk that bug fixes implemented during that period will be problematic. The same holds true for versions that are in the *security* phase of their lives, though generally those have fewer issues on a release-by-release basis, likely because most of the bugs have already been dealt with by then.

- Checking the *Changelog* for a given version (https://docs.python.org/release/3.11.13/whatsnew/changelog.html, for example, for 3.11), or the release notes (https://docs.python.org/3/whatsnew/3.11.html for 3.11 again) may also be useful if there are specific features that are needed or desired in the project, that may not be available or implemented as expected.

As of the end of 2025, assuming that the preference is to avoid versions in their *bugfix* phase, the most current version that fits that criteria is 3.12. Version 3.13 would be viable with the same considerations driving version selection by the end of 2026, and 3.14, expected to be released in October 2025, would be viable by the end of 2027.

Getting and installing Python

Installation of Python varies a bit across operating systems. For macOS and Windows systems, there are installers available for download on the Python website (https://www.python.org/downloads/) that generally take care of everything needed. Those installers include every version of the language going back as far as 2.0.1.

Installation of multiple versions of Python is possible, with caveats

Barring some special considerations for certain Linux distributions, installation of multiple different versions of Python is viable on a single machine. Each installation will typically provide python, python3, python3.xx, and sometimes python3.xx.yy command-line entries that can be used to run it. In cases where there are multiple Python 3.x installations, say 3.11 and 3.12, the most recently installed version will be executed by the python and python3 commands. If a specific version is needed, invoking it with the full python3.xx command will be necessary (e.g., python3.11 or python3.12).

For Linux systems, installation can be more problematic. Many Linux systems have Python installed by default, because some of their programs make use of it. In several cases, those distributions also limit the available versions of Python that can be installed, in order to prevent a user from accidentally breaking system components or programs. Checking the default software installation tools in a Linux distribution is always the best first step: If the specific version of Python that is needed/desired is available, installing it using the standard tools for the distribution is the safest process. The managers of the package repository for the distribution will have made reasonable efforts to prevent installations that can break a system from being available, and anything that is available as an option would be expected to be safe.

In cases where there are no alternative versions available, there are still options worth considering before going down the path of installing from the Python website, or building from source: pyenv and Homebrew.

pyenv (`https://github.com/pyenv/pyenv`) is a command-line tool that allows a user to install, manage, and switch between different versions of Python at will. While switching between versions has many of the same risks as installing other versions, pyenv's ability to download and install minimal, usable Python versions without interfering with the system-level installations makes it a very good candidate for cases where project- and system-level Python version requirements conflict with each other. pyenv is also recognized by at least one Python project management tool, `pipenv`, and integrated well enough that the creation of a new project environment with a new Python version is handled by the project manager almost seamlessly.

Homebrew (`https://brew.sh/`) is a more general-purpose software management tool, capable of installing various Python versions as well as many other software packages. It is not available for Windows, at least as of late 2025, but is a viable option for macOS and Linux systems where multiple Python versions are needed.

If neither of those options is workable, falling back to downloading from the Python website is always possible too. Because of the widely varied package structures across the Linux ecosystem, those downloads are the source code and would require building the local installation from scratch. If this path must be taken, it is important to find a good, step-by-step breakdown of the processes and prerequisites involved. Usually a search along the lines of *{your Linux distro name} build python 3.13 from source* will yield several options.

What's changed in Python since the last edition

The code in the first edition of this book was written in Python 3.6, with an eye toward compatibility with 3.7. The code in this edition was written in Python 3.11, and by the time it sees print, Python 3.14 will have been released. Over each of those versions, there have been a number of changes, many of which will not come into play in the balance of this book, but are, nonetheless, worth knowing about.

Python 3.6

Python 3.6 introduced **f-strings**: strings that allow variable names and operations to be defined within them to be interpreted at run time. F-strings are used frequently in the code in this edition, particularly in log messages where error type names and values are expected to change. For example, here is an error-handling block that catches errors of any Exception type (the error), with any message, and logs the error type and message, along with the current variables (vars()) when the error is caught:

```
except Exception as error:
    logger.exception(
        f'{error.__class__.__name__}: {error} '
        'occurred in function_name'
    )
    logger.error('inputs: {vars()}')
```

Other changes included:

- Allowing underscores to be used in numeric values as readability aids (for example, 1_000_000 instead of 1000000)
- Allowing type annotations to be applied to variables (for example, my_var: int = 12 instead of my_var = 12)
- Support for asynchronous use of generators (https://wiki.python.org/moin/Generators) and comprehensions (https://docs.python.org/3.11/tutorial/datastructures.html#list-comprehensions)

Python 3.7

Perhaps the most significant addition to the language in 3.7 was the addition of the `dataclasses` module (`https://docs.python.org/3.7/library/dataclasses.html`), providing a standard mechanism for defining classes whose primary intention is the storage of data, and tools for working with them. A simple dataclass, representing a person, might look like this:

```python
from dataclasses import dataclass, asdict
@dataclass
class Person:
    given_name: str
    family_name: str
>>> ridcully = Person('Mustrum', 'Ridcully')
>>> print(ridcully)
Person(given_name='Mustrum', family_name='Ridcully')
>>> print(asdict(ridcully))
{'given_name': 'Mustrum', 'family_name': 'Ridcully'}
```

Other new features and improvements for this release are listed at `https://docs.python.org/3/whatsnew/3.7.html`.

Python 3.8

The **walrus operator** (`:=`), more formally known as assignment expressions, became available, allowing the assignment of values to variables as part of a larger, frequently conditional expression.

For example, taken from the *What's New In Python 3.8* page:

```python
if (n := len(a)) > 10:
    print(
        f"List is too long ({n} elements, expected <= 10)"
    )
```

...allows the call to `len(a)` to be used once, assigning the result to n as part of the expression, rather than requiring it to be called again in the `print` statement.

Other new features and improvements are listed for this release at `https://docs.python.org/3/whatsnew/3.8.html`.

Python 3.9

New operators for dictionary types were introduced that allow merging (|) and updating (|=) dictionaries inline.

Other new features and improvements are listed for this release at `https://docs.python.org/3/whatsnew/3.9.html`.

Python 3.10

This release introduced **structural pattern matching** as an alternative to a series of if…elif… structures. For example:

```
match subject:
    case <pattern_1>:        #  if subject == <pattern_1>
        <action_1>           #      <action_1>
    case <pattern_2>:        #  if subject == <pattern_2>
        <action_2>           #      <action_2>
    case <pattern_3>:        #  if subject == <pattern_3>
        <action_3>           #      <action_3>
    case _:                  #  else:
        <action_wildcard>    #      <fallback>
```

Other new features and improvements are listed for this release at `https://docs.python.org/3/whatsnew/3.10.html`.

Python 3.11

The major change in this release was an improvement to execution speed, ranging from 10 to 60 percent faster. A less obvious, but still significant, change was the deprecation of 22 modules, mostly concerned with older data formats no longer in common use. Of those, nine had one or more replacements already defined.

Other new features and improvements are listed for this release at `https://docs.python.org/3/whatsnew/3.11.html`.

> **Annotation changes were made in most of these releases**
>
> Annotation of function and method parameters, and of their return values, is discussed in some detail in *Chapter 7*, along with comparisons of what those changes allowed.

Changes in Python 3.12 onwards

Much of the focus in the more recent releases has been on reducing the requirement for the **Global Interpreter Lock (GIL)** in Python's interpreter. The GIL is a mechanism that allows only one native processor thread to execute Python bytecode at any given time. While that lends a considerable amount of stability to running Python code, by preventing several types of memory-related issues, it also prevents truly parallel execution of Python code. In 3.12, the GIL was attached to individual interpreters, allowing sub-processes that run in their own sub-interpreters to have their own GIL, allowing for more true parallelism. The 3.13 release provided an **experimental** free-threaded build mode, allowing the GIL to be disabled entirely for even more truly parallel processing capabilities.

Another change to keep an eye on is the *experimental* **Just-in-Time (JIT)** compiler, which appears to be (potentially) laying the groundwork for translating Python's bytecode to machine code.

These changes are the ones that I, personally, have found the most significant (or at least the most interesting) and do not represent anywhere near all of the changes that were made for each of these releases. These changes are, obviously, strictly limited to those that have happened to the language itself. There are other changes that have occurred in the time between the first edition and this edition that have little to do with the language, but with how the code gets written. Of those, the one that has made the most waves is undoubtedly the advent of AI for code generation.

The impact of AI on software engineering

As *Chapters 13 and 14* were in progress, there were significant advances in various **Large Language Model (LLM)** tools toward writing and maintaining code. An LLM is a type of **Artificial Intelligence (AI)**, trained on massive datasets to learn patterns and rules of language. Some of the more well-known LLMs as of 2025 include OpenAI's **GPT**, Anthropic's **Claude**, and xAI's **Grok**. While the initial focus of LLMs was more toward natural human languages like English, it was just a matter of time before the idea of similar training for programming languages was considered and added into the mix. Early code generation using LLMs showed some promise, but was typically limited to generating small, independent chunks of code, with little to no reliability for integrating those small code blocks into larger-scoped projects. Over and above that, the code generated was not always reliably representative of what the intent was, as expressed to the LLM through a supplied prompt.

By the beginning of the second quarter of 2025, though, things had improved considerably. By way of example, when **CodeGPT** (`https://chatgpt.com/g/g-cksUvVWar-code-gpt-python-java-c-html-javascript-more`) was given this prompt:

> *I am writing a Python package as an example of AI-generated code. I need a project starting-point that I can download that follows a standard src-directory project structure, as well as having a tests directory with subdirectories for unit tests (unit), integration tests (integration) and system tests (system). Under the src directory, there need to be directories representing a package namespace "hms.core", and there should be corresponding unit-test directories, each prefixed with "test_" for each level of the main namespace under the src directory. The project will use Pipenv to manage package dependencies, and should include, as development package requirements, the pytest, flake8, and coverage packages. Those packages' versions should be pinned to versions less than the next major version; for example, the current version of pytest is 8.3.5, so the pytest installation in the Pipfile should indicate a version less than 9. The package project will eventually be published as a standard Python package, so there should be a pyproject.toml file that captures all the standard information and needs to accomplish that, and package installations for the "build" and "publish" categories of the Pipfile should include the "build" and "twine" packages, respectively. The project will eventually use some cloud- or SCM-resident CI/CD process, but for now, capture the necessary steps and processes in a standard Makefile that will eventually be used to create the final build-and-publish process. That Makefile should include running unit tests and all the other test-suites noted earlier.*
>
> *Please generate this project structure, and provide it as a downloadable file, like a ZIP archive or a TAR file.*

...the resulting project structure was reasonably complete, and was created in less than a minute, with perhaps five to ten minutes needed to write the entire prompt. Iterating over that initial project structure was possible, starting with the addition of functionality using this prompt:

> *Add a data_object.py module to the hms/core directory. This module will contain a class called BaseDataObject, which will use Pydantic Fields to define various properties. Those properties include "oid" an object ID, which will be a UUID value, providing the unique record identifier for objects in a relational database table later on. It will also include "created" and "modified", both UTC dates, capturing the created date/time and last modified date/time of the object's record. It will also include boolean fields called "is_active" and "is_deleted" which keep track of whether the record for a data object is active and deleted, respectively. These fields are all required. The oid field should default to a new UUID value, which can use the built-in uuid4 function. The date/time fields should default to the current UTC date/time. The is_active and is_deleted fields should default to False. All fields should have a description and two or more examples. The module should have an overall description.*
>
> *BaseDataObject will also provide methods to perform CRUD operations: A get method will be used to retrieve one or more objects, and accept zero-to-many oid values (strings or UUIDs), include pagination control parameters that will be used to create a SQL "LIMIT" clause, and "criteria" that will be used to provide other selection criteria, based on equality, inequality, less-than/greater-than, and so on.*
>
> *Update the project code and provide a new download with those changes.*

...generated a reasonable starting point for the `BaseDataObject` and its get method, and continuing with:

> *The get method should be a class method, and should assume the use of parameterized queries with an execute method, following the Python database access API standards. Add a delete class method that accepts one-to-many oid values, that simulates the deletion of one to many records, and an instance method to save an instance's data as well.*

...also yielded reasonable starting-point code for those additions.

Different AIs will generate different results, and have different ways of presenting those results. For example, the same initial prompt, given to Anthropic's Claude (`https://claude.ai`), yielded a Python script that generated the project structure, and the subsequent prompt that GPT Code used to add the get method Claude used to also generate the `create`, `update`, and `delete` methods.

Examples of LLM-generated code are in the chapter repository

The results from each of the LLM code generation efforts noted above are in the repository for this chapter: The Claude Code example is in the `claude-example` directory, and the CodeGPT example in `code-gpt-example` (`https://github.com/PacktPublishing/Hands-On-Software-Engineering-with-Python-Second-Edition/tree/main/CH01-code/claude-example`).

This sort of iterative, AI-assisted code generation has come to be known as **vibe coding** (`https://en.wikipedia.org/wiki/Vibe_coding`), and was a highly contentious topic in April of 2025, judging by the amount and types of discussions around it on LinkedIn and elsewhere on the Internet. The arguments for it include increased speed of output, which is certainly the case, and that the generated code is good enough, which is a very subjective judgment. The arguments against it usually centered around inconsistent and unpredictable code quality, the sheer volume of code that would have to be reviewed by a human engineer, and the lack of decision-making context that a human engineer *just knows to keep in mind* — things like paying heed to security concerns, which CodeGPT had to be told about (...*should assume the use of parameterized queries with an execute method, following the Python database access API standards...* in the second prompt above). Another concern, though its impact will vary from LLM to LLM, is the eventual loss of context by the LLM, leading to **hallucinations**: the generation of incorrect, misleading, or even nonsensical responses and information, typically with no warning or indication that it is happening. This is, ultimately, a function of how much context data a given LLM can keep track of, and that is bound to improve over time, but is a limiting factor whose scope may not be known.

The availability of AI agents — programs that leverage a backing AI system, but are able to keep track of the relevant context they are working in, make decisions, and take actions on their own to achieve specific goals — is another factor worth knowing about. As of this writing, I can only speak to one from personal experience: **Claude Code**. Claude Code appears able to keep track of a lot of context while it is working; I have used it to generate reasonably complete and functional code for creating and managing a REST API using AWS API Gateway that calls SageMaker endpoints, along with the **Infrastructure as Code (IaC)** to manage that API and the SageMaker endpoints it calls. Getting to that point required several days' worth of prompt-writing and iteration over bugs that surfaced, and those efforts cost maybe $35 in Claude token purchases, but the experience was reasonable, most of the time, and the code generated was functional, if brute-forced and occasionally ugly.

Points to consider when using AI code assistants

Stick to one. Don't change to another too frequently, even if there's something much newer and better. Each LLM tends to have its own code style, and shifting between those is likely to be problematic over time.

Iterate in small chunks, and commit changes frequently. There are numerous stories being recounted online along the lines of *[insert AI name here] destroyed my project*, but the common thread among those that I've seen is a lack of tool and code discipline as changes are being made.

Decide on a trust boundary. Depending on how pessimistic you are, either don't trust the AI-generated code at all, or trust it but verify it. In either case, be prepared to review a *lot* of auto-generated code, and tell the AI *how* to fix things that you do not like or agree with.

Be as specific as you can. Tell the AI what you want to accomplish, how it needs to be accomplished, what constraints are in play, etc., etc.

Set limitations on the AI. If there is code that should not be changed, tell the AI that it is not allowed to change that code, and stick to that. Similarly, apply standards as you see fit, even if they are just documentation standards.

TDD with an AI assistant

It seems likely to me that **Test-Driven Development (TDD)**, where the automated tests are written before writing the code that will need to pass those tests, could be usefully combined with AI-assisted code generation. In teams where TDD is already in play, when combined with an agent like **Claude Code** (https://docs.anthropic.com/en/docs/agents-and-tools/claude-code) that can respond to events like test failures, and take corrective actions autonomously, there is real potential for fast, powerful, and *verifiably useful* code generation. Caution would need to be taken to make sure that the agent is not modifying tests to make them pass when modifying code to pass the tests is the approved remedy for those failures.

Is AI here to stay?

If I'm being brutally honest about this, my answer would have to be some variant of *I just don't know*. The ability to generate large blocks of production-ready code quickly, effectively, and **consistently** would have to be among the highest-priority goals in that space. From what I've seen personally, the systems just aren't there yet, not without a lot of review and input from an experienced, competent software engineer. Of those three points, the *consistency* feels to me like it's the most challenging problem still to be solved. I'm not surprised by that, though: Given my admittedly limited understanding of how the LLMs that are behind these efforts work, and a certain amount of empirical observation, that the responses for any given prompt are... random but directed feels like as good a description as anything else. For example, I started two separate sessions with CodeGPT using the same prompt:

> I would like you to generate some starting-point code, in Python, that will be used to keep track of a task-list for a locally-hosted web-application. The target audience is parents of children who have difficulties keeping track of their day-to-day obligations. The system should be able to keep track of those obligations ("chores") and collections of "rewards" that they receive once their cores/obligations are complete.

> Let's start with a very high-level design for the backing logic for the application, concerned with representing the users, obligations, and rewards in the system, without being concerned yet about how those items' data will be stored.

Despite the fact that the prompts were identical, the answers it came up with across those two sessions were significantly different, though there are at least some common elements between them. The class diagrams that were generated by that prompt in each session are shown in *Figure 1.1*, below.

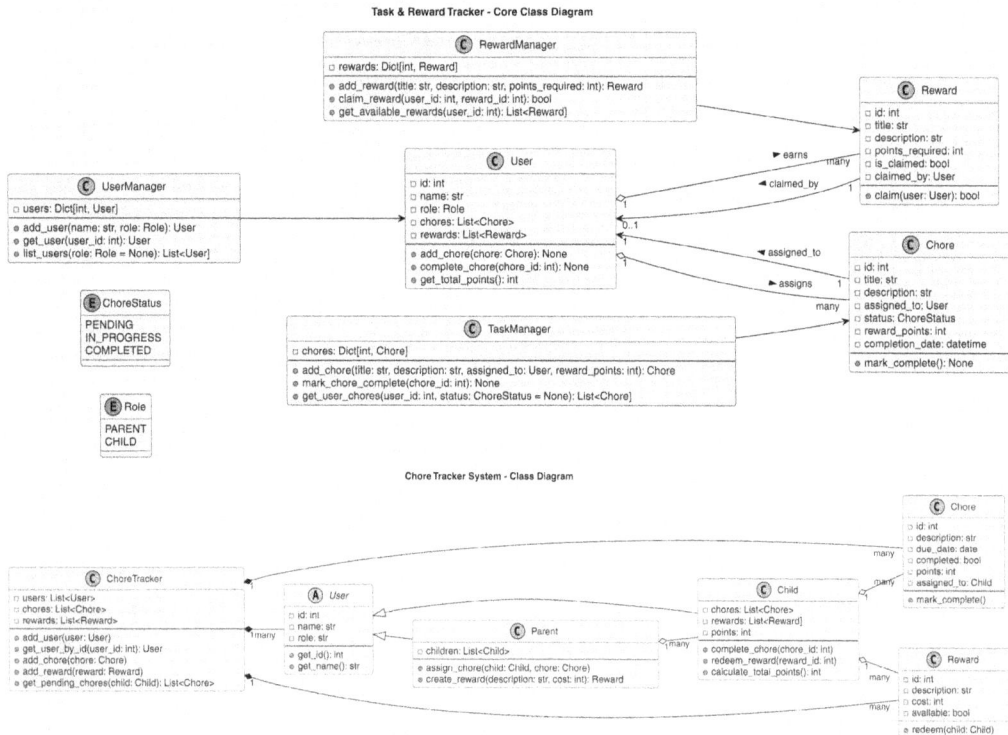

Figure 1.1: The class diagrams from the same prompt in two different CodeGPT sessions

Both of these are viable starting points for the design of the application mentioned in the prompt. Both have significantly different approaches implied just from the class structures that the LLM came up with. At this level, with contexts established for each, progressing deeper into actual functionality would not be difficult, so long as the context doesn't get lost by the LLM somewhere along the way. As soon as that starts happening, though, there will be an even greater need for the kind of software engineering expertise that the balance of this book is about. Without that, the random nature of each prompt will tend to overwrite already-established and vetted code structure, and an inexperienced user will, I suspect, eventually drown in the churn of changes produced (at scale) by the LLM.

Overview of the rest of the book

The rest of this book will examine, in some detail, the skillsets that are, in my opinion, critical to the discipline of software engineering.

Chapter 2 will re-examine the differences between programming — just writing code — and software engineering — knowing *what* code to write, and *why*.

Chapter 3 will discuss the idea of the **Software Development Life Cycle** (**SDLC**), and the kinds of activities and outcomes expected by the phases of that structure.

Chapter 4 will examine the ideas of system modeling and how the varied aspects of it shape system design and development alike.

Chapter 5 will explore the current process methodologies for software development, the paradigms that are commonly in use as code is being written, and various practices that can be leveraged to improve the speed and quality of development outcomes.

Chapter 6 will present common, standard elements of code style, documentation, and commenting, and explore when, why, and how to apply them.

Chapter 7 will focus similar examination and decision-making around *functional* standards for code.

Chapter 8 will show options for several common tools that help manage common Python project concerns and tasks, and some of the more common tools that are actually used to write Python code.

Chapter 9 will mark the beginning of the development story that the balance of the book is concerned with telling: the continuation of the story told in the first edition, about an imaginary company that is starting the process of moving their existing system from a collection of locally hosted services to a cloud-resident web-API-based system.

Chapter 10 will start making some decisions, in the context of the story about the project, based on information and options presented in the previous chapters.

Chapter 11 will go through the process of re-examining the existing Business Object idea in the system that is going to be rewritten, and make a decision about how the system's data is going to be modeled and structured.

Chapter 12 will take the decisions made in *Chapter 11* and determine how system data in Business Objects will be persisted to a back-end data store, after examining the options available for data storage and the criteria that relate to making those kinds of decisions.

Chapter 13 will explore the code structures needed to implement the chosen data persistence mechanism, and how to manage database changes as the needs of those Business Objects change over time.

Chapter 14 will dive into the processes needed to test the Business Objects and their data persistence processes.

Chapter 15 will explore the options available for automating the integration and deployment of code as it is written and approved for promotion to the production system.

Chapter 16 will work through the implementation needed to facilitate local development of an API system, allowing software engineers to work locally with the same code that will be deployed later into the cloud.

Chapter 17 will implement a proof-of-concept level set of API endpoints, using the Business Objects, API requirements, and local development frameworks discussed in previous chapters.

Chapter 18 will walk through the processes needed to actually deploy a functional database and API to an AWS account, leveraging AWS Infrastructure as Code tools, and exploring alternatives when and where they are needed.

2

Programming Versus Software Engineering Revisited

The dividing line between programming and software engineering falls somewhere within the differences between mid-level Software Engineers and Senior Software Engineers, as far as technical capabilities and expertise are concerned. In an Associate-level role, and sometimes in a mid-level role, efforts are often centered around nothing more than writing code to meet whatever requirements apply, and conforming to whatever standards are in play. Software engineering, at a senior developer level, typically takes a bigger-picture view of the same end results. Recently, a new professional level above senior has become available: the Staff Software Engineer. Staff Engineer, as a role, is frequently expected to take a similar bigger-picture view, and apply it across multiple teams, or even whole organizations. There are several facets to this bigger-picture view, some of which will be touched on here: standards, process predictability, and policy and procedure expectations. All of these will also be elaborated upon in later chapters.

In this chapter, we are going to cover the following main topics:

- Roles and expectations
- Looking at the bigger picture
- Asking questions

Technical requirements

The code in this chapter is for demonstration purposes only, showing the application of some of the topics and practices noted in the chapter.

Roles and expectations

Job titles for roles in software development are widely varied, even before accounting for the distinct levels, grades, or ranks indicating seniority in the field. Role titles include variations of *Developer* and *Engineer*, the latter usually prefixed with *Application*, *Software*, or some specific technology focus. Examples of these foci include *Front End*, *Back End*, and *Full Stack* for application-focused roles, and *Infrastructure* or *Network* for roles that relate to those technologies. There are many more variations. Levels, grades, and ranks include *Junior* or *Associate* for those with the least amount of professional experience, *Senior* for those with a substantial amount of expertise, and, more recently, *Staff* variants for those with even more experience. A typical progression, focusing on *Software Engineer* as the base title, might be:

- Associate Software Engineer
- Software Engineer
- Senior Software Engineer
- Staff Software Engineer

Example job/Role titles

See O*NET's *Software Developers* occupation profile at `https://www.onetonline.org/link/summary/15-1252.00` for an example listing of reported job titles. O*NET's occupation classifications change over time, but they have a good track record of providing links to updated pages as older ones are rendered obsolete, or when they deem it necessary to expand into sub-classifications.

Throughout this book, the terms *Software Engineer* and *Developer* should be considered synonymous: they may be used interchangeably, but they are both concerned with a fundamental skill set centering around the processes of writing code. As a Software Engineer advances through the various professional levels, the expectations change in a predictable pattern:

- More involvement with harder and larger-scoped problems, and the code needed to solve them
- More emphasis on higher and higher levels of process design, often independent of the code that is written to implement those processes
- Increasing responsibility for the quality of code across a development team, initially in the form of more peer reviews of code

- More mentoring of less senior software engineers
- More technical leadership in general

The boundaries between title levels may vary significantly across different organizations, but they align in one respect: years of experience. A general, high-level overview of each level's expectations and responsibilities from the list above is presented below for each of the four levels noted earlier.

How these were determined

The expectations and other data presented for each of these levels of software engineering professionals may vary — perhaps wildly — from one organization to another. What is presented below has been gleaned from a combination of the author's personal experience, some informal surveying of peers in various sectors of the industry, and several hours of looking through various online resources to sanity-check the resulting assumptions. The industry changes, though, so by the time this edition sees print, they could very well have changed.

Associate (or Junior) Software Engineers

Associate Software Engineers generally have less than two years of experience in the discipline but have demonstrated sufficient skill in writing code to land the position. That experience might take the shape of formal education, having written enough personal project code to have gotten the attention of a hiring manager, or participation as a contributor to one or more open-source projects. There are several more variations on these themes that would demonstrate the basic skill set and interest in the discipline.

At this **Junior** level, there may not be much autonomy afforded to the software engineer, at least not until they can demonstrate that they can work without assistance or hands-on supervision. Their primary day-to-day goals are likely to be as heavily focused on learning how to apply their knowledge of writing code to the real-world problems their code is expected to solve as on how the development team they have joined executes their work. Odds are good that they will be expected to work closely with a more senior engineer while they learn what they need to know to be given more autonomy, particularly with respect to processes, procedures, and tools in use by the team. This could be thought of as learning and forming good coding habits and practices, at least as far as the norms for the development team are concerned.

They may or may not participate in code reviews, though doing so provides more opportunities to learn the development processes and norms in play. Even when they are participants, they may well not have the authority to approve changes until they can demonstrate their capability to evaluate potential problems in others' code. Their chief responsibility from a code-quality perspective is to learn how to maximize code quality in their own efforts. They will probably not be expected to do any mentoring, though if there are specific areas of expertise that they bring to the table, that is still possible. The same holds true for technical leadership responsibilities.

Software Engineers

A **Software Engineer**, the next level of classification above Associate, generally requires two to five years of experience. At this point, it is reasonable to expect a fair amount of autonomy: a mid-level developer has enough experience that they can be relied upon to write solid code, with little to no supervision, and enough experience to recognize when they need to ask for assistance from someone more senior than they are. Similarly, their experience should lend itself well to peer reviews of code and provide a reliable and trustworthy basis for authority to approve the code changes.

Exposure to more complex problems, requiring more complex code solutions, is also in line with the skills and expectations of a developer at this level. It is also reasonable to expect that those problems will be of a wider scope than those presented to a more junior engineer. Code to provide solutions for problems across the entire scope of an application or a functional domain should not be a surprising occurrence.

Hand in hand with that increase in scope and complexity, more exposure to and responsibility for process design should be expected. By this point in a developer's career, it is reasonable to expect that they would have acquired a fair body of knowledge in how to design and implement code that takes *at least* a slightly *bigger picture* view of a given problem space than an Associate-level peer would be expected to grasp.

Mentoring and technical leadership expectations will be short, informal, and on an ad hoc basis. That does not preclude longer, more formal instances, though: as with their Associate-level peers, if there are specific areas of expertise that they bring to the table, more in-depth mentoring or technical guidance is not out of line.

Senior Software Engineers

Between five and eight years' of experience seems to be the common expectation for a **Senior Software Engineer**. At this level, a software engineer has enough experience behind them to be almost completely autonomous, at least with respect to coding activities. If they are not also acting in some secondary capacity, such as assuming some *Technical Lead* or *Software Architect* duties — natural offshoots of increased code quality and design expectations at this level — that may well be the entire scope of their day-to-day work.

It is common, though, at this level of expertise, for their time and efforts to be better spent on more frequent and more formal mentoring of less-senior teammates, or even across team boundaries within the larger organization. The basic argument in these cases is some variation on the theme of it being more effective to improve the skills of their teammates than to spend their own time writing code. There are only so many hours in a day, and if a senior-level engineer can help *level up* other members of their team, that investment scales better than continuing to write code themselves.

From a technical leadership standpoint, a senior-level engineer is expected to have a solid grasp of not only all the codebases they are associated with but also with how the products or services those codebases define fit into team- and organization-level business goals and objectives. That perspective, along with the expected expert-level understanding of the code itself, and any processes around it, is extremely valuable for peer reviews of changes to the codebase, and a senior engineer can expect to spend more time engaged in those tasks as well.

Staff Software Engineers

Until recently, the general expectation for progression beyond a Senior Software Engineer tended to branch into less code-related areas: *Technical Lead*, *Software Architect*, and *Technical Manager*. These roles were commonly the only promotion options until the idea of a higher-level role that was still focused on the coding side of the work surfaced. That level, **Staff Software Engineer**, is still new, and as such is still very much in flux in organizations where it is an option in the career path of a software engineer. Still, the literature around and about it — Will Larson's *Staff Engineer* (https://staffeng.com) and Tanya Reilly's *The Staff Engineer's Path* (https://www.oreilly.com/library/view/the-staff-engineers/9781098118723/) in particular — along with some research into the expectations around the position indicate that its growth pattern is similar to the changes going from a mid-level to a senior engineering role. The general expectation for years of experience required for a staff-level engineer role seems to be ten or more years with some consistency.

Staff Engineers are frequently expected to be *very* autonomous, finding their own work to pursue, with a corresponding expectation that it will be *important on an organization-wide scale*. That is, while a Staff Software Engineer is certainly more than capable of addressing trivial problems very quickly and efficiently, their time is better spent trying to solve pain points that are experienced by multiple teams, or *all* teams within an organization, or that are simply too complex for less-senior engineers to tackle. Their level of expertise and expected awareness of the bigger-picture goals of an organization also make them logical candidates to take on design tasks of more widely scoped business processes. Expecting more frequent and more formal mentoring of less senior engineers is not uncommon.

A common trade-off for all this increased authority and responsibility is being less involved in the process of actually writing code, in favor of providing more and better technical leadership. There may or may not be opportunities to sit down and write code in the day-to-day work of a staff-level engineer, or it may be limited to stubbing out a basic implementation structure, and then delegating it to a less senior peer to be completed and deployed.

Other branches in the roles tree

Prior to the advent of the *Staff Software Engineer* role, there were a few typical roles that were (and still may be) common paths after reaching a Senior Software Engineer level. Most of these involve moving away from writing code, to varying degrees, and from software engineering as a discipline. They all build on the experience gained by an engineer reaching that senior level, though.

Technical Lead

A **Technical Lead** role frequently moves more toward managing teams of people — engineers in particular — than managing code. Prior engineering experience is important in this role to help ensure better, more complete communication between the people doing the work (engineers) and the people wanting the work done (product owners and more traditional general managers). A Technical Lead may or may not have hiring and firing authority — that may be the line that differentiates it from a *Technical Manager* role — but typically includes both the authority to and responsibility of steering a team's efforts toward business goals, leveraging their technical experience to provide technical direction with respect to *how* those goals should be met.

Software Architect

A **Software Architect** is an extension of the design-related focus of prior roles, focusing more on the *structure* and *interaction* of code elements than on the concrete *implementation* of those elements. They will frequently provide input and direction in technical and coding standards and may participate in code reviews to ensure that those standards are being met. They may or may not write code themselves, or they may only stub out code in the structure they have designed before handing it off to a software engineer to implement and deploy.

Technical Manager

A **Technical Manager**, like the *Technical Lead* noted above, will shift their focus from managing code to managing people. In this role, though, the focus is likely to be far more on people management and business goals than on code management.

Where is the difference between programming and software engineering?

Programming generally implies little more than writing code, with little to no expectation of how that code fits into the scope of a project. It's really more a *given a problem, write code to provide a solution* sort of process, with expectations that most closely mesh with an Associate-level role. As an Associate-level software engineer learns to work with the standards and expectations of a project or a team, they will naturally have more exposure to, and thus awareness of, bigger-picture items like:

- Standards, both technical/developmental and otherwise, including best practices
- The goals that code is written to accomplish, including the business values that are attached to them
- The shape and scope of the project, or the software ecosystem that the code is a part of

As this exposure continues, the day-to-day activities of the Software Engineer would be expected to provide them with the opportunity to learn how those bigger-picture items fit into projects and systems. By the time they have been in a software engineering role for long enough to be considered a mid-level Software Engineer, it's reasonable to expect that exposure to have formed good coding habits that meet the expectations of the systems, projects, or team that they are working with.

The lowest-level software engineering roles start with relatively low expectations around how much attention to bigger-picture items is part of their day-to-day efforts. As a software engineer progresses into more senior roles, those expectations increase accordingly. By the time they have reached a mid-level Software Engineer role, awareness and understanding of those bigger-picture items should have solidified to a point where the engineer can be trusted with more autonomy, and with some design decisions and responsibilities. At a Senior Software Engineer level and above, those same bigger-picture items will likely be among the first concerns of the engineer when handed a project or a problem to solve. So, what does this bigger picture look like, in detail?

Looking at the bigger picture

There are three easily identifiable areas of focus that differentiate software engineering as a discipline from simple programming. A fourth (let's call it **user interaction**) either weaves through the other three or is broken down into its own groups.

Software engineering must pay heed to standards, especially non-technical (business) ones, and to best practices, which are often independent of business needs. These may or may not be *followed* but, since they are standards or best practices for a reason, not following them is something that should always be a conscious (and defensible) decision. It is not unusual for business-process standards and practices to span multiple software components, which can make them difficult to track if a certain degree of discipline and planning is not factored into the development process to make them more visible. On the purely development-related side, standards and best practices can drastically impact the creation and upkeep of code, its ongoing usefulness, and even just the ability to find a given chunk of code, when necessary.

It is rare for code to be written simply for the sake of writing code. There is usually some other value associated with it, especially if there's business value or actual revenue associated with a product that the code is a part of. In those cases, understandably, the people who are paying for the developmental effort will be *extremely* interested in ensuring that everything works as expected (code quality) and can be deployed when expected (process predictability).

Process predictability is mainly a function of the development methodology in play during development, in combination with any other relevant paradigms and processes. The more common options will be examined and compared in some detail in *Chapter 5, Methodologies, Paradigms, and Practices*. Code quality — what it is, how to define it, and how to achieve it — will be discussed in greater detail as the opportunities to call them out surface in *Chapters 9* through *18*.

The remaining policy-and-procedure-related concerns are generally managed by setting up and following various standards, processes, and best practices during the startup of a project. Those items — things such as setting up source control, having standard coding conventions, and planning for repeatable, automated testing — will be examined in some detail in *Chapter 8, Revising the hms_sys System Project*. Ideally, once a set of development, testing, and release processes is in place, the ongoing activities that keep them running and reliable will just become habits. If they are thorough and unobtrusive, they will almost fade into the background until or unless they detect an issue that needs attention from a software engineer to resolve.

Finally, with more of a focus on the code side, software engineering must, by necessity, pay heed to *entire systems*, keeping a universal view of the system in mind. Software is composed of a lot of elements that might be described as **atomic**; they are indivisible units in and of themselves, under normal circumstances. Just like their real-world counterparts, when those atomic units start to interact, things get interesting and hopefully useful. Unfortunately, that is also when unexpected (or even dangerous) behaviors — bugs — usually start to appear.

Though the details of these bigger-picture considerations are forthcoming in later chapters, their potential for impact is already established: standards and best practices shape how problems are solved, with an eye toward those solutions being consistent with system, process, or business needs. Predictability of processes affects the quality of code and various business values like speed of delivery and stability of delivered systems. The holistic, whole-system view expected from more senior software engineers, which may be the most difficult skill to cultivate, provides insight into potential dangers and pitfalls that could detrimentally affect the systems and products those engineers are concerned with. Acquiring this whole-system viewpoint is often just a matter of learning to ask the right questions at the right time, though.

Asking questions

There can be as many distinct questions that can be asked about any given chunk of code as there are chunks of code to ask about — even quite simple code, living in a complex system, can raise questions in response to questions, and more questions in response to *those* questions. If there is not an obvious starting point, these basic questions are a good first step:

- How easily understood is the functionality?
- Who will be using the functionality?
- What will they be doing with it?
- When, and where, will they have access to it?

- What problem is it trying to solve (why do they need it)?
- How does it have to work? If detail is lacking, breaking this one down into the following questions is useful:
    - What should happen if it executes successfully?
    - What should happen if the execution fails?

Teasing out more information about the entire system usually starts with something as basic as the following questions:

- What other parts of the system does this code interact with?
- How does it interact with them?

Having identified all the moving parts, thinking about *What happens if...* scenarios is an effective way to identify risks, dangerous interactions, and potential points where things will break. Examples of these questions include:

- What happens if this argument, which expects a number, is handed a string?
- What happens if that property is not the object that is expected?
- What happens if some other object tries to change this object while it's already being changed?

To help assure that answers to questions are reasonably final, a good habit to get into is to simply ask *what else* whenever any given question has been answered. If something else comes to mind immediately, answer *that*, and continue. If nothing else surfaces, even after a reasonable time spent thinking about it, that is a *reasonably* good indication that the current answer is *reasonably* complete.

To show some of these questions in action, consider this scenario: a new function is being written for a system that keeps track of mineral resources on a map grid, for three resources: gold, silver, and copper. Grid locations are measured in meters from a common origin point, and each grid location keeps track of a floating-point number, from 0.0 to 1.0, which indicates how likely it is that the resource will be found in the grid square. The developmental dataset already includes four default nodes — at (0,0), (0,1), (1,0), and (1,1) — with no values (None) as follows:

(0, 1): gold: None silver: None copper: None	(1, 1): gold: None silver: None copper: None
(0, 0): gold: None silver: None copper: None	(1, 0): gold: None silver: None copper: None

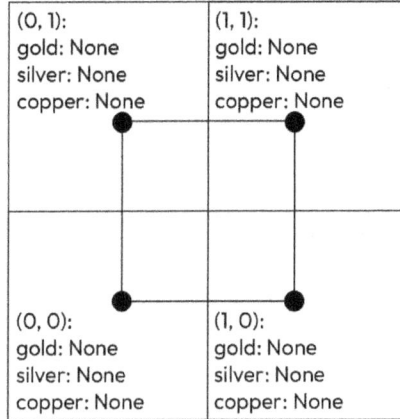

Figure 2.1: The example resource grid

The system already has some classes defined to represent individual map nodes, and functions to provide basic access to those nodes and their properties, from whatever central data store they live in:

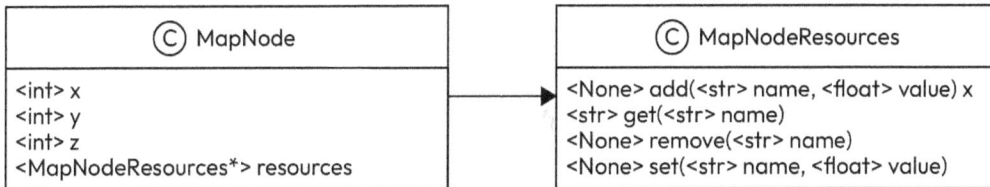

© MapNode
<int> x <int> y <int> z <MapNodeResources*> resources

© MapNodeResources
<None> add(<str> name, <float> value) x <str> get(<str> name) <None> remove(<str> name) <None> set(<str> name, <float> value)

Figure 2.2: The class diagram of the existing code

Constants, exceptions, and functions for various purposes already exist, as follows:

- node_resource_names: This contains all of the resource names that the system is concerned with, and can be thought of and treated as a list of strings: ['gold', 'silver', 'copper']

- NodeAlreadyExistsError: An exception that will be raised if an attempt is made to create a MapNode that already exists

- NonexistentNodeError: An exception that will be raised if a request is made for a MapNode that doesn't exist

- OutOfMapBoundsError: An exception that will be raised if a request is made for a MapNode that isn't allowed to exist in the map area

- `create_node(x, y)`: Creates and returns a new, default `MapNode`, registering it in the global dataset of nodes in the process

- `get_node(x, y)`: Finds and returns a `MapNode` at the specified (x, y) coordinate location in the global dataset of available nodes

A developer makes an initial attempt at writing the code to set a value for a single resource at a given node, as a part of a project. Their initial implementation is:

```python
def SetNodeResource(x, y, z, r, v):
    n = get_node(x, y)
    n.z = z
    n.resources.add(r, v)
```

This code is functional, from the perspective that it will do what it's supposed to (and what the developer expected) for a set of simple tests; for example, executing:

```python
SetNodeResource(0,0, None,'gold',0.25)
print(get_node(0,0))
SetNodeResource(0,0, None,'silver',0.25)
print(get_node(0,0))
SetNodeResource(0,0, None,'copper',0.25)
print(get_node(0,0))
```

Which results in the following output (line breaks and indentation added for clarity):

```
<MapNode (0,0) {'silver': None, 'gold': 0.25, 'copper': None}>
<MapNode (0,0) {'silver': 0.25, 'gold': 0.25, 'copper': None}>
<MapNode (0,0) {'silver': 0.25, 'gold': 0.25, 'copper': 0.25}>
```

By that measure, there is nothing wrong with the code and its functions. Now, let us ask some of our questions:

How easily understood is the functionality? The function, as written, is not difficult to follow from the perspective of what it does with each argument passed to it. However, several argument names are not very descriptive of what they are in the function's context. Using `resource` instead of `r` and `value` instead of `v` would go a long way toward making the function a lot easier to understand without having to track down how it is called elsewhere.

Who will be using this functionality? The function may be called, by either of two different application front ends, by on-site surveyors, or by post-survey assayers. The surveyors may not use it often, but if they see obvious signs of a deposit during the survey, they are expected to log it with a 100% certainty of finding the resource(s) at that grid location; otherwise, they will leave the resource rating completely alone.

What will they be doing with it? Between the base requirements (to set a value for a single resource at a given node) and the preceding answer, this feels like it has already been answered.

When and where do they have access to it? Through a library that is used by the surveyor and assayer applications. No one will use it directly, but it will be integrated into those applications.

How should it work? This has already been answered, but raises the question: Will there ever be a need to add more than one resource rating at a time? That is probably worth noting if there is a good place to implement it.

What other parts of the system does this code interact with? There is not much here that is not obvious from the code; it uses MapNode objects, those objects' resources, and the get_node function.

What happens if an attempt is made to alter an existing MapNode? With the code as it was originally written, this behaves as expected. This is the happy path that the code was written to handle, and it works.

What happens if a node does not already exist? The fact that there is a NonexistentNodeError defined is a good clue that at least some map operations require a node to exist before they can be completed. Executing a quick test against that by calling the existing function with

```
SetNodeResource(0,6, None,'gold',0.25)
```

outputs an error response, because the development data does not have a MapNode object at those coordinates yet:

```
Traceback (most recent call last):etNodeResource(0, 6, None, 'gold', 0.25)
# More error details removed for brevity
map_nodes.NonExistantNodeError
```

If that outcome is satisfactory, then nothing more needs to be done. If it is not — if development standards require raising explicit errors or providing error-logging, for example — then the function would have to be revised to provide an acceptable outcome.

What happens if a node can't exist at a given location? Similarly, there is an OutOfMapBoundsError defined. Since there are no out-of-bound nodes in the development data, and the code will not currently get past the fact that an out-of-bounds node does not exist, there is no effective way to see what happens if this is attempted.

What happens if the z-value is not known at the time? Since the create_node function does not even expect a z-value, but MapNode instances have one, there is a real risk that calling this function on an existing node would overwrite an existing z-altitude value on an existing node. That, eventually, could be a critical bug, and would be worth a deeper examination.

Does this code meet all the various development standards that apply? Without any details about standards, it is fair to assume that any standards that were defined would include, at a minimum, the following:

- Naming conventions for code elements, such as function names and arguments; an existing function at the same logical level as get_node, using SetNodeResources as the name of the new function, while perfectly legal syntactically, may be violating a naming convention standard. The idea of using more verbose names for the resource and value arguments, called out earlier, might also be covered.

- At least *some* effort is made toward documentation, of which there is none.

- Some inline comments (maybe), if there is a need to explain parts of the code to future readers. There are none in the new function as it has been written, although given the simplicity of the function, and how straightforward its approach is, an argument could be made that it is not needed at this point.

What should happen if the execution fails? It should, perhaps, throw explicit errors, with reasonably detailed error messages, if something fails during execution. Again, given how simple this function is, that might be an optional item.

What happens if an invalid value is passed for any of the arguments? Some of them can be tested by executing the current function (as was done previously), while supplying invalid arguments — an out-of-range number first, then an invalid resource name.

Consider the following call, executed with an invalid number:

```
SetNodeResource(0,0,'gold',2)
```

This raises an error:

```
ValueError: set_node_resource expects a float value from 0.0-1.0, or a
value that can be converted to one, for resource_value: 2.0 (float) is not
valid
```

Here is another variant, a similar invalid call with an invalid resource type:

```
SetNodeResource(0,0,'tin',0.25)
```

This raises a similar error:

```
ValueError: tin is not a tracked resource (gold, silver, copper)
```

The function can either succeed or raise an error during execution, judging by these examples; all that needs to happen is that those potential errors must be accounted for.

Other questions may come to mind, but the preceding questions are enough to implement some significant changes. Revising the function to address these starts with the addition of detailed documentation for the function:

```
def set_node_resource(
    x, y, resource_name, resource_value, z=None
):
    """
    Sets the value of a named resource for a specified
    node, creating that node in the process if it
    doesn't exist.
    Returns the MapNode instance used or created.
    Arguments:
    x (int, required, non-negative)
        The x-coordinate location of the node that the
        resource type and value is to be associated with.
    y (int, required, non-negative)
        The y-coordinate location of the node that the
        resource type and value is to be associated with.
    z (int, optional, defaults to None)
        The z-coordinate (altitude) of the node.
    resource_name (str, required)
        The name (a member of node_resource_names) of
        the resource to associate with the node.
    resource_value(float, required)
        The presence (between 0.0 and 1.0, inclusive)
        of the resource at the node's location.
    Raises
     * RuntimeError if any errors are detected.
    """
```

Next is cleaning up the original process, leveraging the system's defined error types and Python's try...except error-handling to ensure that a node is created if it doesn't exist. Once that's in place, it is convenient to handle the optional z parameter to the function. All of that together looks like this:

```
# Get the node, if it exists
try:
    node = get_node(x, y)
except NonexistentNodeError:
    # The node doesn't exist, so create it and
    # populate it as applicable
    node = create_node(x, y)
# If z is specified, set it
if z != None:
    node.z = z
```

Since these revisions do not address possible future error cases or additional resource types, there's not much more that can be done than to add some comments calling out that the possibilities exist.

```
# TODO:
# Determine if there are other exceptions that we can
# do anything about here, and if so, do something about
# them. For example:
#    except Exception as error:
#        # Handle this exception
# FUTURE:
# If there's ever a need to add more than one resource-
# value at a time, we could add **resources to the
# signature, and call node.resources.add once for each
# resource.
```

Handling errors that could be raised from calls to other functionality, and adding some comments about *why* we're doing that, is straightforward enough:

```
try:
    # All our values are checked and validated by
    # the add method, so just set the node's
    # resource-value
    node.resources.add(resource_name, resource_value)
    # Return the newly-modified/created node in
    # case we need to keep working with it.
```

```
        return node
    except Exception as error:
        raise RuntimeError(
            f'set_node_resource could not set '
            f'{resource_name} to {resource_value} '
            f'on the node at (node.x, node.y).'
        )
```

If we ignore the comments and documentation, this does not look much different from the original code — only nine lines of code were added — but the *functional* differences are significant:

- It does not assume that a node will always be available.
- If the requested node does not exist, it creates a new one to operate on, using the existing function defined for that purpose.
- It does not assume that every attempt to add a new resource will succeed.
- When an attempt fails, it raises an error that provides information about what happened.

All these additional items are direct results of the questions asked earlier and of making *conscious decisions* on how to deal with those questions. That kind of result is where the difference between the programming and software engineering mindsets really appears.

There may well be other questions that arise as code takes shape. The ones listed earlier have proven to be good starting points in my experience but should **not** be taken as a complete list. Any question that arises while working on code should be considered valid, and if there's any concern that not knowing the answer to it could lead to problems later on, making an effort to get an answer is almost always worthwhile.

That answer may be some variant of

we don't know, but it's not worth worrying about right now,

and that can be a completely valid answer: knowing that a potential issue exists is the first step in preparing to address it if it does cause problems later on. Identifying potential issues before they become real also makes it considerably easier to recognize those issues if they do arise.

Summary

There is more to software engineering than just writing code. Experience, attention to detail, and asking questions about how the code functions and interacts with the rest of a system are important aspects of evolving from a programming to a software engineering mindset. The time required to acquire experience can be shortened, perhaps significantly, by simply asking the right questions.

There are also factors completely outside the realm of creating and managing code that contribute to that mindset. They focus mainly on what can, or should, be expected from the pre-development planning around a developmental effort, and that starts with understanding a typical software development life cycle. Knowing what the expectations for each successive level are as you progress to more senior roles, and what to pay heed to in order to meet those expectations, will help in achieving those roles. They will also improve your coding skills, helping to form good habits that can be applied even in moving from one team or organization to another.

Many of the bigger-picture considerations mentioned here have their roots in more general, non-functional processes common across the IT industry. The first of those, which we'll examine in the next chapter, is the high-level process by which software is planned, created, maintained, and retired — the **Software Development Life Cycle (SDLC)**.

Get This Book's PDF Version and Exclusive Extras

UNLOCK NOW

Scan the QR code (or go to `packtpub.com/unlock`). Search for this book by name, confirm the edition, and then follow the steps on the page.

Note: Keep your invoice handy. Purchases made directly from Packt don't require an invoice.

3

The Software Development Life Cycle

All software development, Python or otherwise, above a certain level of complexity, follows re-peatable patterns or has a life cycle. A **Software (or System) Development Life Cycle (SDLC)** can be defined as its own distinct development methodology, providing a set of tasks and activities that apply to the development process. That is, even if there is no formal process wrapped around an SDLC, any or all of the activities that comprise one may still take place, and any or all of the artifacts that come out of them may be available during the development of a project.

In this chapter, we are going to cover the following main topics:

- What an SDLC is
- Pre-development phases of the SDLC
- Development-specific phases of the SDLC
- Post-development phases of the SDLC

What an SDLC is

A **software development life cycle**, or **SDLC**, whether followed as a formally defined methodology or informally executed as part of day-to-day business processes, is nothing more than a sequence of activities that occur around and through the development of a piece of software. That software may be an entire system, some sub-system that is part of a larger whole, a single project that adds new features or functionality to some existing system, or any development effort, really. The results of these activities are meaningful in the context of software engineering as a discipline because they can provide structure, definition, requirements, and expectations, both functional and non-functional, for the result of the actual development effort.

Many phases of the SDLC result in *artifacts* of some sort: requirements documentation, development standards, and testing plans are perhaps the most common, but there may be others. From the development effort perspective, not all artifacts resulting from an SDLC may be useful, particularly those coming out of the first few phases of the life cycle's process. Even so, the more knowledge that is available during the development process, the less likely it is that development efforts will go in directions that run contrary to the intentions of the system on a longer-term basis.

To fully explore what an SDLC might provide, we will use one of the more detailed examples found on the internet. It breaks the life cycle down into ten phases, which would be executed in the following order, barring process alterations from a development methodology:

1. Initial concept/vision
2. Concept development
3. Project management planning
4. Requirements analysis and definition
5. System architecture and design
6. Development (writing code) and quality assurance
7. System integration, testing, and acceptance
8. Implementation/installation/distribution
9. Operations/use and maintenance
10. Decommissioning

Many of these individual phases can be merged or might be broken out into smaller sub-phases, but this breakdown — these ten phases — is a useful grouping of similar activities with similar scopes.

The first three phases may all occur before any code is written, defining the high-level concepts and goals, and planning for how to accomplish those goals. The last three phases generally happen after initial development is complete, but as new features or functionality are conceived, or as bugs are discovered, development efforts will be initiated to work through those. The fourth and fifth phases, concerned with the formal definition of requirements and the design and architecture needed to accomplish those requirements, may occur as part of the development process, particularly if development is executed within an Agile methodology. The balance (of the phases), the actual writing, testing, integration, and acceptance of code, are usually the only phases of the SDLC that actually involve the core activity of a software engineer — writing code.

Pre-development phases of the SDLC

The first three phases noted earlier generally do not involve any development or coding. They are sometimes referred to as the *pre-development* phases of the SDLC. Before the first line of code is written, there is the potential for a fair amount of thought and work going into a project. Most of the efforts required for these early SDLC phases center around the high-level concept of the project, and around how development efforts will be managed. Much of it is very high level and abstract, and as such, there may not be many (or any) meaningful artifacts that come from these phases' efforts. Despite that, knowing what outcomes came of them can often provide useful, if simple, context for later efforts, helping to maintain focus on the purpose during the design and implementation phases later.

Phase 1: Initial concept/vision

The very first thing that happens in a project's or system's life is its conception. Behind the scenes, that usually involves the recognition of some unfulfilled need or something that is not working the way it should, though other variations might occur as well. As part of that realization, there will frequently be a collection of capabilities that the conceived system will provide, benefits or functionality that will drive the system's development, and determine when that development is complete. With this initial, very high-level overview, there may not be much in the way of detail. An entire vision might be nothing more than a statement like one of these:

> *We need a better way of managing inventory.*
>
> *We need a way to keep track of fuel efficiency across our delivery truck fleet.*
>
> *We should allow our customers to order our products online.*

The concept and the benefits might come from *anyone* with a stake in the system. Some examples include the following:

- Business staff who are looking for a better way of doing things.
- Developers who recognize that an existing system is not as effective as it could be, or that it is difficult to maintain.
- System administrators might have concerns about how easy it is to manage an in-place system and want a newer, better approach to be taken.

The initial vision might also be for something completely new, at least in the context of the current business setting.

Hopefully, if off-the-shelf solutions or products are available that meet parts of these needs, those options will have been investigated in some detail — maybe even to the point where the vision owner would be able to point to some feature set(s) of those products to provide direction for the development efforts. Having examples of functionality that are close to what is wanted can be a significant time-saver during pre-development design and development alike, and it is almost always worth asking if there are examples of what is wanted as the design and development processes move along. If that sort of investigation was undertaken and no options were found that were even close, that, too, has useful information embedded in it:

- What was missing?
- What did product X do that did not meet the needs of the concept?

If no investigation was undertaken, or if nothing came out of an investigation, it is quite possible that the initial concept would be no more than a sentence or two. That is alright, though, since more details will be extracted later as the concept development starts. This scenario, in the author's experience, happens more frequently than might be expected, particularly in businesses that are heavily invested in the development of their own products, or where there is a desire to *own all the code*.

In more formal processes, other analyses may also take place, looking in some detail at any or all of these:

- **Specific user needs**: What users must be able to do within the system, and what they should be able to do. There may also be a collection of nice-to-have features — things that users would like to be able to do, but that are not a functional necessity.
- **Specific functional needs**: Analyze what problems the system needs to solve, or at least mitigate in a significant fashion.
- **Risks**: Usually, one needs to investigate business-process-related risks, but those may also serve to guide design and development in later phases.
- **Costs (in terms of both money and resources)**: The odds are that this information will not yield much use from a development process perspective, but it is possible for an occasional significant nugget of information to come out of this as well.

- **Operational feasibility**: Examining how well the conceptual system addresses the needs it has been thought up to address. Like with cost analysis, the odds are good that there won't be much that comes out of this that's directly useful for development purposes, but it might identify operational or design areas where there is doubt about feasibility, and those doubts, in turn, may well shape design and/or implementation by the time the system is in development.

At best, then, given either a formal process or sufficient attention to detail through an informal process, the initial concept might produce information or documentation about the following:

- Benefits or functionality expected from the system (usually at a high level, at least to start with)
- A collection of specific, high-level functional needs
- A collection of specific user needs
- Specific features or functionality that were not provided by an off-the-shelf system (thus justifying custom development effort)
- Specific risks to mitigate against
- Specific functional or feasibility concerns to address

All of these have at least *some* value once development is underway and will hopefully make their way into design or requirements, and from there into development.

Phase 2: Concept development

Concept development is concerned mostly with fleshing out some of the high-level *details* that come out of the initial concept, providing details and direction for efforts later in the life cycle. A critical aspect of this step is the generation of various **system modeling** artifacts — a complex enough topic that it will be covered in greater depth in a separate chapter. The balance of the development-related information that comes out of this phase is focused more on marrying business processes and system functionality and providing some detail around system goals. There is also room here for a definition of at least a basic user experience and/or user interface, especially as they connect to the process/functionality.

Defining the business processes embedded in a system includes identifying the business objects that the system keeps track of, the actions that can be taken with respect to those objects, and the outcomes of those actions, at a minimum. Applying the sort of questioning described earlier in *Chapter 2, Programming versus Software Engineering Revisited*, can yield a fair bit of that information if more detail is needed.

This same system concept will be revisited in *Chapter 4*, *System Modeling*, to illustrate how fleshing out the high-level technical design aspects of a system might progress.

By way of example, consider a system whose concept begins with the knowledge that a business needs a way to keep track of fuel efficiency across its delivery vehicle fleet. Working out the business objects and activities from there could answer some very basic questions, such as the following:

What is the system keeping track of?

- The individual vehicles in the fleet
- The mileage on the odometers of those vehicles at irregular intervals
- The *refueling* of those vehicles, at a minimum

What does a refueling activity look like?

- Keeping track of the fuel quantity
- Keeping track of the odometer reading at the time of refueling, to start with

Those two data points would allow for the calculation of fuel efficiency, which is calculated in whatever units each uses (gallons or liters for fuel, and miles or kilometers for the odometer). Fuel efficiency becomes a calculation of any given refueling for any given vehicle, and the current odometer reading for any given vehicle can be retrieved from the odometer reading at its last refueling.

How many refueling activities should be kept for any given vehicle?

If one of the goals of the system is to detect when a vehicle's fuel efficiency has dropped, to flag it for maintenance, or to trigger a review of the delivery schedule associated with it, then there is an obvious need to keep track of more than one such refueling — maybe all of them.

Who will be using the system, how, and where?

There would need to be at least two types of physical access points:

- One from a driver's mobile device (when fueling a vehicle)
- One from in-office computers (for reporting purposes if nothing else)

That set of use cases tells us that we are looking at either a web application or some sort of dedicated phone and computer application set, with access to some common data stores, possibly through a service layer.

There may be other questions that could be asked, but these four alone probably give enough information to make the most of major concept design decisions, though the last may require a bit more exploration before they can be finalized. Similar questioning, asking things such as

What can (a specific type of user) do with the system?

until there are no more users and activities, can also yield more specific system goals, such as:

Various users can log refueling activities, providing the current odometer reading, and the quantity of fuel involved:

- Delivery drivers (at local fuel stations)
- Fleet maintenance staff (at the central office, where there is a company fuel station)

Fleet maintenance staff will be alerted when a truck's calculated fuel efficiency drops to lower than 90% of its average so that the truck can be scheduled for an examination.

Office staff will also be alerted when a truck's calculated fuel efficiency drops to lower than 90% of its average so that the truck's delivery rounds can be examined.

The question of how and where users will interact with the system may well spark some discussion and design decisions around user experience and interface design as well. In this case, perhaps after a discussion about whether the system is a web application or a dedicated phone and desktop application, the decision is made to make the system a web application.

Phase 3: Project management planning

This phase of the life cycle is where all the conceptual items come together, hopefully in a form or fashion ready for the creation of code to start. If there is a formal document as a result, its outline might look something like this:

- Business purpose
- Objectives
- Goals
- What is included
- What is excluded
- Key assumptions
- Project organization

- Roles and responsibilities
- Stakeholders
- Communication
- Risks, issues, and dependencies
- Preliminary schedule of deliverables
- Change management
- Risk and issue management

Developers may not need all of these items, but knowing where to look for various bits and pieces of the information they will need (or, in some cases, who to contact for information) is advantageous.

The *Business purpose*, *Objectives*, and *Goals* phases should, ideally, collect all the original vision information (from the Initial concept/vision phase) with whatever details were added or changes made after the concept design was complete. These will, in all probability, include the starting points for the *Requirements analysis and definition* efforts that go on later, during the development-specific phases of the life cycle. In addition, the *What's included*, *What's excluded*, and *Key assumptions* sections, between them, should expose what the actual scope of development looks like, as well as providing high-level design decisions and any relevant high-level system modeling information. *Risks, issues, and dependencies* may provide specific items of concern or other areas of interest that will help shape development efforts. Finally, *Change management* will set expectations (at a high level, at least) for what processes are expected or planned for as changes to the system are made.

People in a position to answer questions or make decisions about the system's implementation that fall outside the scope of pure development will probably be listed in the artifacts from the *Roles and responsibilities* and/or *Stakeholders* phases, though there may be specific established processes for raising those questions in the *Communication* section.

Even without formal documentation around project management expectations, much of the information noted previously should still be made available to development staff — the less time spent having to track down who can answer a question, the more time can be devoted to writing code.

What should software engineers look for?

By the time all the pre-development SDLC activities are complete, the artifacts they produce should be able to provide high-level direction around questions that will relate to the actual development efforts.

These should include, at a minimum, the following items:

- Who are the users of the system? The **Actors** in use case definitions, which will be explained in *Chapter 4, System Modeling.*
- What do those users need to be able to do with it?
- How are those users going to interact with it (which may include *where* they are using the system)?

Even at the high-level view that these artifacts are likely to represent, there are fundamental decisions that will shape later development efforts.

Development-specific phases of the SDLC

With the widespread adoption of Agile methodologies, the specific shapes of the development-specific phases of an SDLC can vary substantially. Different methodologies make different decisions about what to prioritize or emphasize, and those differences can, in turn, yield significantly different processes and artifacts to accomplish the goals of formal SDLC phases that focus directly on developer needs and activities. Whole books have been written about several of the Agile processes, so a complete discussion of them is well beyond the scope of this book, but all of them address the following activities.

Phase 4: Requirements analysis and definition

Requirements analysis and definition is concerned with discovering and detailing the specific requirements of a system — what the system needs to allow users to do with it. *Users* obviously include end users, ranging from office workers using the system to conduct day-to-day business to external end users such as customers. Less obviously, users should *also* include system administrators, staff who receive data from the system through some reporting processes, and any number of other people who interact with the system in any fashion, or who are affected by it, or by changes to it" — quite possibly including the developers themselves.

The most basic requirements — who is using the system, what they are expected to do with it, and the like — should have been established earlier across the pre-development phases. At this point, those basic requirements may need to be elaborated on to a point where they can be acted upon. In an Agile methodology, that will usually be handled by the creation of **user stories** — informal, general explanations of the functionality to be delivered. Though the specific format may vary, the end goal is the same: to articulate how a software feature will provide value to the user. No matter how those requirements are defined, they should include a more detailed breakdown of the *who is using the system* and *what they are expected to do* mentioned earlier, usually with a tighter focus on specific tasks or user activities in the context of the system.

For example, a high-level requirement that came out of the *Concept development* phase earlier in the SDLC was:

Various users can log refueling activities, providing the current odometer reading and the quantity of fuel involved.

A more specific requirement, focusing on a specific **use case**, might be something like this:

A fleet driver (the user) *must be able to log when they are refueling their assigned vehicle* (the activity), *including the current odometer reading of the vehicle and the amount of fuel purchased* (the relevant data for the activity).

Writing this use case in a common user story format, this might be:

As a fleet driver, I need to be able to log my vehicle's current odometer reading and the amount of fuel being purchased when refueling at a public gas station, so I don't have to keep track of paper receipts for those activities.

The end goal, no matter the format of the requirements, is to provide the developer with enough information to:

- Write code to perform the activity.
- Confirm that the code is doing what it is supposed to, meeting the requirements that relate.

Phase 5: System architecture and design

If requirements analysis and definition are about *what a system provides*, **system architecture and design** are primarily about *how pieces of the system fit together* and *how those capabilities work*. The differences in how various development methodologies deal with architecture and design are less about those *how* questions and more about *when they are defined*. No matter when a set of requirements (the *what it provides* behind the system) is defined, the implementation details (the *how*) will almost certainly be determined by the specifics of how best to implement them in the programming language and how to fit that implementation into the larger system.

System architecture and design at the start of a completely new system or project can be very free-form: There may not be any pre-existing constraints, and if there are they are more likely to be formed by external factors like the environment that the system will run under, the resources required, and the costs involved in the operation of those resources.

For example, there are some structural constraints for systems running as serverless applications in an AWS account that will not apply to systems running as installed software on server hardware. It is important to be aware of and identify any high-level constraints that can impact system design as early as possible, if only to prevent having to re-work large chunks of code because something it needs is not supported in the run-time environment. Beyond any hard constraints a run-time environment might impose, having a high-level design approach, even if it is very loose at first, is a good idea. It need not be anything more complicated than, say, a preference to use only functions, or a preference for classes and an object-oriented design.

System architecture and design will often evolve as a system's development progresses, particularly in an Agile development paradigm. Even in those cases, the end goal is the same, from a developer's perspective; they need to know the following:

- What constraints (if any) they must contend with while writing the code.
- What other pieces of existing code their new code must interact with.
- What those interactions look like — how other functions are called, for example — or what existing classes they need to use.
- What they *can* change in already-existing code, design, infrastructure, or architecture (if a change is needed) to fit their code into the system as a whole.

These items, with the possible exception of the first, also play heavily into system integration concerns, which will be detailed a bit further on.

Phase 6: Development and quality assurance

The development part of this phase probably requires the least explanation: it is when the actual code gets written, using the defined requirements to determine what the goals of the code are, and the architecture/design to determine how to write the code. If the development processes in play do not include **Continuous Integration (CI)**, an argument could perhaps be made that the quality assurance part of this phase should be broken out into its own grouping, if only because many of the activities involved are substantially different — there's less code authoring going on, if there is any at all, in executing a manual test plan than in writing the automated test suites that CI requires.

If CI is in play, writing those automated testing suites may require a substantial amount of up-front code authoring, at least at first. Once those test suites are established, regression testing becomes much simpler and less time-consuming. Development methodologies' concerns with the **Quality Assurance (QA)** aspects of this phase are usually centered around when QA activities take place, while the actual expectations of those activities are usually a combination of development standards and best practices. We will examine CI and the related processes and expectations later, in *Chapter 5, Methodologies, Paradigms, and Practices*, and development standards and best practices in *Chapter 6, Revisiting Development Best Practices*.

Phase 7: System integration, testing, and acceptance

Systems tend to grow, both in size and complexity, over time, as new features and functionality are added. As a result, it is just a matter of time before new code from development efforts must be incorporated into a larger system environment. Attention may also be needed with respect to interactions with other systems and any of the implications raised in those scenarios. In smaller, less complex systems, this integration may be achievable during development. In either case, the integration of new (or modified) functionality needs to be tested to ensure that it has not broken anything, both in the local system and in any other systems that interact with it.

Once whatever integration has been accomplished, the new body of code will need to be tested. Ideally, this will be an automated process. Even if it's not, testing should ideally include execution of new code integrations, regression testing of the system, and end-to-end testing to ensure that the new code works as intended and does not break existing functionality. **User Acceptance Testing (UAT)** may also be relevant, particularly if the new code can be executed through some **User Interface (UI)** interaction. Once all the testing that is needed has been completed, and any issues or errors that surface as a result have been accounted for, the new code is ready to be released.

What should software engineers look for?

As the development-specific phases of an SDLC unfold, they should provide direction with respect to:

- What the required functionality actually *is*.
- How best to implement the required functionality.
- What quality assurance efforts are expected, and what code, if any, is required to those ends.
- How and where their code fits into the larger system, and how to integrate it.
- What testing of the end results is going to involve, how it will be accomplished, and what acceptance of it will involve.

Post-development phases of the SDLC

The portions of the SDLC that happen after the core code of a system is written can still have significant impacts on the development cycle. Historically, they might not involve a lot of real development effort — some code may be written as a one-off for various specific purposes such as packaging the system's code, or facilitating its installation on a target environment, for example. If the structure of the system's code base or, rarely, the language that the system is written in does not somehow prevent it, most of any code that was written in support of post-development activities would probably be created early in the development process to meet some other need.

The last two phases of the SDLC, concerned with the day-to-day use of the system and its eventual retirement, will have less relevance to the core development process in general. The most likely exception to that would be re-entry into the development cycle phases to handle bugs or add new features or functionality (the *use and maintenance* part of the *Operations, use, and maintenance* phase).

Phase 8: Implementation/installation/distribution

As a case in point, packaging the code base and/or the creation of some installation mechanism is likely to be undertaken the first time the code base needs to be installed on an environment for user acceptance testing. If that expectation is known ahead of time — and it should be, at some level — then efforts to write the packaging process or installer may well start before any deployed code is created. After that point, further efforts will usually happen infrequently, as new components need to be added to a package structure, or changes to an installation process need to be undertaken. Changes at that level will often be minor, and typically needed with less and less frequency as the process and the code base installation(s) mature.

The creation and evolution of this sort of process, if it is automated, is part of the foundation for a DevOps process, facilitating both **Continuous Integration (CI)** and either **Continuous Deployment** or **Continuous Delivery (CD)**. These processes, CI/CD, will be examined in more detail in *Chapter 5, Methodologies, Paradigms, and Practices*. For now, the main point to bear in mind is that *some* process to release new versions of the code needs to be in place, whether it's manual, partially automated, or fully integrated into a build-and-deploy process. The shape or flavor of the final deliverable may vary significantly. It could be a package — or a complete application, for that matter — that an end-user installs. That same package or application could also be installed automatically as part of a manual or automated deployment process. There may be other release mechanisms in play, too.

Phase 9: Operations, use, and maintenance

From the perspective of system administrators — the staff responsible for the execution of activities in those phases — developers are *contributors* to the knowledge and processes they need. They relate in much the same way that all of the pre-development contributors to the system's development did with respect to developer knowledge and processes. System administration and maintenance staff will be looking for and using various artifacts that come out of the development process to be able to execute their day-to-day efforts with respect to the system. The odds are good that those artifacts will mostly be knowledge, in the form of documentation, and perhaps the occasional system administration tool.

Usage activities may be undertaken by system administrators and end-users of the system. Of the two, the end-user is likely going to be the more common or frequent type of participant, interacting with the system, and using it to accomplish whatever the system was designed and built to do.

Maintenance activities will usually be one of two basic types of efforts: development of new features and functionality to meet new or evolving end-user needs or tracking down and fixing bugs in the system that someone (probably outside the development team) has discovered.

Phase 10: Decommissioning

Finally, with respect to the process of decommissioning a system, taking it offline, presumably never to be used again: someone, probably at a business-decision level, will have to provide direction or even formal business policies and procedures around what needs to happen. At a minimum, those will likely include:

- Requirements for preserving and archiving system data (or how it should be disposed of, if it is sensitive data).
- Requirements for notifying users of the system's decommissioning.

There may well be more — perhaps a **lot** more — it is very dependent on the system itself, both structurally and functionally, as well as any business policies that might apply.

Knowing how things will be handled during a complete and permanent shutdown may give significant insight into how system processes and data can or should be handled when normal data deletion is executed during normal system operation.

What should software engineers look for?

Only a handful of the post-development items in the SDLC may be significant during the development phase. Most of those are significant only because they can have an impact on how code gets written. That is not to say that the other items aren't important, at least potentially: knowing more about how the system is going to be used, for example, *could* be important, but that is likely to vary across different project types, and have different priorities as a result. The factors that are most likely to have a day-to-day impact on development efforts — and thus be most important to software engineers — are:

- How the code will be deployed to be accessible to end-users.
- What to expect as bugs are reported, triaged, and acted upon.
- What concessions or constraints need to be put in place as code is written with an eye toward eventual decommissioning efforts.

Summary

Even if there is no formal SDLC in place, a lot of the information that would come out of one is still useful for developers. Providing developers with ready access to detailed and accurate information, particularly the pre-development phase concepts and requirements, can make the difference between a project just being programmed and being well-engineered software. Ideally, developers will need to know:

- How is the system supposed to be distributed and installed so that they can plan around those needs, writing code to facilitate them as required?
- What kind of information is needed for post-development activities to provide the relevant documentation or write code to facilitate common or expected tasks?
- What should happen when the system is finally shut down for good so that they can plan and document accordingly?

Another significant contributor to making that difference is the availability of similar information about the system itself, in any or all of several system model artifacts. Those provide more implementation-oriented details that are likely to be more useful than the policy and procedure-level information from the various SDLC artifacts. We will look at those in the next chapter.

Get This Book's PDF Version and Exclusive Extras

Scan the QR code (or go to packtpub.com/unlock). Search for this book by name, confirm the edition, and then follow the steps on the page.

Note: Keep your invoice handy. Purchases made directly from Packt don't require an invoice.

4

System Modeling

The goal of any system modeling process is to define and document a conceptual model of some aspect of a system, usually focusing on one (or many) components of that system. System models may be defined in a formal architecture description language, such as **Unified Modeling Language (UML)**, and can, in those cases, get very detailed, down to the minimum required property and method members of classes.

Details at that level are often fluid — or at least not finalized — until the requirements analysis processes described in *Chapter 3, The Software Development Life Cycle*, are complete. Some of them will be discussed in more detail in *Chapter 5, Methodologies, Paradigms, and Practices*. Additionally, much of the formal documentation discussed here may not be part of the standard practices for a development team. Even in those cases, the questions and practices that are explored here are good skills for a software engineer to cultivate—they will lead to a better understanding of the scope and requirements of a system, even if they are never formally documented. As a software engineer's experience grows, much of what's presented here will become habitual ways of thinking: an almost reflexive understanding of how these relate to each other, and to a system or project.

In this chapter, we're going to cover the following main topics:

- Understanding logical and physical architecture
- Creating and using use cases
- Thinking about data structure and flow
- Planning for inter-process communication
- Putting it all together — system scope and scale

Technical requirements

The code snippet in this chapter is for demonstration purposes only, showing the application of some of the topics and practices noted in the chapter.

Understanding logical and physical architecture

The goal of both logical and physical architecture specifications is to define and document the logical and physical components of a system, respectively, in order to provide clarity around how those component elements relate to one another. The artifacts resulting from either effort may be any combination of text documentation and diagrams, and both have advantages and drawbacks.

Text documentation is often quicker to produce, but unless there is some sort of architectural documentation standard that can be applied, the formats can (and probably will) vary from one team to another, at a minimum. That sort of variance can make it difficult for the resulting artifacts to be understandable outside the team that it originated with. If there is not a lot of movement of developers between teams, or a significant influx of new developers to teams, that may not be a significant concern. It can also be difficult to ensure that all of the moving parts or the connections between them are fully accounted for.

The primary advantage of diagrams is the relative ease with which they can be understood. If the diagram has obvious indicators, or symbols that unambiguously indicate, for example, that one component is a database service and another is an application, then the difference between them becomes obvious at a glance. Diagrams also have the advantage of being more easily understandable to non-technical audiences. If diagrams have a drawback, it's the length of time that it takes to actually generate them. Fortunately, there are tools that can streamline that process greatly, such as PlantUML (`https://plantuml.com`), which generates diagrams from UML text, and Lucidchart (`https://www.lucidchart.com`), which is a very well-designed diagramming application that includes object libraries for most development needs.

In both cases, text-based or diagram-based documents are, obviously, most useful if they are well constructed, and provide an accurate view or model of the system.

Logical architecture

Logical architecture is a view of the components of a system without consideration for where those components reside. A logical component might reside on a specific server or be moved from that server to another as capacity requirements dictate, but the logical, functional aspects of the component will not change if such a move is implemented.

Development is often going to be more concerned with the logical architecture of a system than with the physical. Provided that whatever mechanisms needed are in place for the actual code in a system to be deployed to, live on, connect to, and use the various physical components that relate to the logical components, and that any physical architecture constraints are accounted for, little more information is generally needed, so where any given component lives just isn't as important from that perspective. That often means that a physical architecture breakdown is at best a nice-to-have item, or maybe a should-have at most. That also assumes that the structure in question isn't so commonplace that it needs to be documented. There are, for example, any number of systems in the wild that follow the same common three-tier structure, with a request-response cycle that progresses as follows:

1. A user makes a request through the Presentation tier.
2. That request is handed off to the Application tier.
3. The application retrieves any data needed from the Data tier, perhaps doing some manipulation or aggregation of it in the process.
4. The Application tier generates a response and hands it back to the Presentation tier.
5. The Presentation tier shows that response to the user.

Diagrammed, that structure might look as follows:

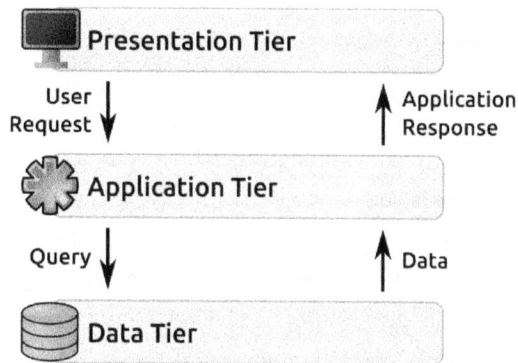

Figure 4.1: A typical process flow in a common three-tier application structure

This three-tier architecture is particularly common in web applications, which have the following properties:

- The Presentation tier, or Frontend tier, is the web server (with the web browser being no more than a remote output-rendering component)

- The Application tier is code called by, and generating responses to, the web server, written in whatever language and/or framework

- The Data tier is any of several backend data store variants that persist application data between requests

Together, the Application and Data tiers may be called a Backend tier. Consider, as an example, the following logical architecture for the refueling-tracking system concept mentioned earlier. It serves as a good example of this three-tier architecture as it applies to a web application, with some specifically identified components:

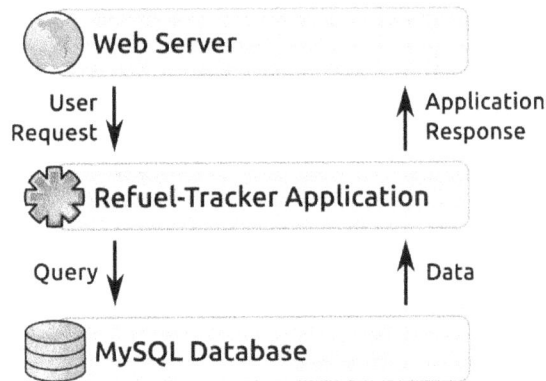

Figure 4.2: The three-tier application process flow applied to the refueling-tracker application

Physical architecture

Physical architecture is often an extension of logical architecture, from a documentation perspective. While logical architecture is concerned with identifying functional elements of a system from the perspective of their roles within that system, physical architecture specifies actual devices — servers and machines — that those logical components live on. Logical components within a system are typically atomic: they cannot be divided. Physical components may not be, though. It's quite possible for multiple logical components to reside on the same physical device. For smaller systems and applications, this may even be a preferred approach; it can reduce, or even eliminate, communications overhead between disparate physical components.

Provided that the physical hardware is sufficient in terms of memory, CPU speed, and so on, *physical* architectures that host the same logical components are *logically* identical. For example, all three of the physical architectures shown in the following diagram are valid implementations of the logical architecture in the preceding diagram:

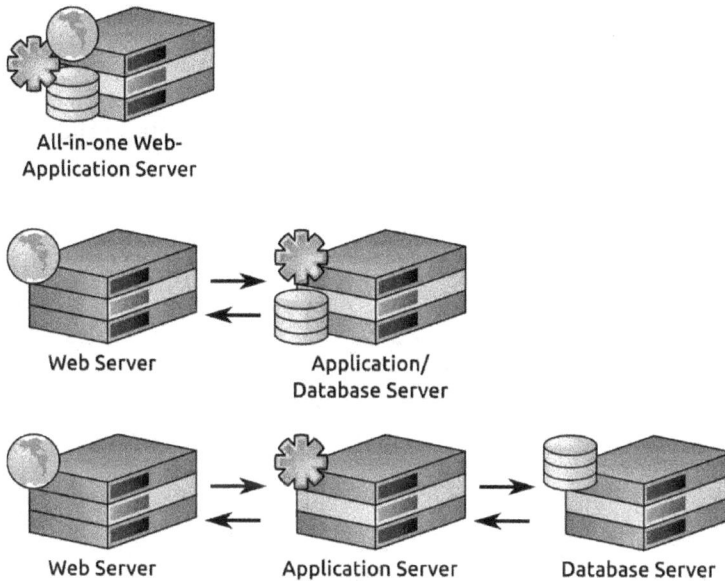

Figure 4.3: Possible physical architectures for the three-tier application shown above

Virtualization with software such as Broadcom's VMware, Microsoft's Hyper-V, and container services such as Docker can blur the line between logical and physical architecture: they allow a single physical machine to host a number of virtual computers, each capable of running its own OS, and with its own dedicated hardware resources. From the perspective of documenting physical architecture, though, these virtual environments should probably be approached as if each were a physical component. The same holds true for cloud-hosted virtual machines, such as those provided by Amazon Web Services' EC2, Google Cloud Platform's Compute Engine, and Azure's Virtual Machines services. Essentially, if it *acts* like a distinct physical server, it can be *treated* as one for the purposes of defining a physical architecture.

Serverless application options, such as AWS Lambda, GCP Cloud Functions, and Azure Functions, may completely remove any need for physical architecture, and thus for documenting it. By their very nature, those services create new environments on demand, with the code that is to be executed: as the need for those environments occurs, a new instance of the environment is created, initialized, and executed. Once there's no longer any need for any given environment, it is removed. It *may* still be useful or desirable to provide physical architecture documentation, though. Should that need arise, it's still *possible* to create meaningful physical architecture information.

So long as a given component *acts* like a real device from the perspective of how it interacts with the other elements, the representation is adequate, for example, in a hypothetical web application that lives completely in some public cloud, where that cloud allows serverless functions to be defined, and functions will be defined for processing requests in the context of business objects, such as Customers, Orders, and Products.

A corresponding physical architecture might look something like this:

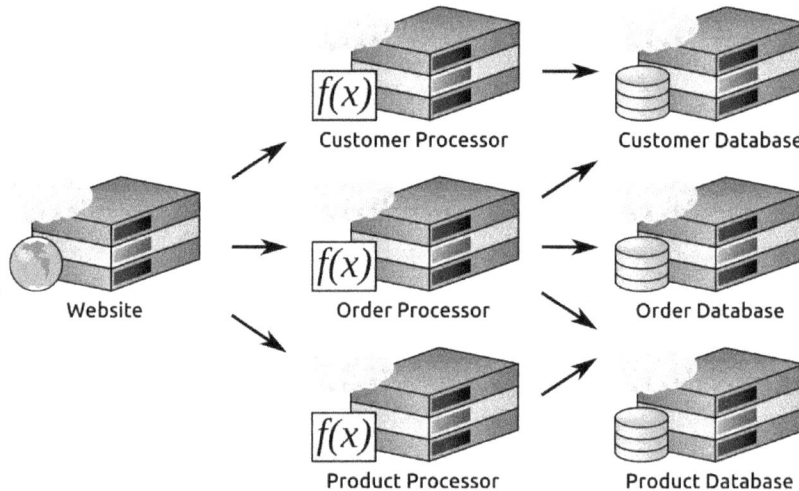

Figure 4.4: A physical architecture for a three-tier application as it might appear in a cloud environment

Collectively, logical and physical architecture specifications provide software engineers with at least *some* of the information needed to be able to interact with non-application tiers. Even if specific credentials will be required but are not supplied in the documentation, knowing, for example, what kind of database drives the Data tier of a system defines how that Data tier will be accessed.

Formal documentation of logical and physical architecture may not be undertaken as part of the SDLC of a system or project. In some cases, particularly in serverless applications, there may not be any real physical architecture to document, and the logical architecture may be implicit simply because of the processes needed and the business objects those processes can be applied to. Even when there is no formal, structured documentation, the architecture involved in a project can affect development efforts. Ultimately, what needs to be known during the development process is all the variations of *what constraints (if any) does the system architecture impose that code has to account for?* Many of those constraints will originate with the specific needs and processes defined in use cases.

Creating and using use cases

In its most basic form, a **use case** is documentation that captures how a user is allowed or expected to interact with a system. Within the context of any given system, the most important thing is whether it's doing what it's supposed to do for all of the use cases that it's supposed to support. Code has to be written for each of those use cases, and each use case corresponds to one or more business processes or rules, so it's only logical that each of those use cases is defined and documented to whatever extent is appropriate for the development process. As with the logical and physical architecture, it's possible to execute those definitions as either text or some sort of diagram, and those approaches have the same advantages and drawbacks that were noted before.

UML provides a high-level diagramming standard for use cases, which is useful mostly for capturing the relationship between specific types of users (**actors**, in UML's terminology) and the processes that they are expected to interact with. That's a good start and may even be sufficient all by itself if the process is very simple, already extensively documented, or known across the development team.

Use cases and Agile methodologies

Use cases are very similar to certain Agile-methodology artifacts. Depending on the scope of the process being captured by the use case, and on an Agile team's preferences around how complex and detailed user stories and epics are, a use case may be functionally equivalent to either. Stories and epics in an Agile context may well capture enough information that formal use case documentation is considered superfluous.

Example use cases — fleet tracking

Using the fleet tracking application concept that was described in the *Concept development* section of *Chapter 3, The Software Development Life Cycle*, as a starting point, we'll imagine some typical activities that the system would be expected to support. From there, we'll generate example use case documentation, both written and diagrammed. Each use case in this example is presented as a simple name, a description, a list of the types of actors who are expected to perform the activity(ies) of the use case, and any data that is expected by the process underlying that use case. It's worth noting that a single use case may well have several process steps behind it, and that those steps may have specific expectations around the sequencing of their execution. Those individual steps may not be documented as part of the use case documentation, though.

The actors that these use cases are concerned with are as follows:

- A **Fleet Manager**, who is responsible for coordinating the addition and removal of vehicles in the fleet, and who approves maintenance requests and the resolution of those requests
- A **Fleet Technician** (or *Fleet Tech*), who performs maintenance on fleet vehicles
- A **Route Scheduler**, who is responsible for defining delivery routes and assigning vehicles to those routes
- A **Fleet Driver**, the actual operator of a fleet vehicle, who drives that vehicle along a delivery route

Actors are frequently associated with specific roles, but they don't *have* to be. In this example, there's no functional reason why a *Fleet Manager* couldn't also be a *Fleet Technician*. If there is a functional difference, it would most likely surface in the implementation of the system's code, perhaps as a set of permissions associated with each individual user, that allows them to act in one or more of these roles.

These use case examples are a fairly small subset of the possible ones for the hypothetical company that the system is running for. They are focused on the activities and interactions that relate to the day-to-day operation of the fleet of vehicles by the Fleet Drivers, and the activities that can have effects on the availability and use of those vehicles. These use cases are as follows:

- **Public Refuel**: A *Fleet Driver* can add fuel to a fleet vehicle at public fuel stations while it's out on its delivery route. They are expected to use the system to log the amount of fuel purchased, the cost of that fuel, which vehicle was refueled, and the vehicle's odometer reading.
- **Home Refuel**: A *Fleet Tech* or *Fleet Driver* can add fuel to a fleet vehicle at the company's fuel depot. They are expected to use the system to log the amount of fuel added, which vehicle was refueled, and the vehicle's odometer reading, but the fuel cost is considered to be free, since it's coming from the company's pre-purchased reserve.
- **Check Fuel Efficiency**: The *system* (as a non-human actor) will, when a refueling activity has been logged for a given vehicle, perform some simple fuel-efficiency calculations, and raise a *Maintenance Alert* if it is below a certain threshold.
- **Maintenance Alert**: The *Fleet Manager* will be alerted when a maintenance need is detected or submitted so that the vehicle can be scheduled for an examination. If the maintenance request is approved, it will be forwarded to a *Fleet Technician*, and the *Route Scheduler* will also be alerted that the vehicle is unavailable.

- **Request Maintenance**: A *Fleet Driver* can log a maintenance request for a given vehicle, which should include the items they feel need attention.

- **Start Maintenance**: A *Fleet Technician* can be assigned a vehicle to perform maintenance on.

- **Finish Maintenance**: A *Fleet Technician* can indicate when the assigned maintenance for a given vehicle is complete. This will also send a notification to the *Route Scheduler* that the vehicle is available.

These seven use cases capture a fair amount of process detail, expressly defining which actors are expected to perform which activities. By themselves, these text descriptions would probably be sufficient to start development against, though specific requirements discovery might be needed as those efforts start. What they *don't* directly show is how the various use cases relate to *one another*. That information *is* present, but the relationships must be teased out by a reader examining enough of the individual use case items to recognize the relationships they imply.

That may not be a concern, depending on various other factors involved in the development of the system. For example, in a serverless application paradigm, or an event-driven system that uses asynchronous messaging to trigger functionality in the system, each of the use cases might be represented by a single chunk of code that knows how to listen for and handle those incoming messages. Diagrams tend to be better at capturing those relationships. Diagrammed, the relationships between these use cases and with their related actors are very clear:

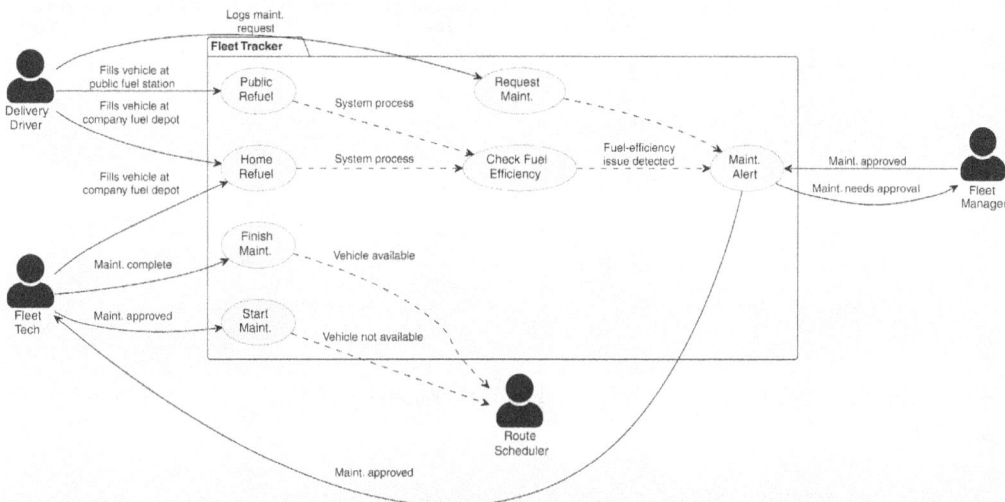

Figure 4.5: Diagram of the example use cases

Use cases tend to be very high level and concerned with *who is allowed to do what* within the context of a system. They often do not capture much in the way of detail about how the process behind the use case works. Even with that limitation, though, they can provide useful information that can shape how code is structured and written. They *may* map out on a one-to-one basis with functions or methods that will have to be implemented, as well as other functions or methods that they will interact with, but *that is not always the case*.

Thinking about data structure and data flow

Between them, basic use case and business process documentation may provide enough information to make the structure and flow of the data through the system obvious, or at least transparent enough that development won't need any additional information. The example processes we've been looking at probably fall into that category, but we'll explore what data structure and data flow diagrams for it might look like anyway.

Structure versus implementation

There are several options for how to implement the data structure, which will be explored in detail in *Chapter 11, Re-Examining Options for Business Objects*. At this point, the main concern is not with how these data structures will be implemented, but with *what they look like at a high level*.

An example data structure

Look at the *Public Refuel* and *Home Refuel* use cases described earlier in *Example use cases: Fleet tracking*:

> *They are expected to use the system to log the amount of fuel purchased, the cost of that fuel, which vehicle was refueled, and the vehicle's odometer reading.*

A data structure for a refueling event can be extracted from those expectations, with the following data points:

- odometer: The current odometer reading (probably an <int> value)
- fuel_quantity: The amount of fuel added to the vehicle (probably a <Decimal> value)
  fuel_cost: The amount of money spent on the fuel (also a <Decimal> value)

- `vehicle_id`: The identifier of the vehicle being refueled (for the sake of this example we'll assume it's an `<int>`)

> **Floating-point versus Decimal types**
>
> Floating-point numbers can be problematic and should be avoided for values where absolute accuracy is essential. At the CPU level, not every floating-point number has an exact binary representation, and just one of those values happening somewhere in the code will cause weird, inaccurate, and annoying behavior. Probably the most common general class of values where this is the case is anything that tracks money. Python, like several other languages, provides a numeric type to more accurately represent currency and other values where a float type would be risky: the `Decimal` type (`https://docs.python.org/3.11/library/decimal.html#decimal.Decimal`).

During the process, a refuel-efficiency value is also being created that might need to be passed along to the *Maintenance Alert* process: `refuel_efficiency`, the calculated efficiency value as of the refueling event, a `<float>` value. Depending on data persistence standards and expectations, a topic that will be examined in much greater detail in *Chapters 11* through *13*, other standard values may be expected. One that seems very likely at this point would be a `date_time` that tracks when the refueling event occurred.

It's also safe to assume that the system will need data objects that represent the individual vehicles in the fleet. There's already a concession to that in the `vehicle_id` field in the refueling event data structure, and while that suffices for that data structure, it would make sense for vehicles to have their own representation. That would allow data points that are associated with a given vehicle to have a single, authoritative value. An initial set of useful data points for vehicles would be as follows:

- `vehicle_id`: The same identifier for the vehicle mentioned earlier in the refueling event data structure
- `last_odometer`: The last recorded odometer reading for the vehicle, following the format and conventions for the odometer value in the refueling event structure
- `efficiency_threshold`: The fuel-efficiency threshold value that will be used to determine whether a *Maintenance Alert* needs to be sent when the *Check Fuel Efficiency* process runs, probably a `<float>` value

These two data structures, diagrammed, look like this:

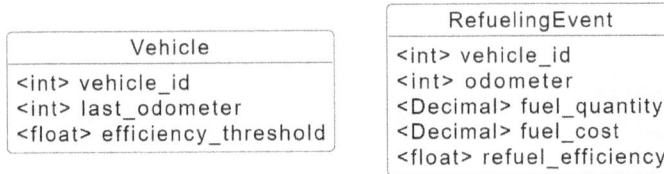

Vehicle
<int> vehicle_id
<int> last_odometer
<float> efficiency_threshold

RefuelingEvent
<int> vehicle_id
<int> odometer
<Decimal> fuel_quantity
<Decimal> fuel_cost
<float> refuel_efficiency

Figure 4.6: The initial example data structure

How were these data elements determined?

The process for working out the design of these data structures hinges on a set of questions, in the spirit of those presented in the *Asking questions* section of *Chapter 2, Programming versus Software Engineering Revisited*. Specifically, starting with the processes described in *Example use cases: Fleet tracking*, we ask the following:

> *What data is needed by this process?*

and

> *Where should that data live?*

In the case of the *Public* and *Home Refuel* use cases, the data points needed were already defined. In order to generate the fuel_efficiency value, fuel_quantity must be present. Since those are properties of individual refueling events, keeping them associated with that data structure was an obvious choice. So, too, should a value calculated from the odometer value in that event, but it must *also* be aware of a *previous* odometer value for the vehicle. At this point, a decision needed to be made, choosing between associating that previous odometer value with the vehicle or associating it with the refueling event. In the interests of preventing the duplication of data, that last_odometer value was attached to the *Vehicle* data structure.

> **Don't duplicate data unless there's no alternative**
>
> The idea of having a single, authoritative source for any given data point in a system — sometimes described as a **single source of truth** — provides several advantages. The most critical one, in the author's opinion, is that when data needs to be written or updated, it only has to happen in one data object or the data store element that corresponds to that object. That eliminates the need for code to handle redundant data writing operations, which keeps code simple and easy to test and manage.

Also, within the scope of the *Vehicle* data structure is a value that keeps track of that vehicle's efficiency expectations: efficiency_threshold. The question that drove that decision was as follows:

Should all vehicles have the same efficiency threshold?

This led to the following question:

What trade-offs happen if they do?

After some consideration, the idea of allowing individual vehicles to have different efficiency_threshold values felt better. That allowed vehicles with known efficiency issues to remain in service without generating a *Maintenance Alert* every time it was refueled.

After a quick review of the use cases described earlier, one more field was added to the Vehicle data structure: a available flag that would be used as part of the *Start Maintenance* and *Finish Maintenance* use cases. The diagram was updated accordingly — if diagrams and other documentation are going to be meaningful, they should be kept up to date — even though the change was trivial:

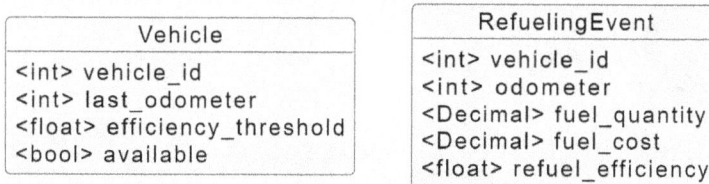

Vehicle
<int> vehicle_id
<int> last_odometer
<float> efficiency_threshold
<bool> available

RefuelingEvent
<int> vehicle_id
<int> odometer
<Decimal> fuel_quantity
<Decimal> fuel_cost
<float> refuel_efficiency

Figure 4.7: The updated example data structure

How does data flow in the system?

Armed with the use cases and data structure, understanding how the data in that structure moves through a system is little more than an exercise in mapping those data points to activities within the use cases. Examining the *Refueling Event* use case discussed earlier, for example, and determining where the data points come into play ultimately yields the following

- A RefuelingEvent is received by the system
- The system uses the vehicle_id provided in that event to retrieve the relevant Vehicle dataset
- The system calculates the refuel_efficiency value that relates to the event, using the last_odometer value for the Vehicle, and updates the RefuelingEvent data
- The system also updates the last_odometer value for the Vehicle

- Finally, the `refuel_efficiency` of the `RefuelEvent` is compared with the `efficiency_threshold` of the `Vehicle`: if the `refuel_efficiency` is below the `efficiency_threshold`, the system generates a *Maintenance Alert* before exiting

Diagrammed, this process looks like this:

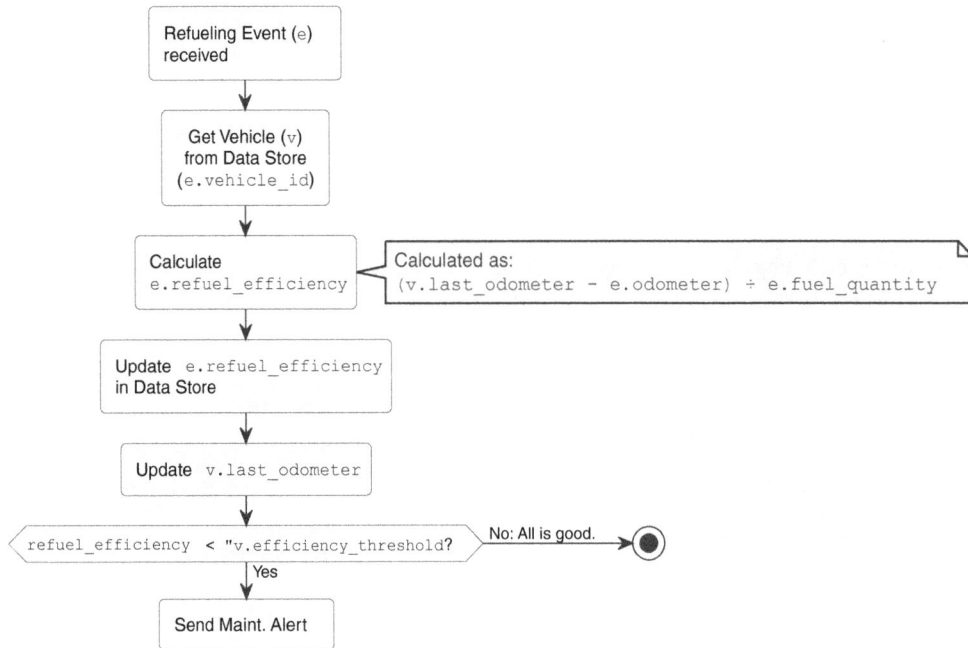

Figure 4.8: The data flow that handles a received Refueling Event

Of the data elements defined earlier, the `Vehicle.available` and `RefuelingEvent.fuel_cost` items are not used in this process, though `Vehicle.available` was already noted as being needed for scenarios that end up sending a *Maintenance Alert*. It's probably a fair assumption, given the data flow shown, that the *Public* and *Home Refuel* use cases, when they are actually implemented, will access the data from some persistent data store, creating a single representation each for the `RefuelEvent` and `Vehicle` involved. That's an implementation detail, though, and could change when the code is actually written. At this point, that detail isn't terribly pertinent; the main concern here is *an awareness of what data is needed by the process as it runs.*

Since this sort of formal documentation is not always a priority for all development efforts, the items discussed here are likely going to be more useful to a software engineer from the perspective of skills to acquire. Learning to think about data structure and -flow *before* any code is written is not difficult, though it may be time-consuming, and may not happen quickly. Getting into the habit of asking questions, or at least thinking through the implications of those questions, is a solid first step going down that path.

Planning for inter-process communication

It's very common for different processes to communicate with each other. At the most basic level, that communication might take the form of something as simple as one function or method calling another from somewhere in the code they share. As processes scale outward, though, especially if they are distributed across separate physical or virtual devices, those communication chains will often get more complex themselves, sometimes even requiring dedicated communication protocols. Similar communication-process complexities can also surface, even in relatively un-complicated systems, if there are inter-process dependencies that need to be accounted for.

In pretty much any scenario where the communication mechanism between two processes is more complicated than something at the level of methods calling other methods, or perhaps a method or process writing data that another process will pick up and run with the next time it's executed, it's worth at least contemplating (if not documenting) how those communications will work. If the basic unit of communication between processes is thought of as a message, then, at a minimum, considering the following will generally provide a solid starting point for writing the code that implements those inter-process communication mechanisms:

- **What the message contains**: The specific data required, expected, and allowed, which may be little more than an elaboration of the concepts presented in *Thinking about data structure and flow*.

- **How the message is formatted**: If the message is serialized in some fashion, converted to JSON, YAML, or XML, for example, that needs to be noted.

- **How the message is transmitted and received**: It could be queued up on a database, transmitted directly over some network protocol, or use a dedicated message-queue system such as RabbitMQ, AWS SQS, or Google Cloud Platform's Publish/Subscribe.

- **What constraints apply to the message protocol**: For example, most message-queuing systems will guarantee the delivery of any given queued message once, but not more than once.

- **How messages are managed on the receiving end**: In some distributed message-queue systems — AWS SQS, for example — the message has to be actively deleted from the queue, lest it be received more than once, and potentially acted upon more than once. Others, such as RabbitMQ, automatically delete messages as they are retrieved. In most other cases, the message only lives as long as it takes to reach its destination and be received.

Inter-process communication diagramming can usually build on data flow diagrams, or on logical architecture and use case diagrams if data flow diagramming was not undertaken. However it is approached, the end goals are the same: to show the flow of messages at the *physical component* level. Pure data flow diagrams are more concerned with the *logical flow* of data and may ignore any *physical architecture* associations. In some cases, a data flow diagram may be sufficient all by itself — this is likely to be the case for applications and services that have a single, monolithic code base, where all the components that send or receive messages live in the same running code space.

There are several options for handling inter-process communication. The monolithic approach, which is essentially functions and methods calling other functions and methods as needed, is one. Another is the creation of services whose sole purpose is to receive and handle messages from other services, whether large-scoped APIs or small, single-purpose microservices. The three approaches that we will examine, each with their own advantages and drawbacks, are as follows:

- A monolithic application, where communication takes the form of functions or object methods (*callables*) calling other functions or object methods
- An API-based approach, where the callables involved have a standard API structure that allows a user request to be accepted and handed off to the core code
- A queue-based, event-driven approach, where the callables act in an event-listener fashion, rather than being explicitly called by other processes

Callables

A **callable**, in this context, may be a function defined in code, or a method of an object defined in code. Python considers *classes* to be callable objects as well, but for the purposes of the current discussion, that variant of a callable definition can be discounted.

The communication process options shown here all live behind a common entry-point that the main process is initiated from a logical component that can be called from an application or web browser from a cell phone or other similar device by a *Fleet Driver* when they refuel a vehicle. There are other common logical components shared between them as well. One is the database that provides the backing data storage for the application. The others are various *Handler* components that execute the actual processes needed by the application. These, the *Refuel Handler* and *Maintenance Handler*, along with any others that might be created as part of the application's overall system, are the code that was written by one or more software engineers.

Each approach described here fulfills the same basic process goal — when a *Fleet Driver* logs that they have refueled a fleet vehicle:

- The data for that effort is collected into a `RefuelingEvent` data structure
- That data structure is sent to the entry-point component
- That component triggers the execution of the *Refuel Handler* code in some fashion, which odes the following:

    - Performs any calculations or data manipulations needed to create a complete `RefuelingEvent` record in the `RefuelingEvents` database table, and writes it to that table
    - Updates the relevant `Vehicle` record in the `Vehicles` table
    - Executes the fuel-efficiency check logic

- If the efficiency check meets the applicable criteria, the *Refuel Handler* code will trigger a process to initiate a maintenance notification; and, finally
- The receipt of a maintenance notification will also trigger a process to a Routing API, which is responsible for handling whatever processes need to be executed to alert routing staff that the vehicle is undergoing maintenance, and is not available for deliveries

Monolithic callables calling callables

The first approach is a monolithic application architecture, containing all of the process-functionality in a single code base, likely running on a single physical device. A monolithic architecture for the refueling application described earlier is shown in *Figure 4.9* diagram:

	Component Type
☑	Activity/use case
⌁	Code
✉	Message
▲	Alert message

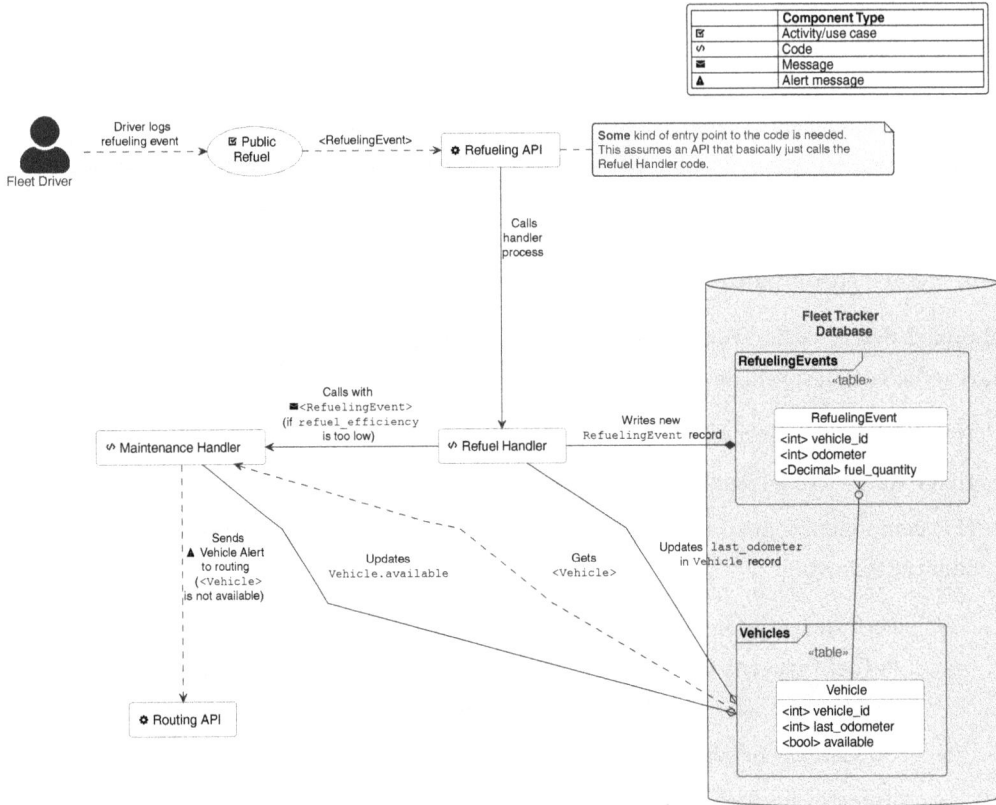

Figure 4.9: Messaging flow in a monolithic application architecture

In this approach, the entry point is an API (the *Refueling API*) that simply calls the *Refuel Handler* code. In turn, that code calls the *Maintenance Handler* code when necessary. The simplest implementation for the *Maintenance Handler* call is for a function in the *Refuel Handler*'s code to call another function in the *Maintenance Handler*'s code.

Monolithic applications and services provide a certain type of efficiency that other approaches frequently lack. Since all of the code lives in the same deployed application or service, communication between components can be very direct — each callable can simply call whatever other callables it needs when required. There is no need for any additional infrastructure to handle those calls, and as a result, there is also no need to worry about creating concrete messages that can live outside the context of those calls themselves.

Monolithic applications tend to be simpler to develop and debug. Since all the code is in one place, tracing a process from start to end is significantly easier than it would be if those processes lived in separate code bases. They are generally also less complicated from a deployment perspective, for similar reasons.

A monolithic structure has several trade-offs that will need to be thought about and accounted for. Perhaps the most significant of these is the potential for an error in the chain of processes leading to a loss of data. For example, if the *Refuel Handler* code in this structure does not take adequate precautions to assure that the RefuelEvent or Vehicle records are well formed before writing them to the database, the process will abort with an error, and some or all of that data could be lost. If that kind of error occurs in a manner that also prevents the *Refuel Handler* from determining that a maintenance notification needs to be sent, it will not be, with still more data loss happening with respect to *those* processes as a result.

Over and above that, if a message that triggers an error is not captured and stored (or at least logged) in some fashion, that message will be lost forever. While recreating lost messages is possible, doing so will be tedious at best, and annoying, particularly if losing messages happens with any frequency.

> **What should happen if the execution fails?**
>
> This question, mentioned in *Chapter 2, Programming versus Software Engineering Revisited*, is *particularly* important to keep in mind in the context of monolithic systems. Well-designed, modern programming languages provide mechanisms for catching errors. Forming habits to leverage those capabilities to *capture* and *handle* errors will save a lot of grief on a long-term basis.

Other trade-offs common to monolithic applications include the following:

- They will tend to be slow to develop, if only because their testing needs to be sufficient to cover the entire code base. In addition, even trivial changes will require the re-deployment of the entire application.
- Their components will tend to be tightly coupled to each other, and that tight coupling will tend to grow over time.

- As a result of this tight coupling, they will need rigorous regression testing. Seemingly unrelated changes may well break something in unexpected ways; the addition of new components, or changes to existing components, may require significant and unexpected changes to other parts of the system.

Monolithic architectures are common for applications that are designed to be run locally by several users. They may still be relatively common as providers of services too, though the growing adoption of cloud-based architectures, and serverless applications in particular, has certainly influenced the popularity of monolithic applications.

APIs calling callables

Using **Application Programming Interfaces (APIs)** is a common pattern, particularly for applications that need to be accessible from the internet. An API is, quite simply, a collection of functions and procedures that allow access to the features and data of an application or service. In the context of an application or service that's accessible over the internet, they typically fall into one of a few common types, with **REpresentational State Transfer (REST)** being one of the more popular options. Other API standards include **Simple Object Access Protocol (SOAP)** and **GraphQL**.

> **Local APIs**
>
> Since an API is, by definition, just a collection of capabilities, the term is also used to describe those kinds of collections that are not accessible over a network — a *local API*. They include installable code packages that are exposed to users through a local, console application.

Regardless of the standard used, the goals of an API are the same: to provide a common, consistent mechanism for accessing the functionality and data of the applications that they expose. APIs that expose functionality over the internet need the messages they accept to be transmissible across a network connection, typically using HTTP and one of several HTTP operations (verbs):

- **POST** to create data
- **GET** to read data
- **PUT** to update data
- **DELETE** to delete data

Collectively, these are commonly referred to as **Create, Read, Update, and Delete (CRUD)** opera-tions. *REST* and *SOAP* APIs may not provide all of these operations but can when the functionality they provide needs those underlying activities to be exposed. GraphQL APIs use POST operations exclusively but provide query, mutation, and subscription processes for retrieving and changing data. An operation that does not change data is a query, operations that change data are mutations, and operations that allow a consumer to wait for the completion of the request are subscriptions.

A REST-format API-backed architecture for the refueling application is shown in the following diagram:

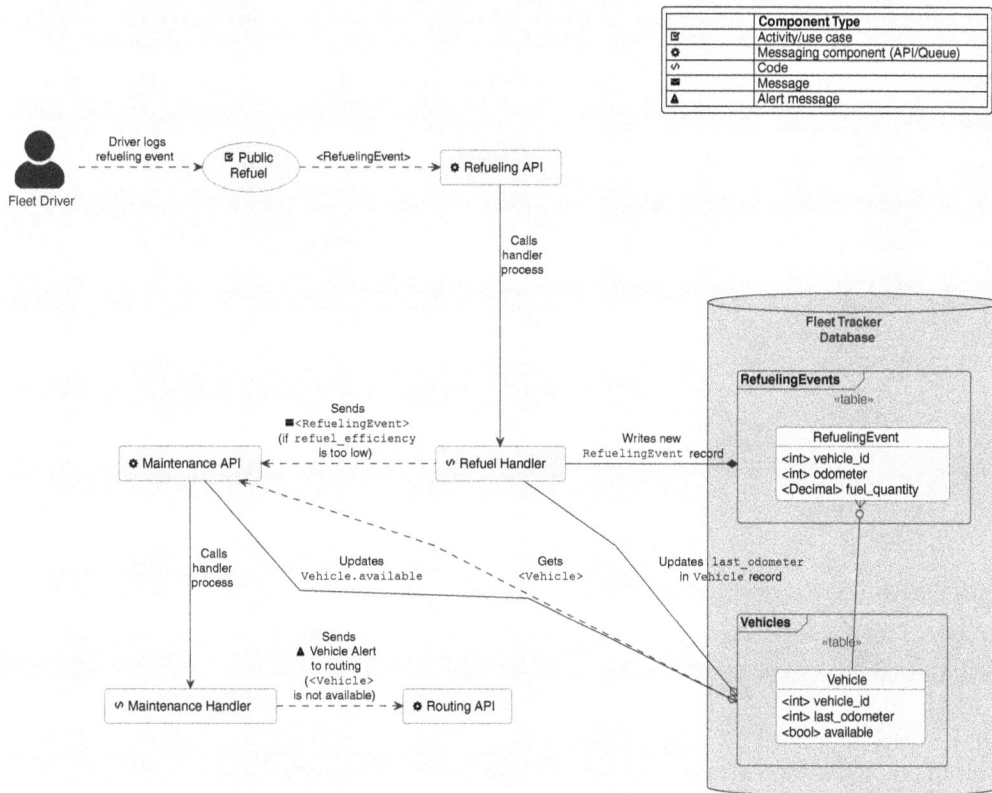

Figure 4.10: Messaging flow in an API-based architecture

The main difference between this architecture and the monolithic variation shown earlier is how it handles the notification process called by the *Refuel Handler* code when the need for a maintenance request is detected. This approach makes a call to a *Maintenance API* that then calls the *Maintenance Handler* functionality, where the monolithic variant *directly* calls the *Maintenance Handler* functionality. This additional API layer allows the request/response process to be wrapped in functionality that accepts a common message format, one that's not tied to any particular programming language or implementation.

Since these APIs accept input from the internet, the common message format needs to be in a format that can be encoded (or serialized) into a text-only representation of the data, sent to the API as part of a request, decoded (or de-serialized) back into native data types and then passed to the code that actually does something with it. The most common format for serializing data is probably **JavaScript Object Notation (JSON)** (https://www.json.org/json-en.html), which is supported across a lot of programming languages. A representation of the data for a `RefuelingEvent` object, for a vehicle with a `vehicle_id` of 12 that had 12.345 gallons of fuel added at a cost of $43.20, and an odometer reading at the time of 12,345, miles would serialize into this JSON (with or without line-breaks and indentation, but presented with both for readability):

```json
{
    "vehicle_id": 12,
    "odometer": 12345,
    "fuel_quantity": "12.345",
    "fuel_cost": "43.20"
}
```

That message would be sent via an HTTP POST request to the API, and from there to the *Refuel Handler* code. If the *Refuel Handler* detected a need for a maintenance notification, that same JSON representation could then be sent to the *Maintenance API*.

The ability of an API to accept well-formed input from any source is a significant advantage of this approach. In this application's structure, there is no *functional* reason why the same *Maintenance API* couldn't accept a maintenance-needed request from a *Fleet Driver*'s device, or from an on-site computer. That would allow users other than a *Fleet Driver* to log maintenance needs. Individual APIs can be much simpler than their equivalent structure in a monolithic application and can be crafted so that they can be deployed independently from each other.

Simpler code for an individual API will generally require less testing, and that testing will also tend to be simpler. Those all assume that each individual API is its own deployable unit — APIs can also be written in a monolithic style, though, separating functionality by different endpoints, often with CRUD operations for specific purposes (refueling versus maintenance, in this example).

The trade-offs for an API-backed architecture include the following:

- Like their monolithic counterparts, API design should pay special attention to capturing and handling errors, for the same basic reasons: if a request fails and the data isn't persisted in some manner, that data will be lost forever
- Observability of API traffic may need to be given serious consideration: APIs that call APIs (which might, in turn, call other APIs, and so on) can make troubleshooting difficult without adequate logging or tools that keep track of those interactions
- Each API may need to be implemented separately, with one API per access point
- Each separate API may have to be accessible at a separate network address, which may require multiple physical servers
- Each separate API may have its own associated physical infrastructure that must be managed

Queue-based event-listener callables

A more recent approach, one that is particularly popular in serverless, cloud-resident applications, is the idea of using a **queue** to capture process inputs. A queue is a mechanism that accepts message inputs and holds on to them until they are retrieved and used by some other process. Depending on the specific queue implementation, those messages may persist until they are actively deleted by the processes that consume them, or they may be deleted by default when they are retrieved by those processes. Queues may or may not be **First In First Out** (**FIFO**), preserving the *sequence* of queued messages.

Queues are the foundation of several event-driven architectural patterns for applications and services. In those implementations, messages accumulate as they are submitted to the queue, and the queue triggers some configured process to read those messages and execute the relevant process, using the message as an input structure.

A queue-backed architecture for the refueling application is shown in the following diagram:

	Component Type
☑	Activity/use case
⚙	Messaging component (API/Queue)
∽	Code
✉	Message
▲	Alert message

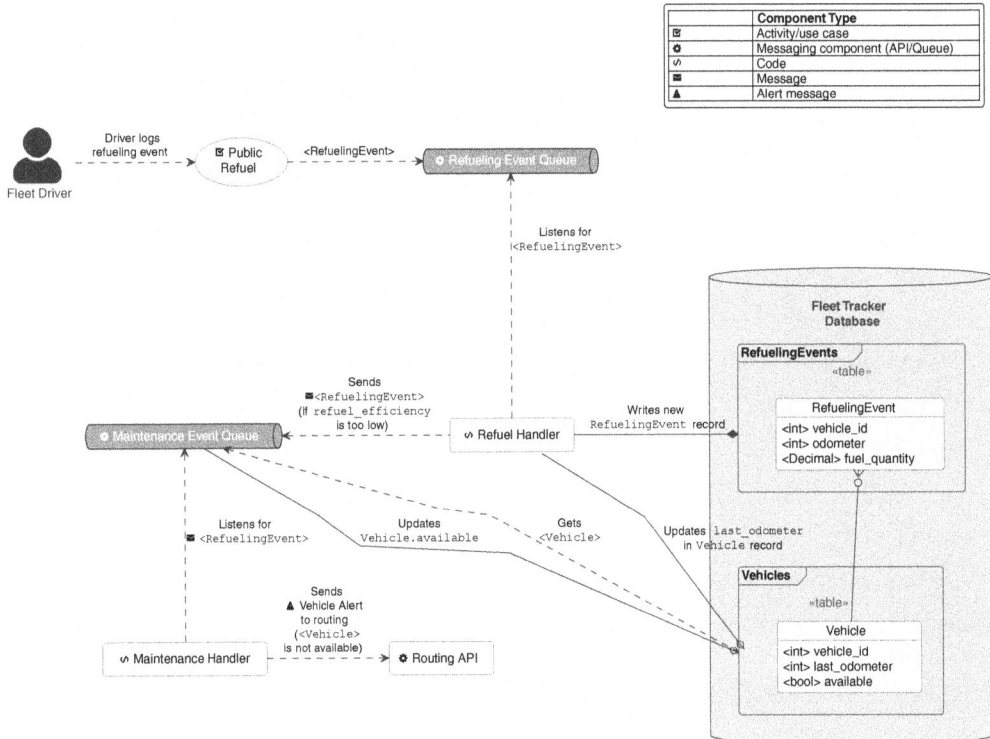

Figure 4.11: Messaging flow in a Queue-based architecture

In this approach, the RefuelingEvent initiated by a *Fleet Driver* is added to the *Refueling Event Queue*, and the *Refuel Handler* code listens for new messages in the queue. When a new message is detected, the *Refuel Handler* process executes, performing the same actions and sub-processes noted earlier, with one critical difference: if a need for a maintenance notification is detected, it sends the original RefuelingEvent data structure to the *Maintenance Event Queue*.

Queue-based applications require some additional infrastructure — the queues themselves — but can provide a significant advantage over their monolithic and API-backed siblings: queues either inherently hold on to messages until they are explicitly removed (even if a process failure occurred), or the processes consuming queue messages can be written to re-insert a failed message into the source queue that it came from. Those possibilities don't *eliminate* the need for capturing and handling errors, but they *do* add a layer of assurance against data loss in cases where errors occur with little to no additional development investment. Because of these traits, queue-based processes tend to scale well, though that scalability may introduce unpredictable and inconsistent process latency as the volume of messages in a queue increases.

The implementation specifics for reading messages from queues vary based on the queue service in play. RabbitMQ and Apache Kafka, for example, rely on a process that actively polls a source queue on a recurring basis, often in an infinite loop, and when a message is received, that loop will call some external function to actually do something with the message. Other queue implementations, such as Apache ActiveMQ, and cloud-resident options such as AWS Simple Queue Service and Google Pub/Sub, either allow configuration of listeners, or configuration that directs messages received by a queue to some other resource, which could be an AWS Lambda Function or a Google Cloud Function.

The main takeaway from a development focus on inter-process communication is how the data identified earlier gets from one point in the system to another.

Putting it all together — system scope and scale

If all of these items are documented and/or diagrammed, if it's done thoroughly and accurately, they will, collectively, provide a holistic view of the total scope of a system:

- Every system component role should be identified in the logical architecture
- Where each of those components actually resides should be identified in the physical architecture
- Every use case (and hopefully every business process) that the system is supposed to implement should be identified in the use case documentation, and any of the underlying processes that aren't painfully obvious should have at least a rough happy-path breakdown
- Every chunk of data that moves from one place or process to another should be identified in the data flow, with enough detail to collate a fairly complete picture of the structure of that data as well
- The formats and protocols that govern how that data moves about, at least for any part of the system that involves more than just passing system objects from one function or method in the code base to another, should be identified
- A fair idea of where and how that data is persisted should be discernible from the logical, and maybe physical, architectures

The only significant missing piece that hasn't been noted is the scale of the system. If the scope is how many types of objects are being worked with or are moving around in the system, the scale would be how many of those objects exist, either at rest (stored in a database, for example) or actively at any given time.

Scale can be hard to anticipate with any accuracy, depending on the context of the system. Systems such as the hypothetical refueling tracker and order-processing/fulfillment/shipping system that have been used for illustration are generally going to be more predictable:

- The number of users is going to be reasonably predictable. All employees and all customers pretty much cover the maximum user base for both of those systems
- The number of objects being used is also going to be reasonably predictable. The delivery company only has so many trucks, after all, and the company running the order system, though probably less predictable, will still have a fair idea of how many orders are in flight at most, and at typical levels

When a system or application enters a user space such as the web, though, there is potential for radical variation, even over very short periods of time. In either case, some sort of planning around the expected and maximum/worst-case scale should be undertaken. That planning may have significant design and implementation effects — fetching and working with a dozen records at a time out of a few hundred or thousand total records doesn't require nearly the attention to efficiency that those same twelve records out of several million or billion would, just as a basic example — on how code might be written. If planning for even potential massive surges in use involves being able to scale out to multiple servers, or load-balance requests, that might also have an effect on the code, though probably at a higher, inter-process communication level.

Summary

All of the components, data, and documentation from this chapter, as well as the previous two chapters, are *potentially* available in any software engineering effort. How much is *actually* available probably depends in part on how much discipline is involved in the pre-development processes, even if there isn't anything formal associated with it. That discipline might only be present because of a singularly talented project or development manager, or a product owner.

With all of the architecture-related artifacts accounted for, in the next chapter, we'll turn our attention to factors that affect how code is written: development methodologies, programming paradigms, and best practices.

5

Methodologies, Paradigms, and Practices

The previous two chapters have been focused on specific questions about a system or project. The first question, from the perspective of a software engineer, is some variation on the theme of *why code is being written* for a given system or project — *what business purposes are being served*, and *who is going to be using it.* Hand in hand with that are questions about *where the code is going to execute* — which plays directly into *how the end users are going to access the functionality it provides* and other, similar facets of the final delivered product.

None of what has been discussed so far addresses a fundamental question that is more significant to the software engineer writing the code: *How is the code going to be written?* That question has at least three major distinctions. One centers around *development methodologies and processes*, what goes on *around* the actual writing of the code. Another is concerned with deciding what the *software architecture* of the code looks like — *how the various code elements interact with each other.* The last question that this chapter will address can be thought of as making decisions about *how the code moves from one state to another* — what needs to happen when it is complete, tested, ready to deploy, and so on. The final question, which will be addressed in detail in *Chapter 6, Revisiting Development Best Practices*, is some variant of what standards are in place that shape how the code itself is written and structured.

In this chapter, we are going to cover the following main topics:

- Process methodologies
- Development paradigms
- Development practices

Technical requirements

The code (what little there is) for this chapter can be found in the GitHub repository for the book, at `https://github.com/PacktPublishing/Hands-On-Software-Engineering-with-Python-Second-Edition/blob/main/CH05-code/`. All of it is expected to run under Python 3.10 or later (it was written with the default Python version for Linux Mint — 3.10.12). Installers for Python can be found at `https://www.python.org/downloads/` for Windows, Linux/UNIX, and macOS.

Process methodologies

It could be argued that software engineering, at least as it is usually thought of now, really came into being with what is widely considered to be the first formally identified software development methodology. That methodology (which was eventually dubbed **Waterfall** in 1976) made people start thinking about not just how the software worked, or how to write the code, but what the processes around writing the code needed to look like to make it more effective. Since then, several other methodologies have come into being, and in at least one case, the collection of various Agile methodologies, there are several distinct sub-variants, though **Scrum** is certainly the most widely known. **Kanban**, a Lean methodology derivative, may be a close second.

At some level, all development process methodologies are variations on the theme of managing development within the boundaries of some common realities that apply to software development teams:

- There are only so many useful working hours per person per day that can be devoted to a project
- There is a limit to the available resources, whether in terms of people, equipment, or money, available to a project
- There is a minimum acceptable quality standard for the project when it is complete

There are two specific development process methodologies worth an in-depth examination in this book's context. A third, Waterfall, will be summarized to provide a frame of reference for the other two: the Scrum and Kanban methodologies. A full discussion of them is well beyond the scope of this book, but the intention is to provide enough detail on each of them to illustrate what their focuses and priorities are, as well as their advantages and drawbacks. At a minimum, this should provide a baseline of what to expect while working any of them. An effort will also be made to tie the phases of each methodology back to the phases of the model SDLC from *Chapter 4, System Modeling*, to show what happens, when, and how.

Waterfall

The **Waterfall** process is a very rigid linear project-management process. In projects following a Waterfall methodology, each step or phase of the project is planned out in significant detail, with requirements for each phase thought out, documented, and ready for a software engineer to pick up and work on. Typically, the high-level phases of a project follow this sequence:

1. **Requirements**
2. **Design**
3. **Implementation**
4. **Verification**
5. **Maintenance**

The **Requirements** and **Design** phases in Waterfall include the activities in the pre-development phases of the SLDC discussed in *Chapter 3, The Software Development Life Cycle*. In a perfect Waterfall plan, every feature, and every potential point of concern that a software engineer would need to be aware of, would be accounted for before a single line of code was written. The **Requirements** phase would account for resource expectations, including the allocation of those resources to specific tasks, the details of those tasks, and the sequence that they would be executed in. As a result, a final timeline for the project could be planned.

During the **Design** phase of the plan, a project schedule and milestones would be defined. The milestones would include exact deliverables at each point in the project schedule. To accomplish those, detailed component-level designs, and more specific, component-level requirements would be defined.

The **Implementation** phase would focus on getting the code written. If there is any preparatory data to be gathered, research to be undertaken, or specific implementation planning that needs to happen prior to the actual construction of the code, this phase is where it would happen. Since this phase is also the first opportunity for the design to be put into practice, it is also the first point in the process where design flaws can truly be proven, or categorically demonstrated as being impossible to implement. If the latter occurs, the process will need to go back to the *Design* phase, at least, to address that scenario.

During the *Verification* phase, the results of executing the code written during the *Implementation* phase are compared with the *Requirements* (and possibly *Design*) phase's expectations. If everything behaves as expected, the code is deployed in some fashion so that it can be used and goes into *Maintenance* mode. If issues surface, the code goes back to the engineers for further *Implementation* work.

Although the specific phases of a Waterfall project are scattered about somewhat in the structure of the SDLC examined previously, they do at least map on a one-to-one basis with elements of that SDLC. Waterfall is an easily understood methodology: Each step is a logical next step from the one that precedes it and builds on the results of that predecessor.

Because it is such a linear process, and because there are such tight dependencies between steps, Waterfall is a very inflexible methodology, and prone to significant delays if some aspect of an earlier step is misunderstood or needs to change while development is underway. Since mid-stream changes are quite common in an imperfect world, and Waterfall simply cannot keep up with them as they occur, it is not, realistically, a viable methodology. These considerations led to the formation of the **Agile** and **Lean** families of development methodologies.

Agile (in general)

By the early 1990s, a sea change was under way in how development processes were viewed. The Waterfall process, despite widespread adoption, started to show more of the flaws inherent to its application to large and complex systems. Other, non-Waterfall methodologies that were in use were also starting to show signs of wear from being too heavy, too prone to counter-productive micro-management, and a variety of other complaints and concerns.

As a result, a lot of thought around development processes started focusing on lightweight, iterative, and less management-intensive approaches that eventually coalesced around the **Agile Manifesto** and the twelve principles that underlie it.

The Agile Manifesto

We are uncovering better ways of developing software by doing it and helping others do it. Through this work, we have come to value:

- Individuals and interactions over processes and tools
- Working software over comprehensive documentation
- Customer collaboration over contract negotiation
- Responding to change over following a plan
- That is, while there is value in the items on the right, we value the items on the left more.
- You may refer to *The Agile Manifesto* at http://agilemanifesto.org/ for more details.

The following are the principles stated in the Manifesto:

- Our highest priority is to satisfy the customer through early and continuous delivery of valuable software.

- Welcome changing requirements, even late in development. Agile processes harness change for the customer's competitive advantage.

- Deliver working software frequently, from a couple of weeks to a couple of months, with a preference for the shorter timescale.

- Business people and developers must work together daily throughout the project.

- Build projects around motivated individuals. Give them the environment and support they need, and trust them to get the job done.

- The most efficient and effective method of conveying information to and within a development team is face-to-face conversation.

Working software is the primary measure of progress

- Agile processes promote sustainable development. Sponsors, developers, and users should be able to maintain a constant pace indefinitely.

- Continuous attention to technical excellence and good design enhances agility.

- Simplicity — the art of maximizing the amount of work not done — is essential.

- The best architectures, requirements, and designs emerge from self-organizing teams.

- At regular intervals, the team reflects on how to become more effective, then tunes and adjusts its behavior accordingly.

In an application, these principles lead to a few common characteristics across different methodologies. There may be exceptions in other methodologies that are still considered Agile, but for our purposes, and with respect to the specific methodologies discussed here, those common traits are as follows:

- Development happens in a sequence of iterations, each of which has one-to-many goals
- Each goal is a subset of the final
- At the conclusion of each iteration, the system is deployable and operational (if only for a given value of operational)

- Requirements are defined in detail in small chunks and may not be defined at all until just before the iteration that they are going to be worked on

Scrum is claimed to be the most popular, or at least the most widely used, Agile development methodology (the 2023 Annual State of Agile Report puts it at somewhere near 70% of Agile methods in use), and as such is worth some more detailed attention.

Kanban is another Agile methodology, though it is not as popular as Scrum (perhaps 10% of Agile methodologies in use, according to the same report). Although there are other Agile methodologies in use in the industry, none of them have even the adoption market share of Kanban, let alone Scrum.

Businesses are also exploring additions and modifications to textbook Agile processes to improve them to meet specific organizational needs that were not encompassed by the original concept.

It is also worth noting that there is at least one methodology that is recognized as being Agile, but that predates the Agile Manifesto by roughly five years: **eXtreme Programming (XP)**. XP introduced several ideas that are still considered to be good practices, and that may be incorporated into non-XP methodologies.

Scrum

Scrum has the following moving parts, broadly:

- The Scrum methodology centers around time-limited iterations called Sprints:
    - A **Sprint** is defined as taking some fixed length of time that the development team (and sometimes stakeholders) can agree upon.
    - Sprint durations are usually the same duration each time, but that duration can be changed, either temporarily or permanently (until the next time it is changed) if there is reason to do so.
    - Each Sprint has a set of features/functionality associated with it that the development team has committed to completing by the end of the Sprint.
- Each feature/functionality item is described by a user story — a short, simple description of a development goal, which may or may not be a complete feature, but is a deliverable and verifiable unit of work.
- The team determines what user stories they can commit to completing, given the duration of the Sprint.
- The priority of user stories is determined by a stakeholder (usually a Product Owner) but can be negotiated.

- The team gathers periodically to groom the backlog, which can include:

  - Estimating the size of stories that do not have one
  - Adding task-level detail to user stories
  - Subdividing stories into smaller, more manageable chunks if there are functional dependencies or size-related execution concerns, and getting those approved by the relevant stakeholder(s)

- The team reviews the Sprint at the end, looking for things that went well, or for ways to improve on things that went less than well.

- The team meets periodically to plan the next Sprint.

- The team has a short, daily meeting (a stand-up), the purpose of which is to reveal what status has changed since the last update. The best-known format, though not the only one for these meetings, is a quick statement from each participant on:

  - What they have worked on since the last stand-up, complete or otherwise
  - What they are planning to work on until the next stand-up
  - What roadblocks they are dealing with that someone else in the team might be able to assist with

Story sizing should not be based on any sort of time estimate. Doing so tends to discount any assessments of complexity and risk that might be critically important and implies an expectation that all developers will be able to complete the same story in the same length of time, which may not be realistic. Use story points or t-shirt sizes (extra small, small, medium, large, extra-large, and extra-extra-large) instead!

From beginning to end, a typical Sprint will unfold something like this, assuming all goes well:

- **Day 1 Sprint start-up activities**:

  Stories and tasks are set up on the task board, whether it is real or virtual, all in a **Not Started** status, in priority order.

  Team members claim a story to work on, starting with the highest priority item. If more than one person is working on a single story, they each claim one of the tasks associated with it. Claimed stories are moved to an **In Progress** status on the task board.

- **Day 1 — N (day before the end of Sprint):** Development and QA
- **Daily stand-up meeting:** (probably skipped on the first day)

- **Development**:

    As tasks are completed, their status is updated on the task board to indicate as much.

    As stories are completed, they are moved to the next status on the task board after development. This column might be **Dev-Complete**, **QA-Ready**, or whatever other status description makes sense given the team's structure.

    If roadblocks are encountered, they are brought to the attention of the **Scrum Master**, who is responsible for facilitating and resolving the blocking issue. If it cannot be resolved immediately, the status of the blocked story or task should be updated on the task board, and the developer moves on to the next task or story that they can tackle.

    As roadblocks get resolved, the items they were blocking re-enter development status, and progress as normal from that point on. There is nothing to say that the developer who encountered the block initially must be the one to continue work on the item after the block is resolved.

- **Quality assurance activities:**

    If QA staff are embedded into the development team, their processes are often like development activities, except that they will start by claiming a story to test from whichever column indicates **Dev-Complete** items.

    Testing a story should verify its acceptance criteria at a minimum.

    Testing may well (and probably should) include *functional tests* that are not part of the acceptance criteria.

- **Story acceptance:** If there are any stories completed that haven't been accepted, they can be demonstrated and accepted or declined by the relevant stakeholder(s). Declined items will go back to the **In Development** or **Not Started** status, depending on why they were declined, and what can be done to resolve the reason for being declined.

- **Sprint-close day:**

    Demonstration and acceptance of any remaining stories.

If time has not been available to do so before, preparation for the next Sprint should take place:

- **Sprint planning:** To prepare the user stories for the next Sprint
- **Backlog grooming:** To prepare and define details and tasks for any user stories that need those details

Acceptance of remaining stories

- **Retrospective meeting**: The team gathers to identify the following:

    - What worked well in the Sprint, to try and leverage what made it work well

    - What worked poorly, or not at all, to avoid similar scenarios in the future

All the daily activities orbit around a task board, which provides a quick mechanism for easily seeing what is in progress, and what the status of each item is:

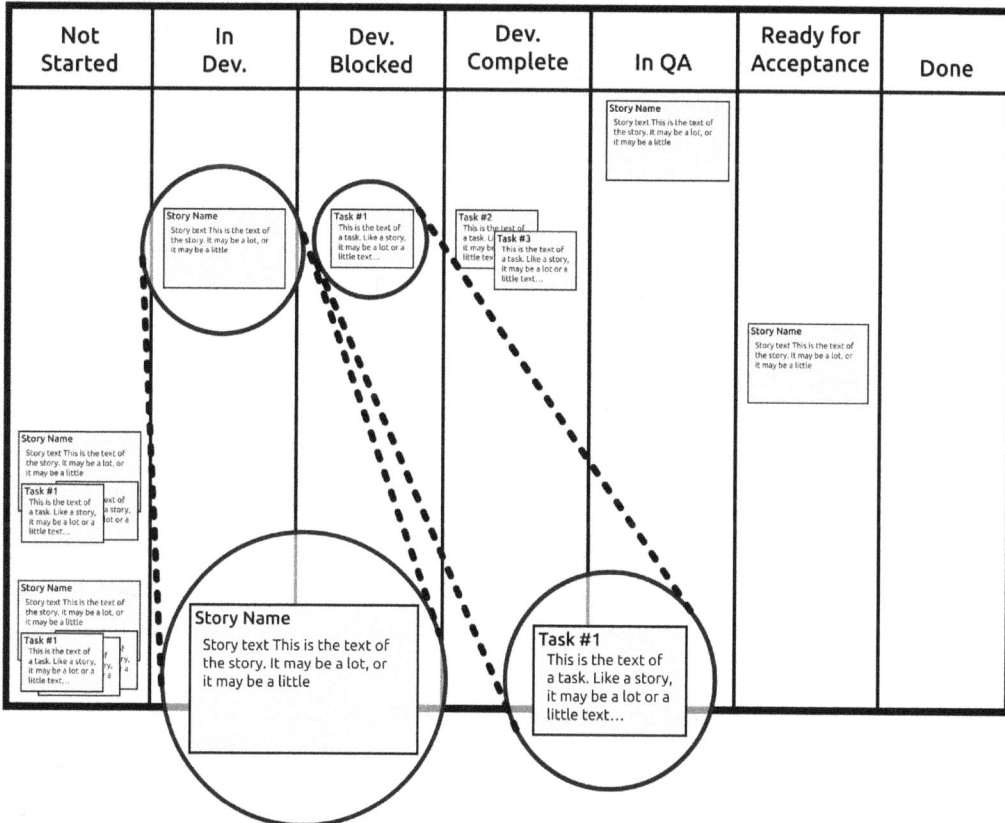

Figure 5.1: An example task board for a Scrum team, showing stories and tasks in various stages of development

The task board shown in *Figure 5.1* has more detailed status columns than are technically required — the bare-minimum column set would be **Stories**, where the top-level stories' details live until they are done, **Not Started**, and **In Progress** for tasks that are part of the Sprint, and **Done**, where tasks (and possibly stories) land when they are complete, tested, and ready for acceptance.

Scrum's priorities are its focus on transparency, inspection, and self-correction, and its adaptability to changing needs and requirements. The task board is a significant part of the transparency aspect of the methodology, allowing anyone with any interest to see immediately what the status of development efforts is. But it does not end there — there is a role known as the **Product Owner**, who acts as the central communications point between the development team and all the stakeholders of the system. They attend the daily stand-ups to have near-real-time visibility into progress, roadblocks, and so on, and are expected to speak for and make decisions on behalf of the entire collection of stakeholders. They are also responsible for connecting team members with external stakeholders if questions or concerns arise that the Product Owner cannot address themselves. Their role is critical in assuring a good balance between providing transparency into ongoing development efforts to the stakeholders and not burdening the development team with ongoing status reporting.

Scrum expects a fair amount of self-inspection in the process itself, and encourages a similar inspection of the results of the process — the software being created, and the practices and disciplines used in creating it — by prioritizing team openness and member intercommunication, providing a mechanism for raising visibility into risks and blocking conditions, and even, to some degree, by encouraging user stories that entail the smallest amount of effort to achieve a given functional goal. When concerns or issues arise, the emphasis on immediate communication and the ready availability of someone who can provide direction and make decisions resolve those issues quickly, and with a minimal degree of interference with the ongoing development process.

Scrum is one of the better methodologies from an adaptability-to-change perspective. Imagine a situation where a development team has been working on parts of a project for the first week of a two-week (or longer) Sprint. At that point, someone at the stakeholder level suddenly decides that a change needs to be made to one of the stories. There are several reasons — good, bad, or indifferent — for that sort of change to be necessary.

Perhaps the functionality that underlies the story is deemed obsolete, and no longer needed at all — if the story has not been completed, then it can simply be removed from the Sprint, and another story from the backlog pulled in to be worked on, if one is available that is no larger than the one being removed. If there's already code written against the story, it may need to be removed, but that is about it in terms of impact on the code base. If the story is complete, then the related code also gets removed, but no new work (additional stories) gets pulled in.

If the story is changed — the functionality behind it is altered to better fit user needs or expectations, for example — the story gets withdrawn from the current Sprint in the same fashion as if it were being removed, at the very least.

If there is time available to re-scope the story and re-insert it into the Sprint, that can be undertaken, otherwise it will be added to the backlog, at or near the top of the list from a priority perspective.

On occasion, it is possible for a Sprint to derail, but the methodology has expectations around how that gets handled as well. If a Sprint cannot be completed successfully for any reason, it is supposed to stop, and a new Sprint is planned to pick up from where that one ended.

Pros of Scrum

Some advantageous aspects of Scrum include:

- Scrum is well-suited to work that can be broken down into small, quick efforts. Even in large-scale systems, if additions to or alterations of the large code base can be described in short, low-effort stories, Scrum is a good process to apply.

- Scrum works well for teams that have consistent skill sets within their domains. That is, if all developers on a team can, for example, write code in the main language of the project without significant assistance, that is a better team dynamic than if only one out of six team members can.

Cons of Scrum

At the same time, because of the structure involved in a Scrum process, there are some caveats:

- Since a Sprint represents a commitment to complete a set of stories and functionality, changing an in-process Sprint, even with a good reason, is troublesome, time-consuming, and disruptive. That implies, then, that whoever is in the position of making decisions that could require in-process Sprint changes needs to be aware of the potential impacts of those decisions — ideally, they would avoid Sprint-disruptive changes without *really* good reasons.

- Scrum may not lend itself well to meeting project- or system-level deadlines until or unless the team has a fair amount of expertise across the entire domain of the system and its code base. Iteration deadlines are at less risk, though they may require altered or reduced scope to deliver working software on an iteration-by-iteration basis.

- Development efforts and outputs become less predictable if the team members change — every new team member, especially if they join the team at different times, will have some impact on the team's ability to be predictable until the new team roster has had time to settle in. Scrum can be particularly sensitive to these changes since new team members may not have all the necessary tribal knowledge to meet an iteration's commitments for a while.

- Scrum may not work well — perhaps not at all — if the members of a team are not all in the same physical area. With modern teleconferencing, holding the daily stand-up is still possible, as are the other varied meetings, but Scrum is intended to be collaborative, so easier direct access to other team members tends to become important quickly as soon as questions or issues arise.

- Unless it's pretty carefully managed not to, Scrum tends to reinforce skill-set silos in a team — if only one developer knows, for example, how to write code in a secondary language that the system needs, that person will be tapped more frequently or by default for any tasks or stories that need that knowledge in order to meet the iteration's commitments. Making a conscious effort to turn silo-reinforcing stories or tasks into a team or paired development effort can go a long way toward reducing these effects, but if no efforts are made, or if there is no support for reducing these silos, they will persist.

Scrum may be challenging if the system has a lot of external dependencies (work from other teams, for example), or a lot of quality control effort that developers must contend with. This last item can be particularly problematic if those quality control requirements have legal or regulatory requirements associated with them. Assuring that external dependencies are themselves more predictable can go a long way to mitigate these kinds of challenges, but that may be out of the team's control.

Scrum and the phases of the SDLC model

The phases of the SDLC model from *Chapter 3, The Software Development Life Cycle* that are important to the development effort happening during specific parts of a Scrum process are as follows:

- Before development starts:

  - **Requirements** analysis and definition happens during the story creation and grooming portions of the process, often with some follow-up during Sprint planning. The goal is for each story's requirements to be known and available before the story is included in a Sprint.

  - System architecture and design items follow much the same pattern, though it's possible for a story in an iteration to have architecture and/or design tasks too.

- The development process itself:

  - **Development**, obviously, happens during the Sprint.

  - **Quality assurance** activities also happen as part of the Sprint, being applied to each story as it is deemed complete by the developers. If testing activities reveal issues, the story would go back to an **In-Development** status, or an earlier status, on the task board, and would be picked up and corrected as soon as possible.

  - **System integration and testing** will likely happen during the Sprint too, assuming an environment is available to execute these activities with the new code.

  - **Acceptance** can happen on a story-by-story basis as each story makes its way through all the QA and system integration and testing activities, or it can happen all at once at an end-of-Sprint demo-and-acceptance meeting.

It is not hard to see why Scrum is popular — from a developer's perspective, with disciplined planning and devoting care and attention to making sure that the developers' time is respected and realistically allocated, their day-to-day concerns reduce to whatever they are working on at the moment. Given a mature team, who have a consistent skill set and a good working knowledge of the system and its code base, Scrum will be predictable from a business perspective. Finally, Scrum, if managed with care and discipline, is self-correcting — as issues or concerns arise, with the process, *or* with the system and code base, the *process* will provide mechanisms for addressing and correcting those items.

Kanban

Kanban, as a process, has a lot of similarities to Scrum, despite a different primary focus: reducing the burden on development teams, allowing them to focus on productivity and efficiency. These derive from underlying Lean principles — providing value through optimization of resources, and promotion of a steady workflow. These similarities include:

- The main unit of effort is a work item that may be roughly equivalent to the user story in Scrum.

- Work items have similar progressive status states as they are worked to their completion, to the point where the same sort of task board, real or virtual, is used to track and provide visibility into work in progress.

- Work items should have all of their requirements and other relevant information ready and waiting before work on them commences. That implies that there is some sort of story grooming process, though it may not be as formally structured as the equivalent in Scrum.

Kanban differs from Scrum in several ways:

- Work items, while they may be time-boxed individually, or sized so that they all represent roughly the same amount of work, are not expected to be completed in a scheduled interval (the Sprint in Scrum).

- There is no expectation or requirement for the daily status/stand-up meeting, though it is a useful enough tool that it is commonly adopted. Other variants and approaches, focusing first on blocked items, then concerns on in-progress items, then anything else, are also viable.

- Kanban does not expect or require that work items be sized, though again it is a useful enough tool and is not uncommon, especially if it is a useful criterion for prioritizing stories for development.

Kanban's primary focus might be described as an effort to minimize **context changes**, which plays out as working on single stories until they are complete before moving on to the next. This frequently results in prioritization of functionality by need, which lends itself well to situations where there are functional dependencies between stories.

What is a context change?

Context changes (or context switching) happen when work on a task is stopped to pick up work on another, different task. Context changes frequently add time to efforts: They require cognitive effort to set aside the task being deferred, more such effort to get into an appropriate mindset for the task being picked up, working on the new task, then more effort again to re-acquire the mindset for the deferred task and resume work on it. If the tasks in question are complex enough that notes or other reminders need to be written, that adds still more time.

That working-until-complete focus may well occur in a Scrum process as well, but it's not actually *expected*: The goal in Scrum is to complete all stories during a Sprint, and assistance from others on the team to complete a story may well be necessary at any point to accomplish that goal.

Kanban's entire process is quite simple:

- Work items (and their tasks) are made ready and prioritized for work.

- An engineer selects a story, and works on it until it is complete, then repeats the process with another story, and another, and so on.

- While development and work against current stories is underway, new stories are made ready and added to the stack of available work as details become available and prioritized accordingly.

Pros of Kanban

Kanban, with different policies and procedures than Scrum, offers different advantages:

- Kanban is well-suited to efforts where there are significant silos of knowledge or expertise, since it's focused on completion of functionality, no matter how long it might take.

- Kanban handles stories and functionality that are both large and not easily divisible into smaller logical or functional chunks, without having to go through the process of subdividing them into Sprint-sized chunks. There are potential trade-offs to this, noted in the caveats below.

- Kanban limits **Work In Progress** directly, which reduces the likelihood of overworking developers, provided that the flow of the work is planned correctly and well.

- Kanban allows the addition of new work by stakeholders at any point in time, and with any priority, though interruption of in-progress work is still best avoided.

- Provided that each story is independent and deliverable, each completed story is ready for installation or implementation as soon as it has been accepted.

> **Work In Progress and WIP limits**
>
> Participants in a Kanban team would be well advised to set a personal **Work In Progress (WIP)** limit, and to avoid taking on more work if they are already at that limit. Similarly, having a team-level WIP limit is useful. The goal for both is to avoid overloading the team, or its members, by reducing the potential for more tasks to be in progress than the team can manage well.

Cons of Kanban

It also has its own set of caveats:

- Kanban can be more prone to bottlenecks in development, particularly if there are large-scale or long-duration dependencies for subsequent stories — an example might be a data storage system that takes three weeks to complete — that is, there is a dependency for a number of small class structures that need it, which could be implemented in a few days if the data storage system were complete.

- Since it does not really provide any concrete milestones at a higher level than individual stories, Kanban requires more direct and conscious effort to establish those milestones if they are needed for external business reasons.

- More conscious thought and effort are typically needed for functionality that is being developed in phases in a Kanban process for it to be efficient — any functionality that has must-have, should-have, and nice-to-have capabilities that are all going to be implemented, for example, needs to provide some awareness of, and guidance on future phase goals from the beginning to remain efficient.

- Kanban does not require that the team be aware of the design underlying the work, which can lead to misunderstandings or development efforts at cross-purposes. Making a conscious effort to de-silo design and raise overall awareness of the larger-scale requirements may be needed, and it may not be apparent that it is needed at first.

There are observations that software teams that use Kanban often have lower-quality results, increases in technical debt, and poorer relationships with customers. Whether these observations relate to teams that use the methodology without any adaptations or customizations is not clear.

> **My own experience with Scrum and Kanban**
>
> Whether because I've simply never been in a position where the concerns about Kanban have surfaced, or for some other reason that I cannot identify, I cannot say that I agree or disagree with these observations. Over the course of seven Scrum-or-Kanban scenarios, across three different organizations, and five different positions, my experience has been that Kanban, or some recognizable derivative of it, has been more successful four times out of those seven. The only potential common denominator I can think of across those successful uses of either Scrum or Kanban was the methodology meshing better with preferred or existing development preferences across the teams involved.

Kanban and the phases of the SDLC model

Many Agile processes, especially those that use stories as a basic unit of effort or work, have a lot of similarities. Since most story-related items have been described in some detail in discussing Scrum, only the points of variation between Scrum and Kanban will be called out:

- **Before development starts: Requirement** analysis and definition, and system architecture and design, work in much the same way as they do in Scrum, for many of the same reasons. The primary difference is that there is a less formal structure expected in Kanban to accomplish the attachment of requirements and architecture details to stories. These are typically undertaken when there's time and/or a perceived need, such as the development team being close to running out of workable stories.

- **The development process itself: Development** and **Quality Assurance** processes are part of the flow of a given story as it is being worked on to completion. System integration, testing, and acceptance must happen during a story's life cycle since there is not an end-of-Sprint meeting to demonstrate development results and acquire acceptance.

With a less formal structure, fewer process rituals, and a readily understandable just-in-time approach to its process, Kanban is easily understood, and easily managed. Some additional care at key points, and the ability to identify those key points, helps in keeping things moving smoothly and well, but if the ability to recognize and address those key points improves over time, so too will the process.

Development paradigms

While the process methodologies discussed earlier were growing and maturing, the increase in computing power also led, eventually, to newer, more useful, or more efficient development paradigms. **Object-Oriented Programming (OOP)** and **Functional Programming (FP)** are the most well-known advances from the original **Procedural Programming** paradigm that dominated the software development scene for decades. That dominance was often shaped by the limitations of hardware and the higher-level languages that were available at the time for simple procedural code. A program, in that paradigm, was a sequence of steps, executed from beginning to end. Some languages supported subroutines and even simple function-definition capabilities, and there were ways to, for example, loop through sections of the code so that a program could continue execution until some termination condition was reached, but it was, by and large, a collection of very brute-force, start-to-finish processes.

As the capabilities of the underlying hardware improved over time, more sophisticated capabilities started to become more readily available — formal functions as they are thought of now, more efficient use of hardware resources, and better flow control options, for example. However, outside a few languages that were accessible only inside the halls and walls of academia, there were few significant changes to that procedural approach in mainstream efforts until the 1990s, when OOP first started to emerge as a significant or even dominant paradigm.

A Procedural Programming implementation

To provide points of comparison, consider a program that needs to perform the following:

- Ask the user for a URL of a web page to retrieve and store
- Check to see if the user is done with the program and exit if they are
- Retrieve the specified page from the URL provided
- Store the retrieved page data in a local, constant file system location.
- Start the entire process over

An example of this process, written in Python in a purely procedural programming fashion, can be found in the GitHub repository accompanying the book. This will be used as a point of comparison against code written in an Object-Oriented fashion, and again with a Functional Programming approach. When run, the resulting output (using the URL for Google as the input) is:

```
Simple procedural code example
Please enter a URL to read, or "X" to cancel: https://www.google.com
Page-data written to /tmp/www.google.com.data
Please enter a URL to read, or "X" to cancel: x
Exiting. Thanks!
```

The code in this example runs from the start of the file to the end, with a loop that handles the process for prompting the user for a URL, or to exit the program. That same loop is used in the object-oriented and functional implementation examples, and the output is virtually identical across them. The significant differences between these examples are in how the main program processes are written.

An Object-Oriented implementation

The distinctive feature of **Object-Oriented Programming (OOP)** is (no great surprise) that it represents data and provides functionality through **instances** of objects. **Objects** are structures of data, or collections of attributes or properties, that may have related functionality (methods) attached to them. Objects are constructed as needed from a **class** that defines the properties and methods that, between them, define what an object *is*, or *has*, and *what an object can do*. An OOP approach allows programming challenges to be handled in a significantly different, and usually more useful, manner than the equivalents in a procedural approach, because those object instances keep track of their own data.

An object-oriented implementation example of the same process noted above can be found in the book's GitHub repository. Although it behaves in *exactly* the same manner as the procedural example, and there are some similarities between the two, how it executes is significantly different:

- There is still a loop that asks the user to input a URL to read, and it still lives in the main execution branch of the code, but it is explicitly only called when the module is run directly (with python `object-oriented-program-example.py` or something equivalent).

- The process for reading the content from the URL lives in a **method** of a PageReader class — `get_page_data`. An instance of the PageReader class is created in each pass through the main loop of the program, and the method of that instance is called during the initialization of each object.

- The data read is stored as an **attribute** of the instance, page_data, which keeps it available to that instance for as long as it exists.

- The process for writing the instance's page_data lives in another method, save_page_data, that is responsible for handling all that process.

- As each pass through the main loop of the program executes:

    - The user is prompted for the URL.

    - If the input indicates that the user wants to end the program, it does so.

    - Otherwise, an instance of the PageReader class is created, passing the URL supplied

    - Then, the instance's save_page_data method is called to save the instance's page_data.

The output from this program, except for the initial title, is identical to the procedural example shown above:

```
Object-oriented code example
Please enter a URL to read, or "X" to cancel: https://www.google.com
Page-data written to /tmp/www.google.com.data
Please enter a URL to read, or "X" to cancel: x
Exiting. Thanks!
```

OOP, as a development paradigm, tends to lead to more modular code, which in turn tends to make both code reuse and troubleshooting easier. It also tends to promote other good code-authoring practices: Since classes can inherit members from other classes, it is easy to define a single method in a single class, then inherit that method in other classes where it is needed, for example. It also typically reinforces thinking of processes in terms of what a given type of thing (a class) can do (methods), and what data is available (properties or attributes).

An FP implementation

FP is a development approach centered around the concept of passing control through a series of pure functions and avoiding shared state and mutable data structures. That is, most functionality in FP is wrapped in functions that will always return the same output for any given input without modifying any external variables. Technically, a pure function should not write data to anywhere — neither logging to a console or file, nor writing to a file — and how the need for that sort of output is accommodated is a discussion well outside the scope of this book.

An FP implementation example of the same process noted above can be found in the GitHub repository accompanying the book. This code, like the previous OOP example, behaves in exactly the same fashion as the original procedural code shown before that. Internally, the processes executed are, again, significantly different:

- The main program calls a function — get_page_to_process — that prompts the user for a URL and ends the program if one is not supplied
- If a URL was supplied, another function is called — process_page — with the supplied URL
- That function calls two other functions: get_local_file_path, which constructs the file path that the data will be stored at, and get_page_data, which is responsible for retrieving the specified page from the URL provided
- The results returned from those functions are passed to yet another function — save_page_data — that writes the data to the appropriate file location

Again, this code performs the exact same function, and it does so with the same discrete steps/processes as the previous two examples. It does so, however, without having to store any of the various data it is using — there are no mutable data elements in the process itself, only in the initial input to the process_page function, and even then, it is not usefully mutable for very long. The main function, process_page, also does not use any mutable values, just the results of other function calls. All the component functions return *something*, even if it's only a None value.

The output from this program, except for the initial title, is identical to the output of the previous examples:

```
Functional Programming code example
Please enter a URL to read, or "X" to cancel: https://www.google.com
Page-data written to /tmp/www.google.com.data
Please enter a URL to read, or "X" to cancel: x
Exiting. Thanks!
```

FP is not a new paradigm, but it did not become widely accepted until relatively recently. It has the potential to be as fundamentally disruptive as OOP was. It is also different, in many respects, so that making a transition to it might well be difficult — it relies on different approaches, and on a stateless basis that is very atypical in or of other modern development paradigms. That stateless nature, though, and the fact that it enforces a rigid sequence of events during execution, have the potential to make FP-based code and processes much more stable than their OOP or procedural counterparts.

Python, though it is an object-oriented language, still allows the creation of free-standing functions. It also does not *require* that functions be created. As a result, Python code can be written as procedural code, using object-oriented structures and paradigms, or using FP paradigms. It is even possible to write code that mixes all three of those paradigms. Procedural code is more likely to appear in simple scripts, initiated by a user or some automated process, that execute some very sequential process. That does not mean that procedural code cannot use functions or objects, just that it is not as likely to. Object-oriented and functional-programming code is more likely to appear in more complex applications than simple procedural code is typically used for.

The methodologies and development paradigms discussed so far can be thought of as wrappers around the processes of writing code, or at least of planning, at a high level, how that code will be written. There are others that focus on what happens with code after it has been written.

Post-development practices

The post-development practices that software engineers are most likely to be participants in are focused on what happens with code, once it is complete — specifically, how the final code is tested, built, packaged, and distributed. Those are most likely to be Continuous Integration and Continuous Delivery or Continuous Deployment.

Continuous Integration

Continuous Integration (**CI**) is a repeatable, automated process for merging new or altered code into a common, shared environment, either on some sort of timed basis or because of some event such as committing changes to a source control system.

Its primary goal is to try and detect potential integration problems as early in the code promotion or deployment process as possible so that any issues that arise can be resolved before they are deployed to a live, production branch. Implementing a CI process, regardless of any specific tools that might be used to control or manage it, has a few prerequisites:

- Code needs to be maintained in a version control system of some sort, and there should be, ideally, one and only one branch that a *final* CI process will execute against.

- The build process should be automated, whether it fires off on a predetermined schedule, or because of a commit to the version control system.

- As part of that build process, all automated test suites should execute. Unit test suites, in particular, should execute and pass, but any integration or system tests that can be usefully executed should at least be considered for inclusion.

When those tests fire off may vary, based on team policies and procedures, functional requirements, or other constraints specific to a given project. There are at least two common strategies, and they both have their advantages:

- Tests executed before the commit and build are complete, if the tools and processes can either prevent a commit or build outright, or roll a commit back to its last good state on a test failure, will prevent code that fails its tests from being committed. The trade-off in this scenario is that it is possible that conflicting changes from two or more code change sources might be significantly tangled and need correspondingly significant attention to remedy. Additionally, if the offending code cannot be committed, that may make it difficult to hand off the offending code to a different developer who might well be able to solve the issue quickly.

- Tests that execute after a build will allow code that has failed one or more tests to be committed to the collective code base, but with known issues at a minimum. Depending on the shape and scope of those issues, it might well break the build — and that can be disruptive to the whole team's productivity.

Other common goals and considerations for a CI process include:

- Some sort of notification process needs to be in place to alert developers that there is an issue — particularly if the issue resulted in a broken build.
- The process needs to ensure that every commit is tested, and builds successfully.
- The results of a successful build need to be made available in some fashion — whether through some sort of scripted or automated deployment to a specific testing environment, making an installer for the new build available for download, or whatever other mechanism best suits the product's, team's, or stakeholders' needs.

With these in place, the rest of the process is just a case of working out some of the process rules and expectations and implementing, monitoring, and adjusting them when/if needed:

- When should commits happen? Daily? At the end of the development of a story, feature, or whatever unit of work might apply?
- How quickly does the commit-test-build process need to run? What steps can be taken, if any, to keep it quick enough to be useful?

The end goal of a CI process is to automate a process that provides confidence that the code considered to be production-ready is, in fact, ready to be deployed. That deployment process could be manual, but if the CI process is fully automated, the next logical step is to automate the next step as a Continuous Delivery or Continuous Deployment process.

Continuous Delivery (or Deployment)

Continuous Delivery or **Continuous Deployment** (CD) are natural extensions of the CI process, taking each successful build, collecting all of the components involved, and either deploying it directly (typically for web and cloud-resident applications and systems) or taking whatever steps would be necessary to make the new build available for deployment — creating a final, end user or production-ready installation package, for example — but *not* actually deploying it.

A complete CD process will allow for the creation, update, or recreation of a production system based solely on information in a source control system. It also likely involves some configuration management and release management tools on the system administration side, and those may well impose specific requirements, functionally or architecturally, or both, on a system's design and implementation.

Summary

These last several chapters have hopefully given you at least a glimpse into all the moving parts outside the writing of code in development efforts that are useful to be aware of as a software engineer. The odds are good that any given team or company will have selected which methodology, and what pre- and post-development processes are going to be in play. Even so, knowing what to expect from them, or what might be causes for concern while working within their various combined contexts, is useful information, and often one of the expectations that divide programmers from software engineers. Each chapter has gotten a bit closer to the actual process of writing code, but without regard to the language involved. The last step, then, before digging into actual code, is to examine the expectations at the code level, including general best practices and best practices that are tied to the development language itself.

6

Code Style and Related Standards

The previous chapter's topics could be loosely grouped as relating to the processes around how writing code is *managed*. In this chapter, we will dig down to a deeper level, discussing practices that shape *what may or will appear in the actual written code itself*: what standards apply to code, why they are relevant or useful, and what factors are involved in the decisions about using or setting aside those standards. Standards that apply to how code is written can be further subdivided by whether they impact how the code executes — **functional standards** — or only impact the readability of the code — **non-functional standards**. This chapter will explore the non-functional standards. The functional standards will be covered in the next chapter. The majority of non-functional standards fall into the following categories:

- Style standards for code — in particular, the community standards set out by the Python maintainers

- Documentation standards — which also include standards around comments in code

The standards chosen provide answers to a single common question that can be phrased as follows:

> *If I were a new member of a development team, tasked with working with this code to add a new feature, optimize its current functionality, or fix a bug in it, what should be in the code itself that I would need to know to make that effort successful?*

Although there is one outlier that has a functional impact, noted in the *Indentation and related formatting* section, these standards focus on how easy it is to *read* and *understand* a given chunk of code.

In this chapter, we are going to cover the following main topics:

- Style standards for code
- Documenting code
- Commenting code

Technical requirements

The code presented in this chapter focuses on providing examples of code and documentation style. Unless specifically noted otherwise, it will run without raising any errors, but will not do anything more than that. All of it is compatible with any Python 3.x environment.

The code can be found at the following GitHub link:

`https://github.com/PacktPublishing/Hands-On-Software-Engineering-with-Python-Second-Edition/`

Style standards for code

Code standards are nothing more than a set of expectations about how code is written, documented, tested, and delivered. When those expectations are adhered to, they lend consistency to the codebase, making it easier for engineers to collaborate, whether working with the existing code, adding new functionality to it, or dealing with a bug within it.

The first of these standards we will examine centers around how code is formatted or styled, and the conventions available and expected in a Python context. For the most part, those are ensconced in a **Python Enhancement Proposal** (**PEP**) that dates back to 2001: PEP 8, the *Style Guide for Python Code*.

PEP 8 standards

Python's official style guide can be found in the **PEP 8** documentation, `https://peps.python.org/pep-0008/`. It currently reflects the original *Style Guide* essay by Guido van Rossum, with additions from a style guide by Barry Warsaw. One of the first and **most important** things that it notes is the following:

A style guide is about consistency. Consistency with this style guide is important. Consistency within a project is more important. Consistency within one module or function is the most important.

However, know when to be inconsistent – sometimes style guide recommendations just aren't applicable. When in doubt, use your best judgment. Look at other examples and decide what looks best. And don't hesitate to ask!

In particular: do not break backwards compatibility just to comply with this PEP!

PEP 8 quotations

The format above will be used to indicate direct quotations from the PEP 8 documentation.

None of the PEP 8 items summarized here should be considered as hard guidelines, then. Code will still run, in many cases, if written without adhering to them. There are reasons and rationales behind them, though, that should be considered before setting them aside, which will be discussed later. The guideline items that are most likely to arise will be summarized and discussed here. The PEP 8 items are particularly significant if there is a need or desire to **lint** code, as they provide the baseline rules for that linting process.

What is code linting?

Code linting (sometimes referred to simply as linting) is an automated process that checks source code for style errors. More advanced linters will also check for certain types of programmatic errors. When a linter is run against a piece of code, it will typically report errors, and terminate with an error condition that can be used to halt an automated build process.

Linters are programs that examine code, checking for various defects. The specific types of defects that they can identify depend on the linter chosen, but the better linters will, at a minimum, look for logical errors as well as stylistic deviations. Among the more common options for linting Python code are the following:

- pycodestyle (formerly pep8): See https://pypi.org/project/pycodestyle/. Checks for deviations from some (but not all) style conventions documented in the PEP 8 Style Guide.

- pylint: See https://pypi.org/project/pylint/. Checks for PEP 8 style deviations, can check for variable name conventions, and has a sizable list of errors that it can identify (see https://pylint.readthedocs.io/en/latest/user_guide/checkers/features.html for a complete list).

- flake8: See https://pypi.org/project/flake8/. Wraps the pycodestyle linter, the PyFlakes linter (roughly equivalent to pylint), and supports checking McCabe code complexity (the number of independent linear paths that can be taken through a body of code).

- pylama: See https://pypi.org/project/pylama/. A full-blown code-auditing tool, combining pycodestyle, the pydocstyle documentation checker, PyFlakes, pylint, and other tools.

The PEP 8 Style Guide covers a lot of ground with respect to what the official standards for Python code are. Of those, there are three that are most likely to be of interest: indentation and related formatting, blank lines in code, and naming conventions. Those are most likely to be noteworthy because they have functional or readability implications for code that can be significant.

Indentation and related formatting

Use four spaces per indentation level.

Spaces are the preferred indentation method.

Tabs should be used solely to remain consistent with code that is already indented with tabs.

Python disallows mixing tabs and spaces for indentation.

Python's syntax uses indentation to indicate logical blocks of code, so indentation is a key item to keep consistent wherever possible. Most code editors that recognize Python will default to this 4-space indentation. It's possible to mix indentation levels, or even mix indentation characters within a module, provided that those indentation levels and characters stay consistent within the body of a function or class. By way of example, these three functions can coexist in a single module:

```python
def space_indented_function_1():
    ... # This is indented with four spaces

def space_indented_function_2():
      ... # This is indented with six spaces

def tab_indented_function():
    ... # This is indented with a single tab
```

However, this function will raise an error when the module it lives in is executed:

```python
def mixed_indented_function():
    ...   # This is indented with a single tab
    ...   # This is indented with four spaces
```

Which raises:

```
File ".../indentation_consistency_example.py", line 12
    ...   # This is indented with four spaces
                    ^
IndentationError: unindent does not match any outer
indentation level
```

The reasoning behind this guideline is ambiguous, but ties back to a fundamental principle behind the design of Python's syntax, also noted on the PEP 8 page (https://peps.python.org/pep-0008/#a-foolish-consistency-is-the-hobgoblin-of-little-minds):

> *One of Guido's key insights is that code is read much more often than it is written. The guidelines provided here are intended to improve the readability of code and make it consistent across the wide spectrum of Python code. As PEP 20 says, "Readability counts".*

Code editor tab settings matter

In a code editor, the difference between the two indented lines may not be apparent, depending on whether tabs have a width equivalent to four spaces. Many code editors have settings that will display spaces and tabs — If you encounter an error like the one shown above, turning that setting on will help with identifying those differences. Indentation errors can surface if the same standard isn't applied by multiple developers working with the same code, even if they are using the same code editor but have different indentation settings.

Limit all lines to a maximum of 79 characters.

For flowing long blocks of text with fewer structural restrictions (docstrings or comments), the line length should be limited to 72 characters.

The rationale for these guidelines is straightforward enough, as noted in the page:

The default wrapping in most tools disrupts the visual structure of the code, making it more difficult to understand. The limits are chosen to avoid wrapping in editors with the window width set to 80, even if the tool places a marker glyph in the final column when wrapping lines. Some web based tools may not offer dynamic line wrapping at all.

This restriction does not really account for newer code editors that can easily accommodate line lengths of greater than 80 characters. That is also accounted for, as follows:

Some teams strongly prefer a longer line length. For code maintained exclusively or primarily by a team that can reach agreement on this issue, it is okay to increase the line length limit up to 99 characters, provided that comments and docstrings are still wrapped at 72 characters.

The limitation of 72 characters for **docstrings** (Python's documentation strings) is presumably a concession to the built-in `help` function `https://docs.python.org/3.11/library/functions.html#help`), which will print the docstring for a named function, method, or class. The `help_function_example.py` module in the book's accompanying GitHub repository, for example, will call the `help` function, showing the name and signature of the function, along with its docstring, as shown in the following *Figure 6.1*.

File Edit View Search Terminal Help

```
Help on function example_function in module __main__:

example_function(str_arg: str, int_arg: int, float_arg: float, bool_arg: bool,
list_arg: list[typing.Any], dict_arg: dict[str, typing.Any], *args: int | float,
**kwargs: Any) -> None
    An example function.

    Parameters:
    -----------
    str_arg : str
        A string value that is used for something.
    int_arg : int
        An integer value that is used for something.
    float_arg : float
        A floating-point value that is used for something.
    bool_arg : bool
        A boolean value that indicates something.
    list_arg : list[Any]
        A list of things.
    dict_arg : dict[str, Any]
        A dictionary of things
:
```

Figure 6.1: The output of the help function from the help_function_example.py module

Since `help` is intended to be used in an interactive session — within a terminal — and that terminal is expected to have an 80-character width, limiting the length of a docstring line, which will always be indented at least four spaces, or eight for a method of a class, ensures that the docstring can be formatted to fit that expected 80-character width.

Because Python is sensitive to indentation, line breaks become important, particularly for functions that have large enough sets of parameters to run past the 80-character break-point (or even the 99-character one noted earlier). That potential is even more likely when annotation is applied. Annotation will be discussed in more detail later in the next chapter, but a simple example function to illustrate the concern and to show the options for handling it is presented in *Figure 6.2*, the code for which is in the `function_indentation_examples.py` module in the repository.

```
 1    from typing import Any
 2
 3  ⊟def example_function_1(str_arg: str, int_arg: int, float_arg: float, bool_arg:
 4  └     ...
 5
 6  ⊟def example_function_2(str_arg: str, int_arg: int, float_arg: float,
 7  ┌                       bool_arg: bool, list_arg: list[Any],
 8  │                       dict_arg: dict[str, Any], *args: int | float,
 9  └                       **kwargs: Any):
10  └     ...
11
12  ⊟def example_function_3(
13  │       str_arg: str, int_arg: int, float_arg: float,
14  │       bool_arg: bool, list_arg: list[Any], dict_arg: dict[str, Any],
15  └       *args: int | float,
16          **kwargs: Any
17  ⊟):
18  │       ...
```

Figure 6.2: Indentation examples for a function with a long parameter list – the red line at the right indicates the 72nd-character position

In the actual code, the line for example_function_1 extends past 160 characters — well past even the longer 99-character line limit suggested above. The PEP 8 page suggests the indentation style used in defining example_function_2, breaking the parameter list up as each parameter crosses the 72-character boundary. The format used for example_function_3 is also a valid variation, grouping the parameters into the same number of lines, but with an indentation level that is closer to the indentation level of the function of the first line of the definition.

Indentation in this book's code

Much of the code in this book will use an indentation approach closer to the one used for example_function_3 shown previously simply because of space constraints on the printed page. I personally like to have individual function parameters on separate lines. I find that easier to read, and it also makes adding, re-ordering, and removing them easier, which I find I have to do with some frequency during early development.

The PEP 8 standards also cover similar indentation concerns outside the context of function parameters. They generally follow the same patterns where there is a wrapping set of parentheses, braces, or brackets. When there isn't such a wrapper, a backslash (\) followed by a new line and one or two indentation levels will handle those cases.

Line breaks and indentation should happen before any operator character (+, -, *, /, and so on), when needed inside the body of a function, method, or other code-process block.

Blank lines in code

Surround top-level function and class definitions with two blank lines.

Method definitions inside a class are surrounded by a single blank line.

Extra blank lines may be used (sparingly) to separate groups of related functions. Blank lines may be omitted between a bunch of related one-liners (e.g. a set of dummy implementations).

Use blank lines in functions, sparingly, to indicate logical sections.

These are all recommendations to improve the readability of code. They have no *functional* impact whatsoever. Note that a line that is just a comment is *not* a blank line, and will contribute to the raising of linting errors, even if it has blank lines before or after them.

Naming conventions

The naming conventions of Python's library are a bit of a mess, so we'll never get this completely consistent – nevertheless, here are the currently recommended naming standards. New modules and packages (including third party frameworks) should be written to these standards, but where an existing library has a different style, internal consistency is preferred.

Naming violations will not be caught by linters

Given the note above, from the PEP 8 standards, it should come as no great surprise that violations of the naming conventions listed here will not raise errors during code linting. There are, perhaps, too many variations to keep track of, several of which are in very mature third-party packages, where changing them would lead to significant breaking changes.

Officially, the naming convention standards are as follows:

- Package, module, function, method, and local variable names should be in lower case, and if there are multiple words, separate those words with an underscore. Examples: `people` (a package), `person_models.py` (a module), `get_person()` (a function or method), and `given_name`, and `age` (variables).

- Class and type names should be in *CapWord* format (sometimes called *PascalCase*). Examples: `Person`, `PersonHome`. User-defined `Exception` elements, as classes, should follow the same convention, *and* be suffixed with `Error` or `Warning` if the exception is an error or warning. Examples: `PersonError`, `BadNameWarning`.

- Global variables that are *not* intended to be used as constants should follow the same conventions as local variables. Global variables that *are* intended to be treated as constants should be named using an all-caps format, with underscores between words when applicable. Examples: `SCOPE`, `GIVEN_NAME_FORMAT`. Environment variables, values that originate from the operating system that the code is running under, are a special case of global variables, and should follow the same conventions, but may be outside the control of the developer.

Constants... aren't

Python does not really support a formal constant the way some other languages do: any name can have a new value assigned to it at run time. The naming convention for these nominal constants is intended to provide a hint that the value behind the name should not be modified, and that doing so may break things in unexpected ways.

In the main, these guidelines are intended to promote code readability. Except for the indentation guidelines, there is little to no functional impact if one or more of them is violated in code. There may be good reasons to adopt standards that explicitly violate some or all of these conventions, which will be examined later in the *What to keep, change, or set aside* section.

Other PEP 8 items

The PEP 8 document makes other recommendations that may not be relevant from a code linting perspective. These include discussion of the following:

- string quoting conventions (use of single- versus double-quote characters);
- whitespace in expressions and statements

- when to use trailing commas
- formatting for block and inline comments
- other naming-convention recommendations
- programming recommendations, including some thoughts on annotations, which will be discussed in greater detail later in this chapter

As with the main conventions called out earlier, there are few functional impacts that would result from violating these. As noted earlier, one of the key tenets of the PEP 8 style guide is that *consistency with the style guide is important. Consistency within a project is more important. Consistency within one module or function is the most important.*

What to keep, change, or set aside

Determining what (if any) standards to apply to code, whether across all code that a team manages, or on a project-by-project basis, is another example of asking questions and making conscious decisions based on their answers. The idea of having a single, consistent set of code styles across an entire team, at least as a default set of standards, goes a long way toward reducing ambiguity and providing a common set of expectations around what code looks like. If some minority number of projects need to break away from those team-level standards, that can be handled by little more than noting those exceptions in the documentation for those projects.

The questions involved in making decisions to break away from PEP 8's conventions are usually few and have simple evaluation criteria behind them.

- Are we going to lint our code?
  - If so, will a linting failure terminate a build process?
  - What linting errors are we prepared to ignore?
- What are the indentation (and related) standards our code will follow?
- What naming conventions are already in play that we would be well served to follow?

Deciding to lint code has benefits. First, it will provide feedback with respect to coding style and standards. It may also catch inefficiencies and even errors in the code being linted if the tool used supports that. If linting is automated as part of a pre-commit process to a source repository, or before executing a build or packaging process, it can also prevent code that does not adhere to the standards, or that bears errors, from making its way into that repository, a production package, or application.

The pycodestyle and flake8 tools noted earlier can both be configured or executed with sets of specific linting errors to ignore. This means that if there are team or project standards that diverge from the PEP 8 standards they are concerned with by default, it is a trivial effort to allow those divergences to pass without error. There are several mechanisms that can be used to ignore specific errors:

- In the code itself, appending an inline comment with the error code that the line raises during linting will ignore that line. For example, appending # noqa: E501

- to the example_function_1 line shown earlier will ignore the *line too long* error linting would raise on that line.

- Errors to ignore, as well as other run-time settings, can be specified on the command line — see the respective documentation for the tools for specific details.

- A setup.cfg or tox.ini file can be created for the project, and the errors to be ignored listed there:

    - For pycodestyle, the file must contain a [pycodestyle] configuration-heading

    - The errors to ignore are specified as a comma-delimited list of codes, for example:

    - ignore = E501,E502

- The configuration for flake8 follows a similar pattern but may also live in a dedicated .flake8 file instead of setup.cfg or tox.ini. The directive in that file to ignore specific errors is extend-ignore, rather than the ignore that pycodestyle uses, but it behaves the same, for example: extend-ignore = E501,E502

Installation of pycodestyle and/or flake8

Both pycodestyle and flake8 are standard Python packages, and can be installed using pip, with

```
pip install pycodestyle
```

or

```
pip install flake8
```

respectively.

An example configuration file, setup.cfg, is provided in the repository for the chapter that provides basic settings with the following standards expectations:

- The team agrees that all project code will be linted, either before allowing a source-control commit to complete, or as part of a build process. In either case, the operation will be terminated if any linting errors are raised.

- The team agrees that flake8 will be their standard linting tool, but that settings for pycodestyle will be maintained in case there is something that it provides that flake8 does not.

- The team agrees that a maximum line length of 95 characters is what they will commit to — this line length is slightly longer than the standard, allowing for longer function names, chains of methods, and other code patterns that they use with some frequency. It also fits nicely in all their development-environment windows, without requiring a large-width monitor.

- The team agrees that the redefinition of names (error code F811) is allowed to pass because those redefinitions occur as part of common inline testing that is executed on modules while they are being written.

This configuration file, then, allows flake8 or pycodestyle alike to be run against a project module (or an entire project). Running those two linting tools against the function_indentation_examples.py module shown earlier yields the following outputs, for flake8:

```
flake8 CH06-code/function_indentation_examples.py
CH06-code/function_indentation_examples.py:4:96:
    E501 line too long (167 > 95 characters)
1   E501 line too long (167 > 95 characters)
```

and for pycodestyle:

```
pycodestyle CH06-code/function_indentation_examples.py
CH06-code/function_indentation_examples.py:96:
    E501 line too long (167 > 95 characters)
1   E501 line too long (167 > 95 characters)
```

Success! Both tools identify the same too-long line, where example_function_1 was defined.

Error-code details and documentation

The list of error-codes that pycodestyle pays attention to can be found in its documentation at https://pycodestyle.pycqa.org/en/latest/intro.html#error-codes. Similarly, flake8 provides a list of errors that can be found at https://flake8.pycqa.org/en/latest/user/error-codes.html.

By understanding what the standard code-style expectations are, and how to override them with various linting tools, defining and enforcing at least some code-style standards becomes a straightforward process. The drivers for those decisions may be a mix of functional and development-environment criteria — the ignored F811 error code and the line-length setting, respectively. Taken together, and with linting enforced by some automated process, at least part of the initial question posed is addressed concerning what stylistic standards are in play.

Style standards focus on what the code *looks like*, in order to provide common structural expectations that, in turn, make it easier for someone new to the code to read through it and identify significant sections of the code. These standards are *not* concerned with the content of the code, or any description of what the code does, how it does it, or why. A significant portion of *those* expectations will be covered in the next chapter, *Internal Standards*, from a more functionally-oriented viewpoint that a developer would need when working with the code itself. Describing what the code does, what its expectations are when called, and maybe how and why it does it for a more casual user of the code — someone who is importing the code as a package, for example — is a function of code *documentation*.

Documenting code

Before deciding how, when, and where to document code, there is another question that needs to be considered: what purpose (or purposes) does code documentation serve? The initial *If I were a new member of the team...* question that this chapter started with reflects one of several possible purposes being served by documentation: Making sure that team members have enough information to do their job without having to track down answers elsewhere. A similar variant might be phrased as follows:

> *If I were a developer using this code for the very first time, is there enough information available that I can use it with a minimum of time spent understanding what I need to do?*

The difference between these is, ultimately, a difference in expectations of who will be using the code, and what shape that use takes. The team-member will have direct access to the code in question, and the information available therein. The external developer will also have access to that code, but that access may not be as easy to work with, depending on how and where the code in question is installed, though they should have access to the help function mentioned in the *Indentation and related formatting* section earlier, and could, thus, retrieve the docstring of any code-element.

It follows, then, that the docstrings of callables are the logical, lowest common denominator for *when* and *where* to document code. Docstrings are available as properties of the code elements that they are associated with and could be extracted as part of an external documentation process as well. There is at least one package that leverages this capability to render external documentation in a variety of formats: Sphinx (https://www.sphinx-doc.org/), though it requires specific elements in the docstrings, and a fair amount of setup to generate the final documentation documents.

The *how* portion of the question is, at this point, only partly answered — putting information into the docstrings of code elements is the *mechanism*, but there is also the implied question of *what should be put in them*. Though there is not an official standard, there is a fair degree of consensus as to what content should be present:

- A brief description of the element being documented, typically what it does
- Optionally, a summary of the element
- Input, output, and error information, if the callable is a function or method:
    - Parameters, by name, often including their expected types, and perhaps a description of their meaning or purpose
    - What it returns, which is frequently little more than a return-type specification, but may also include a brief summary of what that return-value *is*
    - Any errors or other side-effects that can or will occur when executing the callable
    - Any restrictions on when the callable can be called

There are several popular docstring formats in use across packages available in the public Python Package Index (https://pypi.org).

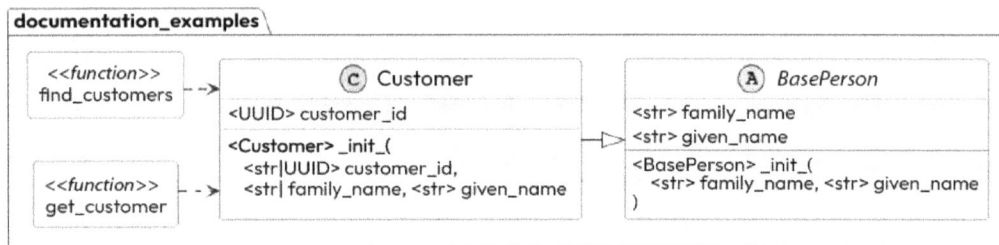

Figure 6.3: The class diagram for the documentation examples

Detailed examples of each are available in the chapter repository for this book; all variations of the structure are shown in *Figure 6.3*. A brief summary of each is presented here as well, showing the documentation for the Customer class and its __init__ method.

A basic format

The **basic format** is plain text covering all documentation items noted earlier:

```python
# From docstrings_example_basic.py
class Customer(BasePerson):
    """

    Represents a Customer in the system.
    """

    def __init__(
        self, customer_id, given_name, family_name
    ):
        """
        Initializes a Customer instance.
        customer_id : UUID | str
            The unique identifier of the customer to
            store in the instance's state.
            Will be converted to a UUID value if one
            is not provided.
        given_name : str | None
            The given_name value to store in the
            instance's state.
        family_name : str | None
            The family_name value to store in the
            instance's state.
        Raises a TypeError or ValueError if customer_id
```

```
                    is not a UUID, and cannot be converted to one.
                    """

            ...
```

The main advantage to sticking with a basic text docstring format is that it does not expect any special formatting. The trade-off is that it will never be anything more than what it is written as — a plain text docstring — which may be sufficient for in-code documentation, and will work with Python's built-in help function, as already demonstrated. If there is a need for external documentation, something that is published to a website for a package, for example, that will either require manual effort to translate (and to maintain as changes are made), or it will be rendered there in a plain text format.

The Epytext format

The **Epytext format** provides mechanisms for identifying parameters of functions and methods, including their expected type and their return type. These specifications, when evaluated with the epydoc command-line tool (https://pypi.org/project/epydoc/), were intended to generate nicely formatted HTML documentation, as well as PDFs using LaTeX.

That tool, the most recent release of which was in 2008, has not been updated to run under Python 3, so the *pretty* output capabilities may not be available. Since the basic formatting differences, originally based on JavaDoc standards, may still be in use, it is worth showing the format. The primary difference between this format and the basic text format is the inclusion of @param and @type tags, as shown in the following example:

```python
# From docstrings_example_epytext.py
class Customer(BasePerson):
    """

    Represents a Customer in the system.
    """

    def __init__(
        self, customer_id, given_name, family_name
    ):
        """

        Initializes a Customer instance.
        @param customer_id: The unique identifier value
            for the customer to store in the instance's
            state.
        @type customer_id: UUID or str
```

```
@param given_name: The given_name value to store
    in the instance's state.
@type given_name: str
@param family_name: The family_name value to store
    in the instance's state.
@type family_name: str
@return: the Customer instance
@rtype: Customer
Raises a TypeError or ValueError if customer_id is
not a UUID, and cannot be converted to one.
"""

...
```

The Epytext format also provided some additional document structuring capabilities in its own markup language, and recognized reStructuredText, allowing for a fair degree of flexibility that can still be useful for complex documentation needs. The format is not difficult to read, though some care needs to be taken to preserve its readability, and it may require some time and practice to get used to its vagaries.

The reStructuredText format

The **reStructuredText (reST) format** was designed to be, in its own words:

> *an easy-to-read, what-you-see-is-what-you-get plaintext markup syntax and parser system.*

Like the Epytext format, it is a plain-text format, with support for text styling, headers, and lists of various types. It also supports preformatted text, useful for code examples, and has at least limited support for images. More detailed information about the content standards can be found in the primer at `https://docutils.sourceforge.io/docs/user/rst/quickstart.html`. reST has been proposed and accepted as a documentation standard in PEP 287 (`https://peps.python.org/pep-0287/`), though that document stresses that it was

> *...proposed as **a** standard, not **the** only standard.*

It has good, solid support, with automatic generation of documentation starting-point content in at least one popular IDE (JetBrains' **PyCharm** — https://www.jetbrains.com/pycharm/), and is the base format used to generate documentation by at least one significant utility in that space (Sphinx — https://www.sphinx-doc.org — which drives much of the documentation available at https://readthedocs.com).

reST uses a tagging syntax similar to the one noted for the Epytext format, with specific tags for parameter and type specifications. This example also shows the use of a bold text style to call out a note about the customer_id parameter:

```python
# From docstrings_example_reST.py
class Customer(BasePerson):
    """
    Represents a Customer in the system.
    """
    def __init__(
        self, customer_id, given_name, family_name
    ):
        """
        Initializes a Customer instance.
        :param customer_id: The unique identifier of
            the customer to store in the instance's
            state.
            **Will be converted to a UUID value if
            one is not provided.**
        :type customer_id: UUID | str
        :param str given_name: The given_name value to
            store in the instance's state.
        :param family_name: The family_name value to store
            in the instance's state.
        :type family_name: str
        Raises a TypeError or ValueError if customer_id
        is not a UUID, and cannot be converted to one.
        """

        ...
```

The reST format allows a fair amount of flexibility for documentation that is intended to be output elsewhere, while maintaining a reasonably readable format in the code itself. Some of the formatting takes a bit of getting used to, but none of that is difficult, particularly if there's already familiarity with similar styling in formats such as Markdown.

The Google format

The **Google format** stresses readability in the code, using indentation to delineate sections within the documentation structure. It also supports inline annotations, though if those annotations are provided, there is no requirement that they are also present in the docstring itself. It also supports reST markup. There is a reasonably standard set of sections that may be present, depending on the context of the documentation:

```python
# From docstrings_example_google.py
class Customer(BasePerson):
    """
    Represents a Customer in the system.
    """

    def __init__(
        self, customer_id, given_name, family_name
    ):
        """
        Initializes a Customer instance.
        Args:
            customer_id (UUID|str): The unique
                identifier of the customer to store
                in the instance's state.
                **Will be converted to a UUID value
                if one is not provided.**

            given_name (str|None): The given_name value to
                store in the instance's state.
            family_name (str|None): The family_name value
                to store in the instance's state.
        Returns:
            An instance of Customer, populated with the
            supplied data-points
        Raises:
```

```
        TypeError: if customer_id is not a UUID or str.
        ValueError: if customer_id is not a UUID, or
            is a str but cannot be converted to a UUID.
    """
    . . .
```

The Google format combines the structural flexibility of the basic text format with the ability to perform at least the basic styling of a docstring for external documentation output purposes. Like the reST format, styling characters may take some getting used to, though, again, that is not likely to be difficult if they are used at all. The type-specification expectations may also take some getting used to, but are cleaner, in many respects, than the corresponding expectations of earlier formats, where there is frequently a separate line needed to specify types.

The Numpydoc format

The **Numpydoc format** extends the Google format, with slightly different handling of sections and parameters. It also advocates for a specific and fairly detailed sequence of sections within a docstring:

- **Short summary**: A one-line summary that does not use variable names or the function name.

- **Deprecation warning (if applicable)**: An indication that the element being documented is being deprecated, including when that deprecation started, when it is expected to be removed, why it was deprecated, and the recommended new way of using the same functionality.

- **Extended summary (if needed)**: A few sentences, providing an extended description.

- **Parameters (if needed)**: A description of the arguments and keywords of a function or method. Type specification may not be needed if the element is annotated but should be as precise as possible when there is a need for them.

- **Returns (if needed)**: What the element returns when called. Note that *Returns* and *Yields* sections are mutually exclusive.

- **Yields (if needed, generator callables only)**: What the element yields when called.

- **Receives (if needed, generator callables only)**: An explanation of parameters passed to the send() method of the generator being documented.

- **Other parameters (if needed)**: Descriptions of infrequently used parameters, intended to be used to document large numbers of keyword parameters, to avoid cluttering the main *Parameters* section.

- **Raises (if needed)**: Details what errors are raised by a callable, and under what circumstances.

- **Warns (if needed)**: Details what warnings are raised by a callable, and under what circumstances.

- **Warnings (if needed)**: Any additional warnings that a user of the function needs to be aware of.

- **See Also (if needed)**: Any references to related code that are expected to be useful or meaningful to the reader.

- **Notes (if desired)**: Any other additional information that might be useful or meaningful to the reader.

- **References (if desired)**: Links to any source materials used in the *Notes* section.

- **Examples (if desired)**: Examples for using the code, which may be checked with the built-in doctest module (`https://docs.python.org/3/library/doctest.html`).

An example of this docstring format, with the variations from previous examples highlighted, is:

```python
# From docstrings_example_numpydoc.py
class Customer(BasePerson):
    """
    Represents a Customer in the system.
    """

    def __init__(
        self, customer_id, given_name, family_name
    ):
        """
        Initializes a Customer instance.
        Parameters:
        -----------
        customer_id : UUID | str
            The unique identifier of the customer
            to store in the instance's state.
            **Will be converted to a UUID value if
            one is not provided.**
        given_name : str | None
            The given_name value to store in the
            instance's state.
        family_name : str | None
```

```
            The family_name value to store in the
            instance's state.
        Raises:
        -------
        TypeError
            If customer_id is not a UUID or str.
        ValueError
            If customer_id is not a UUID, or is a
            str but cannot be converted to a UUID.
        """

        ...
```

The Numpydoc format provides a **lot** of structure guidance for **very** complete documentation. Barring some specific formatting for the *Deprecation warning* section, which is detailed along with all the other sections in the *Numpydoc Style Guide* at https://numpydoc.readthedocs.io/en/latest/format.html, it still allows for considerable freedom in writing docstrings, across a broad range of complexity. The trade-off is, obviously, that larger, more complex docstrings will be needed if the format and structure guidelines are followed.

Shouldn't good code be self-documenting?

The thoughts about documenting code presented here operate under the same assumption: that there is a need for *some* form of documentation separate from the actual code itself. It is certainly *possible* to write good, clean code that requires minimal documentation of this type, at least for those who have access to the code itself. The assertion that any given piece of code is self-documenting, though, *depends on that access*. Consumers of code may not *have* access or may not be able to spare the time to go digging through the code of whatever function, class, or method they are interested in, though. In those cases, some documentation, something that collects all the information those consumers need, is still a good thing.

Writing truly self-documenting code relies on everyone who ever touches that code to follow additional standards. At a minimum, those break down to the following:

- Making sure that *every* identifier (variable, parameter, function-, method-, or class-name) has a clear, meaningful name within the context of the processes the code was written to execute
- Having a good, common understanding of that context, or at least of the problem space that the context lives in

- Adding clear and concise comments where there is any ambiguity in the processes, especially if that ambiguity centers around *why* a process works in a particular way — reading good code should be sufficient to understand *what* it is doing, but why it is being done may not be obvious.

Provided that all of these conditions are met, having a documentation strategy that boils down to *we write only self-documenting code* is a viable strategy. It may not be the easiest strategy to maintain, though, and may not address the needs of *consumers* of that code. Recognizing those needs, when they exist, is a key point for determining and defining a documentation strategy, before even considering how that documentation will be executed.

Defining a documentation strategy is, in a very real way, an exercise in finding a balance-point between the needs for that documentation, and the time required to maintain it. Changes to code that do not have corresponding changes to documentation are counterproductive at best, and over time, can be a worse scenario to deal with than having no documentation whatsoever. The same can be said of comments in code.

Commenting code

Comments are a form of code documentation, with a more specific and limited intended audience: engineers who have access to the code itself. As a result, and bearing that audience difference in mind, many of the same considerations noted earlier about documentation apply to comments as well. Most engineers will agree with the statement that well-commented code is a good thing. Where they will disagree is usually around what, exactly, *well-commented* really means. The following are my own thoughts and opinions about that definition, acquired over the course of my career so far.

> Comments should **explain and clarify** code. If they aren't doing that, there is a problem in either the comment or the code, and that problem should be addressed.

There are several variants of this called out more specifically in later thoughts. The main point here, though, is that if a comment isn't adding value to the code, it should either be altered so that it does, the code should be altered so that a comment can add value, or the comment should be removed.

If a given piece of code **needs** comments, look for ways to eliminate that need. If it cannot be eliminated, the comments should address **why** the code needs to be written the way it was, over and above any other explanation they provide.

A scenario where the need for a comment exists is code that is not *idiomatic*, whether in the context of the language, or a team- or project-standards context. For example, if a team has agreed to use various built-in functions such as map, `filter`, and reduce (see their entries in the *Built-in Functions* page at `https://docs.python.org/3.11/library/functions.html`), those are part of a *team idiom*. If, later, it is discovered that using a **comprehension** (`https://docs.python.org/3.11/reference/expressions.html#displays-for-lists-sets-and-dictionaries`) provides significantly better performance for a specific task, and the code is changed, a comment should be added that explains why the comprehension was used instead.

Idiomatic code

Idiomatic code is simply code that engineers will recognize and be able to read and understand with little to no effort — code that is appropriate to the style(s) associated with Python, or that follows team or project standards.

Write comments with a first-time reader of your code in mind. Don't assume they will know anything about why it does what it does.

This obviously will be a benefit to new hires on a team, but a *first-time reader of your code* can also be someone who has been a member of the same team for a long time and is seeing your code as part of a code review process. If a codebase is rarely touched, that first-time reader could even be the original author — you, even — of code that is going to be modified, months or years after the last time it was touched.

Comments that address **what** is being done should be unnecessary: If reading the code cannot provide a clear understanding of what is happening, consider revising that code until it does, even if that adds additional code in the process.

The code, ultimately (and obviously), is the source of truth with respect to what it does when it is executed. If the only reason a comment is added relating to a particular piece of that code is that it's difficult to follow what is being done, that code should be made more self-explanatory. That may require nothing more than following a naming convention for variables and other code entities, so that the meaning of them is clear, which will be discussed in the next chapter. It might also require significant rethinking of the processes that the code executes. A more specific variant of this commenting rule might be stated as:

> Don't re-state what the code is doing in a comment unless it is not obvious from reading the code, and the code **cannot** be adjusted to make it obvious.

Whether the practice is still taught or encouraged now or not, for some time there was a trend in teaching aspiring engineers to start their code-writing process by writing pseudocode to outline the processes in a function. Comments are a natural way to do that within a codebase, and remnants of pseudocode comments often got left in place after the actual work was complete. Since that approach is often concerned with what the code would eventually be doing, those left-over comments often add no value to the code. An example of a pseudocode outline might look like this:

```python
# We need a function to collect and return the shipping
# status for all of a given customer's orders, and return
# them.
# We'll have a customer ID to work with.
def collect_shipping_statuses(customer_id):
    # Get the customer from the provided ID
    # Get the orders for that customer
    # Set up a variable to add statuses to. This will
    # be returned at the end of the function-call, and
    # may be empty if there are no orders.
    # Iterate over the orders. For each order, call the
    # appropriate API and add the results to the statuses
    # variable:
    # - If the shipper is USPS, call the USPS API
    # - If the shipper is UPS, call the UPS API
    # - If the shipper is FedEx, call the FedEx API
    # Return the statuses variable
```

By the time the actual function is written, if those comments are not adjusted, they add little to no value to the code, simply because they are stating the same thing that the code itself is expressing. Out of the entire body of original pseudocode comments, only one part of one of those comments adds any value, by noting behavior expectations. The rest, highlighted in this example, are noise:

```python
def collect_shipping_statuses(customer_id):
    # Get the customer from the provided ID
    customer = get_customer(customer_id)
    # Get the orders for that customer
    orders = get_customer_orders(customer)
    # Set up a variable to add statuses to.
    # This will be returned at the end of the function-
    # call, and may be empty if there are no orders
    shipping_statuses = {}
    # Iterate over the orders. For each order, call the
    # appropriate API and add the results to the statuses
    # variable:
    for order in orders:
        _id = order.order_id
        # - If the shipper is USPS, call the USPS API
        if order.shipper == 'USPS':
            shipping_status[_id] = check_usps(order)
        # - If the shipper is UPS, call the UPS API
        elif order.shipper == 'UPS':
            shipping_status[_id] = check_ups(order)
        # - If the shipper is FedEx, call the FedEx API
        elif order.shipper == 'FEDEX':
            shipping_status[_id] = check_fedex(order)
    # Return the statuses variable
    return shipping_statuses
```

> When fixing a bug, don't be shy about adding a comment about that change, explaining what the issue was, how the change fixed it, or whatever else feels relevant. Be succinct, though — in the code itself is rarely an appropriate place to write essays about bugs!

If the codebase in question is maintained in source control and has history available for previous versions, comments relating to bug resolution may not be needed at all or could be as simple as a note that identifies the code branch where the bug was resolved. If there is context that is relevant in the code itself, though — say, a comment that warns future readers not to try a previous approach because it led to an issue — that may still add value.

> *Add comments for to-do items, things that need to be fixed later, and other future work anticipated* **if** *there is not a better way to keep track of those. If there* **is** *a better way (a work-ticket system, for example), it does not hurt to link to it (to the relevant work-ticket, for example), but once the source of the comment is no longer relevant,* **remove the comment.**

This is just a more situation-specific variant of a more general idea:

> *Be sure to* **update (or remove) comments** *when they are no longer accurate or relevant.*

Having comments that are inaccurate or irrelevant is worse than having no comments at all. Logically, then, keeping comments accurate and relevant is important, and that effort represents additional work that would need to be done when code relating to a comment is changed. With that in mind, if it is possible to write comments with their eventual removal in mind, where that applies, doing so is advisable.

Linting and comments

There are a handful of comment standards that can be checked by various linters. They break out into spacing-related issues, variations on indentation errors, and variations on having too many leading # characters for both block and inline comments.

The need for comments in code is typically a function of how difficult that code is to read and understand. Writing code that is easily read is a function of using agreed-upon standards, which were already discussed in the *Style standards for code* section earlier. *Understanding* that code relies heavily on making sure that the elements within that code — classes, functions, methods, arguments, and variables — are themselves understandable, which is more likely to be affected by *functional standards* like those discussed in the next chapter.

Summary

This chapter covered a fair number of ideas to consider and make decisions about, but all of them relate, in some fashion, to what sorts of content to expect within the code, and what its structure should look like. Depending on the specific decisions made around each of these ideas, there may be a fair amount of additional work involved to actually follow through on the chosen standards. That's quite possible. At the same time, if those standards are agreed upon by all the developer stakeholders for a project, or within a team, even with the additional work involved, the participants will have agreed that the goals being pursued are worthwhile enough to warrant the additional effort.

None of these standards are a one-size-fits-all decision: different teams and different projects can have wildly different priorities, after all, and even those can change over time. At the same time, each has the potential for significant benefits. Consistent code organization patterns across projects mean that less time will be needed to bring a new person up to speed, even if they are a seasoned professional engineer. The same holds true for consistent, meaningful in-code documentation and comments. Consistent naming conventions, especially if they emphasize meaningful names for code elements, will as well, and would be expected to reduce the number of comments and the amount of content needed in the documentation. Making a conscious decision to use properties, or to use simple attributes — both are viable choices — removes ambiguity from the process of crafting the code and what considerations need to be kept in mind during that crafting, particularly with respect to annotation and type-checking considerations that depend on that choice. Much the same can be said about using or not using data contracts.

The target audience for the standards discussed here is, mainly, users of the code, or perhaps casual readers of it who are looking for more information on how to make use of it. As the project-oriented chapters of this book unfold, starting in *Chapter 9*, *Revising the hms_sys System Project*, the actual application of these standards will be explored, with a substantial focus on how the decisions about them will be made for a project. Depending on the decisions made around documentation, in particular, they may also be of use or interest for engineers who are working with the code at a deeper level — maintaining it, or adding functionality to it — but odds are good that they are going to be more concerned with the topics in the next chapter: the *Functional development standards* that shape what the *content* is that these standards describe the format of, and that can have actual, functional impact on how the code executes.

Get This Book's PDF Version and Exclusive Extras

UNLOCK NOW

Scan the QR code (or go to packtpub.com/unlock). Search for this book by name, confirm the edition, and then follow the steps on the page.

Note: *Keep your invoice handy. Purchases made directly from Packt don't require an invoice.*

7
Functional Code Standards

The next deeper level of standards, and the one that is close to the code itself, concerns making decisions about how the actual functionality is implemented. This chapter focuses on the options and decisions that are most likely to have a significant impact if they were changed after a substantial amount of code was already written. Implied in that description is the idea that making changes to them after development has started introduces risks of breaking changes, or at least a significant amount of rework that could be avoided by making the *right* decision from the start, for whatever value of *right* applies.

Alongside those are some general best practices that are less risk-prone, but that will make the lives of those working with the code, or maintaining it, easier. Taken together, there are a half dozen topics in this set. These may not be the only decision points that can affect a project or the ongoing efforts of an engineering team across multiple projects. Still, the majority of the other decision points are very dependent on the specifics of those projects, or the efforts of those teams.

The six topics that are *global* considerations are:

- How code is organized to make consumption of it as seamless as possible.

- How to structure code, particularly functions and classes, to avoid *cognitive overhead*.

- Why *naming conventions* for code elements are important.

- How to leverage Python's *annotations*, including whether or not to implement *type-checking* with them.

- Deciding whether formal *data contracts* for functions and classes are desirable, or even *necessary* for a project.

- What options are available to ensure that code *observability* meets a project's needs at runtime.

Many of these standards decisions tie back to one or more of the non-functional standards described in the previous chapter. Those standards were concerned with how information about the code is structured, while these are concerned with when those structures should be used, and what the actual content within them is.

Technical requirements

The code in the accompanying repository written for this chapter (https://github.com/ PacktPublishing/Hands-On-Software-Engineering-with-Python-Second-Edition/tree/ main/CH07-code) was written in and tested with Python 3.11, though some examples are written as examples using syntax and structure going as far back as Python 3.0, for the purpose of showing changes across versions of the language. Even in those cases, they will run under Python 3.11, and probably later versions — Python has a good history of maintaining backward compatibility for several years at a time. The code presented in the text of the book may or may not be executable; much of it is for the purpose of illustrating various points discussed in the text.

Installation packages and instructions for Python 3.11 can be found at https://www.python.org/ downloads/, under the *Looking for a specific release?* heading for Windows and macOS systems. Linux systems typically have access to it through their normal package management system (yum or apt/apt-get), though some Linux distributions may require special efforts to install versions other than the default installed with the OS. Those variations are frequently specific to the distribution and are likely to change by the time this book is in print, so searching for specifics online is going to be the best approach to find specific instructions when they are needed for alternative Python versions.

This chapter also assumes a basic familiarity with importing functionality from packages, and with installing third-party packages using `pip` — Python's package installer. The documentation for `pip` can be found at `https://pip.pypa.io/en/stable/`, for any reader who needs to look up specifics on how to use it.

Code organization

The thought process behind deciding how to organize code depends heavily on recognizing how that code is going to be consumed and used. With that in mind, lets walk through the decision-making process for organizing code for a hypothetical company with several specific areas of functional focus (domains) that tie into one or more applications.

> **Domains, formal or otherwise**
>
> The term domains, as used here, does not necessarily mean that the company is following a **Domain-Driven Design (DDD)** paradigm, though in larger organizations that may well be a good fit. In this case, a domain is simply an area of functional focus, as noted. That might be a single software engineer or a team of several that are managing the code behind any number of these domains.

First, an assumption is made that all proprietary code is going to be deployed in some manner that allows access only to the engineering teams within the company. There are four functional domains in the company, for this example:

- **Customers**, concerned with managing customer information
- **Employees**, concerned with managing employee information, specifically as they interact with objects in the other domain
- **Orders**, concerned with tracking and fulfilling orders made by customers of products
- **Products**, concerned with tracking products available to be purchased by customers through the Orders domain

All the objects in the systems that code is being written and maintained for will be persisted to some back-end data store. That may end up being a fifth domain within the engineering structure, or it may not.

Within each of those domains, there are one to three identifiable components that the systems will need to be concerned with, all of which can be loosely classified as being a Person, Place, or Thing of some kind, all of which are also data objects (DataObject). These components, and their relationships to each other, without worrying about any implementation details, can be diagrammed as shown in *Figure 7.1*:

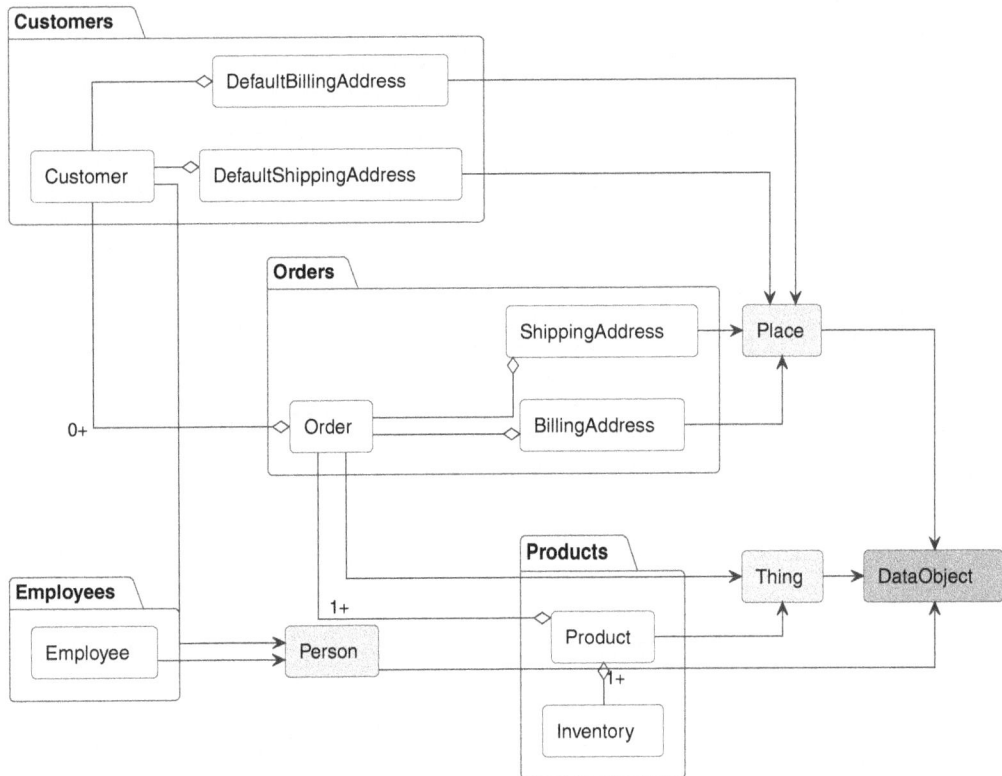

Figure 7.1: The domain-component diagram for Fake Company's systems

This does not require an object-oriented design!

The diagram in *Figure 7.1* is very object-oriented, simply because that approach was easier to diagram in a simple fashion. That should *not* be taken as a requirement for the system design to follow an object-oriented design, though the example will do so because it is simpler to correlate to the diagram.

Outside the organization itself, there may be other domain-like relationships — payment processing, given the commerce-focused nature of this example, would be a likely scenario. With that in mind, a high-level design decision is made to keep all of the organization's proprietary code within a single Python namespace — `fakeco` — to make it easier to differentiate between the organization's own code and third-party packages and modules within the organization's code. For illustrative purposes, we will assume that there is a third-party payment processor whose code is used in the order-handling and order-fulfillment processes that has a top-level namespace of `payment`.

> **Namespaces**
>
> A **namespace**, in Python, is simply a name, which may include dot-notated subsections, that indicates a logical grouping of functionality within a package or module. An example of a namespace in Python's built-in packages is the `http` module collection — `https://docs.python.org/3.11/library/http.html` — which includes child `client`, `server`, `cookies`, and `cookiejar` namespaces to handle various logical groupings of functionality relating to the **HyperText Transfer Protocol (HTTP)**. Another built-in example is the `os` module — `https://docs.python.org/3.11/library/os.html` — which provides functionality relating to interacting with the main operating system that the Python interpreter is running under, and provides at least one child module — `os.path` — that provides functionality for working with file-system paths.

Mapping the diagram's members to namespaces, then, yields the following namespaces and members:

- `fakeco.customers`:

  - `Customer` (type): Represents a customer in the context of the system
  - `DefaultBillingAddress` (type): Represents the default billing address for a customer in the context of the system
  - `DefaultShippingAddress` (type): Represents the default shipping address for a customer in the context of the system

- `fakeco.employees`:

  - `Employee` (type): Represents an employee in the context of the system

- `fakeco.orders`:

    - `Order` (type): Represents an order in the context of the system

    - `BillingAddress` (type): Represents a billing address for an order in the context of the system

    - `ShippingAddress` (type): Represents a shipping address for an order in the context of the system

- `fakeco.products`:

    - `Product` (type): Represents a product in the context of the system

- `fakeco.core_data`:

    - `DataObject` (type): Provides baseline functionality, interface requirements, and type identity for classes that can persist data to and read data from some common back-end data store

    - `Person` (type): Provides baseline functionality, interface requirements, and type identity for classes that represent a person in the context of the system

    - `Place` (type): Provides baseline functionality, interface requirements, and type identity for classes that represent a place in the context of the system

    - `Thing` (type): Provides baseline functionality, interface requirements, and type identity for classes that represent a thing in the context of the system

This structure has been stubbed out in the `namespace-example` directory in the GitHub repository for this chapter. It may not execute, as it is simply an illustration of the results of this namespace design. The structure, however, provides the following advantages:

- Assuming that it was installed, or copied directly into a location where the interpreter can find it, an import of any specific member is as simple a code construct as `from fakeco.{domain_name} import {member_name}` where {domain_name} is one of the domains noted, and {member_name} is a resolvable class, function, or other member.

- Entire related namespaces can be imported in two ways: `import fakeco.{domain_name}` or `from fakeco import {domain_name}` which provides access to any member in that namespace, as `fakeco.{domain_name}.{member_name}` or `{domain_name}.{member_name}` respectively.

The trade-off for this approach is a slightly longer import line than would be needed if the fakeco namespace segment was not included. However, that indicates, unambiguously, that the namespace involved is owned and managed by Fake Company. During development, this namespace can also be explicitly added in any of several ways, which affords the developers the opportunity to write code as if that namespace were already installed, minimizing the potential for differences between the development environment and a production environment, at least as far as import processes are concerned.

Namespaces for individual code entities are only partly defined by the name of the module they live in, and perhaps the package directory that the module lives in. The rest of a full namespace for a code entity like a function or class is controlled by the name of that entity within its parent module.

Structures and standards for classes and functions

There are several questions that can be asked about classes and functions (*callables*) that are worth asking while deciding on standards for code. Though the relationship may not be obvious, many of these questions tie back to a basic psychological factor for humans. Working with code relies, with some frequency, on short-term memory — an engineer needs to keep track of some number of facts or factors about the code that they are working with, and there is a limit to the number of those facts and factors that can live in short-term memory at any given time. The average, as several studies have asserted, is seven items, plus or minus two. To further complicate things, our short-term memory is highly volatile, with new items moving in and replacing older items as new stimuli are encountered. There are several practices common in software development that, while not eliminating this *human memory buffer* restriction, can make it less troublesome by making salient facts easily located, and less likely to flush the entire contents of that buffer. The following questions are intended to generate answers that lead to conscious decisions for standards that relate to those practices:

- How, when, and where do we document (and annotate) callables?
- What are our expectations around the use of comments in code?
- What is our preference around how variables and parameters are named?
- How do we want to handle properties in classes?
- How much code in a single callable do we feel is too much? That is, where is our optimal balance between the amount of code in a callable, compared with what that callable actually *does*?

There may be other questions that surface, based on organization norms, or any of several project-by-project constraints, but these are likely to be common across all those boundaries. Together with these questions is another consideration: how valuable is an engineer's time? The decisions that come out of the answers must also keep that in mind, with an eye toward finding a balance point where an engineer's time is better spent writing new features, or fixing bugs, as opposed to making non-functional improvements to the code they are concerned with.

Having decided on at least some basic guidelines about how to divide functionality into logical subdivisions of functional responsibility, some consideration to how the code entities providing that functionality are named is worth consideration.

Naming conventions for code elements

The naming conventions discussed earlier in the *Style standards for code* section in *Chapter 6*, *Code Style and Related Standards* cover, for lack of a better description, what various code elements' names should look like. They do not really describe what the content of those names should *be*, though. There are several best practices that apply to that facet of code-element naming, which boil down to the following two very basic rules:

- Make the names of all code elements — classes, functions, methods, arguments, and variables — meaningful within the scope that they live in.

- Be aware of where the boundaries between those scopes exist.

Consider, as an example, this function:

```python
def colss(c_id):
    c = gc(c_id)
    ods = gc_o(c)
    ss = {}
    for o in ods:
        if o.shipper == 'USPS':
            ss[o.oid] = check_usps(o)
        elif o.shipper == 'UPS':
            ss[o.oid] = check_ups(o)
        elif o.shipper == 'FEDEX':
            ss[o.oid] = check_fedex(o)
    return ss
```

Functionally, there is nothing *wrong* with this code. Provided that all the classes and functions existed, it would execute just fine. But it is difficult, at best, for a reader to really understand what this function is doing, though the existence of the check_usps, check_ups, and check_fedex function calls might lead the reader to think that it was interacting with some common shipping services.

> **Self-documenting code revisited**
>
> In the *Shouldn't good code be self-documenting?* section of the previous chapter, a key point noted was:
>
> *Making sure that every identifier (variable, parameter, function-, method-, or class-name) has a clear, meaningful name within the context of the processes the code was written to execute.*
>
> The naming-convention decisions made here are fundamental to that goal.

The exact same function, but using meaningful entity names, is *much* easier to understand:

```python
def collect_shipping_statuses(customer_id):
    customer = get_customer(customer_id)
    orders = get_customer_orders(customer)
    shipping_statuses = {}

    for order in orders:
        _id = order.order_id
        if order.shipper == 'USPS':
            shipping_status[_id] = check_usps(order)
        elif order.shipper == 'UPS':
            shipping_status[_id] = check_ups(order)
        elif order.shipper == 'FEDEX':
            shipping_status[_id] = check_fedex(order)
    return shipping_statuses
```

That shows how much of a difference well-named code entities make from the perspective of making code easily understood. Where scopes come into play is understanding that these entity names have no meaning or significance outside the scope they are defined in. Even if multiple functions use the same entity names — customer_id is a very likely candidate for this sort of re-use — that name in each function is distinct from the same name in any other function, and can contain different values, or even completely different value types.

Scopes break down, barring some unusual code structures or various special cases, along specific lines. Member elements of a module, classes, functions, and variables fall within the scope of the module. Elements in a module's scope are also global as far as other module-scope elements are concerned, allowing access to global variables within a module entity without requiring the use of the global keyword. This holds true for any functionality added to the module with an import as well. The scopes of functions behave in a similar fashion: any name defined in a function is available anywhere in that function after the name has been defined. Within the scope of a class, any member name defined by that class can be accessed by any other member of that class, provided that it is identified as being a member (with self).

Other language constructs have their own scopes too. For example, variables defined within any of the various comprehension structures have an existence independent of any identically named variables outside the body of the comprehension, as shown in this console session's use of the variable i:

```
>>> i = 100
>>> print(f'i: {I}')
i: 100
>>> squares = [(i, i**2) for i in range(4)]
>>> print(squares)
[(0, 0), (1, 1), (2, 4), (3, 9)]
>>> print(f'i: {I}')
i: 100
```

Functions or methods defined within other functions or methods also have their own scopes, though they have access to the arguments and variables of their wrapping function, in much the same way that a module-level global is accessible within a function, as shown by the printing of the arg argument in this session:

```
>>> def outer(arg):
...     print(f'outer arg ........ {arg}')
...     def inner(other_arg):
...         print(f'inner arg ......... {arg}')
...         print(f'inner other_arg ... {other_arg}')
...     inner(f'inner: {arg}')
...
```

```
>>> outer('outer')
outer arg ........ outer
inner arg ........ outer
inner other_arg ... inner: outer
```

Within a class definition in a module, all members of the class share the scope of the class, or the scope of an instance of that class. Class-scoped elements, then, have to be accessed through the class itself, using the (global) name of the class, or through a specific instance of a class. That instance-level reference is what the self argument in methods defined within a class provides.

Classes have other capabilities that may be considered for the purposes of defining code standards for a project or a team. Chief among those is their ability to have both simple attributes and managed attributes, also called formal properties.

Deciding between simple attributes and formal properties

In object-oriented programming, classes typically have both methods (what they can do) and properties (what data they have). Methods are straightforward in Python class definitions — they are, in many respects, just functions with a common first argument that provides a reference to the object-instance when the method is called. Properties can be implemented in two different ways, as **simple attributes**, or as **formal properties** or **managed attributes**. Consider the class shown in *Figure 7.2*, representing a person in a system:

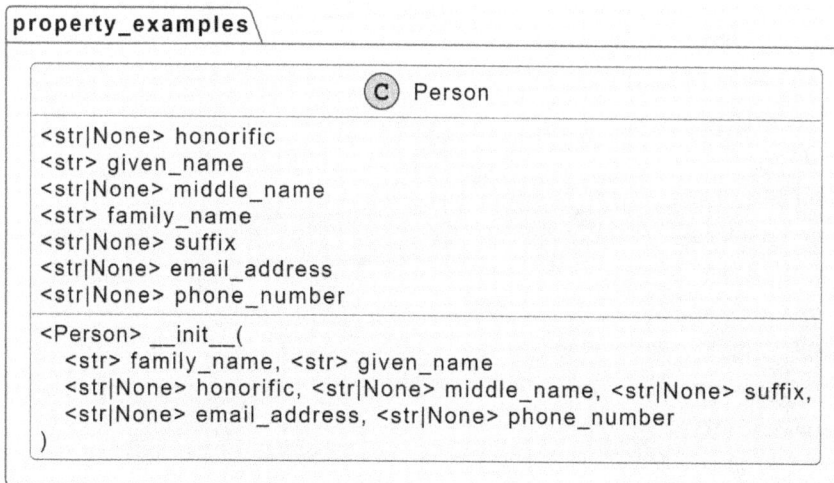

```
property_examples

                        C  Person
  <str|None> honorific
  <str> given_name
  <str|None> middle_name
  <str> family_name
  <str|None> suffix
  <str|None> email_address
  <str|None> phone_number

  <Person> __init__(
    <str> family_name, <str> given_name
    <str|None> honorific, <str|None> middle_name, <str|None> suffix,
    <str|None> email_address, <str|None> phone_number
  )
```

Figure 7.2: A diagram of a class that has several properties

Prior to version 2.2, defining properties for Python classes was limited to simple attributes only. A typical object initialization (the __init__ method) would accept property values in its arguments and set local attribute values based on those arguments. While that works and is still a common process even now, there are drawbacks to it:

- Simple attributes can be added to an instance of a class arbitrarily.

- They can also be *changed* arbitrarily.

- They can even be **deleted** arbitrarily.

- They cannot be meaningfully tested without adding a *lot* of additional complexity to tests elsewhere.

Any one of these means that even if there is *supposed* to be an **interface** for a given class, it's not enforceable without resorting to having dedicated **getter**, **setter**, and **deleter** methods for each property that needs them. That implementation pattern pretty much makes the idea of using simple attributes as properties useless; it doesn't really resolve any of the issues listed above, and adds complexity to the code of a class on top of that.

A typical __init__ method defined for the Person class shown in the earlier diagram, and that simply stores initialization values in simple attributes, would look something like this:

```python
class Person:
    def __init__(
        self,
        family_name,
        given_name,
        honorific = None,
        middle_name = None,
        suffix = None,
        email_address = None,
        phone_number = None
    ):
        self.family_name = family_name
        self.given_name = given_name
        self.honorific = honorific
        self.middle_name = middle_name
        self.suffix = suffix
        self.email_address = email_address
        self.phone_number = phone_number
```

The property decorator (`https://docs.python.org/3/library/functions.html#property`) added the ability to define a collection of methods that would be accessed using the same dot notation as any other attribute of an instance of a class. Instead of simply assigning, reading, or deleting the attribute, that activity would map to a method that would be executed to set, get, or delete the value, respectively. That capability opens the door for some basic type- and value-checking for the value assignment, post-processing (if needed) during value retrieval, and pre-processing (if needed) during deletion.

As an example, here is the implementation for the family_name of the Person class, implemented as a property with **get, set,** and **delete** capabilities:

```python
# From property_decoration_example.py
class Person:
    def __init__(...):
        # The implementation of __init__ does not change
    @property
    def family_name(self):
        return self._family_name
    @family_name.setter
    def family_name(self, value):
        if not isinstance(value, str):
            raise TypeError(
                f'{self.__class__.__name__}.family_name '
                'expects a str value, but was passed '
                f'"{value}" ({type(value).__name__}).'
            )
        self._family_name = value
    @family_name.deleter
    def family_name(self):
        if hasattr(self, '_family_name'):
            del self._family_name
```

The use of properties takes us a significant step toward enforcing an object interface, though it does not, by itself, eliminate the ability to arbitrarily create, alter, or delete simple attributes. The properties themselves, once defined, are no longer simple attributes, though, and only allow that sort of arbitrary activity if the code in the backing methods allows it. They also make it possible to *test* the interface of the class, since it is possible to raise errors when an invalid value type (or value) is passed to a property setter method. The idea of type-checking will be explored in more detail later, in the *Runtime type-checking* section, but the most basic structure and processes needed are simply variations of what has been shown here.

The trade-off for using properties instead of simple attributes is the amount of additional code that is involved. The property_decoration_example.py module, with full get, set, and delete capabilities defined for each of the properties of the Person class, required 130-odd lines of code to implement the 7 properties of the class. Making a conscious decision about whether to use formal properties or just simple attributes, then, becomes a simple cost/benefit analysis: does the code benefit enough from using properties to warrant the additional code that needs to be written for them?

That determination may also be impacted by the functional needs of the backing methods for the property. If handling the constraints or needs of a property requires a lot of code (for whatever value of *a lot* applies), it may be better to break some of that code out into separate methods, functions, or classes in order to strike a comfortable balance between the size of those callables and their capabilities. In that respect, property implementations are no different than implementations of method or function callables, and the separation of responsibilities — and deciding what a good balance is between the size and capability of a property, method, or function — is worth consideration.

Finding a balance between callable size and capability

Another fundamental question that needs to be considered can be stated as *how much code is too much within a single function, method, or class?* The answer to this question is *very* subjective, and may vary wildly across teams, or even across projects within teams. Some of the basic factors to keep in mind include:

- The more a system is built out of smaller, **composable** pieces of functionality, the easier testing will be for each of those pieces, but more (if smaller) tests will need to be written (a minimum of one for each such piece, in all probability).

- At some point, there may be *too many* smaller pieces of composable functionality for an engineer to keep track of at one time, and what exactly *too many* means may vary from one individual to another.

- The most common approach to reducing the size (and thus complexity) of a given callable is to define new subsets of functionality that the original callable then calls a sub-process. For example, a function that calls another function to replace a large block of inline code. This can easily turn into an exercise in trading one type of size-complexity (lines of code in a function) for another (calling a lot of sub-functions).

> **What does composable mean?**
>
> A system with a high level of *composability* provides individual components — functions and classes, typically — that a developer can choose and assemble in whatever combinations are needed to satisfy a set of requirements. **Composable** components must be self-contained, in that they can be used independently of each other, though they may cooperate with other components. They should also allow for any of their dependencies to be replaceable; or, when that is not possible, they should ensure that those dependencies are also available, and handle any requirements for those dependencies without requiring the end user to know about them in any great detail.

As callables get refactored into smaller components, documentation will also likely increase according to the decisions made about that topic. In addition, as the number of callable components increases, the signatures of those callables may start getting difficult to keep track of, even if there are solid naming conventions in place. Another feature of Python, *annotation*, may be able to help reduce any ambiguities when writing code that makes use of larger numbers of callable components.

Annotation and type-checking

Starting with the first release of Python 3, the language provided support for **type annotation**. Specifically, it opened the door for describing, in the code itself, the type-expectations for function and method **parameters**, and of what a given function or method **returns**. Since then, the annotation standard has undergone substantial revision, starting with the introduction of the typing module (`https://docs.python.org/3.11/library/typing.html`) in Python 3.5, and improvements to the syntax allowed for annotation in Python 3.6 through 3.10.

It should be stressed that type annotation in Python, in and of itself, does not provide any direct enforcement of types at runtime. There are packages that can provide runtime type enforcement, but without those additional packages, annotations are little more than additional documentation of the code.

To show the differences, code examples have been written following annotation standards for Python versions from 3.0 through 3.11. As of the time of this writing, Python versions earlier than 3.8 are officially unsupported, and the examples for those versions will not be discussed in great detail. Each example defines and calls a function named example_function, that prints the names, types, and values of the arguments it is called with. The function itself, without any annotations, and without the actual print statements it executes, looks like this:

```
def example_function(
    str_arg, int_arg, float_arg, bool_arg,
    list_arg, dict_arg,
    *args,
    **kwargs
):
    ...
```

The output from each example is the same, except for the module file name, and looks like this (with line breaks and indentation for clarity):

```
{module-file-name}::example_function called:
str_arg ..... (str) str_arg
int_arg ..... (int) 1
float_arg ... (float) 2.345
bool_arg .... (bool) True
list_arg .... (list) ['list', 'values', 6, 7.89]
dict_arg .... (dict) {'name': 'string', 'value': 2}
args ........ (tuple) (0, 1.234)
kwargs ...... (dict) {
                     'kw1': 'kwarg-string',
                     'kw2': 5,
                     'kw3': 6.789
                 }
```

When annotation is encountered, the data provided is collected and attached to the function or method as metadata, which can be retrieved by several means. The examples use the getfullargspec function from the built-in inspect module, and pretty-print the collected annotations of the function, to show what the effects of the annotation are, internally. Each example discussed will present that output as well, for comparison purposes.

A brief history of annotation in Python

The basic structure involved with annotation has not changed significantly since Python 3.0: each parameter in a function can have a colon and some value (a type, by preference) designated after it, and a return type designated after the function's signature, like so:

```python
# from annotations_examples_30.py
def example_function(
    str_arg: str,
    int_arg: int,
    float_arg: float,
    bool_arg: bool,
    list_arg: list,
    dict_arg: dict,
    *args: (int, float),
    **kwargs: object
) -> None:
```

The resulting annotation structure reported by inspect.getfullargspec shows the mapping of parameter annotations, by name, to the types specified for each parameter's annotation:

```
== Annotations of example_function ===========================
{'args': (<class 'int'>, <class 'float'>),
 'bool_arg': <class 'bool'>,
 'dict_arg': <class 'dict'>,
 'float_arg': <class 'float'>,
 'int_arg': <class 'int'>,
 'kwargs': <class 'object'>,
 'list_arg': <class 'list'>,
 'return': None,
 'str_arg': <class 'str'>}
```

Over and above that, it also shows the return type for the function: None in this case.

Annotations can also accept user-defined types. That is, if your code defines a class MyClass, then MyClass can be used as a type designation in an annotation, *provided that the class definition is complete before it is used in an annotation.* That is, MyClass would have to be defined or imported before it was used as a type-designation in an annotation.

What happens if "return" is used as a parameter name?

At first glance, it may seem that return could be accidentally overridden in the annotation structure, by using return as a parameter name. Because return is a reserved word in Python, it's not allowed as a parameter name in a function or method, and will raise a SyntaxError, preventing the collision.

Annotation as of Python 3.5

The introduction of the typing module in Python 3.5 provided a collection of type-annotation designators to make annotating types like list easier, as well as providing mechanisms for specifying what types of members were expected for types that allow any member-type by default — list, tuple, and set types — and for key and member types in mappings like a dict. It also provided a mechanism for specifying multiple expected types for a single argument, in the form of the Union annotation type, and a general-purpose Any type that indicated that there was no specific expected type.

The example_function, annotated with Python 3.5 syntax, differs only in the use of those new typing module items:

```python
# From annotations_examples_35.py
def example_function(
    str_arg: str,
    int_arg: int,
    float_arg: float,
    bool_arg: bool,
    list_arg: List[Any],
    dict_arg: Dict[str, Any],
    *args: Union[int, float],
    **kwargs: Any
) -> None:
```

These designations are straightforward enough. The List[Any] specified for list_arg indicates that the parameter is a list, and that list can contain values of any type. Similarly, the Dict[str, Any] annotation indicates an expected dict type, with string keys, but any member values. The Union[int, float] indicates an expectation that values are expected to be either an int or a float.

The reported annotations structure returned by inspect.getfullargspec shows those changes as well:

```
== Annotations of example_function ========================
{'args': typing.Union[int, float],
 'bool_arg': <class 'bool'>,
 'dict_arg': typing.Dict[str, typing.Any],
 'float_arg': <class 'float'>,
 'int_arg': <class 'int'>,
 'kwargs': typing.Any,
 'list_arg': typing.List[typing.Any],
 'return': None,
 'str_arg': <class 'str'>}
```

This annotation structure remained the de facto standard through Python 3.8.

Annotation in Python 3.6 through 3.8

The bulk of the changes to annotation in Python 3.6 through Python 3.8 centered around the addition of new annotation types to the typing module, providing annotation designations for classes and types in various modules that weren't initially supported. These included representations of classes from the main collections module, along with its child collections.abc. In Python 3.6, the typing module also added support for the annotation of variables *within* functions, methods, and classes. The annotation of variables followed the same basic pattern as the one already established for function and method parameters, for example:

```
def example_function():
    multiplier: int = 2
```

In Python 3.7, an annotations feature was added to the __future__ standard library to facilitate annotations of types whose definitions were not defined or available when the annotation was defined. This relates back to the statement made in the Python 3.0 annotations, earlier:

That is, if your code defines a class `MyClass`, *then* `MyClass` *can be used as a type designation in an annotation,* **provided that the class definition is complete before it is used in an annotation.**

This addition removed that limitation, allowing a custom, user-defined type (a `class`) to be used in an annotation before its definition had been processed. For example:

```
from __future__ import annotations
def some_function(obj: MyClass) -> None:

    ...

class MyClass:

    ...
```

became a valid code-structure, where before that code would raise a `NameError`, because the `MyClass` class wasn't defined before it was used in the annotation of `some_function`. Prior to this, there was no way to work around that other than making sure that the definition of `MyClass` occurred before `some_function` was defined and annotated. Examples of the use of the `__future__` annotations import are provided in the `future_example.py` and `no_future_example.py` modules in the repository, and the latter will raise the `NameError` noted when run.

Annotation in Python 3.9 and later

With the release of Python 3.9 came a significant change in what annotation types were allowed and supported. Until this release, complex types — lists, tuples, and dictionaries in the built-in types, and the types defined in other built-in modules like `collections` and `contextlib` — required specific annotation types that the `typing` module provided. That pattern was shown in the *Annotation as of Python 3.5* section earlier. Python 3.9 included a lot of work to allow the native type names and a lot of the types from other built-in modules to be used directly. That same `example_function` definition could be written like this:

```
def example_function(
    str_arg: str,
    int_arg: int,
    float_arg: float,
    bool_arg: bool,
    list_arg: list[Any],
    dict_arg: dict[str, Any],
    *args: Union[int, float],
```

```
    **kwargs: Any
) -> None:
```

The underlying annotation syntax still required the use of the Union annotation type from the typing module, and the Any type to indicate that the value being annotated could be any type, and thus any value. All of the previous typing module annotation types that this new pattern became supported for were deprecated, but in a manner so that no deprecation warnings would be raised.

> **Deprecation**
>
> **Deprecated** functionality, for readers unfamiliar with the term, is functionality that still exists in a language or system but is expected to be removed in the future. Since that removal will eventually become a breaking change, removal of any deprecated function is something that will eventually have to be dealt with, and the creation of any new code that uses it should be avoided.

In Python 3.10, the annotation syntax changed again, allowing annotations that were previously handled with the Union type to use the pipe operator, |, to join the expected types, like so:

```
def example_function(
    str_arg: str,
    int_arg: int,
    float_arg: float,
    bool_arg: bool,
    list_arg: list[Any],
    dict_arg: dict[str, Any],
    *args: int | float,
    **kwargs: Any
) -> None:
```

Additional annotation types and functions were also added to the typing module in this release, a pattern that continued in Python 3.11. Of particular note in the 3.11 changes is the Self type, allowing annotation to indicate the class that an instance method is a member of as an expected type.

As noted earlier, annotations as Python supports them are little more than additional documentation on functions and methods. However, since the annotation process generates observable data that indicates the expectations for parameters and return values, it's possible to use those data points to enforce type-checks at runtime.

Runtime type-checking

Runtime type-checking in Python code is a subject that many people hold strong, and often conflicting, opinions on. Searching for variations on the topic will lead to all kinds of assertions, including:

- Python code should never execute type-checking — the language is intentionally duck-typed, and the best way to deal with unexpected types is to be rigorous about using try... except blocks to handle unexpected types and values.

- Python code should be annotated so that static type-checking can be executed during a build process, but that is it.

- Properties in Python objects are part of a formal interface and should be type-checked (and value-checked) as needed to preserve the integrity of that interface (a view more commonly held in object-oriented projects).

- My Python code deals with data from external sources; I cannot control the validation of that data before it is passed to my code, so I want to type-check (and value-check) it.

- My Python code costs money to execute. I'd rather catch errors earlier, before they incur unnecessary costs.

As controversial as the idea might be, there are scenarios where run-time type- and value-checking is desirable and scenarios where it is more effort than it is worth. That decision should be made with conscious thought, though, and with an eye toward the practical realities of the code in question: its uses, the run-time context, and where the advantages and trade-offs lie within the field of the code's expected uses.

Assuming there is some need, at some point, to implement type-checking, the annotation structures already described are the starting point for those processes. Annotations define the expectations for input and output of the methods and functions they are attached to. More than that, since they also copy the actual annotation-objects into accessible data structures on their targets, it's possible to write code that accesses those annotations, checks their types, and raises a TypeError if the actual type does not match up with the annotated expectations.

Even without the annotation data, type-checking is not a difficult process, and it can be a very simple one, it just tends to lead to a lot of **boilerplate code** across several functions or methods.

Boilerplate code

Boilerplate code is a piece of code that occurs repeatedly through a codebase. Since it is duplicated code, it tends to make maintenance of the code it lives in a bit more difficult to manage — not because the boilerplate code is complex, necessarily, but because if it needs to be changed everywhere, it's relatively easy to miss one or more instances that need to be changed.

Using the same example_function shown before as a starting point, the type-checking for simple arguments like its str_arg and int_arg is quite straightforward:

```python
# From type_checking_example_01.py
def example_function(
    # Parameters omitted for brevity
) -> None:
    if not isinstance(str_arg, str):
        raise TypeError(
            'str_arg check: Replace this with a '
            'meaningful error-message'
        )
    if not isinstance(int_arg, int):
        raise TypeError(
            'int_arg check: Replace this with a '
            'meaningful error-message'
        )
    ...
```

The values of more complex parameter types — list and dict types in the example, but any parameter that accepts multiple types, really — can be checked in a similar manner. The chief difference is that the types being checked for are passed as a *tuple* of types, rather than a single type:

```python
    ...
    if args and not all(
        [isinstance(arg, (int, float)) for arg in args]
    ):
        raise TypeError(
            'args check: Replace this with a meaningful '
```

```
        'error-message'
    )

    ...
```

So far, these aren't leveraging anything from the annotation structure. Even so, they still do what is expected, raising a `TypeError` if an invalid argument type is presented to the function when it is called:

```
Invalid str_arg:
TypeError: str_arg check: Replace this with a
    meaningful error-message
Invalid int_arg:
TypeError: str_arg check: Replace this with a
    meaningful error-message
Invalid *args:
TypeError: args check: Replace this with a
    meaningful error-message
```

A (probably incomplete) example that actually uses the annotation is presented in the `type_checking_example_02.py` file in the repository for this book. It still ends up being a substantial amount of boilerplate code, but it has the potential to be the exact same boilerplate code everywhere, rather than a potentially different variant for every function. That code, step-by-step:

- Acquires a `name` and `value` for each argument presented to the function
- Extracts the `annotation` for each named parameter
- Acquires the arguments for that annotation if there are any
- Checks and passes validation for the `typing.Any` annotation-type
- Checks types of members of any collection-type arguments — tuples and lists — against the expected types for that, raising a `TypeError` if there is a value that is not one of those types
- Checks the value type against the annotation type for non-collection types, raising a `TypeError` if the argument value is not of the expected type

The basic process is sound, at least as far as the limited testing executed in that example. It behaves in the same fashion as the parameter-by-parameter example described earlier:

```
Invalid str_arg:
TypeError: str_arg check: Replace this with a
   meaningful error-message
Invalid int_arg:
TypeError: str_arg check: Replace this with a
   meaningful error-message
Invalid *args:
TypeError: args check: Replace this with a
   meaningful error-message
```

While that example code is only 28 lines, and could probably be refined into a more robust process, and even made into a decorator that would eliminate the need for multiple copies of the code across a codebase, that work has already been done, and is available as an installable package: typeguard (https://pypi.org/project/typeguard/). The typeguard package pays attention to standard annotations and allows a developer to simply import a single decorator, and then apply it to functions, methods, or even entire classes. Applying it to another variation of the example_function is as simple as this:

```python
# From typeguard_example_311.py
from typeguard import typechecked

...

@typechecked
def example_function(
    str_arg: str,
    int_arg: int,
    float_arg: float,
    bool_arg: bool,
    list_arg: list[Any],
    dict_arg: dict[str, Any],
    *args: int | float,
    **kwargs: Any
) -> None:
    ...
```

The corresponding example code, `typeguard_example_311.py` in the repository, iterates over a collection of *good* argument values (values that will successfully validate by type), then over collections of *bad* argument values (values that should not pass the type-checking validation). When executed, its output shows the expected results for all of the *good* values, and the error details raised (as `typeguard.TypeCheckError` errors) for each bad argument:

```
== invalid str_arg types ====================================
argument "str_arg" (bool) is not an instance of str
argument "str_arg" (None) is not an instance of str
argument "str_arg" (int) is not an instance of str
argument "str_arg" (float) is not an instance of str
argument "str_arg" (object) is not an instance of str
== invalid int_arg types ====================================
argument "int_arg" (float) is not an instance of int
argument "int_arg" (None) is not an instance of int
== invalid float_arg types ====================================
argument "float_arg" (None) is neither float or int
argument "float_arg" (object) is neither float or int
== invalid bool_arg types ====================================
argument "bool_arg" (str) is not an instance of bool
argument "bool_arg" (str) is not an instance of bool
== invalid dict_arg types ====================================
key 1 of argument "dict_arg" (dict) is not an instance
  of str
```

Even if no run-time type-checking is in place, annotation of the input parameters and output serves as a standard mechanism for documenting the expectations of a function or method. When combined with some form of type-checking, that combination allows a function or method to validate its input and output, raising errors at the earliest point that they are happening, which can make debugging easier. It is not unusual for code to have a single function that serves as a point of entry for a process. The validation that type-checking and annotation provide when applied to any function, but particularly to those that serve as entry points, is a starting point for providing and enforcing a *data contract* for those processes.

A first look at the idea of data contracts

While the idea of type-checking and other input validation has obvious implications and advantages in the context of an object-oriented development paradigm, its application is not limited to that context. Any callable, whether it is a deeply nested helper function or method of a class, or an entry-point function that kicks off the processes of a system, can benefit from validating its input. In the context of event-driven systems, and especially systems that rely on serialized input data from sources that are outside the system's control, enforcing validation of inputs is a form of data contract that makes systems more predictable, and more reliable.

> **Data contract**
>
> A **data contract** is simply an enforced definition of a data structure, including its format and any requirements or constraints that apply to the members of that data structure. Those constraints may include minimum and maximum values, expected structures or formats of string values, nested structures, and sequences or collections of values. Collectively, these define a semantic structure for data, setting expectations for what rules apply to that data structure. They may also imply, or even implement, specific units of measurement, if applicable — liters vs. gallons, for example, or kilometers vs. miles.

Implementation of a data contract can take several shapes. When data structures are represented by objects that are defined by classes, and the properties of those classes are formally defined and annotated, and the types and/or values of those properties are checked, the interface of the class serves as a data contract as well. For data structures that are not represented as classes, it is possible to define a schema for that data and apply a check process to the incoming data against that schema. A useful approach for a schema-based input-validation process is to define data structures using a JSON-based schema definition like the components section of the Swagger/OpenAPI Specification — `https://swagger.io/docs/specification/components/` — and use a package like `fastjsonschema` — `https://pypi.org/project/fastjsonschema/` — to validate input data. A more in-depth examination of these options will be undertaken in *Chapter 10, Re-Examining Options for Business Objects*.

The first goal of any input validation process, data contracts included, is to prevent the execution of code that has been supplied with invalid data. Earlier, it was noted that functions and methods could enforce data contracts, and that they were not just an aspect of an object-oriented coding approach. To fully illustrate this, consider this `Person` class:

```python
# From data_contract_function_example.py
from __future__ import annotations
from typeguard import typechecked
@typechecked
class Person:
    def __init__(
        self, given_name: str, family_name: str,
        middle_name: str | None = None
    ):
        self.given_name = given_name
        self.family_name = family_name
        self.middle_name = middle_name
    # Provides a string representation of an object
    def __repr__(self) -> str:
        return f'<{self.__class__.__name__} at '
            f'{hex(id(self))} ' \
            f'given_name={self.given_name} ' \
            f'middle_name={self.middle_name} ' \
            f'family_name={self.family_name}>'
```

This class, as well as the examples of its use, are collected in the `data_contract_function_example.py` module in the chapter's code repository. Using the `typechecked` decorator noted earlier, the `Person` class provides an interface that:

- Requires `given_name` and `family_name` arguments
- Requires the values of those arguments to be string values
- Allows, but does not require, a `middle_name` argument
- Requires that if a `middle_name` is provided, it be a string value as well

At this point, the creation of a `Person` object can be undertaken by passing the given_name and family_name values in a typical manner:

```python
try:
    result = Person('Havelock', 'Vetinari')
    print(result)
except Exception as error:
    print(f'{error.__class__.__name__}: {error}')
```

Which outputs:

```
<Person at 0x7c40f3e53290
  given_name=Havelock middle_name=None family_name=Vetinari
>
```

Python also allows a dictionary of arguments to be created and passed to functions and methods, including the __init__ of the `Person` class, like this:

```python
drumknot = {
    'given_name': 'Rufus', 'family_name': 'Drumknot'
}
try:
    result = Person(**drumknot)
    print(result)
except Exception as error:
    print(f'{error.__class__.__name__}: {error}')
```

Which outputs a similar result:

```
<Person at 0x747bb537a150
  given_name=Rufus middle_name=None family_name=Drumknot
>
```

The type-checking that's in place already prevents the creation of an invalid `Person` object with non-string values passed as its arguments:

```python
try:
    result = Person(1, 2)
    print(result)
except Exception as error:
    print(f'{error.__class__.__name__}: {error}')
```

Which raises and then prints an error:

```
TypeCheckError: argument "given_name" (int) is not an instance of str
```

The data contract expressed by this interface can be usefully carried over to functions that use or create a Person object too. The do_person_things function, brute-force though it is, applies the same typechecked-backed requirements as the __init__ of the Person class, while also accepting an already-created Person object. This example is functional, and illustrates the concept, but may not be the most realistic implementation. Even so, it defines an *in-code* data contract for the function that relates to the Person object it uses.

```python
@typechecked
def do_person_things(
    person: Person | None = None,
    *,
    given_name: str | None = None,
    family_name: str | None = None,
    middle_name: str | None = None
):
    _bad_person_data = 'do_person_things expects ' \
        'either a Person object or a given_name and ' \
        ' family_name value (with an optional ' \
        ' middle_name value) that can create one'
    # Assure that we have a Person, or create one
    if person is None:
        # No person supplied, try to create one
        assert given_name and family_name, _no_person_data
        person = Person(
            given_name, family_name, middle_name
        )
    # Either person was provided, or successfully created
    assert isinstance(person, Person), _bad_person_data
    # Do some computationally-expensive things
    # with the Person created before returning it
    ...
    return person
```

Calling that function with both valid and invalid values allows the function to handle its own expected input rules, as well as allowing the Person class to enforce its interface requirements, using a typical structure:

```
ridcully = Person('Mustrum', 'Ridcully')
try:
    result = do_person_things(ridcully)
    print(result)
except Exception as error:
    print(f'{error.__class__.__name__}: {error}')
```

Which outputs:

```
<Person at 0x727a85869b50
  given_name=Mustrum middle_name=None family_name=Ridcully
>
```

and the dictionary-based argument-structure shown earlier:

```
stibbons = {
    'given_name': 'Ponder',
    'family_name': 'Stibbons'
}
try:
    result = do_person_things(**stibbons)
    print(result)
except Exception as error:
    print(f'{error.__class__.__name__}: {error}')
```

Which outputs:

```
<Person at 0x72d0a6cf5210
  given_name=Ponder middle_name=None family_name=Stibbons
>
```

It can also intercept invalid argument data *before* making the attempt to create a `Person` object, which could be advantageous if that involved some computationally expensive process:

```python
rincewind = {
    'family_name': 'Rincewind'|
}
try:
    result = do_person_things(**rincewind)
    print(result)
except Exception as error:
    print(f'{error.__class__.__name__}: {error}')
```

Which raises, then prints, an error:

```
AssertionError: do_person_things expects either a Person object or a
given_name and family_name value (with an optional middle_name value) that
can create one
```

...and that holds true for argument types that would cause errors if they were passed unchecked to `Person.__init__` as well:

```python
try:
    result = do_person_things(given_name=1, family_name=2)
    print(result)
except Exception as error:
    print(f'{error.__class__.__name__}: {error}')
```

Which also raises, then prints, an error:

```
TypeCheckError: argument "given_name" (int) did not match any element in
the union:
  str: is not an instance of str
  NoneType: is not an instance of NoneType
```

It is typical for a validation process, whether a formal data contract or not, to raise errors. Those errors can get ugly and hard to read, which is why the _bad_person_data error message provides as much detail as it can. More recent versions of Python have made significant improvements in the language's inline error reporting and stack trace display, but even with those improvements, it is often a good idea to issue meaningful and detailed error messages when possible: they can be written to explain exactly what went wrong, as shown in the `AssertionError` output above, and that will make debugging significantly easier.

It is fair to ask the question: *Why should annotations, type-checking, or data contracts be included in code?* They represent additional code that must be tested and maintained, with a corresponding increase in the time required. There are several answers to that question, from different points of focus or emphasis. *Annotations* are additional, but more tightly defined and specialized, documentation that lives in the code itself. Ideally, that means that the next person to pick up the code to try to work with it has more ready access to that information and will not have to context-shift as drastically to understand the relevant code elements. Type-checking, and by extension, data contracts, when applied with thought and discipline, can be leveraged to check inputs to callables before they have a chance to cause significant errors. They can, then, prevent data corruption that is troublesome to remedy. In runtime environments that cost money as code executes, they can also be leveraged to ensure that malformed invocations of callables fail fast. The cost implications per invocation are unlikely to be significant, but in scenarios where thousands or millions of those invocations are happening per second, those trivial costs add up.

The trade-off is that those failures will raise error outputs somewhere along the line, and ugly stack traces with them. Ideally, even in code that has been published or deployed to a production environment, the details of those errors should be visible to the people for whom they are meaningful — the developers who are maintaining that code, in particular. At the same time, it is likely that end users of the code who are using it but not developing in or with it, will not want or need to see those. Finding a balance point in that visibility is a typical concern for *observability*, another topic that is worth considering as an internal standard.

Observability starts with logging

Observability, in a software engineering context, can be loosely defined as having enough visible data about the operation of a piece of software to understand how it is behaving. That ability is most useful when the software in question is behaving badly — generating errors, writing bad data, and so on. There are advantages, though, to having at least some minimal data that shows normal operation and execution, even if it is only useful as a baseline to compare misbehaving executions to.

Barring some sort of active monitoring services, the starting point for most observability concerns is logging the processes being executed at significant and meaningful points. Like most languages, Python provides a logging mechanism, in the form of the built-in `logging` module (`https://docs.python.org/3.11/library/logging.html`). The `logging` module provides a `Logger` object that can issue log messages to any of several output channels, including specific files, and to standard output (a terminal, for example).

Those log messages can be issued by the developer at whatever points seem relevant in the code. They can also be assigned a logging level that maps to how important the log message is. Python's log levels, from most to least significant, are:

- **CRITICAL**, indicating that the code may be unable to continue

- **ERROR**, indicating that a significant, but perhaps non-fatal, error has been encountered

- **WARNING**, indicating that something unexpected has happened, or that a problem might occur in the foreseeable future

- **INFO**, generally indicating some sort of normal operational checkpoint has been reached

- **DEBUG**, used to provide detailed information about what is going on, typically only of use or interest to developers

Even without support from other systems, logging is a useful observability mechanism, but there are some questions to ask, and decisions to make, all variations on the basic theme of *what should be logged? How and when should errors be logged?* is probably the most important thing to ask. Logging errors is invaluable for troubleshooting purposes when code starts failing. *How and when should normal operations be logged?* is important to decide as well. Logging some amount of normal operation through a process, as noted earlier, can provide a useful baseline for troubleshooting purposes, particularly in cases where functions calling functions to any depth can help determine what point of a process is failing. Finally, *what debug-level logging is allowed or expected?* will be useful in run-time environments where logging can be changed without re-deploying the software, in order to gain details of operations when something is going awry.

The answers to these questions will, ultimately, define a logging policy for the code being written. An example of a logging policy that addresses these questions is:

- **All** functions or methods will issue a log message before they exit:

  - A successful exit, with no errors, will log an `INFO` message with the function name and a generic *completed successfully* message: `function_name completed successfully`, for example.

  - A successful exit should also log a `DEBUG` message that captures any relevant, detailed information for state changes, output data structures, etc.

  - An unsuccessful exit, where an error is caught, will log an `ERROR` or `CRITICAL` message, depending on the severity of the error, with the relevant error name and the error message, and include an `exc_info` keyword argument that references the error.

- **Entry-point functions** will log an `INFO` message indicating that they have been called: `function_name called`, for example.

- **Other functions** *may* log a similar message when they are called.

- Simple process checkpoint INFO messages may be logged wherever the developer feels they are useful, but should be limited to simple checkpoint statements — no representation of state, etc. should be present in these messages.

- Detailed process state information DEBUG messages may be logged wherever the developer feels they are useful.

Using exc_info vs. using logger.exception

If logging **CRITICAL** messages is part of a logging policy, passing the error in the exc_info keyword argument will include that error's information in the log output. This is the default behavior for the logger.exception method, but that method logs at an **ERROR** level only.

An example of the application of this logging policy to a very simple function, along with some basic support and setup, leads to this code:

```python
# From observability_logging_example.py
import logging
import os
import pprint
logger = logging.getLogger()
logger.setLevel(logging.DEBUG)
module_name = __file__.split(os.sep)[-1]
class LocalError(Exception):
    ...
def example_function(
    arg1, arg2=None, *args, kwonly1=None, **kwargs
):
    logger.info(f'{module_name}::example_function called')
    logger.debug(pprint.pformat(locals()))
    try:
        logger.debug(
            f'{module_name}::example_function debugging '
            'message'
        )
        # Comment one of these out to see the
        # differences in how they log messages.
```

```
        raise LocalError(
            'Some (recoverable?) error happened'
        )
        raise RuntimeError('Some FATAL error happened')
    except LocalError as error:
        logger.error(
            f'{module_name}::example_function encountered '
            f'{error.__class__.__name__}: {error}',
            exc_info=error
        )
    except Exception as error:
        logger.critical(
            f'{module_name}::example_function raised '
            f'{error.__class__.__name__}: {error}',
            exc_info=error
        )
    else:
        logger.debug(
            f'{module_name}::example_function another '
            'debugging message'
        )
        logger.info(
            f'{module_name}::example_function completed '
            'successfully'
        )
```

After wrapping a call to that function in a __main__ block, with some associated logging configuration, like this:

```
if __name__ == '__main__':
    # Logging to the console
    stdout_handler = logging.StreamHandler()
    formatter = logging.Formatter(
        '[%(levelname)8s] %(message)s'
    )
    stdout_handler.setFormatter(formatter)
    logger.addHandler(stdout_handler)
    logger.info(f'{module_name}.__main__ executing')
```

```
        example_function('arg1 value')
        logger.info(f'{module_name}.__main__ completed')
```

...and running the module, it outputs (with formatting altered for clarity):

```
[    INFO] observability_logging_example.py.__main__
          executing
[    INFO] observability_logging_example.py::
          example_function called
[   DEBUG] {
               'arg1': 'arg1 value', 'arg2': None,
               'args': (), 'kwargs': {}, 'kwonly1': None
          }
[   DEBUG] observability_logging_example.py::
          example_function debugging message
[   ERROR] observability_logging_example.py::
          example_function encountered LocalError:
             Some (recoverable?) error happened
Traceback (most recent call last):
  File "/.../CH06-code/observability_logging_example.py",
    line 21, in example_function
    raise LocalError('Some (recoverable?) error happened')
LocalError: Some (recoverable?) error happened
[    INFO] observability_logging_example.py.__main__
          completed
```

Note

The reader is encouraged to play with the code in this example, particularly the two raise statement lines, and alter the logger.setLevel to a different logging-level from the list above. Even just altering the logging-level to INFO, for example, makes a lot of difference in the output shown above.

Defining and adhering to a logging policy, along with diligence around catching errors with try...except structures in the code, will make the generation of solid, foundational data for observability purposes a known, predictable quantity. In turn, the availability of that data will make troubleshooting easier.

Good, solid observability practices, particularly in large systems or systems that have a high volume of use, will make a lot of difference in the ease of troubleshooting errors when (not if) they occur. Having insight into, at a minimum, where in a long chain of processes a given execution broke down, and how it got there, may even allow specific errors to be reproduced, making them *much* easier to mitigate.

Summary

This chapter covered a fair number of ideas to consider and make decisions about, but all of them relate, in some fashion, to what to expect within the code itself. Depending on the specific decisions made around each of these ideas, there may be a fair amount of additional work involved to actually follow through on the chosen standards. That's quite possible. At the same time, if those standards are agreed upon by all the developer stakeholders for a project, or within a team, even with the additional work involved, the participants will have agreed that the goals being pursued are worthwhile enough to warrant the additional effort.

None of these standards are a one-size-fits-all decision: different teams and different projects can have wildly different priorities, after all, and even those can change over time. At the same time, each has the potential for significant benefits. Consistent code organization patterns across projects mean that less time will be needed to bring a new person up to speed, even if they are a seasoned professional engineer. The same holds true for consistent, meaningful in-code documentation and comments. Consistent naming conventions, especially if they emphasize meaningful names for code elements, will as well, and would be expected to reduce the number of comments and the amount of content needed in the documentation. Making a conscious decision to use properties, or to use simple attributes — both are viable choices — removes ambiguity from the process of crafting the code and what considerations need to be kept in mind during that crafting, particularly with respect to annotation and type-checking considerations that depend on that choice. Much the same can be said about using or not using data contracts. Finally, although logging and error handling can represent a significant amount of additional effort, the benefit they provide during troubleshooting will be self-evident the first time they come into play.

Unlike the *Style standards for code* section in *Chapter 6, Code Style and Related Standards*, there may not be ready-made tools to verify that the standards that derive from these decisions are actually applied. A fair number of them will be verifiable by unit tests, which will be discussed as part of the *Process Standards* chapter, next.

8

Revisiting Development Tools

The last collection of decision points around code projects to discuss is, in many respects, a catch-all of ideas that are important, but that do not neatly fit into one of the groupings in the previous chapters, though they frequently mesh with one or more of those previously explored concepts. These include the following:

- How best to manage package dependencies in a Python project
- What code editor / **Integrated Development Environment** (**IDE**) options are available, and how they handle development needs
- What options are available for facilitating various process standards — managing source code and testing it
- What options are available for delivering code once work against it has been completed

If there is a unifying theme in this chapter's topics, it might best be described as *tools for facilitating development processes*.

Technical requirements

All of the code presented in this chapter was written in a Python 3.11 environment. While most macOS and Linux machines ship with some version of Python, they may not have *this* version installed. Installation packages and instructions for Python 3.11 can be found at `https://www.python.org/downloads/`, under the *Looking for a specific release?* heading for Windows and macOS systems. Linux systems typically have access to it through their normal package management system (yum or apt/apt-get), though some Linux distributions may require special efforts to install versions other than the default installed with the **operating system (OS)**. Since much of this chapter explores options for managing package dependencies and Python virtual environments, installation instructions for those tools are provided or referenced in the body of the chapter; the code examples for each variant require those installations to run.

The code can be found at the following GitHub link: `https://github.com/PacktPublishing/Hands-On-Software-Engineering-with-Python-Second-Edition/`

Package dependency management

It's rare for a project of any size or complexity to not need at least *some* external code. Python's built-in libraries and packages provide a *lot* of ready-to-use functionality, listed on the *Python Standard Library* page (for Python 3.11, see `https://docs.python.org/3.11/library/index.html`), which lists well over two hundred built-in packages and modules. There are more than *ten thousand* additional packages available in the public **Python Package Index (PyPI)** that are compatible with *some* Python 3.x versions (see `https://pypi.org/search/?q=&o=&c=Programming+Language+%3A%3A+Python+%3A%3A+3`).

In a perfect world, any software engineer, working on any project, would be able to assume that the project in question used the same version of Python and that any package dependencies needed by that project would be the same for any other project that needed them. In that setting, package dependencies could be managed with nothing more than built-in tools such as pip (`https://pypi.org/project/pip/`), which is generally installed as a built-in package. Realistically, though, it's not unusual for different projects to have different package requirements or even different Python version needs. Those requirements can (and frequently do) change over time for individual projects as well. Handling different Python versions can be managed with another common Python package — virtualenv (`https://pypi.org/project/virtualenv/`), in combination with another utility — pyenv (`https://github.com/pyenv/pyenv`). Development workflows using these tools are possible, but can be complicated, and tend to be more error-prone; there are more commands to remember for even the relatively simple process of adding a new package dependency to a project.

There are at least two package management utilities that were built with an eye toward making these types of situations easier to manage: pipenv and poetry. Both of these packages provide much of the same package- and virtual-environment management functionality, as shown in *Table 8.1*. They even follow similar command patterns, though the names of the commands vary between them.

Feature	pipenv	poetry
Create and manage virtual environments	✓	✓
Manage development-only packages	✓	✓
Package dependency tracking and management	✓	✓
Package dependency categories/groups	✓	✓
Custom/private package repository support	✓	✓
Execute project code within the virtual environment	✓	✓
Auto-creation of project files		✓
Supports project-specific environment variables	✓	

Table 8.1: Comparison of key features between pipenv and poetry

Both of these options, as might be inferred from their common feature set, provide tools and functionality to create a **Python virtual environment** (**PVE**) that's associated with a code project. They also allow the user to manage package dependencies within the context of that PVE, keeping a clean and specific set of those dependencies separate from any system-wide package installations available through the system's general Python installation.

> **What is a virtual environment?**
>
> In a Python development context, a virtual environment is an isolated instance of a Python interpreter, with its own distinct set of packages. Package management tools such as pipenv and poetry manage packages within the context of their virtual environments, ensuring that a project has the dependencies it needs, but without affecting the system-wide package installations.

The example projects detailed here were set up with a common base of packages: One, flake8, is a linting tool, previously mentioned in *Chapter 6*. Another, pytest, will be discussed later in *Test-framework options*. Both of these are intended to be *development-only* dependencies. In order to demonstrate a normal package-dependency use, each also installs the requests package (https://requests.readthedocs.io), which has several package dependencies of its own.

Why have development-only package dependencies?

The purposes served by many packages — `flake8` and `pytest` in the example projects — are not needed in a final deployed package or application while their capabilities may be desired or needed during development. Shipping a package or an application with packages that aren't actually used by it won't break things, but if all a package dependency does is take up space in the deployed end product, it serves no purpose.

Another typical pattern that the installation of development-only packages is useful for is in cases where a project will be deployed to an environment that will already have a collection of preinstalled packages and access to one or more of those is needed during development. A real-world example of this is writing code for AWS Lambda Functions. Among the preinstalled packages is one, boto3, that provides programmatic access to a host of AWS cloud services and resources. While writing a Lambda function, it's quite common that a developer will need to use the boto3 functionality and be able to in a manner that allows the code in question to be run, if only for testing purposes. In that case, installing boto3 as a development-only package dependency provides that access, without the implicit inclusion of the package in the final deployed code.

These examples also have a simple script, in `scripts/example-run.py`, that shows environment variables available to the script, and the available packages in the Python virtual environment when run.

Managing packages with pipenv

`pipenv` is a general-purpose package-management tool. It makes few assumptions about the goals or intentions behind the code that it is being used with, focusing on management tasks for the virtual environment, and the packages within it. It also provides several utility sub-commands that may be of use during development or a build process, including the following:

- `pipenv check` — Checks installed packages for known security vulnerabilities
- `pipenv graph` — Shows the installed packages, and their dependencies, within the virtual environment
- `pipenv requirements` — Generates the content for a `requirements.txt` for the project's packages
- `pipenv run` — Executes a command in the context of the virtual environment for the project

As of version 2023.4.20, pipenv includes the ability to manage packages within *categories* and to export requirements.txt files for those categories. For projects that combine several deployable units, each of which may have its own package dependencies, this allows considerable flexibility to define a package-dependency workflow for multiple functional components within a single project.

Installation instructions for pipenv can be found on the project's home page at https://pipenv.pypa.io. An example project, pipenv-example, is available in the Git repository for this chapter, which provides a step-by-step breakdown of its use throughout this chapter. For full functionality, including the management of Python versions for each project's virtual environment, the pyenv utility noted earlier should also be installed — if pyenv is installed, pipenv will use it to download and install minimal Python runtimes as needed, setting them up in the project's virtual environment.

Managing package dependencies with pipenv involves three primary commands, with one more that may be needed on occasion:

- pipenv install — Installs one or more packages in the environment
- pipenv uninstall — Removes one or more packages from the environment
- pipenv update — Updates a specific package or all packages in the environment
- pipenv clean — Uninstalls any packages in the environment that are not being actively managed by pipenv (which do not have entries in the Pipfile.lock file used to track package dependencies)

In addition, pipenv run will look for, and incorporate, environment variables (defined in a .env file living next to Pipfile, which pipenv generates), allowing a developer to simulate environment variables that their code uses, without having to create them in the code itself.

A completely manual process for setting up a new project that uses pipenv would involve the following steps, assuming it uses Python 3.11:

- Creating a new directory for the project.
- Navigating to the project's directory in a terminal.
- Initializing the PVE for the project with pipenv --python 3.11. **Note:** Some versions of pipenv, on some platforms, will search for an existing Pipfile in directories above the project's directory. Creating Pipfile first, as an empty file, will alleviate this.
- Installing any common packages needed/desired for the develop-test-build cycle — for example, pipenv install --dev flake8 pytest to install the flake8 linting package and the pytest testing package.

Avoid making changes to the Pipfile directly!

Although it's possible to make changes to the `Pipfile` manually — it is just a specifically-formatted text-file — doing so runs the risk of complicating the environment's package set, requiring clean-up (`pipenv clean`), or even dropping and recreating the virtual environment to remedy any issues that surface as a result. It is almost always better to make changes to the environment using the `pipenv` commands.

At this point, the project is ready for work. As additional dependencies are needed for the project, or deemed not needed, they can be added or removed with the `install` and `uninstall` commands noted earlier.

It is worth noting that `pipenv` supports local files (`.env`) that define environment variables. Environment variables defined in a standard `VARIABLE_NAME="value"` structure in that file will be read and added to the environment for the duration of the interpreter's execution. Among other uses, this facilitates using a `PYTHONPATH` value to point to a project's root directory, for example:

```
PYTHONPATH="src" # Adds the project's src directory to
                 # the import path-set for the project
                 # at run time.
```

pipenv, as noted earlier, is a general-purpose package-management tool for Python. One trade-off when using it is that most types of Python development efforts will require some additional work or setup on a project-by-project basis. Writing Python applications that are deployed to a cloud-based runtime environment (AWS Lambda Functions, for example) will require additional build-process setup. Efforts that are intended to publish Python packages will require different additional setups. For these efforts, there is an alternative that handles a lot of the setup, following the current suggested standards described in the official *Packaging Python Projects* tutorial (`https://packaging.python.org/en/latest/tutorials/packaging-projects/`): the poetry package.

Managing packages with poetry

poetry, like `pipenv`, manages package dependencies in the context of a specific, project-related Python virtual environment. Unlike `pipenv`, `poetry` is more focused on providing that management for the purpose of writing Python packages, suitable for publishing to the public PyPI (`https://pypi.org/`).

Much of its functionality is similar to `pipenv` — the specific command names differ, but the basic toolset provides the same package-management capabilities:

- `poetry add`: This is used to add (install) one or more new packages into the project's environment
- `poetry remove`: This is used to remove (uninstall) one or more packages from the project's environment
- `poetry update`: This is used to update one or more packages in the project's environment

Because poetry is designed for writing Python packages, there are two additional commands that are likely to be relevant:

- `poetry build`: This builds the project as a Python package, in both tarball and wheel distribution formats
- `poetry publish`: This publishes the package to a PyPI-compatible repository, such as the public repository at `https://pypi.org`

Installation instructions for poetry can be found on the project's home page (`https://python-poetry.org`). An example project, `poetry-example`, is available in the Git repository for this chapter, which provides a step-by-step breakdown of its use throughout this chapter. The project setup used for the `poetry-example` project, which is typical for a bare-minimum setup, is as follows:

1. Navigate in a terminal to the directory where the project will be created — unlike `pipenv`, poetry will actually create the project structure, while `pipenv` needs a starting directory created to work within.
2. Create the new project with `poetry new {project-name}` — this creates the project directory and several common and starting-point files.
3. Navigate to the just-created project directory.
4. Install any common development-only packages.
5. Configure the ID to use the project's virtual environment.

At this point, the project is ready for work. poetry creates a minimal project structure but includes enough basic code structure, and all the tools needed to build and publish the project as an installable Python package.

Be sure to test your installations!

Installation of pipenv and poetry alike may not work without some manual tweaks, particularly for certain Windows environments. Be sure to check that your installation works before closing the terminal window where it was executed, and to pay attention to any warnings that the installation process raises.

Deciding which of these two PVE- and package-management tools to use often depends on the final intended output for a project. While poetry provides all the tools needed, and much of the initial project structure involved for writing Python packages, the same tools can be installed in a pipenv-managed PVE. If a project needs to assure deterministic builds, while both provide that capability, the approach taken by pipenv is often easier to understand and follow. Both are relatively easy to integrate into several IDEs and code editors, even to the point of allowing code in the editor to be run within the context of the PVEs that they manage.

IDE options and what to look for

It is technically possible to write and test Python code with nothing more than a basic text editor and a command line. Boiling the development process down to the bare minimum, it really consists of two steps that get repeated until the code does what is intended:

1.   Create new code, or modify existing code.

2.   Run the current code, by whatever means are relevant, to test it.

There is nothing in this process that requires anything more sophisticated, and that basic editor-and-terminal toolset might well suffice for very simple efforts. Once a coding effort reaches a certain level of complexity, though, it is *much* easier to use a tool intended for writing and testing code, integrating as many of the tools as a developer needs into a single IDE. Having all of the necessary tools a click or keystroke away makes the processes of writing and testing code easier to manage, and more efficient, regardless of the programming language involved.

Although there are several IDEs that can be used to write Python code, only three of them will be discussed in detail here. The criteria for their selection include the following:

•   Some form of project-based grouping and management of code

•   The ability to leverage both pipenv and poetry to manage Python run time environments and package dependencies for a project

- Availability across Linux, macOS, and Windows
- A reasonable set of tools, macros, or other facilities to speed key aspects of the development process

The three IDEs that will be compared and contrasted are as follows:

- **Geany**: A lightweight but powerful programmer's text editor with just enough additional functionality available to fall into an IDE classification (`https://www.geany.org/`)
- **PyCharm**: A well-rounded Python-focused IDE, available in both Community (free of cost) and Professional (paid license) editions (`https://www.jetbrains.com/pycharm/`)
- **Visual Studio Code (VS Code)**: A highly extensible and customizable code editor intended to provide just the tools a developer needs for quick write-build-debug cycles (`https://code.visualstudio.com/`)

Unless specifically called out otherwise, each of these can be installed in a reasonably normal fashion on Linux, macOS, or Windows devices. In the cases of macOS and Windows, that generally means that a normal installer program is available. A reasonably normal Linux installation, int this case, means that there is some software-manager package available — a `.deb` or `.rpm` file — that can be manually installed from a download if the IDE program is not available in the relevant software sources.

Generally, the functionality involved in writing and debugging code is very similar across these IDEs. The specific commands, menus, or keyboard shortcuts for tasks relating to those processes will vary, but the basic processes themselves are otherwise almost identical. The most significant differences are in how a new project gets created and configured, which will be examined in detail. Many of the setup and configuration steps for a new project will also apply to cases where a developer is starting work on an existing project for the first time, for example, having cloned a project from a source control repository to work on locally. At a project level, the relevant activities are as follows:

1. **Creating a project directory**: Remember that poetry handles this step during the creation of a new project. This should also be automatically handled when retrieving an existing project from source control.

2. **Setting up a PVE for the project**: This is also handled automatically by poetry during project creation. When retrieving an existing project from source control, the PVE will need to be created and its dependencies installed with `pipenv install` or `poetry install`, whichever is relevant.

3. **Installing any development-only dependencies that are needed or desired for all projects**: The example projects described for each IDE/PVE management combination assume that pytest and flake8 are expected, providing better unit-test discovery and code linting, respectively. Development-only package dependencies may need to be explicitly installed (pipenv install --dev or poetry add --group=dev, as applicable) if the initial PVE setup does not resolve them in projects retrieved from source control for the first time.

4. **Configuring the project within the IDE so that code can be executed, linted, and/or tested as quickly and easily as possible**: Linting and testing configuration may be optional — if the relevant packages are not installed, there would be nothing to configure, or there may be a preference to run them from a command-line rather than from within the IDE.

5. **Allowing access to the environment variables for the system that the code is running on**: This may not be a common requirement for most projects, but the inclusion of this capability will demonstrate the use of a common built-in package within the context of a project. Beyond that, it is one of the major points of variation in one of the IDEs being examined.

Each IDE/PVE-manager combination examined has some variations in the project-creation and project-configuration actions needed. However, each will implement the same bare-bones functionality, captured in the main.py module. There will also be a starting-point stub for a unit-test suite, in a module named test_main.py. Those modules will be identical across all these variants unless the IDE/package-manager combination requires otherwise.

The goals for these examples

These IDEs have more functionality than is being explored here — in some cases, *much* more. The main goal of these explorations is to provide a breakdown of what is necessary to get to the same common point: The ability to write and run/debug code in the IDE in a consistent manner, and with as little effort on the user's part as possible.

The main.py module does nothing more than print some information about what's happening as it executes:

```
Running .../ide-examples/.../example_project/
    src/example_project/main.py
Example using pipenv in Geany
The requests module:
```

```
<module 'requests' from '.../{PVE}/lib/python3.11/
   site-packages/requests/__init__.py'>
A bare-bones project module. All this module does is print that it's being
run, this docstring, and the interpreter that it's running under.
Project Python interpreter: .../{PVE}/bin/python
```

The test_main.py module contains a single test function that will always pass. This test function is in place solely so that running the test module, or the project's test suite, with pytest will not fail for lack of running any tests.

These example projects were written, replicated, and tested across three separate operating systems/platforms: Linux Mint 21.2 (Victoria; based off of Ubuntu 22.04 jammy), macOS 14.5 (Sonoma), and Windows 11 (Home, with updates including PowerShell 7). They were written to run under Python 3.11.

Geany

Geany is intended to be a lightweight IDE, whose main focus is providing enough functionality for a developer to do what they need to do without getting in the way or bogging down the development workflow. The trade-off for this focus is that Geany relies more heavily on other tools and programs available on the machine that it is running on, and on the user knowing how to set configuration to use those tools. Geany is available for download at https://www.geany.org/download/releases/, and there are additional plugins available for download at https://plugins.geany.org/geany-plugins/, which includes the *Project Organizer* plugin that was used while creating the examples here. Some versions of Geany (and its plugin library) are typically available to be installed in Linux software repositories, allowing installation of a supported version for the OS version to be installed like any other software package. This holds true for Ubuntu and at least one Linux distribution derived from it: Linux Mint. Other distributions that do not offer it can still build it from the source code available on the download page.

> **Geany 2.X vs. 1.XX**
>
> Geany released its first major-version change, 2.0, in over a decade in October of 2023. While that version is, obviously, available in general, it is recent enough that there may still be unknown bugs in it, so the example projects presented here were written using version 1.38.

Geany presents an interface layout that is typical of IDEs, as shown in *Figure 8.1*. It includes a project structure display (top left, provided by the *Project Organizer* plugin noted earlier), the editing space, and a Message Window (bottom) that provides access to several tools, including the **Terminal** shown. This display has one custom configuration, placing the file name tabs to the left of the editor, rather than as a tab set across the top of the editor.

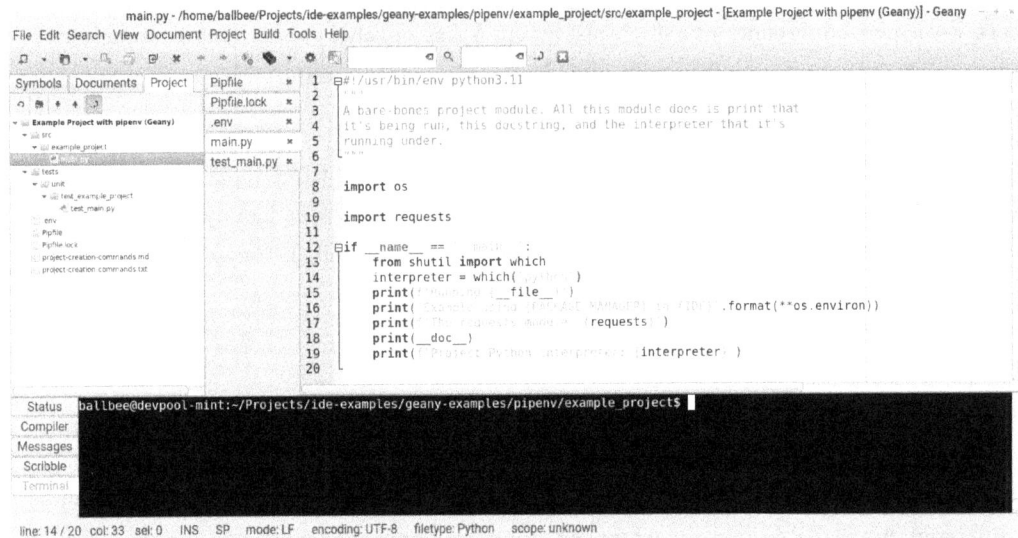

Figure 8.1: Geany's user interface (for visualization purposes only)

When writing Python code in Geany, there are editor configuration settings that can be made to avoid future linting problems. These are shown in *Figure 8.2*, accessed from Geany's **Edit** → **Preferences** menu, under the **Editor** → **Indentation** tab set, and are as follows:

- Set indentation width to 4, conforming to the PEP 8 standard noted earlier
- Set indentation type to use **Spaces**
- Set auto-indent mode to **Current chars**

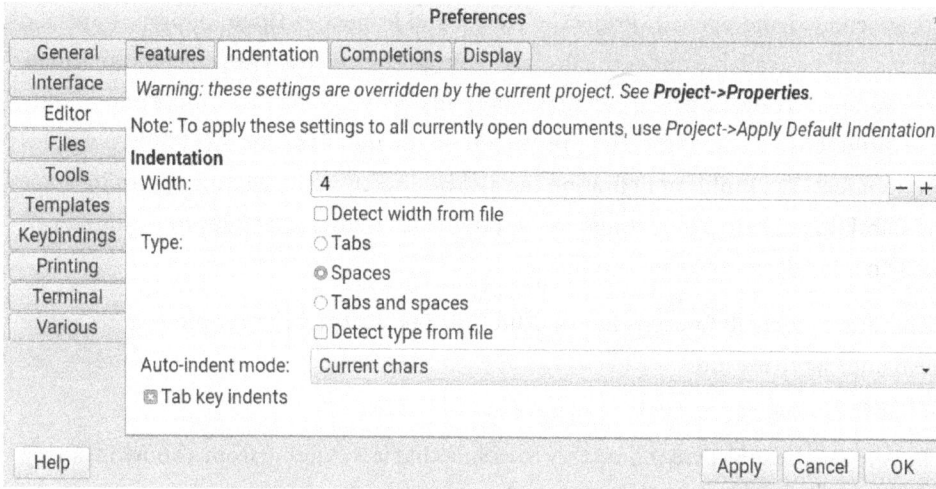

Figure 8.2: Geany's general preferences (configuration) window

Other settings that may be worth examining include the following:

- **General → Startup**, which controls how the IDE behaves when it is opened
- **Interface → Notebook tabs → Tab positions→ Editor** — this is the setting for the custom configuration shown in *Figure 8.1* noted earlier
- **Editor → Display**
- **Tools,** which includes customization of the terminal used to execute code
- **Terminal,** which configures the display settings of the Terminal shown in *Figure 8.1*

These preferences are global to Geany, and will only need to be set once.

Windows-specific Terminal configuration

In the Windows 11 installation that these projects were tested in, which included the most recent version of PowerShell available, **Preferences → Tools → Terminal** needed to be changed to wt cmd /q /c call %c in order for Geany to execute project code from the active editor view. PowerShell also launches multiple tabs during that execution, and if the code executes without error, the tab that execution occurs in is automatically closed, usually before any useful information in it can be read. The example project code shows one possible way to prevent that from happening in main.py.

As projects are created and opened (**Project** → **New...** and **Project** → **Open...**), project-specific configurations will be available under the **Project** → **Properties** menu. These include an **Indentation** tab that can override the global indentations set in Geany's preferences. More importantly, it includes a **Build** tab that allows the user to configure commands to be run for various purposes during development. The **Build** configuration can also be directly accessed from the **Build** → **Set Build Commands** menu item. The settings used for the `pipenv`-based example project are shown in *Figure 8.3*. In more detail, they are as follows:

- Renaming the default **Compile** item as **Run Unit Test Suite** (click the button, and change the name) set to execute

- `cd "%p";pipenv run pytest "tests/unit"`

- (changing to the project root directory to ensure that it is running from a known starting point, and then running `pytest` against the test suite's directory)

- Renaming the default **Lint** item as **Lint Python Module**, which executes `flake8` against the current active module

- Changing the default Execute item to run `cd "%p";pipenv run python "%d/%f"`

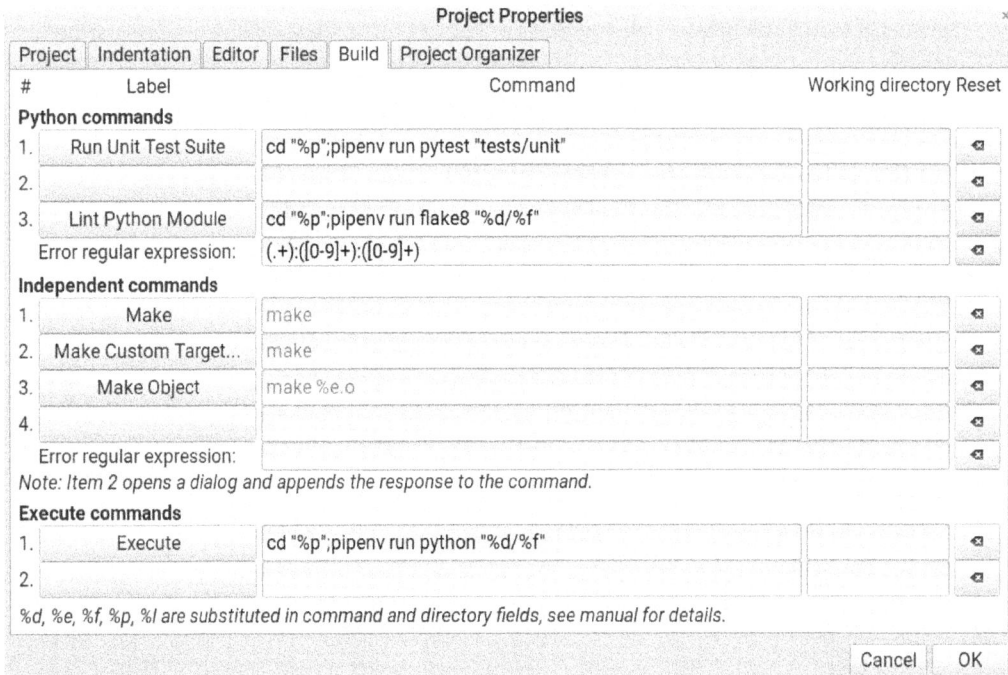

#	Label	Command	Working directory	Reset
Python commands				
1.	Run Unit Test Suite	cd "%p";pipenv run pytest "tests/unit"		⌫
2.				⌫
3.	Lint Python Module	cd "%p";pipenv run flake8 "%d/%f"		⌫
	Error regular expression:	(.+):([0-9]+):([0-9]+)		⌫
Independent commands				
1.	Make	make		⌫
2.	Make Custom Target...	make		⌫
3.	Make Object	make %e.o		⌫
4.				⌫
	Error regular expression:			⌫
Note: Item 2 opens a dialog and appends the response to the command.				
Execute commands				
1.	Execute	cd "%p";pipenv run python "%d/%f"		⌫
2.				⌫

%d, %e, %f, %p, %l are substituted in command and directory fields, see manual for details.

Project Properties — Tabs: Project | Indentation | Editor | Files | Build | Project Organizer — Cancel | OK

Figure 8.3: Geany's project build settings window for the pipenv-based example project; the Independent commands section contains defaults provided by Geany that were not overridden

Project-level configuration should only need to be made once per project, though ongoing tweaks to those settings are obviously possible as new needs are discovered.

> **How does Geany keep track of project settings?**
>
> Project settings are tracked in a `.geany` file, by convention. This file can (and frequently will) contain information that might not allow a project to work as expected across different machines: two software engineers may have different locations where they store project root directories, for example, or might be working with different operating systems that use different file-system path-conventions (Windows vs. MacOS or Linux). If project code is managed in a source control system, these `.geany` files should not be included there, if only to avoid eventual (and perhaps inevitable) conflicts across developer environments.

Because Geany relies extensively on external programs and resources and relies on the user setting anything up that differs from its defaults, there is a fair bit of manual configuration required at first. Once that is complete, though, it is rare that any significant changes will need to be made. At worst, the project-level configuration might need to be set up the first time an existing project is retrieved from source control.

Geany and pipenv

The example project variant running under `pipenv`, and with a full Geany configuration, can be found in the chapter repository, in `ide-examples/geany-examples/pipenv`. The `README.md` file in that directory provides full details of the steps taken to prepare the project, its PVE, and the package dependencies for it. The Geany and project configuration has already been shown in *Figure 8.3*. The creation of the project directory for a `pipenv`/Geany project can be done in any of several ways: Geany's project tools can create it as part of the process of creating the project, or it can be created independently and selected during the project creation process. The PVE set-up, with `pipenv --python 3.11`, must be run from a command line, as must any `pipenv install` needed for any package dependencies.

With the configuration already shown, from within Geany, several basic project activities are ready to use. Any given module can be run, using the Python interpreter associated with its PVE, using the **Build → Execute** menu command (*F5*). The configuration provides a **Build → Lint Python Module** command that will run `flake8` linting against the current active module in the editor. Finally, the entire project's unit-test suite can be run with the **Build → Run Unit Test Suite** command (*F8*).

With only a few changes, a similar process can be used to set up the same capabilities in a project whose PVE is managed by poetry.

Geany and poetry

The example_project variant running under poetry, and with a full Geany configuration, can be found in the chapter repository, in ide-examples/geany-examples/poetry. The README.md file in that directory provides full details of the steps taken to prepare the project, its PVE, and the package dependencies for it. There's little that varies in Geany's project configuration when using poetry versus pipenv: changing that name in the various **Build → Set Build Commands** entries takes care of that after the initial project setup is complete.

That initial project setup varies more, however. Because poetry handles the process of creating the project directory structure, that has to be done manually first. It is not a difficult process, though, all that is required is to navigate to the directory that the new project is going to live in, then execute poetry new with the new project's name, like so:

```
poetry new example_project
```

The resulting project structure is, as expected, more geared toward a Python package development effort — that is, after all, what poetry is optimized for. The addition of the same main.py file to that package directory differs from the structure in the pipenv-based project but is logical and understandable. Similarly, the location of the test module for that main module changes, but is an understandable change within the context of the different project structure. Within the main.py code, since poetry doesn't support .env files by itself, there's also an additional package used (python-dotenv) that needs to be installed to the poetry-managed PVE, and two additional lines of code to import a function from that package and call it to capture the environment variables from the .env file in the project.

Geany is a lowest common denominator, as IDEs go. It can be set up to do everything that a project needs, provided that those needs don't overrun the nine commands that a user can customize under the **Build → Set Build Commands** menu item. Those commands will run, and their results will be displayed, in either a new terminal window or in one of the **Message Window** view panels at the bottom of its UI. Those configurations are little more than menu items that execute commands that the user must know how to define, though, and some of those commands, when they are invoked from the menu, will prompt a user for additional input parameters that may not be relevant for those needs. Other IDEs provide at least some common, desired functionality inline, within their UI. One of those is PyCharm.

PyCharm

PyCharm is a Python-focused IDE by JetBrains, a company that offers nearly a dozen IDEs for various languages. JetBrains describes PyCharm as *the Python IDE for data science and web development*, but it's a perfectly viable option for general-purpose Python development. Over and above the bare-bones functionality that would be expected from any IDE, it offers code completion, real-time detection of errors, and redundancies in code, along with suggestions on how to fix those issues when they have been detected. Its project management allows fast access to all of the code entities in a project, down to the level of module members such as functions and classes. It provides integrations for both `pipenv` and `poetry` package managers, an integrated terminal that automatically runs within the PVEs that provide and integrate with source control management systems such as Git.

PyCharm is available for download from `https://www.jetbrains.com/pycharm/` and is available in two variants: A free *Community* edition and a paid *Professional* edition at $99 for the first year's license for individual use. The Community edition (described as *The IDE for Pure Python Development*) does not include several features offered in the Professional edition, most of which relate to support for web-related technologies. JavaScript and Node.js, along with several frameworks built on those, are the majority of those offerings, but support for the Django web framework (`https://www.djangoproject.com`) and the Flask micro web framework (`https://flask.palletsprojects.com/`) is also in that list. The Professional edition also has built-in database tools and lists **Structured Query Language (SQL)**, a common language for communicating with relational databases, in its supported languages. JetBrains also offers a sizable collection of IDE plugins, many of which might be of use or interest.

Whether a given project uses `pipenv` or `poetry` to manage a PVE and package set, there are several common configuration items to consider as soon as a project is created. These may be addressed after work has started on the actual project code, but if they are going to break anything, it is a better idea to start with those configurations in place: That allows issues that they might raise to be handled as they appear, rather than having to go through a lengthy post-configuration debugging session.

The first step, though, is to create the project. PyCharm's **File → New Project...** menu item is where that starts, which opens a window like the one shown in *Figure 8.4*. This dialog supplies a default project name and may supply a default project location where the new project will be created.

The **Type** options are where the use of pipenv or poetry is specified, once **Interpreter type** is selected and the **Generate new** option for the **Environment** setting is selected. Since both pipenv and poetry need to know what Python version to use, and there may be many Python versions available to choose from, those options are presented in the **Base python** menu, and whichever is appropriate for the project can be selected.

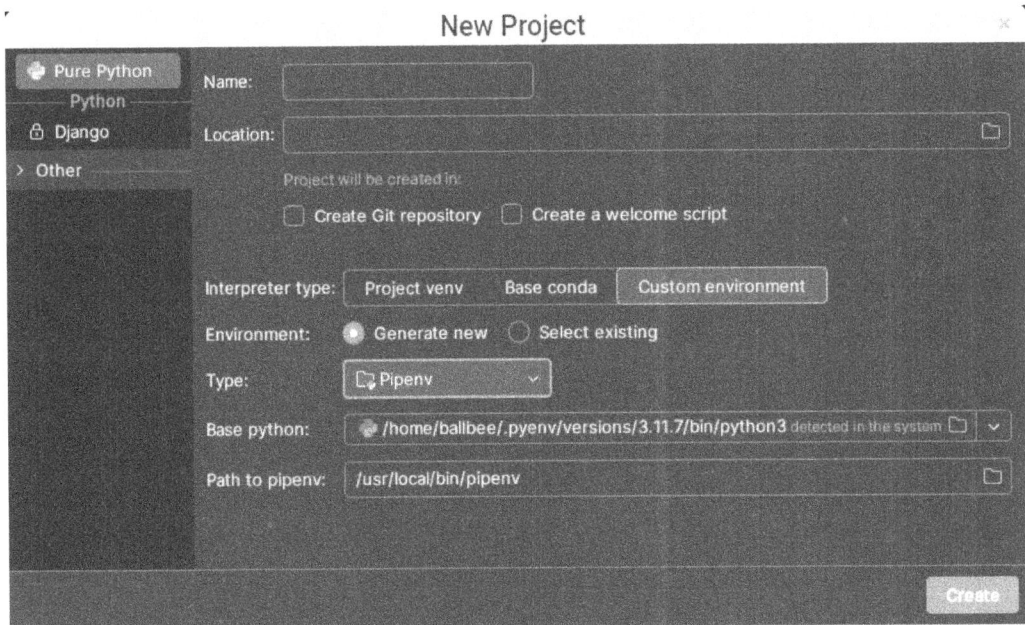

Figure 8.4: PyCharm's New Project dialog

Once all these decisions are made, and the **Create** button is pressed, PyCharm will create a project directory, using the project name specified, at the location specified, along with any standard files that the package manager creates for minimal setup: A Pipfile for pipenv projects, and the project structure described earlier for poetry projects. The initial example_project project created for the pipenv discussion earlier is shown in *Figure 8.5*.

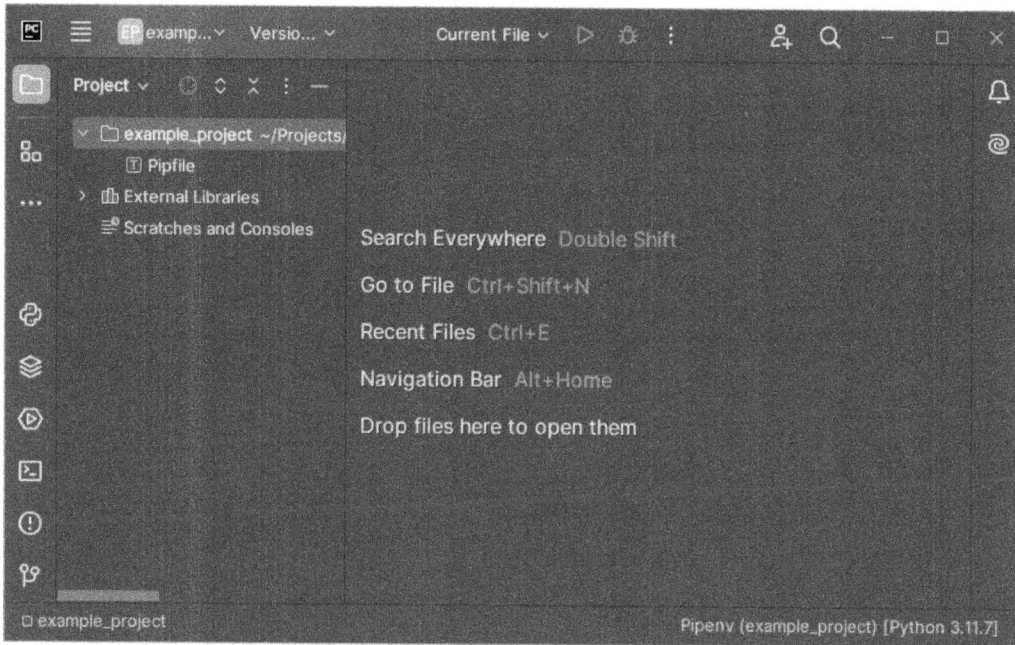

Figure 8.5: A freshly created pipenv-based PyCharm project

At a project level, configuration items to set up for *any* PyCharm project include the following:

- Adding source-code directories to the project, and making PyCharm aware that those directories are *Source* directories. This configuration is under the **File** menu → **Settings**, in the **Project: (project name)** → **Project Structure** group. It presents a file-tree view of the project, where project directories can be selected and marked as **Sources**.

- Setting up a default **Run/Debug Configuration** so that all Python files will, by default, use the same settings when run from the IDE's **Run** menu or its **Run** button (*Shift + F10*). When **Current File** is the option set for that button, **Run** will run the code in the currently active editor window. A starting-point configuration for the example project discussed later is shown in *Figure 8.6*. It includes the following:

  - Setting the **Working directory** to the root project directory, so that all module execution has a single, common starting point for any file-system access needed at runtime

- **Enable EnvFile** and its sub-options are provided by the EnvFile plugin (**File** menu → **Settings** → **Plugins**), which allows the project's .env file to be read and evaluated when a module is run.

- Though not shown in the figure, by default, PyCharm will have an active option shown at the bottom of the panel, **Add source roots to PYTHONPATH**, which tells PyCharm to make the **Sources** directories noted earlier available as import-capable paths when a module is run.

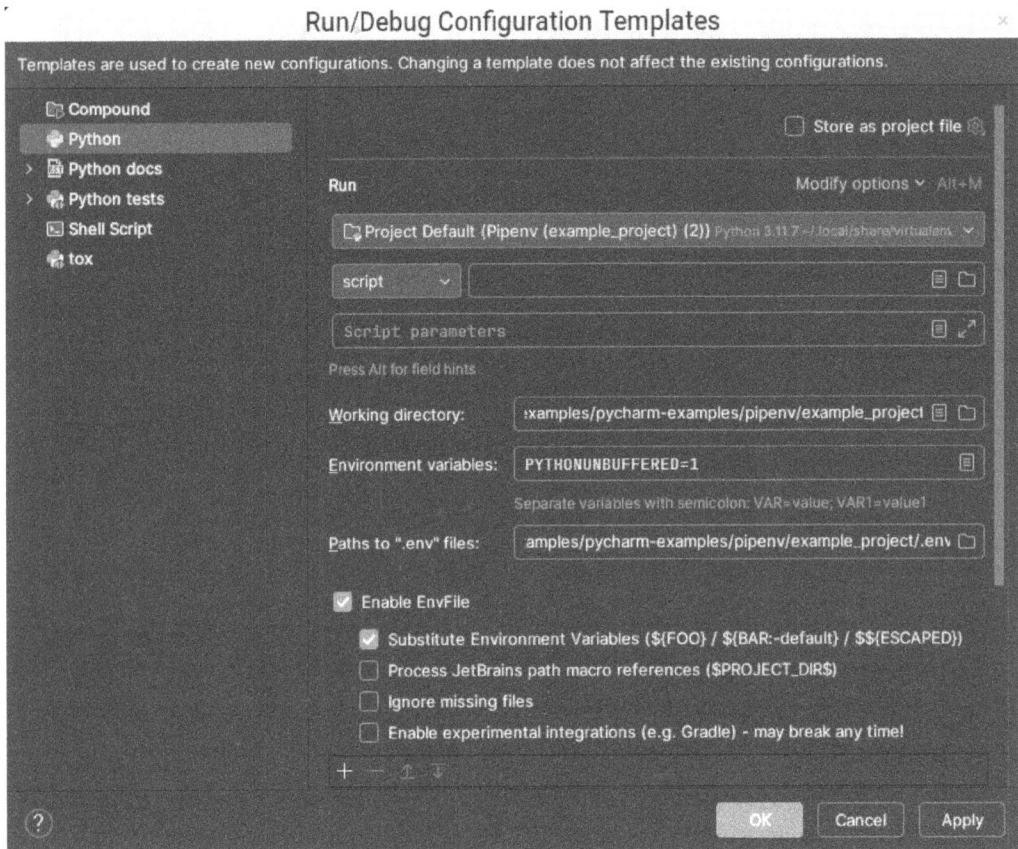

Figure 8.6: A starting Run/Debug configuration in PyCharm

How does PyCharm keep track of project settings?

PyCharm project settings are tracked in files in .idea directories within a project. The project file-system references those files contain are normalized such that they are independent of the location of the project directory on a given user's machine. From that perspective, they should be safe to include in source control, if there is a need or desire to do so, and so long as there are no other environment- or installation-specific data points.

Overall, package management with both `pipenv` and `poetry` works as expected in PyCharm, provided that all activities are executed from PyCharm's **Terminal**. Packages installed even appear in PyCharm's *Python Packages* tool. Installing packages from that tool, though, does not affect the package information files for either — no changes to pipenv's `Pipfile` or `Pipfile.lock` files nor poetry's `pyproject.toml` or `poetry.lock` files occur. In addition, if a project needs to keep different package dependencies separated, using `pipenv`'s `--categories` or poetry's `--group` command flags, there is no apparent way to manage that within PyCharm's UI either. That may not be a common requirement, except for certain types of projects, but when it *is* needed, it *must* be managed using the command line.

PyCharm provides its own built-in linter, which is reasonably good, but may not catch all of the issues that another preferred linter such as `flake8` would, and there is little to no configuration available to customize its settings. While it is possible to add calls to other linters, or to other tools in general, as part of a *Run/Debug Configuration*, that option will only run those tools as part of a run or debug execution. Use of other linters, then, is something that has to be executed manually, or perhaps as part of some external script or process.

PyCharm will auto-detect modules that contain test code, and run those with the detected framework — `pytest`, for example — if it is installed in the PVE for the project, or on the machine in general. That auto-detection has also been known to incorrectly assume that a non-test module that contains a function whose name starts with `test` is a test module. Python tests have their own distinct *Run/Debug Configuration* template, similar to the one shown for a project in *Figure 8.6*. Creating a general *Python tests Run/Debug Configuration* for the test frameworks used by a project should be undertaken before any test modules are executed that generate their own module-specific configuration.

Overall, PyCharm is a solid, usable IDE for writing Python code. It has its own quirks, but provided that configuration is set up when work on a project is started, it will behave in a reasonable and predictable fashion. Of its quirks, the disconnect between its internal package-management tool and both `pipenv` and `poetry` is most likely to cause problems: The fact that it works as expected when changes originate from the command-line tools, but not in the other direction can cause unexpected issues.

PyCharm is a well-established product, with versions going as far back as early 2011. There are newer IDE options that provide similar, higher-level functionality as well. One of the more popular of those is Visual Studio Code.

Visual Studio Code

Visual Studio Code (VS Code) is a source-code editor, distributed by Microsoft under a proprietary freeware license, with over thirty thousand extensions for various languages and development purposes. As of 2024, VS Code was the most popular IDE available, with 14 million installations, and approximately 75% of the market share for IDEs. It is available as a free download at `https://code.visualstudio.com/` and is supported across Windows, macOS, and any Linux distributions that can install from `.deb` or `.rpm` packages.

VS Code is smart enough to recognize when a new file type is created, and whether an additional extension is needed to work with that file type and prompt the user to install the relevant extension. One of those extensions is language support for Python, titled simply *Python* in the VS Code *Extensions* tools. When installed, it also provides *Pylance* (a language server for VS Code) and a *Python Debugger* extension. These extensions can be installed ahead of time, or the user can wait for the prompt, but in either case, the *Python* extension is needed to leverage VS Code's full capabilities with the language.

As with Geany and PyCharm, discussed earlier, the configuration of a project in VS Code is critical in order to run and test code in the IDE. VS Code does not (yet) have UI tools that handle the creation of PVEs with either `pipenv` or `poetry`, but it does keep track of available Python runtime environments on the machine, so the configuration is somewhere between what needs to be done for Geany and PyCharm. The minimal sequence for creating and configuring a new Python project in VS Code is as follows:

1. **Create the project directory**. The choice of PVE-/package-management tool requires different processes for this step:

    - Because `pipenv` does not create any of the project directory structure, a new project folder can be created from the **File → Open Folder...** menu command, which will allow the creation of a new folder before opening it.

    - Because `poetry` creates project directory structure and starting-point files, a project will require less setup effort if the initial creation of its folder is handled *outside* of VS Code. Once that has been completed, the project folder can be opened from the **File → Open Folder...** menu-command.

2. Navigate to the new folder in a terminal, and create the project's PVE with the relevant pipenv or poetry command, as described earlier. This can be done from VS Code's built-in *Terminal*, but the process differs between the PVE managers:

    - For projects that use pipenv, the process of creating the PVE is as described earlier. On completion of the creation of the PVE, pipenv will print a path to the root of the PVE created. This should be noted, as it will be needed to set or verify the PVE's Python executable.

    - Projects that use poetry will not have a PVE created until at least one package dependency is installed (with poetry add). Once that has been done, the path to the Python executable associated with the PVE can be retrieved with poetry env info --executable and should be noted, as it will be needed to set or verify the PVE's Python executable.

3. Create or open a Python (.py) file in the project folder. VS Code may generate a prompt to choose a Python environment in the lower right corner of the UI, or it may have one already selected, found by some auto-detection process:

    - If there is a prompt, click on it, then on **Enter interpreter path...** and paste the path to the PVE's Python executable (ending with bin/python or bin\python.exe).

    - If there is no prompt, click on the **Python 3.XX (...)** item in the lower-right corner of the UI, and verify that the project is using the correct PVE. If it isn't, re-set it with the **Enter interpreter path...** process just above.

4. Install any project package dependencies from the IDE's terminal.

VS Code's configuration has fewer steps than the corresponding configuration in PyCharm, but each step frequently requires more detailed information that the user has to find. Once that configuration is complete, though, Python code in any editor tab can be run as needed.

Like PyCharm, VS Code provides inline linting of code. In VS Code, this is managed by the installation of a linting extension, such as the *Flake8* and *Pylint* extensions published by Microsoft. These linters highlight issues discovered by scanning a file when it is saved and provide the explanation from their underlying linting engines. Some issues discovered by the linting run may have automatic or prompted correction functionality available as well — the functional hooks are present, though there may not be many implemented yet. It is also possible to define **Tasks** in VS Code that can run user-defined commands, such as running the flake8 linter against the entire src tree of a project, or against the current active file. Other task possibilities include running an entire test suite, or running the current active file, with a testing framework such as pytest. The example_project variant has simple examples of all of those tasks.

Others

While VS Code and PyCharm likely dominate the field of Python IDEs, there are several other options that might be worth exploring. They may not have the feature set or capabilities of the two leaders in the field, but as Geany shows, so long as a given code editor supports a certain minimum amount of customization and a reasonable project management structure, it's viable.

Other options include, but are not limited to, the following:

- Sublime Text (`https://www.sublimetext.com/download`)
- PyDev, a plugin for Eclipse-based IDEs (`https://www.pydev.org/download.html`)
- LiClipse, an Eclipse-based IDE that comes with PyDev and other related plugins already installed (`https://www.liclipse.com/download.html`)

Another criterion for the selection of an IDE is the amount of integration that is needed (or even just desired) between an IDE and other systems and processes that can be loosely grouped into process standards for dealing with code in various states when it is not actively in development. Two have been mentioned in passing, or have had code written in the example project that relates to their use: source control, and unit testing. These, along with other automated testing contexts, and with processes for building, packaging, and deploying code, do not have to be integrated with an IDE, but there may be advantages to doing so, depending on engineer or project needs.

Process standards and their tools

Of the multitude of process standards that can be applied to writing and managing code, the two that are most likely to have significant and lasting impact are **source control management (SCM)** and automated testing. SCM provides an ongoing history, tracking all changes made to a body of code over time. Automated testing, and automated unit testing, in particular, provides some measure of assurance that the code is doing what it is supposed to be doing. A mature SCM will also facilitate other process standards, things such as code reviews, and allow still other processes to be integrated when code is made ready for a production deployment or release. It is even possible for an SCM to execute automated test suites prior to allowing changes to be committed or merged to a production-ready state. A more detailed overview of SCM decisions will be explored in *Chapter 10*, and automated testing considerations will be discussed in several chapters as they become relevant or noteworthy. Understanding what these process tools provide at a more abstract level is important enough to cover here first, though.

Source control management options

Source control management (SCM) tools provide a consistent set of mechanisms and processes for keeping track of and managing changes made to code over time in a **repository**. In doing so, they provide a running history of every change made to the code being managed, allowing reversion to older states of the code, should that be needed. Their tools also provide processes to help keep changes made by editors of the code from interfering with, or even breaking, changes made by other editors.

Although there are several options to pick from, the most popular SCM system is Git (`https://git-scm.com`). **Git** is a **distributed SCM**, meaning that it mirrors entire repositories locally for each project, even if there is a main repository somewhere else that is the source of truth for the code being managed. Each mirror contains the entire history of the repository, allowing full access to every change made to the code. Interaction with a source of truth repository copy in a distributed SCM generally only occurs when changes are complete and ready to be made available to other SCM users. Other distributed SCM systems include **Mercurial** (`https://www.mercurial-scm.org`) and GNU **Bazaar** (`https://www.gnu.org/software/bazaar/`).

> **Git integration with IDEs**
>
> Git integration is supported to some degree, if not provided directly, by all three of the IDEs discussed earlier. In Geany, there is a Git Change Bar plugin that highlights changes that have not been committed, but the actual commit, push, and so on, still have to be managed externally. PyCharm has a dedicated **Version control** menu that provides direct and thorough Git integration. In VS Code, there are so many **Extensions** options that the list may be daunting. Starting with extensions published by *GitHub* and *GitKraken* is advisable: They are, at a minimum, easily verified as reputable entities, and their extensions have publication verification.

Other SCM systems, including Apache **Subversion** (**SVN**) (`https://subversion.apache.org`), follow a **centralized SCM** (client-server) approach. In this structure, the repository and its history are stored on a central server, and developers interact directly with that server in every SCM operation. Apart from that implementation detail, many if not all SCM operations will still be available in the more mature centralized SCM options.

Typical SCM activities

A minimal SCM workflow, leveraging the bare minimum of the functionality provided by any SCM, need not be any more complex than these steps:

- A developer checks out the main branch of the repository
- The developer makes and tests changes to the code
- Once all the changes are complete and tested, they are pushed back into the main branch of the repository

This workflow, while functional, is not very robust. It might suffice for small projects, or projects where only one person is making changes to the code. As soon as it is possible for more than one person to be making changes to the same code at the same time, the potential for conflicts in those changes needs to be considered. A more robust workflow that accounts for that kind of scenario would typically look something like this:

1. A developer creates a working branch from the main branch of the repository.
2. They make and test their changes in that working branch, adding them to the changes the branch captures as needed.
3. Once all the changes are ready, they generate a pull request in the SCM.
4. The changes in that pull request are reviewed by peers, the owner of the code base, or whatever other technical stakeholders need to be involved.
5. If the review determines that additional changes are needed, that is communicated back to the developer, who makes and tests changes accordingly, incorporating them into the pull request.
6. Once reviews are complete and changes are all approved, the pull request is merged into the main branch that the working branch was created from.
7. If any **merge conflicts** surface in that process, the developer resolves them, pushing those resolution changes back into their pull request, and then proceeds with the merge.
8. Once the merge is complete, the end result is a new version of the main branch that includes the changes.

This workflow introduces several new terms:

- The **main branch** of a repository is typically the approved, production- or deployment-ready collection of code in a repository. The specific naming of the main branch may vary, but no matter what its name is, it represents this version of the code in the repository.

- A **working branch** is an isolated copy of the code from an SCM repository, which a developer can make changes to without having to worry about altering the main branch of the repository. Code changes following this workflow will start with a single working branch, but other working branches can be created from existing working branches as well. Working branches may also be called **feature branches**, **bug** or **bug-fix branches**, or any of several other names.

- A **pull request** is a collection of proposed changes to be made to the code in a repository that can be reviewed by peers and stakeholders before they are incorporated into the main branch. Pull requests will be associated with one working branch, but might incorporate several working branches, depending on what the SCM allows, and how working branches were created.

- A **merge** simply applies changes from one branch to another branch. This workflow is complete with a successful merge into the main branch of a repository, but merges from one working branch into another are also possible.

- A **merge conflict** occurs when two or more branches are making changes to the same code in a repository, and those changes are mutually exclusive for any of several possible reasons. Merge conflicts will prevent a merge operation from completing; they must be resolved before a merge will be allowed by the SCM system.

An abstract example of this process, including changes requested after a review, but with no merge conflicts, is shown in *Figure 8.7*.

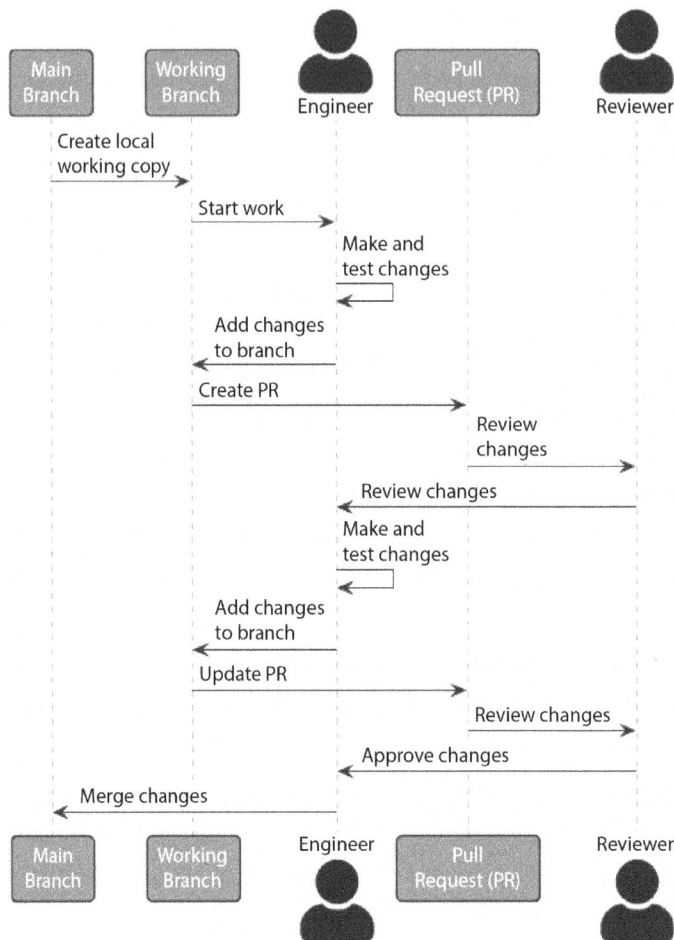

Figure 8.7: A change made to a code base, beginning to end, using the more robust SCM process described previously

This workflow can handle fairly complex combinations of changes made by several engineers. Consider the scenario shown in *Figure 8.8*, where the following is the case:

- Alice needs to make changes to the some_function function, and to the core_function_1 that it uses.

- Bob needs to make changes to the some_other_function function, and to the core_function_2 function that it calls. He does not realize it when he starts the work, but he will also need to make changes to the core_function_3 function.

- Charlie needs to make changes to the `still_another_function` function, and to the `core_function_1` and `core_function_3` functions as well, which may conflict with the changes that Alice and Bob are making.

- Dominic, who owns the package, also needs to make changes to `still_another_function`. He is also responsible for reviewing changes made by Alice, Bob, and Charlie.

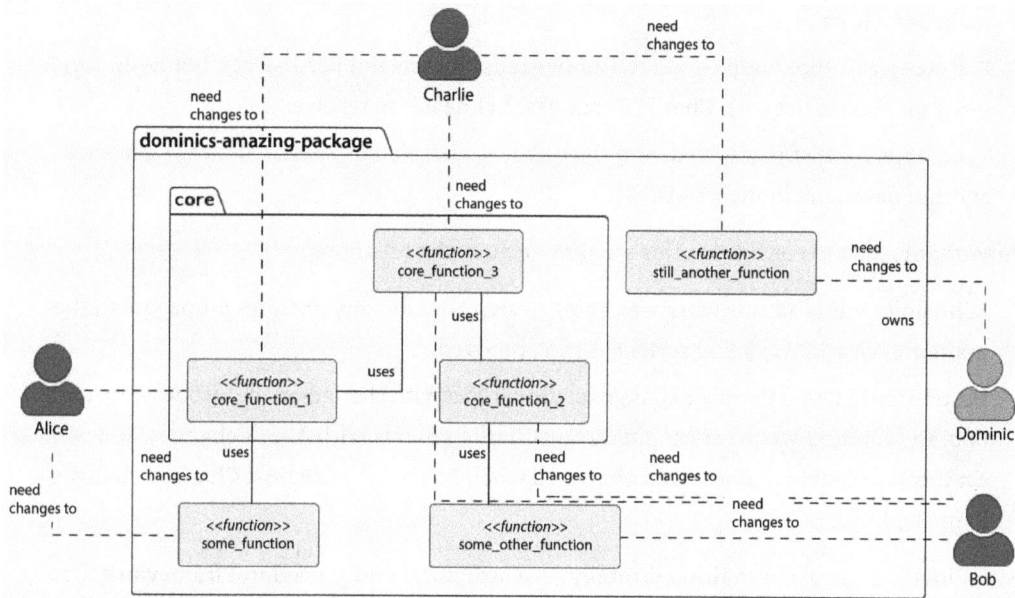

Figure 8.8: An example of changes being made by several developers in a single code base

As these efforts unfold, four new versions of the **main** branch will be created. Versions of **main** will be indicated with `main[#]` through this sequence; at this point, it is `main[0]`:

- All four create their working branches from **main** before anyone else's changes have been completed.

- Dominic completes his changes and merges them. At this point, there is a new main branch: `main[1]`.

- Alice completes her changes and submits a pull request for Dominic to review.

- Alice's pull request is sent back with a minor change request.

- Alice completes the change request, her PR is approved, and she merges, resolving any merge conflicts from Dominic's changes. At this point, there is another new main branch: `main[2]`.

- Bob completes his final change and submits a pull request for Dominic to review.

- Bob's pull request is sent back with a significant change request.

- Charlie completes their final change and submits a pull request for Dominic to review.

- Dominic approves Charlie's change as is, and Charlie merges their branch, resolving any merge conflicts from changes made by Dominic and Alice. At this point, there is a new main branch: main[3].

- Bob completes the change request, Dominic approves it, and Bob merges, but he encounters a merge conflict with Charlie's changes that he has to resolve.

- The merge conflict is resolved, and the merge is completed. This final merge generates another new main branch: main[4].

The important factors to consider in this scenario include the following:

- At no point while all this work was being undertaken did any changes propagate to the **main** branch without being reviewed and approved.

- Despite the fact that Charlie's changes could conflict with changes made by both Alice and Bob, any conflicts would be caught during Charlie's merge with Alice's changes, and one conflict was caught and resolved afterward when Bob's merge against Charlie's changes happened.

This workflow is a simple **branching strategy** — a structural and procedural framework that defines when branches should be created, from where, and when and to where they should merge back into the main branch. More specifically, this is a variant of **feature branching**, where branches are created, worked, and merged based on a specific set of changes needed to add or update a given feature or set of capabilities in the code. In that context, each of the sets of changes made by the actors in the example could be considered a feature. It is not, however, the only branching strategy. Others worth consideration include GitFlow, GitHub Flow, and GitLab Flow. A full exploration of these is beyond the scope of this book, but numerous examples and discussions of them, and where and why they are best applied, can be found on the web.

As important and powerful as these basic capabilities of an SCM are, they frequently offer additional tools that can streamline common processes during development. The most likely to be of use is the ability to automate the execution of processes when specific SCM activities are executed. In Git, these are managed by **hooks** — local scripts that reside in Git's project directory (.git) locally.

A complete list of available hooks for Git can be found in the documentation at `https://git-scm.com/docs/githooks`. Here are a few that can be implemented with little effort, but with potentially significant benefits:

- If there are standards that need to be checked and enforced prior to commits or pushes, activities such as running unit tests to ensure that test suites still pass before those activities are complete, then the `pre-commit` and `pre-push` hooks are good candidates for those. Bear in mind that `pre-commit` fires off locally with every commit, and may be too demanding until a code base is reasonably mature.

- Activities that should take place after retrieving code from the repository, such as running a `pipenv update` or `poetry update` on a fresh checkout, can be triggered using the `post-checkout` hook. The `post-merge` hook can also apply actions to *local* pull commands to similar effects. The `post-merge` hook will not prevent a related merge from completing and thought should be given to logging the results of any activities it triggers.

Of these, the hooks that can execute test suites are probably the more significant, at least from the standpoint of helping to ensure better code quality. That presumes, of course, that the test suites involved are sufficiently rigorous that executing them is going to be meaningful, which is a topic worth some discussion in its own right.

Unit (and other) testing frameworks

Testing of code is *the* critical component of quality assurance in software engineering. The specific types of tests involved, and when and how they are executed may vary, but there are several advantages to capturing test processes in code in some fashion. The first is that tests can be executed with nothing more than a command-line invocation of some sort. Hand in hand with that is the fact that if tests are captured in code, they can be re-run at any point in time, providing ongoing **regression testing** capabilities, and allowing tests to be run after any single change or set of changes. That, in turn, allows those test runs to be automated and integrated into other processes so that a test failure can terminate a build- or deploy process before broken code is released to end users of production systems.

Ultimately, testing is an effort to confirm that all code in a project behaves in a predictable fashion as it accomplishes what it was written to do. The majority of unpredicted behavior is going to fall neatly into categorization as a bug in the code, but whether *every* unexpected outcome is categorized as such is a determination that needs to be made at a team or project level. In a unit testing context, in order to accomplish that confirmation with *absolute certainty*, every line of code needs to be called at least once during the test process.

That absolute certainty may not be feasible, though, particularly if the code being tested uses any external resources that cannot be tested locally. Calls to retrieve data from databases are probably the most common example of this. In those cases, **mocking** results from external calls, essentially generating results as if the mocked functionality had been called, while useful for ensuring that those results are handled in a predictable manner, will often prevent meaningful testing of the database-access code itself. Various approaches to mitigating these kinds of scenarios will be explored later in the project chapters, starting with *Chapter 9*.

Python provides a built-in package, unittest, that provides a reasonably robust set of testing tools. There are several third-party alternatives that can also be considered, the most popular of which is pytest (https://docs.pytest.org), which recognizes and can run test suites written with unittest, and whose test-detection processes and support for additional command-line arguments in test-execution are more robust.

For the purposes of this book, only these two unit testing frameworks will be examined, but there are other testing frameworks, geared for specific testing paradigms that may be relevant for those paradigms. These include behave (https://pypi.org/project/behave/) and lettuce (https://pypi.org/project/lettuce/), which focus on behavior-driven-design, and robotframework (https://pypi.org/project/robotframework/) geared more toward acceptance testing by less technical stakeholders.

For the purposes of comparing and contrasting the expectations for each of these test frameworks, a very basic target module, main.py, was created in the unit-test-examples/src directory under CH08-code in the repository. That module contains a single function, main_function, and a single class, MainClass:

```
def main_function():
    pass
class MainClass:
    def __init__(self):
        pass
    def method(self):
        pass
```

These are the test targets used in each of the unit test examples in the tests directory at unit-test-examples — this is the example test directory referred to in each example.

The primary differences in how tests are implemented under each of these test frameworks are, ultimately, a matter of how tests are *organized*.

Python's built-in unittest package

This example test module is at unittest-example/test_main.py under the example test directory.

The built-in unittest package (https://docs.python.org/3.11/library/unittest.html) provides a solid unit testing framework for Python code. Its test organization relies on the creation of TestCase classes, containing test methods (prefixed with test) that are executed by the test-runner process. The test-discovery process executed by the unittest.main call in that module will only discover TestCase classes. While it would seem logical to create a test function such as test_main_function to test the main_function from the target module, doing so would result in a test function that will not be executed as part of a default unittest.main call.

Creating tests for module-level functions is still possible, though — it just requires that test methods be created under a TestCase class that can be detected and executed. One option that will accomplish this is to create a TestCase class that is intended to test any module-level members that are not, themselves, classes. The test_main.py module for this example does exactly that, with a test_module_functions TestCase class.

The pytest package

This example test module is at pytest-example/test_main.py under the example test directory. The pytest module can be installed like any other third-party module, though in pipenv and poetry development environments, it should be installed as a *development-only* package dependency unless there's a functional need for it in the deployed/published final product.

Test organization under pytest relies on the creation of test functions (prefixed with test) that are discovered and executed during a pytest command-line run. It does not, of itself, provide any type of class-based test organization like the structure expected by unittest. This constraint, then, requires deciding how to organize tests for classes and their members.

At one end of the spectrum for that decision, tests can be organized into one test function for each function or class, and each of those test functions would be responsible for testing everything relevant to its target. At this end of the spectrum, there would be two test functions, one each for the main_function and MainClass members of the example main.py module. The test_MainClass test function would have segments to test each member of the target MainClass class, testing its __init__ and method members. The final result would be a small number of larger (and potentially much more complex) test functions.

At the other end of the same decision spectrum, a test function would be generated for each function, still, *and* for *each member of each class*. That is, for the example `main.py` module, there would be `test_main_function`, `test_MainClass__init__`, and `test_MainClass_method` test-functions. This approach would yield a larger (potentially *much* larger) number of smaller, and simpler, tests. This approach was taken in the `pytest-example` test module.

A hybrid approach

This example test module is at `hybrid-example/test_main.py` under the example test directory.

The `pytest` package will find and execute the test methods of `TestCase`-derived classes in a test suite. That opens the door for a mixture of `pytest`-style test functions, testing source code functions, and `unittest` `TestCase` classes, testing source code classes. The advantage to taking this approach is, arguably, that the test processes for any given code element will more closely mirror the structure and layout of that source element. That is, there will be functions testing functions and classes testing classes. Ultimately, though, as long as the organizational structure of, and testing strategy captured within, those test elements is consistent, the pursuit of that strategy should be consistently applicable.

Testing strategy

Making a conscious decision with respect to what testing strategy should be pursued is important. Without such a decision, test processes are more likely to miss important segments of the source code, increasing the chance of unexpected behavior making its way into the final, production code. If the end goal of a unit-test suite is, as asserted earlier:

> *...to confirm that all code in a project behaves in a predictable fashion as it accomplishes what it was written to do...*

then it follows that a testing strategy should be devised that accomplishes that confirmation for each code element in the source when the test suite is executed.

There are several approaches that can be taken to reach that end goal. Rather than going through all of those permutations, a single approach that shows all of the important facets of a testing strategy will be explored. This example approach assumes that the peer review of code establishes whether the targets being tested were constructed correctly to meet whatever their requirements were. They are only concerned, then, with determining that the *implementation* performs as expected.

The first priority in this strategy is designing tests that prove that a representative set of **happy path** executions behave as expected. The goal of any happy path test is to show that a normal, expected set of inputs to a code element completes without raising any errors, and produces an expected result. Depending on the implementation and the complexity of the inputs, there might be only one happy path test, testing a single collection of inputs, or there could be several, perhaps iterating through several collections of input values, and yielding an expected result for each.

While that meets *some* of the checks for code behaving in a predictable fashion from the goal above, testing for unhappy paths is also part of that equation. An **unhappy path** test calls the target being tested but provides input that is malformed in some fashion. A value could be of an incorrect type, outside an accepted range, malformed in some fashion, or even just omitted. The most common expected outcome for an unhappy path test is that the call to the target will raise an error of some type. If the call to the target does not raise the expected error, that is a failure.

The same structure should be applied to every callable in the code: Every source function should have one or more corresponding test functions, and every source class one or more corresponding test mechanisms (functions or test methods, as dictated by the testing frameworks in use). Between them, those test mechanisms should provide inputs that trigger every decision-point in the source code, and that trigger every error that the code can raise, in order to ensure that all the branches of the code are executed.

Code coverage and how to use it

The collection of inputs and the decisions and errors that are triggered by them during execution will naturally tend to maximize the degree of **code coverage** in tests. Code coverage is a measure of how much of the source code is actually executed by tests when those tests are run. The topic of code coverage is more than a little contentious, but even the detractors of using it as a metric for evaluating code quality (myself included) tend to agree that one of its useful aspects is being able to identify source code that was not executed by any tests.

When source code is not run by a test, that generally means one of two things: The tests are not complete, and need to be modified so that that code is exercised, or the code that wasn't run is *never* going to be run — it is *dead code* — and should be removed. The `coverage` package (`https://pypi.org/project/coverage/`) provides reporting on specific lines of code that were not exercised and is a good starting point for evaluating and remedying those cases.

At this point, this example strategy yields a suite of tests that provides **regression testing** capabilities: as later changes are made to the code, any changes that cause a happy path test to start failing are defects in the code that need to be addressed before the code is released.

Unit tests are expected to have a **reasonable degree of isolation** from each other. What, exactly, constitutes a reasonable degree of isolation is a decision that should be explicitly made. At the *full isolation* end of the range for consideration, each unit test would be completely isolated from all other functionalities that the test target would interact with. For example, if a target function being tested calls another function as part of its process, those calls would be isolated by use of a **mock** of some sort: the actual call to the child function would be intercepted, and predetermined results would be substituted instead. At this level, mocking of calls to child entities can become very complicated, but the trade-off is that there are no dependencies between the test target and any other functionality, so a failure of a given test against a given target can indicate a problem with that target, not with something else that it uses.

At the other end of that range, mocking might be limited to only external resources and their results, for example, results from a database query or a call to a web service — anything where the actual resource may not be available, or where interacting with it could cause changes to data that should not be allowed. Allowing tests to call targets that in turn use other functionality can complicate fixing test failures, but keep the individual tests simpler — sometimes much simpler, especially in cases such as an entry-point function that calls a lot of child functions. This end of that spectrum tends to blur the line between unit testing and integration testing, as discussed later.

Unit testing is the first of several types of testing that can be implemented against a body of source code. It is arguably the most important testing process since it is closest to the smallest units of the code being tested, and as such, it will act as a foundation for other test processes: Knowing that all unit tests have passed provides confidence that other tests that test higher-level capabilities, from simple integration of the unit-tested components to full application-level behaviors, will not be impeded by a component-level failure later on.

Other types of testing

The next step up from unit testing is **integration testing**: tests that demonstrate that all of the components in the code interact with each other in a predictable manner. If the isolation level in unit tests is on the permissive end of the range discussed earlier, integration tests may effectively just demonstrate that different code branches that are *naturally* isolated at the unit-testing level – components that do not directly interact with each other — behave in an expected fashion.

Integration testing will benefit from the same sort of strategy outlined for unit testing: Proving that happy- and unhappy-path executions behave as expected. Mocking of external resources' results is still likely to be valuable, for the same reasons they have value in a unit testing context: avoiding the need for connections to external resources, and/or avoiding manipulation of production data.

Taking a step further from the code, and starting to test the processes that code is designed to perform, gets into the realms of **end-to-end** and **system testing**. The goal for end-to-end testing is to test that one or more inputs into a process within a system execute as expected, yielding the expected results, or handling any errors that might surface from bad inputs. Inputs in these tests are realistic — they should represent an expected input structure. Connections to external services that were mocked out in unit and integration tests may need to be available, perhaps being made against a testing database or other service. Alternatively, they should explicitly remove any data created and persisted by the test process during its execution.

The various types of testing described here can all play a significant part in quality assurance before the code in question is released to its end users. What that release actually looks like will vary based on what the code is intended to provide: It may be a Python package that will be installed and used. It may be built into a downloadable application. It might be deployed as part or all of an online system, a web service, or a full-blown web application. No matter what that process looks like, having test processes that can be run before the release occurs, that are executed with every change merged in an SCM system, or that are part of a build or packaging process provides some measure of confidence that whatever the release process looks like, the code being delivered will behave in a known, expected, and predictable manner.

Delivering Python code

There are any number of distinct delivery paths that Python code can take in order to be made available for end users to consume or otherwise interact with. A short (and incomplete) list would include the following:

- Publishing the code as a Python package that can be installed from the **public PyPI repository** (https://pypi.org), or a private repository such as an **AWS CodeArtifact** (https://docs.aws.amazon.com/codeartifact/latest/ug/using-python.html) instance

- Deploying the code as part of an application using tools provided by any of several Python frameworks such as **Django** (https://www.djangoproject.com/)

- Building, packaging, and deploying the code as a component in a cloud-resident serverless-application structure, such as AWS' **Serverless Application Model** (https://aws.amazon.com/serverless/sam/)

- Deploying the code into some containerized environment, the sort of thing that Docker (`https://www.docker.com`) provides, to be deployed in whatever fashion is relevant for the end use of the code

Regardless of the final delivery path, there are some consistent steps that can be gathered into a single, automated process to ensure that the varied test suites are successfully executed before allowing the rest of that process to continue to completion. For the sake of illustration, assume that the project in question has the following test suites, all written such that they can be discovered and executed by the `pytest` package noted earlier:

- An **end-to-end test suite** that tests complete processes for successful execution, with appropriate guardrails in place to ensure that no production data is persisted for any longer than the duration of the test. This test suite can be executed with `pytest tests/ end-to-end`.

- An **integration test suite** that ensures that all of the individual components (functions and classes) work together as intended, and that does not require access to any real, production resources. This test suite can be executed with `pytest tests/integration`.

- A **unit-test suite** that ensures that each individual component functions as intended. This test suite can be executed with `pytest tests/unit`.

Before any build or packaging process is executed, the *unit* and *integration test* suites can — and should — be run. If either of those fail, that failure is indicative of a problem in the code, and that code should *not* be delivered without *making a conscious decision to allow* the delivery to proceed (skipping the failing tests, perhaps, after creating a bug-fix ticket to deal with it). If these tests pass, then whatever relevant build process is involved in the delivery of the code is safe to execute.

Once that build process has been completed, the *end-to-end test suite* should be executed against it. If this test suite fails, there is a flaw in how one or more processes that the code is trying to accomplish are working, and the delivery process should terminate, preventing delivery of the flawed code. Like failures in the unit and integration testing earlier in the delivery flow, there is always an option to ignore failures in the test suite, but decisions to allow a delivery to proceed anyway are more likely to cause more critical errors, corruption of data, and so on.

Once the end-to-end testing process is complete, the final delivery process will be executed. Since there are so many possible variants, and since each of them could warrant a chapter in their own right, they will not be discussed in detail here, though some examination of them will be undertaken in the project-focused chapters later in this book as they become relevant. A brief summary of each of the options noted earlier, and some references for a more detailed examination will be provided.

Building Python packages

The end goal for this delivery mechanism is, as mentioned, to provide an installable Python package that can be incorporated into other code. The Packaging Python Projects tutorial (`https://packaging.python.org/en/latest/tutorials/packaging-projects/`) provides a comprehensive introduction to the current standard processes and lists several options for specific sub-processes in the overall build flow where they are available. That tutorial, when this chapter was being written, had changed its recommendations in several areas, but mostly in which tools were shown as defaults, and where the metadata for a package project should be defined. The defaults and recommended tools at the time included the following:

- The `build` package (`https://pypi.org/project/build/`) is responsible for creating the structure that the build backend packages into a **distribution package** — a versioned archive that contains the code and resources needed for installation by an end user

- The `hatchling` package (`https://pypi.org/project/hatchling/`), a build backend that assembles the package structure from a build run, along with the project's metadata, into the final collection of *distribution packages*

- The `twine` package (`https://pypi.org/project/twine/`), which is used to upload the distribution packages created to a PyPI repository, where it can be downloaded and installed by an end user

- Defining package metadata in a `pyproject.toml` file (`https://packaging.python.org/en/latest/guides/writing-pyproject-toml/`), along with configuration for build, packaging, and other varied tools

These tools and defaults are the current recommendations, but other, older options were still supported at the time, including the veteran `setuptools` package (`https://pypi.org/project/setuptools/`) that may well still be in use across the majority of packages in the public PyPI index.

Framework-specific delivery systems

Dedicated application frameworks frequently have their own custom test, build, and deploy processes. Django is a good example, providing the following:

- Built-in unit-testing additions (`https://developer.mozilla.org/en-US/docs/Learn/Server-side/Django/Testing`)

- Configuration and deployment options for web applications hosted on some variant of a dedicated server (`https://developer.mozilla.org/en-US/docs/Learn/Server-side/Django/Deployment#getting_your_website_ready_to_publish`)

Other application and API frameworks may also provide test- and build-enhancement utilities that integrate better with the expectations and standards of those frameworks.

Cloud-resident delivery processes

Many of the cloud-resident build and delivery processes follow a similar pattern, at least at a very high level: They wrap the series of commands to be executed in a YAML file, which is read and executed step by step in some sort of temporary compute environment. This basic structure is available in the following:

- **AWS CodeBuild**, which uses a **buildspec** file (`https://docs.aws.amazon.com/codebuild/latest/userguide/build-spec-ref.html#build-spec-ref-syntax`)

- **Bitbucket Pipelines** (`https://support.atlassian.com/bitbucket-cloud/docs/bitbucket-pipelines-configuration-reference/`)

- **GitHub Actions** (`https://docs.github.com/en/actions/quickstart`)

Variations in structure and syntax notwithstanding, these all provide the same basic capabilities needed to execute a build process in a temporary container spun up for that purpose: They provide a mechanism to execute arbitrary commands, one at a time, to install any dependencies that the build process needs, execute tests, build the code in whatever way is relevant for the end delivery goal, execute more tests against that build, and upload it to some final destination, ready to use.

Delivery in Docker containers

Apart from the differences in structure and syntax, a Docker-based delivery process is going to look much the same as one of the YAML-based approaches. A **Dockerfile** (`https://docs.docker.com/reference/dockerfile/`) is just a text file that captures the commands that would be executed by a user to create a final image with the requisite code in place. Those commands would then be executed, in sequence, to create the final container image, ready to run. Resources that the final image would need — such as the code of a project — need to be accessible while that image-generation process is executing, and the final image has to be stored somewhere, but the actual commands needed to test the code are just shell commands, and a copy of the code would be made in the final image, accessible to the task that the container executes when it is started.

There are enough options available for the final delivery of a project's code that deciding what that final delivery needs to be capable of is a critical consideration, driving the final design for delivery of a project. They all have their advantages and drawbacks; some have monetary costs associated, with a certain amount of build time or capacity costing a certain amount of money. Others may lend themselves to local implementation, avoiding those costs, but requiring more time and effort for engineers to manage and maintain them.

Summary

This chapter wraps up all of the factors that require thought, design, and decisions around how projects are developed. Between them (Chapters 5 to 8), they have examined the following:

- Methodologies, paradigms, and practices — *Chapter 5* — that include the following:

    - Basic code structure decisions: procedural vs. object-oriented vs. functional programming

    - Outlining options for handling the code once it is ready to be deployed

- Options and style guidelines within the code itself — *Chapter 6* — to maximize its readability, making it easier to work with over time

- Functional considerations for how code is written — *Chapter 7* — including the following:

    - How to organize code

    - How to effectively leverage features and capabilities of Python to reduce the likelihood of bugs, while further increasing its readability

    - How to keep track of what code is actually doing as it executes, particularly with respect to errors at run time

- Various tools and processes — *Chapter 8* — towards:

    - Managing code dependencies

    - Picking the right tool (IDE) for an engineer's needs and preferred workflow

    - Managing changes to a code base, especially in cases where multiple contributors to the code are working on it at the same time

    - Options for delivering the finished code, and testing it in the process, to help ensure that the end users of the code have the best possible end product

What is lacking in all of this is a single, cohesive example of how those decisions could be made. All of the pieces and parts have been covered, but not how they fit together in a project. That assembly will start in the next chapter, by exploring sweeping changes to the project originally discussed in the first edition of this book.

Get This Book's PDF Version and Exclusive Extras

UNLOCK NOW

Scan the QR code (or go to packtpub.com/unlock). Search for this book by name, confirm the edition, and then follow the steps on the page.

Note: Keep your invoice handy. Purchases made directly from Packt don't require an invoice.

9

Revising the hms_sys System Project

Before starting any code project, some understanding of what it is intended to accomplish needs to be known. That knowledge may be vague, particularly for smaller projects, or for small changes to large projects, and often the implementation details are left in the hands of the engineers who will actually write the relevant code.

For the balance of this book, the project in question is a fairly substantial one — the fictional company whose systems were written about in the previous edition has determined that they need to make some significant changes to the existing system, across several different areas of interest. This chapter will explain how to read some of the material needed to fully understand those changes, before covering, in high-level, the details:

- What those changes are intended to accomplish
- What changes are expected in the context of how the system actually works
- What changes the engineering staff involved want to accomplish, independent of the functional changes needed by the business
- What the basic plan of action is to get from the current state to the new system version

Technical requirements

The relevant portions of the original code from the first edition of this book have been copied to the chapter repository, in the CH09-code directory at https://github.com/PacktPublishing/ Hands-On-Software-Engineering-with-Python-Second-Edition/tree/main/CH09-code. In the process, it was *lightly* cleaned, with most of that effort focused on ensuring that the code could be represented in the text of the book without alteration, should the need arise. All of it can be run in a Python 3.11 environment, though doing so will only show that the syntax and structure are valid — the code itself is little more than a collection of class definitions, with no entry points that actually call any of the functionality that those code elements provide.

As the previous edition's code was not linted, there are several places throughout it that will raise linting errors. These were intentionally left in place so that they could be addressed later when it becomes relevant to the narrative of the book to do so.

Reading the class diagrams in this chapter

Much of the content in this chapter is going to refer to one or more class diagrams. A **class diagram** shows the structure of a system with representations of the classes in the system, frequently including the members — properties and methods — of those classes in a language-agnostic manner. They frequently also capture the relationships between those code elements — classes that inherit from other classes, extending them, or that implement a specific interface — as well as showing the organizational structure of the diagrammed members — packages and namespaces.

Tools for generating class diagrams often do not include specific mechanisms for including functions. They are, after all, diagramming *classes*, and functions are not classes. Since Python code can contain both, and because class diagrams are, ultimately, just component diagrams with specific rules for showing classes, the approach taken here will be to use a generic component to represent functions in code, if and when they are needed. An example of the diagram structure and style used for the rest of this book is shown in *Figure 9.1*, below.

Multiple_Repositories

This is a collection of top-level namespaces.
It is **not** an installable package.

namespace

This is a top-level namespace.
It is **not** an installable package.

package-in-namespace

This is an **installable package**, containing
zero-to-many child **namesspaces**

namespace-in-package

This is a **child namespace**,
installed as part of its
parent package

(**I**) *Interface* ———————————— This is an interface

↑
implements

(**A**) *AbstractClass* ———————————— This is an abstract class

↑
extends

(**C**) Class ———————————— This is a concrete class

↑
uses

«*Function*»
Function(<Class> instance) ———————————— This is a function

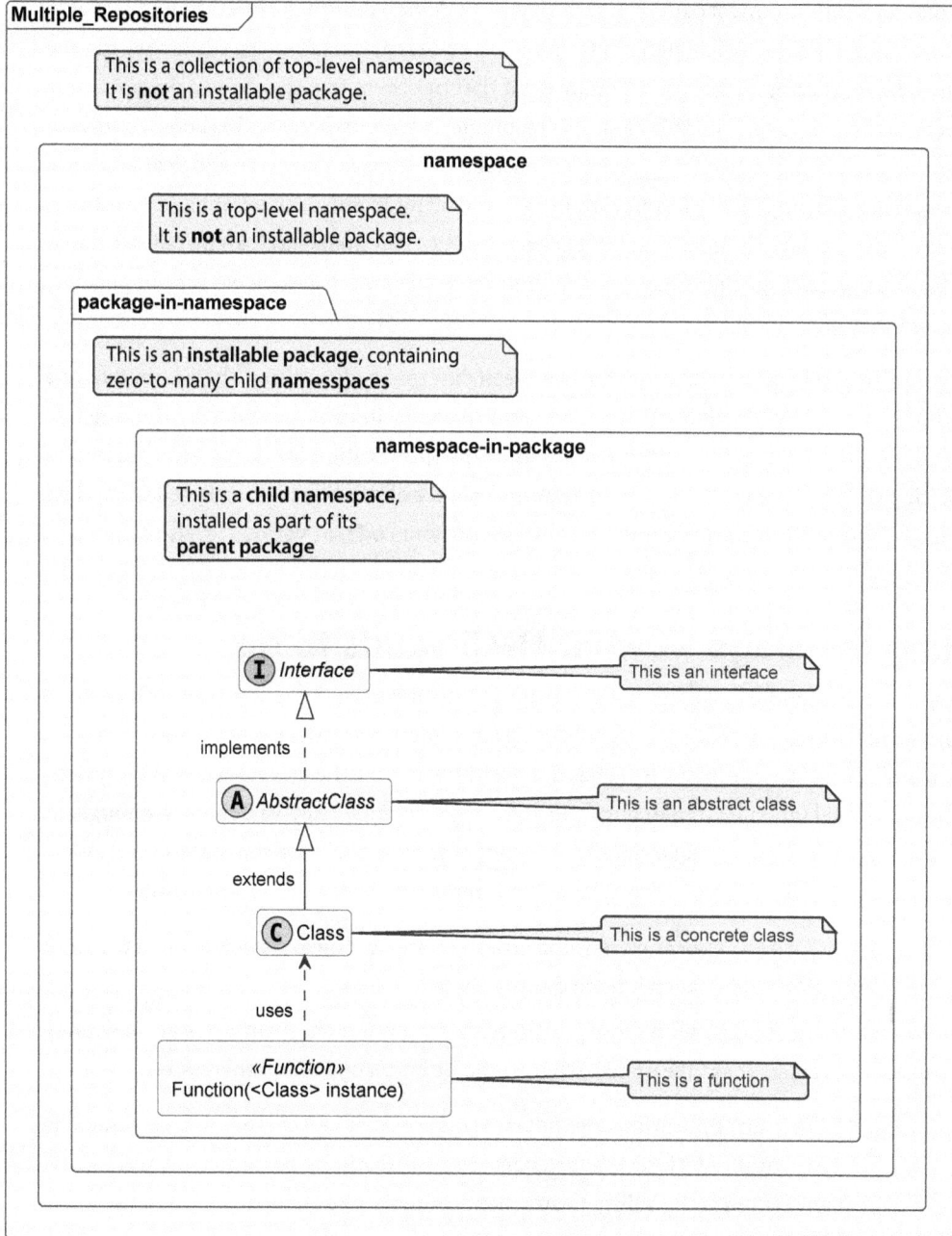

Figure 9.1: The elements used in class diagrams in this book

In this diagram, the outermost container (*Multiple_Repositories*) indicates a collection of packages that do not have a single, logical parent grouping in a code structure. That is, while they may be logically related, there is nothing in the code itself that ties them together from a diagramming perspective. The next layer, bound by a simple rectangle, is a *namespace*. For this book's purposes, namespaces are distinguished from packages in that a namespace may have a logical existence in the structure of a project's code, but cannot be installed by an end user, except as a member of a package. The next layer in from that is a package (*package-in-namespace*), an installable namespace. Within that package there may be any number of child namespaces (*namespace-in-package*), classes, or functions.

This figure also shows several relationships between different code entities: there is an *Interface* that is implemented by the *AbstractClass*. The *AbstractClass* is, in turn, extended by the concrete *Class*, and the *Function* uses that concrete *Class* as a type specification for its instance parameter. After setting the stage for the project work that the balance of this book is concerned with, class diagrams will be used to show various states of the system code, at various levels of detail, in later chapters.

Setting the stage — what HMS wants to do

The project created for the first edition was written for an imaginary company, **Hand-Made Stuff (HMS)**, whose business centers around connecting consumers with artisans who create and sell a variety of unique handmade items. HMS has done fairly well since the first release of their system, with the occasional (and inevitable) bug fixes and improvements. They've done well enough, in fact, that they are looking to make significant changes to how their Artisan and Central Office services will be provided. Some of the ideas and concerns that have been raised include:

- The current Artisan application relies on artisans being technically savvy enough to install the application, and to keep it up to date.

- When artisans struggle with those processes, or simply don't keep up, there are inevitably service desk calls that take up time that would be better spent on other issues.

  - The Artisan application does not currently provide certain functionality that has been requested by several artisans, and indirectly by customers as well. Chief among those is the ability to attach one or more photographs of products.

- Several potential artisans have also decided not to work with HMS because the Artisan application is not available on their smartphone or other mobile device. Management would like to eliminate that concern in order to attract more artisans to their product but has not expressed any particular direction as to how: an artisan-specific web application would suffice, as would a full-blown mobile application. They trust the software engineering team to provide guidance as to the best path forward from a technical perspective.

- IT and Data Administration staff would like to reduce the number of services that they have to maintain, starting with consolidation of the backing databases to a single engine. After some exploration into the options, their mandate to the software engineering team is to move all database use to the relational, SQL-based database that the main customer website already uses.

- Software staff *will not* have to worry about the actual implementation of that database or the migration of current data.

    - They *will* have to adjust any application code that makes use of any other databases.

    - They *may* also be tasked with defining formal schemas for the new database tables needed.

- In a related effort, there is considerable interest by IT, Data Administration, and Management staff to move their entire system into the cloud.

- The decisions around this have not yet been made, but the software engineering staff have been advised to keep this eventual move in mind as they re-work whatever parts of the current code base are relevant.

    - There is some interest in moving to a serverless architecture in the process, and investigations into the capabilities of AWS' Serverless Application Model (SAM, see `https://aws.amazon.com/serverless/sam/`), Azure Functions (`https://azure.microsoft.com/en-us/products/functions`) and Google Cloud Platform's Cloud Functions (`https://cloud.google.com/functions`) has been started.

- Whether a serverless architecture is the eventual direction or not, the Software Engineering team *does not* need to be concerned with front-end work for the eventual solution: there is a front-end developer that will handle all of that work.

- They *will*, however, need to be concerned with providing a single, web-accessible API that the front-end code will make calls to, which implies standard HTTP request/response processes, and data structures that can be issued and consumed by front-end code easily.

- There are a number of other general fixes and updates that the software engineering team would like to make, in order to improve the maintainability of the code base, and to make their ongoing work easier in general. These include, but are not limited to:

  - Bringing the code up to the standards and structures expected for the most current Python release that is supported across the three cloud providers being considered (3.11 as of this writing).

  - Taking advantage of more modern tools for managing package dependencies and automated testing.

  - Reorganizing the code base to follow more standard delivery practices — specifically, if it's feasible to have *some* kind of standard Python package installation process, with all of their code in a single, top-level namespace, that would be preferred.

- More rigor in the documentation of the code — like most software engineering teams, the current software engineering team has had to deal with a fair amount of turnover in the last five years, and better documentation would make onboarding new engineers easier and faster.

In order to come up with even a basic, high-level roadmap of how to proceed, the first step is to take a look at what the code looks like now and evaluate what needs to change. With those determinations made, and some thought about how to work those changes in with as little disruption as possible, the roadmap can start taking shape, and more details can be elaborated as needed.

Reviewing the current codebase

In many respects, the entire body of project changes presented here is little more than a system-wide collection of refactoring efforts. **Refactoring** code is the process of restructuring it to improve operation, efficiency, or maintainability, *without* changing what the code does when it is executed. It is quite possible, perhaps even inevitable, that refactoring efforts will make changes to *how* the code does what it does in the process. While the software engineering team is waiting for the decision to be made about whether the new API-based version of the system will reside in the cloud or on-premises, they can still undertake many of the improvements that they want to. So long as there is some attention paid to the potential constraints that any new API would introduce, there is nothing that prevents them from moving forward in the meantime.

Defining the roadmap for those changes involves, at a minimum, a more in-depth examination of the current state in the code base of:

- Projects and processes, in particular:

    - Project structures

    - Management of package dependencies

- The current Business Object structures
- Separately, how those Business Objects' data persistence operates now, and how to convert them, when necessary, to use the required SQL-based back-end data store
- Testing strategies and practices, and team standards around them
- Build and delivery processes for the code in the projects

Each of these examinations will be discussed briefly here, and in more detail in one or more chapters later in the book. Each summary here, and a chapter later, will address where things stand at the start of the work — its current state — what the team wants or needs to accomplish, what needs to happen to get to that goal, and what constraints need to be kept in mind while that work is being done. All of these efforts are being considered with another goal in mind: to at least *try* to allow each step of the process to arrive at a deployable package set that can be used in existing applications and services with as little change of code as possible within those consumers of those packages.

Projects and processes examination

The current state of the code base, before any of this refactoring is started, is shown in *Figure 9.2*, below.

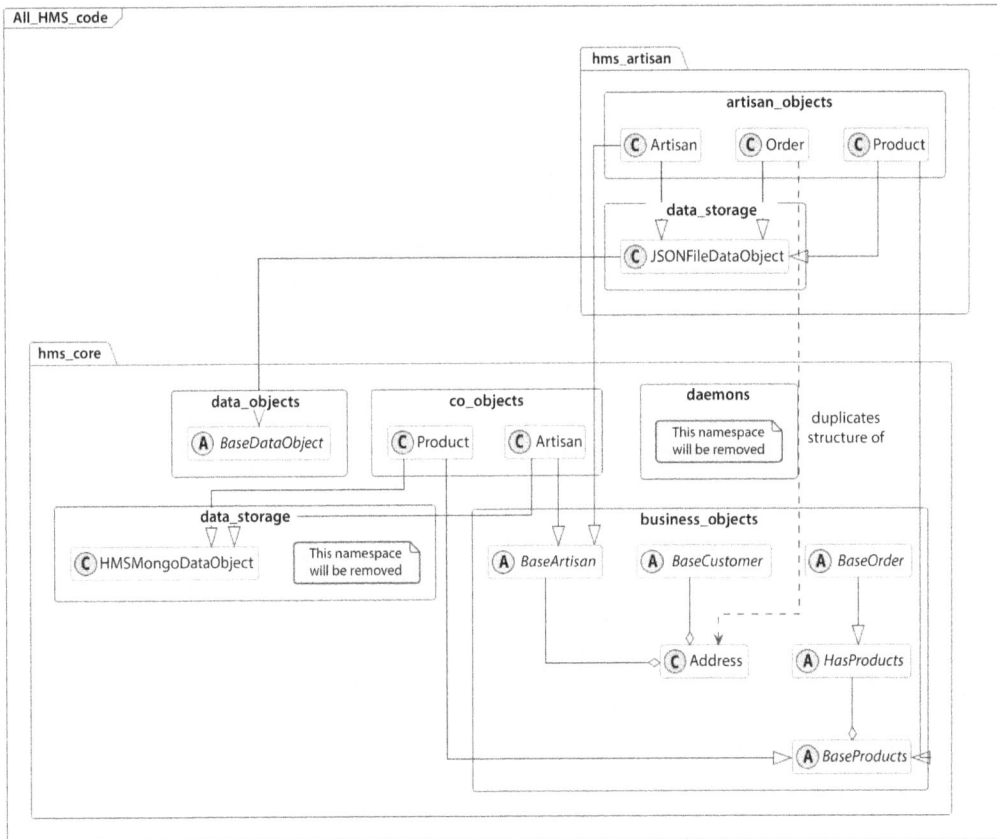

Figure 9.2: The current structure of the HMS code base. Class members — properties and methods — are omitted for clarity of the overall structure of the code base

Current state code

The current state of the code has been reproduced in the repository for this chapter. In the process, that code was reformatted to fit a narrower maximum line width, so that it could be copied into the text of the book as is when needed. In the process, several code-formatting errors — things like missing or extra whitespace, and indentation — were corrected, but original style, format, and logical errors discovered by more modern linting were left in place, to be addressed in later chapters. Documentation-string content was also frequently left alone. Since testing will be re-examined, the test code from the first edition was not converted. Neither were several of the original code's support directories that were not expected to serve any purpose in the revised code.

One of the development team's goals for the entire refactoring is to reorganize the code base into a more logical package namespace. From a functional perspective, this namespace reorganization isn't really *required*: it is a convenience thing, when it comes right down to it, that is intended to make life easier for first-time users and maintainers of the package set. There *is* a single relatively small functional improvement that will come of this effort, though: the current codebase has some duplicated code, shown in *Figure 9.2* as a dashed line between the `Order` class in `hms_artisan.artisan_objects` and the `Address` class in `hms_core.business_objects`.

The examination and decisions to be made in this effort include:

- What the new namespace's structure will look like
- How package dependencies will be managed
- How the new namespace's code will be managed in **Source Control Management (SCM)**
- What, if any, SCM hooks could be usefully applied across the repositories across the entire package set, and for each package individually
- Whether the organization of automated tests, unit tests in particular, will need to change according to the new namespace structures, and what those changes will look like if they are needed or desired
- Where, in the unit test suites, there will be external services that will need to be accounted for, and how they will be accounted for
- How the code for each package will be built and packaged, and where it will be deployed to, even if that is a temporary, interim process

These will be examined in much greater detail in *Chapter 10*. The initial goal of this reorganization of code is to make no changes to either what that code does, or how it does it; it is merely a change in where the individual code entities reside within the structure of the new namespace. There will be some changes needed in how those entities are imported, and those changes would have to carry across to any code outside the context of the new namespace that uses them. As such, the changes made during these efforts should be able to ignore any of the constraints and requirements that will affect later stages of the overall effort, though keeping them in mind as the reorganization is in progress may lead some decisions down specific paths that would not be considered without that context.

Winnowing out the constraints

There are two constraints from the list of goals and requirements presented in the *Setting the stage — what HMS wants to do* section earlier that are likely to have significant or wide-ranging impacts on the balance of the efforts after the reorganization. In no particular order, they are:

- The end goal of providing a single, web-compatible API, which has strong potential to shape the implementation of data objects, discussed in *Chapter 11*.

- In addition, the persistence of those data objects, moving as it will from the original code's NoSQL database back-end to the required SQL-based **Relational Database Management System (RDBMS)**, will also tie into those Business Objects to some degree but will have an even more significant impact on the implementation of the data persistence processes themselves. *Chapter 13* will examine those in detail.

The general fixes and updates that the software engineering team wants to undertake will also have a variety of impacts, particularly around the business object implementations in *Chapter 11*. There may also be other points in the code base changes where update items will come into play that cannot be anticipated at this point.

Bringing testing standards up to something more current can be assumed to have impacts on how tests are written and executed, which will surface in several of the following chapters already mentioned, as well as in *Chapter 15*.

Business Objects examination

The data structures that need to be represented in the context of the revised packages and the systems that use them are not expected to change much, if at all. However, a significant point of consideration in that area is how, or perhaps whether, to implement a formal data contract for the business objects, while keeping the database and API constraints in mind. There are a number of options available that could be used to implement a data contract, and they will be examined in detail in *Chapter 11*.

Data persistence examination

Given the requirement to change the back-end data store provider, a deeper examination of both current expectations and how best to future-proof an implementation will occupy much of the discussion and decision-making presented in *Chapter 12*. This will also lead in to more concrete implementation in *Chapter 13*.

Of particular importance in this examination will be the options for managing a concrete, formal database schema, and what cues and signals can be gleaned from the code — Business Objects in this system — that bridges between the data store and the consumer of the data through the API.

Given the probable decision to move the HMS systems into the cloud in the foreseeable future, at least a brief examination of cloud-resident NoSQL options is appropriate, even though the expressed intention at this point is to move away from that data store type. If only because their availability raises the probability that there will eventually be a shift in data storage preferences, knowing what their implementation would look like, and making sure that a SQL-based implementation would not preclude the possibility of eventually changing to a NoSQL backing data store needs to be kept in mind.

Testing strategies and practices examination

The majority of the changes expected with respect to testing processes are the evaluation and probable adoption of a different testing framework — pytest, specifically — which may or may not lead to significant restructuring of the original code's tests. As part of that evaluation, reviewing the high-level testing strategy in place, and determining if any changes are needed or desired, will be undertaken.

The original test suites were concerned, in the main, with unit testing, and not with integration, end-to-end, or system testing in general, though the basic strategies were at least defined in the previous edition.

Build and delivery processes examination

Because the final deliverable after all of these efforts involves both common code — Python packages, probably, but there may be other alternatives — and API code, thought needs to be given to what the build and deployment processes need to do. The decisions made around these processes may affect, or be affected by, the decisions made with respect to the package management processes. They will also be affected by where the final deliverable API is hosted, to some extent: any delivery process, in particular, needs to be compatible with whatever mechanisms are required to put the final API code in place, whether that's in a server-based or cloud-resident serverless context.

The considerations and decisions that will need to be made here will be affected by the project structure revision: each deployable component must be deployed with whatever dependencies are relevant, including other packages in the HMS code base. Over and above that, the question of what needs to be deployed, and how those deployments will need to happen, will have to be considered. That will depend, to some degree, on the final hosting and run-time structure of the final API, which will, in turn, depend on a decision that the software team may not be in charge of making.

These half-dozen major groupings of changes, considerations, and constraints, *and* the decisions around them, have a fair amount of cross-over between them. Figuring out the sequencing required, especially if there is a need or desire to allow the new refactored and reorganized code to start replacing the existing code sooner rather than later, is worth a more in-depth exploration.

Drawing the roadmap

There are a lot of decision points and considerations in this effort that live in one category that affect or will be affected by decision points and considerations in other categories. The software team brainstormed together to try and identify the ones that were obvious to them, or that they felt were critical. The results, though they may be incomplete, are shown in *Figure 9.3*, below. There is one decision that is outside their control: the choice of cloud provider, shown in the *External decisions* grouping in the diagram. There are others, grouped in *Team decisions*, that are, if not totally their decisions to make, at least not dependent on external decisions. There are also some that are already made and are not represented in the diagram at all. These include the choice of an SCM provider, which is already in place, and that the team is comfortable with.

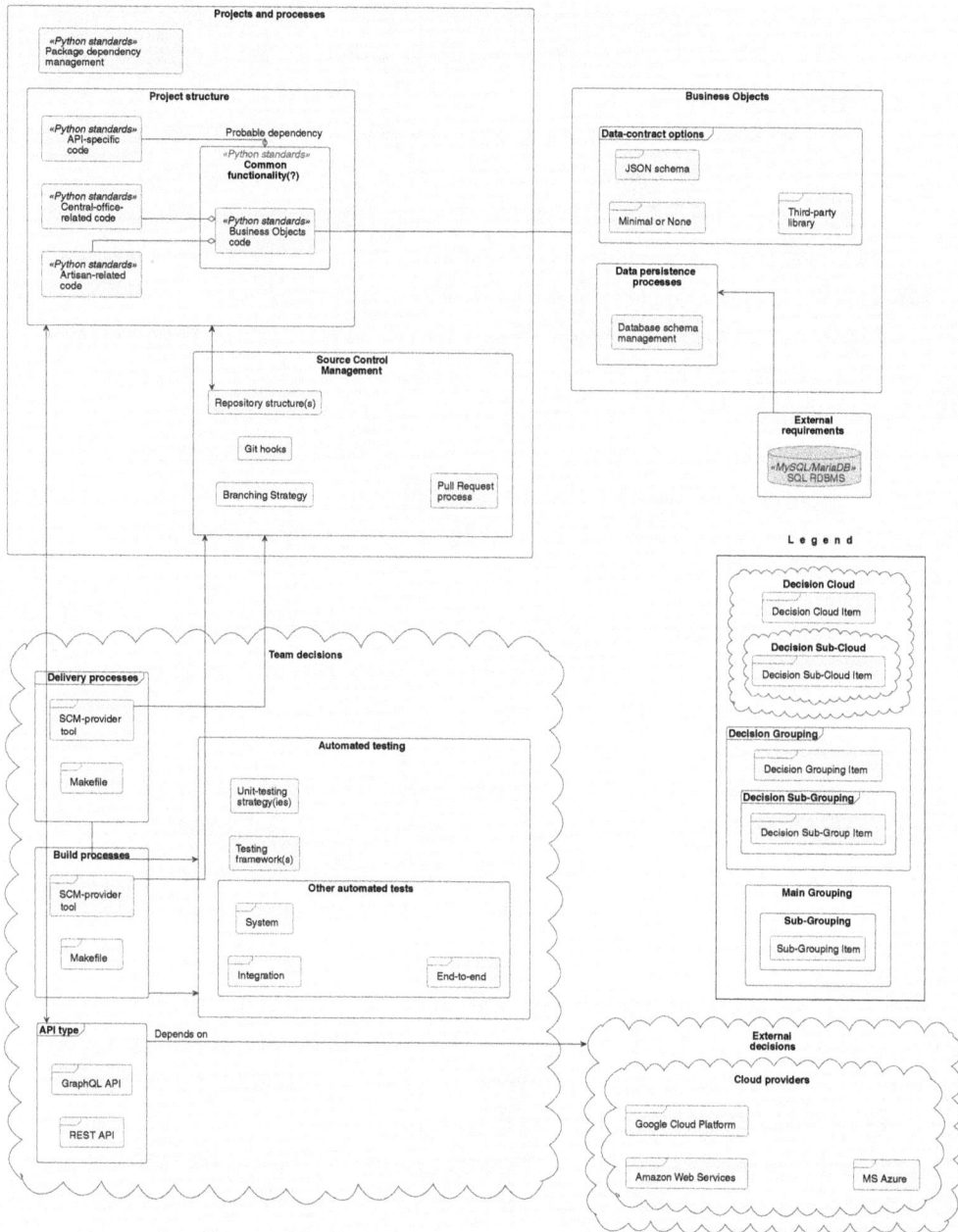

Figure 9.3: The relationships between the various decision points in the next several chapters

(This image is for visualization purpose only. Check the graphic bundle for a high resolution version.)

The remaining items can be grouped into the examination categories already mentioned — *Projects and processes, Business Objects, Testing strategies and practices,* and *Build and delivery processes.* With the exception of the *API-specific code* node in the *Projects and processes* grouping in the diagram, which depends on which of the *API types* items is selected, and which in turn is likely to depend on the *Cloud providers* decision that they will not be making, but will hopefully have input on, the items in the *Projects and processes* group have the fewest external dependencies to contend with. There is one such dependency, through the Business Objects group, that ties to the SQL RDBMS that has been called out as an *External requirements* item, but work on that can be deferred, or undertaken with a temporary, throw-away database if needed. These items will be addressed in *Chapter 10.* The bulk of these changes are expected to be *organizational,* rather than *functional* — they will affect how the package code is accessed, and how packages interact with each other, but not what the components within those packages actually *do.* Some attention will also be paid to the *Automated testing* items under *Team decisions* in the diagram, with at least some concrete, complete test implementations fleshed out after making the *Unit-testing strategy(ies)* and *Testing framework(s)* decisions noted there.

Changes to the *functionality* of the existing *Business Objects* are the next item to address. The rationale behind that decision is straightforward enough: data persistence is already known to be a mission-critical piece of functionality — if data cannot be reliably read and written, the entire system is useless. The Business Objects in the system will provide the API's interface to those processes. There are two major points of interest in this effort. The first is how (or whether) to implement any formal data contracts for those business objects. The second, which may depend on the first, is how to create and manage the corresponding database schemas for those business objects — what that process looks like, where it starts and ends, and all the details in between. Those bases will be discussed in *Chapter 11.*

Once any common expectations for Business Objects have been established, the process of actually *writing* data to the database needs to be worked out. This is the other half of the concern noted above: *If data cannot be reliably read and written, the entire system is useless.* The previous version of the system had a set of basic architectures that handled that for local file-based data storage and for access to a different back-end database system. Those need to be consolidated and implemented in a manner that, ideally, allows them to be added to Business Object definitions wherever needed so that the state data of those objects can be stored in the back-end database, and retrieved and modified as needed by the final API. This implementation will be examined in *Chapter 12.*

With the database persistence processes worked out, and the code elements implemented that provide Business Object representation of the data structures that the API will be concerned with, marrying the two together will be covered in *Chapter 13*. As the back-end data store will have changed in that implementation, the testing of those data persistence processes will need to be re-examined in some detail. The previous version's tests may be meaningful from the standpoint of showing what kinds of tests are needed or desired, the backing implementation will have changed, and those tests will no longer be useful. Re-working the data persistence tests, whether they actually test against a functional database engine or simply mock that functionality out, will be explored in *Chapter 14*.

Once the implementations for the decisions listed so far are complete, the remaining *Team decision* items that are not tied to the API types decision can be addressed. These will determine which of the *Build processes* and *Delivery processes* items are best suited to the new API. *Chapter 15* will examine those options and their implications in detail, leaving the examination of the new API's code and deployment processes for the next series of chapters.

This sequence is only one possible roadmap for the project to take. It was selected, in the context of the story being told about this project's efforts, because it would provide the most opportunity to allow the existing code to be replaced as new, improved functionality was developed. In a real-world context, this sort of development sequence would reduce risk to an established project: each incremental change made could be designed and executed to replace some existing functionality with as little change as possible at each step. It would not be without some additional effort, but those additional efforts would, generally, be smaller, and less prone to breaking large chunks of existing functionality.

If the context of this development story were different, for example, if the cloud decision had already been made, it might well make more sense to start at the API design level and work down through the functionality needed until everything was changed and ready. That is also a perfectly viable roadmap, it simply has different costs, risks, and implications. The most significant of those, in all probability, would be the need to maintain two separate code bases for the duration of the effort until the entire new API version was ready to use. At that point, the switch could be made, and the older code base retired.

Other variations are not difficult to imagine. Starting with the required backing database change, for example, could start with working out the Business Objects from there, along with the (probably manual) translation process from database schema to Business Object class. From there, deriving an API request/response structure would complete this approach. This would also, almost certainly, require maintenance of two versions of the code base for some period.

Summary

This chapter focused on determining what needs and requirements have to be accommodated in making the changes involved in HMS' next steps for their systems, and at least a rough, high-level assessment of the specific work to be done. In mapping out the logical sequence of efforts to undertake, several caveats and considerations have been exposed, at the same high level. The details of each of these high-level groups will be explored in the relevant chapters that follow, starting with the basic reorganization of the current package structure into a new namespace. Along with that, we will examine and address various decision points that relate to how the code is managed.

Subscribe to Deep Engineering

Join thousands of developers and architects who want to understand how software is changing, deepen their expertise, and build systems that last.

Deep Engineering is a weekly expert-led newsletter for experienced practitioners, featuring original analysis, technical interviews, and curated insights on architecture, system design, and modern programming practice.

Scan the QR or visit the link to subscribe for free.

https://packt.link/deep-engineering-newsletter

10

Updating Projects and Processes

This is the last chapter that will focus on systems and processes that affect how code is managed and handled. Writing code is only a part of the entire process ecosystem of software engineering. That ecosystem also has to make decisions about how the code is structured, how it is managed when multiple engineers are expected to be interacting with it and making changes to it, how it will be tested, and what is involved in making the final code available for others.

In this chapter, we're going to cover the following main topics:

- Reviewing and revising project structure
- Making source control management decisions
- Planning for unit testing
- Working out a build process
- Interim and final deployment considerations

The decisions that will be discussed should be made *consciously*, with intent and an understanding of their implications and trade-offs. To do otherwise is to open the door for ambiguity in processes that will, given time, cause issues or concerns that an engineering team will have to fix.

Technical requirements

The code for this chapter was written for Python 3.11 and assumes that it is available on your machine. Download and installation instructions are available online at https://www.python. org/downloads/ for Windows, Linux/Unix, MacOS, and other systems. This chapter will also examine several other installable utilities and packages for various purposes: installation instructions will be provided for them as they are discussed or will follow typical Python package installation practices.

All of the code mentioned or discussed in this chapter is available in the CH10-code folder in the GitHub repository for this book, at https://github.com/PacktPublishing/Hands-On-Software-Engineering-with-Python-Second-Edition/tree/main/CH10-code.

Reviewing and revising project structures

The first substantial chunk of work that the software team wants to accomplish is the reorganization of the current codebase into a namespace structure that is easier to understand, and more consistent in naming than the original structure. As part of these efforts, at least some of the following goals initially noted in *Chapter 9* will be addressed, though perhaps only in part, initially.

Bringing the code up to the standards and structures expected for the most current Python release that is supported across the three cloud providers being considered (3.11 as of this writing).

Taking advantage of more modern tools for managing package dependencies and automated testing.

Reorganizing the codebase to follow more standard delivery practices — specifically, if it's feasible to have some kind of standard Python package installation process, with all of their code in a single, top-level namespace, that would be preferred.

The end goal of the namespace reorganization is to arrive at a collection of smaller, composable packages that all live under a single common namespace segment: hms. By the time the effort is complete, that namespace is expected to look something like this:

hms — The root namespace that all the packages live in.

- artisan — The namespace that contains classes and functionality relating to Artisan activities and data structures.

    - data_storage — Data-storage functionality specifically for Artisan use.
    - objects — The classes that represent Artisan-specific data structures.

- central_office — The namespace that contains classes and functionality relating to Central Office (business) activities and data structures.

    - data_storage — Data-storage functionality specifically for Central Office use.

    - objects — The classes that represent Central-Office-specific data structures.

- core — The namespace where common base classes for all of the other namespaces will live. This package is going to be an internal dependency for many (perhaps all) of the other packages in the namespace.

    - business_objects — The collection of abstract base classes and other common functionality needed to provide representations of those business objects in other packages' objects modules.

    - data_objects — The collection of abstract base classes and other common functionality needed to provide common processes for reading, writing, and otherwise working with object state-data persisted to a back end data store.

This new package structure is shown in *Figure 10.1*, below.

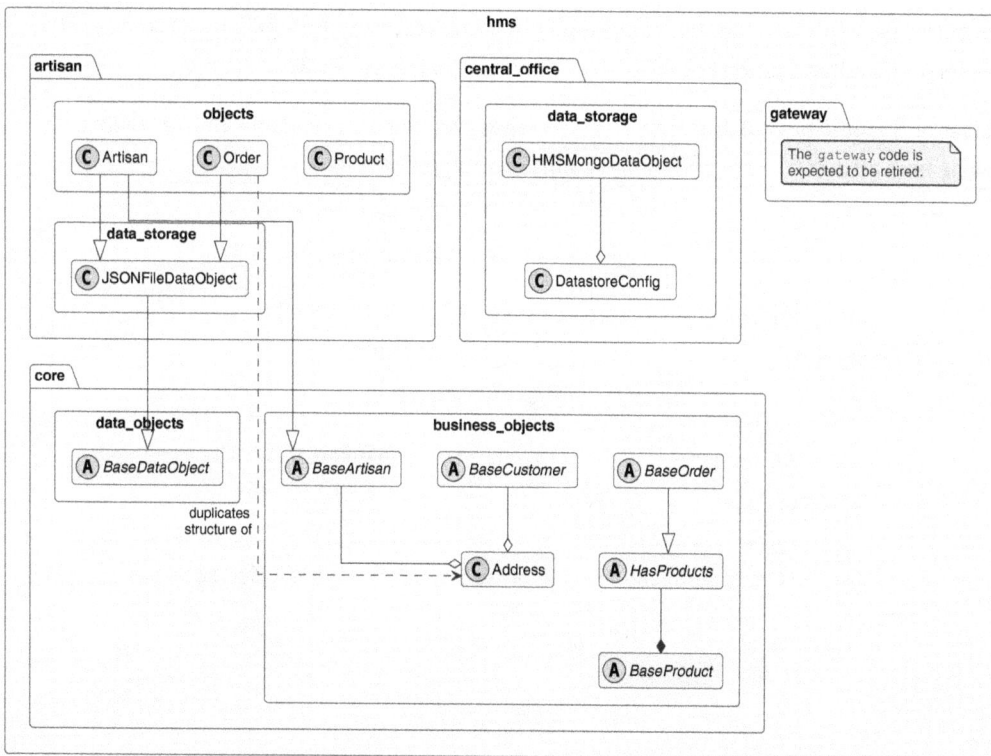

Figure 10.1: The final structure of the revised namespace

Ignoring the gateway namespace member

Because the expectation is that a new API of some flavor is going to be created as part of the entire project revision effort, the code in the gateway namespace segment is going to be set aside for the time being. If there were a real *need* to convert it before the final API efforts were underway, it *could* be converted, but there is no expected need to do so at this point in the story.

This revision, then, provides three of the aforementioned **composable packages** desired, facilitating the installation of only the functionality that is needed for any given purpose. For example, assuming that the final API is going to have discrete deployed functionality for individual endpoints for both Artisan and Central Office use, the Artisan-related endpoints could install only the `hms.artisan` namespace package, and its dependency on the `hms.core` package would be taken care of automatically. In this scenario, there would be no access to any of the code in the `hms.central_office` package because it would never have been installed in the first place. A similar installation scenario for the Central Office endpoints, installing `hms.central_office` and its dependencies, while leaving the functionality in `hms.artisan` out of the picture completely. The results of these installation scenarios are shown in *Table 10.1*, below:

Packages and modules available after installing hms.artisan	Packages and modules available after installing hms.central_office

• `hms`
    • `artisan`
        • `data_storage`
        • `objects`
    • `core`
        • `business_objects`
        • `data_objects`
	• `hms`
	    • `central_office`
	        • `data_storage`
	        • `objects`
	    • `core`
	        • `business_objects`
	        • `data_objects`

Table 10.1: The results of installing the hms.artisan and hms.central_office packages, side by side

The new structure is known in Python terms as a **namespace package**: a collection of separate *distributions* that can be independently installed, and that live in the same top-level namespace directly once they *are* installed. This is the mechanism that will provide the smaller, composable packages that were noted earlier, allowing the installed-package sets shown in *Table 10.1* to be used as shown.

Testing that the reorganization is functional is quite simple: given any single module, it should be possible to execute that module individually without it raising any ImportError or ModuleNotFound errors. There are several tasks that will have to be executed against each of the modules before those simple tests can succeed. The first two are:

- The original modules need to be moved into a new directory structure that mirrors the final package namespace for each module.

- A decision about how to manage package dependencies will need to be made so that a mechanism for allowing modules in one package directory to import modules from another package directory.

The namespace changes are shown in *Table 10.2*, below:

Original location		Move to	
Namespace	Module	Namespace	Module
hms_artisan	artisan_objects	hms.artisan	objects
hms_artisan	data_storage	hms.artisan	data_storage
hms_core	business_objects	hms.core	business_objects
hms_core	co_objects	hms.artisan	objects [1]
hms_core	data_objects	hms.core	data_objects
hms_core	data_storage	hms.core	data_storage

[1] This will eventually involve merging Artisan and Product classes that exist in both the current hms_artisan and hms_core namespaces into single classes in the hms.artisan namespace. The thought here is that Artisans own their own object-representations and the definitions of their products.

Table 10.2: The high-level namespace changes to be implemented

The basic process for accomplishing these changes is straightforward, if somewhat tedious:

1. Set up a directory structure that follows the namespace segments. The full directory structure for the new hms.core namespace, within the context of the codebase, will involve creating an hms directory at whatever location makes sense in a standard project structure and a core directory within that.

2. Move the original files into their new namespace-related directory.

3. Change any `import` statements to point to the new namespace for the relevant module or code entity being imported.

4. Test the change by executing the module.

Could this process be automated?

In a very real way, this entire effort is an exercise in **refactoring** the codebase: restructuring the source code to improve its operation without changing its functionality. There are several refactoring tools available that could be used to automate at least *some* of these — a quick search online for *refactoring tools for python* will yield several of them.

Once the initial file move and namespace change are complete, the modules in the new `hms.core` namespace pass this simple test. The modules in the other namespaces, though, do not. They raise a `ModuleNotFound` error...

```
ModuleNotFoundError: No module named 'hms'
```

...because nothing has been done yet that allows the Python interpreter to know where to look for the top-level `hms` namespace. A brief sidebar to explore Python's import process will explain what is going on.

Python's import process

Python's import subsystem follows a set of simple rules, but those rules can be leveraged in several ways to allow these imports to succeed. When a Python module is run, behind the scenes, the interpreter generates and keeps track of a collection of file-system paths that it will search in for import-capable entities. To illustrate this, change the code at the end of one of the modules in the new `hms.core` namespace to:

```python
if __name__ == '__main__':
    import sys
    from pprint import pprint
    pprint(sys.path)
```

When the module is run, it pretty-prints (with the imported pprint) something like the following:

```
[
    '/{local-path}/CH10-code/hms-core/src/hms/core',
    '/{python-version-path}/lib/python311.zip',
    '/{python-version-path}/lib/python3.11',
    '/{python-version-path}/lib/python3.11/lib-dynload',
    '/{python-version-path}/dist-packages',
]
```

The first item in this list will always be the path that the module being run lives in. If there is no module — for example, if the import sys through the pprint(sys.path) above were run in a Python session in a terminal — that first item will be an empty string that will resolve to the file-system path where the terminal session was started. Each item after that is a standard path that the Python interpreter knows to add; they provide paths to the various built-in packages that ship with the Python version installed.

If the system has a PYTHONPATH environment variable set, any of the path values it provides will also be included in the sys.path list. For example, running...

```
# Note the addition of the PYTHONPATH
PYTHONPATH="flobnar:quasmo:$PYTHONPATH" python3.11
>>> import sys
>>> from pprint import pprint
>>> pprint(sys.path)
```

in a terminal session outputs:

```
[
    '',
    '/{local-path}/flobnar',
    '/{local-path}/quasmo',
    '/{local-path}',
    '/{python-version-path}/lib/python311.zip',
    '/{python-version-path}/lib/python3.11',
    '/{python-version-path}/lib/python3.11/lib-dynload',
    '/{python-version-path}/dist-packages',
]
```

The content and resolution of the first line remain unchanged from the previous example. The second and third lines in the list include the flobnar and quasmo paths specified in the PYTHONPATH that was issued prior to the interpreter being launched. The remaining lines also remain unchanged.

These paths, as noted earlier, tell the Python interpreter where it is allowed to look for items when it encounters an `import` statement. Given an import like this, from the `hms.central_office.objects` module...

```
from hms.core.business_objects import Address
```

... the interpreter starts at the first entry of the list, looking for an hms directory, then a core directory within that, if it exists, and finally a business_objects module-file or package-directory within that. If all of those can be found, it proceeds with the `import` specified. If the `import` *cannot* be resolved, because any one of the items it was looking for didn't exist, then it goes to the next item in the `sys.path` list and tries again starting there. This process repeats until the `import` needed is found, or until the end of the `sys.path` list is reached, at which point an error is raised.

Knowing all of that, then, all that is necessary to get past the earlier error...

```
ModuleNotFoundError: No module named 'hms'
```

...is to come up with a way to add the appropriate paths to the command that actually executes the module. That process, whatever shape it takes, should be consistent within the scope of every package codebase, and a strong argument can be made that it should be consistent across all projects that a given software team is responsible for.

It is technically possible to manage this, at least in some of the more popular IDEs used in writing Python code, without having to bring the package-management processes into the question. So long as the execution of a module within the IDE can be controlled, and an additional PYTHONPATH can be specified as a prerequisite before running the module, the addition of one or more appropriate PYTHONPATH values will take care of the issue. That said, the combinations of IDEs and package-management tools discussed in the *IDE options, and what to look for* section of *Chapter 8* have already provided information about how to incorporate environment variables in their execution processes, and ultimately, that is all that is required — PYTHONPATH can be set up as an environment variable, using whatever mechanism works best for the combination of tools in use. That still leaves the question of how to manage package dependencies unanswered, though, and that decision may affect how best to provide the environment variables that would include PYTHONPATH, so let's look at that next.

Deciding on a package management tool

Arguably, the most critical factor in making a decision about a package management tool is what the final output of all the code in a project is going to need. The two mentioned earlier — *Package dependency management*, in *Chapter 8* — are pipenv and poetry. Each has its advantages for certain project contexts.

poetry is designed and optimized for writing Python packages. In setting up a poetry-backed project, all of the requisite standard tools for building a package will be automatically installed in the **Python Virtual Environment** (**PVE**) for the package project, and the basic configuration those tools need will also be created. If the bulk of a team's work is centered around writing and publishing Python packages, poetry is an obvious choice for consideration.

On the other hand, if the scope of a project includes code that is not intended for package-centric distribution, poetry may introduce additional work and constraints to write custom build processes to handle those exceptions. An alternative is to approach the structure of the final project output with the idea of everything in it being provided by packages. This is a perfectly valid approach as well, generally speaking, though in certain contexts it may introduce additional complexity in testing. In some contexts — cloud-resident serverless-function-based APIs, for example — it may also add a layer of obfuscation to the code that may make troubleshooting more difficult. Neither of these precludes the use of poetry for codebases that mix packages and non-package code. At worst, they require more care, thought, planning, and discipline to avoid complicating things too much.

pipenv is a more general-purpose package management solution: it makes no significant assumptions about what the final output of a project is, be it a package, a free-standing command-line program, a web application, or whatever else. Since the processes for building Python packages are well documented and actively maintained (see the *Python Packaging User Guide* at https:// packaging.python.org/), and can almost certainly be templated out to some degree, there is not much lost in choosing pipenv over poetry even in scenarios where a significant portion of a codebase is expected to generate packages as its final deliverable.

In making the decision about package management for the HMS revision that we're concerned with, poetry seems like an obvious choice given what has been discussed so far: all the revisions of existing code are centered around the creation of packages that will be installed and used in a still-to-be-designed API. However, as was noted in the *Setting the stage* section of *Chapter 9*:

There is some interest in moving towards a serverless architecture in the process, and investigations into the capabilities of AWS' Serverless Application Model (SAM), Azure Functions, and Google Cloud Platform's Cloud Functions have been started.

In these contexts, after a brief investigation into their typical structures and best practices, it seems likely that the API implementation will need to provide a full set of **Create**, **Read**, **Update**, and **Delete** (**CRUD**) functionality for at least four distinct business-object types: Artisan, Order, Product, and Address. Search-like functionality also seems likely for Product and Order business objects, and a similar need for other business objects cannot be ruled out at this point. Even if the CRUD (and potential Search) functionality is grouped by those business objects in the final API codebase, the code that could be classified as non-package outputs outnumbers the packages that have been defined so far.

Choosing pipenv would also provide a few additional tools that would have to be added as additional dependencies to a poetry-based project. The ability to use pipenv check to check for known security vulnerabilities, rather than having to manually track down the relevant packages, and write a wrapper script to perform those checks, is an example of the first scenario.

The decision-making process for the HMS around this question boiled down to discussing the options, weighing the risks of the choice impacting the API code that hasn't even been designed yet, and examining the existing, if older standard, build processes in place in the current code. Since the API implementation is still a substantial unknown, but there's a strong possibility that it would need sixteen or more separate functions defined, possibly each with its own deployment path and process, the team felt that there was more risk of problems or additional work to go with poetry. Those risks were not significantly offset by poetry's tool-chain for package development. The team committed to at least starting a package-project template for future use, possibly even one generated by poetry, that would still use pipenv for its package management. The clincher was that pipenv had built-in security checking facilities, the inclusion of which in a build or publishing process for a public-facing API felt like a significant advantage. Their choice was pipenv.

Having made that decision, the simplest path forward to resolving the ModuleNotFoundError issue that was occurring is to include a PYTHONPATH in a local environment file (.env file) in each package's code. As noted in *Chapter 8*'s *Managing packages with pipenv*, pipenv automatically looks for and uses a supplied .env file to set environment variables. Since PYTHONPATH can be set in that context, that provides a single, common location where that value can live for all the members of the software team.

The only trade-offs are that the individual .env files may need to differ from one team member to another, and that it's likely that secret information will eventually live in those files as well. Both of these would be solid reasons to not include the .env file in the repository — using whatever facility the **source control management (SCM)** provides to ignore them — to avoid collision of values across team members, and to prevent secret information from being stored in an SCM repository.

> ### Another option for development purposes
>
> Since `pipenv` was chosen, it is worth calling out that there is another option to allow cross-project dependencies to be managed: using *editable dependencies* (`https://pipenv-searchable.readthedocs.io/basics.html#editable-dependencies-e-g-e`). This will allow a development-only dependency to be attached to a given `Pipfile`, pointing to some other location, such that the other location is installed. At this stage in the process, that may not be viable — the various `setup.py` files that would be used have not been checked yet — but once they are operational, a command like
>
> ```
> pipenv install '-e ../hms-core' --dev
> ```
>
> within the other two package projects should allow them to reference the `hms-core` package code, along with its dependencies, according to the `pipenv` documentation (`https://pipenv-searchable.readthedocs.io/basics.html#editable-dependencies-e-g-e`).

The final set of changes made to finish the namespace reorganization, implement the `pipenv` package management, and provide common starting points for the local .env files for each project were:

- Creating a `pipenv` PVE with `pipenv --python 3.11`
- Installing `flake8` and `pytest` with `pipenv install --dev flake8 pytest`
- Creating a `template.env` file that the software team members can use as starting-points for their own local .env files
- Creating a local .env file from the `template.env`, one in each local copy of the package projects, and testing that all of the package modules run without raising the `ModuleNotFoundError` error that was encountered before

The collected changes at this point have been tagged in the book repository with Chapter-10-reorganization-complete and can be examined in detail there. These include the main Pipfile file for each package project, the corresponding Pipfile.lock, and a template.env file that is intended for developer use when they first check out any given package project.

The Pipfile files are human-readable collections of the package dependencies associated with the project. They include, at this point, any package dependencies required for the package project when it is published, as well as a collection of development-only packages. The hms-central-office package's Pipfile includes the pymongo package as a dependency, for example, and all of them include both flake8, for code linting, and pytest, for automated test discovery and execution.

Avoid modifying Pipfile manually!

Though it is technically possible to manually modify a Pipfile, it is also *very* easy to cause problems by doing so. pipenv has all the functionality needed to undo a mistake when adding or installing a package dependency, and less time will be spent executing pipenv uninstall / pipenv install commands, for example, than will be required to undo a bad manual change.

The Pipfile.lock files capture details about *every package* that is associated with a given PVE for a project. These include any dependencies or requirements for those packages, and their dependencies, in turn. They also include specific versions of packages, SHA-256 hashes for the packages (used to verify that packages have not been tampered with before allowing them to be used or updated), and what **Python Package Index (PyPI)** they were installed from. These details allow pipenv-managed projects to generate **deterministic builds** — builds where specific versions of specific packages are known and used consistently — and can also be used to generate requirements.txt files that are the lowest common denominator for specifying package dependencies for Python code (see the documentation for the pipenv requirements command for details).

> **Keep Pipfile.lock or requirements.txt files in SCM, but not both!**
>
> Both `Pipfile.lock` and `requirements.txt` files are intended to be unambiguous sources of truth for package dependencies for a project. If both are stored in SCM, there is a risk that those dependencies would be changed in one, but not the other, leading to inconsistencies, or even conflicts. Since `pipenv` can install from `requirements.txt` files, and can generate them on demand, it is better to decide which will be the source of truth for a project, store only that file in SCM, and leverage `pipenv` to generate the other when needed by an engineer or a build process.

The `template.env` file is exactly what it sounds like: a template file for a local `.env` file for developer use. The intent behind it is to provide a common starting-point for local `.env` files, without requiring that those files be stored in the SCM. For this set of package projects, they are almost identical, containing:

```
# Template .env File
# Make a copy of this file, named ".env" in your local
# development directory, and change the values as needed.
# NOTE: The PYTHONPATH assumes, by default, that all repos
# will be checked out under a single, common directory.
# The entries in it (delimited by a ":") are:
# * The "local" src directory of this project;
# * The "local" src directory of the hms-core project;
# We shouldn't need to have the explicit :$PYTHONPATH in
# it. though.
PYTHONPATH="src:../hms-core/src"
```

The exception, for this set of package projects, is in the copy for the `hms-core` package project, which only needs a reference to its own local `src` directory.

Having selected `pipenv` as the package management tool of choice for these projects, there are several tools that are available, many of which can be incorporated in hook scripts for the SCM. They will be explored in the next section.

At this point, the project structure has been revised and restructured into package projects that can each support their own distinct set of dependencies and requirements. Each package project is set up so that their final build-and-publish process will generate the individual package as a member of the new, common hms namespace. The interaction between those packages during local development has been accounted for, leveraging the PYTHONPATH environment variable in the local .env file so that Python's import mechanism knows how to find them. Each package project could have been created in a new SCM repository, or they could have been worked out locally and added to an SCM repository as they were completed — the sequencing is really more a decision based on what was convenient while these pieces were put in play. In any event, it is safe to assume that they would all be in SCM by the time all of these efforts were completed, which means we can now take a closer look at how to take advantage of the decisions made here in an SCM context.

Making source control management decisions

The fundamental decisions about SCM really boil down to only a few items: what the SCM engine is (Git, https://git-scm.com/ vs. Mercurial, https://www.mercurial-scm.org/ or some other option), where the actual main repository is going to live, and, perhaps, what kind of branching strategy will be used to manage changes to a codebase. In HMS' case, the first two of these have been made at the management level: they are using a cloud-resident Git system, **Bitbucket** (https://bitbucket.org/), provided by Atlassian. Branching strategies are decisions that each software team can make on their own, and can even differ from one project to another if a team feels that is the best approach. Similarly, the use of SCM functionality hooks, in particular, is a team-level decision. Up to this point, the only constraint has been focused on ensuring that a reasonable amount of discipline and quality assurance is in place to minimize the potential of broken code being deployed to an end user.

Since the new versions of the packages are expected to be used as part of a public-facing API, there are a few areas where that basic principle could be improved: checking package dependencies for known vulnerabilities with pipenv check is one that the team identifies in short order. None of them want to be pulled in to a support call if a security incident surfaces. They also liked the idea of not allowing changes to be pushed to the repository, even if those changes are not going into the main, production-ready branch of the repository, without passing at least some of the unit test suite first.

How the SCM is going to be used

The team has been successfully using a very basic branching strategy for some time now, and do not see any pressing need to change that, or their typical workflow. Typically, that workflow is:

1. Create a branch for a feature, bug, or whatever other change is needed.

2. Make the requisite code changes in that branch, committing and pushing as needed to keep the changes clean and purposeful.

3. Once everything that needs to be changed has been done, start a pull request for the branch.

4. Review each other's work in those pull requests, asking questions and suggesting (or even requiring) changes before the pull request is approved.

5. Once there are enough approvals, including at least one technical lead and one other engineer familiar with the codebase, merge the pull request into the main branch.

6. If the change needs an immediate build — more commonly for bug fixes — start a process to build, test, and publish the code that was just changed.

The final step, building, testing, and publishing the package, will be addressed later — there are other considerations that need to be examined before any changes to that process can be defined and decided upon. The rest, after some discussion between team members, led to a list of needed and desired process items that they agreed on. In no particular order, they were:

- We should make sure that we're updating package dependencies, if there are any that need it, every time we work on a package.

- We need to make sure we're at least aware of any dependent packages with security issues, and we need to make conscious decisions about not addressing them when they show up if we aren't going to address them.

- We need to require that the unit test suites, at a minimum, pass before allowing code to be pushed, even to a pull request. Alternately, we need to require them to pass within a pull request before allowing changes to be merged.

- We should also be able to require other test suites — integration testing, for example — to pass before allowing a code push.

- If we're going to lint our code, we should probably require that to succeed before allowing a push as well.

Why these are relevant in a discussion about SCM is because they can be accomplished through the use of hooks.

What Git hooks make sense

A **hook** is a collection of one or more programs or scripts that an SCM can execute automatically as part of some standard action. Git has, as of August of 2024, twenty-eight options for hook functionality (`https://git-scm.com/docs/githooks`), and other SCM options have at least some basic hook capabilities as well, though their names and the specifics of where they live in a project, and when and how they are triggered, will vary. These hook programs and scripts, in Git, live in the local `.git/hooks` directory of a project, one file per supported hook. Each is triggered by one or more specific processes within Git itself.

The processes in the earlier list all center around only a couple of the available hook options. The desired update to package dependencies when work on a project starts will be best served by implementing a `post-checkout` hook that executes `pipenv upgrade`. With that hook in place, any time that `git checkout` is executed, the package dependencies for the project will be updated. It might also be useful to execute when a `git pull` is executed, which would trigger the `post-merge` hook. This would trigger if an engineer needed to pull in changes from the main repository made after their own updates and changes had already been started, provided that the `pull` activity happens within the local repository scope at some point after a remote or origin pull action has done its thing. The `post-checkout` hook file could be as simple as this:

```
# post-checkout
# A Git Hook to execute after checking something out from
# a repository: git-checkout or git-switch
# If the version of pipenv installed does not automatically
# update --dev and --categories sections' dependencies,
# they can be explicitly called by specifying
# --dev
# or
# --categories {category names}
# as needed.
pipenv update
```

The other items on that list all hinge on the idea of doing something before allowing a push action to succeed, which is exactly what the `pre-push` hook is intended to do. A bare-bones implementation for the `pre-push` hook could be as simple as this:

```
# pre-push
# Check for security issues with any package dependencies.
pipenv check
```

```
# Run the project's unit-test suite
pipenv run pytest tests/unit
# Lint the project's source and test code
pipenv run flake8 src
pipenv run flake8 tests
```

However, the `pipenv check` it contains will eventually raise an issue:

it's possible (almost certain, actually, given enough time) that a vulnerability will surface from `pipenv check` that cannot be mitigated by a package update. In that case, ignoring a given vulnerability can still be done in-line in the hook's script, but since those hook scripts are in the `.git` directory, and that directory is not included in the main repository's tracked files, changes to them will not propagate to the repository itself. That means that every engineer needs to update their own local hook script every time a vulnerability falls into this category.

An alternative to that would be to write the actual hook-scripts elsewhere in the project's code, somewhere that will be persisted in the repository as code is committed and pushed, and reference that script from the actual hook script in the local file system structure. That would also allow some degree of record-keeping of vulnerabilities that were being ignored, along with some documentation of the rationale behind those decisions. A fairly basic approach that accomplishes this is shown in the `hook-scripts/security-scans.py` module added to each of the package projects (tagged as `Security-scan-script-example` in the book's accompanying repository). With the required functionality available outside the `.git/hooks` directory, revising the local pre-push hook script to:

```
# pre-push
# This should be copied (not moved) to the .git/hooks
# directory, and made executable
# Check for security issues with any package dependencies.
pipenv run python hook-scripts/security-scans.py
# Run the project's unit-test suite
pipenv run pytest tests/unit
# Lint the project's source and test code
pipenv run flake8 src
pipenv run flake8 tests
```

will allow it to be called locally, while allowing changes that need to be made to it over time to live in the project's repository, where any engineer can add to or remove from it as needed.

There are at least two separate caveats to keep in mind when creating Git hook scripts for a project. The first is that if the operating systems in use by the members of a project's development team are not all the same, those scripts may well need to accommodate OS-specific command execution differences. It may be possible to mitigate the risks of differences across operating system script versions by simply managing one variation of each for each OS in play. That will not eliminate the risk of drift between different versions for any purpose, but it will minimize it.

The second is that because these scripts reside in a standard directory that is not, itself, tracked in the SCM by default, *something* has to be done to ensure that the scripts that *are* tracked are applied as hooks. In Git, that can be managed by setting the local configuration to point its core. hooksPath to a tracked directory, for example:

```
git config core.hooksPath hooks
```

to point to a tracked hooks directory. This would have to be configured for every local copy of the source repository in use by any engineer: a minor task, but one that would be easily missed. Having a back-up process, in the form of some sort of test-process when creating a pull request, and not allowing direct pushes to the repository — good ideas anyway — would at least prevent changes from propagating past the final push to the main branch, in case that configuration change were missed. If that were not feasible for some reason, make sure that everyone who might work with the repository knows that they need to make their own copies of the various hook scripts. This is, obviously, more prone to human error.

In the case of HMS's software team, after some discussion, they decide that the following hooks will be used, to establish the following checks and balances in their workflow. Their result is in the book repository, tagged as Final-git-hooks-structures in the *Chapter 10* code:

- A post-merge and identical post-checkout, which execute when code is pulled from a repository, to update local package dependencies, and run a security check. The goal here is to at least *try* to keep package dependencies as current as possible, and to catch any needed security updates before work is done that might be impacted by them. If security issues are raised, they should be examined and either fixed or ignored with documentation about *why* they are being ignored.

- A pre-push that executes the same security check, followed by the project's unit test suite, and ends with linting of the project's source code with flake8. This is what was provided in the pre-push example shown earlier. During their discussion, the team also considered the idea of using the exact same hook-script code as a post-commit hook, allowing all of the same checks to execute when a commit is fired off, but without the possibility of a failure from the hook's execution preventing the commit. This scenario would provide notification on every commit that the commit would, if pushed, pass or fail the checks.

Thoughtful implementation of hooks in an SCM process opens the door for a number of checks and guardrails to be applied locally before local changes are pushed into a production-ready branch. One of those guardrails has already been noted in the pre-push hook script shown earlier: executing a unit test suite. Defining expectations about those test suites, including how rigorous those test suites should be, how they are expected to be written, when they are expected to be used, and what their structure expectations are is a topic all on its own.

Planning for unit testing

Unit testing is the foundation of a disciplined testing process for code. The intent behind a unit test suite is to test individual code components within a codebase, at some acceptable level of isolation from *other* components in the codebase, in order to verify that each of those components behaves in a *predictable fashion*. Note that nowhere in that definition did the terms **bug** or **defect** (or any other synonym for them) appear. The distinction between *unpredictable* behavior and *undesirable* behavior (a bug or defect) is subtle, but noteworthy. Odds are good that unpredictable behavior will also be undesirable behavior, but the two are not always the same: it's possible, however unlikely, that unpredictable behavior will not be unwanted.

The idea of testing for predictable behavior also includes the potential for code to raise errors under certain circumstances. For example, if a chunk of code is written so that it with some variant of the supported try … except … else … finally structure (see https://docs.python. org/3.11/tutorial/errors.html), so that certain types of exceptions are caught and handled, and unexpected exceptions are re-raised, it is useful and meaningful to write tests that verify that those exceptions are handled (or re-raised) as expected. If a test target is called with inputs that *should* raise an exception, but that exception is *not* raised, that represents a failure result for the test.

That leads, then, to the idea of setting expectations for how rigorous a test suite should be, that is, how thoroughly should the members of the test suite test their respective targets, and how strictly any testing expectations are adhered to. Obviously, the more thorough the sets of test inputs are, the more thorough the actual test executions will be. There are limiting factors, though. It is impractical, at best, to generate test inputs for every possible integer value for every function or method that uses one or more integer inputs, as an example. Even if the range of values were to be limited to the nominal maximum value allowed by the underlying operating system, that would involve $2^{64}-1$ distinct values to test for each integer input to each test target, which would involve so many test inputs that the first such test would not complete before the engineer who wrote it had retired! Additionally, there would be little benefit to that extreme level of rigor in a test: most of the individual integer values would share certain properties with a large set of others. They could all be classified as positive numbers, non-zero numbers, even or odd numbers, and so on.

It makes more sense to tie the test-input expectations to the code in some manner and limit the inputs accordingly. Using the same integer-based value, and assuming that the execution of the target being tested branches in only three cases, a negative value that raises an error, a zero value that raises a different error, or a positive value that executes to completion without error, the meaningful test inputs are easily represented by three values: -1, 0, and 1. Taking a similar approach for other values and types is a straightforward exercise in evaluating the expectations of a given test target. Consider, for example, this create_person function:

```python
def create_person(
    given_name: str, family_name: str,
    birth_date: datetime|int
):
    """
    Creates and returns a Person object, populated with
    the supplied input data.
    Parameters:
    -----------
    given_name : str (required, non-empty)
        The given name of the Person to create.
    family_name : str (required, non-empty)
        The family name of the Person to create.
    birth_date : datetime or int timestamp (required)
        The birth date of the Person to create, expressed
        as either a datetime (preferred) or a timestamp
        (int) that can be converted to one.
    Raises:
    -------
    ValueError:
        - If supplied an empty string value for either
          given_name or family_name.
        - If supplied a birth_date in the future, or too
          far in the past (over 150 years)
    """
    # The body of this function isn't needed, so long as
    # its implementation is as documented/annotated above.
    # That said, we'll want to see what is coming in to
    # it later, so let's print the parameters:
```

```
print('create_person called:')
print('='*40)
print(f'given_name .... {given_name}')
print(f'family_name ... {family_name}')
print(f'birth_date .... {birth_date}')
print('-'*40)
```

The initial members of the test suite that test this target can be easily broken down into eight distinct test processes:

- A *happy path* test that passes a non-empty string value for the given_name and first_name parameters, and a birth_date value that is a datetime for a date and time in the past, but less than 150 years ago.

- A *happy path* test that passes an int value (a timestamp) instead of a datetime for birth_date, as well as non-empty strings for given_name and first_name parameters.

- An *unhappy path* test that passes an empty string value for given_name, but happy path values for the other parameters.

- An *unhappy path* test that passes an empty string value for family_name, but happy path values for the other parameters.

- An *unhappy path* test that passes a datetime representing a date/time in the future for birth_date, but happy path values for the other parameters.

- An *unhappy path* test that passes an int timestamp representing a date/time in the future for birth_date, but happy path values for the other parameters.

- An *unhappy path* test that passes a datetime representing a date/time too far in the past for birth_date, but happy path values for the other parameters.

- An *unhappy path* test that passes an int timestamp representing a date/time too far in the past for birth_date, but happy path values for the other parameters.

Happy and unhappy paths

A **happy path** is a call to a function, method, or other callable that provides arguments or parameters that fall within normal, expected constraints, and that returns a normal, expected value. A happy path is, essentially, the normal behavior that the test target was written to implement, under typical (or even ideal) circumstances. An **unhappy path**, then, is a path through the code that does not meet those conditions, and that might be expected to raise an error.

In a happy path test, it can be useful to provide a collection of parameter values that are expected to work without error, one set for each parameter, iterate over that collection, and execute the target function with each set of parameters. For example, you could set up a collection of given_name, first_name, and birth_date parameter values (including the datetime and int-timestamp variations) with the following values:

```python
from datetime import datetime, timedelta
given_names = ('John', 'Jane')
family_names = ('Smith', 'Jones')
past_offsets = (
    timedelta(days=-120),        # several months
    timedelta(days=-21*365.25)   # 21 years ago
)
now = datetime.now()
birth_dates = tuple(
    [now + past_offset for past_offset in past_offsets]
    + [
        int((now + past_offset).timestamp())
        for past_offset in past_offsets
    ]
)
```

...then doing something that will yield all possible combinations of those values in this case, using the built-in itertools.product function (https://docs.python.org/3.11/library/itertools.html#itertools.product) to create a sequence of argument tuples:

```python
[
    ('John', 'Smith', datetime(2024, 5, 10, 12, 14, 7, 0)),
    ('John', 'Smith', datetime(2003, 9, 8, 6, 14, 7, 0)),
    ('John', 'Smith', 1715364847),
    ('John', 'Smith', 1063023247),
    ('John', 'Jones', datetime(2024, 5, 10, 12, 14, 7, 0)),
    ('John', 'Jones', datetime(2003, 9, 8, 6, 14, 7, 0)),
    ('John', 'Jones', 1715364847),
    ('John', 'Jones', 1063023247),
    ('Jane', 'Smith', datetime(2024, 5, 10, 12, 14, 7, 0)),
    ('Jane', 'Smith', datetime(2003, 9, 8, 6, 14, 7, 0)),
```

```
        ('Jane', 'Smith', 1715364847),
        ('Jane', 'Smith', 1063023247),
        ('Jane', 'Jones', datetime(2024, 5, 10, 12, 14, 7, 0)),
        ('Jane', 'Jones', datetime(2003, 9, 8, 6, 14, 7, 0)),
        ('Jane', 'Jones', 1715364847),
        ('Jane', 'Jones', 1063023247)
    ]
```

An example of this kind of process is provided in the `scratch-space/create_person_iterations.py` module in the chapter repository. The primary advantage provided by this approach for generating arguments for iterations of test-target calls is that it allows the values that are expected to work to be defined in one place in the test code, allowing them to be reused as needed. Because the values live in one place, adding a new value, or removing an existing one, is very easy, and will apply automatically to any test that uses the set of values. So long as each source collection has at least one member in it, the end result (all possible combinations of all inputs) will still be returned — it would, for example, be possible to reduce the `given_name` and `family_name` collections to one member each, so that only `'John'` and `'Smith'` values were represented, but still providing all the permutations of `birth_date`.

That approach would provide a strategy for testing a reasonable set of happy path values with a fair degree of thoroughness. What about unhappy paths, though? A similar approach, grouping collections of invalid values for one parameter with valid values for the others, is a good first step, and may be sufficient by itself if there is no pressing need to test *multiple* invalid values. A complete example of this approach is provided in the `scratch-space/create_person_unhappy.py` module in the chapter repository. In the interest of making variable names descriptive, using the `given_name` parameters, good and bad (valid and invalid) values are broken out separately like this:

```
# Define the valid values here for each parameter name
good_given_names = ('John', 'Jane')
...
# Define some invalid values -- and types - for
# unhappy path testing purposes
bad_given_names = ('', 1, True, object())
```

Since the test parameters will need to include mixes of good values that should not trigger any failures and bad values that should, separate functions to create parameter-sets that include all possible combinations of the good and bad values needed, like this:

```
def get_bad_given_name_parameters():
    return (
        args for args in product(
            bad_given_names,
            good_family_names,
            good_birth_dates
        )
    )
```

Executing calls to the target function then becomes a simple matter of calling that target with each of the parameter-set generator functions:

```
# Call the function once with each of those
# argument-sets
for parameters in get_bad_given_name_parameters():
    create_person(*parameters)
# These functions follow a similar pattern
for parameters in get_bad_birth_date_parameters():
    create_person(*parameters)
for parameters in get_bad_family_name_parameters():
    create_person(*parameters)
```

In the context of a unit test, this approach would make calling the test target with a collection of parameters that should raise predictable errors very easy. Each of those calls, as a test, would be expected to raise a predictable error, and if the error is not raised, the test fails. Between this and the happy path parameter sets, all of the test permutations noted earlier can be easily implemented. This sort of approach also tends to maximize code coverage in a test suite.

> **Code coverage — is it good, evil, or somewhere in between?**
>
> In simple terms, code coverage is a metric that helps with understanding how much
> of the target source code is actually executed by a test suite. Tracking code coverage,
> and being able to identify code that has not been exercised during the run of a test
> suite, is beneficial for identifying code that either still needs to be tested, or that
> will never be executed. Using coverage as a target measure of quality is likely to be
> misleading. The most widely used Python module for tracking and reporting on
> code coverage is the `coverage` module (`https://coverage.readthedocs.io/`).

The HMS software team decides that this strategy is how they would prefer to approach unit
testing. This decision, they feel, maximizes the rigor of the tests, while keeping the management
of tests relatively simple. They also plan to use code coverage reporting as a signpost for closer examination of both test and source code, making sure that code flagged as untested is, at minimum,
examined closely. If that code needs to be tested, tests will be altered accordingly, hopefully by
simply adding new valid or invalid values to their parameter collections. If untested code reveals
paths through the source code, that code will be examined in closer detail to determine whether
it serves a purpose or not and pruned out if it does not. This decision also raises questions about
how individual test functions or methods will be named, as well as other, more general test suite
organization concerns. That, in turn, requires making a decision about what testing framework
is going to be used.

Although there are other options, the HMS team feels that there are only two testing frameworks
that they would consider: Python's built-in `unittest` (`https://docs.python.org/3.11/library/`
`unittest.html`) and the third-party `pytest` package (`https://docs.pytest.org/`), or some
mixture of the two (since `pytest` will execute `unittest` tests). There are details that they want
to examine for both, including what test modules' members and structures would look like and
the level of effort required to test targets in sufficient isolation from other targets.

To illustrate the code differences required by each testing framework, we'll build out a reasonably complete test module using unittest and pytest both for the class and function shown in *Figure 10.2*, below:

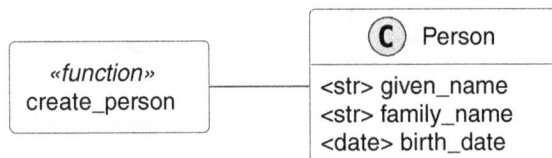

Figure 10.2: The class and function being used in the example person.py module to show how tests differ between unittest and pytest

A unittest test implementation

The test module for the unittest-based test module can be found in the chapter repository at scratch-space/unittest-exploration/test_module.py.

Python's built-in unittest module is the lowest common denominator of unit testing frameworks for Python code. It is a built-in module that ships with any Python installation, and as such is available without any additional installations. It takes a class-based approach, defining a TestCase class that identifies collections of test methods to be executed when the corresponding test suite is run. Implementation of a test suite in a unittest context, then, consists of:

- Defining one to many test classes, derived from the TestCase class.
- Adding one to many test methods to that class, each prefixed with test, which defines the tests to be executed by the TestCase-derived class during the execution of the test process.

Since a unittest execution only recognizes TestCase-derived classes during the discovery of tests, *every* test that needs to be executed must be defined as a member of one of those classes. Testing of functions, then, relies on the presence of a TestCase-derived class, which may feel awkward to software engineers or their teams. The trade-off here is that the test case classes provide a single point in the organization of a test suite that keeps all of the presumably related test methods together.

The TestCase class defines more than two dozen types of assertions that can be used to define very precise test evaluations, which can be a daunting task to remember, though many of them can be replaced with simple self.assertEqual or self.assertNotEqual method calls, at the expense of having to write a bit more code to make those comparisons work. Some of those assertion methods are *too* precise, even — assertions for raised exceptions accept only a single exception type to be specified, for example.

Tests that need to check for any of several exception types require additional test code either to arrange for specific expectations, or an alternative approach that checks results from the target callable and explicitly calls `self.fail` to *force* a failure. Alternately, the built-in `assert` statement can be used, with a similar level of additional effort. The assertions provided by the `TestCase` class include an `assertRaises`, which can be used to check for a *single, specific* type of exception being raised. Testing for any of several possible types (`TypeError` and `ValueError` in this example) requires a more brute-force approach, `try`-ing the execution of the target, and using `except` to catch the expected errors. If more or better visibility or messaging for tests that fail to raise an expected exception type is desired, the `fail` method can be used to explicitly cause a failure and to provide more detailed messaging about that failure.

Given the earlier emphasis on generating an iterable collection of test-target arguments, another capability of particular interest is its support for a `subTest` context, allowing each iteration being tested to pass or fail in its own right and provide better insight into those individual failures when they do occur. That is, if a test method iterates over, say, six different sets of parameters, and the third and fourth raise failures for whatever reason, each of those failures will be displayed individually, while the others behave as simple successful tests.

A final note, before moving on to the equivalent test module built with pytest: Because unittest relies on the `TestCase` classes mentioned earlier, the example test module includes a `test_get_person` class, derived as required from `TestCase` class. In a `unittest`-based test process, this is one of the cleanest ways to handle tests for functions — probably *the* cleanest way. As would be expected, it keeps the test methods relating to the function grouped as methods of the test case class, eliminating any potential risk of the relevant test processes being scattered through the test module.

A pytest test implementation

The test module for the pytest-based test module can be found in the chapter repository at `scratch-space/pytest-exploration/test_module.py`.

By contrast, implementing testing processes that are based only on pytest require nothing more than the creation of a test module and the creation of a test function (whose name would be prefixed with `test`) for each test case that is needed. Because pytest does not directly support the sort of class-based test structures that unittest does, a *pure* pytest implementation of tests against *class* targets would be broken up into test functions for each member and scenario that needs to be tested.

Depending on how granular those target testing scenarios need to be, that is, how many distinct test functions need to be defined, there is significant potential for a *lot* of test functions to be defined. In all fairness, the same could be said of a unittest-based implementation, but that proliferation would happen within the scope of the test case classes, lending a bit more structure to the organization of the test methods.

When pytest runs a test suite, it performs a discovery operation that finds and keeps track of test functions in modules within the specified path. The default process finds modules whose names begin with test, and any functions *within* those modules whose names begin with test. Every function thus discovered will be executed within the context of the module it resides in.

The discovery process provided by pytest is simpler and more intuitive than the equivalent in unittest. By way of comparison, here are the equivalent commands for each, using the pipenv environment set up for the entire CH10-code repository:

```
# pytest
pipenv run pytest pytest-exploration
# unittest
pipenv run python -m unittest discover \
    -s unittest-exploration
```

The reporting provided by pytest in the event of a test failure is almost always sufficient without any additional effort: It identifies the assertion that actually caused the failure, and enough of the context of the code executed leading to that failure to identify where in the target code the failure originated, providing a fair chance of identifying the cause of a test failure without leaving the results of the test.

Writing the assertions for tests in a pure pytest context is frequently simpler than the equivalent in a unittest suite: it simply uses the built-in assert statement, and any failed assertion equates to a failed test. The trade-off for this simplicity is the requirement for the test author to figure out how to handle anything that is more complex an assertion than a simple equality check.

Testing for exceptions being raised is similar in pytest and unittest, differing only in the name of the function used to capture the results of the target call before checking for the expected error type. Unfortunately, it still only allows a single exception type to be specified, so testing with an iteration of calls that may raise different exception types still requires the kind of structure that a similar unittest-based approach requires, as noted earlier.

A hybrid approach

It is worth noting that the test detection processes in pytest will find and execute unittest. TestCase classes. This means that using a mixture of the two test frameworks is possible, which would allow class-based test structures to be defined for classes being tested, and function-based test structures for target functions. A pytest execution of unittest test structures will honor most unittest functionality. The notable exception is the unittest.TestCase.subTest structure, used to test over iterations of parameters. By default, when pytest encounters a failure in a subTest structure, it will detect that failure and immediately terminate the test run, without executing any other sub-tests in the iteration. There is an add-on package for pytest, pytest-subtests (https://pypi.org/project/pytest-subtests/), that allows a pytest run to fully honor those.

There are several criteria that the HMS team considered before making a decision about what test framework to use:

- They liked that pytest supports both its own test structures and the unittest structures that they already have defined for the previous version. Their hope is that this will allow them to reuse a substantial amount of test code that has already been written.

- The simpler function-based approach of pytest will, they hope, lend itself to other automated testing that will be needed later: end-to-end testing in particular, was raised, but *any* testing process that could benefit from a simpler function-based structure is fair game.

- pytest appears to have a richer ecosystem of plug-ins that may be needed, or at least useful as their efforts unfold.

- The one potential concern that surfaced, the limited pytest support for unittest subTest functionality to iteratively test larger sets of parameters against test targets for more thorough and rigorous tests, can be accommodated if it becomes annoying with one of those plug-ins.

After examining the options and their pros and cons, they decide that they will use a hybrid approach in writing their unit tests:

- Test elements may be written using either unittest or pytest constructs.

This will, they feel, provide the best balance of flexibility and convenience in writing, maintaining, and executing tests for their code.

Other unit testing expectations and decisions

With the decision made about the tool set to be used made, the remaining test-related decisions can be addressed, to come to what might be thought of as a *testing policy*. Those are, in the main, decisions about:

- What the expectations are about what *must* be tested, what *should* be, and what criteria apply, if any, to allow a test to be skipped.

- How much isolation of components being tested is needed or desired.

- How tests will be organized within the code — where they will live in the project's code, their naming conventions, and other, similar organizational details.

Deciding what *must* be tested also includes some thoughts about what the goals of a test suite are, and how tests will accomplish those goals. Ideally, the goals for a unit test suite are some variation of the idea that the tests should exercise all source code in a project, checking that all code behaves in an expected fashion. Realistically, as already noted, that may not be technically feasible: there may be an essentially infinite number of permutations that can be passed to a target code element. The idea of defining a reasonable subset of values designed to accomplish that *exercise all source code* goal has already been described from an implementation perspective, including providing values that are expected to raise errors.

The easiest logical testing policy statements that relate to this, that lend themselves naturally to accomplishing the goal of exercising all source code, is to require that all source code elements must have one or more corresponding test-code elements and that all tests exercise a meaningful, reasonable subset of inputs. This was discussed in some detail in the examples earlier. What has not been addressed yet is the idea of when (or if) it is reasonable to *skip* testing some path through the source code. Given the stated goal of testing all paths through the source code, the idea of intentionally not testing some of it may not seem rational, but there are viable reasons for doing so. From a testing policy perspective, the question of how much isolation is expected in tests is a key consideration. The logical extreme of the idea that unit tests are intended to test individual source components in isolation from other source components leads to the idea that a unit test for a function that calls one or more *other* functions should **patch** each of those other functions, and possibly **mock** the results of those calls. That extreme may be *too* extreme for some teams or projects: it tends to lead to separate code for each variation of those calls being tested, each of which is, itself, code that has to be maintained.

What is patching and mocking?

In both `unittest` and `pytest`, a **patch** is a mechanism that intercepts a call to some identified function or method, allowing any calls to the patched entity to proceed as if the original function were called. A **mock** is a simulation of the results of a call to a patched function or method that can be assigned as a return value for a given patch during a test. Taken together, they allow calls that are made by a target code element being tested to be simulated, with whatever results are needed within the context of a test, without actually calling the original target code elements. Mocking and patching will be shown in more detail in later chapters during the implementation of tests against project code. As Martin Fowler notes in his *Mocks Aren't Stubs* article (`https://martinfowler.com/articles/mocksArentStubs.html`), there are several other terms that may be equivalent to *mock* and *patch* in various languages.

Certain common software design practices require mocking or patching, though, if *any* isolation is expected. Typically, these scenarios involve functionality that requires access to some resource that is not part of the project itself, or that may not be accessible when a test suite is executed. A common pattern is some variation of a system where:

- Application or state data is persisted in a back end data store of some sort, like a database.
- The code contains functionality to handle reading, writing, and deletion of that data, wrapped in one or more functions or methods.

There are a variety of reasons why access to the actual data store might be discouraged or even prohibited. Perhaps the data itself is sensitive — personally identifiable information, financial or health data, or trade secrets, for example — and the liability risks are unacceptable. Another, more common variation on this theme is a policy of not storing access credentials in a code repository, in case it gets compromised. Or maybe the process of writing data kicks off other processes that are expensive, financially or computationally, and it's just not worth the additional time or money spent. Whatever the reason, all of the functionality that would normally use that data store could be patched, and the results of those calls mocked so that the tests could run without requiring that access.

If all of that data access functionality is patched, though, the next question is how does that functionality itself get tested? Whether there is no way that it *can* be tested, or if other reasons dictate that it *should not be tested*, the end result is the same: tests for them need to be *omitted* in some fashion. The easiest way to accomplish that is to simply not write those tests in the first place, but that leaves no indication in the code that the missing tests *should* be omitted.

Both unittest and pytest provide a mechanism for skipping tests using a skip decorator that can be attached to a test element. When skip is applied, the test element it decorates still exists, and will be discovered by the test framework, but the execution of the decorated test item will be skipped, displaying in the test output that it *was* skipped, and a *reason* for it being skipped. This allows test code to be defined, even if the target that would be tested cannot be *meaningfully* tested, or not tested at all for some reason, but showing that a conscious decision was made to not test the target, and what that reason was.

Always provide a reason when skipping tests!

Though a reason is an optional argument in the pytest version of the skip decorator, it is always a good idea to provide one anyway. That acts both as inline documentation concerning why the test was skipped, and information output during the execution of a test suite.

The question of how much isolation should be involved in tests that do not use any external functionality is, ultimately, a team preference decision. Deciding in favor of more isolation, all the way up to full isolation, leads, as noted earlier, to more patching and mocking of the child elements, and may well add a lot more test code as a result. Allowing tests of a source code element to make actual calls to its child elements reduces that complexity, but with a trade-off: if one of the child elements stops functioning, or even just starts behaving in a way that causes the test to fail, that increases the likelihood of having to do more in-depth examinations of why a given test is failing.

The HMS team's test policies with respect to what their goals and related expectations for tests are, and what should be tested, are:

- Unit tests will be written for all code elements in the project's source code.
- Unit tests that rely on external resources, particularly data storage, will use patching and mocking so that no actual connections are created or needed.
- Unit tests are not expected to patch or mock code entities' calls or results if those entities are part of the project unless they fall into an external resources category.
- Unit tests may be skipped if they cannot yield meaningful test results. Any skipped test code must provide a reason that it was skipped.
- Unit tests will at least make an attempt to execute all reasonable combinations of happy path values, with the expectation that each of those combinations, passed to the test target, will execute without error, and yield expected results.

- They will also execute a similar set of reasonable combinations of unhappy path executions, each of which is expected to raise some type of predictable error, raising a test failure if the expected error does not occur.
- Code coverage reporting will be used to identify code that has not been executed during the execution of a test suite, and efforts will be made to address any substantial gaps, but coverage will not be used as criteria for whether code can be released.

The last two items that the HMS team wants to consider are what the structure of a test suite looks like — where the suite lives, how modules and their members are named, and the like — and when tests will be executed. The first item they already have a *de facto* policy for that carries over from the previous version's code:

- Test modules will live in a `tests/unit` directory.
- The standard prefix for a test-module name, as well as for the members of those modules, will be `test_`.

This section discussed a lot of thoughts to be considered and decisions to be made to establish what unit testing for Python code can and should do. The current state of the decisions that the HMS team made are documented in the book's repository, at `tests/unit/README.md` within the individual projects. Without knowing precisely what the build, package, and deploy processes will look like yet, defining where in those processes the unit tests will run cannot be completely identified. Even so, there is consensus that they should execute successfully before allowing code to merge into the production-ready branch for any given project, and the `pre-push` Git hook discussed earlier is already set up to run the unit test suite, provided that individual engineers configure their local copies to run them.

Working out a build process

Once a project's code has been successfully tested, it's ready to be packaged and published to a PyPI repository. From there, anyone who has access to that repository can install the packaged code, whether with the built-in `pip` tool, `pipenv`, or `poetry`. At a high level, the process is only two activities:

- Building the package, which creates an installable package in one or more standard formats in a directory structure within the project's existing directory structure.
- Publishing the resulting package files to the target PyPI repository.

The process is relatively straightforward — there are tools to handle all of the steps needed for each activity — though there are a few items that can be confusing until they are fully understood.

The Packaging Python Projects tutorial

The official Packaging Python Projects tutorial at https://packaging.python.
org/en/latest/tutorials/packaging-projects/ has improved significantly
since this book was started, and provides most of what a software engineer would
need to know to successfully package and publish a Python project to the public PyPI
(https://pypi.org/). This section will mostly cover variations from that tutorial
that relate to using a private PyPI-compatible package repository, examining local
project considerations that relate, and addressing any gaps that the tutorial did not
cover when this chapter was written.

The first thing that needs to be decided is which of the various build back end options will be used.
When this chapter was written, there were four listed in the packaging tutorial to select from:

- setuptools (https://pypi.org/project/setuptools/), which has been active and
  maintained since late 2013.

- hatchling (https://pypi.org/project/hatchling/), a newer, extensible entry in the
  field, available since early 2022.

- flit (https://pypi.org/project/flit/), touted as a simple tool for simple package
  publication purposes, available since early 2018.

- pdm (https://pypi.org/project/pdm/), a modern package and dependency manager
  supporting the latest PEP standards, available since early 2021.

Each of these tools relies on a standard pyproject.toml file to define project metadata. Using
the setuptools build back end, a pyproject.toml file with a minimal collection of useful or
meaningful data for the hms-artisan package would look like this:

```
[build-system]
requires = ["setuptools>=61.0"]
build-backend = "setuptools.build_meta"
[options]
package_dir =
    =src
packages = find_namespace:
[options.packages.find]
where = src
[project]
name = "hms-artisan"
```

```
version = "0.0.1"
description = "The Artisan package for Hand Made Stuff (HMS)"
readme = "README.md"
requires-python = ">=3.11"
```

> **Additional pyproject.toml options**
>
> There are several additional options available in a `pyproject.toml` file — see `https://packaging.python.org/en/latest/guides/writing-pyproject-toml/` for a complete description of them.
>
> Each project in the book repository, starting with the code for this chapter has a slightly more detailed `pyproject.toml` file.

The `[build-system]` section of the file defines a build back end to use, and any required packages that the build process will need. The `setuptools` build back end was selected partly for its maturity, and partly because it is typically already available in a `pipenv` PVE. All of the build back ends listed above are compatible with the Python Packaging Authority's `build` package (`https://pypi.org/project/build/`), which will also need to be installed. For the HMS projects, they were installed with:

```
pipenv install --categories build_publish build
```

The `build_publish` category passed as `--categories` was added to keep the package dependencies needed for building and publishing a package separate from the normal development-only package dependencies. That is not a functional requirement, but it does help keep package dependencies easier to track down in a project's `Pipfile`, particularly for projects that have a lot of development or other dependencies. That category also includes the `twine` package (`https://pypi.org/project/twine/`), which collects various utilities needed to actually publish a package to a PyPI repository.

The `[project]` section defines project-level data. Of those data points, only the `name` and `version` fields are required:

- `name` is the name of the project as it will appear in a PyPI repository package list. It must consist of ASCII letters, digits, underscores "_", hyphens "-" and periods ".". It must not start or end with an underscore, hyphen, or period.
- `version`, unsurprisingly, is the version of the package as of the time it gets published to the PyPI repository that it can be installed from.

Version is important!

Depending on where the package is published to, the PyPI repository may or may not allow an existing version to be replaced. It is a good idea to make *sure* that as new versions are ready to publish, the version in the `pyproject.toml` file is updated accordingly! This is something that might benefit from an additional automated test; it's that important.

The `dependencies` metadata (see the *Dependencies and requirements* section of the tutorial) is also important if the package being built has any dependencies. In the context of the HMS packages being discussed here, any package that gets installed to a project's working environment that is not a development-only dependency, and that is not part of the already-established `build_publish` category) where `build` and `twine` were installed) should be represented in the project's `dependencies`.

Once all of the above is accounted for, the actual build process can be executed from the project root directory with:

```
# NOTE: This assumes a pipenv-based project; alter
# accordingly for poetry or if neither is in use!
pipenv run python -m build –sdist --wheel
```

The `--sdist` and `--wheel` flags specify that the build should create a **source distribution** and a **wheel distribution**, a ZIP-format archive with a `.whl` file extension, respectively. Both formats can be installed with tools like `pip`, but it's considered good practice to upload both the source distribution, for users who may need a simple source package and a built distribution (a wheel). The build command assumes, by default, that the project source is in a `src` directory, but a different directory can be specified if needed. For example:

```
pipenv run python -m build my_custom_src –sdist –wheel
```

would look for the package source in a `my_custom_src` directory.

Once the build process is complete, the project directory will contain some new directories and files:

- A `build` directory that will contain a `lib` directory with a copy of the package source. It may also have build-process directories for your specific operating system, or other artifacts.

- A dist directory that contains the final package files. In this example, the build created:

    - hms_artisan-0.0.1.tar.gz — the source distribution package.

    - hms_artisan-0.0.1-py3-none-any.whl — the built distribution wheel package.

- A src/project_name.egg-info directory, where project_name is the same package name that appears in the dist-directory items, where the standard package metadata files are gathered by the build process before being incorporated into the final packages in dist.

Barring unusual circumstances, these new items should be added to the project's .gitignore file, so that the project repository isn't tracking various packaged versions of the code, or any artifacts from the build process — they would be overwritten with the next build anyway. An example_gitignore file, containing the additional items that should be added to a project's .gitignore, is provided for each project.

Python's standard build processes for packages, though they may be something of a moving target over time as they are being improved, are fairly straightforward. There are additional considerations, mostly centering around managing package dependencies, that will be examined in more detail later — the *Data persistence and BaseDataObject* chapter, which relies on at least one third-party package, is the first place that will provide that opportunity. Once the package build is complete, there will be a local copy of the packaged code, ready to be published (uploaded to a PyPI repository), or deployed in whatever fashion applies. The shape of that publication process will vary depending on where the package ends up, and whether that destination has a supported process for installation by standard Python tools.

Interim and final deployment considerations

The process of publishing a package to make it available in the public PyPI (https://pypi.org/) is actually quite simple, though it requires some setup first. The core package used to publish packages is twine (https://pypi.org/project/twine/), mentioned earlier in the build and publish packages installed earlier. Once the build process is complete, all of the distribution packages that it created will be available in the dist directory that was created. From there, assuming that the uploader has credentials for the target repository server, the actual upload can be as simple as:

```
pipenv run twine upload -u USERNAME -p PASSWORD dist/*
```

twine credentials can also be stored as environment variables, TWINE_USERNAME and TWINE_PASSWORD, allowing the upload command to be further simplified:

```
pipenv run twine upload dist/*
```

That's all well and good if the intent for a package is that it be made publicly available. For the HMS codebases, that's not desirable, though. Fortunately, depending on the still-pending cloud-provider decision, there are ready-made options available for private PyPI repository hosting:

- Amazon Web Services' *CodeArtifact* (`https://aws.amazon.com/codeartifact/`)
- Azure's *Azure Artifacts* (`https://azure.microsoft.com/en-us/products/devops/artifacts`)
- Google Cloud Platform's *Artifact Registry* (`https://cloud.google.com/artifact-registry`)

Based on what AWS' CodeArtifact provides, it is reasonably safe to assume that similar capabilities exist in the competitor services, in which case:

- They provide a private PyPI-compatible package index that can be used to install custom, private packages.
- If a requested package cannot be found in the private repository, the request will be forwarded to the public PyPI service, a process called *fall-through* in official Python documentation.
- They will accept standard `twine`-based package publication requests.

There are also several projects that provide PyPI hosting capabilities in some fashion in the Python Packaging User Guide at `https://packaging.python.org/en/latest/guides/hosting-your-own-index/`.

Some of these PyPI services may allow a package to be uploaded over an existing version of the same package. This can be problematic for consumers of the package, since the signature for the new package is unlikely to match the signature of the previous version, resulting in a security warning during an update of the package, and preventing that update from completing.

Even without access to a PyPI-compliant service, there are other options that may work. The built-in `pip` tool, `pipenv`, and `poetry` all support installing from a Git repo URL, allowing package installations directly from Git. Keeping package versions distinct, if needed, will require some discipline when new versions are merged into the main branch, but can be managed by tagging versions within the structure of the Git repository. The most basic implementation of a private package repository, as described in the Python Packaging User Guide, is little more than a website that provides access to the package files in the site structure expected by the various installation tools.

For development purposes, this decision can be deferred: all that a developer really needs, with respect to how private packages behave during development, is that those packages be accessible to the import processes that they need locally. If a team can agree that they will keep full copies of all the relevant code locally, then making them available for import is as simple as assuring that the PYTHONPATH environment variable includes all of the relevant directories. For example, if one of the HMS engineers has the following local structure:

- $HOME/hms_code

    - hms-artisan

        - src

    - hms-central-office

        - src

    - hms-core

        - src

...then their local PYTHONPATH can provide access to all of those package projects by simply including the relevant paths, like this (line breaks added for clarity):

```
PYTHONPATH="src:
~/hms_code/hms-artisan/src
~/hms_code/hms-central-office/src
~/hms_code/hms-core/src"
```

The HMS team decides to take this last approach, at least until other decisions are made by management that will determine what their other options are. It will require some discipline on their part as they work on the code, at least until another option becomes available, but it is not terribly onerous, since they are only concerned with three package projects going forward. Using a local copy of all packages in their code ecosystem also allows them to make changes across multiple packages, should the need arise: if some work in the hms-artisan package requires changes in hms-core, for example, the engineer can simply make those changes when needed, remembering to start pull requests for both packages when they are done.

While the decisions around how code will be published are important on a longer-term basis, they are not critical for development to take place. There are a lot of options available for managing access to private package code to choose from.

Summary

This chapter has covered the last of the systems and processes that affect how code is managed and handled. Options have been presented, and decisions made and explained in the context of the HMS projects, for managing Python Virtual Environments and package dependencies, for Source Control Management, for and expectations about unit testing the project code. The processes and considerations for building, packaging, and deploying the final code have been discussed, though decisions on these topics were not explicitly made, or were deferred, awaiting more information yet to come.

At this point, we can (finally) turn our attention to the actual code. We'll start in the next chapter by examining options for defining and implementing the actual data structures needed in the HMS system packages. That research will also keep the idea that the code is being written to provide a REST API in mind and discuss some best practices and documentation options as a preparatory step for defining how those data structures will be persisted to a back end data store.

11

Re-Examining Options for Business Objects

The idea of a business object — a representation of the individual data points for a given record that allows information about a person, place, or thing — requires some design decisions to be made about how those will be implemented. Each approach that is considered has its own advantages and drawbacks, and it is important to recognize, at least at a high level, what those are, and how they will be likely to impact the work and the resulting code. There are several options available to write code that can validate the structure and content of those business objects, some of which are available using nothing more than built-in Python capabilities. Other options, with common third-party packages, provide more or better capabilities, and those will also be examined, particularly with an eye towards providing API documentation using a common standard for such things.

In this chapter, we're going to cover the following main topics:

- Why use business objects?
- Modeling an artisan — exploring several approaches to implement business objects with a simple subset of the overall HMS code
- The decision-making process for the selection of a business object strategy

Technical requirements

The code for this chapter was written in Python 3.11, using `pipenv` (https://github.com/PacktPublishing/Hands-On-Software-Engineering-with-Python-Second-Edition/tree/main/CH11-code) for package and Python virtual environment management, as described in the previous chapter. Each option is individually represented in the `hms-core` directory in the chapter directory of the book's repository, and the chapter repository's `Pipfile` has all the required package dependencies across all of those options.

Why use business objects?

For the purposes of this book, a **business object** is a representation of some logical grouping of data that is relevant to a product or service. That data is generally atomic, in that it cannot be broken apart without losing the meaning that it has in the context of the overall data structure. Business objects may be **composed** of other objects — an object representing a person might have one or more distinct mailing-address data structures associated with it; for example, a mailing address and a billing address, either of which might not be set. They might also have collections of other objects. An `Order` object might well be expected to have one or more `Product` objects associated with it.

If business objects are defined so that they *validate* their data — not just that a given object property name exists, but that it is of an accepted type, or even of an appropriate value — they make working with application data faster and more consistent across the entire application. One example is an `email_address` field, defined so that it must be populated, must be a string value, and must be a well-formed email address. Another example is an optional date or date-time field that must be a date in the past, if it is populated at all.

To explore the options available for defining business objects, we will focus on two related object types in the HMS service: defining a type that represents an artisan, and another that defines an address, a physical location where mail could be sent.

Modeling an artisan

To provide a context for the options we will be exploring, consider the classes shown in *Figure 11.1*. They include a concrete `Address` class, representing a physical mailing address, and an abstract `BaseArtisan` class, which provides the interface requirements and common functionality for classes that will represent an artisan in the context of the system. The `BaseArtisan` class includes an `address` property, which is an instance of the `Address` class, allowing an `Artisan` object to incorporate a single address for an artisan that it represents.

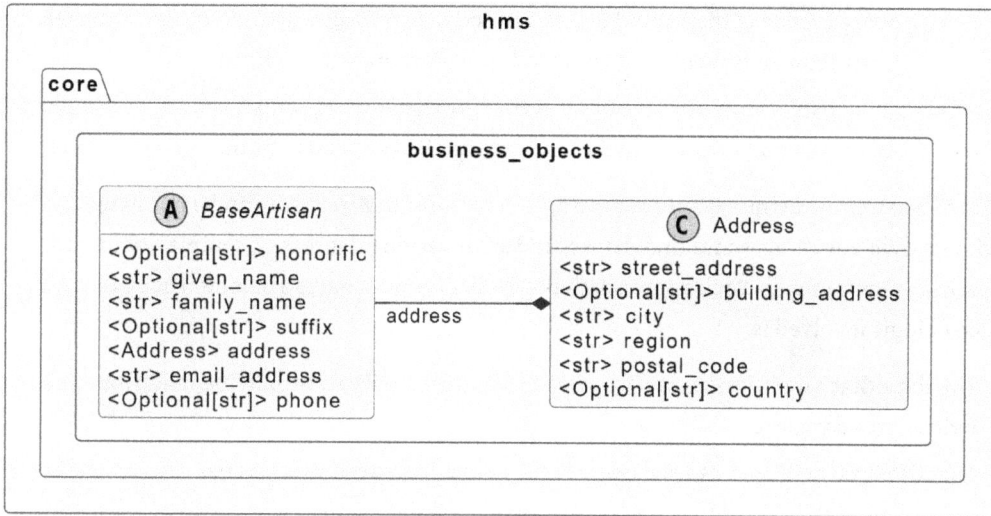

Figure 11.1: The business objects to be implemented using different approaches

The diagram in *Figure 11.1* also indicates some constraints for several of the object fields:

- BaseArtisan

    - honorific is an optional string value, used to store honorifics like Mr., Mrs., Ms.

    - given_name is *required*, and stores the given name of the artisan the object represents (the "first" name, in western societies).

    - family_name is also *required*, storing the family (or "last") name of an artisan

    - suffix is *optional*, storing strings like Sr., Jr, and so on.

    - email_address (required) and phone (*optional*) are self-explanatory.

- Address

    - street_address is the *required* street address for the address. It could also be used to store post-office box numbers.

    - building_address is *optional*, and intended to store information like apartment numbers, office suite numbers, and so on.

    - city, *required*, is the name of the city.

    - region is the state, for United States addresses, or the equivalent in other countries. It is currently *required*, though that may need to be examined in more detail later.

- `postal_code` is the United States ZIP code, or the equivalent in other countries. Like region, it is *required* at present, but may change in the future.

- `country` is the *optional* country name for the address, only needed for artisan addresses that are outside the country that HMS operates from.

There are at least three distinct ways that the data structures in *Figure 11.1* can be implemented, each with its own advantages and drawbacks, and with varying degrees of complexity or additional package requirements. Each approach that we will examine shares a common goal, though. The chain of logic involved is:

- The data that any instance of these objects contains will eventually be read from and written to a database

- That database will have at least some fields defined as specific data types

- Some fields will have additional constraints

It makes sense, then, to at least try to carry field types and other constraints into the objects that will use those records. That provides continuity from the data layer of the API, through the software that interacts with it, and out to the responses that will be returned by requests to the API. Essentially, the goal is to promote higher levels of data integrity at the software layer, reducing the potential of invalid data making it to the persistent storage that the backing database provides. That goal is going to be accomplished by validating the data that is used to generate the business object instances, raising errors when that validation fails, and providing at least some data quality assurance built into the software layer.

Another goal coming out of a business object definition process is more documentation-oriented: Providing a standard set of documentation for any other developers who are writing code to *consume* the API. At the time this book was written, the most popular standard was the **OpenAPI Specification** (**OAS**, `https://swagger.io/specification/`), which provides a standard structure for defining the behavior and data structures of a REST API as a **JavaScript Object Notation** (**JSON**) document. It is not uncommon for these documents to be defined in YAML (`https://en.wikipedia.org/wiki/YAML`) — YAML is sometimes easier to read and work with, can be used in Python code with the addition of a single package (PyYAML, `https://pypi.org/project/PyYAML/`), and supports comments in the document. The business objects, acting as they do as a bridge between the data layer of the system and the API itself, will eventually need to be represented in that documentation, in its standards `components.schemas` section.

A final goal, at least for now, is to provide a consistent output of the business objects' data structures that can be relayed back through the API to the consumer that requested that data. Since the API for HMS is intended to be a REST API, and it is expected to be consumed by a web browser, the idea of returning a JSON structure is very appealing. JSON is *very* easy to work with in front-end code (because it is widely supported across platforms, languages, and frameworks), while still providing meaningful structure in the data being returned.

Each of these implementations will show the strengths and weaknesses of their approach to these goals, while providing a functional implementation of the classes shown in *Figure 11.1*, and honoring the constraints shown in the diagram.

Dictionaries and a JSON schema

The code for this exploration can be found in the *Chapter 11* repository, in the json-schema/src/ hms/core/business_objects.py module (https://github.com/PacktPublishing/Hands-On-Software-Engineering-with-Python-Second-Edition/tree/main/CH11-code). This approach uses the third-party fastjsonschema module (https://pypi.org/project/fastjsonschema/), which would add about 370 kB of third-party package dependencies to a project that uses it. It is a mature package, with a 2.X.X major version dating back to late 2018.

Python provides a basic built-in data type that can be used to represent structured data: the dictionary (dict). A representation of an artisan object, with an address, can be represented quite easily, looking something like this:

```
example_artisan = {
    # Omitting the optional honorific, suffix,
    # and phone values
    "given_name": "John",
    "family_name": "Smith",
    "email_address": "john.smith@test.com",
    "address": {
        # Omitting the optional building_address
        # and country values
        "street_address": "1234 Main Street",
        "city": "Springfield",
        "region": "Some Place",
        "postal_code": "98765-4321"
    }
}
```

Python's dict types can be directly converted, with some limitations, to JSON representations of the same data structure. This makes them a natural choice for APIs that return JSON payloads. These limitations are not complex. A JSON representation of an object (a Python dict) must obey the following constraints:

- The keys of the dict must be one of a few types: str, int, float, or bool values. They can also be None.

- The keys should be *unique*, which means that only one True, False, or None value should be used. It is technically possible to create a dict with multiples of any of these key values, but only the last key/value pair encountered in the dict will be available.

- The values in the dict must be JSON compatible: they must be one of the types mentioned above, or a list (an array in JSON terminology) or a dict (an object in JSON).

Dictionaries, by default, do not *care* what types of values are in their members. That is, there is nothing preventing the values in the example artisan dictionary shown from being assigned any non-string values: booleans, other dictionaries, random objects, or whatever else. Similarly, there is nothing preventing a value of the right type from being set to an invalid value: setting the value of the email_address key to not-an-email-address would be allowed. This is the fundamental issue that any validation effort would have to address.

This approach handles that issue by defining a **JSON schema** (https://json-schema.org/) — a data structure expressed in JSON that describes the structure, types, content, and constraints of a data structure to be validated — and using that schema to compile a validator object. The resulting validator object can be called like a function, passing the data structure to be checked. If any validation errors are encountered, the validator will raise an exception (a JsonSchemaValueException, defined by the fastjsonschema package) that can be caught and handled in a try...except code block, or simply allowed to terminate the running process. That schema definition can be stored in its own file, read in, and converted to the dict structure that fastjosnschema.compile needs using Python's built-in json module. It could also be expressed as a native Python dict in a module, and imported wherever needed, or a module could even define the schema, compile it to a validator, and *that* could be imported. An example of the schema for this discussion is defined as ARTISAN_SCHEMA in the business_units.py module, and compiled into a validator, artisan_validator, for ease of reference to all the moving parts in that module.

Initially, the JSON schema for the `BaseArtisan` data structure can be defined with little more than simple string-type specifications. Setting aside the `address` field for the time being, every field is a string type and can be defined with a structure like this:

```
{
    "type": "object",
    "properties": {
        "field_name": {
            "type": "string",
        },
        ... more properties/fields as needed
}
```

The JSON schema specification allows fields to be defined as *required* — By default, all fields are *optional*. Making the `given_name`, `family_name`, and `email_addresses` required, while leaving the `honorific`, `suffix`, and phone fields optional, is as simple as defining them, then adding the names of the required fields to a list of `required` fields, like this:

```
{
    "type": "object",
    "properties": {
        "honorific": {
            "type": "string",
        },
        "given_name": {
            "type": "string",
        },
        "family_name": {
            "type": "string",
        },
        "suffix": {
            "type": "string",
        },
        "email_address": {
            "type": "string",
        },
        "phone": {
            "type": "string",
        },
```

```
        },
        "required": [
            "given_name",
            "family_name",
            "email_address"
        ]
    }
```

JSON schemas can also apply various constraints and requirements to the contents of the fields. Applying the following field constraints:

- honorific and suffix, if they exist at all (they are optional fields), must be at least two characters in length, and no more than seven.

- given_name and family_name must be at least two characters.

- email_address must be a well-formed email address.

- phone must be a well-formed phone number.

yields this schema structure.

```
    {
        "type": "object",
        "properties": {
            "honorific": {
                "type": "string",
                "minLength": 2,
                "maxLength": 7
            },
            "given_name": {
                "type": "string",
                "minLength": 2
            },
            "family_name": {
                // Same as given_name
            },
            "suffix": {
                // Same as honorific
            },
            "email_address": {
                "type": "string",
```

```
            "pattern": "^[a-zA-Z0-9._%+-]+@[a-zA-Z0-9.-]
                       +\\.[a-zA-Z]{2,}$"
            // pattern value is on two lines here, see
            // the code in the repo
        },
        "phone": {
            "type": "string",
            "pattern": "^(\\+\\d{1,2}\\s)?\\(?\\d{3}\\)
                       ?[\\s.-]\\d{3}[\\s.-]\\d{4}$"
            // pattern value is on two lines here, see
            // the code in the repo
        },
    "required": [
        "given_name",
        "family_name",
        "email_address"
    ]
}
```

It is worth noting that the email_address and phone fields use a pattern to define a **regular expression** (abbreviated hereafter as a **regex**, https://en.wikipedia.org/wiki/Regular_expression) that will be applied to their values. If a value supplied to either of those fields does not generate a match against that regex, that value is not valid.

Handling the address field, which is another required value, but is a complex structure of its own, adds the following to the schema:

```
{
    "type": "object",
    "properties": {
        // Fields/details omitted here for space reasons
        "honorific": { ... },
        ...
        "phone": { ... },
        "address": {
            "type": "object",
            "properties": {
                "street_address": {
                    "type": "string"
```

```
                    },
                    "building_address": {
                        "type": "string"
                    },
                    "city": {
                        "type": "string"
                    },
                    "region": {
                        "type": "string"
                    },
                    "postal_code": {
                        "type": "string"
                    },
                    "country": {
                        "type": "string"
                    }
                },
                "required": [
                    "street_address",
                    "city",
                    "region",
                    "postal_code"
                ]
            }
        },
        "required": [
            "given_name",
            "family_name",
            "email_address",
            "address"
        ]
    }
}
```

By default, an object defined with a JSON schema accepts values for fields that have no definition in the schema but does not validate them. For example, if a field named `additional_field` were added to the `example_artisan` structure, with any value at all, validation would still pass, and the `additional_field` would still be represented in the underlying Python `dict`.

If that behavior is not desired or acceptable, it can be overridden like this:

```
{
    "type": "object",
    "properties": {
        ...
        "address": {
            "properties": {
                ...
            },
            "additionalProperties": false,
            "required": [
                ...
            ]
        }
    },
    "additionalProperties": false,
    "required": [
        ...
    ]
}
```

At this point, barring a formal schema version specification, the schema is complete. It can be read and passed to fastjsonschema.compile, and the resulting validator object can then validate any Python dict (representing a JSON object) passed to it:

```python
import json
import fastjsonschema
artisan_validator = fastjsonschema.compile(ARTISAN_SCHEMA)
try:
    artisan_validator(example_artisan)
    print('Valid Artisan data-structure:')
    print(json.dumps(example_artisan, indent=4))
except Exception as error:
    raise
```

The example_artisan shown earlier passes validation:

```
Valid Artisan data-structure:
{
    "given_name": "John",
    "family_name": "Smith",
    "email_address": "john.smith@test.com",
    "address": {
        "street_address": "1234 Main Street",
        "city": "Springfield",
        "region": "Some Place",
        "postal_code": "98765-4321"
    }
}
```

If the same example_artisan has a field value changed, say setting given_name to None with:

```
example_artisan['given_name'] = None
```

then the validation fails:

```
fastjsonschema.exceptions.JsonSchemaValueException:
    data.given_name must be string
```

So, too, does an attempt to pass any fields that are not part of the defined structure in the schema:

```
example_artisan['additional_field'] = True
```

Output:

```
fastjsonschema.exceptions.JsonSchemaValueException:
    data must not contain {'additional_field'} properties
```

Passing an invalid email address also causes validation to fail:

```
example_artisan['email_address'] = 'not an email address'
```

Output:

```
fastjsonschema.exceptions.JsonSchemaValueException:
    data.email_address must match pattern
    ^[a-zA-Z0-9._%+-]+@[a-zA-Z0-9.-]+\.[a-zA-Z]{2,}$
```

Finally, passing an empty dict/object also fails validation:

```
example_artisan = {}
```

Output

```
fastjsonschema.exceptions.JsonSchemaValueException:
    data must contain ['address', 'email_address',
    'family_name', 'given_name'] properties
```

This approach, using a JSON schema to validate values stored as a simple Python dict, is powerful, fast, and relatively simple, provided that the schema definition is well understood and managed with care and discipline. It does have some drawbacks that may not be obvious at first though. The one that is most likely to raise issues is that the validation process only happens when the validator is explicitly called. That means that it is quite possible for a dict to come into a block of code, validate successfully, then have a value changed to something that is not valid. In order to prevent that, the validation process would need to be called any time that a change is made to the dict. An example of one approach to work around that issue is presented in the chapter repository, in the json-schema/src/hms/core/dict-subclass-with-schema.py module. The approach taken there is fairly straightforward:

- A new class is defined (SchemaBoundDict) that inherits from Python's built-in dict type.
- An override of the normal __init__ is defined that checks for a schema definition attached to the class, and that creates the validator object, before calling the __init__ of the dict that it derives from.
- A __setitem__ method is defined, overriding the one that exists in the built-in dict, that calls the original method, then validates the current state of the object.

The same series of simple tests was included in that example, and they all behaved as expected. As an additional benefit, because the class is derived from the built-in dict, Python's built-in json module has no trouble rendering it to JSON.

Another consideration is that schema definitions on an object-by-object basis will tend to lead to duplication of schema structure across a codebase. The BaseArtisan structure that we've delved into so far could just as easily apply to other classes that represent different types of people: A Customer, for example, might well have the exact same structure that we've seen up to this point, while an Artisan might also have an associated collection of Product objects.

It would make sense to define some common, generic structure that collects all of the fields in a Person, then derive Artisan and Customer from that — that is how an object-oriented design might approach it, at any rate. The problem that surfaces in this scenario is that the Address is likely to be identical for any of those Person-derived types. The JSON schema specification supports this sort of inheritance (see the description of $defs and $ref at https://json-schema. org/understanding-json-schema/structuring), but it more or less requires that either all of a schema's object definitions be in the same location, or that the individual schema definitions be available in separate sources, one per object type, and that the schemas cross-reference those extensively. It is not an insurmountable challenge, but it will lead to more complexity that may not be desirable.

A final consideration is the assembly of the final API documentation in the expected OAS version. The JSON schemas we've been working with are not always fully compatible with the OAS schema that is expected for the final API documentation. The gaps between the two will depend on whether the current version of the fastjsonschema package supports the current version of the OAS. Even when the two are in sync, the question of how to assemble the final OAS documentation from the various object schemas, possibly across several different locations, will have to be examined and implemented, possibly as a manual effort. Since that will be a recurring concern, it will be discussed later in the chapter, once all of the other options have been examined.

A Python class structure

The code for this exploration can be found in the *Chapter 11* repository, in the class-based/src/ hms/core/business_objects.py module (https://github.com/PacktPublishing/Hands-On-Software-Engineering-with-Python-Second-Edition/tree/main/CH11-code). This approach relies on the typeguard package mentioned earlier to provide runtime type-validation of arguments being passed to functions and methods, as well as validation of their return values. Including typeguard adds roughly 75k worth of third-party package dependencies.

Classes in an object-oriented language have the ability to define a data structure, and Python is no exception to that. However, since Python is dynamically typed, using simple attributes will not provide any leeway for the sort of validation that is being sought. That is, while a typical (if simple) Python implementation of the __init__ for a BaseArtisan class that leverages the typechecked decorator from the typeguard package to make *some* attempt at type validation might look like this:

```
@typechecked
class BaseArtisan(metaclass=abc.ABCMeta):
    def __init__(
```

```
    self, given_name: str, family_name: str,
    # This assumes that there is a defined Address
    # type available
    address: dict | Address,
    email_address: Optional[str] = None,
    honorific: Optional[str] = None,
    suffix: Optional[str] = None,
):
    """
    Object initialization
    """
    self.honorific = honorific
    self.given_name = given_name
    self.family_name = family_name
    self.suffix = suffix
    self.address = address
    self.email_address = email_address
```

... there is nothing in this (yet) that performs anything more than basic type-checking of the values passed to the class to initialize an object. In order to actually validate any of those values, we need to turn to Python's property decorator (https://docs.python.org/3.11/library/functions.html#property). The property decorator allows a class to define methods that are executed automatically by the Python interpreter when an object member with a given property name is called. Assuming a class (SomeClass) with a single property (some_property) that allows the value to be set, retrieved, or deleted, a bare-bones property-based implementation would look something like this:

```
class SomeClass:
    def __init__(self, some_property: str):
        self.some_property = some_property
    @property
    def some_property(self) -> str:
        # Gets the value of the property
        return self._some_property
    @some_property.setter
    def some_property(self, value: str) -> None:
        # Sets the value of the property
        self._some_property = value
```

```
@some_property.deleter
def some_property(self) -> None:
    # Deletes the value of the property, if it exists
    if hasattr(self, '_some_property'):
        del self._some_property
```

When an instance of SomeClass is created, the some_property parameter is required, and the __init__ method sets the self.some_property to the value of the parameter. The Python interpreter recognizes that some_property is a property object, and calls the *setter* method defined — the second method named some_property. That sets an internal storage attribute (self._some_property, note the leading underscore) to the value. Later, if instance.some_property is requested, the Python interpreter again recognizes that some_property is a property object, and calls the *getter* method defined — the first method, decorated with @property — and returns the value of the internal storage attribute. Similarly, if the instance is asked to delete its some_property value (del instance.some_property), the *deleter* method is called.

Defining properties is a very powerful capability of the language. Because each property, under the hood, is a collection of whatever methods are defined in the class, those methods can perform whatever processes are desired before completing their execution. That can include checking the type of the incoming value (though typechecked already does that in the BaseArtisan example), checking the value itself, or whatever else is needed.

An important trade-off to note is the amount of additional code that is involved. Before adding any validation logic, and assuming that all of the properties needed for BaseArtisan are allowed to be deleted, there would be 140-plus lines of code just to provide a minimally functional set of properties, and a similarly bare-bones Address function would add another 140-plus lines of property code. The basic @property-decorated getter-methods are almost identical, differing only in the method names and the names of the internal storage attributes, and are unlikely to change. The net result is that there is a *lot* of boilerplate code at this stage, roughly a third of which will *always be* boilerplate code.

To illustrate the advantages of this approach, we will focus on four properties in the BaseArtisan class: given_name (a required string property), honorific (an optional string property), email_address (required, with special validation), and address (required, with special input handling). For the time being, the assumption is that none of these properties need to implement any sort of deletion logic: Once they are set, they cannot be removed. We'll also assume that the getter methods for each can remain as simple as possible, just returning the appropriate storage-attribute value, and letting the typechecked decorator on the class handle any invalid return values.

The given_name property is an example of one of the simplest patterns of property behavior. It is required during object initialization, it must be a string value, and that value must be at least two characters long. It also seems logical to assume that given_name cannot be all white space characters and that any leading and trailing white space should be removed, if only to make sure that sorting by them would yield the expected results later on. With all of that in mind, the initial implementation of given_name, with validation and the other rules noted, looks like this:

```python
@typechecked
class BaseArtisan(metaclass=abc.ABCMeta):
    ...
    @property
    def given_name(self) -> str:
        """
        Gets or sets the given_name of the
        Artisan that the instance represents
        """
        return self._given_name
    @given_name.setter
    def given_name(self, value: str) -> None:
        """
        Setter method for the given_name property
        """
        # Pre-process the value to remove leading
        # and trailing white space
        value = value.strip()
        # Validate the length of the value string
        if len(value) < 2:
            raise ValueError(
                f'{self.__class__.__name__}.given_name '
                'must be at least two characters long'
            )
        # If this point is reached, the value is valid,
        # so store it
        self._given_name = value
```

The only real differences introduced are the use of the built-in str.strip() method, which removes whitespace from the start and end of a string value, used to preprocess the incoming value, and the five lines of code that check that value against the minimum length accepted for it. Though this is a personal preference on the author's part, there is a reasonably detailed error message attached to the ValueError that is raised if the validation checks fail. The thought behind that is that when validation fails, it is better to provide some concrete, actionable information about *why* the failure occurred than to just raise a generic error.

The honorific property is, superficially, going to behave much like the given_name property, though it has a bit more length-validation details to implement. An important decision needs to be made here too, though. Specifically, how should optional properties be handled, bearing in mind that somewhere down the line we'll need to convert instances of this object into JSON, or at least into JSON-ready dict values that, themselves, can be converted into JSON. The point of concern is whether that JSON representation, given an object instance that never had an honorific specified, should include the field (probably as a null value), or omit the field entirely. Since an API payload that contains an artisan object will presumably be read by JavaScript code in a client browser, and since JavaScript will allow a reference to a non-existent field name without throwing any errors, allowing the JSON payload to omit fields that have no value would save a trivial bit of bandwidth for every response processed.

On the other hand, if other *Python* code in the back-end system needs to read a non-existent field, it is a bit more efficient to explicitly include fields even when they have a null value: Any field that exists in the data contract is *guaranteed* to be present in the JSON payload, so no special checking for those fields' existence needs to happen beforehand. The trade-off, making sure that any property will return something, even if it is a None value that becomes a null in JSON, doesn't need to be anything more complicated than using Python's built-in getattr function, which will return the value of an attribute if it exists, or some known default value (None) otherwise. That implementation, safer for other Python code, would look something like this:

```python
@property
def honorific(self) -> Optional[str]:
    """
    Gets or sets the honorific of the Artisan that
    the instance represents
    """
    return getattr(self, '_honorific', None)

@honorific.setter
```

```python
def honorific(
    self, value: Optional[str] = None
) -> None:
    """
    Setter method for the honorific property
    """
    # If the value is None, set it and be done
    # with it
    if value is None:
        self._honorific = None
        return
    # Otherwise, pre-process the value to remove
    # leading and trailing white space
    value = value.strip()
    # If what's left is an empty string, we
    # can also set it to None, then exit
    if not len(value):
        self._honorific = None
        return
    # Otherwise, validate the length of the value
    if len(value) < 2 or len(value) > 7:
        raise ValueError(
            f'{self.__class__.__name__}.honorific '
            'must be two to seven characters long'
        )
    # If this point is reached, the value is valid,
    # so store it
    self._honorific = value
```

Note that the docstring provided on the initial getter method (the plain @property decorator) will be applied to the property created at that point, even though the setter method (the @honorific. setter decorator) has not been attached yet.

The same basic structure can be applied to any validation processes or mechanisms needed, provided that they can run as part of a property's setter method. It is even possible, for setter methods that share common validation requirements, to write helper functions or other callables, keeping the common validation logic in a single location in the code, and calling it from each setter method that shares the validation ruleset. The suffix property in this example could leverage that capability.

More complex validation processes can check for patterns in string values, using the same regex shown in the JSON schema-based approach shown earlier. Using the email_address property as an example, after importing the built-in re (regular expressions) module, and creating a common, global EMAIL_PATTERN regex object to use as a validation process, we land on:

```
import re

...

EMAIL_PATTERN = re.compile(
    r'^[a-zA-Z0-9._%+-]+@[a-zA-Z0-9.-]+\.[a-zA-Z]{2,}$'
)
@typechecked
class BaseArtisan(metaclass=abc.ABCMeta):
    ...
    @email_address.setter
    def email_address(self, value: str) -> None:
        """
        Setter method for the email_address property
        """
        # Validate of the incoming value
        if not EMAIL_PATTERN.match(value):
            raise ValueError(
                f'{self.__class__.__name__}.email was '
                f'passed "{value}", which did not match '
                f'the pattern "{EMAIL_PATTERN.pattern}".'
            )
        # If the value passes (there is a match), store it
        self._email_address = value
```

The advantage this approach provides, in exchange for the sheer volume of boilerplate code involved sometimes, is putting the control of validation in the code itself. The email_address property setter method code is a typical example of that, allowing flexible validation with the regular expression shown, and the ability to provide more human-readable error messaging when validation fails. It also allows the classes to store Python data types in those properties: For example, a modified_date property could use an actual datetime object, allowing that property's value to be modified or worked with using its built-in capabilities, or other built-in Python functionality. Generating an actual Address object during the execution of the address setter method is another variation of the same theme.

That implementation might look like this:

```
@address.setter
def address(self, value: dict | Address) -> None:
    """
    Setter method for the address property
    """

    if isinstance(value, dict):
        value = Address(**value)
    self._address = value
```

There is a noteworthy drawback to this class-based approach, though: It is not JSON serializable without additional code and some standards that would have to be decided upon and implemented. The same inline test code that was used to test the dictionary-based approach:

```
try:
    instance = BaseArtisan(**example_artisan)
    print('Valid Artisan data-structure:')
    print(json.dumps(instance, indent=4))
except Exception as error:
    print(f'{error.__class__.__name__}: {error}')
```

...fails with this error:

```
Valid Artisan data-structure:
TypeError: Object of type BaseArtisan is not JSON
    serializable
```

Python's built-in json module provides two mechanisms for customizing the capabilities of its dump and dumps functions. The first is using custom JSONEncoder objects (https://docs.python.org/3.11/library/json.html#json.JSONEncoder). These can be defined to handle any custom types needed before handing the serialization process back to the default provided and passed as the cls argument to json's dump and dumps functions. If this approach is used, it is a good idea to have a single encoder class that knows how to handle all of the object types in the codebase. That may be problematic in cases where there are multiple, distinct packages that provide objects in need of serialization: The custom JSONEncoder class will need to keep track of all of those classes, raising a strong possibility of circular import problems (modules needing to import from each other) in the future. The second built-in approach is to provide a custom function, passed in the default argument of the dump and dumps functions, that knows how to deal with the various custom types.

This raises the same concerns as the custom `JSONEncoder` type. In both of these cases, any serialization of a business object would need to pass whichever of those customizations were implemented in every call to either of those `json`-module functions.

Circular imports

A "circular import problem" in programming, particularly in Python, occurs when two modules attempt to import each other, creating a loop where neither module can fully initialize because they are both waiting for the other to be loaded first, resulting in an error as the interpreter gets stuck in this circular dependency loop.

An alternative approach is to require that all objects that need JSON serialization capabilities provide some common process to provide that serialization directly, or at a minimum, generate a JSON-safe `dict` of their data that can be passed to the dump and dumps functions. One such implementation would involve creating an Abstract Base class that requires that capability in other classes derived from it, then implementing that required method in each of those derived classes:

```python
class IsJSONSerializable(metaclass=abc.ABCMeta):
    """
    Requires derived classes to implement a common
    json_safe_dict method to facilitate
    """

    @abc.abstractmethod
    def json_safe_dict(self) -> dict:
        """
        Generates and returns a JSON-safe dict of the
        object's state-data.
        """
        raise NotImplementedError(
            f'{self.__class__.__name__}.json_dump has '
            'not been implemented, as required by '
            'IsJSONSerializable.'
        )
    ...
@typechecked
class BaseArtisan(
    IsJSONSerializable, metaclass=abc.ABCMeta
```

```
    ):
        ...

        def json_safe_dict(self) -> dict:
            return {
                'address': self.address.json_safe_dict(),
                'email_address': self.email_address,
                'family_name': self.family_name,
                'given_name': self.given_name,
                'honorific': self.honorific,
                'suffix': self.suffix,
            }
@typechecked
class Address(IsJSONSerializable):
    """

    Represents a physical address, where mail could be sent.
    """

        ...
        def json_safe_dict(self) -> dict:
            return {
                'building_address': self.building_address,
                'city': self.city,
                'country': self.country,
                'postal_code': self.postal_code,
                'region': self.region,
                'street_address': self.street_address,
            }
```

The inline testing used earlier has to be modified to show that the new json_safe_dict method works as expected:

```
try:
    instance = BaseArtisan(**example_artisan)
    print('Valid Artisan data-structure:')
    print(json.dumps(instance.json_safe_dict(), indent=4))
except Exception as error:
    print(f'{error.__class__.__name__}: {error}')
```

...but it *does* work as expected:

```
Valid Artisan data-structure:
{
    "address": {
        "building_address": null,
        "city": "Springfield",
        "country": null,
        "postal_code": "98765-4321",
        "region": "Some Place",
        "street_address": "1234 Main Street"
    },
    "email_address": "john.smith@test.com",
    "family_name": "Smith",
    "given_name": "John",
    "honorific": null,
    "suffix": null
}
```

This is a fairly common solution to the challenge of making objects JSON serializable. The primary advantage of this sort of solution is that it puts the responsibility for handling the serialization process solidly in the realm of the class definitions for those objects. So long as the interface for getting the JSON-ready dictionary is consistent across all such objects, it is a fairly easily remembered variant too. If, for some reason, the addition of a JSON-related helper method is not viable, there is another alternative that might work better: Defining the business object classes as sub-classes of Python's built-in `dict` type.

Using a dict as a basis for a class

The code for this exploration can be found in the *Chapter 11* repository, in the `dict-class-based/src/hms/core/business_objects.py` module (`https://github.com/PacktPublishing/Hands-On-Software-Engineering-with-Python-Second-Edition/tree/main/CH11-code`). Like the Python class approach, it relies on the typeguard package to provide type-checking and leverages the same @property decorator to define formal properties for the classes. Where it differs is in how the class is defined (what its parent classes are), where the property values are stored, and how they are set and retrieved.

Python's built-in classes and types can be used as parents of classes in user code. The built-in types have their own methods that can be overridden in derived classes to modify the behavior of those methods, and thus the behavior of a custom class derived from those built-in types.

For the purposes of defining business object classes, defining those so that they inherit from Python's built-in dict type provides several benefits:

- Any dict object may be passed to the json module's dump and dumps functions.

- So long as the keys and values of that dict are JSON compatible, the dict will be converted to JSON successfully.

- The same @property decoration shown earlier can still be used to define formal properties, and to perform validation as needed for the values passed to them.

- The methods that are provided by a dict to access, set, and delete values within the dict by other Python code can be overridden to prevent their use outside the context of a @ property execution.

The first thing that has to be done is to implement code that prevents general-purpose dictionary value manipulations. The methods that provide those capabilities to other Python code are __getitem__ (gets an item identified by its key from the dict), __setitem__ (sets an item value in the dict identified by a key), and __delitem__ (deletes an item identified by its key from the dict). These methods are automatically called by the Python interpreter when it encounters a relevant code structure — for example, something = a_dict['key'] will call the __getitem__ method of the a_dict dictionary, passing the key, and that method will look up the key, and return the related value. Similarly, a_dict['key'] = 'some_value' will call the __setitem__ method, passing the key and some_value, and that method will set the key/value pair in a_dict accordingly. Creating a class that overrides those methods, that can be used later as a parent class for the business objects, will take care of preventing *unwanted* dict-style access to the object's data:

```python
class PropertyOnlyDict(dict):
    """
    Overrides the __getitem__, __setitem__ and __delitem__
    methods of the built-in dict type, to prevent them
    from being used.
    """
    def __delitem__(self, *args, **kwargs):
        # Don't allow del property_only_dict['name']
        raise TypeError(
            f"'{self.__class__.__name__}' object "
            'does not support item deletion'
        )
    def __getitem__(self, *args, **kwargs):
```

```
        # Don't allow property_only_dict['name'] access
        raise TypeError(
            f"'{self.__class__.__name__}' object "
            'is not subscriptable'
        )
    def __setitem__(self, *args, **kwargs):
        # Don't allow property_only_dict['name'] = 'value'
        raise TypeError(
            f"'{self.__class__.__name__}' object "
            'does not support item assignment'
        )
```

At the level of the properties, the implementations are, mostly, identical to the implementation for a regular class. The main differences, as noted earlier, are in where and how the values received by the property setter methods are stored. So long as the class inherits from the PropertyOnlyDict class shown above, it will not allow getting, setting, or deleting values using standard dict syntax for those operations. However, because PropertyOnlyDict itself inherits from dict, the setter methods defined for properties in child classes can call the methods explicitly using the dict type itself to provide their functionality. The same four properties in the previous BaseArtisan class examples, given_name, honorific, email_address, and address, are shown here to illustrate how this would work:

```
@typechecked
class BaseArtisan(PrivateDict, metaclass=abc.ABCMeta):
    ...
    @property
    def given_name(self) -> str:
        # Docstring and comments removed for space reasons
        return dict.__getitem__(self, 'given_name')
    @given_name.setter
    def given_name(self, value: str) -> None:
        # Docstring and comments removed for space reasons
        # Validation is identical, and removed for
        # space reasons.
        return dict.__setitem__(self, 'given_name', value)
    @property
    def honorific(self) -> Optional[str]:
        # Docstring and comments removed for space reasons
```

```python
        return dict.__getitem__(self, 'honorific')
    @honorific.setter
    def honorific(
        self, value: Optional[str] = None
    ) -> None:
        # Docstring and comments removed for space reasons
        # Validation is identical, and removed for
        # space reasons.
        return dict.__setitem__(self, 'honorific', value)
    @property
    def email_address(self) -> str:
        # Docstring and comments removed for space reasons
        # Validation is identical, and removed for
        # space reasons.
        return dict.__getitem__(self, 'email_address')
    @email_address.setter
    def email_address(self, value: str) -> None:
        # Docstring and comments removed for space reasons
        # Validation is identical, and removed for
        # space reasons.
        return dict.__setitem__(
            self, 'email_address', value
        )
    @property
    def address(self) -> Address:
        # Docstring and comments removed for space reasons
        return dict.__getitem__(self, 'address')
    @address.setter
    def address(self, value: dict | Address) -> None:
        # Docstring and comments removed for space reasons
        # Validation is identical, and removed for
        # space reasons.
        return dict.__setitem__(self, 'address', value)
```

Stepping through the process: when an instance's given_name is *set*, the *setter method* is called with the value passed to it, it performs the validation, then calls dict.__setitem__ to set the given_name key of the instance (self) to that value.

Both of these class-based implementations for business objects have one potential concern: If an OAS schema document is needed or desired for a deployed API, that would require that it be created manually. The dictionary-and-schema approach that this section started with has the same concern, to be fair, but at least has a schema defined as part of the implementation. Even if those JSON schemas require some manual tweaking to fit into an OAS structure, those changes are likely to be minimal — they may even be scriptable. There is one final option to examine that addresses that goal: creating model classes with another third-party library: Pydantic.

Using Pydantic BaseModel

The code for this exploration can be found in the *Chapter 11* repository, in the pydantic-based/ src/hms/core/ modules (https://packt.link/UMeUe). This approach relies on a third-party package named pydantic (https://pypi.org/project/pydantic/), which provides classes that can be used to define data objects or *models* in pydantic's terminology. These models can have *fields*, which are roughly equivalent to the methods decorated with @property shown in the Python class structure examples earlier in the chapter. pydantic is a fairly large package, adding roughly 770k to a project's package dependencies, but it provides a *lot* of functionality in exchange, and there are a lot of support and extension packages that can be used to enhance the baseline functionality that pydantic provides.

A *very* minimalistic approach for implementing the Address and BaseArtisan classes that were shown in the previous two sections is very simple. All that needs to be done is to import the BaseModel class that pydantic provides, then define as many classes as are needed for data or business objects, each with named fields annotated with their data types. At this bare-bones level, only eighteen lines of code are required to define those classes with basic type checking of their fields:

```python
import abc
from typing import Optional
from pydantic import BaseModel
class Address(BaseModel):
    street_address: str
    building_address: Optional[str] = None
    city: str
    region: str
    postal_code: str
    country: Optional[str] = None
class BaseArtisan(BaseModel, metaclass=abc.ABCMeta):
    honorific: Optional[str] = None
```

```
        given_name: str
        family_name: str
        suffix: Optional[str] = None
        address: Address
        email_address: str
```

The full code of this example, including some inline testing, can be found in the minimal_example.
py module (https://github.com/PacktPublishing/Hands-On-Software-Engineering-with-
Python-Second-Edition/tree/main/CH11-code). Each field uses standard Python annotation
structures (https://docs.python.org/3.11/howto/annotations.html) to indicate the type of
value that the field expects. Fields can be annotated as *optional* of one or more types — Address.
building_address, Address.country, BaseArtisan.honorific, and BaseArtisan.suffix show
an optional string value variant, using the built-in Optional[type] annotation provided by Python's built-in typing module. That is sufficient for the class to enforce value-typing rules during
the creation of an instance. For example, this will create a BaseArtisan instance without raising
any errors:

```
inst = BaseArtisan(
    given_name='John',
    family_name='Smith',
    email_address='john.smith@test.com',
    address=Address(
        street_address='1234 Main Street',
        city='Springfield',
        region='Some Place',
        postal_code='98765-4321',
    )
)
```

...while this:

```
inst = BaseArtisan(family_name=False, email_address=12345)
```

...will raise validation errors, with *very* detailed error information, for all of the missing required
field/property values, or the values whose types are not valid (with some irrelevant error data
omitted for space reasons):

```
pydantic_core._pydantic_core.ValidationError:
    4 validation errors for BaseArtisan
given_name
  Field required
```

```
    [type=missing, input_value={'family_name': False,
     'email_address': 12345}, input_type=dict]
family_name
  Input should be a valid string
    [type=string_type, input_value=False, input_type=bool]
address
  Field required
    [type=missing, input_value={'family_name': False,
     'email_address': 12345}, input_type=dict]
email_address
  Input should be a valid string
    [type=string_type, input_value=12345, input_type=int]
```

Model classes can also be passed a dictionary of values, including whatever mixture of model classes, or the values needed to create those model classes, is needed. That is, both of the examples shown below will also create a BaseArtisan instance without error:

```python
artisan_params = {
    "given_name": "John",
    "family_name": "Smith",
    "email_address": "john.smith@test.com",
    "address": {
        "street_address": "1234 Main Street",
        "city": "Springfield",
        "region": "Some Place",
        "postal_code": "98765-4321",
    }
}
inst = BaseArtisan(**artisan_params)
artisan_params = {
    "given_name": "John",
    "family_name": "Smith",
    "email_address": "john.smith@test.com",
    "address": Address(
        street_address='1234 Main Street',
        city='Springfield',
        region='Some Place',
        postal_code='98765-4321',
```

```
    )
  }
inst = BaseArtisan(**artisan_params)
```

Model classes created with `pydantic.BaseModel` keep track of enough information about their fields to be able to generate a JSON schema with a class method called `model_json_schema`, inherited from the `BaseModel` class, that can be used elsewhere to validate or document those models' interface expectations. Focusing on the same four `BaseArtisan` properties examined in the previous explorations, `given_name`, `honorific`, `email_address`, and `address`, the schema generated from the `pydantic`-based class shows some significant differences from their equivalents in the manually created schema from the *Dictionaries and a JSON schema* exploration. Omitting the generated `title` of each property, which is more a documentation concession than any sort of functional element, and details of some properties that exist in one schema but not the other, the comparison for these four properties is shown in *Table 11.1*. A complete schema rendering of both models is provided in the `minimal_example.schema.json` file in the repository.

`pydantic`-generated Schema	Manual Schema

"given_name": {
 	
  "type": "string"
 	
},
	"given_name": {
	
	  "type": "string",
	
	  "minLength": 2
	
	}

"honorific": {
 	
  "anyOf": [
 	
    {"type": "string"},
 	
    {"type": "null"}
 	
  ],
 	
  "default": null,
 	
},
	"honorific": {
	
	  "type": "string",
	
	  "minLength": 2,
	
	  "maxLength": 7
	
	}

"email_address": {
 	
  "type": "string"
 	
}
	"email_address": {
	
	  "type": "string",
	
	  "pattern": "^ ... $"
	
	}

``json
"address": {
 	
  "$ref": "#/$defs/Address"
 	
}
``
	``json
	"address": {
	
	  "type": "object",
	
	  "properties": {
	
	    // ...
	
	  },
	
	  "required": [
	
	    // ...
	
	  ]
	
	}
	``

Table 11.1: Comparison between pydantic-*generated schema elements and their equivalents in the manually generated schema*

The generated given_name does not have the minLength constraint, enforcing a minimum length of the value for that field. There is a similar gap, with both minLength and maxLength missing in the honorific property. The generated honorific also more explicitly allows either a string value or a null, as well as specifying a default null value specification. The generated email_address property is missing the entire pattern that the manual schema uses to enforce a well-formed email address value for that property. Finally, the address property, rather than relying on an explicit object type definition, uses a $ref to point to the location in the current schema of that object definition as an independent schema.

Python annotations, pydantic, and optional fields

The combination of how Python Optional[type] annotations work, how pydantic handles those, and the required property specifications of the JSON Schema standard lead to an odd scenario: When a model field is specified as Optional, but doesn't provide a default value (None is typical), the schema will not *report* it as required, but it will be *treated* as a required field, albeit one that will accept a default of the type specified in the Optional annotation.

The most obvious pattern of missing property settings in the generated schema are those that have some validation purpose. In cases where validation can be limited to simple type checking — string values for string fields, int values for integer fields, and so on — this may be acceptable. In scenarios where more detailed or rigorous validation is required, pydantic provides a solution: use of the Field function (https://docs.pydantic.dev/latest/concepts/fields/), which provides settings for all of the missing items noted, and more. A complete implementation of the Address and BaseArtisan classes using Field to specify the same validation implemented in the previous examples can be found in the business_objects.py module, along with its complete JSON schema dump, in business_objects.schema.json.

The actual implementation of the same four focal fields, with the addition of those validation field settings and some additional field settings for additional documentation output in the schema, looks like this:

```
honorific: Optional[str] = Field(
    title='Honorific', default=None,
    description='The honorific of the Artisan that '
    'the instance represents',
    min_length=2, max_length=7,
    examples=[None, 'Mr.', 'Ms.', 'Mrs.', 'Dr.',]
)
given_name: str = Field(
    title='Given Name',
    description='The given name of the artisan that '
    'the instance represents',
    min_length=2,
    examples=['John', 'Jane',]
)
email_address: str = Field(
    title='Email Address',
    description='The email address for the Artisan '
    'that the instance represents',
    pattern=r'^[a-zA-Z0-9\._%+\-]+'
    r'@[a-zA-Z0-9\.\-]+\.[a-zA-Z]{2,}$',
    examples=['jsmith@gmail.com',]
)
address: Address = Field(
    title='Mailing Address',
```

```
        description='The mailing address for the Artisan '
        'that the instance represents'
)
```

The title and description additions to these field definitions are purely documentation; they will have no functional impact, though they will provide further details for published schemas used by others. The examples items are, not surprisingly, example values for each field. While the examples also do not have any direct functional impact, they will provide a ready-made set of test values when the time comes to write unit tests for the business objects.

The schema output generated by pydantic's model classes is a *JSON* schema and is not directly compatible with the **OpenAPI Specification** (**OAS**, see https://swagger.io/docs/specification/ v3_0/about/) that will eventually be used to provide API-level documentation. When this book was being written, Pydantic did not provide a ready-made mechanism for generating OAS-compatible schema documentation, but the changes needed are not difficult to script:

- OAS only allows a single example value for any given object property, while JSON Schemas allow multiple examples items. If examples is defined, setting an OAS-compatible example to the first examples item, and removing the original examples specification will generally suffice.

- OAS organizes model types into several categories, including entries in its components namespace for schemas (general reusable object definitions), responses (objects that define responses returned from an API), and requestBodies (objects that define request expectations for an API's endpoints). While there is no functional requirement for the responses and requestBodies namespaces to exist, using them does provide additional clarity.

- JSON schema output of Pydantic model definitions will frequently attach models that are used as types for a model's properties to the definitions of the models that use them. For example, the BaseArtisan definition generated by Pydantic will include the Address model as a definition item in a $defs section of the BaseArtisan schema and refer to that section from the address property of the BaseArtisan definition. While that may be functionally allowed in an OAS schema, it does break from OAS conventions and may lead to bloat if the same process happens for every use of a model property type. Scripting a process to move any of these $defs items into a standard location like components/ schemas is not difficult either.

Many of these can be addressed with the addition of a third-party extension to Pydantic: the openapi-pydantic package (https://pypi.org/project/openapi-pydantic/). This package also provides tools for defining a full OpenAPI specification for an API purely in Python code. Even without that, generating a collection of model-object schema definitions that comply with OAS standards is not difficult, and the results can be verified easily with online tools like Swagger's Editor (https://editor-next.swagger.io/), as shown in *Figure 11.2*.

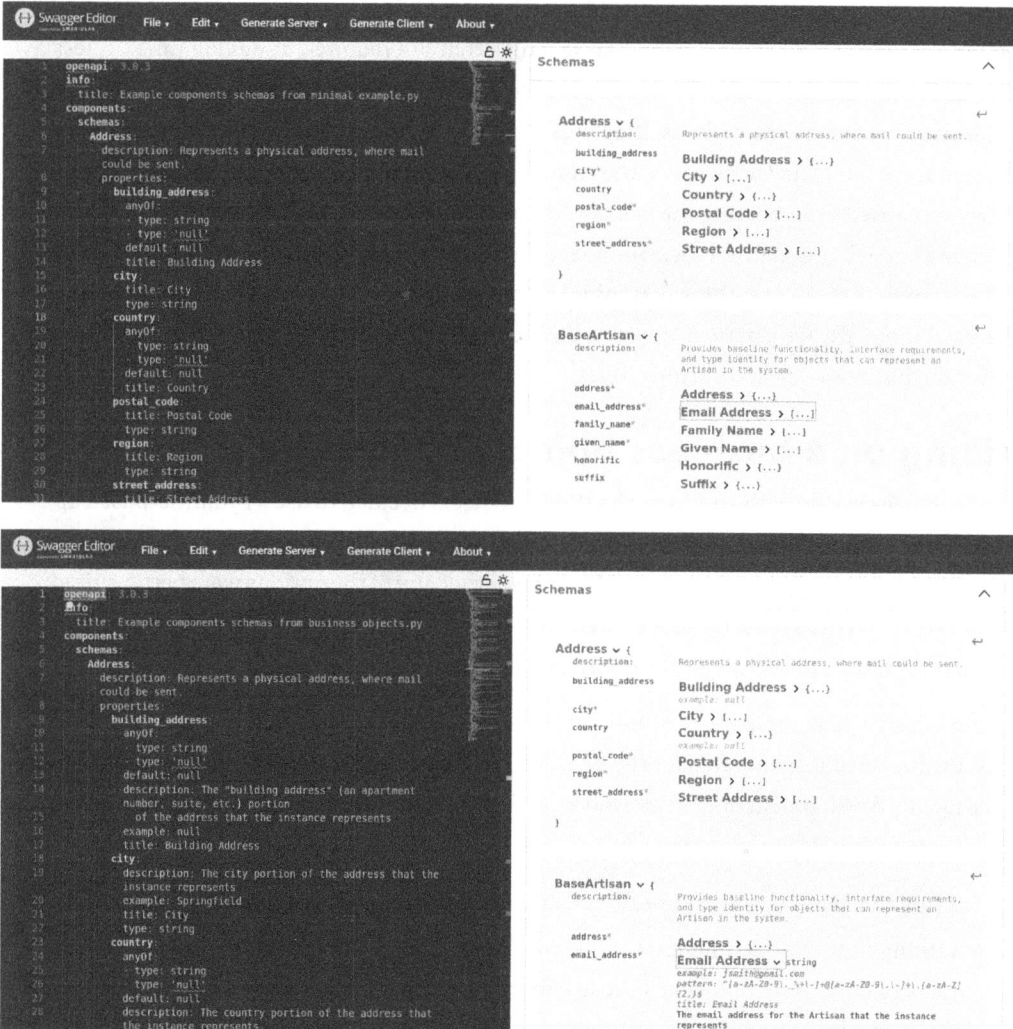

Figure 11.2: The Swagger Editor views of the minimal_example and business_objects modules' schema outputs

All of the approaches shown in this section have their advantages and drawbacks when it comes to making a decision about how to define and manage business objects in the context of an application or API. The primary considerations involved in making a decision about which to use will vary across products based on their requirements and constraints. Products operating with severely constrained space for additional package installations will benefit from using pure Python class structures or using `fastjsonschema` to validate native Python dictionary data structures. The trade-off in those cases is the need for additional engineer time to create and maintain those classes and any external documentation like schemas that are required at deploy time. In less constrained deployments, a more advanced approach, like the one provided by `pydantic`, may be preferable, if only because the code itself defines all of the documentation elements needed for those external elements. In those cases, the trade-offs will include some slight increase in processing speed caused by importing the package in the first place and the increase in the amount of underlying code that executes when a model object is created or used. These options are the most robust, though there are others that might be pursued. Knowing what the advantages and drawbacks of them are, we can turn our attention to making the decision about what the architecture for the business objects will look like.

Deciding on a business object architecture

After a lengthy discussion of the options, the HMS engineers decided to use a Pydantic-based approach for their business objects. Much of the discussion centered around whether they wanted to follow a **design-first approach** for their API, and whether any of the options were better suited to that, or even prevented it outright. A Design First Approach is a methodology that prioritizes the design of a product or service — the final API in this case — before any development of it.

From a pure design-first perspective, it follows that the OAS documentation mentioned earlier would be the first artifact generated for the final API. That documentation would then serve as a guideline for any development of or future modification to the final API and its capabilities. There are advantages to following this approach:

- The functional requirements are all well-defined before any real code work is undertaken.

- Assuming that the documentation includes both data contracts for operations and examples of data that conform to those contracts, many of the testing requirements are also already documented, which should simplify some of the testing expected for the API.

- Other teams working towards using the API can simply refer to that specification and start their work sooner as a result, even if they have to fall back on mocked responses from the API while the actual functionality is being developed.

On the other hand, the simple fact of the matter is that if there are discrepancies between what an API specification *says* the code does and what the code *actually* does, the code *wins*. That means that there is some risk of a discrepancy between the two. In those cases, there may not be a good way to test for those kinds of discrepancies without writing much more intricate testing processes, and the odds are good that it will be necessary to implement testing of those testing processes.

The *Dictionaries and a JSON schema* approach, at first glance, feels like a very natural approach under a design-first methodology; after all, it starts with a schema already. However, if the schema standard used for validating business object data isn't directly compatible with the schema expectations for the API, that requires translation from one to the other, introducing a risk of errors in translation. The HMS engineers are planning to provide OAS documentation for their APIs consumers, and while there are not a *lot* of discrepancies that could cause those kinds of translation errors, they felt that the ones they could identify — lack of support for more than one example value on object properties in particular — were too limiting, or would require more effort to keep up with than doing so was worth.

The *Python class structure* approach, whether using standard Python classes or following the *Using a dict as a basis for a class* approach have all of the same issues, but to a greater degree: A final OAS schema would have to be created and managed with a completely manual process, barring a *lot* more development work to create the kinds of schema-output processes that Pydantic already provides. There would be no need for an object-level schema to be created or managed, at least, and that would reduce the risk of translation errors and eliminate some additional work required to keep multiple schemas in sync.

The *Using Pydantic BaseModel* approach, though it does not seem at first glance to support a design-first methodology, *can* be used in a way conducive to that methodology. The main constraint of design-first is that the design happens first. It makes no assumptions about *how* that design is built. That, then, means that so long as the design involved can be altered without making functional alterations to the processes, how that design is achieved is simply not a consideration. With that in mind, the HMS engineers' discussion landed on these agreements:

- The API design will be managed in code, using the openapi-pydantic package (https://pypi.org/project/openapi-pydantic/) to define the OpenAPI specification for the API as a whole.

- The API definition will live in the same repository as the API implementation itself and will rely on the other business-unit packages to provide the OAS component models when necessary.

- OAS components will be represented in the design using Pydantic models to define data structures and the relevant validation.

Though there may be additional considerations that have to be addressed later, this will allow the design-first priorities to be maintained with a fair degree of independence from the actual implementations for the service later on. The actual assembly of the API definition will happen later, in the *Anatomy of a Service* chapter, but the decisions made at this point, and some of the initial project structure that will relate to them can be created now (the `hms-backend-api` directory in the chapter repository).

Summary

This chapter has taken an in-depth look at several options for representing application or service data in a consistent fashion within the code itself. Each of these options provides assurance that, provided that the code is actually used, the data that the code is working with will be validated according to any constraints associated with it. That assurance holds for data that comes from user input through the API, and that those constraints and requirements — the data contract for those objects — can be documented in a common, industry-standard manner.

Those data contracts can also be applied to reading data from and writing data to a back-end data store. The fact that a standard schema document can be generated for them also means that the data structure that will be persisted is a known quantity, though no investigation has been done yet into the mechanics of how that data will be read and written. That will be the next chapter's primary focus.

12

Reviewing Business Object Data Persistence

While it is technically possible for applications and services to not need to persist data, that need is more common than not, particularly in scenarios like the HMS API that is being discussed through this book. The specific shapes and needs for data storage can vary wildly, based on several variables, including the underlying storage mechanism and the specific needs for an application or service. As a result, there are several considerations and decisions that can be made. This chapter is intended to provide the information needed to understand what those decisions are, what trade-offs are involved in making one decision over another, and several high-level principles that shape those trade-offs.

In this chapter we're going to cover the following main topics:

- The need for data persistence
- Common data store concepts and terminology
- The ACID principles behind **Relational Database Management Systems (RDBMSes)**
- Some of the popular options available for RDBMS and NoSQL databases
- How to select a data store technology
- Development and testing implications once that selection is made

Technical requirements

There are no specific requirements. The code in this chapter is provided for illustrative purposes only.

The need for data persistence

Not all applications and services require data persistence, though it is far more common than not: the ability to keep track of data between processes that live in code is important even in relatively simple cases, and critical in scenarios where there is no user state tracked over time. This is particularly critical in web-based applications and services: the HTTP protocol that underlies all web-based applications and services is inherently **stateless**: web-servers and services neither know nor care who is making a request. Though there are mechanisms that can be used to provide *some* state information, their capacity is limited. Browser cookies are limited to 4 kilobytes *total* for any given domain, and there should not be more than 50 of those. Query-strings in a URL — the key/value pairs after a ? in a URL — are technically not limited according to the official standards, but different browsers and servers may limit them; those limits are often not well documented, and they may not be consistent from one browser/server case to another. Even if those limitations did not exist, data that is only present during user requests is not accessible outside that context without doing something to save it — to persist it so that it can be read and used outside that context.

In order to persist in a meaningful fashion, then, application data must be stored somehow. There are several possible solutions to the basic problem, but we will focus on using a back-end database system. Other options were explored in the first edition of this book, but they do not lend themselves well to the sort of data persistence that would be expected for a web-based application or service, for several reasons. To fully explore the reasons why they are less desirable solutions, we will first need to consider what data can (and should) look like when it is stored, what operations can be undertaken with data, and what characteristics of a data store make them more stable and more desirable.

Common data store concepts and terminology

At the heart of the sort of data store that the hms project is concerned with are several concepts: the first concept is the idea of a **record**, which contains data about a particular object. Records are stored in **tables**, which are simply collections of records with the same defined structure: a **schema** much like the schemas discussed in the previous chapter.

Schemas for tables define one-to-many **fields**, which provide a name for the data-segment, and at least a basic data type for the field. Table schemas are also responsible for defining fields about the table's records: a unique identifier that allows any given record to be unambiguously identified for retrieval, alteration, or deletion is the most common, but other possibilities include fields that keep track of when a record was created or modified, and sometimes whether the record is active or not.

The second is a **transaction**: an operation that reads, writes, or deletes one-to-many records from one-to-many tables in a data store. Even the most basic operations, ones that read or affect only a single record in a single table, are transactions whose activities succeed or fail as a whole. Most databases that use **Structured Query Language (SQL)** to provide a **Relational Database Management System (RDBMS)** also provide a mechanism to define transactions that are collections of simpler operations, allowing those collections to succeed or fail based on whether all of the child operations succeed, or any of them fail, and allowing any successful operations whose changes would be invalid because of some failure to be rolled back. This capability will be discussed in more detail a bit further on, in the *Data characteristics* section.

The last concept that will be discussed here is the idea of an **operation**. A database operation is a specific action that performs some function with or against one or more records, to achieve a specific result. There are four basic operations in the context of a data store that are carried out through the software that interacts with a data store, and out to an API that provides access to that data. Collectively, they are often referred to as **CRUD**, which stands for **C**reate, **R**ead, **U**pdate, and **D**elete.

> **Available API types**
>
> This chapter will focus on a **Representational State Transfer (REST)** API approach, since that is the expected focus for the project being described. There are other options, though: of particular potential interest is **GraphQL** (`https://graphql.org`), which allows an API caller to designate what fields and data sub-structures will be returned, created, or manipulated during an API operation. GraphQL APIs also provide a formal schema definition that expresses what data names and types are available through it, and that schema can be leveraged in code to perform run-time type-checking of requests made to the API. The `qlient` package (`https://pypi.org/project/qlient/`) has proven to be a reliable, high-performing workhorse for GraphQL API access in my experience.

A **Create operation** accepts incoming data, and creates one or more new records in the backing data store. In a REST API, this data is typically provided through an HTTP POST request. Assuming a JSON payload and a SQL data store, an example POST request to create a new person might contain data that looks like this:

```
{
    "given_name": "Brian",
    "family_name": "Albee"  // Note the typo in this name
}
```

That payload would be sent in a POST request to a URL like:

```
https://some-api.com/people/
```

Once accepted, the data is written to the relevant tables with a SQL INSERT statement. Assuming a table named People, with given_name and family_name fields, the INSERT corresponding to the JSON payload above would look something like this:

```
INSERT INTO People (given_name, family_name)
VALUES ('Brian', 'Albee');
```

Create operations are typically responsible for generating unique identifiers for the records being created. Whether that happens in the code that runs before the database call or within the database itself is a design decision that needs to be considered. There are advantages to both approaches: if the code is responsible for generating that identifier, it will be available to the code without having to make any additional requests to the database, or any special arrangements within it to build a custom transaction that returns it as part of the database call. Assuming that the code is responsible for generating the identifier, and that record identifiers will be **Universally Unique Identifier (UUID)** values, the SQL generated would change to something like this:

```
INSERT INTO People (person_id, given_name, family_name)
VALUES (
    '59b691bf-b603-4c18-bdad-e3fe7a12bdc0',
    'Brian', 'Albee'
);
```

...where the person_id value (59b691bf-b603-4c18-bdad-e3fe7a12bdc0) is generated with a uuid.uuid4() call, and converted to a string value as part of the generation of the SQL statement.

Why use UUID values for identifiers?

UUID values are more secure than the typical serial numbering of records as identifiers. A UUID value can represent any one of 16^{32} different values — that is 3.4×10^{38} different values that a potential bad actor would have to attempt in order to access a single record. Even accounting for the reduction of those possible values using code that leverages the birthday paradox, that translates to 1.8×10^{19} combinations that would have to be checked to access a single record. At a million attempts per second, finding a single record would require thousands of years. In comparison, that same million attempts per second could find a serially numbered record ID in a matter of *seconds*. Even in cases where there are thousands or millions of potential records to access, the time required to find and potentially compromise even one record is significant.

A **Read operation**, in its simplest form, accepts a unique identifier of a record, and returns the data for that record. In a REST context, read operations are typically executed with HTTP `GET` requests, such that a request like:

```
https://some-api.com/people/{person_id}
```

...would return the record data for the record with the `person_id` supplied. In JSON, using the `person_id` value from above (`59b691bf-b603-4c18-bdad-e3fe7a12bdc0`), that would be expected to yield a JSON response like this:

```
{
    "person_id": "59b691bf-b603-4c18-bdad-e3fe7a12bdc0",
    "given_name": "Brian",
    "family_name": "Albee"
}
```

The SQL generated by the code to return that result could be as simple as:

```
SELECT * FROM People
WHERE person_id='59b691bf-b603-4c18-bdad-e3fe7a12bdc0';
```

Decide what data should actually be returned!

This example SQL query is very broad — possibly too broad — in that it will return *all* the fields from the record in question. If the structure of the table includes fields that should not be returned in response to an API request, or that do not have an identified use, it is better to remove those from the response data, whether by specifying field-names in the query itself, or generating specific data-responses in the API code for specific use cases.

There are several potentially useful variations of read requests that are common in REST API implementations. One such is the idea of providing a listing of all records that match some criteria — a search or filtering operation, for all practical purposes. In that scenario, a request searching for or filtering results down to records with a `family_name` value of `'Albee'` could look something like this:

```
https://some-api.com/people/?family_name=Albee
```

...and would return a list (or an `array`, in JavaScript terms) of matching results:

```
[
  {
    "person_id": "59b691bf-b603-4c18-bdad-e3fe7a12bdc0",
    "given_name": "Brian",
    "family_name": "Albee"
  }
]
```

The data store behind an API might well contain hundreds, thousands, or even millions of records that could be returned in this kind of list. With that in mind, allowing the request to specify pagination controls like a page number and a number of items per page, and adjusting the response data structure accordingly, should be considered. A request similar to the one shown earlier, but listing all the available records in the backing `People` table, and using those pagination parameters, might look like this:

```
https://some-api.com/people/?page=1&max_responses=10
```

...and return a structure like this:

```
{
  "people": [
    {
      "person_id": "59b691bf-b603-4c18-bdad-e3fe7a12bdc0",
      "given_name": "Brian",
      "family_name": "Albee"
    },
    // This example assumes that there are more than
    // ten records found, but those have been omitted
    // for space reasons.
  ],
  "page": 1,
  "max_responses": 10,
  "next_page": 2
}
```

In this response-structure, the presence of a next_page value indicates that there are more re-cords available, and provides a value for the next page that could be substituted in the page parameter of the original request. Providing the current page number and the max_responses value is not *required*, but would make things easier to troubleshoot on the API consumer's end. The change to the JSON response structure still allows easy access to the data requested (in the people field), while allowing additional data about the response to be provided in the response itself. This flexibility of response structure is a significant advantage to using a response format that can accommodate structured data. Additional query-string parameters controlling sorting are also common in APIs.

Why use JSON?

JSON is an easier data-format to use in JavaScript code that would run on a browser if API data were being accessed directly. It is not the only option, but using a single JSON.parse() call in client-side code to generate a single object with field-names and their data is much less code than, for example, reading members from a DOM object in an XML response.

An **Update operation** presented to an API does exactly what it sounds like: updates a back-end record with new data from the request. In a REST API context, this involves an HTTP PUT or PATCH request. The semantics of these two HTTP verbs are worth some discussion. A PATCH is intended to *partially update a resource*, altering only the specified fields from the request, while a PUT is intended to *replace an entire resource*. Following these semantics strictly, a PUT request will *always* be **idempotent** — that is, the same request, repeated multiple times, will always have the same effect — while a PATCH might not be, depending on the specifics of the changes being requested.

At first glance, idempotency might seem like a desirable characteristic of a system that writes data to a data store: after all, if the same transaction yields the same resulting data in a record, that is probably desirable behavior. However, when different data changes can occur from different sources, that needs to be examined in more detail before deciding that a fully idempotent data change process is really what is needed. Consider, for example, two people making different changes to the same record through an API that's being served over HTTP:

- One needs to change the family_name to correct a typo.

- Another needs to alter a different field; for this example, we'll use a phone_number that hasn't been shown in previous examples yet.

Assuming that both of the actors making these changes retrieve the record data before any changes have been made, they are working with data that was returned from the API as:

```
{
    "person_id": "59b691bf-b603-4c18-bdad-e3fe7a12bdc0",
    "given_name": "Brian",
    "family_name": "Albee",
    "phone_number": "303-555-1212"
}
```

The family_name change is submitted first, with a complete payload that looks like this:

```
{
    "person_id": "59b691bf-b603-4c18-bdad-e3fe7a12bdc0",
    "given_name": "Brian",
    "family_name": "Allbee",   // The fix added an "l" here
    "phone_number": "303-555-1212"
}
```

The phone_number change follows after the family_name change has been completed, with this payload:

```
{
    "person_id": "59b691bf-b603-4c18-bdad-e3fe7a12bdc0",
    "given_name": "Brian",
    "family_name": "Albee",
    "phone_number": "720-555-1212"   // Area-code change
}
```

If both of these changes are handled in a way that writes the entire data structure as a change, and the original retrieved data isn't updated before the second payload is sent, the phone_number change will happen, but the family_name change from the previous update request will be *undone*, overwritten with the original data that was retrieved at the start of the process. That is, the SQL that would be generated as each request was processed would look like this:

```
UPDATE People
SET
    given_name='Brian', family_name='Allbee',
    phone_number='303-555-1212'
WHERE person_id='59b691bf-b603-4c18-bdad-e3fe7a12bdc0';
UPDATE People
SET
    given_name='Brian', family_name='Albee',
    phone_number='720-555-1212'
WHERE person_id='59b691bf-b603-4c18-bdad-e3fe7a12bdc0';
```

The back-end code will not be able to determine what fields have been changed without the front end doing something to indicate changed vs. unchanged state. From a back-end processing perspective, the easiest way to accomplish that is to simply not include any unchanged field-values in the payload for an update — which is the kind of payload structure that is implied in a PATCH request. Those same requests, then, would look like these:

```
{
    "person_id": "59b691bf-b603-4c18-bdad-e3fe7a12bdc0",
    "family_name": "Allbee"
}
```

and

```
{
    "person_id": "59b691bf-b603-4c18-bdad-e3fe7a12bdc0",
    "phone_number": "720-555-1212"
}
```

Handling updates in the hms project

Given the decision made by the team in the previous chapter to use a Pydantic-based approach for their data-models in code, even before defining how the data persistence will actually function, there is an approach that can be taken to keep updates consistent, without having to rely on writing a lot of SQL-generation code to test. An update could retrieve the specified item from the data-store, update (and validate) any specified fields from the request in that instance, then update the record in the database with the complete state data of the instance. That would not absolutely guarantee that concurrent updates would not encounter problems, but it would reduce the length of time that they could happen in to the length of time it would take to process the updated fields and write the data. Even for very complicated data structures updating over slow database connections, that can be kept fast, given some care in how the process is designed and implemented.

Taken together, all of this implies that updates should be handled using PATCH requests if the semantics and intentions of the HTTP verbs are going to be honored. Using processes that follow the intentions of the HTTP PUT verb should be used sparingly, if at all: only when there is a reasonable degree of confidence that complete overwrites will not cause issues.

The last CRUD operation is the **Delete operation**. Like the update operation just discussed, it does exactly what would be expected given the name: deletes a resource. In a REST API context, delete operations are handled by sending HTTP DELETE requests, with an identifier for the resource to be deleted. A delete request generally follows the same URL structure as a read/GET request; the difference is in the type of request being made — which HTTP verb is in play when the request is sent — so a delete request for a Person record through the same hypothetical API will look the same as the corresponding GET request:

```
https://some-api.com/people/{person_id}
```

An additional point for consideration from an implementation perspective is whether a delete action *really* deletes the relevant record, or simply sets some flag-value that prevents it from being accessible to future requests of the other CRUD operation types. Certain types of data — financial information, commonly, though there are others — may have data-retention policies that require records to be preserved even after they are nominally deleted.

The CRUD operations discussed here provide an operational chain, from an API request through the code that processes the requests, into the backing data store. In some cases the response from the data store will return data to the code that, in turn, can be relayed back to the API as a response. There are other HTTP verbs that an API may handle, but these are the ones that relate directly to the data store integration. The backing data store can be of several different types, though this project will be concerned with implementing a data store that uses a SQL-based RDBMS. Good, reliable data stores will have tools to facilitate or enforce a variety of characteristics on their activities and the data being stored and worked with that at least start with another acronym: compliance with ACID principles.

ACID principles

ACID is a set of principles that, when followed, are intended to ensure that database transactions are processed consistently and reliably. A transaction, in a bit more detail than was summarized earlier, is a single, logical unit of work, whether it is a single read or write operation, or multiples of those operations, yielding a single result. There are four key concepts in ACID:

- Transactions are **Atomic**, meaning that an entire transaction is treated as a single unit of work.
- Transactions are **Consistent**, following whatever validation rules apply, and ensuring that the database is always in a valid state.
- Transactions are **Isolated**, allowing multiple transactions to be processed at the same time without affecting one another.
- The results of completed transactions are **Durable**, and will not be lost if the database system fails.

Not all SQL databases are inherently fully ACID compliant, though the majority of the popular ones are. A notable exception is MySQL, though it provides a storage engine option, **InnoDB**, which *is* ACID compliant alongside its **MyISAM** engine, which is *not*.

At a database system level, simple, single-statement operations like selection or deletion of one or more records and creation or update of a single record are atomic. In cases where multiple SQL statements need to be treated as a single transaction — they all must succeed for the entire set of changes to be committed — most SQL-based databases provide some mechanism to create multi-statement transactions, though the specific syntax varies from database to database (see *Table 12.1* below for some common variations).

A commonly mentioned example of a multi-statement transaction is transferring money from one bank account to another. The process involved is simple enough:

- Subtract the transfer amount from the source account's balance.
- Add the transfer amount to the destination account's balance.

If either of those steps fails, something undesirable happens: the balance in one of the accounts is not updated, and the money involved is lost, or is incorrectly credited to the destination account. Implementing a transaction around the two updates, and rolling back to the last known good state for both records if either of those updates fails, ensures that if the transfer fails for *any* reason, both accounts are still unmodified.

RDBMS	Start	Rollback	Complete
MS SQL Server	`BEGIN [TRANSACTION]`	`ROLLBACK [TRANSACTION]`	`COMMIT [TRANSACTION]`
MySQL	`START TRANSACTION`	`ROLLBACK [WORK]`	`COMMIT [WORK]`
Oracle	`BEGIN`	`ROLLBACK`	`END`
PostgreSQL	`BEGIN`	`ROLLBACK`	`COMMIT`
SQLite	`BEGIN [TRANSACTION]`	`ROLLBACK [TRANSACTION]`	`COMMIT or END [TRANSACTION]`

Table 12.1: The SQL variations for creating multi-statement transactions by database

Why is SQLite included?

SQLite (`https://www.sqlite.org/`) is a small, fast, self-contained SQL database engine that can be run and used locally for development purposes. It is not suitable as a production database system, but can provide enough local database functionality to remove the need for a full local development database installation in many cases.

If the RDBMS supports table definitions that allow data to be validated, and that will reject data creation or changes that do not conform to those validation rules, then the *system* is consistent, for whatever value of consistent can be applied. The ability to define valid data types, require data in a field, and enforce basic data sizes is typical of SQL table definitions, but different SQL variants might not support more sophisticated value checking. At a minimum, the specific implementation of a SQL CHECK constraint can vary across databases (see *Table 12.2*, below, for examples using an age field that must be a positive integer value).

RDBMS	CHECK constraint syntax
MS SQL Server	`age int CHECK (age>=0)`

MySQL	`age int,`
	
	`' … other table fields`
	
	`CHECK (age>=0)`

Oracle	`age int CHECK (age>=0)`
PostgreSQL	`age int CHECK (age>=0)`
SQLite	`age int CHECK (age>=0)`

Table 12.2: The SQL variations for CHECK constraints by database

When designing an application or service that needs data constraints applied to data in a back end data store, there are three basic possible approaches:

- Apply constraints in the code, but not the database.
- Apply constraints in the database, but not the code.
- Apply constraints in the code and the database.

If the code is solely responsible for data constraints, the database becomes little more than a persistent storage mechanism for the data. Some very basic constraints on the database side may be unavoidable: fields in SQL tables require a type specification at a minimum, and some of those types, string data in particular, may require a maximum length to be defined as well. The most significant trade-off in taking this approach is that data may be modified without the benefit of the code that enforces data constraints and integrity.

If only the database is responsible for the validation of data, then the code cannot validate data without making a call to the database. That may degrade application performance to some degree, and will require some consideration of how to handle validation errors that originate from there. In the case of API development, where the deliverables include schema documentation, additional effort will need to be undertaken to create and maintain those schemas based on the structure of their data from the table definitions, since that definition exists only in the database.

If constraints and validation occur in both the code and the data store, the primary trade-off will be in the ongoing need to keep those constraints synchronized between the two. Some thought should be given, and a decision made, about which of the two is closer to being a formal source of truth with respect to those constraints. Additionally, thinking out (and probably documenting) what that synchronization process actually looks like would be advisable.

There is little that software engineers need to be concerned about with respect to the isolation and durability principles of ACID. Both are functions of the database system itself, in the main. There are some basic, common-sense considerations that could apply, like avoiding database transactions that take unreasonable lengths of time to complete, but those will generally be caught by reviews of code as it is written.

Knowing what the data store will be charged with doing, and what the implications of the ACID characteristics of a data source involve, the selection of a database service to provide the data source is the next consideration.

Data store options

There are dozens of SQL database engines available to pick from. Of those, there are five that are generally available in some fashion across the major cloud providers, some of which may also be available in serverless variations. Those five are:

- MS SQL Server (`https://www.microsoft.com/en-us/sql-server`)
- MariaDB (`https://mariadb.org/`) / MySQL (`https://www.mysql.com/`) — two different database engines that share the same SQL syntax
- Oracle (`https://www.oracle.com/database/`)
- PostgreSQL (`https://www.postgresql.org/`)

These are not the only cloud-based options — creating a cloud-resident server as a **Virtual Machine (VM)**, or perhaps using a container-based service, is also an option. These five have some degree of built-in support and maintenance in the form of automatic updates, integrated backup processes, and other various features that may vary from one cloud provider to another.

SQL-based relational databases are also not the only type of data store solution available. Another option is one of several NoSQL engines, including:

- Apache Cassandra (`https://cassandra.apache.org/`)
- Apache CouchDB (`https://couchdb.apache.org/`)
- MongoDB (`https://www.mongodb.com/`)

- Neo4j (https://neo4j.com/)
- Redis (https://redis.io/)

There are also purely cloud-resident options across the larger cloud providers: Amazon Web Services offers DynamoDB, Google Cloud Platform offers Bigtable, and Microsoft Azure's offering in the space is called Cosmos.

Although there have been advancements: new and improved features, functionality, and capabilities to both types of databases in general, as well as to the specific engines within those groups, their general characteristics, advantages, and trade-offs remain largely unchanged.

Relational (SQL) databases

Relational Database Management Systems (RDBMSes) are one of the more mature data storage approaches available for applications, with options that have been in common use for decades. They typically store data as individual records (sometimes called **rows**) in tables (or relations) that define field names (**columns**) and types for all member records. Tables often define a primary key field that provides a unique identifier for each record in the table. A simple example of a table that defines user records might resemble the following:

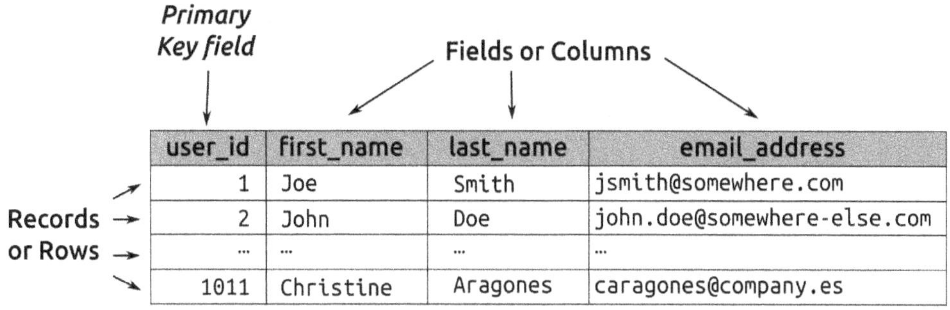

Figure 12.1: An example table structure storing user data

Each record in a table is, then, a consistent structure of data — all users in the preceding example would have user_id, first_name, last_name, and email_address values, though the values for the fields other than user_id might be empty, or NULL. The data from any table can be accessed or assembled through a query without having to change the tables themselves, and it's possible to join tables in a query so that, say, users in one table can be associated with records that they own in another — orders, perhaps.

This structure is often referred to as a schema, and it both defines structure and enforces data constraints such as value type and size.

The most common query language for relational databases is the **Structured Query Language (SQL)** — or at least some variant of it. SQL is an ANSI standard, but there are a number of variants available. There may be others, but SQL is almost certainly the most popular option, and is very mature and stable.

SQL is a complex enough topic in its own right, even setting aside its variations across database engines, to warrant a book of its own. We'll explore a little bit of SQL as hms_sys iterations progress, though, with some explanation of what is happening.

Advantages and drawbacks

One of the more significant advantages of a relational database data store is its ability to retrieve related records in a single query request — the user/orders structure mentioned earlier, for example. Most relational database systems will also allow multiple queries to be made in a single request, and will return a collection of records for each of those queries as a single result set. The same user- and orders-table structure could, for example, be queried to return a single user and all of that user's orders, which has some advantages in application object structures where one object type has one or more collections of objects associated with them.

Another potentially significant advantage to most relational database engines is their support for transactions — allowing a potentially complex set of changes, or insertions of data, to roll back as a whole if any single data manipulation fails for any reason. This is virtually guaranteed to be available in any SQL RDBMS, and is a very significant advantage when dealing with financial systems. Support for transactions may be a functional requirement for systems that deal with moving money around — if it isn't, it's probably worth asking why it isn't. Support for transactions that encompass multiple operations is a key aspect of full ACID compliance — without it, the atomicity, consistency, and (to some extent) isolation criteria will be suspect. Fortunately, almost any relational database system that's worthy of being called one at all will provide transaction support sufficient enough for any need likely to arise.

Many relational database systems also support the creation of views and stored procedures/ functions that can make data access faster and more stable as well. Views are, for all practical purposes, predefined queries, often across multiple tables, and are often built to retrieve specific data subsets across the tables they are tied to. Stored procedures and functions can be thought of as approximate equivalents to application functions, accepting certain input, performing some set of tasks, and perhaps returning data that was generated by the execution of those tasks. At a minimum, stored procedures can be used in place of writing queries, which has some performance and security benefits.

The schema inherent to tables in most relational databases is both an advantage and a drawback, potentially. Since that schema enforces data constraints, there is less likelihood of having bad data living in a table. Fields that are expected to be string values, or integer values, will always be string or integer values, because it's simply not possible to set a string field to a non-string value. Those constraints ensure data type integrity. The trade-off for that, though, is that value types (and sometimes the values themselves) may have to be checked and/or converted when going into or coming out of the data store.

If relational databases have a downside, it's probably that the structures of the tables containing data are fixed, so making changes to those requires more time and effort, and those changes can have effects on the code that accesses them. Changing a field name in a database, for example, may well break application functionality that references that field name. Most relational database systems also require separate software installations, and server hardware that is operational at all times, like associated applications are. This may or may not be a concern for any given project, but can be a cost consideration, particularly if that server lives in someone else's infrastructure.

Scaling an RDBMS may be limited to adding more horsepower to the server itself — improving the hardware specifications, adding RAM, or moving databases to new, more powerful servers. Some of the aforementioned database engines have additional packages that can provide multi-server scale, though, such as scaling horizontally into multiple servers that still act like a single database server.

Support for JSON data types

Since the previous edition of this book, spurred by an increased focus on the use of JSON in application and service development, several of the five databases listed earlier have added some type of support for JSON data types. Though the specifics of that support, and its actual capabilities, vary from database to database, there are opportunities to leverage them that will be discussed in the *Data access design strategies* section later in this chapter.

In the same order as listed earlier, here are the pertinent facts about those database options. The various connector packages listed, unless otherwise noted, are compliant with the *Python Database API Specification* (`https://peps.python.org/pep-0249/`), which defines a programmatic standard for accessing databases in Python code.

Microsoft SQL Server

Microsoft SQL Server (**MS SQL**) is a proprietary SQL-based DBMS, using its own variant of standard SQL (T-SQL). The differences are generally trivial, at least for simple to somewhat complex needs.

MS SQL also has clustering and replication options for high-availability and load scenarios, with the same need for discrete servers to maximize the effectiveness of horizontal scaling.

There are at least two Python options for connecting to and working with MS SQL databases:

- `pymssql` (`https://pypi.org/project/pymssql/`): This specifically leverages the **Tabular Data Stream** (**TDS**) protocol used by MS SQL, and allows more direct connection to a back-end engine.
- `pyodbc` (`https://pypi.org/project/pyodbc/`): This provides database connectivity through the **Open Database Connectivity** (**ODBC**) protocol.

As of late 2024, Microsoft has placed its testing efforts and confidence in the pyodbc package.

MySQL and MariaDB

MySQL is a popular RDBMS that started as an open source project in the mid-1990s. MariaDB is a community-maintained fork of MySQL, intended to serve as a drop-in replacement for MySQL, and to remain available as an open source option in case MySQL (now owned by Oracle) ever ceases to be released under an open source license. MySQL and MariaDB remain functionally interchangeable with minimal adjustment needed.

Both use the same variant of SQL, with mostly trivial syntax differences from standard SQL that are typically very straightforward. MySQL is — and MariaDB is presumed to be — more optimized for reading/retrieving data than for writing it, but for many applications, those optimizations will likely not be noticeable.

MySQL and MariaDB can be horizontally scaled through the use of clustering and/or replication software additions to a base installation to meet high availability or load needs, though for this to really be effective additional servers (real or virtual) are necessary.

There are specific recommended Python packages for connecting to and interacting with each of these options:

- The `mysql-connector-python` package (`https://pypi.org/project/mysql-connector-python/`) is the officially supported solution for MySQL connectivity.
- The `mariadb` package (`https://pypi.org/project/mariadb/`) is the officially supported solution for MariaDB connectivity.

There are several Python libraries for connecting to and interacting with MySQL, and since MariaDB is intended to be able to directly replace MySQL, those same libraries are expected to work without modification for MariaDB access.

Oracle

Oracle is one of the earliest RDBMS options, dating back to the late 1970s. It is usable on a variety of operating systems, including Windows, Linux, and Mac OS X. It has its own SQL variant, PL/SQL, that varies significantly from the published SQL standards. It is a popular enterprise database solution, though its licensing may be prohibitively expensive for smaller organizations.

Python connectivity to Oracle databases is provided by the cx-Oracle package (`https://pypi.org/project/cx-Oracle/`). It also requires the installation of the *Oracle Instance Client* packages (either the Basic or Basic Light variant, according to the documentation available when this chapter was written: `https://www.oracle.com/database/technologies/instant-client.html`), which will complicate the setup somewhat for operating systems that do not support the **Red Hat Package Manager** (**RPM**) format.

PostgreSQL

PostgreSQL is another open source database option — an **Object-Relational Database System** that is designed with an emphasis on standards compliance. As an **ORDBMS**, it allows data structures to be defined in a more object-oriented fashion, with tables that act like classes with the ability to inherit from other tables/classes. It still uses SQL — its own variant, but again, with mostly trivial differences for most development purposes — and has several Python options for connecting to and working with a database. It also has replication and clustering support, with the same sort of caveats noted for previous options. The recommended Python package for connecting to and using a PostgreSQL database is psycopg2 (`https://pypi.org/project/psycopg2/`).

Local development options

All of these options allow some sort of local installation that can be used for development purposes. The open-source databases — MySQL, MariaDB, and PostgreSQL — can be installed on Linux, macOS, and Windows systems directly, with full features and functionality. The proprietary options — MS SQL and Oracle — have developer installation options, which provide enough similarity to a full, licensed installation to make them viable to work with during development. They may not have the *full* functionality of their fully licensed equivalents, though. Historically, one of the more common restrictions in development versions of proprietary database installations is that access to the tables and data is limited to the local machine only. There may be different or additional constraints in place for those by the time this book is published.

If there is a need for a local development database, but functional or policy reasons prohibit a local installation, there is another option: **SQLite** (`https://www.sqlite.org/`). SQLite is a C library that implements a small, fast, self-contained SQL database engine, and is installed with Python. Its implementation of SQL is not the same as the SQL implementations for any of the other databases discussed; some variations between them have already been noted in *Tables 12.1* and *12.2*, earlier in this chapter. It may be a viable option, though, if the data structures and interaction with the data are simple enough. It does not support stored procedures, but can handle both transactions and query parameterization.

A better option, if a *local* database installation is not viable, is to set up development-only copies of a database, perhaps one for each developer, on some database server. That would allow full access to the features and functionality of the actual database engine, and would eliminate any possible need to translate from one SQL implementation to another (from SQLite to MySQL, for example).

NoSQL databases

There are dozens of NoSQL database options available, both as standalone/local service installations and as cloud database options. The driving factors behind the designs of most of them include an emphasis on the following:

- **Support for massive numbers of users**: Tens of thousands of concurrent users, maybe millions — and supporting them should have as small a performance impact as possible
- **High availability and reliability**: Being able to interact with the data even if one or more database nodes were to go completely offline
- **Supporting highly fluid data structures**: Allowing structured data that isn't bound to a rigid data schema, perhaps even across records in the same data store collection

From a development perspective, the last point in this list is perhaps the most significant, allowing almost arbitrary data structures to be defined as needed.

If the concept of a table in an RDBMS is a storage model, there are a number of alternative storage models across the NoSQL database continuum:

- **Document stores**: Each record equivalent is a document containing whatever data structure it was created with. Documents are often JSON data structures, and as such allow for some differentiation between different data types — strings, numbers, and booleans as simple values, nested lists/arrays and objects for more complex data structures — and also allow for the use of a formal `null` value.

- **Key/value stores**: Each record equivalent is simply a value, of whatever type, and is identified by a single unique key. This approach could be thought of as a database that is equivalent to a single Python dict structure.

- **Wide column stores**: Each record could be thought of as belonging to an RDBMS table with a very large (infinite?) number of columns available, perhaps with a primary key, or perhaps not.

There are also some variants that feel like they combine aspects of these basic models. Creating a data store in Amazon's DynamoDB, for example, starts by defining a table, which requires a key field to be defined, and allows a secondary key field to be defined as well. Once those have been created, though, the contents of those tables act like a document store. The net result, then, acts like a key/document store (a key/value store where each key points to a document).

NoSQL databases are typically non-relational, though there are exceptions to this. From a development perspective, this implies that one of at least three approaches needs to be taken into consideration when dealing with application data that is stored and retrieved from a NoSQL data store:

1. Never use data that relates to other data — ensure that every record contains everything it needs as a single entity. The trade-off here is that it will be difficult, if not impossible, to account for situations where a record (or the object that the record is associated with) is shared by two or more other records/objects. An example of that might be a user group that multiple users are members of.

2. Deal with the relationships between records in the code that works with those records. Using the same users/groups concept just mentioned, that might involve a Group object, reading all the relevant User records and populating a users property with User objects from that data during instantiation. There might be some risk of concurrent changes interfering with each other, but not significantly more than the same sort of process would risk in a RDBMS-backed system. This approach also implies that data will be organized by object type — a distinct collection of User object data and a distinct collection of Group object data, perhaps — but any mechanism that allows the different object types to be differentiated will work.

3. Pick a back end data store engine that provides some sort of relational support.

NoSQL databases are also less likely to support transactions, though again there are options that do provide full ACID-compliant transaction capabilities, and the criteria/options for dealing with transactional requirements at the data store level are very similar to those mentioned previously, that is, dealing with relational capabilities. Even those without any transaction support are still going to be ACID-compliant for single records — at that level of complexity, all that is required to be compliant is that the record is successfully stored.

Advantages and drawbacks

Given the high availability and concurrent user focus behind most NoSQL options, it should come as no great surprise that they are frequently better suited than their RDBMS counterparts for applications where availability and the ability to scale are important. Those properties are even more important in big data applications, and applications that live in the cloud — as evidenced by the fact that the major cloud providers all have their own offerings in that space, as well as providing starting-points for some well-known NoSQL options:

- Amazon (AWS)

    - DynamoDB (`https://aws.amazon.com/dynamodb/`)

- Google

    - Bigtable (`https://cloud.google.com/bigtable`, for big data needs)

    - Datastore (`https://cloud.google.com/products/datastore`)

- Microsoft (Azure)

    - Cosmos DB (`https://azure.microsoft.com/en-us/products/cosmos-db`)

    - Azure Table storage (`https://learn.microsoft.com/en-us/azure/storage/tables/table-storage-overview`)

The ability to more or less arbitrarily define data structures can also be a significant advantage during development, since it eliminates the need for defining database schemas and tables. The trade-off for that, potentially, at least, is that since data structures can change just as arbitrarily, code that uses them has to be written to be tolerant of those structure changes, or some sort of conscious effort may have to be planned to apply the changes to existing data items without disrupting systems and their usage.

Consider, as an example, the User class mentioned earlier — if a password_hash property needs to be added to the class, in order to provide authentication/authorization support, the instantiation code will likely have to account for it, and any existing user-object records won't have the field already. On the code side, that may not be that big a deal — making password_hash an optional argument during initialization would take care of allowing the objects to be created, and storing it as a null value in the data if it hasn't been set would take care of the data storage side, but some sort of mechanism would need to be planned, designed, and implemented to prompt users to supply a password in order to store the real value. The same sort of process would have to occur if a similar change were made in an RDBMS-backed system, but the odds are good enough that there would be established processes for making changes to database schemas, and those would probably include both altering the schema and ensuring that all records have a known starting value.

Given the number of options available, it should also not be surprising that there are differences (sometimes significant ones) between them with respect to performing similar tasks. That is, retrieving a record from the data, given nothing more than a unique identifier for the item to be retrieved (id_value), uses different libraries and syntax/structure based on the engine behind the data store:

In MongoDB (using a connection object):

```
connection.find_one({'unique_id':'id_value'})
```

In Redis (using a redis connection):

```
connection.get('id_value')
```

In Cassandra (using a query value and a criteria list, executing against a Cassandra session object):

```
session.execute(query, criteria)
```

It's quite possible that each different engine will have its own distinct methods for performing the same tasks, though there may be some common names that emerge — there are only so many alternatives for function or method names, like get or find, that make sense, after all. If a system needs to be able to work with multiple different data store back-end engines, those are good candidates for designing and implementing a common (probably abstract) data store adapter.

Since relational and transactional support varies from one engine to another, this inconsistency can be a drawback to a NoSQL-based data store as well, though there are at least some options that can be pursued if they are lacking.

NoSQL BASE principles

NoSQL databases have a different set of principles than the ACID principles noted earlier for RDBMSes. Those principles are referred to as **BASE**:

- **B**asic Availability: The database is generally available.
- **S**oft state: Data stores do not need to be write-consistent, and replicated data may not be consistent at all times.
- **E**ventual consistency: Data stores will *eventually* reach a state of consistency, whether by internal synchronization of some sort, synchronization at the next read, or by some other mechanism.

MongoDB

MongoDB is a free, open source, NoSQL document store engine — that is, it stores whole data structures as individual documents that are, if not JSON, very JSON-like. Data sent to and retrieved from a MongoDB database in Python uses Python-native data types (`dict` and `list` collections, any simple types such as `str` and `int`, and probably other standard types like `datetime` objects).

MongoDB was designed to be usable as a distributed database, supporting high availability, horizontal scaling, and geographic distribution out of the box. It is an open source project, and can be installed locally for development purposes.

Like most NoSQL data storage solutions, MongoDB is schema-less, allowing documents (roughly equivalent to a record in an RDBMS context) within a MongoDB collection (roughly equivalent to a table in an RDBMS) to have totally different structures.

Redis

Redis is an open source, in-memory data store that can be used as a NoSQL database. It is formally considered a key/value store, providing a very simple data model where all values have corresponding keys, and the engine does not know anything about the values other than their related key names. Data living in Redis, at least in the *Community Edition*, is limited to `String` primitives, though various types of collections of those values are also supported, including `Hash` (roughly equivalent to a Python `dict`), `List`, and `Set` types. Python code relying on Redis as a back end data store may need to be responsible for converting from Redis' `String` values into Python types like `bool`, `float`, `int`, and so on.

Since Redis is an *in-memory* data-store, data persistence has to be accounted for in some fashion: if a Redis store crashes or restarts, the data it is persisting would otherwise be lost. Redis provides two options to handle data persistence, which may be combined:

- **RDB** (Redis Database), which executes point-in-time snapshots of the data set on a defined schedule

- **AOF** (Append Only File), which captures every write operation received by the server, allowing those to be replayed to rebuild the data set

These are documented online, starting at `https://redis.io/docs/latest/operate/oss_and_stack/management/persistence/`.

An open source version of Redis can be installed locally for development purposes, though that version does not provide the same level of functional convenience as the paid versions.

Other NoSQL options

The cloud-resident options noted earlier have local development options as well, though with the exception of AWS DynamoDB, they are described as emulators, and generally require the installation of other system components. The details for each can be found online:

- AWS DynamoDB local: `https://docs.aws.amazon.com/amazondynamodb/latest/developerguide/DynamoDBLocal.html`

- GCP Bigtable emulator: `https://cloud.google.com/bigtable/docs/emulator`

- GCP Datastore emulator: `https://cloud.google.com/datastore/docs/tools/datastore-emulator`

- Azure Cosmos DB emulator: `https://learn.microsoft.com/en-us/azure/cosmos-db/how-to-develop-emulator`

- Azure Azurite emulator (Table Storage and other Azure Storage options): `https://learn.microsoft.com/en-us/azure/storage/common/storage-use-azurite`

Despite the differences and trade-offs inherent to any of the NoSQL options available, they remain a viable option for applications and services. For certain types of applications and services, they may be a *better* option, as NoSQL data stores are generally better for high levels of **horizontal scaling**. Horizontal scaling traditionally increases service capacity by adding more machines or nodes to a system. Traditional RDBMSes *can* scale horizontally, through techniques like sharding — breaking a database into smaller units, each living on a separate server — or replication — copying data from a primary database to one or more replicas. Most NoSQL databases are designed to take advantage of additional resources more easily as a primary design decision. Selection of a data store technology has a number of decision points and considerations that need to be examined.

Selecting a data store technology

A key decision for any data persistence implementation is choosing a back-end database system to store the data. The advantages and drawbacks of the high-level groups of those options — RDBMS (SQL) vs. NoSQL — have been discussed earlier. At a system-by-system level there will be features available that may also contribute to the decision. That decision may be encompassed entirely by the selection of a specific database system outside the control of a development team. For the project being discussed in this book, that decision was outside the development team's control.

The HMS project's data persistence decision

The HMS software engineers don't actually get to decide what database system their code has to use. It's not uncommon for this sort of decision to be made by development teams as part of a project, but it's also not uncommon for these kinds of decisions to be made outside the context of a project. In this particular case, they are required to use the existing database system that the rest of the company's systems use. In this case, that system is MySQL, one of the RDBMSes described earlier.

A more thorough, if dated, example of designing data persistence using a NoSQL back-end database can be found in the first edition of this book.

The RDBMSes discussed here were chosen, at least in part, because they are supported across several of the major cloud providers. Not all of them are available through all of those providers, but even in those cases, it would be possible to host a database with a dedicated virtual machine, or perhaps a container-based solution. Over and above that, Amazon Web Services provides serverless options for two of the open-source options — MySQL and PostgreSQL — making them worth additional consideration if a serverless implementation is advantageous.

From a security perspective, one of those features that should be given serious consideration is support for query parameterization. **Query parameterization** is a type of prepared statement process that defines the process of a query separate from the data that will be used in the execution of the query. Those data points are represented by placeholders in the text of the query, and the query text is sent as a separate chunk of data to the database.

The query data, though it may be sent in the same request as the query text, is *separate* from the query, allowing it to be validated by the database API or the database engine itself. Using parameterized queries is a recommended pattern to limit the possibilities and/or impact of **SQL injection attacks** (https://owasp.org/www-community/attacks/SQL_Injection).

This practice is not foolproof — it cannot guard reliably against the use of dynamic identifiers in a query name without being very conscientious about how those identifiers are provided, for example — but it is a solid step toward making data access more secure in a code base.

> **Availability of query parameterization in Python**
>
> Any database access library that adheres to the *Python Database API Specification* (https://peps.python.org/pep-0249/), implementing an execute method for Cursor objects, provides at least *some* degree of query parameterization support.

Another RDBMS feature that has become more common in recent years is support for a JSON data type. JSON has become pervasive in web applications as the preferred format for transferring data between front-end web pages and their components and back-end data stores, frequently through an API. While JSON itself can be represented as nothing more than a string data type in a back-end data store, some database systems provide a dedicated JSON data type, along with some degree of support for typical database functionality against those fields. Support for JSON data types and selected key functionality for them across the RDBMSes discussed earlier is shown in *Table 12.3*:

RDBMS	Has JSON field type	Indexable JSON fields	Constraints available?
MS SQL Server	No (expected soon)	No (may change soon)	No (may change soon)
MySQL	Yes	Yes	Yes (JSON schemas)
MariaDB	Yes	Yes (special)	Minimal (well-formed)
Oracle	Yes	Yes	Minimal (well-formed)
PostgreSQL	Yes	Yes (limited)	Yes
SQLite	Yes (limited)	Yes (special)	No (may change soon)

Table 12.3: Support for JSON field types across RDBMS options

Support for formal JSON types is worth consideration because it opens up different data-structure design possibilities on the database side. Consider a design that must provide data access for the Artisan and Address classes discussed in the previous chapter, for example. Adding to that some common database fields — a unique identifier (object ID, or oid) and fields that track when a database record was created and last modified in a `BaseDataObject` class — yields the possible classes shown in *Figure 12.2*.

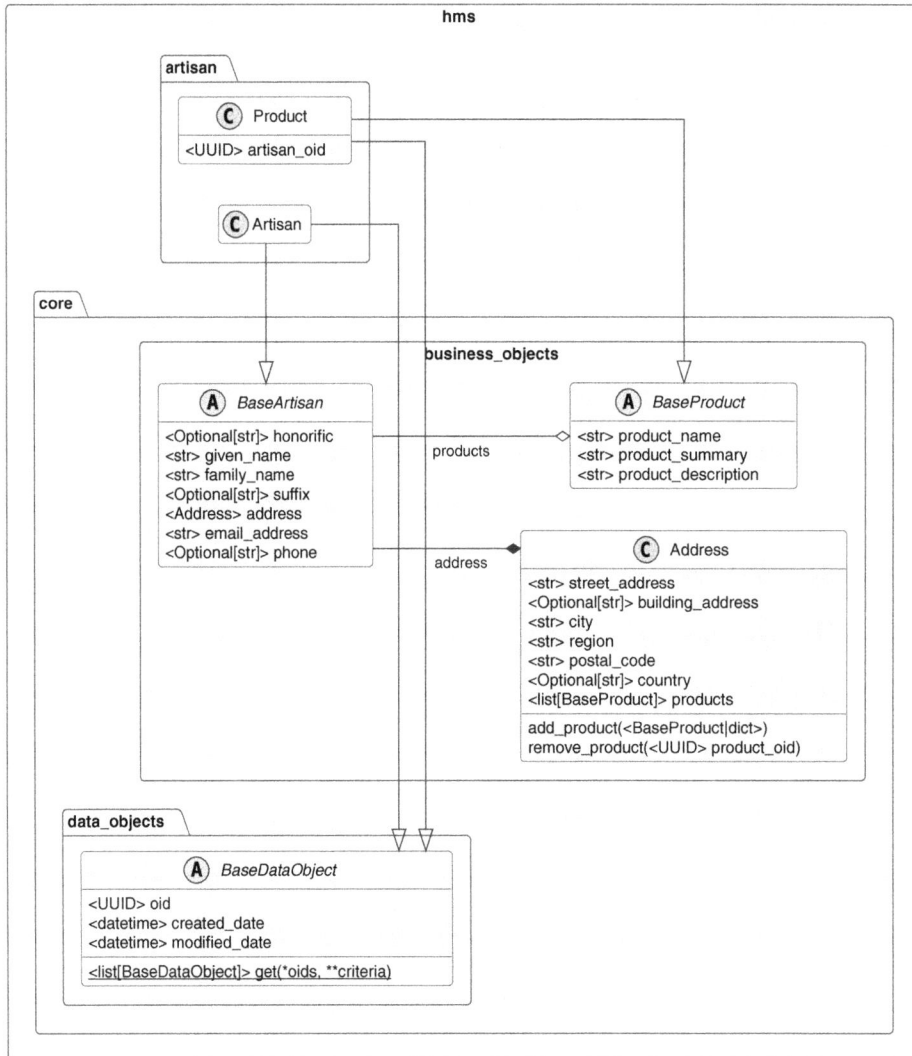

Figure 12.2: A possible set of relationships between Artisan, Address, and Product types in HMS' system

The traditional approach to defining table structures to store the state-data for instances of these classes would be to define those tables with individual fields for each property of the final classes. For example, the table that stores data for instances of the hms.artisan.Product class could be created like so:

```
/**
 * Define the table structure for hms.artisan.Product
 */
CREATE TABLE `Product`(
    -- Fields from BaseDataObject class
    `oid` CHAR(36) NOT NULL,
    `created_date` DATETIME DEFAULT CURRENT_TIMESTAMP,
    `modified_date` DATETIME ON UPDATE CURRENT_TIMESTAMP,
    -- Fields from Product class
    `artisan_oid` CHAR(36) NOT NULL,
    -- Fields from BaseProduct class
    `product_name` VARCHAR(120) NOT NULL,
    `product_summary` VARCHAR(4096),
    `product_description` VARCHAR(65535)
);
```

If, at some point in the future, new fields needed to be added to the Product table, the most basic process for performing those additions would involve altering the existing table with an ALTER TABLE statement. For example, adding a price field would look something like this:

```
ALTER TABLE `Product`
ADD `price` DECIMAL(10,2) NOT NULL;
```

Those ALTER TABLE statements would need to be tracked over time, so that they could be reconciled across changes made by several engineers working on code that needs to make those changes. A similar scenario would play out for changes required for fields that originate from the BaseDataObject class in the code, but *those* changes would need to be applied, tracked, and reconciled across *multiple* tables — any table that stored BaseDataObject data.

An alternative approach, storing the `Product` data as a `JSON` field in the table, would simplify the initial creation of the table, as well as making the table schema immune to many changes made in the `Product` class:

```
CREATE TABLE `Product`(
    -- Fields from BaseDataObject class
    `oid` CHAR(36) NOT NULL,
    `created_date` DATETIME DEFAULT CURRENT_TIMESTAMP,
    `modified_date` DATETIME ON UPDATE CURRENT_TIMESTAMP,
    -- Fields from Product class
    `artisan_oid` CHAR(36) NOT NULL,
    -- A JSON field could store *all* the product data!
    `product_data` JSON
);
```

In this example, the `artisan_oid` field is stored explicitly in its own field, making it easier to link a record from an `Artisan` table to the `Product` records that relate. Strategically, ensuring that any `Product` field that was needed or useful for any data retrieval use case is available as a dedicated field in the table, even if it were also present in the `product_data` JSON field, would preserve the advantages of dedicated fields in tables, while reducing the need for extensive schema modifications for data that is only needed for read or display purposes. If the JSON data is validated by the code, as expected from the business object definition strategy in the previous chapter, the impact of changes to those business object classes on their corresponding database tables can be reduced to accounting for new fields that have database operation significance in the code. This data structure approach is essentially a mixture of traditional, normalized RDBMS data management practices and a NoSQL-style document storage concept, reducing or removing the need for formal, detailed data structure definitions for fields where they are not needed.

Another relatively new feature of some RDBMSes' SQL implementations is the ability to execute an **upsert** query: essentially, a mechanism for allowing a single query to either insert a new record or update an existing one as a single statement. As might be expected, given the variations noted earlier in more mature SQL expectations like transactions and field-level constraints, there is little consistency for this functionality across the RDBMSes examined, as shown in *Table 12.4*:

RDBMS	Insert-or-update syntax

MS SQL Server	`MERGE INTO …`
	
	`https://learn.microsoft.com/en-us/sql/t-sql/statements/merge-transact-sql`

RDBMS	Insert-or-update syntax
MySQL	`INSERT … ON DUPLICATE KEY UPDATE …`
MariaDB	`INSERT … ON DUPLICATE KEY UPDATE …`
Oracle	`UPSERT INTO …`
PostgreSQL	`INSERT INTO … ON CONFLICT …`
SQLite	`INSERT OR REPLACE INTO …`

Table 12.4: Support for insert-or-update capability across RDBMS options

The ability to perform either record creation or alteration in a single statement allows code that is writing data to have a single process to perform either of those actions. It would be possible, for example, to write a single save() method for any given business object class that would perform whichever operation made sense. An example upsert for the Product table defined earlier might look like this:

```
INSERT INTO `Product` (
    `oid`,
    `created_date`, `modified_date`,
    `artisan_oid`,
    `product_name`,
    -- These are optional fields still
    `product_summary`, `product_description`
)
VALUES (
    '61e4232e-1c76-4562-bb7e-8d1f487803b4',
    '2024-12-21 13:29:02', '2024-12-21 13:29:02',
    '0dbb4aa9-0744-419d-80a3-902dc4ba6f3e',
    'My Product Name',
    NULL, NULL
)
ON DUPLICATE KEY UPDATE
    `created_date`='2024-12-21 13:29:02',
    `modified_date`='2024-12-21 13:29:02',
    `artisan_oid`='0dbb4aa9-0744-419d-80a3-902dc4ba6f3e',
    `product_name`'My Product Name',
    `product_summary`=NULL,
    `product_description`=NULL
```

There are certain concessions that need to be made and considerations to be kept in mind if an upsert-based data-writing strategy is pursued:

- All fields must have values accounted for, including NULL values (or whatever is appropriate) for any given empty field.

- To minimize the chance of conflicting updates, each upsert data-writing operation should retrieve the current record, modify the data in each relevant field, but **not** in any primary key fields, then perform the upsert query.

- Upsert queries can get very large very quickly, since they must account for the data values in both the INSERT and UPDATE sections of the SQL involved.

Special handling may be needed for removal of data from fields — for example, resetting the product_summary and product_description fields shown above will likely require checking that those fields exist in an update request, and only setting a NULL value if those fields exist *and* contain a NULL (or equivalent) value. This may be needed whether an upsert-based process is used or a more traditional separation of record insertion/creation and alteration/update is used. In that more traditional structure, a possible approach would be to have both create() and update() methods available for a business object, each of which uses a smaller, dedicated SQL statement to perform the relevant operation against the database. Those queries would look much like the sections of the upsert example shown earlier:

```
/**
 * Traditional INSERT
 */
INSERT INTO `Product` (
    `oid`,
    `created_date`, `modified_date`,
    `artisan_oid`,
    `product_name`,
    -- These are optional fields still
    `product_summary`, `product_description`
)
VALUES (
    '61e4232e-1c76-4562-bb7e-8d1f487803b4',
    '2024-12-21 13:29:02', '2024-12-21 13:29:02',
    '0dbb4aa9-0744-419d-80a3-902dc4ba6f3e',
    'My Product Name',
    NULL, NULL
```

```
)
/**
 * Traditional UPDATE
 */
UPDATE `Product` SET
    `created_date`='2024-12-21 13:29:02',
    `modified_date`='2024-12-21 13:29:02',
    `artisan_oid`='0dbb4aa9-0744-419d-80a3-902dc4ba6f3e',
    `product_name` 'My Product Name',
    `product_summary`=NULL,
    `product_description`=NULL
WHERE `oid`='61e4232e-1c76-4562-bb7e-8d1f487803b4';
```

The HMS team, armed with all these considerations and knowing that the database engine they will be required to use is some version of MySQL, made the following decisions about how they will plan to implement their data access code and the tables behind the business objects:

They will use *parameterized queries* whenever possible. While there is some additional overhead involved while writing the code for the API, it is a good security precaution. Even though they do not feel like there is much risk of their database being compromised, and the impacts if it should happen feel small, it is the right approach to take.

They will use *JSON fields* to store all business object data, for ease of retrieval and integration with the Pydantic-based business object decisions made earlier. Additional dedicated fields will be provided for those objects, and may duplicate fields and their values in the JSON representation of the object data, where there is a need or an advantage to doing so. The examples that they could identify included:

- The unique identifier of the object's record in the database (oid, a UUID value).
- Any related object identifiers, like the artisan_oid noted above, which relate objects in one table to objects in another (a Product record to the *Artisan* record for the artisan that owns the product, in this case).
- Any status data controls and flags. Having flag-fields that indicate whether a Product record is available (is_available), or an Artisan record is active (is_active), along with a flag that indicates that a record should be *treated* as deleted even if it hasn't *really* been deleted (is_deleted), are examples that they could come up with.
- Other data points about a record, including a created_date and modified_date.

Much of the rationale behind this decision was based on the simple recognition that the Product items that are already in the live systems have an extremely variable structure. Some have materials specifications, like wood, wood and brass, and various mixtures of fabrics and other materials. Others may have one or more colors, some have physical dimensions, others clothing sizes, and so on. All of this variation across products would be amazingly troublesome to manage in a conventional approach, with fields for each material, color, measurement, or size; a flexible structure, using a JSON field for those, led to the realization that there was little advantage in having dedicated fields for those values for the use cases they could anticipate.

At the same time, until the ability to query with data in a JSON field is verified and tested for speed, the need for at least some fields to live outside the JSON data structure was assumed to be important. The advantage of having a single JSON field that could be passed to a business object constructor was obvious to them as well, and worth the additional effort needed to make sure that field values that needed to live both in the JSON field and outside it would be handled appropriately.

With respect to making a decision about whether to use *upsert* or traditional query structures for creation and updating of records in the data store, the initial thought was to try the upsert approach initially, until or unless it proved too troublesome to maintain. While there are some trade-offs, the basic paradigm of an upsert approach is closer to the paradigm that the development team is accustomed to: writing entire documents to the data store has been the baseline process in the current NoSQL-based store that is being replaced with this new effort.

These decision points cover the options and the decisions that need to be made for code implementations in an application or service. Even limiting design decisions to the handful of options discussed here, there are a lot of possible combinations available, each with its own set of advantages and drawbacks. There is another significant consideration that has not been discussed yet, though: how and when the data persistence capabilities and functionality will be tested.

Additional testing needs for data persistence operations

Data persistence is a mission-critical piece of any application or service that uses it. As such, it is just as critical to make intentional, defensible decisions about how and when data persistence functionality is going to be tested. At a unit testing level, since those are intended to run in isolation from other systems, data persistence functionality tests will typically be written with mocked or patched functionality, so that they can execute within that isolated context. Those tests, then, are intended to prove that the software components function as expected *given known data inputs*.

They do **not** prove that actual data inputs are, themselves, valid, or that any of the processes that use the software components with actual data are behaving as expected. Those fall into the realm of other types of tests:

- System tests
- End-to-end tests

As noted earlier, **system tests** focus on systems as a whole, which would include interaction between an application or service and any data persistence layers. They are, then, a logical type of test for verifying that data can be written, read, and otherwise manipulated for each software component that has those capabilities. **End-to-end tests** are concerned with the *processes* that an application or service executes. Their goal, put simply, is to verify, given a known input to a specific process, that the end results of that process' execution are as expected.

System and end-to-end tests are important guardrails in CI/CD processes. When set up so that a failure of those tests will terminate a build and/or deploy process, they go a long way toward ensuring that new or altered code will not be released with the capability of corrupting system data. Axiomatically, data is more important than the code that works with it. Code can be changed or even replaced in its entirety without affecting data integrity, or revenue generated by the systems the code implements. If data gets corrupted or destroyed, on the other hand, the system that uses it may be useless.

Summary

This chapter has focused on the decisions and design principles behind data persistence, with only theoretical and example code structures to illustrate those principles. Along the way, the needs and rationales for those principles have been discussed, along with options and their trade-offs. While there may be other considerations that surface while designing data persistence for applications and services, the ones discussed here are the ones that will have the highest impact on the actual implementation of those applications and services. Armed with these concepts, and having decisions made about high-level implementation strategies, the actual implementations can be worked out, which will be the focus of the next chapter.

Get This Book's PDF Version and Exclusive Extras

Scan the QR code (or go to packtpub.com/unlock). Search for this book by name, confirm the edition, and then follow the steps on the page.

Note: Keep your invoice handy. Purchases made directly from Packt don't require an invoice.

13

Data Persistence and BaseDataObject

With the decisions from the previous chapter made, the final design, on both the software and data store side, involves defining the data structures in the service code, the table structures that will store those data objects in the back-end store, and the processes involved in reading and writing data to and from the store. These are all connected: a field that exists in the business objects defined in software code must be represented in the table structure where those objects' data are stored, and SQL has to be defined to get the data into and out of those tables.

In this chapter, we're going to cover the following main topics:

- Setting up a development database
- Figuring out where to start with use cases
- Reviewing and revising the BaseDataObject ABC
- Defining a management process for database changes
- Implementing the business objects

Technical requirements

The code for this chapter was written in Python 3.11, using `pipenv` for package and Python Virtual Environment management, as described earlier in this book. The chapter repository's `Pipfile` has all the required package dependencies across all of those options, and a functional PVE can be initiated by running the following from the `CH-13-code/hms-core` project root directory:

```
pipenv sync –dev
pipenv sync
```

Verification that the packages needed are all installed can be accomplished by running

```
pipenv graph
```

...which should output something similar to this (though the versions may vary, and sub-dependencies have been omitted here):

```
email-validator==2.2.0
flake8==7.1.1
mysql-connector-python==9.2.0
pydantic==2.10.6
PyYAML==6.0.2
typeguard==4.4.1
```

Database setup will require a functional installation of MySQL 8.x (the version in play while the chapter was being written was 8.0.41). Installers for MySQL are available online at `https://dev.mysql.com/downloads/installer/`.

Follow along with tags in the GitHub repo

There is so much code generated in this chapter that it would not fit in the text of the chapter without **significantly** exceeding space limitations. The detailed code for each major chunk of work can be found in the GitHub repo's tags (`https://github.com/PacktPublishing/Hands-On-Software-Engineering-with-Python-Second-Edition/tags`), prefixed with CH-13, and called out at the beginning of each section.

The entire collection of code for the chapter is in the repository at `https://github.com/PacktPublishing/Hands-On-Software-Engineering-with-Python-Second-Edition/tree/main/CH13-code`

Setting up a development database

These changes are tagged in the GitHub repo as `CH-13-Database-set-up`

As HMS engineers already know that the production service's database will be MySQL, they will install a local MySQL instance to develop against, and since the setup of a development database is generally going to be a one-time exercise, they decide to simply document the steps that are needed to accomplish it, capturing what they can in some `.sql` scripts (in the `hms-core/database/HMS/set-up` directory in the chapter repository):

- Installation of MySQL.

- Creation of a local development database (named `HMS_DEV` for everyone): `001-create-application-database.sql`

- Creation of a database account that the service will use to access data (`hms-service-user`): `002-create-application-user.sql`

- Granting basic permissions, for `INSERT`, `SELECT`, `UPDATE`, and `DELETE` SQL operations, to all tables and views, and `EXECUTE` for any functions or procedures in the `HMS_DEV` database for the `hms-service-user` account: `003-grant-application-user-permissions.sql`

- Granting full administrative permissions to the `HMS_DEV` database for the user whose machine it lives on. This couldn't be easily scripted because the user name isn't a constant: each user has their own local user name on their development machine.

Once the documented process has been followed, the database will exist, though it will not have any tables or data yet. Those will be defined later. It is still possible to verify that the database exists at this point, though, as well as defining the environment variables that will be used to make the database connections in code, and even creating a function that will create, cache, and return a connector object as the first code in the new `data_objects.py` module. With all of those changes in place, a simple inline test in that module, using this code:

```python
# Code to run if the module is executed directly
if __name__ == '__main__':
    with get_env_database_connector() as db:
        with db.cursor() as cursor:
            cursor.execute('SHOW TABLES;')
            print(
```

```
        'SHOW TABLES results: '
        f'{cursor.fetchall()}'
    )
```

runs without error, though its output is not terribly dramatic:

```
SHOW TABLES results: []
```

Database setup scripts may be safe to re-run

These scripts are safe to re-run for the MySQL database engine that the HMS team is concerned with, though they are *noisy*. That is, they will report errors in several cases, like failing to create the database or the user if those already exist, but they will not overwrite those existing items. Even when they report those errors, any further processes in the SQL script files will still execute, even if they, too, report errors of their own. That may not be the case for all database engines, and it would be worth checking before assuming that similar processes would work for, say, MS SQL Server or PostgreSQL.

The setup process documentation is stored in the project code for at least two reasons. The first is that anyone who is working on the project's code would presumably want or need their own development database, and they would already have access to the repository with the relevant code, so the documentation would also be available. The second reason is that if there are any changes that need to be made to the setup processes as development progresses, those changes can be captured in the SQL scripts and will be available to everyone else in the team when needed. This hints at a need for some standards around how database changes will be managed on an ongoing basis, and that topic will be explored in more detail later in this chapter.

This setup makes some assumptions about how the final production database will be accessed. The set of specifications and credentials noted in the documented process is a fairly typical arrangement for most RDBMS access libraries: The specifications have to identify where the database lives (a host and port), and what database is actually being used on that host (the database name). The credentials (account/user name and password) identify a database user or account that will be executing database operations, and provide authentication for that user to allow those operations to take place. All of these have to exist in some fashion in both the development and production environments, though they will almost certainly differ between those environments. Ideally, from within the code base, the acquisition of those values should use the same code. That, then, implies that the production environment will have its own set of environment variables, the values of which the engineers do not need to know, or might not be *allowed* to know.

Whoever is managing the database server and whatever production environments the code is running in will have to set those up.

Although there will be a functional (if empty) database available once the setup scripts have been run, there are two design items to consider first. The first relates to the expectation that there will be common fields for business objects, which need some sort of common structures for both code and table definitions. The second is determining where to start those definitions — choosing a business object/table combination to start defining fields for. There may be obvious candidates for this latter decision, but if there aren't, a good starting point is to simply take stock of the use cases that are needed, determine what, if any, dependencies are involved for them, and pick a subset of that use case functionality that has no dependencies.

Figuring out where to start using use cases

There are a number of ways that these designs can be approached — starting from the code, or starting from the tables, for example — but ultimately, all of these resolve to examining one or more use cases for the data in question. A **use case** is simply a description of how a user interacts with a system to achieve some goal, in enough detail to identify any required process steps, any data points that need to be accounted for, and any functional requirements or prerequisites involved.

To illustrate how use cases can guide both implementation details and the priorities for those implementations, consider the following apparently basic use case that the HMS engineering team will need to implement:

> *A Customer needs to be able to view a list of the most recently available Products available on the site, including the Product name, a summary description of the Product, a link to a Product detail view, and at least one image, if one is available, for the Product in question.*

The *criteria* for retrieving *Product* listing items — searching for Products — is a separate, future concern; this initial use case is simply getting a list of recent *Product* data sets, sorting by most to least recent, and returning those. Ideally, the listing process will use the same code and the same data set, but if there is a future need to have separate processes because of unexpected technical requirements later on, that will be handled as those requirements surface.

HMS has some business rules that affect this: A *Product* has to be created by the *Artisan* that owns it, and the *Product* listing has to be approved by someone in the main office. *Product* items also have to be active, not flagged as deleted, and not be part of an existing Order. These lead to two more use cases that will need to be accounted for as prerequisites for the first use case:

> *An Artisan needs to be able to create a Product.*

> *A Product Approver (a member of the HMS staff) needs to be able to approve a Product for inclusion on the site.*

There is also an implicit use case to allow an Artisan to edit their existing *Product* items, but that is not a hard prerequisite for the initial use case being pursued, so long as the *Product* creation allows the creation of an active *Product* item that is not flagged as deleted during its creation. A similar argument could be made for an approved status for a *Product*, but because there is potential for liability if a *Product* that doesn't meet HMS's standards for inclusion were to be included on their site, that approval process is considered important enough to warrant implementation sooner rather than later.

The prerequisite for an *Artisan* to exist in order to create and own a *Product* is self-evident, and leads to another prerequisite use case:

> *An Artisan needs to be able to sign up as an Artisan on the site.*

Because there are potential liabilities involved if an *Artisan* sign-up is not verified and approved, there is one more use case that needs to be considered, for reasons similar to the *Product* approval use case noted earlier:

> *An Artisan Activator (a member of the HMS staff) needs to be able to activate an Artisan after verifying their information.*

There are, then, four prerequisite use cases that need to be addressed before the simple product-view use case can be accommodated. The relationships between these use cases are shown in *Figure. 13.1.*

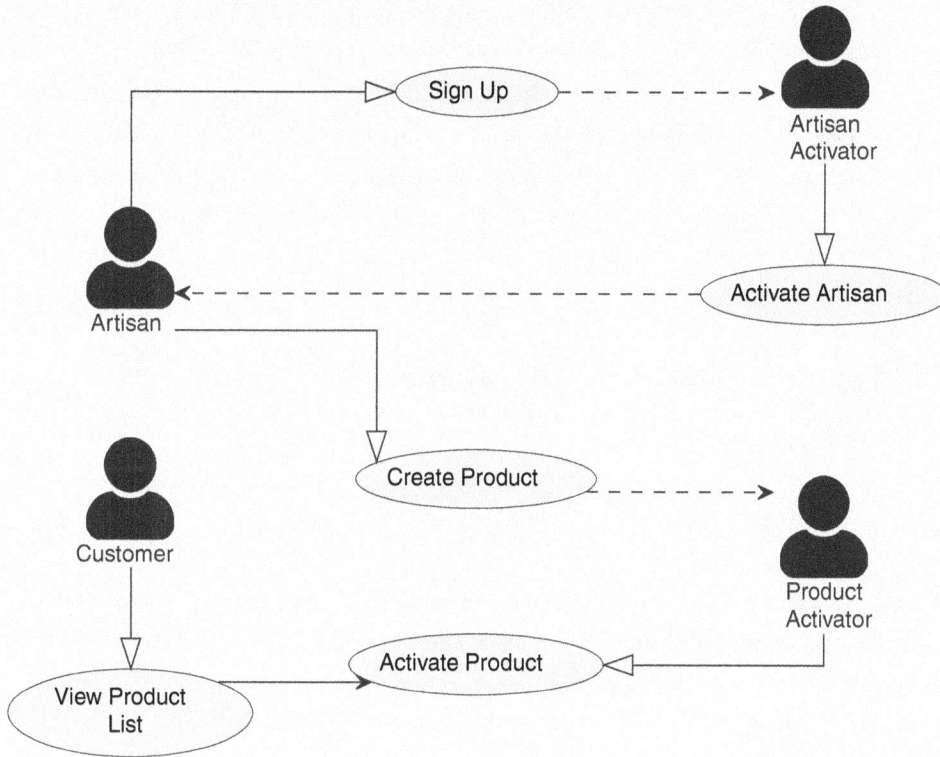

Figure 13.1: The use-case dependencies behind the first main use case

For purposes of implementing the *View Product List* use case noted earlier, these additional use cases may need to be implemented first, at least in part.

Unblocking prerequisite use cases

Complicated prerequisite use cases *can* block efforts that depend on them, but they may not *have* to, provided that some subset of the final implementation can be worked through sufficiently to provide whatever functional dependencies are involved. In these example use cases, that could be accomplished by implementing a minimal *Artisan* business object, with whatever fields are needed for the *Artisan*-to-*Product* relationships, and the fields involved in determining active, deleted, and approved statuses for *Artisan* and Product objects. There would still be more work needed later to finish those objects, but they could be used in their incomplete states in any work efforts that rely on those dependencies.

Over and above those four use case dependencies, there are *functional* requirements common to them all: the *Product* and *Artisan* business objects need to be defined in code, with the fields that relate to them, and they need to be made ready for data persistence operations. As a first step, addressing that last need requires defining a common field-set in the database for all business objects to use, and implementing a class that provides those fields, along with any instance or class methods that can be identified as necessary. The common fields and functionality can be implemented in a revised `BaseDataObject` class, which can then be used as a mixin base class for the actual business-object classes.

Reviewing and revising the BaseDataObject ABC

These changes are tagged in the GitHub repo as `CH-13-BaseDataObject`

The purpose of the original `BaseDataObject` class that the HMS engineering team is revising was to provide a common definition of data-object fields and functionality that could be applied to concrete business object classes as a mixin. A **mixin** is simply a small class designed to provide specific functionality that can be *mixed in* with other classes through the inheritance capabilities provided by an object-oriented language. In Python, since it supports multiple inheritance, using a mixin class is as simple as adding the class name to the parent classes in a child class definition. For example, once the `BaseDataObject` and `Artisan` classes are defined, the `Artisan` class' definition will look something like this:

```
class Artisan(BaseDataObject):
    ...
```

In more traditional OO languages that do not support multiple inheritance, the use of mixins is still feasible; it simply requires determining where in an inheritance chain the mixin needs to occur in order to provide the common functionality provided.

To start with, the design of the `BaseDataObject` class is going to be concerned *only* with providing field definitions that are common across all business objects, and one class method that can be used to create and return an instance of a `BaseDataObject`-derived class given data in the two standard formats that are returned from a database connection: a `dict` that maps field names to their values, and a `tuple` of `tuples` that contain those key/value pairs.

Those field names and value types will also be leveraged to define a common set of database table field definitions that can store the common field values in the data store, providing a template or starting-point for the definitions of tables for specific business object types later. The initial fields in the BaseDataObject class and their corresponding database field definitions are shown in *Figure. 13.2*.

> These changes are tagged in the GitHub repo as CH-13-BaseDataObject-and-related. The changes committed in that tag contain more detailed code and SQL than are presented in the text here.

Class Diagram	Related common SQL

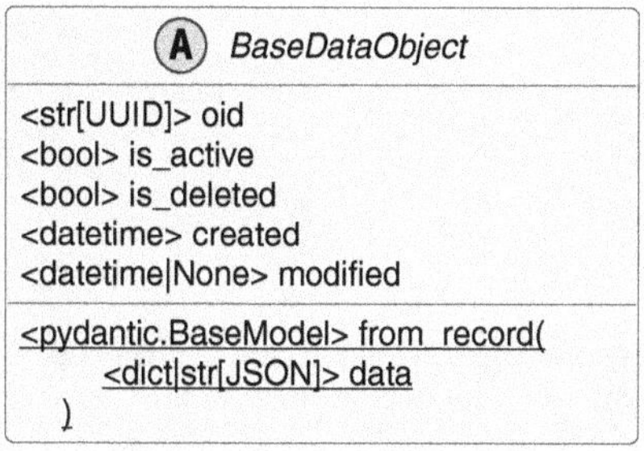 **Ⓐ** *BaseDataObject*
 	
<str[UUID]> oid
<bool> is_active
<bool> is_deleted
<datetime> created
<datetime|None> modified
 	
<pydantic.BaseModel> from_record(
    <dict|str[JSON]> data
)
	`oid CHAR(36) NOT NULL,`
	`is_active TINYINT(1)`
	`   DEFAULT 1 NOT NULL,`
	`is_deleted tinyint(1)`
	`   DEFAULT 0 NOT NULL,`
	`created DATETIME`
	`   DEFAULT CURRENT_TIMESTAMP`
	`      NOT NULL,`
	`modified DATETIME`
	`   ON UPDATE CURRENT_TIMESTAMP`
	`      NULL`

Figure 13.2: The common data fields for business objects defined in the BaseDataObject
class, and the common SQL corresponding to them for use in business object tables

Earlier (*Chapter 11*), the HMS team decided to use Pydantic (https://pypi.org/project/pydantic/) as the foundation for data modeling in their business object classes. With that in mind, and limiting the field definitions to the functional necessities, the implementation of the BaseDataObject class is quite simple (docstrings, method type annotations, and class-scope comments have been omitted for space reasons):

```
# Built-In Imports
import abc

from datetime import datetime
```

```python
from typing import Any
from uuid import UUID, uuid4
# ...
# Third-Party Imports
from pydantic import BaseModel, Field
# ...
class BaseDataObject(metaclass=abc.ABCMeta):
    oid = Field(default_factory=uuid4, frozen=True,)
    is_active = Field(default=False)
    is_deleted = Field(default=False)
    created = Field(
        default_factory=datetime.utcnow, frozen=True,
    )
    modified = Field(default=None,)
    @classmethod
    def from_record(cls, data) -> BaseModel:
        if isinstance(data, tuple):
            data = dict(data)
        return cls(**data)
```

When applied through the mixin inheritance the class was designed for, these fields define the following consistent set of properties:

- oid: The unique identifier of the record for the instance's state data in the back-end data store.
- is_active: A flag indicating whether the object is active or not, which can be used as a high-level filtering constraint to differentiate between records that are publicly accessible and those that are not.
- is_deleted: A similar flag, indicating that a given record is *logically deleted* — meaning that it should be treated as deleted even though it still exists, possibly pending an actual record deletion from the database.
- created: The UTC date/time that the record was created.
- modified: The UTC date/time of the last modification (from a SQL UPDATE) to the record.

Logical vs. actual deletion

There are scenarios where an actual record deletion may not be permitted, or needs to be deferred until other activities outside the control of an application or service have been completed. To support those cases, a flag field like the is_deleted shown here can be used as criteria to remove records from query results until an actual deletion is executed, if that is even permitted. In the context of the HMS system, logical deletion is expected to be used to support scenarios like an *Artisan* closing their account, where an actual deletion might prevent any close-out activities like payment of money due for orders that have not been completed yet.

The corresponding fields that would be expected for any table that provides back-end data storage for objects that derive from BaseDataObject were shown in summary in *Figure. 13.2*. A more complete treatment of them, including MySQL COMMENT information can be found in the database/examples/base-business-object.sql file in the repository.

Since BaseDataObject is defined using the same Field mechanism that was shown in *Chapter 11*, it is possible to extract a JSON schema document that captures the details of that implementation. Since BaseDataObject is not, itself, derived from Pydantic's BaseModel class, a new class derived from both must be created to access both the defined fields and the BaseModel.model_json_schema method that provides the JSON schema structure. This is implemented in the scripts/write-base-data-object-schema-file.py script in the hms-core project, and when executed, it writes that schema document to the file at documentation/BaseDataObject-schema.yaml in the same project.

With BaseDataObject defined and reasonably final for the time being, the HMS team can turn their attention to the implementation of the concrete business object classes, starting with the Artisan class that had no other dependencies in the use cases examined earlier, and working up to the Product class. The creation of these classes will require the creation of corresponding table definitions for the database, and that will require some thought to be given to how database changes will be managed on an ongoing basis.

Defining a management process for database changes

These changes are tagged in the GitHub repo as `CH-13-Database-management`

Managing changes to the structure of a relational database is a process that should be carefully considered and designed in order to at least reduce — and preferably *eliminate* — any risk of losing data when changes need to be made. There are several tools available that may be able to simplify the creation and modification of database tables and data, including:

- **SQLAlchemy** (`https://www.sqlalchemy.org/`), in 2.X.X versions as of this writing, with older versions going back almost two decades (2006).

- **Tortoise ORM** (`https://tortoise.github.io/`), which is described as a young project, though it has nearly two hundred released versions, dating back to 2018.

These are **Object-Relational Mapper (ORM)** tools, providing ways to map between objects — instances of classes, which could include the Pydantic `BaseModel`-derived classes expected in this project — and back-end relational databases. These ORMs provide both database management facilities, allowing modification of a back-end database to be managed in code, and mechanisms for executing queries against databases. They also provide their own mechanisms for defining model classes, roughly equivalent to the Pydantic model classes discussed earlier.

This last item is a critical consideration for the design that the HMS engineers have decided on. To fully leverage an ORM, they would have two options to choose from. The first would be to abandon the Pydantic model decision in favor of using ORM-supplied model classes. This would involve them writing code for their business objects to serialize those objects into JSON for output to the API that they will be building. While that is not a difficult challenge to solve, it would be time-consuming. Another consideration is that validation for fields would have to be explicitly created and maintained, something that the Pydantic approach does with trivial effort on the engineers' parts. A final trade-off is the loss of the automatic JSON schema documentation generation capabilities that all Pydantic model classes provide. This last item tips their decision against using ORM models: manually managing documentation that another team will be relying on, while not difficult, is tedious and more likely to be a source of errors that they would rather not have to deal with.

Another option that would still allow most or all of both an ORM's and Pydantic's capabilities to be used advantageously would be to separate the data-access processes — and the database management processes too — from the business object model definitions. In short, using the ORM and the model classes that would be built for it to handle the data access and database structure management tasks, passing query results managed by the ORM's tools to the Pydantic models, and working with those model instances as they already expect to. The trade-off in this scenario is the need to create and manage copies of model structures in two places, increasing the potential for discrepancies between them that could lead to errors. While they are reasonably confident that tests could be written to mitigate this potential, they represent more work that they are not confident is technically necessary, though the idea of separating data-access and business-object code is appealing.

Since the HMS engineers are expecting the table structures in their database to be very simple, they decide to manage those tables manually, at least for the time being. If, at some point in the future, integration of an ORM to handle data access and database structure management feels needed or desirable, they feel that re-examining that is a viable option.

When an ORM-based approach would be better

The decision made in this case is shaped significantly by the fact that the bulk of an object's data will be stored in a single JSON field. Fields that will be used in queries — the unique identifier, created and modified dates, and any fields that provide hooks for relationships to object records in other tables — are, in this design, the only ones that really need to be explicitly defined outside that JSON field context. In scenarios where most or all object fields need to be available as distinct fields in a database table, an ORM-based approach would provide significant advantages and would be worth consideration.

That manual process needs to accomplish several key things, all of which fall into a high-level concept that might be described as *keeping track of changes to database objects*:

- It needs to capture the initial creation of tables, and tables relating to business objects in the code in particular. The same holds true for any other database objects that might be needed later — views, stored procedures, or functions, and so on — but the initial priority is the tables.

- It needs to capture any changes made to database objects (again, prioritizing tables for now), with an eye towards making sure that those changes can be applied in a consistent fashion, and *in the sequence that they need to be applied in to account for any dependencies that are part of those changes.*

- It needs to be able to keep changes made for different purposes isolated from each other. For example, if two engineers need to make changes to the same table, and those changes do not have any interdependencies between them, those should be captured separately.

- It needs to be capable of applying all the database changes needed, in the sequence they are needed in, regardless of whether those changes are being applied to a local development database, to a production database, or to databases in any environments between those.

To accomplish all of these, the HMS engineers decide to capture the SQL that creates or modifies database entities in a collection of `.sql` files in the `hms-core` project (in the `hms-core/database/HMS/implementation` directory in the chapter repository). Those will keep track of the SQL needed to create or update any API database instance, following some relatively straightforward rules:

- Each file will be named so that executing them in a basic sort order will apply changes in a predictable and repeatable sequence. File names will also give some indication of what executing the file does, or if that is not feasible, what ticket in their work-tracking system those changes relate to — a *ticket file*.

- Initial creation of tables will be defined first, with tables that have no dependencies on other tables being defined before those that do.

- Alterations to tables that do not involve dependencies on other tables may be made in the original table-definition file. Alterations that have dependencies will be made in ticket files.

- A repeatable scripted process will be written that will read and apply *all* of the SQL in *all* of the `implementation` directory files when executed.

- Periodically, as time allows and when the collection of files is getting difficult to manage or keep track of, the team will *squash* the SQL code down in some fashion, allowing them to consolidate changes into single files. That process is still to be thought out and defined at this point.

This manual process is less complicated than it might sound

Although the potential for a lot of `.sql` files accumulating is real, each individual file should be reasonably tightly focused on accomplishing a single change, or a small set of related changes, to the database. The main challenge in following this process is likely going to be figuring out the best balance between assuring that changes are happening after all dependencies involved are accounted for. That potential glut of files over time is part of the reason why the *squash* process was called out above as a rule, even if it is not implemented immediately.

In MySQL, at least, re-running these SQL files will not damage an existing database under normal circumstances. A SQL script that executes a CREATE TABLE, for example, will succeed if the table does not already exist, and fail without interrupting the process if the table *does* exist. Similarly, any ALTER TABLE statements will succeed the first time they are applied to a table. By way of example, consider this SQL:

```sql
-- example-table.sql
CREATE TABLE Example (
    oid CHAR(36) NOT NULL PRIMARY KEY
);
ALTER TABLE Example
    ADD COLUMN name VARCHAR(32);
ALTER TABLE Example
    MODIFY COLUMN name VARCHAR(120) NOT NULL;
```

When executed the first time against a MySQL database, it outputs the following:

```
mysql> SOURCE /.../example-table.sql
Query OK, 0 rows affected (0.04 sec)
Query OK, 0 rows affected (0.04 sec)
Records: 0  Duplicates: 0  Warnings: 0
Query OK, 0 rows affected (0.10 sec)
Records: 0  Duplicates: 0  Warnings: 0
```

If it is executed again, it outputs the following:

```
ERROR 1050 (42S01): Table 'Example' already exists
ERROR 1060 (42S21): Duplicate column name 'name'
Query OK, 0 rows affected (0.03 sec)
Records: 0  Duplicates: 0  Warnings: 0
```

In this example, the attempt to create the Example table failed because that table already existed, but it did *not* stop the following statements from executing. The next statement, adding the name field to the Example table, *also* failed, for a similar reason: that field already existed. It did not prevent the next statement from executing, though. The final statement, modifying the same name field to change its size, did *not* fail. Instead, it re-applied that same modification to the field, which did not *change* anything because it had already been modified.

This approach still has some risk — back databases up before changing them!

The alteration of existing fields in a table can result in loss of data in several ways: Changing from one data type to another may alter data in undesirable ways. Altering any of the various string-type fields (VARCHAR in the example above) to make their allocated size smaller will, at best, truncate any existing data to fit into that new, smaller size. To avoid accidental permanent loss of data, even during development, it is always a good idea to back up a database before applying any changes. If all goes well, that backup can be deleted later, but if something goes awry, the database can be restored to its last state before those changes were attempted.

In general, so long as changes made are not removing data, whether by removing the fields that those data reside in or changing the field type to something that is not compatible with some or all of the existing data in a table, this process is *reasonably* safe.

This safety may not exist in other databases!

Though MySQL handles this sort of re-running of SQL with a fair degree of grace and safety, that may not hold true for other database engines. If in doubt, check first before adopting this kind of process!

For example, using the dependencies described earlier, in the *Figuring out where to start with use cases* section, and focusing on the tables for storing Artisan and Product business object data:

- The SQL needed to define an Artisans table will be created in a file named 000010-Artisan-table-definition.sql.
- The SQL defining a Products table will be created in 000020-Product-table-definition.sql, with the expectation that the Product objects in that table will have a relationship to objects in the Artisans table.

The SQL field definitions shown in *Figure 13.2* (and written in more detail in the chapter repository at hms-core/database/examples/base-business-object.sql) provide a good starting point for the initial creation of tables in a back-end data store for the business objects that relate in the code. The fields listed there and defined in the example SQL file are common to all classes that derive from BaseBusinessObject.

Capturing these table definitions in code in some fashion allows those definitions to live in the project that they relate to, next to the application code that will use those tables. That will make keeping changes that need to be made in both application and database code in sync considerably easier. All that remains, once those SQL files are in place and ready to be applied to the database, is a mechanism to actually do that. The HMS engineers decide, as a starting point, to simply write a Python script that will handle that. That script (`hms-core/database/HMS/implementation/apply-sql.py`) handles executing a backup of the database, then applying all the SQL files in the directory it resides in. This same script can also be executed as part of a build process, allowing database changes to be made as part of a build. Depending on how any shared databases are hosted, it may need to be tweaked to save the backup files it generates to a permanent location, but that is a problem that can be solved later.

> **There are other tools available**
>
> While this scripted approach is viable, there are tools available that may be a better fit for more complex scenarios. One such is HashiCorp's Terraform (`https://www.hashicorp.com/products/terraform`), which can also manage cloud infrastructure and resources, and offers a free tier that allows up to 500 resources to be managed per month as of early 2025. Even when some other tool is available, understanding how database changes can (and should) be propagated in a less automated fashion is important to understand.

The final consideration with respect to managing database entities is recognizing that changes made to a database used by application and service code should be tested. Like unit tests written against code, tests against the database operations should ideally be repeatable and able to be run locally, even if only against an engineer's local development database. Unlike unit tests, these tests must be able to connect to and work with the actual database in order to prove that all database operations executed by the code perform in an expected manner. If the ability to execute the test suite against a production database is needed, they should also take steps to limit the exposure of test data to end users and to clean up any test data generated when the suite is run. At a minimum, checking that columns created or altered exist, are of the correct type, and have all the desired constraints associated with them can be tested by examining them directly in the database. In MySQL, that will be facilitated by using the `SHOW COLUMNS` statement (`https://dev.mysql.com/doc/refman/8.4/en/show-columns.html`), and all of the RDBMS discussed here have an equivalent mechanism to retrieve table column details.

With these decisions made, the HMS engineers have all the pieces they need to be able to implement the business objects needed for the use cases described above: The strategy for defining those business object classes was determined earlier (in *Chapter 11*). Database set-up for local development has been defined. A basic data structure within the database has been defined that will be used as a starting point for creating the tables that relate to each business object. The processes for making and managing database changes have been defined, and some basic tooling for executing those changes has been written. All that remains at this point is defining the business objects' structures, creating the database elements that relate to them, implementing the business object classes, and testing them with an eye towards the use cases that need to be supported.

Implementing the business objects

There are two business object classes that need to be defined with data persistence, Artisan and Product. In order for those to have data persistence, following the current design intention, they will need to derive from a common BaseDataObject class, which will be defined as an **Abstract Base Class (ABC)**. The Artisan class, since it represents an artisan user, and business policy requires that artisans' addresses need to be available, will also need to incorporate an address data structure. The kind of data that an address object would store and manage — a simple mailing address — is not limited to being associated with an Artisan. It could also be part of an order later, so the data structure, while not a business object, will be defined as a separate Address class that can be composed or aggregated into other classes as needed.

Composition and aggregation

Composition in an OOP context means that one object is considered to be part of another. The implication in that relationship is that the composed object cannot exist without the object that it is composed into. The Artisan/Address relationship described is a composition relationship.

Aggregation, on the other hand, means that one object can own or access another object, and that owned object is independent of the owner. The Artisan/Product relationship that will be developed here is an aggregation relationship: Even though there are business rules that do not allow a Product to exist without an owning Artisan, the objects themselves are distinct from each other.

The HMS engineers also know that future use cases will include a detail view of a product on the site, and the ability for a customer end user to be able to search for products. The detail view page use case will have a need for zero-to-many product images that relate to the Product. Those images can also be treated as business objects, and will eventually be defined as a ProductImage class. The search use case implies a need for some sort of metadata storage that will tie characteristics like what a product is made of, what kind of product it is (furniture vs. clothing, perhaps), and other descriptive data points. Those considerations for the future use cases, they feel, will not need to have the complexity of a full-blown business object implementation, but they will be eventual requirements, so the engineers include them in their planning documentation now.

Their approach to implementing the business objects that do relate to the initial use cases they they will work on

- Define the business-object classes, inheriting from BaseDataObject, and including all the descriptive elements that will eventually be needed, like title and description properties.

- Generate a JSON schema that captures the data-structure requirements, saving the schema for each object as a reference document.

- Use those JSON schema documents to define table fields/columns in the relevant SQL file that defines the table.

- Write several different varieties of tests for each business object class, including unit tests, some level of system/integration testing that checks that data is persisted correctly, and an end-to-end test for each use case.

Their initial design, accounting for all the fields that the engineers can identify that various classes need, is shown in *Figure 13.3*. Since the Artisan class is a dependency for the Product class, that will be the first business object class they address. Since the Artisan class needs to persist data, it needs to derive from the BaseDataObject ABC, and that is where the actual implementation efforts will begin.

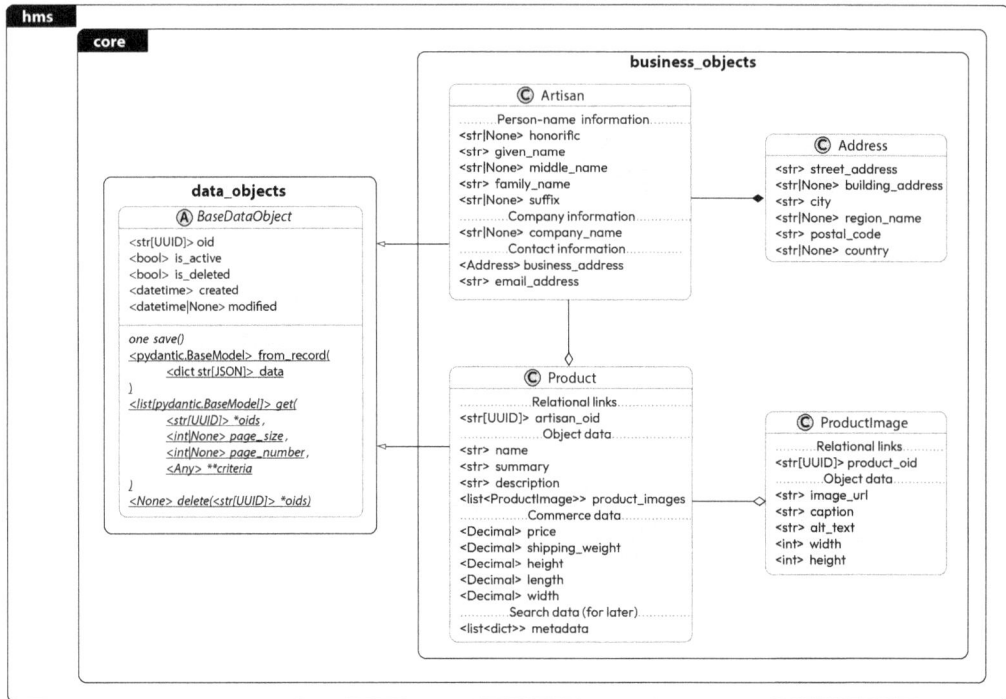

Figure 13.3: The business object classes, with data persistence, being built in this chapter

Finalizing the BaseDataObject implementation

These changes are tagged in the GitHub repo as `CH-13-Final-BaseDataObject`

The field implementations for the `BaseDataObject` ABC were established earlier, in the *Reviewing and revising the BaseDataObject ABC* section, so all that really remains is working out the methods shown in that class in *Figure 13.3*. Those methods provide the baseline **C**RUD (**C**reate, **R**ead, **U**pdate, **D**elete) functionality for business objects, or at least the requirements for their implementation in derived classes.

In the order they are shown in the BaseDataObject class in the figure, those methods are:

- save — an abstract instance method that will be called to write the state data of the object to the database, whether that operation is the creation of a new record or an update to an existing record.

- from_record — a class helper method that provides a mechanism for converting a record data structure retrieved from the database into an instance of the class.

- get — an abstract class method that will be called to retrieve any number of business objects whose state data is populated from their corresponding records in the database. This method is intended to be a general-purpose retrieval, supporting filtering, sorting, and pagination of records retrieved from the database, and thus of the corresponding business objects retrieved.

- delete — an abstract class method that will be called to perform actual, physical record deletions of one or more business object records in the database.

- Initially, the save method is defined as an abstract method more because it is expected to need different inner workings for each business object, in the form of a different SQL query string for each concrete business object type. Making save an abstract method, and thus requiring each derived class to implement its own version of that method, is the simplest method of both requiring the functionality and **encapsulating** those differences, keeping the differences for each class associated with the classes themselves. It would also be possible, technically, to make the SQL query string the point of encapsulation, and have a single, concrete save method defined in BaseDataObject that would build the create-or-update query using that string as a template. Implementing that approach instead would reduce the amount of additional code needed for the derived, concrete classes, but would not change how much testing would be needed for them: Each concrete class would still need, at a minimum, a set of database tests for the creation and update of records. It would also add to the testing needed for the BaseDataObject class. For the initial implementation, the HMS engineers decide that taking a brute force approach is a better use of their time.

Don't be afraid to go down a brute force path!

Taking a brute force approach is not necessarily a bad thing, for all that **elegance in code** is commonly touted as a desirable thing. While elegant code — code that is clean, concise, and easily understandable — *will* be easier to read and maintain, at the end of the day, an engineer's initial goal is *working* code. It can always be refined later!

The process for creating an instance of a class that derives from `BaseDataObject` is captured in the `from_record` class method. This method is intended to accept query result input in two forms: One is expected in database connection packages that follow the *Python Database API Specification* defined in PEP-249 (`https://peps.python.org/pep-0249/`): a `list` of `tuple` values, each containing the *name* of the field and its *value*, in that order. An example of just such a result for a `BaseDataObject`-derived class with no additional fields is:

```
LIST_OF_TUPLES = [
    ('oid', UUID('175f29e8-889a-466f-b0ab-7691fba25237')),
    ('is_active', False),
    ('is_deleted', False),
    ('created', datetime.datetime(2025, 1, 25, 16, 51)),
    ('modified', None)
]
```

This structure can also be converted directly to a `dict` — each `tuple` in the `list` captures the key (field name) and value needed for that — and the conversion of results into a `dict` is a common feature in many database connector APIs, even though it is *not* part of the PEP-249 standards (see *Frequently Asked Questions* there for the reasons why: (`https://peps.python.org/pep-0249/#frequently-asked-questions`). The example above, converted to a `dict`, looks like this:

```
# The conversion of the list of tuples above to a dict
# with dict(LIST_OF_TUPLES)
{
    'created': datetime.datetime(2025, 1, 25, 16, 51,),
    'is_active': False,
    'is_deleted': False,
    'modified': None,
    'oid': UUID('175f29e8-889a-466f-b0ab-7691fba25237')
}
```

Since the business object classes are defined as Pydantic models, and Pydantic models can accept dict values during object creation, the entire process implemented in the from_record class method reduces to nothing more than creating a dict from a list of tuples when needed, then creating an instance of the class using that dict, like this:

```python
@classmethod
def from_record(
    cls,
    data: dict[str, Any] | list[tuple[str, Any]]
) -> BaseModel:
    if isinstance(data, tuple):
        data = dict(data)
    return cls(**data)
```

The get method for the BaseDataObject class is, hands down, the most complex method that will need to be implemented for any concrete class that derives from that class. Consider, again, the first use case noted earlier:

> *A Customer needs to be able to view a list of the most recently available Products available on the site, including the Product name, a summary description of the Product, a link to a Product detail view, and at least one image, if one is available, for the Product in question.*

Combining that with some of the business rules also noted earlier, that Product items in the list need to be approved (is_active), not deleted (is_deleted), *and* related to an Artisan that meets those same criteria, leads to a very complex query for this apparently simple use case. While Python's support for complex filtering is very good, and could be applied to this use case either as a list comprehension or some custom function applied to an iterable using the built-in filter function, there would be trade-offs.

List comprehensions

A **list comprehension** (https://docs.python.org/3.11/tutorial/datastructures.html#list-comprehensions) is a built-in syntax for generating lists whose members can be filtered and manipulated during creation. They are, in many ways, just an alternative to the built-in filter() function (https://docs.python.org/3.11/library/functions.html#filter).

The first, and potentially most significant trade-off relates to an expected requirement for this use case: that the results for any given retrieval of a `Product` list should be in pages of data — subsets of all of the available items, of some predetermined length — that the end user customer can move through on the site. Though that was not explicitly noted in the use case, it is a safe assumption: if retrieving ten products to display takes half a second, for example, then retrieving a hundred products taking fifty seconds is not an unreasonable assumption.

That sort of delay is not a good user experience, and paging the results is a typical solution to that problem. However, that means that the back-end query, in order to provide all possible records that *might* apply to the filtered results before reducing the results to those for a given page, would have to either get *every* record, or the code would have to make *multiple* queries, and assemble the final results from the filtered results of those queries. Those are both feasible approaches, but they will become less efficient over time, as the number of records grows.

A more efficient approach would be to leverage the database's capabilities to handle the business rules involved — databases are *good* at that sort of thing, so it just makes sense. A typical approach would involve the creation of a **view** — a virtual table that makes some subset of the data in one or more tables available to be queried in the same manner as a regular table. Taking that approach would mean adding a new parameter to the get method, something that would allow it to query from the main table, or from some known view that returns the same data structure, but that applies the relevant business rules as filters. The HMS engineers decide to call that parameter `db_source_name`, and add it to the get method, but it will not be used until the first concrete business object class is defined, so, for the time being, that is all that they need to do about it.

Filtering and sorting also have to be addressed in some manner. That first use case specifically mentions *most recently available Products available on the site*, which is a good indicator that sorting is in play there, even if the filtering is all handled by targeting a use-case-specific view instead of the main table. There are at least two ways to handle both filtering and sorting with respect to the get method. The first way is to write separate methods, as many as one per use case, that provide the needed functionality for any given use case. That is a very brute force approach, and while it is not categorically a bad approach, it has some significant trade-offs. The first trade-off is that if there are changes made to the backing database structure, there is a good possibility that every use-case-specific method would have to be altered accordingly.

At a minimum, each and every one would have to be examined to determine if changes were needed. The second trade-off is that it would very likely require a fair amount of duplication of code, though if the design of the methods involved is approached with discipline and caution, that possibility may be significantly reduced, or even eliminated. Duplication of code is not necessarily a bad thing: if the needs driving the duplicate code are distinct, forcing a single body of code to serve those multiple needs introduces dependencies that may complicate changes later as those driving needs' requirements change. Duplicating code instead, preserving the isolation of the code responsible for serving them, will eliminate that concern.

Another approach that could be taken, that leverages the original design of the method, would be to allow filter- and sort-criteria values to be passed with specifically structured names to indicate what the related field is, what the criteria value is, and what the criteria operation for that field and value is. For example: Assume there is a `Person` business object class defined, deriving from `BaseDataObject`, that the class defines `given_name` and `family_name` fields, and that it already has all of the database entities required for it in place. Given the current signature for the get method, and ignoring the `oids`, `db_source_name`, `page_size`, and `page_number` parameters for illustration purposes, the already-defined criteria parameter already supports direct equality criteria like these examples:

```
# Retrieve all Person objects named John Dough
people = Person.get(given_name='John', family_name='Dough')
# Retrieve all person objects with family_name of Dough
people = Person.get(family_name='Dough')
```

By allowing specific variations of field names like `sort_given_name`, the calling code could indicate that the results should be sorted by the field or fields that `sort_` was prepended to, and the direction of that sort — ASC for ascending or DESC for descending — could be indicated:

```
# Retrieve all person objects with family_name of Dough
# and sort (alphabetize) them by given_name
people = Person.get(
    family_name='Dough', sort_given_name='ASC'
)
```

Similarly, appending what might be called an operation tag to a field name — _neq for **not-eq**ual, _lt for **less-than**, _lte for **less-than-or-equal-to**, and so on — could allow calling code to make fairly complex queries. For example, getting every Person object created during January of 2025, and sorting them by family (last) name, then given (first) name would look like this:

```python
# Retrieve all person objects created in Jan-2025, and
# sort them by family_name then given_name
people = Person.get(
    sort_family_name='ASC', sort_given_name='ASC',
    created_gte='2025-01-01', created_lte='2025-01-31'
)
```

> **This approach is version-sensitive!**
>
> This approach, at least for the sort_ field prefix, will behave unpredictably in Python versions earlier than 3.7. Prior to that version, the sequence of keys in the built-in dict type (which is all that the **criteria parameter is, ultimately) was arbitrary. Starting with Python 3.7, the sequence of keys, whether printed or iterated over, was preserved. For example, if a function or method were called with the keyword arguments second=1, sort_second=2, first=3, sort_first=4, they would print (but *not* pprint) in that order, and iteration over them would also be in that order. Since the sort_-prefixed names would be used to create a SQL ORDER BY second, first clause, that sequence difference could easily result in unexpected sort-order results in earlier Python versions.

These aspects of the get method open up an interesting possibility: If the main SQL needed to retrieve records regardless of the filtering (a WHERE clause) and sorting (an ORDER BY clause) is moved into its own class-specific entity, then the get method can be written in such a way that it no longer needs to be abstract — the exact same processes can be applied to the varied SQL source, wherever it comes from, to add filtering criteria and sorting instructions, before the SQL is executed and the resulting records are used to create the list of objects that will be returned.

After some discussion and debate about the best path forward, the HMS engineers decide to alter BaseDataObject as shown in *Figure 13.4*.

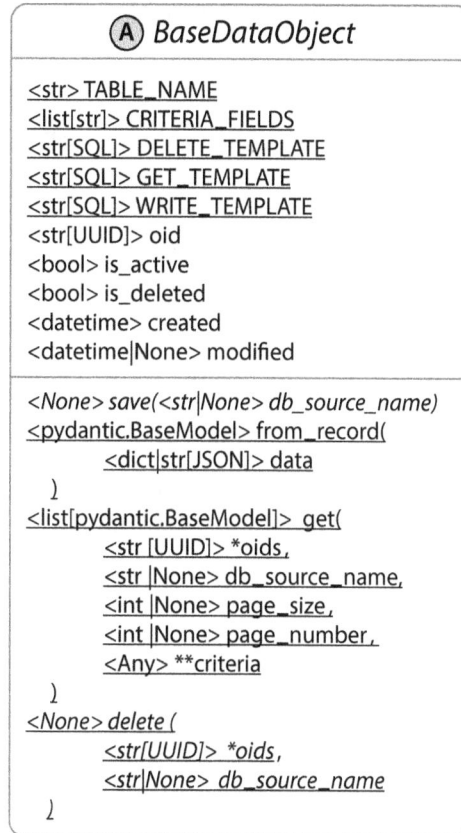

Figure 13.4: The revised BaseDataObject

Their changes are:

- Adding a TABLE_NAME class attribute that will store the default table name in the database that the get, delete, and save methods will use, but that can be overridden by passing a different table name in db_source_name.

- Adding a CRITERIA_FIELDS class attribute, a list that keeps track of the names of the fields that are available outside the JSON field, and that are available to be used as filtering or sorting criteria.

- Adding DELETE_TEMPLATE, GET_TEMPLATE, and WRITE_TEMPLATE class attributes that will be used to provide SQL templates for the delete, get, and save methods, respectively, to use as a starting point to build queries.

- Defining a common object_state field to be defined in the database tables for business objects that will store the object state data, serialized to a JSON value.

- Adding the build_limit_clause, build_order_by_clause, and build_where_clause helper functions, which will be called by the get method to create the related SQL clauses for a query. The build_where_clause helper function will also be used to provide common criteria handling for the delete method.

- Converting the delete, get, and save methods to concrete methods, and implementing them in BaseDataObject, making use of the changes above.

- Defining criteria variations for the get method to allow checks for equality, inequality, greater- and less-than variations, sub-string criteria, and value-membership criteria, as well as record sorting.

These changes allow the BaseDataObject ABC to provide all of the basic structure for the CRUD operations methods needed in one location, while providing options for overrides in specific business object classes should the need arise.

See the complete changes in the repository

The collected changes made here came to nearly 400 lines of code — far too many to reproduce in the book, but they are all available in the chapter repository's data_objects.py module, committed in the CH-13-Final-BaseDataObject tag.

Note that the get method changes define criteria prefixes and suffixes that allow the code to specify the various selection criteria and sort-ordering noted in the list above.

With the final implementation of BaseDataObject complete, the process for implementing a specific, concrete business object class involves only four steps, the first three of which are either very simple or involve code structures already shown:

- Define the class, deriving from both BaseDataObject and Pydantic's BaseModel Abstract Base Classes.

- Add any additional fields needed for the concrete class, providing any constraints and field properties needed.

- Add any of those fields that are expected to be needed for some query use case to the new class' CRITERIA_FIELDS class attribute.

- Write the SQL that will create the table for the class, and add it to the SQL files in the project.

The last item is worth a more detailed examination, but the first three can be worked through for the Artisan and Product business object classes, independent of that. Using the diagram in *Figure 13.3*, there is enough information to implement those classes with the data persistence provided by BaseDataObject as fully functional business objects.

The Artisan business object implementation

> These changes are tagged in the GitHub repo as CH-13-Artisan-and-Address

In the context of HMS' systems, an **Artisan** is a person or company that creates one-of-a-kind, hand-made products. The diagram in *Figure 13.3* captures those variants by allowing both personal names — given_name, family_name, and so on — and an optional company_name that is intended to be displayed instead of the personal names if it exists for a given Artisan.

HMS, as a company, needs to be able to contact an Artisan, usually by email, but they can also envision a need for sending physical mail. Artisan objects and their records, then, need to keep track of both an email and a physical mailing address. The email address is a simple string value, though it should be validated as being well-formed, ideally.

> **Email validation and Pydantic**
>
> Email validation comes in two forms: validating that an address is well-formed, following the expected structure, and actually verifying that the email address exists and that someone is paying attention to it. For the first validation type, Pydantic provides two string types that validate email addresses in at least two standard forms. See https://docs.pydantic.dev/2.0/usage/types/string_types/ for the EmailStr and NameEmail types it provides. The second validation requires sending an email to the address and having the recipient verify that it was received in some fashion. A typical approach is to send a validation link to the email address, and when that link is followed, the address is flagged as validated in some fashion. This latter approach is outside the scope of this book, but examples are easily found online.

The mailing address is, itself, another complex data structure, with its own fields and rules for the validation of those fields' values. This implementation will use a separate Pydantic model, an Address class, that does not, itself, need to be persisted to the database, and **compose** it within the Artisan class so that it has an Address object within it. Address objects, at present, are not expected to ever need to be stored except as members of other classes: An Artisan has one address, and an Order would be expected to have one or two — one for shipping, and one for billing — but none of these need to exist as distinct database records, or thus as BaseDataObject-derived classes.

The products field has some similarities to the business_address field, in that it is composed in the Artisan class. There are other considerations, though, since products is a *list* of objects. The first consideration is that each Product is its own business object instance, relating to an Artisan by matching the Artisan.oid to the Product.artisan_oid shown in *Figure 13.3*. As time goes on, especially if there is no active effort to delete Product records from the database, any process for getting any number of Artisan objects that also includes all of their related Product objects will get slower and slower as more and more Product objects are associated with their Artisan objects. As it turns out, implementing that sort of field structure in a Pydantic model class is more complicated than might be assumed. That is, while it is possible to define the products field in a way that looks like it should work, like so:

```
products: list[Product | None] = Field(
    title='Products',
    default_factory=list,
    description='The collection of Products, active '
    'or not, deleted or not, associated with the '
    'Artisan.'
)
```

... creating a meaningful examples attribute on the field definition is complex, and can become more time-consuming than it is worth. An alternative that would allow Artisan.products to fetch the relevant Product objects when necessary, and store those so that only one database query would need to be made for the products of any given Artisan object is not difficult to achieve. It might look something like this:

```
@property
def products(self) -> list[Product]:
    """
    Gets and caches the list ofProduct objects
    associated with the instance.
```

```
    """
    if getattr( self, '_products', None) is None:
        self._products = Product.get(
            artisan_oid = self.oid
        )
    return self._products
```

This approach would work, but it would not solve the potential volume-of-records concern noted earlier. It would also tend to lead to multiple database requests, any of which could return large result sets, running through the single database connector object that has been defined already. That, in turn, would eventually lead to slow-performing data loads for use cases where multiple Artisans with large collections of Products need to be fetched. It also breaks the JSON schema generation functionality of the Artisan object that Pydantic provides for classes deriving from the BaseModel class shown earlier.

After thinking on the use cases that they are concerned with now, and looking ahead to the potential use cases where multiple Artisans with their complete collection of Products might be needed, the HMS engineers decide that the process of joining lists of Artisans and Products is really a function of the API endpoint being called, not of the business objects themselves. In those cases, the process they envision would involve:

- Using the get method of the main business object to retrieve the relevant main list of objects — for example, calling Product.get() to get the first page of the most recent products.
- Collecting the relational ID field values from that object list and using it as an _in criteria field for the get method of the related business object type to retrieve all the objects that are related to any object in the first list — for example, calling Artisan.get(artisan_oid_in=(artisan_oids).
- Collating those results into a single, final result set, using a new API-specific model class to define and validate the data structure, and to provide the JSON schema that will be used to publish the OAS data contract for the endpoints that it relates to.

A preliminary (and, at this point, untested) implementation that does all this looks like this:

```
from hms.core.business_objects import Product, Artisan
class APIProductListItem(Product):
    artisan: Artisan | None = Field(
        title='Artisan', default=None,
        description='The Artisan related to the Product'
    )
```

```python
def get_recent_products(
    db_source_name: str | None = None,
    page_size: int | None = None,
    page_number: int | None = None,
    **criteria: Any
) -> list[APIProductListItem]:
    # Make a single query to get the relevant products
    products = Product.get(
        db_source_name = db_source_name,
        page_size = page_size,
        page_number = page_number,
        **criteria
    )
    # Gather the artisan oids to use to fetch the
    # related artisans
    artisan_oids = tuple(
        set([product.artisan_oid for product in products])
    )
    # Get those artisans, storing them as a dict by
    # their oids
    artisans = {
        artisan.oid: artisan
        for artisan in Artisan.get(*artisan_oids)
    }
    # create the list of APIProductListItem results
    results = [
        APIProductListItem(**product.model_dump())
        for product in products
    ]
    # associate the related artisans
    for result in results:
        result.artisan = artisans.get(result.artisan_oid)
    return results
```

This implementation strategy, they feel, is more flexible and will be easier to work with on a longer-term basis, even though it means adding new model classes for API results and new functions to create the relevant results.

The final implementations of the Address and Artisan classes, with docstrings, comments, and optional field parameters removed for brevity, are:

```
class Address(BaseModel):
    street_address: str = Field()
    building_address: str | None = Field()
    city: str = Field()
    region_name: str | None = Field()
    postal_code: str = Field()
    country: str | None = Field()
class Artisan(BaseModel, BaseDataObject):
    honorific: str | None = Field()
    given_name: str = Field()
    middle_name: str | None = Field()
    family_name: str = Field()
    suffix: str | None = Field()
    company_name: str | None = Field()
    business_address: Address = Field()
    email_address: EmailStr | NameEmail = Field()
```

The next step, then, is to finish defining the Product business object class and any additional classes relating to it. In the main, there is little that needs to be considered there that has not been examined in working through the Artisan class definition, though there are some variations on the themes explored during the creation of the Artisan class.

The Product business object implementation

These changes are tagged in the GitHub repo as CH-13-Product-and-ProductImage

The Product business object shown in *Figure 13.3* is a bit more complex than the Artisan class, and illustrates some new concepts for handling data structures in the context of a business object's design:

- It has an additional field, artisan_oid, that provides the relationship key between a Product and the Artisan that the Product is associated with.
- It also has a list of ProductImage data structures that are expected to be stored in their own table, and have to be integrated into the data retrieval processes for a Product.

- Finally, it captures a metadata structure that, while only loosely defined at this point, also has to be accounted for.

Although there is no explicit use case defined yet that requires that artisan_oid be available as a criteria parameter name that the get class method will recognize, it is a safe assumption that there will be one somewhere along the line. Making it available as a criteria name will allow queries that start with an Artisan, and retrieve that Artisan's Product items — the inverse of the data access example for the API Product listing shown earlier. It is not difficult to imagine use cases that could take advantage of this capability: variations of an Artisan page that show all of the Products that an Artisan has available could be useful to customers, and would almost certainly be useful for site administrators responsible for managing Artisan user accounts.

The implementation required to allow the artisan_oid field as criteria for query purposes in the get method is relatively trivial. BaseDataObject already defines a class attribute, CRITERIA_FIELDS, that captures the standard fields, so all that really needs to happen is to add artisan_oid to the Product class attribute, like this:

```python
from typing import ClassVar
class Product(BaseModel, BaseDataObject):
    CRITERIA_FIELDS: ClassVar[list[str]] = \
        BaseDataObject.CRITERIA_FIELDS + ['artisan_oid']
```

Why annotate this as a ClassVar?

Pydantic models assume that any attribute that *looks* like a field needs to be *handled* as one. If the ClassVar[list[str]] annotation shown here is not applied, or if it follows the list[str] pattern of the attribute in BaseDataObject, it will, respectively, raise an error, or include the CRITERIA_FIELDS attribute in the schema for the class, which is not desired behavior.

Handling of product images in the system faces similar challenges to the Artisan-Product relationship that was discussed in the design and implementation of the Artisan class. Specifically, there is a one-to-many relationship from a given Product to its related ProductImage objects, though in their experience, the HMS staff feel confident that it is less likely for a single Product to have related images to the same degree that Artisans have Products.

There is also a much stronger possibility that an Artisan may want to change out one or more product images, and the review process anticipated for that is expected to be much simpler — all that is really needed is for someone on the HMS staff to look at the image, make sure it is acceptable, and approve it. All of these, taken together, lead to storing image data structures separately from the products they are associated with, in their own database table. That will make the image-approval process faster and easier to implement, when it comes time to implement it, and keep that implementation very simple.

However, that also means that the Product class has to change how it retrieves data. Consider three basic permutations of Product records:

- One that has *no* associated images.
- One that has *one* and only one associated image, intended for use as the display image for the product in product listings and detail views.
- One that has *multiple* images that will be used in a product detail view to create an image carousel, with *one* of those images also being designated as the display image for product listings.

In the first case, the standard query that is supported by the default get method would suffice. That is, ignoring pagination needs for illustrative purposes, making a call like:

```
Product.get(sort_created_date='desc')
```

...would retrieve all of the product records, but no images. It would be possible to build the Product creation and update processes so that they would accept image uploads, handle storing them where they would be accessed by a customer's browser, *and* populate the relevant Product record with a copy of the relevant ProductImage records. Taking that approach would require duplication of data across those two tables, though, which would have to be managed carefully to avoid discrepancies between the data in those tables. Going down that path would, though, allow the default get method to retrieve all of the images associated with a Product in a single query, solving for all three of the permutations listed above.

Another approach would be to change the SQL that is used by the default get method to retrieve both the Product record and *one* ProductImage record that relates, if one exists. That would involve overriding the default BaseDataObject.get, so that Product.get has its own code that handles both of the first two permutations, extracting and creating the single ProductImage object, and including them in each Product record as needed. That does not address the third permutation at all, though, as it would limit the number of related images retrieved to one record.

After some reflection on how the proposed approach for fetching and joining lists of Artisans and Products described earlier works, the HMS engineers come to the conclusion that the same approach could be implemented in all of the various get methods where there are source records for the main business object type that have related records of some other type associated with them. An expected trade-off using this approach is that instead of making one query with the current parameters supplied to the get call, there would be two or more — one for the main object, and one more for each related type. Using the Artisan → Product → ProductImage types as an example, and assuming that get parameters yield two or more Artisan objects, the process breaks out into ten steps:

- The get method retrieves the relevant Artisan records, just like it does currently, with an interim result that is a list of Artisan business objects.

- The artisan_oid values that need to be passed to Product.get are extracted from the interim list of Artisan objects.

- The collection of all products that relate to any of the artisans in the interim results is retrieved by passing the collection of artisan_oid values to Product.get(artisan_oid_in=artisan_oids).

- The Product.get method collects all of the product_oid values that need to be passed to ProductImage.get, and calls that method, returning interim product objects.

    - Those results are grouped into lists for each product_oid value.

    - The interim product results are finalized by adding the grouped product image results that correspond to a given product oid to those products.

    - Those results are returned.

- Those results are grouped into lists for each artisan_oid value.

- The interim results are finalized by adding the grouped product results that correspond to the oid value for each Artisan to those Artisans.

- Those results are returned.

Another trade-off that may not be obvious or expected is that *any* Artisan.get call that is made will return the entire tree of related objects, which may be more data than some use cases need, and may needlessly slow the process of returning simpler results for use cases that do not need the entire data set. For example, a simple listing of all Artisan names should be achievable with a single query, even if that query is made using the Artisan.get method.

With all of these factors in mind, the HMS engineers decide that it would be a better idea to create use-case-specific functionality, probably as freestanding functions, to handle the specifics for any given use case.

That leaves only the metadata field. This field was part of the original NoSQL data structure of Product objects in the system that is being replaced, and was intended and designed to allow products to be classified by any number of different key/value pair items. Some examples of metadata in the original system included classifications like:

- Material: various types of wood (*Cherry wood*, *Oak*, and *Pine*), metal (*Brass*, *Steel*), and fibers/fabrics (*Wool*, *Cotton*).
- Department: high-level classifications like *Clothing* and *Furniture*.
- Type: a basic name for the product, indicating what it is, including things like *Table* and *Scarf*.
- Color (self-explanatory)

In the original system, having metadata available as properties of individual product objects was an easy decision: To the database engine in question, it was just more structured data, and was available to be queried like any other structured data in the individual object records. In the current relational database design, it may or may not be fully supported; the team had not determined that by this point in the design process. Even if it is supported, a more pertinent question is whether it should be included or not.

The use cases where the metadata comes into play are all centered around the idea of being able to find similar products based on those metadata values. For example, if a customer is looking at a wool scarf product, and wants to find other scarves, they would click on a *Scarf* link on the page and be taken to a product-listing page with all of the products in the system that have been tagged with the *Scarf* metadata Type value. If queries based on metadata structures are not possible, or if they are, but there is a significant performance impact because of the nature of the query, the idea of moving metadata for all products into its own table structure just makes more sense. That table could be only a few fields:

- The metadata category name (Material, Department, Type, and Color from the list above, and any others that apply to any other products).
- The metadata value (see the examples in the list above).
- A product identifier oid that ties that metadata key/value pair to the product that it applies to.

With some specific index structures to optimize for specific use cases, indexing on product oid for product detail views, on the category_name and value fields for metadata-based search queries, and maybe a unique index across all three of those fields to assure that any given category_name/value combination can only be applied once to a given product oid, metadata retrievals for all of the expected use cases become very simple queries. The metadata details query for a single product would simply retrieve all key/value pairs for the product's oid. The search query would only need to return the relevant product oid values for any given set of key/value pairs, which would be fed into the Product.get class method to retrieve the relevant products.

With those thoughts in mind, the HMS engineers decide to move the metadata out of the Product structure entirely. Had they decided to keep it as a Product class property, the implementation would not have been difficult, looking something like this:

```
metadata: Optional[dict[str, str]] = Field(
    title='Product Metadata',
    description='The metadata names/values associated with the Product',
    default={}
)
```

...but the benefits they expect to gain outweigh that implementation, even though it is simple. Really, there are only two functional downsides they can envision related to taking this approach. The first is that an additional Product method will have to be implemented to handle the metadata items. The second is that it is simply easier when metadata is being saved for a product to delete all existing metadata and write a new, complete set. While it is possible to retrieve existing metadata, alter it, then save it back to the database, along with any new items, and to remove any metadata that is not part of the new set, the code and processes involved in doing that are significantly more complex, and probably not worth the effort and potential for ongoing maintenance of that code.

Now that the code-side business objects' definitions are complete, the time has come to implement the database tables that correspond to those classes, to store the state data for objects that the system will use. Because of the design decision made earlier, to store all object data in a single JSON field in the database, and only define separate, explicit database fields where there is a use case that needs to execute queries that use them, the process is simple enough that it is only barely worth describing, but there are permutations that bear closer examination.

Creating the tables for business object classes

These changes are tagged in the GitHub repo as `CH-13-Table-Definition`

Because the business objects are defined as Pydantic models, and because Pydantic models can generate JSON schemas that reflect their structure and constraints, those schemas provide an excellent starting point for defining table structures. An example of the schema-elements provided by the `BaseDataObject` class is in the chapter repository, in the `documentation/BaseDataObject-schema.yaml` file. Since a table definition would only really require the names, types, and default expectations for the fields that need to be created, stripping that file down to just those elements leads to this structure:

```yaml
title: BaseDataObject-schema-members
properties:
  oid:
    type: string
    format: uuid
  is_active:
    type: boolean
    default: false
  is_deleted:
    type: boolean
    default: false
  created:
    type: string
    format: date-time
  modified:
    anyOf:
    - type: string
      format: date-time
    - type: 'null'
    default: null
```

Using this schema as a starting point, a table template file was generated in the database/
examples/base-business-object.sql file in the repository. Stripped down to the functional
essentials, that definition looks like this:

```
CREATE TABLE BaseBusinessObject (
    oid CHAR(36) NOT NULL PRIMARY KEY,
    is_active TINYINT(1) DEFAULT 0 NOT NULL,
    is_deleted TINYINT(1) DEFAULT 0 NOT NULL,
    created DATETIME DEFAULT CURRENT_TIMESTAMP NOT NULL,
    modified DATETIME ON UPDATE CURRENT_TIMESTAMP NULL
)
```

The table-definition process that led to this follows some very simple rules:

- Every property name in the JSON schema is used as the field name in the table (the oid
  field in the class is represented in the database by a field called oid, for example).

- Where JSON schema formats are specified, those will affect the field type and/or the field
  size. For example:

  - The oid field in the schema has a format: uuid specified, which means that the
    database oid field needs to accommodate that structure. Since UUIDs are all 36
    characters long, that led to the CHAR(36) definition for the database oid field.

  - Similarly, the created field specifies a format: date-time, which is best repre-
    sented by the DATETIME field type for the database field of the same name.

  - The modified field is similar, but because the JSON schema specifies that it may
    either be a date-time value or null/None, it is allowed to have a NULL value in the
    table definition, unlike the other fields defined.

- Other types, like the type: boolean specifications for the is_active and is_deleted
  fields in the JSON schema, may not have a direct database-type equivalent, or may allow
  fields to be defined using a convenience type-name (BOOLEAN), but be converted to another
  equivalent type by the database itself (the TINYINT(1) specification is how MySQL prefers
  to define Boolean fields, for example).

What if the JSON field needed to be broken out into individual fields?

The same basic approach, starting with the JSON schema and defining table fields
accordingly, could be applied to table definitions.

The only field definition remaining that is not accounted for is the JSON field where the complete instance data is stored. That field, named object_state in the BaseDataObject.get class method defined earlier, simply adds a line to the field definitions shown above, leading to a final table template as:

```
CREATE TABLE BaseBusinessObject (
    oid CHAR(36) NOT NULL PRIMARY KEY,
    is_active TINYINT(1) DEFAULT 0 NOT NULL,
    is_deleted TINYINT(1) DEFAULT 0 NOT NULL,
    created DATETIME DEFAULT CURRENT_TIMESTAMP NOT NULL,
    modified DATETIME ON UPDATE CURRENT_TIMESTAMP NULL,
    object_state JSON NOT NULL
)
```

In cases where the business object classes do not add any new fields outside the object_state, all that will generally need to be done is to copy this template to a new SQL file and alter the table name. In cases where there are additional fields that need to be accounted for on the database side — in the case of the Products table, where the Product class introduces the artisan_oid field, relating a Product to its Artisan owner, for example — those additional fields will need to be added to the table definition, following the same rules for identifying field types and constraints noted earlier. Examples of the final table definitions for Artisan, Product, and ProductImage object records are provided in the chapter repository, in the database/implementation directory, numbered so that they will be run in the correct order by the apply-sql.py module in that same directory.

Summary

This chapter has walked through a lot of significant decisions, designs, and implementations, taking the project from virtually nothing implemented to fully fleshed-out implementations for the main business objects that were targeted as initial priorities. Those implementations include at least starting, if untested, implementations for persisting business object data in the back-end data store, and thoughts about how to manage changes to that data store have led to policy and procedure decisions and definitions to handle expected types of changes across the entire stack.

Although it did not dive deeply into verifying the identified use cases, that is, ultimately, a discussion that is better suited from the perspective of how the testing of code is implemented, and what those tests' goals are. That will be the primary focus of the next chapter, as it works through verification of the activities in those use cases.

Get This Book's PDF Version and Exclusive Extras

UNLOCK NOW

Scan the QR code (or go to packtpub.com/unlock). Search for this book by name, confirm the edition, and then follow the steps on the page.

Note: Keep your invoice handy. Purchases made directly from Packt don't require an invoice.

14
Testing the Business Objects

Testing source code is a critical piece of any mature software project. Rigorous testing, starting with unit tests, and with the addition of integration, system, end-to-end, and user acceptance tests where needed, can make or break the success of a project, providing assurance that the project's code is doing what it was designed to, and continues to perform in an expected manner as changes are made. What *rigorous* means, specifically, can vary from project to project, and from team to team — it can be very context-sensitive. Too much testing, too much rigor, can take time away from developing new features and functionality, with time being spent writing new tests and maintaining old ones. Too little testing opens the door for more bugs that have to go through whatever troubleshooting and remediation processes a team has in place. Finding the balance, making the decisions that define what the optimum level of testing rigor is for a project, requires understanding what tests do, how they work, what constraints should be in place, and a host of other factors.

This chapter will describe those factors, including:

- The purposes of, and goals for, testing
- The different types of testing that are likely to relate to a project
- What considerations need to be made and acted upon to establish testing standards for a project or a team
- Implementing a unit test suite for the HMS project

Technical requirements

The code for this chapter was written in Python 3.11, using `pipenv` for package and Python Virtual Environment management, as described earlier in this book. The chapter repository's `Pipfile` has all the required package dependencies across all of those options, and a functional **Python Virtual Environment (PVE)** can be initiated by running the following from the `CH-14-code/` `hms-core` project root directory:

```
pipenv sync –dev
pipenv sync
```

Verification that the packages needed are all installed can be accomplished by running

```
pipenv graph
```

...which should output something similar to this (though the versions may vary, and sub-dependencies have been omitted here):

```
coverage==7.6.12
email-validator==2.2.0
mccabe==0.7.0
mysql-connector-python==9.2.0
pycodestyle==2.12.1
pydantic==2.10.6
pyflakes==3.2.0
pytest==8.3.5
PyYAML==6.0.2
typeguard==4.4.2
```

Database setup will require a functional installation of MySQL `8.x` (the version in play while the chapter was being written was `8.0.41`). Installers for MySQL are available online at `https://dev.mysql.com/downloads/installer/`.

The complete collection of code for this chapter is provided in the chapter repository at `https://github.com/PacktPublishing/Hands-On-Software-Engineering-with-Python-Second-Edition/tree/main/CH14-code`.

The purposes of and goals for testing

The testing of code has one basic purpose: to prove that the code being tested behaves in an expected, predictable fashion. Unexpected or unpredictable behavior is almost always going to be classified as a **bug** in the code: something that needs to be fixed because it will lead to unwanted effects. The nature of those effects can fall into a number of categories, including violation of business rules or data expectations — usually high-priority concerns — user experience issues, gaps in process logic, and more. It is technically possible for unexpected behavior to *not* be a bug as well: perhaps the unexpected behavior is not going to cause any issues, it is just... unexpected. Tests that fail should terminate the execution of a test suite, in a manner that can be used to terminate a build process where they are being executed. Similarly, tests that raise errors should also terminate any processes that are relying on them to complete successfully.

Testing for expected results with valid input structures, commonly called a **happy path**, is important and is likely to be the first and most obvious target for test processes. Happy-path testing, as a quality assurance process, verifies that the planned scenarios and processes behave predictably, and that is important to verify. The predictable behavior being verified by test processes can — and probably should — also include verification that when code is presented with invalid inputs, it handles those as intended, or, at a minimum, reports those failures in an expected fashion. These tests are variously described as **unhappy path** or **sad path** tests.

Test processes should be **repeatable** and executable **on demand**, ideally in a manner that allows their execution to be integrated into software management, publication, and deployment processes. When that repeatable, on-demand goal is met, it opens several possibilities for performing quality assurance checks throughout the life of any body of work being executed against the code, including:

- Requiring tests to pass before the code is deployed to a production environment or distributed to end users
- Requiring tests executed against the results of a build and/or packaging process
- Requiring tests to pass before the code is run through build and/or packaging processes
- Requiring tests to pass before allowing it to be promoted to internal environments, where other teams would consume it for their own projects' purposes

- Requiring tests to pass before allowing changes to be merged in a Source Control Management (SCM) system, typically managed as a **pull request**

- Requiring tests to pass before allowing changes to be pushed to an SCM system, typically preventing the creation of a pull request

- Allowing spot-checks of changes to be made locally by an engineer as they are working through changes to the code

All of these provide checkpoints where code that is not meeting expectations can be prevented from progressing toward a final production deployment or publication. There is no reason why *all* of these checkpoints cannot be implemented. If there is no possibility for changes to occur as code gets promoted, built, packaged, or deployed, requiring additional tests in the transitions from one process to the next is going to be redundant and *functionally* not necessary.

Tests are typically organized into **suites**: collections of tests of a common type, intended to be run in their entirety, and that will collectively pass or fail as a single operation. A single test suite is intended to systematically evaluate the features and functionality of a code base, given some common purpose for the tests in the suite.

Test suites should ideally be executable with a single command, one that can be executed from a command line in a terminal. That capability allows tests to be run at any point in time, in any environment where the test code and the source code it tests are both available. That, then, allows engineers to run tests locally, during development, to test their work, as well as allowing test-execution processes to be run as part of SCM operations, build/packaging processes, and publishing/deployment processes.

These characteristics are common across a number of different types of test processes, despite some significant differences in what those process types are intended to test. The most common types of test processes, which we will examine next, include unit testing, integration testing, system testing, and end-to-end testing. All of these would benefit from being constructed as repeatable processes, being able to be executed on demand. Depending on what the code being tested actually *does*, there may be avenues available to automate at least *some* user acceptance testing as well.

The different types of testing

Each of the five basic categories of testing noted earlier has its own specific goals, though in certain types of software projects, or if a team managing the code and its test suites allows it, there may be a certain amount of overlap between those goals. In general, testing categories vary mainly in two areas:

- What scopes or processes those tests are concerned with
- What resources they are expected or allowed to have access to

It may be useful to think of the scopes and processes of tests in relation to their proximity to the original source code. That is, unit tests are closest to the source code in many respects, being concerned with individual software elements in the code, while integration tests are concerned with collections of those units, system tests are concerned with the entire collection of those units, and end-to-end tests are concerned with subsets of the system — including non-code resources — that work together to achieve some result. With that breakdown in mind, we will start by examining unit tests.

Unit testing

The goal of a unit test suite is to verify that every *individual unit of code* — every function, and every class member that has code involved in its implementation — functions as intended. Ideal, if not always realistic or mutually compatible, goals for unit tests include items from the **FIRST principles** of unit testing (from https://medium.com/pragmatic-programmers/unit-tests-are-first-fast-isolated-repeatable-self-verifying-and-timely-a83e8070698e). Specifically, following those principles, unit tests should be Fast, Isolated from (or Independent of) other units, Repeatable, Self-verifying, and Thorough.

The desire for unit tests to execute quickly (the *fast* item listed previously) is straightforward enough: If tests run quickly, then they will not slow down development, packaging, builds, or deployment when the test suite is integrated into one of those processes. The *fast* and *thorough* principles can conflict with each other, though. It is a good idea to make a conscious decision early on around which of those two is the more important consideration, if that prioritization can be made at all.

The *isolation* principle, taken to its logical extreme, would more or less require that tests for individual functions be written such that they are completely independent of other units in the source code. That would advocate, for example, that if the source code contains a function (A) that calls three other functions (B, C, and D), the tests for the A function should **mock** or **patch** calls to the B, C, and D functions so that they are not actually called as part of the test for the A function.

Mocking and patching

Mocking, in a unit testing context, involves the creation of a fake version of some object that mimics the behavior of a real object that is used in the context of the target code being tested. Patching temporarily replaces an actual implementation of a function, method, or object with something that the test process can control, allowing the target code to be called by a test without actually calling the element being patched. In Python, patching usually involves the creation of a mocked object, whose behaviors can be controlled in order to simulate specific outputs or values, which can then be used to test specific execution scenarios for the target code being tested.

This degree of isolation has one noteworthy advantage to it: If a given test fails, it is a *given* that the cause of the failure is within the target of the test, not in some dependency of that target. That is, in the example with functions A, B, C, and D, if a fully-isolated test executing against function A fails, it will *not* be because of some failure in functions B, C, or D. There are trade-offs, though: First, in order to thoroughly test the interactions between functions A, B, C, and D, a separate integration test will be needed. Secondly, the test for A may become substantially more complicated, since it would have to mock or patch results coming back from functions B, C, and D for *all* of the scenarios that the test of A is executing tests for. As isolation between source code units is relaxed, a unit test suite will start to overlap more and more with *integration testing* principles.

How much isolation is really needed (unit- and integration-testing overlap)?

Consideration should be given to how much isolation is really needed or useful in unit tests, and whether the inclusion of integration testing between source-code components is tolerable, or perhaps even desirable. Purely as a statement of opinion, I prefer to allow the implicit integration testing that comes with not mocking/patching all of a test target's in-code dependencies, but I *also* advocate mocking/patching external dependencies when it is useful to do so — and *always* in cases where those dependencies are external systems.

Unit tests being *repeatable* has already been discussed as a common characteristic of all test suites. The only additional consideration that feels worth mentioning in this context is the idea that the execution of a given unit test should reach the same pass/success every time it is run.

If a test fails intermittently, that may be a clue that some part of the code being tested would benefit from adding more *isolation* — mocking or patching some dependency that behaves in an unpredictable fashion — or that the dependency itself needs some attention to make it behave more reliably.

The idea of tests in a suite being *self-verifying* is as much a removal of human evaluation as anything else. That is, tests should pass or fail on their own, without needing evaluation or interpretation by a human being. If there are specific paths through the code that require human evaluation, and that need for evaluation cannot be removed by altering the code, that is worth consideration for implementing as a variant of a user acceptance testing process.

The final item (that tests should be *thorough*) is one that has a surprising amount of negotiation potential, depending on team-level and organizational priorities. Under ideal circumstances, *every* piece of code should be tested, and tested with every possible combination of inputs. That is not a realistic approach, though: it is not difficult to come up with examples of tests for very simple functions that would take years, centuries, or even millennia to execute completely. Remember that the goal of a unit test suite is simply to show that every unit in the code being tested behaves as intended. A more specific approach to reaching that goal would be to write tests that exercise every line of the code being tested. That would entail providing test parameters that hit every decision point present in that target code, which implies examining the target code and crafting parameters to use during testing that will make all of those decisions. Ultimately, this is simply an exercise in *generating a reasonable, meaningful subset of parameter values* to execute tests with.

Code coverage: What to make of it

The idea of exercising every line of code in the target code being tested is just another way of expressing the idea of **code coverage** in testing. Code coverage is, simply, a measure or metric that shows how much of the source code is actually exercised by a test suite. It is a contentious subject, at best: Detractors argue, with some justification, that it does not guarantee code quality in any reliable way, that it can mask underlying issues with poorly written or inefficient tests, and that it eats more time than it is worth. The one advantage that tracking code coverage provides that is generally useful is the identification of code that was not exercised during testing, which can be examined to improve tests, or with an eye toward whether the missed code is actually needed or whether it could be removed.

At an organizational level, there may be other priorities that shape which tests are expected, which are optional, and which will probably never be implemented. If an organization is mostly concerned with speed of delivery, testing will likely be limited to happy-path testing initially, and new tests will be introduced as needed when resolving bugs that surface later. If the organization is concerned more with data or process integrity, common concerns in medical and financial circles, the testing priorities are likely to be more aligned to the other extreme, where *everything* is tested, happy- and unhappy-path scenarios alike, including what errors are raised, and how errors are handled by the code. The establishment of testing standards, including examination of these priorities, and how best to accomplish the desired degree of testing, will be covered in more depth later.

In the Python ecosystem, there are two main players in the testing tools space: the built-in unittest package and the third-party pytest package.

The unittest package

The unittest package (https://docs.python.org/3.11/library/unittest.html) is a built-in package, shipping with any standard Python distribution. It takes a class-based approach, providing a TestCase class that engineers will use to construct their own **test case classes**, grouping relevant tests together for the test targets in the source code being tested. The actual test processes are implemented as **test methods** — methods attached to a TestCase-derived class that are executed when the test suite is run, and that call the target code being tested.

This class-based approach lends itself well to certain organizational patterns of tests in a suite: It lends itself well to defining a test case class for each source function or class being tested, with test methods defined in those classes to execute specific test scenarios. This structure keeps related tests bundled neatly, without requiring much in the way of additional naming conventions. The TestCase class provides a large list of assertion methods (https://docs.python.org/3.11/library/unittest.html#assert-methods), including assertions that check for equality, inequality variations, near-equality variations, presence of errors and warnings, and some process-logging checks. It also provides various set-up and tear-down hooks that can be used at test module, test case class, and test method levels, and a facility for implementing sub-tests that makes testing across iterations of values easier to manage and report on.

Under the same namespace, Python also provides the unittest.mock package (https://docs.python.org/3.11/library/unittest.mock.html), which provides functionality for mocking and patching in the context of a test method.

While unittest provides command-line tools to discover and run tests, the syntax is more complicated than the equivalent in pytest (see below). A typical execution of a unit test suite in a project structure that has a tests/unit directory would look like this:

```
pipenv run python -m unittest discover -s tests/unit
```

The pytest package

The third-party pytest package (https://pypi.org/project/pytest/) is a popular alternative to the built-in unittest package. It is designed to simplify writing small tests, while allowing those tests to scale to support larger, more complex testing for applications and libraries. Tests in a pytest suite can be written as functions or classes. Those classes are defined as simple, generic Python classes, with no special inheritance required. By default, any function whose name starts with test, and any class whose name starts with Test (note the case difference!), will be found by the test-discovery process. Test methods in those classes follow the same default discovery rules as test functions, so a test* method will be found and executed, while a Test* method will not.

The availability of functions in a pytest suite can simplify writing tests considerably for tests that do not need the more detailed structure provided by test classes: writing test functions for source functions and test classes for source classes is a natural, logical division, for example.

pytest does not have an extensive collection of special-purpose assertions like unittest, but uses a detailed introspection process that allows it to rely on just the built-in assert Python keyword, which makes test assertions considerably easier to work with.

pytest does not have built-in mocking and patching, but that is available as a plug-in, provided by the pytest-mock package (https://pypi.org/project/pytest-mock/). The pytest ecosystem also has over one thousand other plug-ins available to provide other capabilities (see https://docs.pytest.org/en/stable/reference/plugin_list.html for an automatically compiled list).

The pytest execution and test-discovery process is simpler than unittest, and its output may be easier for some to understand and follow when test failures occur — pytest handles inline print and logging calls more gracefully than unittest does.

Executing a test suite with pytest from the command line is as simple as this, for a typical project with a tests/unit directory:

```
pipenv run pytest tests/unit
```

Execution of a test suite written with unittest using pytest is almost fully supported — there are a few features of unittest that behave differently when run with pytest, but the tests still pass or fail the same way.

Which testing tool to use?

A team should consciously decide what testing tools they will use, and how those will be used, but be ready to adapt as needed if circumstances warrant. The safest bet, generally speaking, is to write tests using unittest, since that is part of every standard Python distribution, and pytest will honor those test constructs. That said, pytest is a perfectly viable alternative, provided that it meets all the needs and desires a team has for testing purposes, or that a plug-in can be found that provides something that unittest has but isn't part of the base installation of pytest. The tests written for this book will use unittest to define tests, but may be run at the level of the whole suite using pytest, since it handles outputs for failures better (in my opinion).

The coverage package

Even if the idea of using code coverage as any sort of quality metric is undesirable, being able to see what code was not exercised during the execution of a test suite is useful information. The coverage package (https://pypi.org/project/coverage/) provides reporting capabilities that include showing lines of code that were missed during the execution of a test suite, and it works with both unittest and pytest test suites. The commands for each are:

```
# Running coverage to monitor a unittest suite
pipenv run coverage run -m unittest discover -s tests/unit
# Running coverage to monitor a pytest suite
pipenv run coverage run -m pytest tests/unit
```

Generating the final coverage report, and explicitly showing the source lines that were not executed (the -m flag) is the same regardless of the test runner used:

```
# Reporting on the results of the test suite run
pipenv run coverage report -m --include "src/*"
```

The report generated by this command shows missing lines — lines of code that were not executed by the pytest run that generated the data — and filters those to the src directory only. The default output (without --include "src/*") will also include the code executed in the test suite, which can be useful, but if the primary focus for missing line metrics is the source code itself, that may also be a distraction. The output of this command after the unit testing, shown later in this chapter, was completed is:

```
Name                                Stmts   Miss    Cover
----------------------------------------------------
src/hms/core/business_objects.py      58      10      83%
src/hms/core/data_objects.py         180       9      95%
----------------------------------------------------

 TOTAL 238 19 92%

# Missing lines (extracted from display above):

business_objects.py ... 355-357, 365-379, 498
data_objects.py ....... 149-150, 341, 345, 474,
                        498, 672, 689, 698
```

As noted earlier, even if the coverage percentage in these reports is ignored, the collection of missing lines that is included is useful information. Examination of those lines can point to missing test scenarios, whether they take the shape of missing parameters that need to be used while executing a test, or modifying the source code itself. Changes to source code made as a result of coverage reporting might include removal of **dead code** — code that will never be executed, no matter what parameters are in play — or reworking of the source code so that the code missed *becomes* testable.

Unit tests are the foundation of code testing and a significant factor in any quality assurance process. The decisions made about how they will be implemented are correspondingly significant, and can make or break the successful implementation of an automated QA process, so they should be made with care and consensus across a team wherever possible: if the unit testing standards are too strict, or involve too much tedious make-work, they will tend to be glossed over, or cause friction within a team. The advantages of having well-designed tests, though, will eventually yield significant benefits, especially if they are integrated into key points in the processes for promoting and deploying code. Those benefits may not be obvious as they occur.

The fact that tests continue to pass as code is changed over time, or bring to light issues that get fixed before they get published or deployed, is not as obvious as dealing with the bugs that would surface otherwise. The ongoing reduction of bugs to fix, though, may be apparent over a long enough period of time. There are other quality assurance processes and tools to facilitate those, which are also worthy of consideration at the same proximity to the code: linting, complexity checking, and detection of gross errors.

Other close-to-the-code quality assurance options

Though they do not fall into the same level of quality assurance as unit testing, in that they will not have any functional effect on the usability or performance of the code, there are other code quality checks that can be run against the code itself that will, over time, tend to improve the quality of life for software engineers working in a code base. The three that will be highlighted here are all provided by a single package, flake8 (https://pypi.org/project/flake8/), which provides:

- Linting of Python code
- Complexity checking of Python code
- Detection of gross errors in Python code

Several of these may also (or already) be provided by plug-ins or extensions to an engineer's IDE, but they can be useful tools to report on potential concerns as part of automated code-handling processes — builds, packaging, and deployment.

Linting is a static analysis of source code that checks for potential errors, deviations from coding guidelines, and stylistic inconsistencies. Linting typically does not involve execution of the code being examined, but may parse it for the purposes of tracking things like variable names that are not used, checking line lengths in the code, and so on.

Complexity checking evaluates and quantifies the intricacy of a given unit of code, identifying when the code is too complex — making too many decisions — or other factors that can lead to the unit being difficult to maintain or test, or problematic for multiple engineers to work on at the same time.

Gross error-checking will look for errors that may not have been caught during local development testing. Of these additional items, this is the least likely to be of concern in a Python context, since most of these kinds of errors will immediately surface when any local execution of code is undertaken, or the first time a related test suite is executed.

Like the code coverage metrics discussed earlier, linting and complexity checks may not be sufficient grounds for preventing code from being promoted, but they provide useful pieces of information that engineers can use to address potential concerns. By way of example, the initial copy of the code for this chapter from *Chapter 13*, when checked with:

```
pipenv run flake8 --exit-zero --max-complexity 8 src/
```

...yielded the following items:

```
src/hms/core/business_objects.py:33:1:
    C901 'get_examples' is too complex (9)
src/hms/core/business_objects.py:445:21:
    F821 undefined name 'get_env_database_connector'
src/hms/core/business_objects.py:449:39:
    W291 trailing whitespace
```

The --exit-zero flag forces flake8 to run without returning a status that would terminate a build or other processes. Essentially, this is telling it to report on issues, but don't stop anything else from happening as a result of any issues that are detected. The --max-complexity 8 specified tells flake8 to run a McCabe cyclomatic complexity check (https://en.wikipedia.org/wiki/Cyclomatic_complexity) against the code being checked (all of the src directory), with a maximum complexity of 8. According to McCabe, anything over a complexity value of 10 is too complex, so the selection of 8 as a value is really more intended to show when things are getting too close to being too complex. The get_examples function in the report is getting there, but is not crossing that threshold.

The *undefined name* item in that output is an example of a gross error. In this particular case, the underlying error would have been caught by a test process, or an error would have been raised if the code that calls the get_env_database_connector function were executed, but neither of those had happened by the end of the previous chapter.

The last item in that output is a linting failure. In this case, flake8 is picking up a stylistic issue in the code that is accounted for in the PEP-8 standards (https://peps.python.org/pep-0008/, under *Other Recommendations*):

> *Avoid trailing whitespace anywhere.*

Neither the complexity nor linting items would present any functional concerns were this code to deploy as it stood when the check was run. The *undefined name* issue could, but since this chapter is going to test that, and fix the issue in the process, it would normally be a non-issue in a more realistic situation.

These additional checks are merely options that can, over time, contribute to the stability, maintainability, and overall quality of the code they are executed against. Moving back to a test-oriented focus, and a bit further away from the code in some cases, leads to the idea of integration testing.

Integration testing

An integration test suite is intended to verify that different software components — typically packages or modules in a Python context—work together as intended. Test cases in an integration test will usually be concerned with checking data flow between components, or how those components communicate with one another, and identifying compatibility issues and data-handling problems. As a whole, an integration test suite is designed to validate overall system functionality from the perspective of the interactions between its components.

Depending on how extensive the isolation of unit test implementations are, there may well be a fair bit of integration-like testing within the bounds of a unit test suite: functions in a code base calling each other as unit tests execute is not necessarily a bad thing, though the context for making that determination may vary from project to project, team to team, etc. Take, for example, the A, B, C, and D functions given as an example in the unit testing isolation discussion earlier.

If those relate to each other and to an external resource — an API call or database, perhaps, the specifics do not really matter, just that it is a resource that is not part of the code base — then those relationships might be diagrammed as shown in *Figure 14.1*.

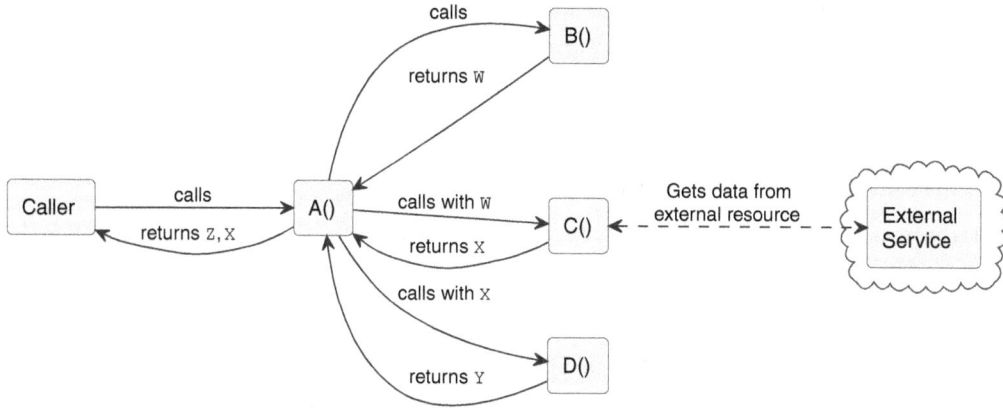

Figure 14.1: Elaborating the unit test connectivity from the previous function example

The dotted line between the C function and that external resource represents an external dependency that would need to be mocked or patched in a unit test, regardless of whether the other relationships are allowed (the solid lines in the diagram) or those relationships were also mocked or patched in the tests. With that level of isolation, the diagram would look almost identical, only the connections would differ, as shown in *Figure 14.2*.

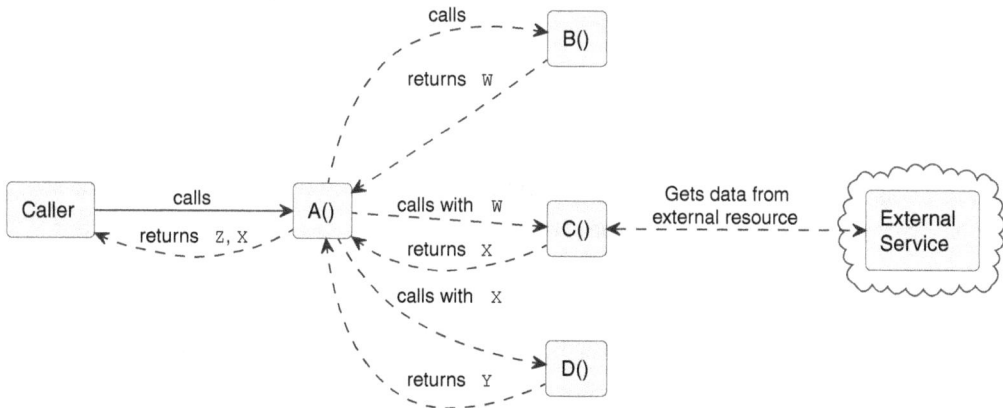

Figure 14.2: The same functions, unit tested with complete isolation

The real question, then, as far as integration tests are concerned, is whether there is anything gained by unit testing in complete isolation, or if it is better, in whatever way, for those tests to allow actual calls to their dependencies. Those actual calls are what an integration test would be testing, by definition, and if they are already sufficiently tested (for whatever value of *sufficiently* might apply), with the lack of isolation in *Figure 14.1*, then there is little point in doing more testing. The value of *sufficiently* could vary quite a bit, though, and might include any or all of the following across each of the *calls/calls-with/returns* connections:

- Is the call tested with good and bad inputs?
- Is the response from the call tested for a failure scenario of the function being called, and does the caller handle that scenario as expected?
- Is the chain of connection values tested adequately? That is, are the W, X, and Y values returned from B, C, and D verified, in general, and are the calls that use those returns verifying that they are using those values when they actually occur?

If the answer to any of those is no, then one of three things needs to happen:

- The unit tests need to be updated to accommodate the missed test scenario.
- An integration test needs to be written to handle the missed test scenario.
- A decision needs to be made to not test that scenario, and documented if the team's agreements for handling specifically skipped tests require it.

It is worth noting, in this example, that if there is an active integration test for the A to C function call, which relies on an external resource that doesn't exist in the code at all, that the call involved to that resource is still mocked/patched, just like it would be for the unit test of C. Like unit tests, integration tests should have a certain degree of isolation, it is just less restrictive than the extreme isolation case for its unit test counterpart: barring some very unusual circumstances, they should still be executable without any connections to any external services. Testing that includes connections to external services falls into one of two other categories, depending on what the test process is intended to verify. If it is verifying general system component communications and interaction, it falls into the category of a *system test*. If it is testing a specific process that involves connections and processes within the system, but not the system at large, it likely falls into the category of an *end-to-end test*.

System and end-to-end testing

Formally speaking, a system test suite is intended to comprehensively check and verify the functionality of an *entire software system*, including interactions (integrations) with *other* systems. End-to-end tests are, in many ways, simply subsets of a full system test suite, focusing on a specific real-world user scenario, and verifying that it executes to completion with the expected results. In the interests of efficiency, or even just eliminating as much redundancy as possible, it may be a better approach to construct end-to-end test suites as needed, determine what system connections were not tested across those, and build additional system-segment tests to cover any of those gaps.

Tests that fall into either of these categories can be expected to make actual connections to external systems: APIs, databases, and so on. Since that implies the capability to make actual changes to system data, some thought needs to be given to managing those changes. If they have the potential to change what a user is seeing on a live system — a web application that suddenly reads test-scenario data that has been added is perhaps the most likely example currently — then some sort of safeguards need to be put in place to avoid presenting test data to an end user.

A common solution to address this sort of concern is to have one or more intermediate environments somewhere between the code changes and the production system where those kinds of test changes can be made with impunity. A common arrangement for those is environments for:

- **Development**, where developers can work with code changes in a controlled, isolated area. System and end-to-end testing here can happen as part of a development cycle, and the entire environment can be considered safe (if inconvenient) to completely destroy if needed.

- **Testing** is intended to provide a clean environment where code that has been approved for promotion can be tested at a system level.

- **Staging** is typically as close a replica of the current production environment as can be managed, often with data copied from production on some recurring basis. Manual user acceptance testing, when it exists, is typically carried out here, and performance and load testing (to determine how much user activity/traffic the system can support) are also commonly executed here. In some organizations, when there are multiple teams that interact with each other's systems, this is the designated integration point for those cross-team service calls.

- **Production** is where the end users actually interact with the system and its software.

Provided that each of the pre-production environments is isolated from the other environments, that isolation affords both developers and build/deploy processes the freedom to test whatever is necessary without fear of contaminating other environments' data. An engineering team can safely test changes to data, or even to the database itself, at the development and testing levels, without fear of impacting the systems or work of other teams. Other teams can safely make calls into a system at the staging environment level without having to be concerned about whether those will impact the team whose system they are calling, or the production environment, where actual user data resides. In a worst-case scenario, if a system in a given pre-production environment is hopelessly broken, it can be dropped and reconstructed from its last known good state's code, while allowing the team that owns it to track down the root cause of the breakage.

User acceptance testing

User Acceptance Testing, or **UAT**, focuses on testing the behavior of a system to confirm that it does what is expected from the perspective of an end user. Although that typically means that it is more of a specialized system or end-to-end test process, it is possible for UAT efforts not to need the sort of real data access that is implicit there. Even so, if UAT can be automated, even in part, it will be safer to either group those automated tests so that potentially destructive tests are kept separate from those that are non-destructive or to simply execute all of a UAT suite in a context where destructive tests will not have adverse impacts.

UAT is frequently a manual process, though for certain types of applications, there are tools that can automate those. One such, for web-based systems, is the suite of web browser automation tools provided by Selenium (`https://www.selenium.dev/`). Those tools include a user interface that allows user browser activity to be recorded and saved for replay later — Selenium IDE — and a collection of WebDriver installables that provide the underlying functionality for almost all of the popular web browsers, installable on Windows, macOS, and several flavors of Linux. Selenium is free, has an installable package (`https://pypi.org/project/selenium/`), and can even export recorded browser activities to code that can be run as a test with the `pytest` package mentioned earlier in the *Unit testing* section. That export, since it is just code itself, can be stored in a project's repository, and updated and tracked just like the project's code, or its other test suites.

Selenium is not the only option for web-related UAT. Other alternatives, which may or may not have free plans or pricing available, include Cypress, Playwright, and Puppeteer. There are also automation tools for Selenium-based testing that can simplify the creation of UAT suites, including WebDriverIO and Katalon.

Outside the area of web-related applications and services, UAT suites may need to be built specifically for the UI being tested, and the shape and flavor of those processes will vary, perhaps significantly, depending on the UI framework that is in play in the application. That is, if a console GUI application is written in Python using the built-in `tkinter` package (`https://docs.python.org/3.11/library/tkinter.html`), the implementation of those tests, using the methods available for UI objects to control or simulate user actions, are going to look very different than the implementations for testing applications using PyQT (`https://www.riverbankcomputing.com/static/Docs/PyQt5/installation.html`), wxPython (`https://wxpython.org/`), Kivy (`https://kivy.org/`), or any of the several other options available for building GUIs for applications running on a user's machine. The underlying test processes — if a user does *x*, the expectation is that *y* will happen — may not change, but the processes involved in actually *simulating* the *user does x* part and verifying the expectation of *y* happening are going to look as different as the UI code itself would.

These types of test processes are, hands down, the most common that will apply to any random software project. Not all of them will usefully apply to all projects — if there is no UI, for example, then UAT is unlikely to be needed: The sorts of verifications it would provide will probably be more usefully built in additional end-to-end or system testing. Of them all, unit testing is the most likely to be needed and useful, if not outright required. Those tests are, after all, testing *the code itself*, and the existence of code that can be tested is the only consistent factor in software projects. Deciding on whether any of the others will be implemented, when any given test suite will be executed, and what the effects of a failure in a suite of tests are, taken as a whole, is a decision about testing standards.

Establishing testing standards

As noted earlier, the goal of any collection of tests for a software project is to provide some degree of assurance that it performs as expected. Those expectations are captured in tests as collections of arguments to pass to functions and methods, and chains of function or method calls to simulate actual user activity. Defining standards for testing is a higher-level set of expectations, defining what processes should be tested, and thus what tests an engineer needs to write as they work on the code that will eventually be deployed.

When testing standards are defined not just in terms of what they test, but *where* and *when* those tests are executed, and what the effects of test failures are, they provide a blueprint for how changes to code get deployed. That definition, coupled with automation of most of the processes involved in building and deploying code, is the foundation for a **Continuous Integration/Continuous Delivery** (or **Deployment**) (**CI/CD**) process.

For the purposes of this book, the question of what should be tested, and what those tests actually look like, breaks out into nine main guidelines:

1. At a unit-testing level, the base guideline is that everything in the source code must have a corresponding test process. That process may not be *implemented*, but it must at least *exist*. A more detailed breakdown of this intention is:

    - Each function should have a corresponding happy-path test that uses a large enough rational subset of argument values to exercise all the branches in the code that would execute for all happy-path scenarios.

    - Each function should have a corresponding unhappy-path test for each of its arguments, intended to exercise all the branches in the code that would execute for all unhappy-path scenarios.

    - Each class should have corresponding happy- and unhappy-path tests, following the pattern described above for functions, for each method of the class.

    - Any managed attribute members of a class that have executable code behind them — any @property attributes, or any Pydantic Field members, for example — should have corresponding tests as follows:

        - Setting a value will follow the function/method pattern.

        - Getting a value should be tested for each value-setting process or operation.

        - Deletion of a value should test that a get operation afterward behaves as expected.

    - All happy-path tests should be implemented, unless there is a good reason not to, one that the team agrees on.

    - Unhappy-path tests should be implemented where they relate to formal or implied data contracts — class properties and entry-point functions in particular — anywhere that data external to the code itself is being received and acted upon.

2. Unit tests should be completely isolated from external systems and dependencies. That applies even to the system database, even though each engineer is expected to have one available. This decision allows unit tests to run in non-local environments without fear of contaminating those environments' systems.

3. Unit tests may also act as integration tests for other code elements in the same project. That is, testing of functions that call other functions is allowed, so long as those functions being called do not have any external systems or dependencies.

4. Reporting on coverage must be available for unit tests, and should be executed in any automated process that runs those tests, to identify any significant gaps in coverage. No formal coverage metric will be mandated, though — the point of this reporting is to identify areas that have not been tested, with an eye toward improving coverage, or removing code that is not executed.

5. Integration tests should verify the behavior of the project's code with respect to external systems and dependencies. They should also clean up after themselves, such that there are no lasting changes to data in those external systems as a result of the tests. In cases where that is not possible, those should, at a minimum, be documented as existing, and if there is a way to manually undo those effects, that should be documented as well.

6. End-to-end tests should be implemented for all processes that are deemed significant by the engineering team or by any other stakeholders. They should follow the same lasting-changes rules as integration tests.

7. System tests should be implemented to address any identified gaps after end-to-end tests are in place. They should also follow the same lasting-changes rules as end-to-end or integration tests.

8. User Acceptance Testing will be automated wherever possible, assuming that it is even needed.

9. All test suites should be executable locally, so that engineers can run them on demand.

These standards are very stringent for a reason

These testing standards lean very significantly toward a *test-everything* mentality that may not be realistic outside certain product circles that inherently have very strict testing requirements, like medical or financial software. They are presented here and acted upon in the project code for this book, partly because it would be easier for the reader to not apply all of these standards in test code than it would be to present less strict tests and have the reader try to work out how to make those tests more strict. They are also partly presented because I feel that rigorous testing is a hallmark of professionalism as a software engineer.

With these standards defined, it is possible to define a code promotion process that takes advantage of them. That process, for the project in this book, is shown in *Figure 14.3*. The basic flow is:

- *Software Engineers* make changes in their *Local Environment*, testing and debugging as needed to complete that unit of work.
- When work is complete, it is committed and pushed to the *SCM* as a *Pull Request*.
  - Unit tests *may* be run locally as a pre-push action, at the discretion of the engineer who is working on the code.
- The SCM will execute the suite of *Unit Tests* against the version of code in the pull request:
  - Those tests **must** execute and **not fail** before a pull request is allowed to be merged.
  - The pull request must be approved by a *Reviewer* (someone other than the engineer who made the changes) before it is allowed to be merged.
- Approved and tested changes will be merged into the *Main Branch* in the project repository.
- Changes to the *Main Branch* will kick off a build process in the *Development Environment*:
  - *Unit Tests* will run again to ensure that there are no environment differences that will cause a test failure: they **must** execute and **not fail** before continuing.
  - The current *Main Branch* code will be built and deployed to a *Development Instance*.
  - *Integration Tests* **must** execute and **not fail**.
  - *System Tests* **must** execute and **not fail**.
- If no tests fail, a *Tested Build* artifact will be created that can be used in later environments to drive deploy processes in the *Staging* and *Production Environments*.
- The *Tested Build* will be deployed to the *Staging Environment*:
  - This will result in a *Stage Instance*.
  - *UAT Tests* **must** execute against that instance and **not fail**.
- If no tests fail, a *Deployment Approver* will be notified that there is a deployment ready for the *Production Environment*.
- Once the deployment is approved, the tested build artifact will be used to deploy the newest version of the system to the production environment.

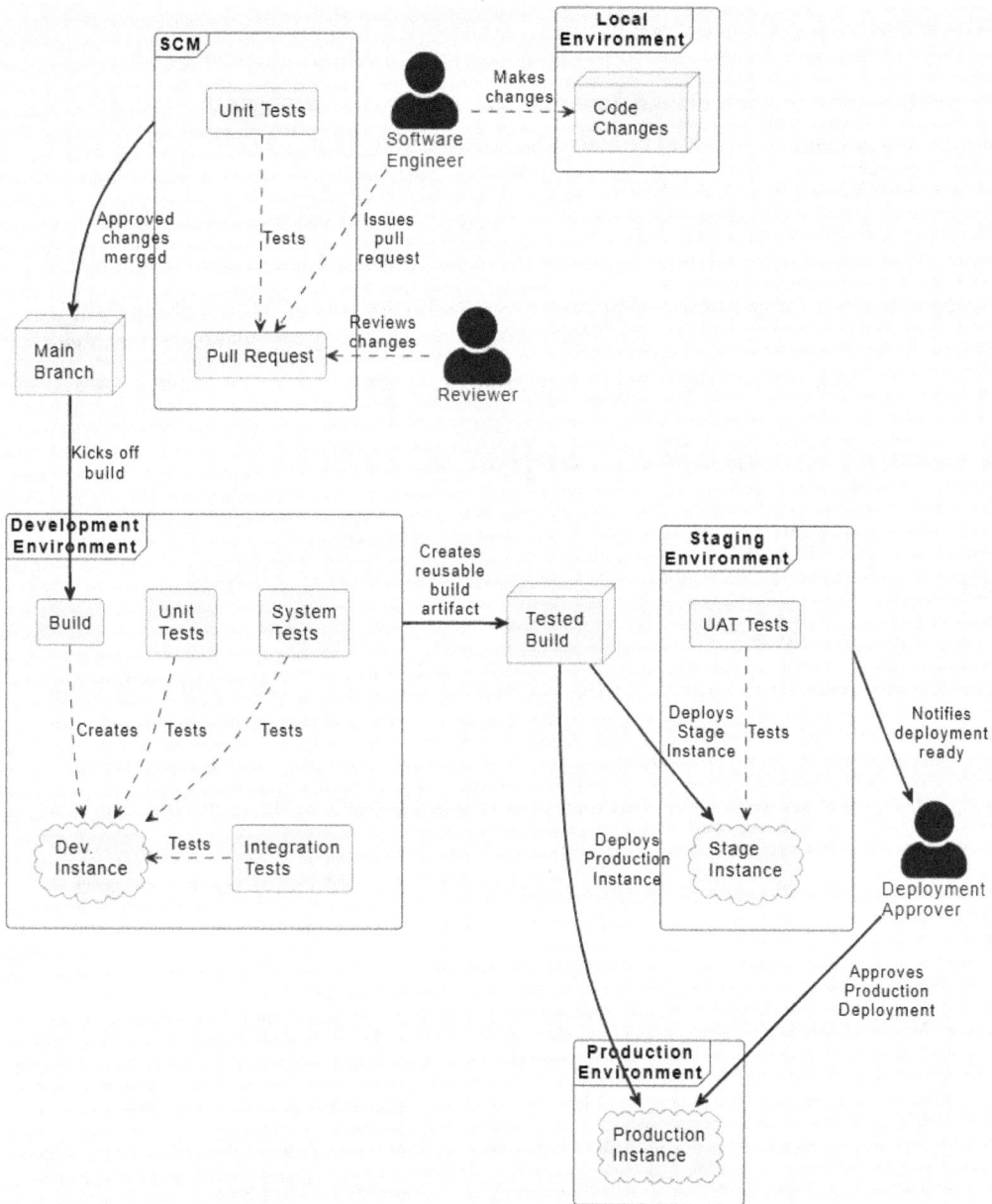

Figure 14.3: The code-promotion workflow for the HMS service

This code-promotion process implies some degree of automation that hasn't been discussed in detail yet. Those details, how it would be implemented to automate as much of the process as possible, are dependent on the tools and systems available to an engineering team, but there are a lot of options available. Online SCM providers like GitHub and Bitbucket provide automation options that can be triggered when a pull request is created or modified, and when a merge or push to a main branch is executed. All of the major cloud providers have some kind of build-/deploy automation services that can be triggered by the same SCM activities. For now, though, our main concern is actually implementing the tests — deciding how (or if) they will be integrated will depend on decisions that do not really impact the implementation of the tests themselves. With all that said, then, it is time to start implementing those tests, starting with the unit tests.

Unit testing the business object classes

These changes are tagged in the GitHub repo as `CH-14-Test-Stubbing`.

Achieving the end goals for the unit-test suite that were defined in the testing standards starts with making sure that every source code entity has a corresponding test suite entity. Specifically, every source module should have a corresponding test suite module, and every member of each source module should have a corresponding test case in the test suite. Once those module members and their corresponding test members have been identified, the happy- and unhappy-path rules noted above also need to be checked. To that end, the HMS team found a third-party package that at least identifies missing test entities for standard Python classes: `goblinfish-testing-pact` (`https://pypi.org/project/goblinfish-testing-pact/`).

Following the instructions in the `MANUAL-SETUP.md` file in that package's documentation, they were able to quickly generate test modules for all of the source modules in the project, and identify and stub out test case classes and test methods for the `data_objects.py` module. The package did not yet support the necessary live code analysis needed to handle the Pydantic `BaseModel` classes, though. As a result, although the initial identification of test cases for the `business_objects.py` module was possible, there were complicating factors that required manual efforts to reach the point where all of the business objects' test methods were accounted for. Those efforts were started with a pair of scripts (in the `temporary-scripts` directory in the chapter repository) that automated the bulk of the basic test structure creation. Most of the manual effort after that was correcting linting issues that inevitably arose from automating that much test-stub creation.

> **The goblinfish-testing-pact package is a work in progress**
>
> Disclaimer: The goblinfish-testing-pact package is a project that the author is working on. It is expected to progress, perhaps significantly, by the time this book is published, but the version in use for this project has been pinned to the 0.0.5 version that was the current state when this chapter was written.

At this point, most of the test processes were explicitly skipped, looking much like the test_street_address_get_happy_paths test method shown here:

```python
class test_Address(unittest.TestCase):
    """Tests the Address class."""
    @unittest.skip('Test stubbed but not yet implemented')
    def test_street_address_get_happy_paths(self):
        """
        Tests the get process of the street_address field
        of the Address class
        """

        self.fail(
            'test_street_address_get_happy_paths has '
            'not been implemented yet'
        )
```

They were also stubbed out with a default forced failure (the self.fail shown above), with the intention that implementation of any given test method would follow a pattern like this:

- Remove the unittest.skip decorator, so that the test method would actually be run if the test module was executed.
- Change the message presented in the self.fail to indicate that the test was not complete.
- Implement the test method, re-running the test module or the specific test method as needed until that test method is complete.
- Removing the self.fail.

At this point, there are 184 test methods present, 177 of which were skipped. The implementation of the actual tests will be discussed in an increasing approximate order of complexity, at least as source code entities exist in the current project's structure, starting with functions, then Abstract Base Classes, standard or concrete classes, and ending with classes based on Pydantic BaseModel, including the concrete classes in the business_objects namespace of the project.

Unit testing functions

These changes are tagged in the GitHub repo as `CH-14-Function-test-patterns`.

There are five functions that need to be tested in the current code. The first that will be focused on is the `get_env_database_connector` function in the `data_objects.py` module, simply because it has no parameters. This function's sole purpose is to wrap the process for creating a connection to the service database, using environment variables to provide the parameters for that connection, and caching the results so that calls to the function will return the same database connection. On the surface, this sounds like it would be really simple to test: simply make the function call, and verify that a connection object is returned. It is not as simple as that, however. Making a database connection, at least with the MySQL connection library that is used in the project, actively tries to make a connection to an external service, which is something that the testing standards prohibit. It also relies on environment variables to actually make that connection, and those are data points that are outside the code itself.

Python's built-in `unittest` packages have at least two possible ways to provide the level of isolation that the testing standards require: the `unittest.mock` built-in (`https://docs.python.org/3.11/library/unittest.mock.html`) allows mocking objects with either a `Mock` or `MagicMock` object, or using the `patch` function it also provides to automatically create one of those objects. The `patch` function, used as a decorator, sets up the resulting mock object as a context manager: an object that takes control of program flow, allowing resources to be used and managed within a specific, temporary context.

Mocking and patching: The *Quick Guide* in the Python documentation

Mocking and patching are complex subjects, and a complete explanation of them could easily occupy the rest of this chapter, so readers are encouraged to see the *Quick Guide* section of the `unittest.mock` documentation at `https://docs.python.org/3.11/library/unittest.mock.html#quick-guide`.

Understanding how these relate to a test process is going to be easier to understand with an example and explanation, so here is what the final implementation of the test_get_env_database_connector_happy_paths test method looks like:

```python
@patch.dict(
    os.environ,
    {
        'MYSQL_HOST': 'some-database-host',
        'MYSQL_PORT': '1234',
        'MYSQL_DB': 'some-database-name',
        'MYSQL_USER': 'some-user-name',
        'MYSQL_PASS': 'super-secret-password - really',
    }
)
@patch('mysql.connector.connect', autospec=True)
def test_get_env_database_connector_happy_paths(
    self, patch_connection
):
    """Test getting a cached database connection."""
    # INITIAL connection retrieval: Arrange
    patch_connection.return_value = CMySQLConnection()
    # Act - initial connection retrieval
    connector = get_env_database_connector()
    # Assert
    patch_connection.assert_called_with(
        host=os.environ['MYSQL_HOST'],
        port=os.environ['MYSQL_PORT'],
        user=os.environ['MYSQL_USER'],
        password=os.environ['MYSQL_PASS'],
        database=os.environ['MYSQL_DB'],
    )
    # CACHED connection retrieval: Arrange
    patch_connection.reset_mock()
    # Act
    cached_connector = get_env_database_connector()
```

```
# Assert
patch_connection.assert_not_called()
self.assertTrue(
    connector is cached_connector,
    'Second and subsequent calls to get_env_'
    'database_connector should return the same '
    f'object, but {connector} and '
    f'{cached_connector} are not the same object.'
)
```

The `patch.dict` decorator sets up a context that lasts for the duration of the execution of the test method. For the duration of that context, the `os.environ` dictionary, which is where the function being tested gets its MySQL connection parameters, will have those parameters replaced with the entries specified. All other keys in the patched dictionary remain unchanged. By providing well-formed, but utterly invalid values for those keys during the execution of the test, there is no chance that any real connection could be made, even if steps were not taken to prevent that with another patch.

That patch adds another context to the execution of the test method. Within *that* context, all calls to the specified `mysql.connector.connect` function will be replaced by calls to a mocked object that allows the test to run without making calls to the actual function, allows the values returned by those calls to be controlled, and provides methods that can be called to verify certain types of activities that the mocked object was subjected to. It also passes that mock object to the original test method, which is why that method has an additional parameter: `patch_connection`.

As the test executes, it follows a typical pattern for unit tests, though it does so twice:

- **Arrange**: Arranging data for input, expected results, and whatever else is necessary before the target of the test is called.

- **Act**: Making the actual calls to the target of the test, often capturing the results returned in a variable for later comparison. In this particular case, the results of the two calls being made to the target `get_env_database_connector` function need to persist so they can be compared, but when there is no need for multiple values to be tracked, it is not unusual for the actual response from the target to just be named `actual`.

- **Assert**: Comparing the actual response to the expected response is the most common activity for this phase, but any other assertions — checks that will raise some sort of error that will bubble up to the test process to indicate a test failure — are possible too.

The initial *Arrange* phase in this test sets the result of the patch_connection mock object to an actual MySQL connector object. If that were not possible, for example, if the MySQL connector type required an actual database connection, it could be replaced with a Mock or MagicMock object.

The *Act* phase that immediately follows calls the target function being tested, which in turn calls the patched function that simulates calling the real function that would create the database connection, and that call uses the os.environ dictionary values that were patched earlier. The mock object that is called instead keeps track of the calls that are made to it, allowing the following *Assert* phase to verify that the function call being simulated was called with the expected parameters from the patched os.environ as well — that is what the assert_called_with call does in that phase.

Because the target function uses the @cache decorator (see https://docs.python.org/3.11/library/functools.html#functools.cache), the first call made to it will store the results in memory, using the arguments passed to it as a key to look up previous results. In this case, since there are no parameters for the function, any call will result in the results of the first call being returned. That is testable behavior too, and the second *Arrange* phase sets the stage for that by resetting the patch_connection mock object (reset_mock), so that any calls from that point on behave as if the mock object had just been created. The second *Act* phase, then, is expected to retrieve the cached database connector that was returned the first time it was called, which should skip the call to the patch_connection mock object. Both of those expectations are verified in the second *Assert* phase, completing the verification of the expected behavior. Mocking and patching are very powerful tools for writing tests with whatever degree of isolation is needed. The patch function can also be used within the body of a test as a context manager, which would allow the test code above to be written in a form like:

```
def test_get_env_database_connector_happy_paths(self):
    with patch('mysql.connector.connect', autospec=True):
        # Arrange, Act and Assert
        ...
```

if that form were preferable.

Testing the build_limit_clause function follows a more typical pattern. That function, in the data_objects module with the previous test target, does not depend on any external functionality; it simply accepts two number values (page_size and page_number) to build a SQL LIMIT clause used in the BaseDataObject.get class method. There are three specific test methods expected for the function, based on the testing standards defined earlier: One that tests happy path calls, and one each for unhappy path scenarios for each of its two parameters.

All three of these tests can benefit from having common collections of arguments for both parameters, both valid and invalid values, so the test case class defines those as class attributes:

```python
class test_build_limit_clause(...):

    ...
    valid_arguments = {
        'page_size': (1, 2),
        'page_number': (0, 1)
    }
    invalid_arguments = {
        'page_size': (0, 1.2, 'three'),
        'page_number': (-1, 2.3, 'four'),
    }
```

The happy-path test is the most complex of the test methods that use those, since it should, ideally, execute a test against all of those possible combinations. To ensure that failures of any combination will allow later combinations' tests to proceed, while still reporting an overall test failure, it leverages the subTests context provided by the unittest.TestCase class (https://docs.python.org/3.11/library/unittest.html#unittest.TestCase.subTest). The final test method implementation, with comments and test failure messaging removed for space reasons, is:

```python
def test_build_limit_clause_happy_paths(self):
    for page_number in \
            self.valid_arguments['page_number']:
        for page_size in \
                self.valid_arguments['page_size']:
            with self.subTest(
                msg=f'Testing page_size {page_size}, '
                f'page_number {page_number}'
            ):
                offset = page_size * page_number
                expected = (
                    f'LIMIT {page_size} '
                    f'OFFSET {offset}'
                )
                actual = build_limit_clause(
                    page_size, page_number
                )
                self.assertEqual(actual, expected)
```

Apart from the subTest context, which just adds the message provided to the test failure output reporting — [Testing page_size 2, page_number 1], for example — this is a fairly straight-forward variation of the *Arrange, Act, Assert* approach noted earlier. All three phases occur in each subTest as the test method iterates through the combinations being tested, but they are still present.

The unhappy-path tests initially revealed an issue: while the function's implementation *did* check for values below certain thresholds, it did not check for *integer* values, which allowed two of the three invalid values to pass when they should have failed. Since the project already uses Pydantic to define model classes, and Pydantic installs the typeguard module (https://pypi.org/project/typeguard/), it was decided to simply add the typechecked decorator provided by typeguard to all of the functions in that module, like so:

```python
@typechecked
def build_limit_clause(page_size: int, page_number: int):
    ...
```

With that change in place, the final test methods for the unhappy paths ended up as:

```python
def test_build_limit_clause_bad_page_number(self):
    page_size = self.valid_arguments['page_size'][0]
    for page_number in \
            self.invalid_arguments['page_number']:
        with self.subTest(
            msg=f'Testing page_size {page_size}, '
            f'page_number {page_number}'
        ):
            with self.assertRaises(
                (AssertionError, TypeCheckError)
            ):
                build_limit_clause(page_size, page_number)
def test_build_limit_clause_bad_page_size(self):
    page_number = self.valid_arguments['page_number'][0]
    for page_size in self.invalid_arguments['page_size']:
        with self.subTest(
            msg=f'Testing page_size {page_size}, '
            f'page_number {page_number}'
        ):
            with self.assertRaises(
```

```
        (AssertionError, TypeCheckError)
    ):
        build_limit_clause(page_size, page_number)
```

The unhappy-path test methods do not need to care about the result returned, since the expectation is that an exception will be raised. That expectation is handled by the assertRaises context manager, also provided by the unittest.TestCase class. That context needed to account for all of the error types that could be raised (AssertionError and TypeCheckError) as well.

The happy-path test for the build_where_clause function, also in the data_objects module, uses a similar iteration-and-subTests pattern, iterating over the SQL_OPERATORS collection in the module, and altering the expected value in the test if the operator suffix being tested requires it. The unhappy-path tests are, in the team's opinion, not usefully testable at this point in time: Even if invalid criteria or criteria_fields values are passed to it, it should always return a well-formed response that will not prevent the get method that is calling it from running. Examination of the function from that perspective exposed that it would return a broken SQL-string fragment in those cases, and that was fixed, returning the same empty results that were returned if there was no criteria supplied. The results retrieved by the calling get method may not be what was expected, and that may be an issue later on, so they added that to their technical debt to address, but left the unhappy paths untested for now. A similar situation occurred with respect to the tests for the build_order_by_clause function, and it was handled in the same manner after implementing some simple, brute-force tests for the happy-path scenarios.

The final function to be tested, get_examples, was originally a member of the business_objects module, where it was used to generate examples of Pydantic BaseModel-derived classes in other such classes (for example, ProductImage examples in the Product.product_images field). Apart from the fact that it was moved to the data_objects module, and the corresponding tests were moved accordingly, its process was fairly straightforward, in the main. The one exception to that was testing the randomization that the function provides, which involved iterating over several attempts to compare the randomized sequence with the non-randomized sequence to show that the randomization was functional. It is also worth noting that the unhappy-path test for the BaseModel class-type was such a simple test that there was no real need to implement the *Arrange, Act, Assert* structure that has been used in previous tests.

It may not be obvious, but there is an underlying pattern to all of these example tests that is at least hinted at in the happy- and unhappy-path test requirements that have been implemented in these examples. That pattern, simply put, is to identify decision points and potential ways that calls to a function can go wrong, and make sure to implement tests against those scenarios, or at least identify them and plan for them later. The identified points of interest included the caching and environment variables in the first function, identifying and testing valid and invalid data types and values in several others, iterating over collections of those values to make sure that any decision points based on their variations would be acted on, and making sure to test for expected errors from the functions when an invalid value was presented. This sort of examination of the processes within a function will rarely fail to identify useful, meaningful variations to test for any function, and though there are other patterns that may prove more useful for functions with different needs, that initial identification — simply asking *What could go wrong here, and how could it be tested?* — will go a long way toward writing good, solid tests regardless of the specifics of the function being tested.

Unit testing classes, both concrete and abstract

The same analysis and implementation patterns that apply to writing tests for functions will apply to writing tests for the methods and manage-attribute properties of classes. The only structural difference between a function and a method member of a class is the expected reference for the scope of the method's operation when it is called. By convention, those scopes are `self` for a method called against an instance of a class, or `cls` for a method called against a class itself. Class methods are indicated by using the `@classmethod` decorator (see `https://docs.python.org/3.11/library/functions.html#classmethod`). Those scopes are implicitly provided when the method is called. That is, given an instance of a class, `instance`, that has a method, calling `instance.method()` passes the `self` argument automatically, providing an object reference that the method can use to refer to the object instance. A similar mechanism for class methods provides the `cls` argument for class methods, such that `my_class.classmethod()` automatically knows that the `cls` involved is `my_class`. Those automatic argument passing processes are part of the basic processes in Python, and are trustworthy to the point where the `self` and `cls` arguments rarely need to be explicitly tested. In those rare cases, though, they are just another argument, and the related code analysis and test implementation will almost always suffice.

Managed attributes, created with the @property decorator, effectively just wrap up to three methods into a standard data descriptor object (see https://docs.python.org/3.11/howto/descriptor.html). Individually, testing of those methods would follow the same analysis and implementation as a function or method. The only real difference is that there are up to three of those methods whose behavior would need to be tested, one each for getting, setting, and deleting the value of the property. Those variations can be accounted for in detail by simply breaking the related tests into distinct test methods for each logical subset of possibilities. For example, given a class that defines a name property, with get, set, and delete actions, test methods should cover, at most, the following scenarios (using a simple variation of the naming convention established for functions for the individual test method names):

- A happy-path test for the get action (test_name_get_happy_paths)
- An unhappy-path test for the get action (test_name_get_unhappy_paths)
- A happy-path test for the set action (test_name_set_happy_paths)
- An unhappy-path test for the set action (test_name_set_unhappy_paths)
- A happy-path test for the delete action (test_name_del_happy_paths)
- An unhappy-path test for the delete action (test_name_del_unhappy_paths)

Not all of these permutations may be needed for any given property, though: A property that does not *allow* a delete action could simply not include those tests, or have a single test that verifies that trying to execute del instance.name to delete the name of an instance fails in an expected manner. Setting aside the testing of the Pydantic BaseModel Field types for the moment, which can be written with some attention to leveraging capabilities that are available to those constructs, but not to a standard @property, the balance of the happy- and unhappy-path testing for standard class constructs follows recognizable variations of these patterns.

Mocking, patching, and context managers

Mocking and patching objects that act as **context managers** — objects that define some runtime context for the duration of their execution (see https://docs.python.org/3.11/reference/datamodel.html#with-statement-context-managers) — will often require mocking and patching of those objects' __enter__ and/or __exit__ methods. The database cursor objects used in this project follow that pattern, and required mocking of the __enter__ method rather than the context object itself during the implementation of the test_save_happy_paths test. These changes are tagged in the GitHub repo as CH-14-Mocking-context-managers. The balance of the tests created against BaseDataObject methods are tagged in the repo as CH-14-Method-test-patterns.

Because the fields of the business objects are defined as Pydantic `Field` objects rather than standard built-in `@property`-decorated method sets, there are some alternative approaches available for testing those. The basic approaches can all be illustrated with the tests against the `BaseDataObject` fields.

Unit testing Pydantic BaseModel classes

These changes are tagged in the GitHub repo as `CH-14-Pydantic-model-tests`.

Recall that part of the reason that Pydantic models and their fields were chosen as an implementation mechanism was that a JSON schema for each model could be retrieved from the class definition. Part of that is the ability to define `examples` values for each field. Those `examples` values provide a ready-made collection of rational happy-path values that can be used to test the fields that they are associated with. Using those as testing values also has the side benefit of verifying that all of the examples that appear in the JSON schema are verified as being valid for the fields. That approach will, in the majority of the time, cover the happy-path testing needed for those fields/properties.

The question of how much and what kinds of unhappy-path testing should be undertaken is a decision that needs to be made based on several factors. In general, if the underlying processes for properties and fields come from the Python language itself (the `@property` decorator) or from a well-tested and trusted third-party package (Pydantic's `Field`), the processes themselves can be considered trustworthy. That is, if the processes for setting a property and retrieving its value again have no other logic associated with them, the tests for those properties and fields are safe to skip, or even not implement, at least until the addition of any process logic. In many cases, tests should still be written simply to verify that the expected types and values are supported, and that unexpected types and values are handled in an expected fashion, but those tests rarely need to be anything more than setting a value and confirming that it can be retrieved. When there are additional constraints, whether those are implemented as part of a property setter method, or as constraint settings on a Pydantic `Field` (for example, `min_value` and `max_value` for a `Field` that tracks an `int` or other number), *that* is where the need for additional, more detailed testing surfaces.

The three classes in the `business_objects` module that inherit from `BaseDataObject`, by definition, inherit the members defined in `BaseDataObject`. Since those will be tested against the class that they are defined in, testing them in the business object classes would be redundant, at best. However, having tests that will start to fail if that relationship changes might be useful. For example, testing that `Artisan.oid` is the same `Field` defined in `BaseDataObject.oid` can be explicitly tested, or set up so that the test method will be skipped if that condition is true, or executed if it is not, with a preset failure and messaging to explain what the cause of that failure is. That latter implementation is arguably more elegant, and looks like this:

```python
class test_Artisan(unittest.TestCase):
    """
    Tests the Artisan class.
    """
    # Tests of the inherited fields
    @unittest.skipIf(
        Artisan.oid is BaseDataObject.oid,
        'The oid field is inherited from BaseDataObject'
    )
    def test_oid(self):
        self.fail(
            'Artisan.oid was originally inherited from '
            'BaseDataObject, but that has changed, and '
            'it needs to be tested in relation to the '
            'Artisan class'
        )
```

The majority of the remaining tests across the business object classes follow patterns similar to the ones put in place in the chapter repository. The set of tests pushed to the repository for this section is not complete — there are a number of tests that were simply not implemented because of time constraints, but they would, in the main, follow similar patterns to those established by the ones that were completed and pushed.

Although there are no specific coverage metrics goals associated with this project, it is worth noting that simply taking this approach has already provided reasonably solid code coverage, which can be shown by running the test suite with the coverage package tool and generating a report.

Those commands are:

```
pipenv run coverage run -m pytest tests/unit/
pipenv run coverage report -m
```

The results are:

Name	Statements	Miss	Coverage	Missing
business_objects.py	58	10	83%	355–357, 365–379, 498
data_objects.py	180	9	95%	149–150, 341, 345, 474, 498, 672, 689, 698

The bulk of the missing lines shown here are in the save_metadata method of the Product class, which was discussed earlier, but set aside for the time being.

This section has covered the implementation of unit tests for every basic object type present in the project code: Functions and classes based on Pydantic's BaseModel. It has also described unit-testing patterns and processes for standard Python classes, both concrete and abstract. The main focus has been toward testing as much of the source code as possible, with the understanding that testing to these extremes may not be the approach taken by the reader or the reader's team(s). How much testing is implemented, and what strategy is followed to meet the standards and requirements for testing, is ultimately a team decision, guided by product needs and the team's recognition of the trade-offs that will determine how much testing is too little or too much.

Summary

The amount of space taken to discuss unit testing precludes going into too much detail for the other types of testing that would come after in a CI/CD process: *Integration*, *System*, *End-to-End*, and *User Acceptance Testing*. However, those have many shared characteristics and goals with unit testing; only the scope, focus, and constraints of those test types vary. For the purposes of this project, given the source code in place at this point, it is a safe bet that the following will hold true:

- Integration testing will be focused mostly on the interaction between business objects and the back-end data store. These tests will generally not need to do much more than create a business object instance, save it, read it, assert that the data was saved correctly, and delete the object's record. Those tests will look much like the unit tests, but without the patching and mocking of database resources that are so prevalent in the unit test suite.

- System and end-to-end testing will probably need to wait for the design and implementation of the API and of specific processes that API endpoints wrap. These tests will define sequences of activities in code that are executed, wait for those processes to execute to completion, and verify that the end results are within expected boundaries. Whether they will need to clean up after they are executed will depend on the specifics of the system segments or processes being tested, but they are not expected to need much more than the deletion of records created during the execution of the test.

- The shape and flavor of potential User Acceptance Testing will vary significantly depending on how users interact with a system. Projects with substantial front-end UI implementations will need more than projects that do not have those implementations. API projects, like the one being discussed here, may benefit from some degree of UAT executed through the UIs that call them, but those tests may be owned by another team if the UI in question is owned by another team.

Other types of testing that will not be addressed in this book but that are worth consideration include **Load Testing** and **Stress Testing**, concerned with assessing the performance of a system under high but reasonable conditions, and unreasonable conditions, respectively. **Security Testing** and **Vulnerability Testing** processes, concerned with finding and mitigating security risks — unauthorized access, data protection, known vulnerabilities in package dependencies, and more — are also well worth implementing: A good starting point for determining what kinds of risks are commonly found is the **OWASP Top Ten** list (`https://owasp.org/www-project-top-ten/`).

Regardless, all of the varied types of testing discussed here, starting with the unit test suite, can be integrated into a Continuous Integration/Continuous Delivery (or Deployment) (CI/CD) process. What implementing that integration looks like will depend heavily on what the backing CI/CD process implementation looks like, which is the focus of the next chapter.

15

CI/CD Options

Testing, building, and deploying code is a task that has to be undertaken every time changes to the code are approved for end user access. The previous chapters have covered how project code is structured and written, and both what tests can and should be written, and how they work. Putting all of those items together, it is possible to build automated processes that take the current code in a project, test it, generate one or more deployable artifacts, and deploy those artifacts. Automating these processes, so that they are repeatable with little to no human interaction (and thus little to no risk of human interaction introducing process errors), takes the discussion into the realm of CI/CD.

In this chapter, we're going to cover the following main topics:

- What purposes a CI/CD process serves
- CI/CD implementation options

Technical requirements

The code provided for this chapter, in the CH15-code directory of the book's repository (https://github.com/PacktPublishing/Hands-On-Software-Engineering-with-Python-Second-Edition), is for illustration purposes only, and does not actually execute in any meaningful fashion. The various CI/CD processes in the CH15-code/cicd-processes directory there, with the exception of the Makefile example, require an active account and repository with the relevant SCM provider (Bitbucket or GitHub), or an active AWS account in the case of the aws-codebuild-buildspec.yml file. The Makefile requires installation of the GNU Make program, available at https://www.gnu.org/software/make/. Readers are encouraged to fetch and play with the CI/CD process definitions as they see fit, but be aware that some of them, particularly the AWS resources, will cost money if they are left active and used for long periods of time.

What purposes a CI/CD process serves

Continuous Integration and **Continuous Delivery** or **Deployment** (**CI/CD**) are a set of practices intended to automate the handling of changes made to code, improving collaboration capabilities between contributors to that code in the process. *Continuous Integration* focuses on facilitating the ability of code contributors to merge their changes into a shared repository and executing the same set of automated processes every time that occurs. *Continuous Delivery*, one of the two possible meanings of the *CD* in the abbreviation, focuses on processes that result in a ready-to-deploy state as code is promoted from the current version or branch in the repository to whatever the production state is, whether that be deployed into a user-accessible application or service, a code package that end users can install and use, and so on. Continuous delivery often has at least one manual approval requirement in that process, acting as a final safety measure before allowing code changes to be promoted to a state where they can be consumed by an end user.

Continuous Deployment takes those automated processes a step further, allowing code changes to propagate to their final production state or environment without manual intervention. It is common for Continuous Deployment processes to require that additional tests pass against the deployable code artifacts from the preceding CI processes. In scenarios where the final deployed result is an application or service that is immediately accessible to (and used by) end users, it is not unusual to have post-deployment monitoring in place that will roll back deployed changes to a previously known good state if the newly deployed code encounters too many errors or other unwanted conditions.

Taken together, the automation of these processes has several beneficial effects. The fact that they are automated, and thus repeatable, reduces the amount of time that would be required to manually execute the same processes. It also reduces, or even eliminates, the possibility of manual errors in a deployment process: if a human is not managing the build and deploy process, they cannot forget to run the unit test suite for the project, for example. Automated CI/CD processes also enforce consistency of the processes needed to promote code changes, running the same processes with every change. As an added benefit, the CI/CD processes can almost always be expressed in some sort of code, or code-like content, and kept with the project, which makes it easier for engineers making changes to the code to keep the CI/CD definitions up to date if corresponding changes are needed.

A typical progression for a full CI/CD process includes most of the following processes, though some may not be relevant or needed on a project-by-project basis:

- Compiling the code
- Unit testing the code

- Building/packaging the code into a deployable artifact
- Promoting the deployable code to specific environments
- Integration, system, and user acceptance testing of the promoted code
- Publishing the deployable artifact
- Deploying the artifact

The actual sequence might vary as well, depending on specific needs or requirements for a given project. Each of these has specific goals that they are intended to accomplish, and the failure of any individual step in the sequence should normally cause a failure in the CI/CD process, rather than allow code that was broken in some manner to be promoted to end user accessibility.

Compiling the code

A formal compile step is unusual in Python projects, partly because Python is in something of an odd space as far as compiled vs. interpreted code is concerned. When code is compiled in languages like C and C++, the end result is binary code that is tailored to the CPU and possibly the operating system of the machine that the compile process was executed on. Java behaves in a similar fashion, creating **bytecode** — a representation of source code that can be run or interpreted by a virtual machine — that will execute natively when run by a **Java Virtual Machine (JVM)**, and the JVMs are compiled for specific CPUs and operating systems as needed.

Python code can, technically, be compiled into its own type of bytecode. If you've ever seen .pyc files, usually living in a __pycache__ directory, that is what those files are. Those files are automatically created and cached whenever a module is imported. If there is a functional need to explicitly generate those .pyc files, they can also be created with the built-in py_compile module (https://docs.python.org/3.11/library/py_compile.html). That bytecode, whether automatically generated or not, is *interpreted* by the Python runtime. Python's bytecode-compile process is quite fast, though, and there is rarely a need to explicitly perform a compile step, even as a test in a CI/CD process: If the project has sufficient unit testing in place, enough to import every module in a project at least once while those tests run, then every module in the code will have been compiled the first time it was imported or executed.

Note that this compile process, even in languages other than Python, may or may not result in a free-standing executable, a package, or anything other than a new collection of compiled code entities. In Python, the generation of a command-line program, an installable package, or a deployed service is typically a build/package operation, later in the CI/CD workflow.

Unit testing the code

This phase of a CI/CD workflow is exactly what it sounds like: running the relevant unit test suites associated with the project. What the actual execution of the test suite looks like will be determined by what testing frameworks are available, with the two noted in the previous chapter — unittest and pytest — being the most likely candidates. Assuming that the test suite has been written with forethought about it being used in a CI/CD process, regardless of which test framework is used to run them, the tests should be executable with a single command. For unittest and pytest, those commands are:

```
python -m unittest discover -s tests/unit
```

and

```
pytest tests/unit
```

respectively, without taking the potential need to include a pipenv run, or some other PVE-specific command prefix, to use the PVE's installed version of Python.

As noted in previous chapters, unit test suites should be written with sufficient isolation that they can be run *anywhere*, and without access to *any* resources or processes that are not part of the project code. Their execution in the context of a CI/CD process is a significant part of the reason why this is desirable: If the tests are being run, for example, in an environment that does not have access to a database, and the tests require access to that database, those tests will fail. Correcting those failures would involve either reworking the tests to make them isolated enough to work, or adding access to the resource — the database in this example — solely so that the tests will pass. While that latter option is possible, it may be the more complex of the options, especially as code changes that have corresponding database changes start to be undertaken.

Unit tests should be executed and required to pass at least once in a CI/CD process. If they are not executed *somewhere*, the effort that went into creating them was wasted, after all, and if they are not run as part of an automated process, then the consistency and predictability that go hand in hand with that are lost. Their ability and expectation to be executed with every pass through a CI/CD process also provides ongoing **regression testing**, raising test failures if changes to the source code break previously established functionality. It is a good idea, whenever possible, to set up SCM pull requests so that they will also execute the same test suite as changes are committed and pushed to a pull request. With that additional test run in place, pull requests will detect test failures before the changes that cause them have been merged into a branch where they will fail anyway.

Unit tests, and perhaps others that are similarly independent of external resources, are the logical first step in any CI/CD process. The reasoning behind that is straightforward: If the tests fail, then none of the other processes' outputs are trustworthy, or should be used anyway under any reasonably normal circumstances. The time saved in not building, packaging, and testing in less isolated contexts, and compute costs for those processes when they are applicable, may be trivial, but even that small efficiency gain is worthwhile over time.

Building/packaging the code into a deployable artifact

The specifics involved in a build process will vary depending on what the final output of the CI/CD process actually is. Projects that are intended to provide an installable package, something that can be installed with `pip install` or any of the equivalents in a PVE manager, will have different processes than those that are, for example, being deployed to some cloud infrastructure to provide API functionality, and those will differ from a deployment where the code is installed into a Docker container image. The common denominator, no matter what the deployment mechanism looks like, is to end up with a usable copy of the code, an artifact that can be promoted, published, or used in subsequent steps in the CI/CD process. Many of these artifacts are, in some fashion, the result of some sort of packaging process.

Packaging for projects that will be published as installable Python packages, whether they are published to the public PyPI repository (`https://pypi.org/`) or to a private repository that provides the same installation capabilities, has been thoroughly described in the official *Packaging Python Projects* tutorial (maintained by the Python Packaging Authority at `https://packaging.python.org/en/latest/tutorials/packaging-projects/`). This process relies on the `build` package (`https://pypi.org/project/build/`), which provides a common, standard build process for Python packages, and one of several build backend options, documented there. It also requires the creation of a configuration file, `pyproject.toml`, which defines the properties and requirements for both building the package and installing it, along with package metadata: the name of the package, its version, and a plethora of other options described in the *Writing your pyproject.toml* documentation (`https://packaging.python.org/en/latest/guides/writing-pyproject-toml/`). The end result of a package build process is one or more standard Python package files, with options including **source distribution** (a `.tar.gz` file, a gzipped tar archive), and **wheel distribution** (a `.whl` file, which is, ultimately, just a ZIP archive) outputs. The `build` process also assembles metadata from the `pyproject.toml` file, and from other files that are specified therein, to provide things like the package's PyPI documentation (typically a `README.md` file in the project), a short description of the package, and any of a host of classifiers (`https://pypi.org/classifiers/`) that are standard metadata elements for common characteristics of packages.

The actual build command for a Python package is typically little more than

```
python -m build
```

and the resulting build output artifacts will be collected in a single common directory (dist) for use later in the publishing process.

Python's import processes are capable of reading and importing from a ZIP archive file. That means that it is possible, for deployed end results where it would make sense, for a project's code and dependencies to simply be gathered and zipped into a file. An end user of that packaged code would simply download the archive, make sure it was present in their PYTHONPATH, and treat it normally otherwise. This sort of packaging can get a bit more complicated, since it may need to account for package dependencies being shipped with the ZIP file. Using the zip-package-example in the chapter's repository as an example, those commands would be:

```
# From the directory that the zip-package-example
# directory lives in:
# - Create the directory that will be used to zip
# the package up
mkdir my-package
# - Copy the source code from the project
cp zip-package-example/my_code/example.py my-package
# - Install the package dependencies into the new directory
pip install -r zip-package-example/requirements.txt \
    --target my-package/
# Zip the directory into the package file
zip my-package.zip my-package/*
# Remove the package directory
rm -fR
```

ZIP archives are commonly used in certain cloud contexts

For example, a variation of this process is used by the AWS SAM build command (https://docs.aws.amazon.com/serverless-application-model/latest/developerguide/sam-cli-command-reference-sam-build.html), to package up the code and dependencies for certain compute resource types (Lambda functions in particular, though there may be others).

Python code can also be packaged by composing it into a Docker image. In this scenario, that image file is the deployable artifact. It is not unusual for Docker-based implementations to need to provide environment variables that are used by the code at runtime, and a common approach to solve that need is to use .env files and read them with a dedicated library like python-dotenv (https://pypi.org/project/python-dotenv/). Although container-based Python deployments are frequently focused on providing longer-running services — web services and even applications — container-based deployments where the container remains active just long enough to complete some task before going idle or even being deleted until the next time it is needed are not uncommon. The documentation for Docker provides a reasonably detailed example of how to containerize a Python application based on the FastAPI package (https://fastapi.tiangolo.com/) at https://docs.docker.com/guides/python/, including details on how to use both a Dockerfile to create the image and how to compose several images into a collection of containers that provide an entire application.

Regardless of the specific mechanisms involved in a build or packaging process, the end goal is the same: To generate a collection of files that contain whatever is needed to allow the code to be deployed in some fashion. Further changes to the code itself should be avoided after a build/packaging process has completed, so that the file artifacts created — which have already had at least some code testing executed against them — can be deployed as-is from this point forward. There may be additional testing executed after the build/packaging is completed, before any deployment as well: a Python package build could be further tested by actually installing it into a new, disposable Python Virtual Environment to verify that it is, in fact, installable, and any tests that were run prior to this point should still run without error, for example.

Promoting the deployable code to specific environments

Once deployable build artifacts are available, it is not uncommon for deployment processes to go through installation and execution processes across one or more environments for a variety of reasons. An **environment**, in this context, is simply a logical collection of systems and their related resources — including the code that is being deployed — with some baseline expectations about who those systems and resources are expected to be used by, and the purposes that are being served. A common pattern for environments provides several focused copies of a deployed system, though the names may vary across organizations or even teams. The end goal of deploying across multiple environments is to provide guardrails and risk mitigation as updates to systems are undertaken.

The first of these is the **development environment**, where the system's users are the engineers and other members of a team. Development environments are where all of the individual engineers' changes first come together, and provide a safe space where testing of changes can be executed to verify that all the current changes still behave as expected in the context of entire systems. Development environments are where breaking changes should ideally be caught before they propagate to other environments where other teams or users would see issues. A development environment may be a logical place for integration and system testing to take place, particularly since they are not expected to have production-level quantities or quality of data (though they may have both). They are also intended to be relatively safe to tear down and rebuild should the need arise: doing so would affect only the team itself, and while it might be inconvenient and/ or time-consuming to undertake, it would not block other teams or systems that rely on those systems being operational.

The next environment in the sequence is often a **test environment** (or **QA environment**), intended to be where thorough testing of a system takes place. If integration and system tests are not undertaken in a development environment, the test environment is the logical place for them to be executed. Performance and load testing are also commonly undertaken in test environments, particularly if they would slow a system down to the point where it is unusable. Security testing is also a common effort at this point.

Testing environments may be optional (though testing should not be)

Depending on team or organization standards and expectations, a development environment may be where all of these tests take place. A test environment is still intended for a team to use, not other teams in an organization, and consolidating those efforts in a development environment may be preferred for any of several reasons: It may be less expensive in terms of servers or cloud resources needed, or it may reduce the complexity of the deployment process, for example. If testing processes are time-consuming or frequently block other development efforts for other reasons, that is a strong argument for the implementation of a dedicated test environment.

A **staging environment** is typically the final environment that changes must pass through successfully before being deployed to end users. Ideally, a staging environment should be a nearly identical replica of the production environment that a system runs under for end users, particularly in terms of hardware, quantities of system data, and so on. At a minimum, the data available at a staging environment level should be realistic, or at least valid — well-formed but nonsensical data may be acceptable — and if the sheer quantity of data available is not equivalent, extrapolation of performance metrics and expectations should be easily accomplished.

Staging environments are frequently the first point of contact for the interactions between systems owned by multiple teams in organizations where there are multiple teams. By the time that a system has been deployed to a staging environment, it is expected to be *functionally* equivalent to the production system and thus safe for another team to use for development purposes. It is typical for **User Acceptance Testing (UAT)** to be executed in a staging environment.

The final environment in a deployment process is the **production environment**, where end users actually interact with the systems, applications, or services being deployed. If there is automated testing in this environment, it is likely to be some sort of **canary test** process, where if certain criteria are met — too many errors, an unacceptable increase in system latency, or a decrease in performance, for example — the deployment is **rolled back**: reverted to a previous accepted version of the system.

The use of various environments in a deployment process is associated with entire systems, applications, and services, for example. It is rarely a useful construct for projects like Python packages or user-installed applications, where the end user is actively installing the code in some manner. Multiple environments for application or service deployment provide a useful framework where integration, system, and user acceptance testing can be implemented as part of the deployment process to reduce the risk of broken code making it to an end user's experience. Non-system projects like packages and other user-installable items should still be evaluated for the need for any or all of those types of tests, though, and those needs should be accommodated as best they can, typically as part of a build or packaging process.

Publishing the deployable artifact

Projects like Python packages or locally installed applications typically need to be published in some fashion so that end users can install or update the project's end result. Container-based deployments may also have a publication activity associated with them, making the container image available to end users or systems that make use of the container. In both cases, the basic process is similar, involving uploading the deliverable package or container image to some repository where an end user can retrieve and install it, using whatever standard tools apply. The standard *public* Python package and application repository is *The Python Package Index* (`https://pypi.org/`), but there are private options available as well, including the *Hosting your own simple repository* options (`https://packaging.python.org/en/latest/guides/hosting-your-own-index/`) and paid options like *Cloudsmith* (`https://cloudsmith.com/product/formats/python-repository`) and *Jfrog Artifactory* (`https://cloudsmith.com/product/formats/python-repository`).

AWS, Google Cloud Platform, and Microsoft Azure all provide some degree of support for hosting private PyPI-compatible repositories as well. For Docker images, the standard public repository is *Docker Hub* (https://hub.docker.com/), and the same paid services noted above both support private image registries, as do the same cloud providers.

These activity phases are a reasonable breakdown of the most common expected activities in a CI/CD process for Python development efforts, though there may be others that apply to less general development efforts. The sequence they are presented in is typical, with each new action building on or depending on the success of the one before it. All that remains are the specific commands needed for the different variations, and some way to orchestrate those commands so that they run in the right order and yield the expected results.

CI/CD implementation options

In order to fully explore what is needed for a CI/CD implementation, it is first necessary to know what is being deployed and what the final result needs to be. The project example so far has focused on code that is intended to be deployed as a Python package that is designed to be incorporated into the back-end functionality of an API, but at this point in the story of the HMS work, there has been no discussion of the API code itself, beyond setting an expectation that it would need to be a serverless implementation of some kind, with an API resource of some type calling serverless functions to handle requests and generate responses for each endpoint therein.

All three of the most popular cloud providers provide **command-line interfaces** (**CLIs**) for working with resources in their cloud spaces, so the actual deployment processes presented in this discussion will take a CLI-based approach in order to keep the same basic paradigm throughout. One of those providers, **Amazon Web Services** (**AWS**), also offers several dedicated cloud-service options that allow **Infrastructure as Code** (**IaC**) definitions of cloud resources and their configurations and options. The other two, **Google Cloud Platform** (**GCP**) and Microsoft's **Azure** rely on other technologies like HashiCorp's **Terraform** (https://developer.hashicorp.com/terraform) to provide that functionality outside the context of command-line tools and scripting.

No matter what the implementation is that actually drives the build, test, and deploy processes, the process steps will be the same for every CI/CD process execution on a project-by-project basis. The CI/CD for the hms-core package that has been the main focus so far must execute the following steps, with a failure of any given step terminating the entire process:

1. Test that the current specified version of the package in the code does not already exist in the repository where it will be retrieved from later.

2. Run the unit test suite.

3. Build the package.

4. Upload the package to the repository.

The commands to accomplish these steps are very straightforward, though the test for the current version in the second bullet point will require some additional work. In the order that they need to be executed, they are:

```
# Run the package-version test
pipenv run pytest tests/packaging
# Run the unit test suite
pipenv run pytest tests/unit
# Build the package
pipenv run python -m build
# Upload the package to the target repo:
# $TWINE_REPO is the URL of the repo,
# $TWINE_USERNAME is the username used to authorize there
# $TWINE_PASSWORD is the password used to authorize there
pipenv run twine upload dist/* -r $TWINE_REPO \
    -u $TWINE_USERNAME -p $TWINE_PASSWORD
```

On the API side, since the tools for building and deploying cloud resources vary from one provider to another, there are differences in certain actions and processes, and there may be differences in how the API code itself needs to be written, so the HMS team needs a decision to be made about which cloud provider is going to be chosen.

The cloud provider decision

The decision made and used for the balance of this book is to go with AWS. Though Azure and GCP are both viable contenders as well, AWS has been in the business for longer and has consistently been the market leader in the cloud space for years. The functional differences between the cloud services needed for this project are relatively minimal, but the processes involved in getting the project operational are too significant to delay the decision any longer.

With that decision made, there are still several implementation options to choose from. The initial expectation is that the packages discussed up to this point will have their own CI/CD processes, resulting in an installable package, and the API code and infrastructure that has not been discussed yet will have its own, which will include the installation of the custom packages as needed. There are two key workflows that need to be accommodated: A **local build** that executes all of the test and build processes, but does not actually publish or deploy anything, and a **CI/CD build** that does all that the local build does, but also publishes or deploys the final artifacts.

CI/CD with GNU make

The GNU make program (https://www.gnu.org/software/make/) is a tool that orchestrates collections of processes or **target**s, identified by a name, in a Makefile — a text file that the program can read and execute target commands from in a reproducible fashion. Using make and a Makefile is a very portable approach: any operating system that can run the make program can execute the target specified, running the commands and dependent targets as needed to achieve the desired results. The processes it defines are straightforward, but easier to follow with the targets easily referenced. With that in mind, here is a complete Makefile starting point for any of the HMS package code discussed up to this point, or expected in the balance of the book, which is also provided, with more comments and friendlier outputs, in the chapter repository at cicd-processes/Makefile:

```
PYPI_REPOSITORY_URL = $(PYPI_REPOSITORY_URL)
TWINE_USERNAME = $(TWINE_USERNAME)
TWINE_PASSWORD = $(TWINE_PASSWORD)
IGNORED_PIPENV_CHECKS = \
    --ignore 123 \   # Ignore known vulnerability ID 123
.PHONY: cicd-build local-build init test packaging-test build verify check
upload clean
local-build: packaging-test test build verify check clean
cicd-build: init packaging-test test build verify check upload clean
init:
    @cp template.env .env
    @pipenv --venv >/dev/null 2>&1 || pipenv sync --dev  || pipenv sync
--categories build, publish
packaging-test:
    pipenv run pytest tests/packaging
test:
    pipenv run coverage run -m pytest tests/unit
```

```
        pipenv run coverage report -m
build:
        pipenv run python -m build
verify:
        @TMP_ENV=$$(mktemp -d) && \
                python -m venv $$TMP_ENV/venv && \
                . $$TMP_ENV/venv/bin/activate && \
                pip install dist/*.whl && \
                pytest tests/unit && \
                deactivate && \
                rm -rf $$TMP_ENV
check:
        pipenv check $(IGNORED_PIPENV_CHECKS)
upload:
        twine upload --repository-url $(PYPI_REPOSITORY_URL) \
                -u $(TWINE_USERNAME) -p $(TWINE_PASSWORD) dist/*
clean:
        @echo "Cleaning up build artifacts..."
        # Remove build output and metadata
        rm -rf build dist *.egg-info
```

With this `Makefile` at the project root, there are two main targets that can be used to execute the CI/CD process locally:

```
make local-build
# Or just make; local-build will be used by
# default if no target is specified
```

and

```
make cicd-build
```

Each of those targets has a list of other targets that make will execute before running the commands under the target being called. Both include the packaging-test, test, build, verify, check, and clean targets, and the cicd-build target also includes the init target before executing those. Each of those targets serves a specific purpose in the overall CI/CD process.

The order of execution for those targets is:

- `init` initializes a CI/CD build environment by making a copy of the project's `template.env` file in a `.env` file that the environment's pipenv-managed PVE will use, before checking for an existing PVE. If the PVE is not found, it is created, and the project's `Pipenv.lock` file is used to install the package dependencies for the project's code. The `pipenv sync --dev` command installs development and non-development requirements alike, and the `pipenv sync --categories build,publish` installs the `build` and `twine` packages.

- `packaging-test` runs any packaging-related tests, from the `tests/packaging` directory in the project, which are intended to check for potential conflicts with the current code's package version being published to the target package repository. That repository is specified in the `PYPI_REPOSITORY_URL` environment variable, and the process may not need any credentials: It's simply going to look to see if the current package version is listed there.

- `test` runs the unit test suite in tests/unit, using the `coverage` package (a `--dev` package dependency) to keep track of the actual lines executed by those tests, then outputs a coverage report to show which source lines were not executed during the tests.

- `build` builds the project, creating package files in a `dist` directory at the project root, and various files under a `build` directory next to `dist`, and an `*.egg-info` directory in the `src` of the project. The package files under the `dist` directory are the artifacts that will eventually be published in cases where that is part of the process.

- `verify` creates a temporary directory and a related PVE, installs the freshly built package into it, re-runs the unit test suite to make sure that nothing in the packaging process introduces any errors, then cleans things up, removing the PVE.

- `check` executes a `pipenv check` command (https://pipenv.pypa.io/en/latest/commands.html#check), which looks for known vulnerabilities in the package dependencies in the project. Those vulnerabilities can be explicitly ignored by adding their identifiers to the `IGNORED_PIPENV_CHECKS` value. The intention here is to raise a vulnerability warning, prompting an examination of the vulnerability, before deciding whether to add it to the ignored list (if it is not relevant or critical), to update the vulnerable dependency, or to try to find an alternative to the vulnerable package.

- `upload` is only used in the `cicd-build` target, and is responsible for uploading the built package files to the PyPI repository that the packaging-test target examined earlier. The credentials for accessing that repository are the `TWINE_USERNAME` and `TWINE_PASSWORD` environment variables at the top of the file.

- clean removes all of the build artifacts from the environment where the make process has run. In a CI/CD context, it may not be needed, particularly if the process runs in a container that is deleted after each execution.

Processes managed by make are as portable as the commands and file specifications that the Makefile includes. The make program itself can be installed and run on all the major operating systems available today: Linux, macOS, and Windows. If make-based processes have any drawback, it is that when an execution fails (or if the clean target does not clean everything up correctly, or doesn't exist), the project may be left in an *unclean* state that can lead to unexpected and unwanted effects on later executions. By design, make pays attention to the presence and timestamps of files generated by each target, and to the timestamps of files used by those targets, to determine if a given target needs to be re-run. That process is not foolproof, though, and can lead to incorrect builds when it misses something. Forcing each target to execute every time is an option, and is accomplished in this example by using the .PHONY pseudo-target to specify which other targets will always execute.

Installation of other software

This example does *not* install the relevant Python version, even in the init target intended for use in CI/CD environments. The baseline assumption is that all the software needed to execute any given make target is already available in the environment that the make command is being run in. For the local-build, designed to run on an engineer's machine, those installations are managed by the engineer themselves. In other environment contexts, the installations would have to be managed in some other fashion.

It is possible to incorporate a make-based test/build/deploy process inside other CI/CD systems, allowing a single Makefile in a project to provide all the requisite logic and processes for any build under any environment. With a well-thought-out Makefile in place, other build processes can simply use the relevant target to do all that needs to be done. Most **Source Control Management (SCM)** providers also provide some sort of build-process tooling that could take advantage of this approach, though they also provide their own ways of issuing the same commands as part of their processes.

CI/CD with SCM tools

At least two separate online SCM providers offer CI/CD services that can be attached to individual code repositories:

- Bitbucket Pipelines (`https://www.atlassian.com/software/bitbucket/features/pipelines`) offers 50 free build minutes per month on their free accounts, with 1,000 additional minutes costing $10. That may be per repository, per project (repository grouping), or per account; their pricing documentation is not clear.
- GitHub Actions (`https://docs.github.com/en/actions`) offers 2,000 free CI/CD minutes every month on their free accounts, and (apparently) unlimited free build minutes for public repositories.

Both use a similar definition process, at a high level, though the specific formats and structures vary. Both represent the CI/CD process in a YAML file. Those YAML files define the sequence of activities to be executed in a temporary build environment running in some sort of containerized compute, along with information about what types of repository activities trigger those processes. When a trigger is detected, the build process kicks off, creating a container that the commands will execute in, configures it as needed with any related information in the YAML file, and runs the commands until the process completes or reports an error.

Because these processes will need access to various secrets — the `TWINE_USERNAME` and `TWINE_PASSWORD` noted earlier fall into this category, and others will be needed for deployments into various types of environments for application and service code — they also provide some mechanism for storing those secret values, associated with the repository. That allows any secret needed by the build process to be stored **with** the repository, but not **in** it.

Do not store secrets in a repository!

Secrets should **never** be stored in a repository. Doing so poses significant security risks that can lead to compromises of systems or unauthorized (and maybe undetected) use of resources with monetary costs involved. Though SCM providers make efforts to keep their systems secure, secrets can be leaked by accident, sometimes by cloning or forking repositories, or if a user account that has repository access gets compromised.

Of the two variants noted earlier, the **Bitbucket Pipeline** format is simpler, at least for the package build and deploy process being examined. It lends itself well to a single-step process that can accomplish everything necessary to test, build, and publish a Python package without having to worry about passing the results of a given step in the process to later step entries. An example of a Bitbucket Pipeline definition that accomplishes the same ends as the previous make-based process is available in the chapter repository at `cicd-processes/bitbucket-pipelines.yml`. Without most of the comments in that file, it looks like this:

```yaml
image: python:3.11.11-bullseye
options:
  max-time: 2
pipelines:
  branches:
    main:
      - step:
          name: Test, build and publish the package
          variables:
            IGNORED_PIPENV_CHECKS: "--ignore 123"
          script:
            # Show build environment info
            - uname -a
            - pwd
            - ls *
            - python3.11 --version
            - python3.11 -m pip install pipenv==2023.12.1
            - cp template.env .env
            - pipenv sync -dev
            - pipenv graph
            - pipenv run pytest tests/packaging/
            - pipenv run coverage run -m pytest tests/unit
            - pipenv run coverage report -m
            - pipenv sync --categories build
            - pipenv graph
            - pipenv run python -m build
            - TMP_ENV=$$(mktemp -d)
            - python -m venv $$TMP_ENV/venv
            - $$TMP_ENV/venv/bin/activate
```

```
- pip install dist/*.whl
- pytest tests/unit
- deactivate
- rm -rf $$TMP_ENV
- export IGNORED_PIPENV_CHECKS="--ignore 123"
- pipenv check $(IGNORED_PIPENV_CHECKS)
- pipenv sync --categories publish
- pipenv graph
- twine upload
    --repository-url $PYPI_REPOSITORY_URL
    -u $TWINE_USERNAME
    -p $TWINE_PASSWORD dist/*
```

The bulk of these commands are identical to the ones used in the previous make-based example. Each item in the script list of the step in the definition will be executed by the process when a push to the main branch is detected. Additional branches can also be defined, with a name or wildcard, its own step (or several, if needed), and a script list to execute.

A significant addition here is the collection of commands under the # Show build environment info comment. These are intended to provide information about the build environment itself. If the build pipeline fails for some reason, having the build process report each of the following can be immensely useful in troubleshooting issues:

- uname -a reports the operating system, the name of the machine, the kernel version of the operating system kernel, and the CPU type that's running, among other things.

- pwd prints the current working directory that the build process is executing in, which can be used to correct relative path issues, if they arise.

- ls * lists all of the files and directories in the directory shown by the pwd command, which can also help in correcting relative path issues, if they arise.

- python3.11 --version shows the specific version of the Python installation.

- python3.11 -m pip install pipenv==2023.12.1 installs a specific version of pipenv in the build environment, overwriting any previously installed version if needed.

Consistency in `pipenv` versioning

The versioning scheme for `pipenv` follows a date-of-release strategy rather than **semantic versioning** (`https://semver.org/`). Typically, with semantic versioning, changes in specific fields of the version number indicate whether breaking changes to the software are likely or expected. For example, a version change from `1.2.3` to `2.0.0` indicates that there are breaking changes across those two versions, while a change from `1.2.3` to `1.3.0` is intended to indicate that new functionality has been added, but compatibility with the previous version is expected. Similarly, a change from `1.2.3` to `1.2.4` typically indicates a backwards-compatible bug-fix. Since `pipenv` doesn't use that convention, looking for breaking changes across versions typically means reviewing the changes, which is tedious at best and can be very time-consuming. In general, it is a good idea for teams to standardize on a single version of pipenv and update that version everywhere when there is a need or desire to.

From that point on, the commands shown, and the sequence that they are shown in, are the same as the ones in each of the targets in the make-based example, though there are a couple of noteworthy items there too. There are `pipenv sync --category` installations broken out separately in this definition: the `build` and `publish` categories are not installed until they are needed. The intention with those is to avoid installing those package groups until the tests prior to their use have passed. That is expected to save a few seconds of *chargeable build-time* for each pipeline execution if they would not be called anyway. After each of those installations, the pipeline also executes a pipenv graph to show the current installed packages at that point, for troubleshooting purposes should the need arise.

GitHub Action structure and syntax are recognizably similar to an equivalent Bitbucket Pipeline definition, though there are some significant structural differences. A GitHub Action definition that is directly equivalent to the Bitbucket Pipeline just shown would look like this, minus some name values that are shown in the `cicd-processes/github-actions-build.yml` file in the chapter repository:

```
name: Test, Build, and Publish Package
on:
  push:
    branches:
```

```yaml
        - main
  jobs:
    build-and-publish:
      runs-on: ubuntu-latest
      timeout-minutes: 2
      container:
        image: python:3.11.11-bullseye
      env:
        IGNORED_PIPENV_CHECKS: "--ignore 123"
      steps:
        - uses: actions/checkout@v4
        - run: |
            uname -a
            pwd
            ls *
            python3.11 --version
        - run: python3.11 -m pip install pipenv==2023.12.1
        - run: cp template.env .env
        - run: |
            pipenv sync -dev
            pipenv graph
        - run: pipenv run pytest tests/packaging/
        - run: |
            pipenv run coverage run -m pytest tests/unit
            pipenv run coverage report -m
        - run: |
            pipenv sync --categories build
            pipenv graph
            pipenv run python -m build
        - run: |
            TMP_ENV=$(mktemp -d)
            python -m venv $TMP_ENV/venv
            source $TMP_ENV/venv/bin/activate
            pip install dist/*.whl
            pytest tests/unit
            deactivate
            rm -rf $TMP_ENV
```

```
    - run: pipenv check $IGNORED_PIPENV_CHECKS
    - env:
        TWINE_USERNAME: ${{ secrets.TWINE_USERNAME }}
        TWINE_PASSWORD: ${{ secrets.TWINE_PASSWORD }}
        PYPI_REPOSITORY_URL: \
          ${{ secrets.PYPI_REPOSITORY_URL }}
      run: |
        pipenv sync --categories publish
        pipenv graph
        twine upload \
          --repository-url $PYPI_REPOSITORY_URL \
          -u $TWINE_USERNAME -p $TWINE_PASSWORD dist/*
```

The chief differences between this structure and the Bitbucket variation are the use of the run keys, which allow the commands to be grouped in a more natural fashion, one command per line, rather than requiring each of them to be a distinct item in the list of commands.

These SCM-based CI/CD processes and the techniques for defining them are not limited to SCM providers. At least one cloud service uses a very similar approach to define reusable build processes for testing and building code: AWS and its CodeBuild service.

CI/CD in the cloud: AWS CodeBuild

AWS' **CodeBuild** (`https://aws.amazon.com/codebuild/`) works in much the same way that the Bitbucket and GitHub processes do: a container is created from some common, relevant image, dependencies get installed, and a process starts up to execute a series of commands. If all those commands execute successfully, the resulting artifacts can be published or deployed as needed, or passed along to the next step in a larger **CodePipeline** (`https://aws.amazon.com/codepipeline/`) process for whatever disposition is relevant. Because CodeBuild resources live in AWS's infrastructure, an external triggering mechanism is needed to kick off the build process. The most common approach is to create a **webhook** — a lightweight, event-driven communication method that allows applications and services to notify each other when a specific event occurs. The processes for each of the SCM providers are described in their respective documentation:

- Bitbucket: `https://support.atlassian.com/bitbucket-cloud/docs/manage-webhooks/`
- GitHub: `https://docs.github.com/en/webhooks/using-webhooks/creating-webhooks`

These webhooks, once created, can be used as the trigger mechanism for a CodeBuild resource, kicking off the process that it was built to execute. That process is defined, once again, by a YAML file that provides commands to be run, in sequence. The file structure for a CodeBuild is called a **buildspec**, and is documented at https://docs.aws.amazon.com/codebuild/latest/userguide/build-spec-ref.html. A buildspec that will execute the same test, build, and publish processes as the previous examples would look like this:

```yaml
version: 0.2
env:
  variables:
    IGNORED_PIPENV_CHECKS: "--ignore 123--ignore 456"
  # Uncomment if you want to use AWS Secrets Manager
  # secrets-manager:
  #   TWINE_USERNAME: twine:TWINE_USERNAME
  #   TWINE_PASSWORD: twine:TWINE_PASSWORD
  #   PYPI_REPOSITORY_URL: twine:PYPI_REPOSITORY_URL
phases:
  install:
    runtime-versions:
      python: 3.11
    commands:
      - echo "Installing pipenv"
      - pip install pipenv==2023.12.1
  pre_build:
    commands:
      - echo "Environment info"
      - uname -a
      - pwd
      - ls *
      - python3 --version
      - echo "Setting up environment"
      - cp template.env .env
      - pipenv sync --dev
      - pipenv graph
```

```
    build:
      commands:
        - echo "Running packaging tests"
        - pipenv run pytest tests/packaging/
        - echo "Running unit tests with coverage"
        - pipenv run coverage run -m pytest tests/unit
        - pipenv run coverage report -m
        - echo "Building the package"
        - pipenv sync --categories build
        - pipenv graph
        - pipenv run python -m build
        - echo "Verifying the built package"
        - TMP_ENV=$(mktemp -d)
        - python -m venv $TMP_ENV/venv
        - source $TMP_ENV/venv/bin/activate
        - pip install dist/*.whl
        - pytest tests/unit
        - deactivate
        - rm -rf $TMP_ENV
        - echo "Running pipenv check"
        - pipenv check $IGNORED_PIPENV_CHECKS
    post_build:
      commands:
        - echo "Publishing the package"
        - pipenv sync --categories publish
        - pipenv graph
        - twine upload -repository-url
            $PYPI_REPOSITORY_URL -u $TWINE_USERNAME
            -p $TWINE_PASSWORD dist/*
```

A buildspec can break actions out into several phases, including the install, pre_build, build, and post_build phases shown in the example. They also have access to secret storage in AWS Secrets Manager (https://aws.amazon.com/secrets-manager/) and can automatically retrieve and decrypt those secrets into environment variables to be used in the process.

Other commands of interest for builds

Depending on needs, desires, and team standards, there are other commands that might be usefully incorporated into a build process. If code linting is a concern during a build, that can be accomplished with several linting tools. The `flake8` package (`https://pypi.org/project/flake8/`) provides linting, PEP-8 conformance checking, and McCabe code-complexity checking all in one package, for example, and could be integrated as a check process that would terminate a build when any issues are detected with:

```
pipenv run flake8 src --max-complexity 10
```

If the preference is to run the checks but not terminate a build, that can be accomplished with a very similar command:

```
pipenv run flake8 src --max-complexity 10 --exit-zero
```

These would both check all of the code in the `src` directory, looking for code style issues (PEP-8 style-guide compliance), various types of code issues (including imports and variables that are not used), and functions and methods that are too complex, and should be refactored (see `https://en.wikipedia.org/wiki/Cyclomatic_complexity` for a detailed description of code complexity).

It might also be useful or desirable to incorporate additional testing processes against the code, including integration, system, and end-to-end test suites that have been discussed previously. Another possibility is testing that docstrings in the code that provide examples of use provide *valid* examples of use. Python's built-in `doctest` package (`https://docs.python.org/3.11/library/doctest.html`) can do just that.

Summary

All of the examples presented here so far have focused on the test/build/publish processes for Python packages, mostly because that has been the focus of the project code exploration so far in this book. As mentioned in the *Building/packaging the code into a deployable artifact* section earlier, there are other packaging and deployment processes that will apply to application and service projects, though they will depend heavily on how and to where those projects' code is deployed. With the cloud-provider decision made in this chapter, the next chapter can finally focus on how the API implementation will take shape.

16

API Options

Python's third-party package ecosystem provides several popular and robust options for creating several types of web-based APIs and even full-blown applications. Outside of those options, there are standard cloud-resident mechanisms for providing the same API or service functionality. There are even options that mix the two basic approaches, for example, using a third-party package to implement an API or application, but deploying the result in a container living in the cloud. Choosing between these options can be a daunting task — they all have their advantages and drawbacks. The intent of this chapter is to provide enough information on each of the major players in that space to make informed decisions about the best path forward for a set of requirements.

To that end, this chapter will discuss the following:

- What standards and options are available for providing an API, independent of the frameworks required to implement them
- A functional (if simple) example application and API in two of the simpler popular server-based frameworks
- How those server-based approaches can be implemented with popular containerization systems
- What an equivalent implementation would involve in a purely serverless, cloud-resident implementation

Technical requirements

The code for this chapter was written for Python 3.11 and assumes that it is available on your machine. Download and installation instructions are available online at https://www.python.org/downloads/ for Windows, Linux/Unix, macOS, and other systems. The functional examples presented here have different package dependency requirements, which are captured in the Pipfile or requirements.txt files for each example. Running them will also require a complete local development database installation, as discussed in *Chapter 13*.

Code for this chapter is provided in the chapter repository at https://github.com/PacktPublishing/Hands-On-Software-Engineering-with-Python-Second-Edition/tree/main/CH16-code/.

Moving from services to APIs

Prior to the development story that this book has been telling, HMS was focused on providing various **services** — self-contained programs running in the background — that provided specific capabilities for the Artisans and HMS operations. The changes to that approach that have been described in this book have focused on moving from that kind of service-based implementation to an API-based approach. An **API**, short for **Application Programming Interface**, is a set of rules and protocols that provide a common set of processes that allow different software applications to communicate and exchange data. In this particular case, the HMS API being discussed could be more precisely described as a **Web API** — an API that is accessible using standard HTTP requests and responses, accepting and returning data in a manner that is compatible with that protocol. APIs that do not use a web request/response exist; it is not uncommon for packages to be described as providing an API, for example, even if it has no relevance to any web or HTTP use context.

There are several options to choose from when providing a web-based API. The most widely used is **REST (REpresentational State Transfer)**, providing a simple, flexible, and scalable model that is directly compatible with all of the common HTTP request types. REST as an API standard is also very mature, dating back to the early 2000s, and typically uses JSON to represent the data going to and coming from the API.

A newer option that is becoming popular is GraphQL. **GraphQL** (https://graphql.org/) is a query language that is processed by server-side runtimes that allow requests to specify what data is to be returned at an object-by-object and field-by-field level, and supports multiple concurrent operations in a single request. GraphQL provides two basic operation types: **queries** that return data, and **mutations** that create, alter, or delete data. GraphQL requests, whether queries or mutations, can also be made in a **subscription** context that allows a client to make the request and be sent the data when it is complete.

These are not the only options available for the provision of web-based APIs. Other options include **Remote Procedure Call (RPC)** implementations that could be thought of as web interfaces for making function calls on an API server, and **Simple Object Access Protocol (SOAP)**, an XML-based API protocol that can support client/request state — awareness of who a client making a request is, and their previous interactions with the API — and provide more robust security based on that.

For HMS's purposes, REST is the preferred option for several reasons:

- A GraphQL implementation would require an additional server to be created to interface between client requests and the relational database that actually stores the data. There are other considerations that make it worth looking at as an option in the future, and the HMS team will keep those in mind as the REST API is being developed.

- The various RPC options, even the ones that allow for JSON payload responses, all focus on *actions* to be executed rather than *resources* or *objects* whose data is to be returned. While that's not inherently problematic, it doesn't really add much value (if any) and has the potential to complicate front-end implementations.

- SOAP is XML-based, and the front-end team that will be consuming API response data would strongly prefer that API data be returned in JSON, to avoid over-complicating their front-end code or slowing their efforts as they learn how to accommodate XML response data.

- A REST implementation is just easier, conceptually, to understand. The resource objects that will be returned are represented in the request URLs by their name, and the HTTP actions/verbs indicate what is being done in the context of those resource objects.

Making a decision about what type of API to implement relies on several factors. A key consideration is knowing how the data from an API is going to be consumed, and what constraints, if any, need to be kept in mind. Those constraints may be *hard* (functional) ones, such as the need for additional server systems cited for the GraphQL option, or *softer* ones that might be resolvable with thorough documentation or training for whoever is working on the consumer side of the API requests. Equally important is understanding the use cases for the data being returned. What data is required and what data is optional is a good starting point in that space, as is what kinds of actions will be taken in the context of that use case: what CRUD operations, and what other operations are needed. Knowing those, the next step is to consider the design of the API.

Designing the API

Before diving into the design of the REST API, there are some terms that should be defined in relation to how a REST API functions. The first are typical **HTTP methods** (also commonly called **actions** or **verbs**) that determine what is expected in a request structure, and what kinds of response data are required or expected for them.

GET requests simply ask for data, and the responses to them will include that data, if it is available. GET requests are what browsers send when requesting a web page, and a GET request is no different from that perspective. GET requests are only allowed to send one content type (x-www-form-url-encoded), which is likely sent by default by a browser, if it is sent at all. Responses to GET requests should include a content-type specification, with application/json, indicating JSON data, being the most relevant for the current discussion.

HEAD requests are identical to GET requests, except that they return no response content, just the header information that would be returned for an equivalent GET request. HEAD requests are useful for determining whether the response for a given request has changed, provided that they return a Last-Modified header in their response, allowing a client to determine whether a full request of some other type would return new data.

POST requests submit a data payload intended to be used to create a new resource. In HTML forms, they may supply a content type to specify how the submitted data needs to be handled (multipart/form-data), with a default indicating that the payload is URL-encoded data (application/x-www-form-urlencoded). In the context of making an API request, an explicit Content-Type header should be sent to indicate the type of data supplied in the payload. REST APIs that communicate through JSON will expect a JSON payload in the body of the request, and an application/json content-type header, and will return a JSON response payload, with the same content-type header, if they return anything.

PUT requests and **PATCH requests** submit a data payload intended to change existing data in a resource, with a PUT expected to replace the existing resource in its entirety, and a PATCH expected to change only the data specified in the payload submitted. These methods are not supported in HTML forms, but otherwise have the same expectations as the POST method.

DELETE requests, unsurprisingly, request the deletion of one or more resources. In a REST API context, it is safest to implement DELETE requests so that they require the explicit resource identifier(s) of the resource(s) being deleted.

Other HTTP methods

There are four other HTTP methods available, but they are unlikely to be needed or useful in the context of simple APIs. A complete list can be found online at `https://developer.mozilla.org/en-US/docs/Web/HTTP/Reference/Methods`. One that is noted there, but which will not be discussed here, is the `OPTIONS` method, which is a key capability needed for implementing **Cross-Origin Resource Sharing** (**CORS**) for APIs that do not live under the same top-level URL as the pages or applications making requests to them. See `https://developer.mozilla.org/en-US/docs/Web/HTTP/Guides/CORS`.

These methods mostly map in a straightforward manner to the **Create**, **Read**, **Update**, and **Delete** (**CRUD**) processes noted in previous chapters, though certain API types may constrain the HTTP request types, requiring them to be used even for CRUD actions that would logically make more sense to be handled as described here:

- A **Create** action will be implemented using a **POST** request.
- A **Read** action will be implemented using a **GET** request.
- An **Update** action will be implemented as either a **PUT** or **PATCH** request, perhaps supporting both actions.
- A **Delete** action will be implemented as a **DELETE** request.

The last common concept shared across API types is the idea of a **resource** — a discrete piece of data, or an object, that can be accessed and manipulated using the API. In a very real way, API resources can be thought of and treated as equivalents to records in a back-end data store. They will have a unique identifier, which may simply be the URI of the resource in the API's context, but more often is the same unique identifier that uniquely identifies that object's data in a back-end data store. The resources that will be discussed here are also **objects**: instances of the classes defined in the hms-core code, which has been the focus of the last several chapters.

Designing the REST API

Using the terms discussed above, a REST API is not much more than a set of URL paths under a common root URL location that group resources and allow actions to be requested within those groups. That common root-URL location could be a dedicated API server (api.hand-made-stuff. com, for example), or a path under a URL for a website (www.hand-made-stuff.com/api). Functionally, there is no difference in the code involved, though the latter option would avoid having to contend with CORS requirements mentioned earlier. Below that, it is a good practice to include a version as part of the path, allowing future versions to coexist with current versions for as long as the older version is in use.

Below that root URL, whatever shape it takes, the actual organization of the API starts with path segments named after the resources that they relate to. In the case of the HMS API, those path segments map requests received to operations and functionality relating to the business object classes defined earlier:

- artisans would interact with Artisan objects, allowing direct interactions with those objects and their records in the back-end data store.
- products would interact with Product objects in a similar fashion.

REST APIs typically have a nested structure available when there are relationships between resources. In the case of the HMS API, these nested paths, including an {oid} in the path that identifies the object of the type preceding it in the URL, would be logical examples:

- artisans/{oid}/products would relate to all of the Product objects relating to an Artisan identified by the {oid}.
- artisans/{oid}/products/{oid}/images would relate to all of the ProductImage objects associated with a Product identified by its {oid}, and that Product, in turn, would relate to the Artisan object identified by *that* {oid}.
- products/{oid}/images would also relate to all of the ProductImage objects associated with a Product identified by its {oid}, but without the Artisan relationship.
- products/{oid}/artisan would relate to the Artisan associated with the Product identified by the {oid}, perhaps returning a subset of the Artisan data rather than the entirety of it.

At least in theory, each of these six paths, with their methods as **endpoints**, would be able to accept requests using any of the HTTP methods described earlier, resulting in 30 HTTP-verb/endpoint combinations that would require code behind them in order to do anything useful.

Realistically, though, given the use cases mentioned several chapters back, that number can be reduced significantly, at least at first, to these six path/method combinations:

Use Case	Endpoint	HTTP Verb
Artisan: Sign Up	`artisans`	POST
Admin: Approve Artisan	`artisans`	PATCH
Artisan: Add Product	`artisans/{oid}/products`	POST
Artisan: Edit Product	`artisans/{oid}/products/{oid}`	PATCH
Artisan: Delete Product	`artisans/{oid}/products/{oid}`	DELETE
Admin: Approve Product	`artisans/{oid}/products/{oid}`	PATCH
General: View Products	`products`	GET

Table 16.1: The simplified endpoints needed for known use cases

Between them, working from the bottom up, those endpoints provide the following:

- A collection of *Product* data structures, suitable for use in generating an end-user-focused product list
- The approval of a specific *Product*, *Artisan* management of *Product* objects (including creating, editing, and deleting Product data)
- Administrative approval of an *Artisan* to be active on the site
- The initial *Artisan* sign-up

REST is first and foremost a standard for defining uniform interfaces for accessing data with standard HTTP methods. In combination with easily understood resources — artisans and products, for example — it allows endpoints to be defined so that the end user needs only to understand the intentions of those interfaces. For example, the `products` endpoint, since it is the general retrieval endpoint in the products resource path, will probably be built to return all data for `Product` objects, which may be more data than is necessary for the product list page that was noted in the original discussion of use cases. If a more limited dataset were desired, there is nothing functionally preventing another endpoint — `product-list`, perhaps — from being defined that retrieves all of the same `Product` objects, but reduces the JSON results to only fields and child objects that are relevant for that specific use case.

The freedom and flexibility of REST come with at least one trade-off, though: Documentation of anything that is not a standard data retrieval or manipulation process, even if it is as simple as not supporting a field in one endpoint that is available in another, becomes increasingly important as more of those variations accumulate.

There are at least two widely used standards for documenting REST APIs: the **JSON API Specification** (`https://jsonapi.org/format/`) and the **OpenAPI Specification (OAS)**, formerly known as **Swagger** (`https://swagger.io/specification/`). Both are standard ways to define schemas for APIs and their operations, and data structures as JSON or YAML documents. Those schema documents may include data about the schema elements — descriptions of endpoints, names for them, example data for object fields, and more — that can be rendered into more human-readable formats with various tools and online services. A partial example of such a schema is included in the chapter repository in the file at `documentation/example-oas-schema.yaml`. That schema, if pasted into the new **Swagger Editor** page at `https://editor-next.swagger.io`, shows how much detail can be provided in a schema, and how it can be rendered, with a screen capture of part of that rendered documentation shown in *Figure 16.1*.

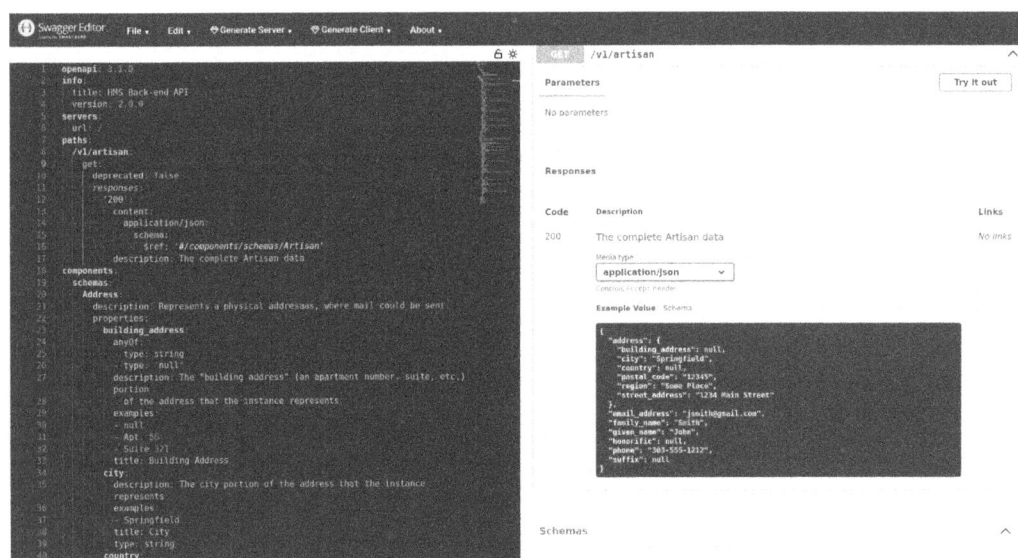

Figure 16.1: The Swagger Editor view of the example-oas-schema.yaml file in the chapter repository

Although REST is a very popular API approach and has a lot of flexibility, it also has limitations. Because REST is based on a request/response process model, it cannot be used in scenarios requiring constant real-time data updates without actively repeating requests, a practice commonly known as **polling**.

The data structures returned by a REST endpoint are, by default, consistently structured and may return more data than is actually needed for a given use case as a result. In a similar vein, if a response object does not contain all the data that a given use case requires, but that data is available through some other endpoint, retrieval of all the requisite data can involve multiple requests and multiple responses. There are ways to work around these, including the creation of custom-purpose endpoints as already described, and allowing the request to specify fields and child objects in some fashion, but both of those require additional development effort: more code to write, test, and maintain over time.

REST is inherently **stateless**: no information about any client is maintained across multiple requests, requiring any state-related data to either be passed with each request or managed in some other fashion, often on the client side, adding complexity *somewhere* in the stack. That state information frequently also includes authentication and authorization data that has to be planned for and implemented, with the potential for different requirements on a per-endpoint and/or per-method basis. Potential authentication and authorization concerns are significant enough that they will be addressed later in this chapter.

REST is a strategy, or a set of architectural guidelines, at most, not a formal protocol. As a result, considerable variation in REST implementations can be found across different APIs, even in the same organization or team. It is even possible for wide variations to occur across different endpoints in the same API. Standardization and documentation will both go a long way towards reducing these variations, or at least reducing their impact, but those efforts can also add time to development efforts.

All of the various drawbacks of REST APIs noted here led to the design, development, and release of another common, popular API alternative: GraphQL.

An equivalent GraphQL API

GraphQL was developed internally by Facebook in 2012 to address several of the drawbacks of REST noted earlier, and released to the public in 2015. Like REST, it is consumed over an HTTP connection and uses one of the HTTP protocol's methods/verbs (GET or POST) to submit requests. They both provide a number of endpoints where requests can be made to work with API data. A GraphQL API has only one endpoint, though, typically /graphql, while a REST API can have several, and may have dozens. That is pretty much where the similarities end.

GraphQL APIs rely on, and are defined by, a **schema** — a definition of the structure of the data that is accessible through the API, and the specific operations that are available through that API. Using the business object classes defined in *Chapter 13* as an example, the definitions for Artisan and Product objects in a GraphQL API should look familiar:

```
scalar DateTime
scalar Decimal
interface BaseDataObject {
  oid: ID!
  isActive: Boolean!
  isDeleted: Boolean!
  created: DateTime!
  modified: DateTime
}
type Artisan implements BaseDataObject {
  oid: ID!
  isActive: Boolean!
  isDeleted: Boolean!
  created: DateTime!
  modified: DateTime
  honorific: String
  givenName: String!
  middleName: String
  familyName: String!
  suffix: String
  companyName: String
  address: Address!
  emailAddress: String!
  products: [Product!]!
}
type Product implements BaseDataObject {
  oid: ID!
  isActive: Boolean!
  isDeleted: Boolean!
  created: DateTime!
  modified: DateTime
  artisanOid: ID!
  name: String!
```

```
    summary: String!
    description: String!
    productImages: [ProductImage!]!
    price: Decimal!
    shippingWeight: Decimal!
    height: Decimal
    length: Decimal
    width: Decimal
    artisan: Artisan!
}
```

The GraphQL schema in the chapter repository

The full GraphQL schema document is available in the chapter repository at `documentation/example-graphql-schema.graphqls`. It has comments and documentation omitted here, as well as all of the schema representations for all of the business object classes defined earlier, and additional operations.

This collection of object/type definitions uses two **custom scalars**, `DateTime` and `Decimal`, to provide a more meaningful, descriptive type in the schema. A **scalar** in GraphQL is a value type that has no children, and thus no way to retrieve anything deeper in the type hierarchy. In contrast, the `Artisan.products` field, returning an array of `Product` objects, and the `Product.artisan` field, returning a single related `Artisan` object, have their own hierarchies that can be used: every `Product` in `Artisan.products` would allow a query to retrieve any fields defined in the `Product` type. The availability of this hierarchy is important in defining queries to be executed against a GraphQL API. For example, assume that there is a use-case for some consumer of this GraphQL API to fetch a given `Artisan`, along with all of their available, active `products`, but limiting the data that comes back to the `Artisan`'s `companyName` or the collection of `givenName`, `familyName`, and other *person-name* fields, the `country` from `Artisan.address`, the `oid`, `name`, `summary`, `price`, and the first active, non-deleted `ProductImage` for each `Product`. A GraphQL query, based on the schema shown above, that meets those needs would look like this:

```
# The final query, with comments, is in the chapter repo at
# documentation/example-use-case-graphql-query.graphql
query GetActiveArtisanWithProducts($artisanId: ID!) {
  artisan(oid: $artisanId) {
    honorific
```

```
        givenName
        middleName
        familyName
        suffix
        companyName
        address {
          country
        }
        products {
          oid
          name
          summary
          price
          productImages {
            imageUrl
            caption
            altText
            width
            height
          }
        }
      }
    }
  }
```

If the use case that this query was written for changed, for example, to add the `Artisan.address.postalCode` field and remove the `Artisan.products.productImages.caption` field, those changes are easily made in the query content.

Once a query is constructed, all that needs to be done with it is to make a request with the query body and the variables (if any) needed. In JSON, that payload (with the whitespace and newlines reduced for brevity) would look like this:

```
{
    "query": "query GetActiveArtisanWithProducts
        ($artisanId: ID!){artisan(oid:$artisanId)
        {honorific givenName middleName familyName
        suffix companyName address{postalCode country}
        products{oid name summary price
        productImages{imageUrl altText width height}}}}",
```

```
    "variables": {
      "artisanId": "00000000-0000-0000-0000-000000000000"
    }
  }
```

A significant advantage that GraphQL provides over REST equivalents is that the consumer of the API gets to decide what data elements they want. As long as those fields are available in the relevant object schemas, they can be read by the consumer without requiring any change to the API or any of its backing code. That allows the consumer to fine-tune what data they are requesting, without having to worry about **over-fetching** — retrieving data through the API that will not be used by the consumer — which is a common concern in REST APIs.

GraphQL provides only two basic operations: queries to retrieve data, and mutations to create, alter, or delete data. Those operations are also defined in the schema for the API. Some examples of the queries and mutations that might be expected in the example schema discussed are as follows:

```
### Queries ###
# Root-level query type for retrieving domain objects
type Query {
  # Retrieve a single Artisan by its oid (UUID)
  artisan(oid: ID!): Artisan
  # Retrieve a paginated list of Products
  products(
    offset: Int = 0,
    limit: Int = 10,
    includeInactive: Boolean = false,
    includeDeleted: Boolean = false,
    sortBy: ProductSortField = CREATED_DESC
  ): [Product!]!
}
# Enum to control sorting options for product queries
enum ProductSortField {
  CREATED_ASC     # Oldest first
  CREATED_DESC    # Newest first (default)
  PRICE_ASC       # Lowest price first
  PRICE_DESC      # Highest price first
  NAME_ASC        # Alphabetical by name
  NAME_DESC       # Reverse alphabetical
```

```
}
### Mutations ###
# The various *Input types below are shown
# in the full schema in the chapter repository.
type Mutation {
    """Create a new artisan."""
    createArtisan(input: CreateArtisanInput!): Artisan!
    """Update an existing artisan by oid."""
    updateArtisan(input: UpdateArtisanInput!): Artisan!
    """Create a new product."""
    createProduct(input: CreateProductInput!): Product!
    """Update an existing product by oid."""
    updateProduct(input: UpdateProductInput!): Product!
}
```

In a very real way, GraphQL can be thought of as an API abstraction for working with a back-end data store. The consumer gets to define what data they are retrieving, creating, or altering, and provided that the request is valid according to what is defined in the schema, the request will execute without error, creating, altering, or retrieving the data accordingly.

Given all of these advantages, a natural question to ask is, Why not use GraphQL instead of REST? There are several reasons that a REST implementation might be better than GraphQL, based on the data structures and expected use cases for them:

- REST is good for simple data sources, where the objects being returned are well-defined. In contrast, GraphQL is better suited for large, complex data, particularly if it is interrelated.

- REST, focused as it is on resource objects, is often easier to understand: The idea of a single URL where a request can be made that could be thought of as *get me all Artisans* or *get me the Artisan with this ID* is a simpler concept than having to write a query for the same object set, or learning how to read and understand the relevant GraphQL schema, though that should not need to happen more than once, ideally.

- REST is, in many ways, more flexible, particularly when there's a need to generate custom data structure responses that need to be controlled at the API side in some fashion.

- Because REST allows for (or even requires) a number of different endpoint URLs, it is often easier to apply authentication and authorization restrictions: in a REST context, it is not unusual for authorization to be a simple pass/fail. For example, if a user is authorized to get a response from an endpoint at /api/artisans/{UUID}, writing code that handles that check is far easier than writing code that checks whether they can access every field being requested through the single /graphql endpoint that a GraphQL API provides.

GraphQL is still a viable alternative for API provision, though, and is worth examining as an option, particularly when data complexity is significant. Most of the complexity that is added to an API solution for GraphQL is on the development side of the service, where software engineers who are typically more used to dealing with it will be well-suited to doing so. The balance, particularly for consumers of API data, will be easily mitigated by the simple expedient of providing adequate documentation, including examples, in particular.

This discussion only focused on two of the available types of APIs. The others mentioned earlier, at the beginning of the chapter, may also prove to be better options for other needs, but REST and GraphQL are likely to provide all that is needed for typical web-based APIs. Since the focus for the HMS API that has been building up through this book is a REST implementation, development of a REST API solution will be discussed in more detail later in this chapter, but it is worth examining the several ways of implementing both REST and GraphQL APIs using Python.

Common API options

The Python ecosystem has several options available for implementing API services and full-blown web applications, even before adding the cloud-resident options into the mix. Those options can be usefully grouped into local and containerized implementations, and cloud-resident implementations. The local and containerized implementations include both REST and GraphQL service options.

It is worth mentioning that the REST API providers can also be used to construct and return web pages. From the perspective of the request/response processes involved, there is little to no difference between endpoints that return HTML text content and endpoints that return JSON data structures. The underlying processes may be significantly different in how they do whatever it is that they do to generate their responses, assuming the responsibility for generating any of the HTTP data that is needed to differentiate between HTML and JSON responses, or whatever other data formats are involved.

Web browsers have a very limited set of HTTP actions/verbs that they can use when making requests in the context of what a user is allowed to do on a page. Those are limited to GET and POST, even in HTML <form> elements. Specifying any other actions, such as PATCH and DELETE, simply will not work. Client-side scripts, however, can use any of the available HTTP actions/verbs, opening up the potential for dedicated, meaningful CRUD-operation requests like the ones shown earlier in *Table 16.1*.

Local, server-resident, and containerized implementation options

The common theme between local, server-resident, and containerized API options is that the code is running as a process on some machine, whether it is a virtual (container or virtual computer) or a physical (local or server) machine. A local implementation could run on a workstation or laptop during development, and a dedicated server once it has been deployed to a production environment. It could also run inside a container in the same physical device context, using a containerizing service like Docker, Podman, or Kubernetes. Regardless of how the system is executed, it has some running process that waits for requests, routes those to whatever back end logic is relevant, processes the request, generates a response, and returns that response.

REST-compatible services written in Python provide either a **Web Service Gateway Interface** (**WSGI**) or **Asynchronous Service Gateway Interface** (**ASGI**) implementation that accepts a standard, translated HTTP request from a dedicated web server system suc as **Apache** (using mod_wsgi) or **NGINX**, into a request structure that is more directly usable by Python code, and passes that to an associated Python callable to be processed. The results of those processes are then converted back into a standard HTTP response and returned to the web server, and from there to the client making the request. This type of setup, where the web server is responsible for handling the incoming requests and sending back the responses for those requests, is a **reverse proxy** implementation. Reverse proxy options also include **Gunicorn**, **Waitress**, and **uWSGI**.

On the Python code side of that arrangement, there are some variations in what the code looks like that associate a given HTTP request path (an **endpoint**) to a given function that handles requests to that path. The two API frameworks that will be examined in any detail here are **Flask** and **FastAPI**. There is also a REST API extension for the Django web-application framework, but that will not be examined in much detail here, for reasons that will be explained later.

To show the similarities and differences between Flask and FastAPI implementations, examples of both have been provided in the chapter repository, implementing a very simple web application page and REST API. The root of the site (/) maps to a function named website_home, which provides an HTML page that shows all of the Artisans in the application database, and a form that allows the user to create a new Artisan. The HTML of that page is defined as a template file, and the content is populated dynamically using the popular Jinja2 templating package (https://pypi.org/project/Jinja2/). The various page components that are shown and hidden rely on calls to the API that is provided in the application.

These examples implement two API endpoints, using GET, POST, and PATCH methods to differentiate between how each endpoint behaves for each method, with a total of four action/endpoint combinations:

- `/api/v1/artisans/` (GET) maps to the get_artisans_root function, and returns a list of every Artisan object in the database, whether it is active or not.

- `/api/v1/artisans/` (POST) maps to the post_artisans_root function, which accepts Artisan data as key/value pairs, creates a new Artisan object with the supplied data, and saves it to the database.

- `/api/v1/artisans/<oid>/` (GET) maps to the get_artisan_by_oid function, and returns a single Artisan object, identified by the oid value (<oid>) in the path.

- `/api/v1/artisans/<oid>/` (PATCH) maps to the patch_artisan_by_oid function, which accepts Artisan data as key/value pairs, retrieves the Artisan specified by the oid in the path (<oid>), updates the retrieved Artisan object, and saves it to the database.

API implementations using Flask and FastAPI are provided in the chapter repository to make it easy to compare and contrast the code required for each. These implementations provide a very basic front-end page, using a common templating engine (jinja2, see https://pypi.org/project/Jinja2/) and using Bootstrap (https://getbootstrap.com/) to provide some reasonably modern layout and styling for that page. The rest of the functionality they provide is all focused on implementing some of the basic CRUD operations for Artisan objects, including creation of new Artisans, updating existing ones, and two variations of reading existing objects (one at a time, or as a collection) using built-in JavaScript functionality.

Flask (REST)

> *Flask is a lightweight WSGI web application framework. It is designed to make getting started quick and easy, with the ability to scale up to complex applications.*
>
> *from* https://flask.palletsprojects.com/

Package: https://pypi.org/project/Flask/

Flask's implementation centers around the creation of an **application object**: an instance of the Flask class provided by the package. That application object (app) provides a decorator method, route, that defines the endpoint path and HTTP method associations for individual functions, and registers them with the application object. In summary, the code for the Flask implementation of the endpoints and methods described earlier is the following:

```python
from flask import Flask, request
# Module "Constants" and Attributes
app = Flask(__name__)
@app.route('/api/v1/artisans/<oid>/', methods=['GET'])
def get_artisan_by_oid(*args, **kwargs):
    # The **kwargs is where the oid can be found
    ...
@app.route('/api/v1/artisans/', methods=['GET'])
def get_artisans_root():
    ...
@app.route('/api/v1/artisans/<oid>/', methods=['PATCH'])
def patch_artisan_by_oid(*args, **kwargs):
    # The **kwargs is where the oid can be found
    payload = json.loads(request.data)
    ...
@app.route('/api/v1/artisans/', methods=['POST'])
def post_artisans_root():
    payload = json.loads(request.data)
    ...
```

The complete code for this example is available in the CH16-code directory of the book's repository on GitHub, in the flask-example directory.

Once the Flask application is run, its home page (shown with some Artisan objects added locally during testing) should look something like the screen capture shown in *Figure 16.2*.

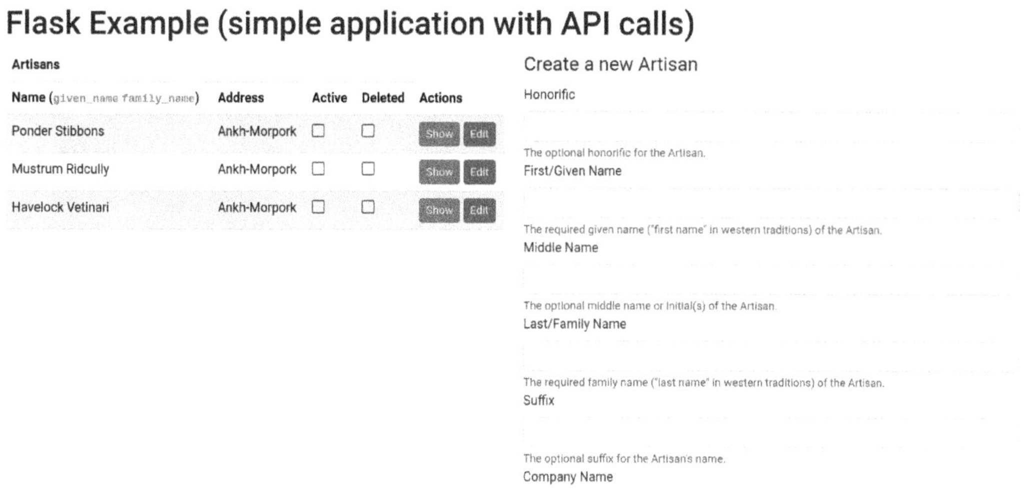

Flask Example (simple application with API calls)

Figure 16.2: The home page of the Flask example from the chapter repository

Each *Artisan* shown has a **Show** button that triggers a display of the complete set of fields for that object, and an **Edit** button that triggers a form display that allows its data to be edited. Those triggered views also trigger a **Show Create a new Artisan form** button at the bottom of the *Artisan* list, allowing the user to return to the view shown in *Figure 16.2*.

FastAPI (REST)

> *FastAPI is a modern, fast (high-performance), web framework for building APIs with Python based on standard Python type hints.*
>
> *from* `https://fastapi.tiangolo.com/`

FastAPI claims speeds comparable with TypeScript and Go implementations, and credits that to tight integration with Pydantic (for data modeling) and `starlette` (`https://pypi.org/project/starlette/`), a lightweight and low-complexity web framework designed for asynchronous web services. The approach it uses to define endpoints in HTTP services is very similar to the approach taken by Flask, using decorators to associate specific Python functions to specific endpoint paths and HTTP methods within the context of an application object.

FastAPI's decorators are specific to HTTP methods, though, while Flask allows a single function to handle any specified HTTP methods. A summarized view of the same endpoints provided in the Flask example, using FastAPI's functionality, is the following:

```python
from fastapi import FastAPI
app = FastAPI()
host = os.getenv('FASTAPI_RUN_HOST', '127.0.0.1')
port = int(os.getenv('FASTAPI_RUN_PORT', '5000'))
@app.get('/api/v1/artisans/{oid}/')
async def get_artisan_by_oid(oid: str):
    # Note that oid is an explicitly defined parameter!
    ...
@app.get('/api/v1/artisans/')
async def get_artisans_root():
    ...
@app.patch('/api/v1/artisans/{oid}/')
async def patch_artisan_by_oid(oid: str, payload: dict):
    # Note that oid is an explicitly defined parameter!
    ...
@app.post('/api/v1/artisans/')
async def post_artisans_root(payload: dict):
    ...
```

The complete code for this example is available in the CH16-code directory of the book's repository on GitHub, in the fastapi-example directory.

FastAPI is geared towards asyncio

Another significant difference, and probably one that contributes significantly to FastAPI's speed advantage over Flask, is its support for the built-in asyncio library (https://docs.python.org/3.11/library/asyncio.html). asyncio provides built-in handling for concurrent (or parallelized) execution of I/O-bound operations, where the primary constraint on the execution time of that code is the time spent waiting for input and output operations to complete. Examples of I/O-bound processes include interaction with external resources such as APIs and databases. CPU-bound, or process-bound operations, in contrast, are mostly constrained by the CPU performing computations.

Because the functionality within each of the endpoint functions is the same, as well as the templating for the HTML output and the client-side scripts and styles, the page looks and behaves in exactly the same manner as the Flask example noted earlier — only the specific decoration to assign functions to endpoint/method combinations has changed.

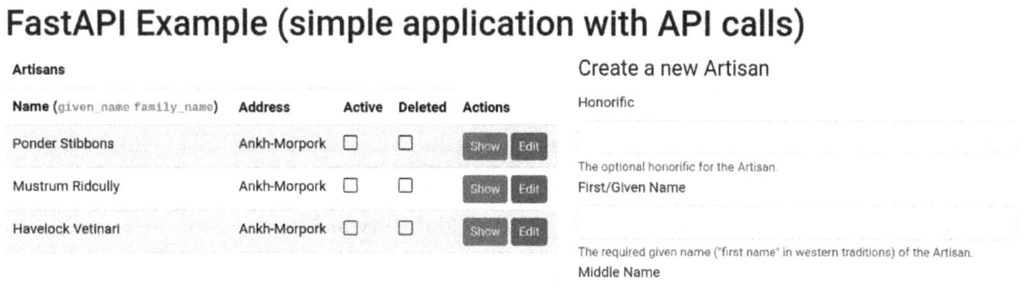

FastAPI Example (simple application with API calls)

Artisans					
Name (given_name family_name)	**Address**	**Active**	**Deleted**	**Actions**	
Ponder Stibbons	Ankh-Morpork	☐	☐	Show Edit	
Mustrum Ridcully	Ankh-Morpork	☐	☐	Show Edit	
Havelock Vetinari	Ankh-Morpork	☐	☐	Show Edit	

Create a new Artisan

Honorific

The optional honorific for the Artisan.
First/Given Name

The required given name ("first name" in western traditions) of the Artisan.
Middle Name

Figure 16.3: The home page of the FastAPI example from the chapter repository

FastAPI and Flask are both designed with APIs as a primary deliverable. There is no reason, as shown by the examples for each, why they cannot return HTML content, scripts, styles, or even serve images for a full-blown website. Ultimately, the only differences between an API response and responses that return those other data types are how they are handled in the structure of the code and what additional code needs to be written to generate that data, if any.

Django REST framework (REST)

Django (`https://www.djangoproject.com/`) is a high-level Python web application framework that is designed to facilitate rapid application development. Although it is designed for full-blown application development — web pages with content driven by a back-end data store — its ecosystem also includes a package that allows Django applications to provide REST APIs: the **Django Rest Framework (DRF)** (`https://pypi.org/project/djangorestframework/`).

> **Be sure to install the right DRF package**
>
> There is a `django-rest-framework` package available in the public PyPI repository; that is not the package in question, though it appears to have been an effort by one of the maintainers of the actual package.

Because the DRF leverages Django's core functionality, including an ORM and robust model-class and model field definitions that are substantially different from the design direction taken for the HMS project discussed here, no example code has been provided. Django, in conjunction with the DRF, is a perfectly viable option for creating APIs, though, and may be an *extremely* good choice for a new project: Django's ecosystem of third-party applications/packages has *thousands* of options to add commonly needed capabilities for Django systems (see `https://djangopackages.org/`). Those include authentication and authorization, alternatives to the DRF, GraphQL API provision, and much, much more.

Other options for providing REST APIs include Falcon, Bottle, Eve, and Tornado, all of which can be found on the public PyPI repository. Their implementation expectations vary somewhat from the examples shown for Flask and FastAPI, but appear straightforward enough.

In the GraphQL space, there are at least two packages that appear to be popular: Graphene and Ariadne. Examples of implementations for both are provided in the chapter repository, but it is worth noting that these do not have an HTML front-end, even though they both use FastAPI as the connector between the ASGI server (`uvicorn`) and the API services themselves. Both examples can be started as local services using the same command as a result:

```
pipenv run uvicorn src.app:app -reload
```

They can be queried with the same `curl` commands from a terminal, for example:

```
curl -X POST http://localhost:8000/graphql/ \
    -H "Content-Type: application/json"\
    -d '{"query": "{ getArtisans { oid givenName familyName } }"}'
```

That command will return the same results, shown here formatted for ease of reading:

```
{
    "data":{
        "getArtisans":[
            {
                "oid":"645c068c-4a3c-4cfa-90ac-659b99e5034b",
                "givenName":"Ponder",
                "familyName":"Stibbons"
            },
            {
                "oid":"88b637f7-8d10-4437-89b8-6fad350b96ba",
                "givenName":"Mustrum",
                "familyName":"Ridcully"
```

```
        },
        {
            "oid":"fd709d83-438d-4b8f-8911-daa9797dc03b",
            "givenName":"Havelock",
            "familyName":"Vetinari"
        }
    ]
  }
}
```

GraphQL prefers camelCase over snake_case naming

Despite the fact that the field names defined in the models being used by these examples are defined using snake_case, both of the GraphQL implementation examples convert those to camelCase equivalents across the board, as can be seen in the preeciding example output. The Graphene example did this all by itself, while the Ariadne example at least allows the field-names to be defined using either. Both examples use camelCase naming for consistency.

Graphene (GraphQL)

Graphene's implementation focuses on defining classes for the GraphQL input and object types that are expected. Incorporating the business objects, defined as Pydantic models earlier, is not supported by Graphene itself, but by an additional package, graphene-pydantic, which provides additional classes that make that integration quite easy. The input and object type classes automatically define GraphQL **resolvers** — functions that resolve a value for a given field or type within the schema — for both the classes as object types and the properties/attributes of those classes as fields. Resolvers can also be defined to override that built-in functionality, or to handle custom requirements for a given field. The implementation of the GraphQL type for an Artisan, with a custom resolver for the email_address field, would look something like this:

```python
from graphene_pydantic import PydanticObjectType
from hms.core.business_objects import Artisan, Address
class ArtisanType(PydanticObjectType):
    class Meta:
        model = Artisan
        exclude_fields = (
            # Custom handling
            "email_address",
```

```
            # Ignoring Product associations for now
            "products"
        )
    email_address = graphene.String()
    # Custom resolver to handle the two email-address
    # types allowed in the Pydantic model
    def resolve_email_address(parent, info):
        return str(parent.email_address)
```

> The complete code for this example is available in the CH16-code directory of the
> book's repository on GitHub, in the graphene-example directory.

Graphene's approach, simply defining classes and letting the framework it provides handle the
creation of the required resolvers, will be quick and easy to implement, so long as there are no
incompatibilities with the field types those resolvers use. In cases where there are incompatibilities, the creation of custom resolver methods to handle those is an option, as is customizing
resolver methods for other reasons.

Ariadne (GraphQL)

Ariadne's approach starts with the definition of a GraphQL schema document like the one shown
earlier in this chapter. That schema is used by the main application (the app.py file in the example), along with query and mutation resolver items (defined in resolvers.py), to create and
mount a GraphQL ASGI process that actually handles the request/response processes when the
GraphQL API is called. Conversion of the data returned by the business object processes is handled
by various converter functions (converters.py), which is where the field-name changes for this
example noted earlier take place. The portions of the various files relating to the Artisan query
shown earlier are as follows:

```
# resolvers.py
from ariadne import QueryType
from hms.core.business_objects import Artisan
from converters import artisan_to_dict, input_to_artisan
query = QueryType()
# -- Query Resolvers --
@query.field("get_artisans")
def resolve_get_artisans(_, info):
    artisans = Artisan.get(db_source_name='Artisan')
```

```
        return [artisan_to_dict(a) for a in artisans]
# converters.py
def artisan_to_dict(artisan: Artisan) -> dict:
    return {
        "oid": str(artisan.oid),
        "honorific": artisan.honorific,
        "givenName": artisan.given_name,
        "middleName": artisan.middle_name,
        "familyName": artisan.family_name,
        "suffix": artisan.suffix,
        "companyName": artisan.company_name,
        "emailAddress": str(artisan.email_address),
        "businessAddress": artisan.business_address
        .model_dump(mode="json")
    }
```

> The complete code for this example is available in the CH16-code directory of the book's repository on GitHub, in the ariadne-example directory.

All of these options, as shown by the examples in the chapter repository, can be run locally, making local development easy to accomplish. With appropriate ASGI/WSGI services to bridge the connection between a client request and the service itself, there is nothing that would prevent the exact same code from being deployed to a server, whether physical or virtual, on-premises, or in a public cloud. Paying for cloud-resident servers can be expensive, though, may not be supported in all cases, and may be more difficult or complicated with respect to load-balancing or providing automatic rollbacks of services that fail runtime testing. In those cases, another option is to build those services into a container and deploy those containers instead.

Containerizing API services

The idea of containerizing applications — packaging applications up with all of their dependencies like libraries and configuration, allowing them to be run on any infrastructure — is not new. Virtualization solutions like VMware, allowing different versions of a service to be deployed to different virtual machines, and controlling access to those versions by simply activating and deactivating the relevant virtual machines, were possible early in the 21st century. Enterprise-scale virtualization of servers on premises was common enough by 2010 that even companies that had minimal to no formal Information Technology departments could (and did) make use of the idea.

The first production-ready release of **Docker** (https://www.docker.com/), in late 2014, represented a sea change in the idea of virtualization. Docker allowed much more portable and efficient virtual machines to be created and managed as containers rather than virtual machines. A Docker container could be run anywhere that Docker could be run, sharing host-machine resources, reducing the need for at least some resources to be defined in each container/virtual machine, and requiring less memory and disk space. These efficiencies also significantly improved boot-up time for the container: A container typically starts in seconds, whereas an equivalent virtual machine might take minutes. The portability containerization provides also allows a developer to build and work with a containerized application locally, and be able to deploy that exact same code base and application to other environments, reducing the need for environment-specific configuration and other environment-related concessions in many cases.

A complete rundown of how to build and deploy a containerized Python application is beyond the scope of this chapter, but there are ample resources and references online for those readers who are looking for more details. One of the best starting points is in the official Docker blogs, at https://www.docker.com/blog/how-to-dockerize-your-python-applications/. A very basic example, implementing the FastAPI-based version of the example application shown earlier, is provided in the chapter repository.

The process of creating a container in Docker, in its simplest form, can be little more than making sure that all of the relevant code and associated resources are in a common directory, then telling Docker to build an image — the actual data and files needed, along with any configuration and environment settings — then running that image as a container. The simplest process for defining an image is through the use of a Dockerfile that provides instructions for the image build process to execute. The Dockerfile for the example is very simple:

```
# Start with an image that provides a bare-bones
# Python installation.
FROM python:3.11-slim
# Set working directory
WORKDIR /app
# Copy the source code and related resources into
# the working directory
COPY . /app
# Install dependencies
RUN pip install --no-cache-dir -r /app/requirements.txt
# Expose port for FastAPI so the application can
```

```
# be reached by a browser
EXPOSE 5000
# Run FastAPI app with uvicorn
CMD ["uvicorn", "app:app", "--host", "0.0.0.0", "--port", "5000"]
```

The project structure used here is slightly different, since it is easier to collect all the items that Docker needs in one directory and simply copy that directory into the working directory for the image. In this case, the code of the hms-core package has been added directly to the app directory that is copied into the working directory, alongside all of the FastAPI-specific files from the earlier example. If the hms-core package were available as an installable package, that would not be needed. There is also a requirements.txt file that captures all of the package dependencies for the application and the hms-core package. This was created in the hms-core project with the following:

```
pipenv requirements > requirements.txt
```

Then, it was copied to the example application directory so that it could be used to install the package dependencies for the example. This example also provides a Makefile that provides build, run, and rebuild targets to make building the image, running a container with the current images, and rebuilding and running the container more convenient.

> The complete code for this example is available in the CH16-code directory of the book's repository on GitHub, in the fastapi-docker-example directory.

This example can be run locally, and behaves and appears exactly the same as the non-containerized FastAPI example, barring a title change in the main page it provides.

FastAPI Example (Containerized simple application with API calls)

Artisans							Create a new Artisan
Name (given_name family_name)	Address	Active	Deleted	Actions			Honorific
Ponder Stibbons	Ankh-Morpork	☐	☐	Show	Edit		
							The optional honorific for the Artisan.
David Kibner	San Francisco	☐	☐	Show	Edit		First/Given Name
Fletcher Christian	Adamstown	☐	☐	Show	Edit		
							The required given name ("first name" in western traditions) of the Artisan.
Mustrum Ridcully	Ankh-Morpork	☐	☐	Show	Edit		Middle Name
Havelock Vetinari	Ankh-Morpork	☐	☐	Show	Edit		
							The optional middle name or initial(s) of the Artisan.

Figure 16.4: The home page of the containerized FastAPI example from the chapter repository

Image creation with a Dockerfile is limited to creating a single container image. That image can be used to create any number of running containers, allowing other processes to spin up additional copies of an application or service automatically, for load-balancing purposes. Those containers are independent of one another, unless they are built to share resources in some fashion, so that a failure of one container that terminates the main process it is running will not affect any other containers executed from the same image. When applications need multiple containers, for example, one container that provides a database and one or more application containers that use that database, there is another mechanism available to make the creation and management of suites of containers easier: Docker Compose. As multi-container applications fall outside the scope of this book, they will not be discussed in any detail, but a useful starting point on that topic is the *Docker Compose Quickstart* (`https://docs.docker.com/compose/gettingstarted/`).

All of the options discussed here are, as noted, viable for both local development, testing, and troubleshooting purposes, and for deployment to a production environment that uses physical or virtual servers. Physical and virtual servers could be on-premises. Virtual servers are also an option in public clouds, whether using a virtual computer service like Amazon **Elastic Compute Cloud (EC2)**, a wrapping service like AWS **Elastic Beanstalk** that adds support for commonly desired capabilities like auto-scaling and monitoring, or a container-based service like Amazon's **Elastic Container Service (ECS)** or **Elastic Kubernetes Service (EKS)**. Public cloud providers also frequently provide *serverless* options — collections of services that allow code to be run on demand, rather than through some type of constantly available virtual machine.

Serverless options

The idea of serverless computing is straightforward enough — it is an execution model where developers write and deploy code, typically as functions or microservices, without having to manage the underlying infrastructure where that code runs. In a cloud context, cloud providers' systems handle provisioning and scaling of the runtime resources that the code is deployed to and executed on. They also typically maintain baseline software versions, things like the version of Python available to a deployed body of code to run under.

Historically, the predecessors to the current serverless approach included various **Platform as a Service (PaaS)** offerings. In the early 2010s, AWS offered Elastic Beanstalk (`https://aws.amazon.com/elasticbeanstalk/`), and Google Cloud Platform offered Google App Engine (`https://cloud.google.com/appengine`). Both of these follow a common PaaS model where the provider delivers the (virtual) hardware, software, and infrastructure needed for developing, running, and managing applications. Both of these services still involved deploying application code to a virtual machine of some sort — Elastic Beanstalk to an Amazon EC2 machine, and Google App Engine to a container that would run in some cluster.

In both cases, those deployed applications' servers would run constantly, costing money even when the applications themselves were completely idle.

In late 2014 or early 2015, AWS introduced **Lambda functions** (`https://aws.amazon.com/lambda/`) — a serverless, **event-driven** compute service that defines a body of code with an entry-point function that is executed when an event trigger indicates that the function needs to be executed, passing the event that triggered it with data needed for the function to execute successfully. By the end of 2016, Google Cloud Functions (`https://cloud.google.com/functions`) and Azure Functions (`https://learn.microsoft.com/en-us/azure/azure-functions/`) were also generally available, following similar if not identical basic concepts. These offerings share common serverless application themes, centering around the idea of a **Function as a Service (FaaS)**, where the deployed code is a collection of modules with a defined entry-point function that is executed when an event is detected that a given function is expected to handle. That event-driven approach is a common theme even outside the FaaS context, with any number of cloud resource types capable of generating events, though for events to be usefully consumed, there generally must be some kind of compute resource involved — something that *receives* events, and actually *does something* with them. For the purposes of this book, the type of event that is most relevant is an event that is generated by a resource that accepts HTTPS requests to an API endpoint, and routes that event to a function that handles that event, returning a response that the API then returns to the calling client. Because serverless application implementations are triggered by events, their compute resources do not need to be constantly running, allowing them to follow a pay-as-you-go pricing model, making them much more cost-effective than a dedicated server.

In the years since, the basic approaches behind the varies FaaS offerings have not changed, though there have been improvements in various areas like **cold-start** times — how long it takes for a new instance of a function to be ready to accept events — provisioning concurrency — keeping one or more already-warm function-instances in reserve to avoid cold starts — and faster or more reliable access to other resources like network interfaces, various data-store services, and services that provide better observability into the execution of those FaaS entities.

The most common pattern, for the purposes of providing an API as needed for the HMS project being discussed, is composed of an *API Service* that accepts HTTP requests, and one-to-many serverless functions designed to handle the events generated by the API service when a request is received. The *API Service*, upon receiving a request, determines whether the request matches a registered endpoint path. If there is a match, that path will also have a configuration that identifies what handler function is intended to handle those requests, creates an event data structure that includes any of the HTTP parameters that can be passed along to the handler function, and invokes the related handler function, passing the event data along.

The target function accepts that event, executes whatever logic is involved in processing the request, and generates a response payload that is sent back to the API Service, which then transforms the response into an HTTP standard response and returns that to the calling client. An example flow diagram, using the Artisan object type and indicating the HTTP methods and corresponding serverless functions, is shown in *Figure 16.5*. That flow assumes that each HTTP method has one and only one handler function that relates to a given API operation, though some of the functions may handle more than one HTTP method — both PUT and PATCH are, ultimately, intended to update an API object, for example.

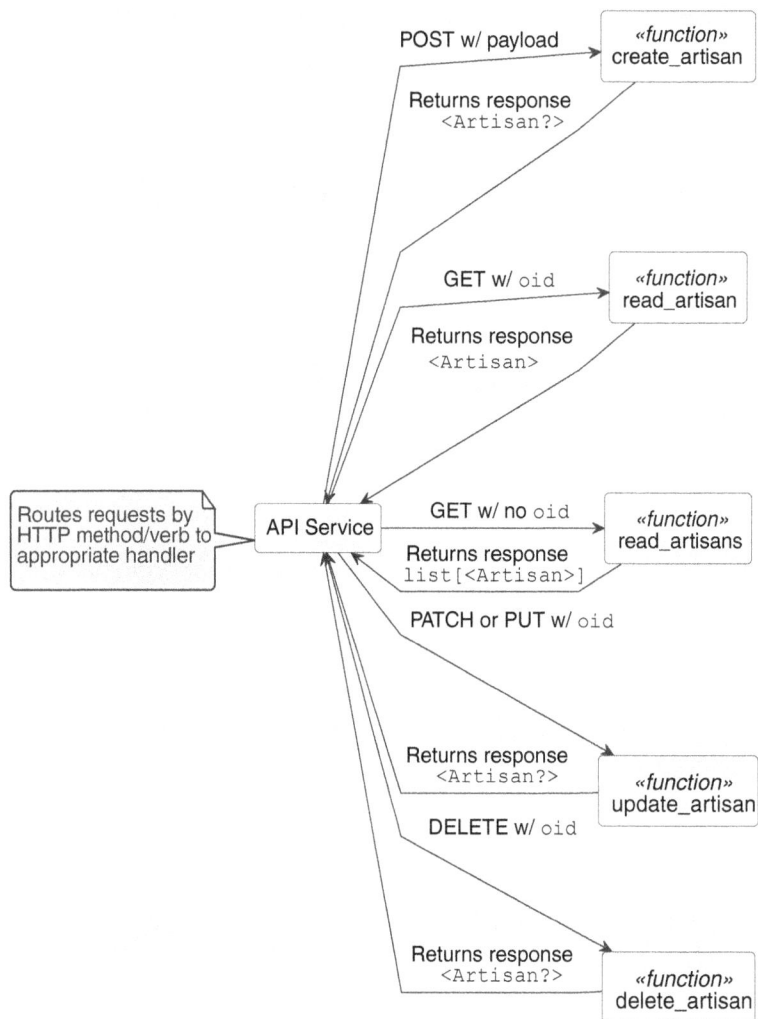

Figure 16.5: The flow of requests to and responses from the handler methods in a simple serverless architecture

All three of the main public cloud providers have services that can be used to create serverless APIs.

Amazon API Gateway (REST)

The API Gateway service is the primary serverless API mechanism offered by AWS. It is a fully managed service, requiring no upkeep or maintenance activities by developers apart from any that are needed for new or changed connections to other services, or changes in backing code. At its most basic, it is an approximate equivalent to the FastAPI and Flask applications described earlier, providing a mechanism to map incoming requests, using specific HTTP methods and made to specific API endpoints and paths, to a backing function. API Gateway also provides hooks to integrate with a wide range of other services, allowing it to act as an HTTP proxy for resources as varied as S3 buckets (for files), AppSync GraphQL APIs (allowing a single API to provide both REST and GraphQL capabilities), and DynamoDB tables (for direct data operations against a table).

API Gateway provides two basic variations of APIs supporting the full range of HTTP methods: a REST API service type and a more limited HTTP API service type. The REST API variant is generally more performant, with built-in automatically generated CloudFront **Content Delivery Network (CDN)** service instances. This variation also provides a broader range of security, authorization, development, and monitoring features. A complete breakdown of the differences between the two can be found in the API Gateway documentation online at https://docs.aws.amazon.com/apigateway/latest/developerguide/http-api-vs-rest.html.

Both variations support integrations to AWS Lambda functions to provide request-handling processes. Lambda functions all share a common input signature, accepting an event dictionary and a context object:

```
def lambda_handler(event: dict, context: LambdaContext):
    ...
```

For API implementations, there is a standard **Lambda Proxy Integration** structure for the event (https://docs.aws.amazon.com/apigateway/latest/developerguide/set-up-lambda-proxy-integrations.html) that incorporates several common variable values derived from a standard HTTP request. Using a request to http://my-api/v1/artisans/00000000-0000-0000-0000-000000000001 as an example, these include the following:

- The path of the request, along with the resource definition that notes any placeholders for path variables, and any pathParameters that can be extracted:

    - path: /v1/artisans/00000000-0000-0000-0000-000000000001
    - resource: /v1/artisans/{oid}
    - pathParameters: {'oid': '00000000-0000-0000-0000-000000000001'}

- The headers sent with the request, as well as a multiValueHeaders field that captures the same data, but as lists of header values.

- The queryStringParameters sent with the request, as well as a multiValueQueryStringParameters field that captures those items, but as lists of query-string values.

- A requestContext that captures most, if not all, of the values of the context object.

- The body of the request, a string that will contain the payload sent with the request. Requests other than POST, PATCH, and PUT methods will still have a body value, but it will be sent as an empty string.

- A Boolean flag, isBase64Encoded, that indicates whether the body is encoded as a Base-64 string.

The Lambda Proxy Integration standard also defines a response structure that includes isBase64Encoded, headers, multiValueHeaders, and body fields that follow the same conventions as the input structure. It also includes a statusCode field, intended to return the numeric value of the applicable standard HTTP status code for the response (https://developer.mozilla.org/en-US/docs/Web/HTTP/Reference/Status).

The context object (an instance of a class named LambdaContext) sent is also documented online (https://docs.aws.amazon.com/lambda/latest/dg/python-context.html), though most of its properties will be represented in the requestContext noted above. LambdaContext objects also provide a single method, get_remaining_time_in_millis, that returns the number of milliseconds remaining for a given Lambda function before it will time out.

The actual implementation within a Lambda function handler can be quite simple, though it is generally a good idea to include some error-handling at the entry-point function level. Handling errors there allows any calls to child functions to simply execute or raise errors as needed, leaving the handling of those errors to the wrapper around the entire process. Examples of POST and GET handler Lambda functions show this approach:

```python
# Imports omitted for space reasons
def handle_artisan_post(
    event: dict, context: object
) -> dict:
    """
    Handles a POST request to create a new Artisan
    object, returning the newly created object.
    """
```

```python
    try:
        artisan_data = json.loads(event['body'])
        new_artisan = Artisan(**artisan_data)
        new_artisan.save(db_source_name='Artisan')
        response = {
            'statusCode': 200,
            'body': new_artisan.model_dump_json()
        }
    except KeyError as error:
        logger.error(
            f'{error.__class__.__name__}: {error} while '
            'trying to create an Artisan'
        )
        response = {
            'statusCode': 400,
            'body': 'No artisan created for request '
            f'{context.aws_request_id}.'
        }
    except Exception as error:
        logger.exception(
            f'{error.__class__.__name__}: {error} while '
            'trying to create an Artisan'
        )
        response = {
            'statusCode': 500,
            'body': 'No artisan created for request '
            f'{context.aws_request_id}.'
        }
    finally:
        return response
def handle_artisan_get(
    event: dict, context: object
) -> dict:
    """
    Gets and returns a single Artisan object,
    identified by the oid in the request path
    """
```

```python
try:
    oid = event['pathParameters']['oid']
    artisans = Artisan.get(
        oid, db_source_name='Artisan'
    )
    if len(artisans) == 1:
        result = {
            'statusCode': 200,
            'body': artisans[0].model_dump_json()
        }
    elif len(artisans) == 0:
        msg = (
            'Could not find an Artisan identified '
            f'by {oid}'
        )
        logger.error(msg)
        result = {
            'statusCode': 404,
            'body': msg
        }
    else:
        msg = (
            f'Retrieved {len(artisans)} Artisan '
            'records, when only one should be '
            'returned'
        )
        logger.error(msg)
        response = {
            'statusCode': 400,
            'body': msg
        }
except KeyError as error:
    logger.error(
```

```
            f'{error.__class__.__name__}: {error} while '
            'trying to retrieve an Artisan'
        )
        response = {
            'statusCode': 400,
            'body': 'No artisan retrieved for request '
            f'{context.aws_request_id}.'
        }
    except Exception as error:
        msg = (
            f'{error.__class__.__name__}: {error} while '
            'trying to reetrieve an Artisan'
        )
        logger.exception(msg)
        response = {
            'statusCode': 500,
            'body': f'{msg} in request '
            f'{context.aws_request_id}.'
        }
    finally:
        return response
```

These functions handle a number of failure conditions in a reasonably graceful manner: If required data — the body data required to create a new Artisan, or the oid that identifies an existing one — is not provided, or cannot be resolved for some reason, the functions return a **400 Bad Request** status code. If some other unexpected error prevents the functions from doing what they are intended to do, they return a **500 Internal Server** status code. If, in the case of a GET request, an oid is supplied that does not resolve to an Artisan record in the database, a **404 Not Found** status code is returned. Any requests that return an error statusCode value also log those errors in some detail, and they return an error message to the calling client that describes *what the error was*, and *what AWS request was involved*, making troubleshooting a bit easier if the logs for the function have to be examined. The details of the errors are *not* issued back to the client, though, for security reasons.

Always return relevant HTTP status codes

There are many HTTP status codes available to indicate all kinds of response situations. A complete reference list of them can be found online (`https://developer.`
`mozilla.org/en-US/docs/Web/HTTP/Reference/Status`), grouped to include client error responses (the caller did something wrong) and server error responses (something went wrong in the code). Returning relevant status codes allows consumers of an API to make decisions based on those values, opening the door to a better user experience overall. Note that the list behind that link includes a status code that was originally proposed as a joke — **418 I'm a teapot** — which may not be accepted in certain HTTP contexts, and should not be used without verification that it will not cause issues.

Any successful response returns a **200 OK** status, along with the data that relates: the newly-created Artisan data for the `POST` handler, and the data for the requested Artisan for the `GET` handler. The data returned in the body of the response is a JSON representation of the relevant Artisan model.

REST API provision in other cloud providers

The focus on serverless implementation patterns presented so far is focused on using AWS services — API Gateway and Lambda functions — but there are equivalents in the other two main public cloud providers:

- Google Cloud Platform provides GCP API Gateway and Cloud Functions
- Azure provides Azure API Management and Azure Functions

Though space in this chapter makes a detailed discussion of either or both of those impractical, there will be common aspects and reasonable assumptions that can be used to start an exploration of those by the reader:

- The API Gateway equivalents will have to solve the same problems: routing requests to the backing function logic.
- There will be a standard input structure that provides relevant HTTP request data to the functions that handle request/response processes for a given endpoint.
- There will be a standard output/response structure that functions should apply to the data they return, that the API Gateway equivalents can process and return to the calling client as a standard HTTP response.

Taking a container-based approach and implementing an API with packages like FastAPI and Flask, as shown earlier, may be a better approach, depending on the needs and requirements driving that API. Containerized solutions are inherently capable of being deployed to any cloud provider, so the same code base could be built, containerized, and deployed to any production environment, in any public cloud, without having to contend with differences between Lambda functions, Cloud Functions, and Azure Functions expectations and requirements along the way.

GraphQL API provision in the cloud

All of the major public cloud providers also offer at least one GraphQL API solution. Since the primary focus of the project being discussed in this book is a REST API, those GraphQL options will not be discussed in great detail, but they can at least be identified for readers who have a need or interest in exploring them:

- AWS's offering in this space is **AppSync**. AppSync is a dedicated, managed, serverless GraphQL API service, which can be implemented as a distinct API or attached to API Gateway as a proxied resource.

- In Google Cloud Platform, the service to start exploring is named **Apigee**. Apigee can provide both GraphQL and REST APIs.

- Azure's offering in the API space is its **Azure API Management** service. Like GCP's Apigee, it can provide both GraphQL and REST API implementations.

Local development of serverless implementations

The advantages of a serverless approach noted earlier come with a trade-off: The code being written is intended to run in the context of those cloud services, and that context may not be easily replicable, or replicable at all, for local development. While local copies of some types of resources — the local database mentioned earlier, for example — and configuration that is tied to the environment that code is running in can go a long way towards mitigating those, there may not be local equivalents for everything needed for local development purposes.

For applications that will run under AWS, there are at least a few options to work around those constraints. The first, assuming that the deployment process for an application allows it, is to set up individual development environments in the cloud and write code and configuration so that it can make use of those resources in a local context. This works well for applications that are deployed with AWS's SAM templating and tools (and CloudFormation, by extension, should be viable as well), and could reasonably be expected to work with other CI/CD processes like Terraform. There are two main considerations to bear in mind. The first is the need for some sort of environment specification that can be used to differentiate between a developer's environment and any of the standard environments (development, quality assurance, staging, production) that are created or updated as work on the application is complete. The second is that the developers' accounts will need to be able to access cloud-resident resources from a local development environment. This is usually mainly a matter of configuring developer permissions. Once those are sorted out, standard tools and packages like boto3, which will be needed to interact with other cloud resources, should work just like they would in the actual cloud environments.

AWS also provides, through its SAM tools, the ability to run serverless applications locally, provided that those applications are defined using SAM/CloudFormation templating and that they do not use services that are not available in the local SAM implementation. This approach leverages Docker containers to provide resources that can be created and updated locally and executed. It is not (in this author's experience) a fast process, though, frequently requiring rebuilding resources every time a code change is made, and on every request made to a local instance of an API.

Another option is to provide a full cloud context locally. There is at least one option available in this space: **LocalStack** (https://www.localstack.cloud/localstack-for-aws), which provides emulation of 100+ AWS services as of this writing. LocalStack has both free and Pro tiers, but the free tier provides enough service capabilities to handle common API development needs. Like AWS's local SAM tool, it uses Docker to provide services and may have similar speed/performance constraints.

If the deployment process can be directly tied to the code of a project, the chalice package (https://pypi.org/project/chalice/) may also be a viable option. chalice is a framework for writing serverless applications in Python. Functionally, it looks much like the FastAPI and Flask examples shown earlier, defining an application object and using route decorators provided by that object to associate specific Lambda function code with API endpoints and other AWS resource types. Once defined, that application can be run locally with a single command — chalice local — and a running application can be told to monitor for changes. chalice can also deploy a project, though that deployment process may not be compatible with deployments of/for other resources that it cannot define.

As a final option, for cases where the project doesn't need any more local functionality than running an API, it is possible to wrap a collection of Lambda functions with routes that are part of a FastAPI or Flask application.

Local Lambda-backed APIs with FastAPI/Flask

This is my preferred option, personally. I found it to be useful enough that I've written a package to provide that functionality without requiring the alteration or decoration of the Lambda handler functions themselves: `https://pypi.org/project/goblinfish-aws-local-lpi-apis/`. It is very much a work in progress as this is being written, but I fully expect that I'll have it to a usable `1.0.0` version by the time this book is published.

There are a lot of options available for implementing and deploying an API service, as can be seen by all of the examples and topics covered in this chapter so far. Despite the number of variations available, the high-level design of APIs is relatively simple to work through, since it is really more concerned with defining the endpoint paths, methods, and I/O expectations for the data being exposed through the API. There are a couple of other considerations for the approaches that have not been discussed, but that need to be considered as well.

The first of these is Authentication and Authorization (sometimes abbreviated as **AuthN/Z**). **Authentication** processes are concerned with allowing an end user to unambiguously and securely identify themselves, verifying their identity with respect to their access to a system. **Authorization** builds on that identification, allowing the system to determine in some fashion what access permissions any given authenticated user has to parts of that system. There are several Authorization options, each with its own strengths and trade-offs.

Use of **JSON Web Tokens (JWTs)** is a popular option. A **JWT** is a compact, URL-safe token used to securely transmit information from a client to a service. It is an encoded JSON object containing **claims** — information about the user that is associated with the token — including their identity, and their membership in various groups or roles. JWTs are validated against a service endpoint belonging to the service that issued the JWT to the user in the first place. If the token validates successfully, it is considered trustworthy, and the token can be decoded, and the claims used to make decisions about whether the bearer of the token is allowed to access a given resource in the system. If the token does not validate successfully for any of several reasons, that is an indicator that the request should not be allowed. Issuing JWTs typically requires a backing service, with any associated.

API keys are another option. An **API key** is simply a unique string that is sent with requests as header values (x-api-key is a commonly used header name), or as form- or query-string values. On receiving a request with an API key, the service is responsible for checking whether the key is valid and allows or denies the request accordingly. API keys are much simpler to implement, but are less secure: They can be easily compromised if they are not handled and used with care and discipline, though they may be sufficient for internal API use, or for scenarios where end-users are allowed or expected to maintain their own API keys, a practice that is common for APIs intended for system-to-system use.

Another common option, particularly for smaller, self-contained systems, is to keep track of user permissions as part of a user session. In this approach, every user is issued a unique session identifier when they first connect to the service. As a user logs in, system logic and data stores are used to keep track of the user associated with that session, and authorization decisions are made by examining the session itself or the data of the user that the session belongs to. Sessions are a server-side solution, and though they may be easy to implement, they may not scale well without considerable thought and discipline in their design, since they must maintain some level of user state as the user moves through the system.

Other AuthN/Z options include **OAuth** variations and **Mutual TLS (mTLS)**, with varying degrees of increased complexity. The selection of an AuthN/Z approach for a system really depends on the needs of the system and the sensitivity of the data accessed through it. For low-risk systems, an API key may be sufficient. For more complex scenarios, especially those involving third-party (user) access or sensitive data, JWTs or OAuth are more commonly used if maintenance of user state in a session-based approach would be too expensive or introduce too much latency. mTLS is often considered to be the best option for critical applications, providing highly secure processes with strong authentication and encryption of traffic, but it comes at a price, in the form of additional certificate management and a more complex setup.

Caching of responses is another facet of APIs and other systems that is worth consideration. **Caching**, whether on the server or client side, is simply storing copies of frequently used data in a known storage location. In a server-side context, caching can remove the need to make slow data store connections and requests for data that has already been retrieved, improving performance and, where applicable, reducing data access costs. In a client-side context, caching improves the performance of an application by removing the need to wait for a new copy of already-retrieved data if it has not changed since it was last fetched.

In a complete HTTP application context, where both client and server are providing enough information for client-side caching to be available, there is little more that needs to be done than generating or reading and acting on a handful of header instructions:

- The ETag (entity tag) response header (https://developer.mozilla.org/en-US/docs/Web/HTTP/Reference/Headers/ETag) uniquely identifies a specific version of a given resource. There is no standard mechanism defined for creating the value returned in this header. Common mechanisms include generating a hash of the content with md5 (see https://docs.python.org/3/library/hashlib.html#hashlib.md5) or a more recent algorithm, and simply keeping track of version numbers, or perhaps a date/time string, or even a simple timestamp number.

- The Last-Modified response header (https://developer.mozilla.org/en-US/docs/Web/HTTP/Reference/Headers/Last-Modified) provides a client with a date/time that the resource was last modified.

- The If-None-Match request header (https://developer.mozilla.org/en-US/docs/Web/HTTP/Reference/Headers/If-None-Match) tells a server that a response to the request should only return a new response if none of the ETag values that were passed in the header's value match the current ETag value. If any requested version can fulfill the request, the server is expected to return a 304 Not Modified HTTP status, telling the client to use its cached version of the resource instead.

- The If-Modified-Since request header (https://developer.mozilla.org/en-US/docs/Web/HTTP/Reference/Headers/If-Modified-Since) tells a server that the request should only return a new response if the resource in question has been modified after the date/time value sent in the header. If that condition is not met, the server is expected to return a 304 Not Modified HTTP status, telling the client to use its cached version of the resource instead.

These are not the only caching-related HTTP headers...

There are others that provide other controls for how and when resources are cached in a typical browser-server request/response process. The *HTTP Cache Headers – A Complete Guide* article at https://www.keycdn.com/blog/http-cache-headers provides a good overview of the others that are commonly used.

Between them, these four headers can provide very robust caching capabilities for web-based APIs. An initial request, sent with none of those headers, would receive the first response, which would have both `ETag` and `Last-Modified` headers in the response. Those values would be stored as data points associated with the resource in the local cache. Any subsequent requests made for that resource could then look up the last known values for each, populate them in the `If-None-Match` and `If-Modified-Since` headers of the request, and make the request.

On the server side, the `ETag` and modified-date values would be compared with their current values, and if they indicate that the resource has not been modified, a simple `304 Not Modified` response would be sent back. These checks would need to be implemented in the service code if they are not provided by the framework that the service code is running under (FastAPI, Flask, AWS API Gateway, etc.).

Summary

This chapter has shown several options for implementing web-based APIs, showing the basic code structures required for each. It has also explored the options for the environments that those implementations can execute in, and at least touched on various advantages and trade-offs for each option. Armed with the understanding of these options that this chapter has explored, it is time to decide on a high-level definition of the HMS Artisan and Product API and implement it. That will be the focus of the next chapter.

17

Assembling the API

Starting back in *Chapter 12*, this book has been assembling information and thinking through the designs behind the various moving parts needed to implement the final API. In *Chapter 13's Figuring out where to start with use cases*, a set of processes and goals for what might be considered a **Minimum Viable Product (MVP)** design was described, and the chapters after that focused on the implementation details for key aspects of the processes that would be integrated into the final API. Finally, at this point, all of those moving parts have been at least thought through, and in some cases implemented to the point where they can be assembled into a demonstrable MVP API, providing enough functionality to be useful for the entire process flow described.

This chapter, then, will focus on assembling all of those moving parts into a demonstrable, locally executable API. The code written to that end will be shaped by several decisions made about where it will eventually run, what constraints will have to be kept in mind as a result, and what the implications of those constraints are. They will play out as only two major sections, but the latter will dig deeply into several variations of common themes and implementation patterns needed to provide the final API:

- Designing the HMS API implementation
- The implementation sequence, implementing endpoints for specific end-user/business object combinations for the standard CRUD operations:
  - Create
  - Read
  - Update
  - Delete

Follow along in the repository

Each significant iteration of the code in this chapter has been tagged in the chapter's GitHub repository. Those tags will be called out in the chapter text, and can be found in the repository's *Tags* page at `https://github.com/PacktPublishing/Hands-On-Software-Engineering-with-Python-Second-Edition/tags`.

Technical requirements

The code for this chapter was written for Python 3.11, and assumes that it is available on the reader's machine. Download and installation instructions are available online at `https://www.python.org/downloads/` for Windows, Linux/Unix, macOS, and other systems. The package requirements for the chapter's code are captured in the `Pipfile` or `requirements.txt` file, and can be installed as described earlier in this book. Running them will also require a complete local development database installation, as discussed in *Chapter 13*.

This chapter focuses heavily on being able to make and view the results of requests to a local API instance, initially without any concerns for a front-end UI. To that end, there are several tools available, including Bruno (`https://www.usebruno.com/`) and Postman (`https://www.postman.com/`), both of which provide a developer-friendly UI for making HTTP requests and seeing the responses to those requests.

Code for this chapter can be found in the repository at `https://github.com/PacktPublishing/Hands-On-Software-Engineering-with-Python-Second-Edition/tree/main/CH17-code`.

Designing the HMS API implementation

There have been several decisions made in earlier chapters that contribute to the design of the API that will be implemented in this chapter. The mapping of requests made to the API to their back-end components is shown in *Figure 17.1*, below, but there are several other decision points that may not be represented in that diagram. The collection of the decisions involved that will impact the implementation in this chapter includes:

- The API will be implemented using AWS Serverless Application Model resources, with an API Gateway resource accepting requests, running back-end processes, and returning responses to the requester.

- The back-end processes will be implemented as Lambda Functions, using AWS' Lambda Proxy Integration standards for input and output data structures.

- The API will be versioned, with a /v1/ path segment indicating the first released version. Future versions that involve breaking changes will be versioned as /v2/, /v3/, and so on.

- The main resources that the API will be concerned with are the Artisan, Product, and ProductImage objects defined several chapters back.
- The CRUD operations that will (or may) be implemented will use standard HTTP methods as follows:

  - POST requests for creating new objects. POST requests may return the data of the created object, or a simple HTTP 201 Created status code (https://developer.mozilla.org/en-US/docs/Web/HTTP/Reference/Status/201) and an empty body if the specific use case does not need the data.

  - GET requests for reading one or more objects. When reading a single object, the oid of the object will be passed in the path to identify the specific object requested.

  - PATCH requests for updating single objects, identified by their oid value as a path parameter. PUT requests would also be technically viable, but since PATCH requests are intended to allow updating any or all fields of an object, while PUT requests are intended to replace the entire object, PATCH just feels semantically better.

  - DELETE requests for deleting single objects, identified by their oid value as a path parameter.

- At a high level, different types of users will be allowed to perform various CRUD operations through the API:

  - A *Logged-in Administrator* will typically be able to *read* and *update* any fields of any object, even if they do not *own* that object. They may or may not have the ability to *create* objects as well, in the future. They will also have the ability to *delete* any object in the system, but that will be limited by business rules that apply to specific use cases.

  - A *Logged-in Artisan* is expected to be able to *create* Product and ProductImage objects. They generally will also be able to *update* any field that they were allowed to create in any object that they own.

  - Public users, including *Logged-In Users* (customers) and *Anonymous Users*, will be allowed to read specific subsets of Artisan, Product, and ProductImage objects, defined for specific use cases.

- **Authentication and Authorization (AuthN/Z)**, at least for local development purposes, do not need to be accounted for. When deployed to an AWS account, the API Gateway for any given environment will implement a Lambda authorizer (https://docs.aws.amazon.com/apigateway/latest/developerguide/apigateway-use-lambda-authorizer.html), and that will eventually need to be accounted for, but the specific AuthN/Z requirements are not known at this point.

- Although the specific requirements have not yet been fully defined for logging and provision of data points for operational metrics, observability, and monitoring purposes, there are some agreed-upon standards for logging functions' processes during execution, and some baseline expectations for tracking how long each function takes to execute.

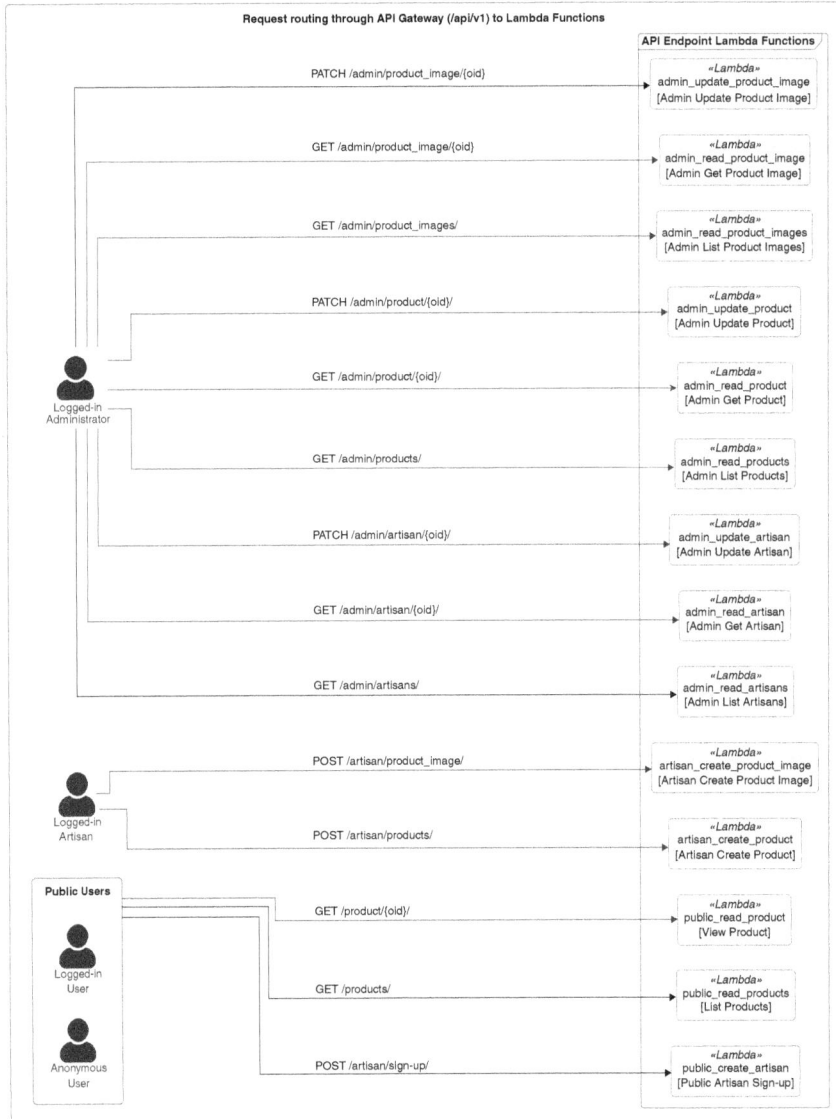

Figure 17.1: How requests will be passed to Lambda Functions in the API Gateway implementation of the HMS API

(This image is for visualization purpose only. Check the graphic bundle for a high resolution version.)

For ease of local development and testing, the Lambda Function code will be accessed through a local FastAPI application using the `goblinfish-aws-local-lpi-apis` package (`https://pypi. org/project/goblinfish-aws-local-lpi-apis/`).

The implementation sequence

> The initial state for the project code is tagged as `Ch17-Initial-code-stubs` in the project repository.

The implementation goals for the chapter are derived from the processes that need to be implemented, and the order that they need to be executed in, for an Artisan to sign up in the system and add a product to the public-facing product list view page. These were noted in an earlier chapter, but in the interests of keeping them close at hand for this chapter, they are worth listing again, with some elaboration:

- An end user, either anonymous or already a customer, signs up to be an **Artisan** (the *Public Artisan Sign-up* endpoint in *Figure 17.1*).

- An **Artisan Reviewer** (someone on HMS' staff acting as a *Logged-in Administrator*) reviews new `Artisan` sign-ups, either by starting with a list and clicking through to individual `Artisan` pages that need review and activation, or by going straight to an individual `Artisan` page (the *Admin List Artisans* and *Admin Get Artisan* endpoints).

- The **Artisan Reviewer** activates the new `Artisan` (*Admin Update Artisan*).

- An **Artisan** creates a new `Product` (*Artisan Create Product*).

- A **Product Reviewer** (someone on HMS' staff acting as a *Logged-in Administrator*) reviews new `Product` submissions, either by starting with a list and clicking through to individual `Product` pages that need review and activation, or by going straight to an individual `Product` page (*Admin List Products* and *Admin Get Product*).

- The **Product Reviewer** activates the new `Product` (*Admin Update Product*).

- An **Artisan** creates a new `ProductImage` (*Artisan Create Product Image*).

- A **Product Reviewer** reviews new `ProductImage` submissions, either by starting with a list and clicking through to individual `ProductImage` pages that need review and activation, or by going straight to an individual `ProductImage` page (*Admin List Product Images* and *Admin Get Product Image*).

- The **Product Reviewer** activates the new ProductImage (*Admin Update Product Image*).
- A **Public User** views the Product list page, possibly clicking on an item there to a Product detail page (*List Products* and *View Product*).

Although the sequence listed is the logical sequence of events, endpoints that are used to return list or detail data for items created earlier in the sequence will be developed first, in order to allow for visibility into the data being created. For example, the *Admin List Artisans* and *Admin Get Artisan* endpoints will be built out before the *Public Artisan Sign-up* endpoint that actually *creates* Artisan objects.

These processes account for fourteen endpoints in the API, just under one-third of the total logical endpoints that the API could implement for basic CRUD operations. Between them, they will show common patterns for GET, POST, and PATCH HTTP operations against the API. The remaining thirty-one endpoints, along with their backing Lambda Function code, have been stubbed out as well, but will not be discussed here, with one exception: an example *Artisan Delete Product* endpoint that was not included in *Figure 17.1* will be used to explore how to handle operations that need data for multiple objects to be managed in the context of a database transaction.

The starting point code for the Lambda Functions

The stubs for each Lambda Function were created with a script to provide a common starting point for each Lambda Function. That common starting-point function, with placeholders for various names, minus the supporting imports and other items that can be seen in the stubs/lambda-function.py file in the chapter repository, looks like this:

```
@tracker
def api_handler(
    event: LambdaProxyInput, context: LambdaContext
) -> LambdaProxyOutput:
    """
    The {operation} handler for {object} targets
    in the {scope} scope.
    Parameters:
    -----------
    event : LambdaProxyInput (dict)
        The API event to be handled.
    context : LambdaContext
        The standard Lambda context object provided
        by AWS during a Lambda invocation.
```

```
    """

    try:
        logger.info(f'{module}.api_handler called')
        logger.debug(f'event: {json.dumps(event)}')
        logger.debug(f'context: {repr(context)}')
        # TODO: Replace this with actual logic
        result = {
            'statusCode': 501,
            'body': 'Not Implemented '
            f'({context.aws_request_id})'
        }
    # TODO: Add other exception-handling if needed
    except Exception as error:
        logger.exception(
            f'{error.__class__.__name__}: {error} '
            'occured in api_handler'
        )
        logger.error(f'event: {json.dumps(event)}')
        logger.error(f'context: {repr(context)}')
        result = {
            'statusCode': 500,
            'body': 'Internal Server Error: '
            f'({context.aws_request_id})'
        }
    logger.info(f'{module}.api_handler complete')
    logger.debug(f'result: {json.dumps(result)}')
    return result
```

This function stub provides a ready-to-use structure that incorporates the logging and process-monitoring data points expected so far. The default return that it provides is a standard HTTP 501 Not Implemented status, allowing endpoints to be defined locally that return that status initially, until code is written to actually implement whatever processing needs to happen for those endpoints. The **highlighted block** of code is expected to be the only consistent, substantial change in any of these function stubs: that is where the actual logic for the process will be implemented.

The Admin List Artisans endpoint

These changes are tagged in the chapter repository as `Ch-17-admin-list-artisans-endpoint`.

The use cases for this endpoint center around generating a list of `Artisan` names, with their current statuses (`is_active`, `is_deleted`). The `Artisan`-name data displayed is expected to be either the `company_name`, if it is populated, or the collection of contact name fields (`honorific`, `given_name`, `middle_name family_name`, and `suffix`) values. Each element in the response will also include the `oid`, which can be used by the caller/client to generate a URL to another API call, or to a page, where the details of the Artisan are provided. In the context of the first set of use cases that the endpoint is being implemented for, the data will be used to populate a list of `Artisan` objects, each linking to an `Artisan` detail page/view where an administrator can review a given `Artisan` and activate them in the system.

The implementation of this endpoint leverages the `criteria` keyword arguments of the `BaseDataObject.get` class method, and that method's pagination parameters, `page_size` and `page_number`, to allow a calling client to filter and sort the results by any of the supported criteria fields of the `Artisan` class. It omits the `business_address` and all of the child fields of that structure, as well as the `email_address` and `products` list: None of these fields are currently expected to be needed in an `Artisan` list displayed to an administrator.

A change for the future

The current Artisan object does not allow sorting or filtering by any of the `*_name` fields, or the `is_active` or `is_deleted` fields. While those are not critical for establishing the basic functionality of the endpoint, they will be very important for the main use case that this endpoint is intended to serve. These updates will be addressed in the following chapter, along with the deployment process for the API, since they represent a change to the database structure that will need to be deployed as well.

The actual logic is relatively simple, though there are aspects of how various request data points are retrieved that are worth calling out. The Lambda Function module defines a constant (`LIST_FIELD_NAMES`) early in the code that controls what fields are returned in the results.

```
LIST_FIELD_NAMES = (
    'oid', 'is_active', 'is_deleted', 'created',
```

```
    'modified', 'honorific', 'given_name', 'middle_name',
    'family_name', 'suffix', 'company_name'
)
```

The query string data of a request is passed as a dictionary named querystringParameters in the Lambda Proxy Integration input structure — the event passed to the function. The logging after the initial try statement in the original function stub code remains unchanged, following the standard logging approach that the HMS engineers agreed to follow.

```
def api_handler(
    event: LambdaProxyInput, context: LambdaContext
) -> LambdaProxyOutput:
    # ...
    try:
        logger.info(f'{module}.api_handler called')
        logger.debug(f'event: {json.dumps(event)}')
        logger.debug(f'context: {repr(context)}')
```

After that, the real implementation starts. Any query strings for pagination purposes need to be converted to int values, replacing the str values that they were originally. All other query string values are left alone and passed to the Artisan.get class method in order to retrieve the relevant Artisan object data, and that process is time-tracked for metrics collection and reporting purposes:

```
        get_params = event.get('queryStringParameters', {})
        pagination_params = {
            key: int(get_params.get(key, 0)) or None
            for key in ('page_size', 'page_number')
        }
        get_params.update(pagination_params)
        logger.debug(f'get_params: {get_params}')
        with tracker.timer('artisan_db_access'):
            artisans = Artisan.get(
                db_source_name='Artisan', **get_params
            )
```

Once the collected results are available, the final results are filtered down to only the field names specified in the LIST_FIELD_NAMES collection defined earlier, and the final body is generated by serializing the results before being returned in a Lambda Proxy Integration output structure:

```python
results = [
    {
        key: value for key, value
        in artisan.model_dump(mode='json').items()
        if key in LIST_FIELD_NAMES
    }
    for artisan in artisans
]
body = json.dumps(results)
result = {
    'statusCode': 200,
    'body': body
}
except Exception as error:
```

The results, retrieved with the Admin List Artisans Bruno collection (at bruno/hms-api-collection/Admin List Artisans.bru in the chapter repo), using a page_size of 1 and a page_number of 0, retrieved one Artisan item, created during the previous chapter's examples:

```json
[
    {
        "oid": "645c068c-4a3c-4cfa-90ac-659b99e5034b",
        "is_active": false,
        "is_deleted": false,
        "created": "2025-05-24T20:26:43.009467",
        "modified": null,
        "honorific": "",
        "given_name": "Ponder",
        "middle_name": "",
        "family_name": "Stibbons",
        "suffix": "",
        "company_name": ""
    }
]
```

The output also included a JSON representation of the collected metrics, latency times for the api_handler function as a whole, and the artisan_db_access time captured in the code shown above.

```
{
    "latencies": {
        "artisan_db_access": 1.503,
        "api_handler": 2.036
    },
    "metrics": {}
}
```

This breakdown of the first endpoint is fairly long, with a fair bit of detail into how the changes were made, what the implementation does, and how it does it. Other, later endpoints that perform similar operations are expected to follow very similar patterns, varying mainly in which business object they use to retrieve their data.

The Admin Get Artisan endpoint

These changes are tagged in the chapter repository as Ch-17-admin-get-artisan-endpoint.

The other endpoint needed by a site administrator for purposes of viewing an Artisan is the *Admin Get Artisan* endpoint. The focus of this endpoint is the retrieval of *all* Artisan data for a given Artisan, identified by a specific oid value that is presented to the API as part of the request path (that is, /api/v1/admin/artisan/{oid}/). That data includes a list of Product objects associated with the Artisan, with the expectation that an administrator page for an Artisan will display a list of those products.

Because a specific, identified resource is being requested, there are additional checks that should be implemented for incoming requests to this endpoint, and failures of those checks should return specific HTTP status codes. Perhaps the most basic of those checks is whether, given a well-formed oid value, the back-end process can retrieve an Artisan whose oid value matches. If that is not the case, REST API and HTTP conventions would at least strongly suggest that the response returned would have a **404 Not Found** status, indicating that the process executed without error, but the requested resource could not be found.

In order to provide a distinct exception that can be used for those scenarios, a new, custom exception class is defined in the business_objects.py module: ArtisanNotFoundError.

```python
class ArtisanNotFoundError(Exception):
    """
    An exception to be raised if Artisan.get does not
    return an expected collection of Artisan objects.
    """
```

The process for retrieving a given Artisan and their associated Product objects, leveraging the get method of those classes inherited from BaseDataObject as described several chapters back, is not complex in and of itself. Accounting for the varied error possibilities adds some small degree of complexity, mostly because of the variations of HTTP status codes that need to be returned for different types and causes of errors. The additions to the starting point code for the endpoint to fetch the related Artisan and Product list, living in the try block of the starting point code, are:

```python
# Get the Artisan oid to retrieve
artisan_oid = event.get('pathParameters', {}).get('oid')
if artisan_oid is None or len(artisan_oid.split(',')) != 1:
    raise ValueError(
        f'{module}.api_handler requires a single '
        'oid, but that path parameter resolved to '
        f'"{artisan_oid}" ({type(artisan_oid).__name__}).'
    )
# Get the Artisan objects, keeping track of how
# long the process takes for metrics purposes
with tracker.timer('artisan_db_access'):
    artisans = Artisan.get(
        artisan_oid, db_source_name='Artisan'
    )
# Raise an error if no Artisan could be found
if len(artisans) == 0:
    raise ArtisanNotFoundError(
        'Could not retrieve an Artisan '
        f'identified by "{artisan_oid}".'
    )
artisan = artisans[0]
# Get the Product objects associated with the Artisan
```

```
# and store them in the Artisan's products field
with tracker.timer('product_db_access'):
    artisan.products = Product.get(
        artisan_oid=artisan_oid,
        db_source_name='Products'
    )
result = {
    'statusCode': 200,
    'body': artisan.model_dump_json()
}
# ...
```

There are only a few specific types of errors that are explicitly handled in this code. The first is
when no Artisan can be found in the database whose oid matches the oid passed in the request.
In that case, the API should return a standard HTTP **404 Not Found** status, after logging the error
and the input (the event and context) that caused it to occur. The code for handling that error
case looks like this:

```
except ArtisanNotFoundError as error:
    # This "standard" logging structure will
    # be repeated for all error-handling
    logger.exception(
        f'{error.__class__.__name__}: {error} '
        'occured in api_handler'
    )
    logger.error(f'event: {json.dumps(event)}')
    logger.error(f'context: {repr(context)}')
    result = {
        'statusCode': 404,
        'body': 'Not Found: ({context.aws_request_id})'
    }
```

As there is nothing preventing a request from being made with an invalid oid value in the
URL — a request made to /api/v1/admin/artisan/this-is-not-a-valid-oid/ under the API's
root path, for example — the potential for invalid requests also needs to be handled. In this
endpoint, the only input that can cause that sort of error is an invalid oid in the request path.
If the oid is not a well-formed UUID string, it will fail in being converted to a UUID, raising a
ValueError in the process.

There are also checks in the code to make sure that an `oid` is present in the path, and that it is a single value. If either of those checks fails, it explicitly raises a `ValueError` as well, which is handled with this code, returning a standard HTTP **400 Bad Request** status:

```
except ValueError as error:
    # "Standard" logging shown above...
    result = {
        'statusCode': 400,
        'body': 'Bad Request: '
        f'({context.aws_request_id})'
    }
```

Those two errors are the only types that are expected that a caller of the API would be able to take action to remedy. Other, unexpected errors also need to be accounted for, though, in a manner that allows an API client to determine whether the response received is usable or not, and in a manner that allows the team that owns the API to troubleshoot issues when they arise. To that end, a final except statement, handling any error that has not been handled previously, logging the details of the error, and returning a standard HTTP **500 Internal Server Error** status is put in place:

```
except Exception as error:
    # "Standard" logging shown above...
    result = {
        'statusCode': 500,
        'body': 'Internal Server Error: '
        f'({context.aws_request_id})'
    }
```

HTTP status codes are important!

In the context of a web API, returning the appropriate HTTP status code for any given request is *important*: consumers of an API, faced with an error response and a non-error status code like **200 OK**, will be faced with having to interpret the error results in order to cope with unexpected response data. At best, this will be frustrating, and it will create more work for those consumers that should not be necessary. The HTTP standard has status codes for all kinds of scenarios — a full list is available online at https://developer.mozilla.org/en-US/docs/Web/HTTP/Reference/Status — and there is no good excuse for not using them when appropriate.

With these first two endpoints implemented and providing some visibility into the Artisan and Product data that will be generated and manipulated with later endpoints, we can turn our attention to the first of the endpoints that actually serve an end-user need: the *Public Artisan Sign-up* endpoint.

The Public Artisan Sign-up endpoint

These changes are tagged in the chapter repository as `Ch-17-public-artisan-sign-up-endpoint`.

The *Public Artisan Sign-up* endpoint will be used to create an `Artisan` record from input submitted by a user who wants to sell products through the system. A prospective artisan will be presented with a form that allows the submission of `Artisan` data after they have gone through an initial account set-up process that is managed by another team. By the time the end user reaches the form page, they will have created and logged in to an initial artisan account, including an `email_address` that has been verified by that sign-up process. Once the remainder of the `Artisan` data has been submitted, the initial `Artisan` record will be created, and any authentication/authorization information updates that relate will be made.

> **Authentication and Authorization are unknowns at this point**
>
> The specifics of how **Authentication** and **Authorization (AuthN/Z)** interact with this endpoint are not defined yet. For purposes of discussion, the assumption is that the relevant `oid` for the new artisan is something that is accessible through whatever AuthN/Z data structure is provided with the request. Any functionality needed to retrieve that, or to reconcile it after the `Artisan` creation is complete, will be stubbed out with placeholder functions called `_authnz_preflight` and `_authnz_reconcile`.

Once the submission completes successfully, an HMS staff member will be responsible for approving it (using an endpoint that will be covered later). On the front end of the process, the page that the user will use to supply their artisan information will contain a standard HTML form, but the submission process will gather data from the form's fields, create a JSON payload, and send that to the API with an HTTP `POST` operation. That payload, by the time it is processed by the API's code, will follow the conventions of the `Artisan` object, with a structure that looks like this:

```
// Values represented as null here.
// Required values will be discussed later.
```

```
{
    "oid": null,
    "honorific": null,
    "given_name": null,
    "middle_name": null,
    "family_name": null,
    "suffix": null,
    "company_name": null,
    // The Address data points may require special
    // consideration in front-end code
    "business_address": {
        "street_address": null,
        "building_address": null,
        "city": null,
        "region_name": null,
        "postal_code": null,
        "country": null
    },
    "email_address": null
}
```

Because this endpoint is concerned with creating new data, the requirements for that data need to be kept in mind by the front-end developers: Any required fields must be supplied, as must any requirements for fields that have specific format, type, or value expectations. Front-end validation is optional — the API is expected to perform validation, and report back any fields that are missing, or that have invalid values, identifying the fields that are in error, and providing some indication of what the error is. Assuming that all of the input is valid, the main process behind the endpoint is really nothing more than creating and saving an Artisan object. That code, in the standard try block provided in the starting point code, is:

```
_authnz_preflight()
artisan_data = json.loads(event['body'])
new_artisan = Artisan(**artisan_data)
new_artisan.save(db_source_name='Artisan')
_authnz_reconcile()
result = {
    # HTTP 201 Created status
    'statusCode': 201,
```

```
    # Return the Artisan data created
    'body': new_artisan.model_dump(mode='json')

}
```

Lambda Functions' event.body

Lambda Functions' event inputs from a Lambda Proxy Integration invocation by an API Gateway will contain a body field, which will be a JSON-serialized representation of the actual data that was received by the API. The json.loads(event['body']) shown in the code above is where the JSON payload is converted into a Python dict for use in the remainder of the function.

Because the save method of the Artisan class implements a create-or-update query process when writing data to the database, no special consideration needs to be made for handling errors if a duplicate create-effort is made. The only process-specific errors that need to be handled so far center around validation issues with submitted fields, and sending back useful error information. The error-handling code for that is:

```
except ValidationError as error:
    # Gather up the error information from
    # the Pydantic ValidationError
    invalid_fields = {
        '.'.join(invalid_field['loc']).split('[')[0]:
            invalid_field['msg']
        for invalid_field in error.errors()
    }
    # Standard error-logging (omitted for brevity)
    # Also log the fields that caused problems...
    logger.error(f'invalid_fields: {invalid_fields}')
    # ...and include them in the response:
    reponse_body = {
        'message': 'Bad Request: '
        f'({context.aws_request_id})',
        'fields': invalid_fields
    }
    result = {
        'statusCode': 400,
```

```
        'body': json.dumps(reponse_body)
    }
```

An example response, from the submission of the example JSON payload above, is:

```
{
    "message": "Bad Request: ({aws_request_id})",
    "fields": {
        "oid": "UUID input should be a valid string",
        "given_name": "Input should be a valid string",
        "family_name": "Input should be a valid string",
        "business_address.street_address":
            "Input should be a valid string",
        "business_address.city":
            "Input should be a valid string",
        "business_address.postal_code":
            "Input should be a valid string",
        "email_address.function-after":
            "Input is not a valid NameEmail"
    }
}
```

The balance of the error-handling for the endpoint function is essentially identical to the examples shown earlier, generating a **500 Internal Server Error** response: Any general errors will be logged using the exception logging method to include a stack trace, and the event and context values that caused the error logged with the error logging method immediately after.

With the base process and error-handling in place, a submission can be made using the *Public Artisan Sign-up* request (bruno/hms-api-collection/Public Artisan Sign-up.bru in the chapter repository) with the following data:

```
{
    "oid": "00000000-0000-0000-0000-000000000000",
    "given_name": "Sybil",
    "family_name": "Vimes",
    "business_address": {
        "street_address": "Ramkin House",
        "building_address": "Scoone Avenue",
        "city": "Ankh-Morpork",
        "postal_code": "N/A"
```

```
    },
    "email_address": "sybil.vimes-ramkin@twurps.org"
  }
```

That request completes successfully, returning this response (omitting null values for brevity):

```
{
  "oid": "00000000-0000-0000-0000-000000000000",
  "is_active": false,
  "is_deleted": false,
  "created": "2025-07-05T15:43:36.023521",
  "given_name": "Sybil",
  "family_name": "Vimes",
  "business_address": {
    "street_address": "Ramkin House",
    "building_address": "Scoone Avenue",
    "city": "Ankh-Morpork",
    "postal_code": "N/A"
  },
  "email_address": "sybil.vimes-ramkin@twurps.org",
  "products": []
}
```

The same data is also returned from a request to /api/v1/admin/artisan/
00000000-0000-0000-0000-000000000000/, and the expected summary data from a request to
/api/v1/admin/artisans/.

The next endpoint to be examined, following the sequence of processes outlined above, is back
on the administrative side: the endpoint that HMS staff will use to activate an Artisan after it
has been created and reviewed.

The Admin Update Artisan endpoint

These changes are tagged in the chapter repository as Ch-17-admin-update-
artisan-endpoint.

The primary use case that this endpoint is designed to accommodate is the approval of a newly created `Artisan` in the system. That approval process is only expected to be an update to a single field, `is_active`, but the process is being built such that it can handle updates to *any* field in the `Artisan` object structure, in order to allow future modifications if they are determined to be needed. Because this is an update to an existing object's data in the database, there are some standard rules that apply:

- The pattern established earlier with the *Admin Get Artisan* endpoint is for the `oid` of the related object to be supplied in the request path. For example, an update request for the example `Artisan` created in the *Public Artisan Sign-up* endpoint would be made to `/api/v1/admin/artisan/00000000-0000-0000-0000-000000000000/`.

- That endpoint pattern already exists, but only responds to HTTP `GET` requests so far. The update process will use the same path, but an HTTP `PATCH` method will be used instead, indicating a change to one or more of the target object's field values.

- HTTP `PATCH` requests, like the `POST` request used in the *Public Artisan Sign-up* endpoint, expect a payload to be submitted in the body of the request.

These are all common patterns and rules for REST APIs. REST API operations executed against a specific resource identify that resource in the request, and use an HTTP method that indicates what *kind* of action is being executed against that resource. The expectation for a `PATCH` request to provide a request body is part of the HTTP standard for that request method.

Update operations, whether in an API context or not, frequently require more checking of their input data than the other CRUD operations. Like Create operations, they have to be concerned with types and values of data in a request's payload being valid, but it is common for Update operations to have constraints on *which* fields can be altered, whereas a Create often does not need to check those. Read operations may also have restrictions applied with respect to which fields are returned, but since they do not alter data, those restrictions are typically more concerned with limiting fields returned to those that are needed for a specific purpose. Over and above that, the only consistently expected field from an input perspective is the identifier of the resource. Delete operations have that same baseline expectation, an identification of a resource to be deleted, but there is no payload that needs to be checked at all.

For the purposes of the *Admin Update Artisan* endpoint, the check processes need to implement input checks based on a simple set of decisions and the rules that come out of those:

- What fields in the resource data is a user allowed to change?
- How are those validated?

- How are those field restrictions managed?

- What should happen if none of those fields are supplied, or they are passed with invalid values?

- What should happen if fields that are not in the allowed list are submitted?

- When an update request is successful, what will be returned?

- How is general access to the endpoint controlled, so that unauthorized changes will not be allowed?

For the purposes of this endpoint, the answers that the HMS engineers land on for these questions are:

- Administrators are allowed to change the is_active and is_deleted fields only, at least for now. The emphasis of the system is to allow as much self-service capability as possible to the artisan users, so all that administrators really need to do is activate/deactivate Artisan objects, and be able to flag or un-flag them for deletion.

- Field validation will be handled by leveraging the built-in validation provided by the business object models' implementations: Pydantic's validation is already available, so leverage that. Validation failures will raise a ValueError internally, and return an HTTP **400 Bad Request** response.

- The list of fields that the endpoint is allowed to alter will be a simple list of field names stored in the Lambda Function module, either as a handler function variable, or a global in the module, whichever feels easiest to manage.

- If no allowed fields are specified, that will also raise a ValueError internally, and return an HTTP **400 Bad Request** response.

- If fields are sent in the request that are not in the collection of allowed fields, that too will raise a ValueError internally, and return an HTTP **400 Bad Request** response.

- A successful update request will return the complete data set for the Artisan object that was changed, with a **200 OK** HTTP status.

The last item in their list of decisions to be made, regarding access control, is part of a larger question that needs to be addressed for all endpoints of an API that are not intended for public consumption. A more in-depth examination of that question and some of the options available to implement answers to it will be presented later in this chapter.

Everything needed to call the *Admin Update Artisan* endpoint is provided in the *Admin Update Artisan* request in the chapter repository (at `bruno/hms-api-collection/Admin Update Artisan.bru`). Because it is a `PATCH` request type, it expects a request body, and because a request is expected to update only a single `Artisan` object, it expects an `oid` in the request path to identify *which* `Artisan` object is going to be modified. The most common typical use case, activating an artisan by setting the `is_active` of the related `Artisan` object to `true`, would look something like this:

```
/*
 * Sending this as a JSON payload/body to the endpoint at
 * /api/v1/admin/artisan/{oid value goes here}/
 */
{
    "is_active": true
}
```

The data returned by that `PATCH` request (omitting fields with null values again, for brevity) applied to the Artisan created in the *Public Artisan Sign-up* example shown earlier is:

```
{
    "oid": "00000000-0000-0000-0000-000000000000",
    "is_active": true,
    "is_deleted": false,
    "created": "2025-07-05T15:47:32.631246",
    "given_name": "Sybil",
    "family_name": "Vimes",
    "business_address": {
        "street_address": "Ramkin House",
        "building_address": "Scoone Avenue",
        "city": "Ankh-Morpork",
        "postal_code": "N/A"
    },
    "email_address": "sybil.vimes-ramkin@twurps.org",
    "products": []
}
```

These first four endpoints have at least started to establish some potential implementation patterns for business object operations: There is an object creation operation, a couple of variations of object read operations, and an object update operation so far. Those approaches for the `Artisan` objects can be used as examples and guidelines for the implementation of similar operations for `Product` objects.

The Admin List Products endpoint

These changes are tagged in the chapter repository as `Ch-17-admin-list-products-endpoint`.

The use case that this endpoint is intended to serve is very similar to the one for the *Admin List Artisans* endpoint discussed earlier: An HMS product approver needs to be able to retrieve a list of `Product` objects that are pending approval — the default state for a `Product` is to have an `is_active` value that is `False` — and drill down from that list into the individual `Product` objects' details in order to approve them. With that goal in mind, the data points in the list of objects in the response really does not need to be much more than the `oid` of the `Product`, which will be used as a parameter to generate a link to the details, and the `name` of the `Product`, though providing the `is_active` value and maybe the `is_deleted` value would allow those to be displayed: they are potentially useful information in a product listing.

> **Populating test `Product` data**
>
> The initial development of `list` and `get` operations for `Artisan` objects was facilitated by there already being data in the local database left over from previous chapters. To similarly facilitate the development list and get operations for `Product` objects, a few example products were created, associated with the Artisan created in the *Public Artisan Set-up* endpoint described earlier. Those initial objects were created with a throw-away script that created new `Product` objects, then saved them. Creation of one or more new `Product` objects using the endpoint intended for artisans to do that will be covered in more detail shortly.

Using the same approach taken for the artisan list endpoint, defining a module attribute that is used to filter the full field set of each `Product` object returned down to only the ones that are relevant to the use case is simple:

```
# The list in the code contains *all* of the fields
# available, but has many of them commented out, for
# ease of adding them in later if desired.
LIST_FIELD_NAMES = (
    'oid', 'is_active', 'is_deleted', 'name',
)
```

The actual business object retrieval code for Product objects is almost identical to the code already written for Artisan objects. The business object name is different (Product instead of Artisan), some internal variable names were changed to reflect that change, and the db_source_name used to indicate where the data is being retrieved from was changed to point to the Products table. All of the query-string handling is the same, as is the handling of errors.

Everything needed to call the *Admin List Products* endpoint is provided in the *Admin List Products* request in the chapter repository (at bruno/hms-api-collection/Admin List Products.bru). The results of that call, with the Product objects created to test the endpoint, look as they are expected to, given the field names specified earlier:

```
[
  {
    "oid": "00000000-0000-0000-0000-000000000000",
    "is_active": false,
    "is_deleted": false,
    "name": "Swamp Dragon Eggshell Brooch"
  },
  // ... additional items truncated for space reasons
]
```

The data returned here is sufficient for a front-end process to build a link to a detail page for a specific Product item: all that is needed is a way to identify which product is being viewed — the oid field provides that — and some meaningful text to populate that link with — the name of the Product. The oid, since it identifies a specific Product, is also used to retrieve data for a specific Product in the endpoint that retrieves that detailed data.

The Admin Get Product endpoint

> These changes are tagged in the chapter repository as Ch-17-admin-get-product-endpoint.

This endpoint is intended to provide the complete, detailed data for a specific Product, in much the same way as the *Admin Get Artisan* endpoint shown above returns Artisan data. Like the *Admin List Products* endpoint just above, this endpoint's implementation is similar enough to its Artisan-related equivalent that the final code is identical, barring changes to object, variable, and database table names.

A Bruno request example for the endpoint has been provided in the chapter repository (at bruno/ hms-api-collection/Admin Get Product.bru). The results of that call, passing the oid of the Product shown in the previous endpoint's output in the path, yield the following data, omitting the height, length, width, and size fields, which had null values, and truncating the summary and description fields for space reasons:

```
{
    "oid": "00000000-0000-0000-0000-000000000000",
    "is_active": false,
    "is_deleted": false,
    "created": "2025-07-12T14:36:15.628507",
    "artisan_oid": "00000000-0000-0000-0000-000000000000",
    "name": "Swamp Dragon Eggshell Brooch",
    "summary": "Delicate brooch crafted from real ...",
    "description": "This exquisite piece of jewelry...",
    "product_images": [],
    "price": "120.0",
    "shipping_weight": "0.05"
}
```

It is worth noting that, at this point, with one or more Product objects associated with the example Artisan, the *Admin Get Artisan* endpoint's products results are being populated now. The fields returned there are unfiltered, including all the fields for each products entry associated with an Artisan, and not limited, so an Artisan with dozens or hundreds of products could be a larger data set than is needed or desired.

With both of the administrative endpoints relating to Product objects implemented, the implementation of the artisan-accessible endpoint to create those products can be implemented and tested.

The Artisan Create Product endpoint

These changes are tagged in the chapter repository as Ch-17-artisan-create-product-endpoint.

This endpoint is public-facing in the sense that it is intended for use by external users, specifically logged-in artisan users. The use case being served by the endpoint is the creation of a new `Product` object associated with an existing `Artisan` object. There are authentication and authorization concerns that would apply to the endpoint, which will be examined later in this chapter: If a request being made to this endpoint is not made with credentials expected for a logged-in artisan user, it must be denied.

Structurally, the endpoint's Lambda handler has code that has already been used in previous endpoints, with changes to variable names as appropriate for the change in the target business object involved in the process. Within the `try` block provided by the starting-point code template, the first significant chunk of functionality is the same acquisition and checking of an `oid` for the related `Artisan` object:

```python
# Get the oid of the Artisan that the
# new Product will be created for
artisan_oid = event.get(
    'pathParameters', {}
).get('artisan_oid')
if artisan_oid is None \
        or len(artisan_oid.split(',')) != 1:
    raise ValueError(
        f'{module}.api_handler requires a single '
        'artisan_oid, but that path parameter '
        f'resolved to "{artisan_oid}" '
        f'({type(artisan_oid).__name__}).'
    )
```

Like any endpoint in the system that is expected to have authentication and authorization constraints, this endpoint will define `_authnz_preflight` and `_authnz_reconcile` placeholder functions that will be called before allowing any data read or write operations to take place. Those functions will eventually either raise an error that can be translated to standard HTTP **401 Unauthorized** or **403 Forbidden** status code responses. If the overall authorization processes defined later in this chapter make them unnecessary, they will be removed.

AuthN/Z function additions

The addition of the AuthN/Z-related functions was missed in previous endpoints before they were committed to the chapter repository, but were put in place along with the changes specific to this endpoint.

The actual process for creating and saving the new Product object to the system database is very simple, looking much like the process for creating a new Artisan in the *Public Artisan Sign-up* endpoint:

```python
# Create the new Product object from the payload,
# and write it to the database.
_authnz_preflight()
product_data = json.loads(event['body'])
product_data['artisan_oid'] = artisan_oid
new_product = Product(**product_data)
_authnz_reconcile()
new_product.save(db_source_name='Products')
result = {
    'statusCode': 201,
    'body': new_product.model_dump_json()
}
```

The chapter repository has a Bruno request for this endpoint (at bruno/hms-api-collection/ Artisan Create Product.bru) with a minimal payload structure and the payload used to test this endpoint under its *Docs* tab. The result of that call, omitting null value fields and the product_ images that have not been addressed yet, was:

```json
{
  "oid": "134456ed-7767-4b23-8010-f6a81aabfa5d",
  "is_active": false,
  "is_deleted": false,
  "created": "2025-07-12T20:26:35.321372",
  "artisan_oid": "00000000-0000-0000-0000-000000000000",
  "name": "Fireproof Dragon-Cradle Blanket",
  "summary": "Handwoven blanket with...",
  "description": "Perfect for young swamp dragons...",
  "price": "89.0",
  "shipping_weight": "1.2",
}
```

Application of common, recurring patterns

There is nothing substantially new in the implementation of several of the remaining endpoints in the original sequence. Established patterns for the **Create**, **Read**, and **Update** aspects of **CRUD** operations, even those with the placeholders for AuthN/Z constraints, reduced the initial creation of the following endpoints to little more than copying and pasting the basic structure, and altering business object, variable, and data source names accordingly. The endpoints that only had to follow these patterns are:

- The *Admin Update Product* endpoint, intended to allow an HMS administrator to approve newly created `Product` items.

  > Code changes for this endpoint are tagged with `Ch-17-admin-update-product-endpoint` in the chapter repository, and the corresponding Bruno collection is at `bruno/hms-api-collection/Admin Update Product.bru`.

- The *Admin List Product Images* endpoint, intended to provide HMS administrators with a simple, summary-level list of `ProductImage` objects in the system.

  > Code changes for this endpoint are tagged with `Ch-17-admin-list-product-images-endpoint` in the chapter repository, and the corresponding Bruno collection is at `bruno/hms-api-collection/Admin List Product Images.bru`.

- The *Admin Get Product Image* endpoint, intended to provide the complete, detailed data for a specific `ProductImage` object, for detailed review by HMS administrators when there is a need for that data in the review process.

  > Code changes for this endpoint are tagged with `Ch-17-admin-get-product-image-endpoint` in the chapter repository, and the corresponding Bruno collection is at `bruno/hms-api-collection/Admin Get Product Image.bru`.

- The *Admin Update Product Image* endpoint, intended to allow HMS administrators to approve a ProductImage object for display on the site.

> Code changes for this endpoint are tagged with Ch-17-admin-update-product-image-endpoint in the chapter repository, and the corresponding Bruno collection is at bruno/hms-api-collection/Admin Update Product Image.bru.

The observant reader may have noticed that one of the endpoints in the implementation sequence noted earlier was skipped: the *Artisan Create Product Image* endpoint. That endpoint has additional needs that there are no established patterns for, and warrants a deeper examination.

The Artisan Create Product Image endpoint

> These changes are tagged in the chapter repository as Ch-17-artisan-create-product-image-endpoint, and the corresponding Bruno collection is at bruno/hms-api-collection/Artisan Create Product Image.bru.

This endpoint is intended to serve the use case of a logged-in Artisan submitting an image file to be associated with a Product object as one of its ProductImage elements. Because this process involves uploading a file from the Artisan's local file system, there are several considerations that need to be examined and decided upon to define the actual implementation for the endpoint. A number of those are reliant on how the front-end UI is going to implement the file selection and submission process, while others are best-practice concerns that should be applied to any file-upload process. At a very high level, the process involves an upload of the file itself, and the data elements for the image file that are defined as fields in the ProductImage model class. In summary, the fields that are provided, directly or indirectly, by the Artisan user are:

- product_oid: The unique identifier of the Product that the ProductImage is associated with. This field is provided indirectly by the page that the upload form lives in.
- caption (user input): The optional caption for the image.
- alt_text (user input): The required alt-text for the image.

There are other fields in the structure that the Artisan simply *cannot* provide, or that they are not *allowed* to provide, for various reasons. Those include the fields that are common to all business object classes (provided by the BaseDataObject class), and fields whose values will be calculated during the upload process:

- oid (a BaseDataObject field): The unique identifier of the record for the instance's state data in the back-end data store
- is_active (a BaseDataObject field): Flag indicating whether the object is "active"
- is_deleted (a BaseDataObject field): Flag indicating whether the object is "deleted" (pending an *actual* deletion later, perhaps)
- created (a BaseDataObject field): The date/time (UTC) when the object was created
- modified (a BaseDataObject field): The (optional) date/time (UTC) when the object was last modified
- image_url (calculated): The required URL of the image
- width (calculated): The width of the image, in pixels, as originally uploaded
- height (calculated): The height of the image, in pixels, as originally uploaded

It is worth noting that *none* of these fields account for the actual image data — the intent for the image upload process is to accept that data, along with the user-supplied data values, and:

- Perform whatever processes are needed to verify the image data itself.
- Modify the image if needed to meet display standards and expectations.
- Calculate the values for the fields from the list above as needed.
- Save the (possibly modified) image to a location that can be resolved by a browser from the image_url field.
- Reconcile all of the fields needed to create the ProductImage object, and create it.
- Write the ProductImage object record.

The entire process, just like the previous endpoints that implement HTTP POST functionality, starts with a payload. The HMS engineers would prefer that the payload be a JSON object, if only because that follows the same pattern as every other endpoint implemented so far. That JSON payload, including the fields explicitly supplied by the Artisan end user, and the ones that would be supplied by the page that the UI lives in, would look like this:

```
{
    "caption": "Optional caption for the image",
    "alt_text": "Required alt-text for the image",
```

```
        "image_data": "{Base64-encoded binary data: The image}"
    }
```

This approach puts the responsibility for generating the image_data field value on the front-end UI: That UI will use standard JavaScript functionality (FileReader.readAsDataURL, see https://developer.mozilla.org/en-US/docs/Web/API/FileReader/readAsDataURL) to read the contents of the file locally and generate a data:URL representation of the image (see https://developer.mozilla.org/en-US/docs/Web/URI/Reference/Schemes/data). That data will look something like this (truncated for space reasons):

```
data:{MIME type};base64,iVBOR ... ggg==
```

The image_data value is the string segment that follows the base64, portion of the data — everything else can be discarded: The MIME type (see https://developer.mozilla.org/en-US/docs/Web/HTTP/Guides/MIME_types/Common_types), while potentially useful, could be faked by a malicious actor, and will be determined in the endpoint code by examining the actual image data submitted. The base64 indicator serves no purpose in the endpoint code receiving the data; the endpoint will attempt to base-64 decode the image_data field's value, and if that fails, the submission will terminate.

Non-JSON payloads are also an option

Though this example focuses on using JSON payloads for consistency, there are other options: A standard HTML <input type="file"> field, in a <form> with an enctype="multipart/form-data" attribute, will generate an HTTP payload that can be parsed with libraries like python-multipart (https://pypi.org/project/python-multipart/) to yield a usable data structure.

The processing for a ProductImage POST request has to account for two separate operations. The first is the creation of a new ProductImage record, which looks very similar to the POST processing from previous endpoint examples. The second is performing all of the activities needed to store the image file in a location where a client can access it. In the final deployed API system, this storage location will almost certainly be an **AWS S3** (https://aws.amazon.com/s3/) **bucket**, which will be attached to the deployed API as an endpoint that allows the API to read and return those uploaded images' data.

The image storage process has a lot of potential sub-processes that may be desirable or necessary to implement as well:

- Checking that the image does not contain a virus should be given serious consideration
- Cropping and resizing an image to fit into one of several prescribed sizes and/or aspect ratios
- Verifying that the image is in a web-compatible format: PNG, JPEG, etc., and a format that is intended to be used in the context of the system, which might include conversion of an unsupported image format to one that is supported in the process
- Creating **thumbnail images** — smaller-sized copies of the original images that require less network bandwidth to transmit — for use in list views of products

Executing some kind of virus scan on any files uploaded to a system on the web is always a good idea. Files that are distributed through the web can be a significant risk to any end users who read those files, and the potential for an infected file to be distributed to hundreds or thousands of victims makes uploads an attractive target for bad actors. Although images displayed through a web browser, as these product images are expected to be, are not a common attack vector, they are still a potential attack vector. There are several services available that can be used to perform virus scans, including:

- **Cloudmersive's Virus Scan API** (`https://cloudmersive.com/virus-api`)
- **Verisys Antivirus API** (`https://www.ionxsolutions.com/products/antivirus-api`)
- **attachmentAV** (`https://attachmentav.com/`)

It would also be feasible to implement virus scanning in a **Lambda Function using a Docker image** instead of a simple package. AWS provides ample documentation to guide engineers down that path, should it be desirable (see `https://docs.aws.amazon.com/lambda/latest/dg/python-image.html#python-image-instructions`). The Docker image would need to include an installation of an antivirus application, and some way to call that antivirus process, for example, using **ClamAV** (`https://www.clamav.net/`) and the `clamav-client` package (`https://pypi.org/project/clamav-client/`). While this approach might be less expensive than paying for an antivirus service, it would also require working out a process to keep virus detection current: Viruses and antivirus software both change very quickly; even ClamAV, an open source project, tends to have multiple updates on a daily basis to keep up with new viruses, and those updates can take anywhere from a few seconds to several minutes.

Implementing the starting point for a virus-check process adds several elements to the code. The first is a custom `Exception` class, which will be used later to raise an error if a virus scan fails:

```python
class VirusScanFailedError(Exception):
    """
    An error to be raised if an external virus-scanning
    API detected a virus.
    """
```

Without knowing yet exactly how the virus scan process will be implemented, the best short-term option, which allows the process to be defined later, while still allowing it to be called and testable now, is to stub out a helper function that will eventually contain the actual implementation:

```python
def _call_virus_check_api(image_base64_str: str):
    """
    Submits the supplied base64-encoded string to an
    external virus-checking API. If the results of
    the check indicate a virus, raises a
    VirusScanFailedError
    """
    # TODO: Implement the actual API call.
    ...
```

within the try...except block that is common to all of the Lambda handler implementations, which allows the process to be put in place for later use. The addition of a new except that handles any `VirusScanFailedError` exceptions raised completes that part of the process:

```python
except VirusScanFailedError as error:
    logger.exception(
        f'{error.__class__.__name__}: {error} '
        'occured in api_handler'
    )
    logger.error(f'event: {json.dumps(event)}')
    logger.error(f'context: {repr(context)}')
    result = {
        'statusCode': 422,
        'body': 'Unprocessable Content: '
        f'({context.aws_request_id}). '
        'The submitted file did not pass a virus check'
    }
```

422 Unprocessable Content

From `https://developer.mozilla.org/en-US/docs/Web/HTTP/Reference/Status/422`:

The HTTP `422 Unprocessable Content` client error response status code indicates that the server understood the content type of the request content, and the syntax of the request content was correct, but it was unable to process the contained instructions.

Using this status code will allow the front end receiving the response to alert the artisan end user that there was a virus detected in their upload attempt.

```python
try:
    # Standard logging omitted for space
    _authnz_preflight()
    # Get the event body and make sure it's
    # what's expected
    body = json.loads(event.get('body', 'null'))
    assert body is not None, (
        'No "body" present in event'
    )
# Get and check the image data
image_base64_str = body['image_data'] \
    .split(',')[-1].strip()
assert image_base64_str, (
    'No "image_data" present in event.body'
)
# Use the string representation for virus
# checking with external API calls
_call_virus_check_api(image_base64_str)
```

Only allowing specific image formats to be uploaded requires being able to examine the image's properties. Since there are other properties of an uploaded image that will also need to be examined later, a local in-memory copy of the image will be created using the `pillow` package (`https://pypi.org/project/pillow/`), and asserting that the format of the image is in a collection of accepted image formats.

The code to manage that starts with the collection of accepted image formats, as a `dict` object with the format names and MIME type:

```python
ALLOWED_MIME_TYPES = {
    'JPEG': 'image/jpeg',
    'PNG': 'image/png'
}
```

Within the `try...except` block provided by the starting-point code, it is then a simple matter to create an `image` object and check that it is of an appropriate file type:

```python
# Decode the Base 64 string to get the
# actual binary data for the file
image_base64 = bytes(image_base64_str, 'utf-8')
image_bytes = b64decode(image_base64)
image_io = io.BytesIO(image_bytes)
image = Image.open(image_io)
# Debug logging removed for space
assert Image.MIME.get(image.format) \
    in ALLOWED_MIME_TYPES.values(), (
    'Uploads must be one of '
    f'{list(ALLOWED_MIME_TYPES.keys())} '
    'file types.'
)
```

That same image object can be used to generate the standard-sized final images that will be presented to end users in the system's front end pages. Standardizing images to fit common sizes, resolutions, and/or **aspect ratios** (the ratio of an image's width to its height) helps to ensure that when images are presented to the front end that is responsible for displaying them, they will not result in inconsistent appearances and a bad user experience. There are at least two standardizations that are applicable to the HMS system: One will generate an optimal image for a product detail page, and another will generate a thumbnail image to be used in product list pages. Without knowing the parameters for those images — what size constraints must be applied to them, chiefly — and how the front-end UI will allow an artisan user to define things like the main point of interest in the image, the specific process cannot really be defined yet.

As a further complication, also needing definition by the front-end developers, there may be significant differences in the process based on whether the list displays will use a typical list view, one of two masonry grid layouts, or something completely different (see *Figure 17.2* for examples of these layout options).

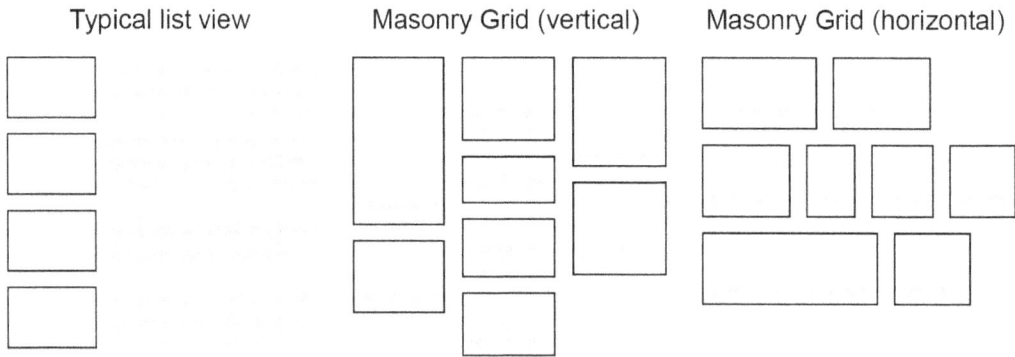

Figure 17.2: Some common layout variations for collections of images on the web

The idea of having both detail and thumbnail images, for product detail views and product list views, respectively, was not accounted for in the original design of the ProductImage business object. After some discussion, the rules for handling the various image sizes (and purposes) were decided to be:

- The original image upload would be saved in case of future need to perform large-scale recreation of the detail and thumbnail images — for example, if the front end changed from a typical list layout to one of the masonry grid layouts shown in *Figure 17.2*.

- Thumbnail and detail images would be saved to specific path locations that would be accessible relative to the root of the site, and their final URLs could be calculated from the oid associated with the ProductImage. For example, an image upload that resulted in an oid of 00000000-0000-0000-0000-00000000000a would have the following URLs calculable as:

    - `{site root}/product_images/details/00000000-0000-0000-0000-00000000000a.png` for the detail view's image
    - `{site root}/product_images/thumbnails/00000000-0000-0000-0000-00000000000a.png` for the thumbnail

- All images would be converted to and saved as PNG images.

- The original, detail, and thumbnail image sizes would be stored as properties of the main ProductImage.

The final image sizes for detail and thumbnail images are not yet defined, so in the interim, the best that can be done is to set up placeholder functions that at least return a copy of the original image provided. At this point, apart from the function names, they are identical, looking like this:

```python
def _create_detail_image(original_image: Image) -> Image:
    """

    Placeholder code

    """

    # TODO: Handle the maximum size, scaling, cropping,
    #        etc. based on business rules for detail
    #        images that are TBD.
    # For now, just return the original image and its
    # width and height.
    return original_image
```

Those are called in the main body of the try...except block of the function:

```python
# Resize and convert the image as needed to
# create a product-detail image
detail_image = _create_detail_image(image)
# Resize and convert the image as needed to
# create a product-thumbnail image
thumbnail_image = _create_thumbnail_image(image)
```

Saving the resulting images is handled by a common helper function (logging, comments, and documentation omitted for space reasons) that uses environment variables to provide path information:

```python
# Environment variables for image uploads
ORIGINAL_IMAGES_LOCATION="file:///{API_ROOT_DIR}/product_images/original"
DETAIL_IMAGES_LOCATION="file:///{API_ROOT_DIR}/product_images/detail"
THUMBNAIL_IMAGES_LOCATION="file:///{API_ROOT_DIR}/product_images/thumbnail"
```

The local FastAPI application defines the `API_ROOT_DIR` environment variable, which will be used to populate the `{API_ROOT_DIR}` placeholders in these variables:

```python
environ['API_ROOT_DIR'] = str(Path(__file__).parent.resolve())
```

The function that actually executes the file-saving process is relatively straightforward:

```python
def save_image(
    image: Image, location: str, oid: str
) -> None:
    image_name = f'{oid}.png'
    if location.startswith('s3://'):
        raise NotImplementedError(
            'Saving images to an S3 bucket is not yet '
            'supported.'
        )
    elif location.startswith('file:///'):
        save_path = Path(
            location[8:].format(**os.environ)
        )
        if not save_path.exists():
            save_path.mkdir(parents=True)
        image_path = save_path / image_name
        image.save(image_path)
```

This function is then called once for each image — original, detail, and thumbnail — that needs to be saved, after retrieving the oid from the body of the submission, or creating a new oid value if one was not supplied:

```python
# Use a common oid for each
new_image_oid = body.get('oid', str(uuid4()))
save_image(
    image,
    os.environ['ORIGINAL_IMAGES_LOCATION'],
    new_image_oid
)
save_image(
    detail_image,
    os.environ['DETAIL_IMAGES_LOCATION'],
    new_image_oid
)
save_image(
    thumbnail_image,
```

```
        os.environ['THUMBNAIL_IMAGES_LOCATION'],
        new_image_oid
    )
```

Since the layouts for thumbnail images may require those images to have different aspect ratios than the detail images, and both of those might vary from the size of the original image, the HMS engineers decided to keep track of the height and width of each image. To do that, a new child class/data structure was defined to capture those data points for each image variant and added to the ProductImage class:

```python
# Comments, documentation, and duplicated info
#omitted for space
class ProductImageSize(BaseModel):
    ...
    width: int=Field(
        gt=0,
        examples=[320, 240],
    )
    height: int=Field(
        gt=0,
        examples=[320, 240],
    )
...
class ProductImage(BaseModel, BaseDataObject):
    ...
    original_image_size: ProductImageSize = Field(
        examples=[
            ProductImageSize(width=900, height=1600),
        ]
    )
    detail_image_size: ProductImageSize = Field(
        examples=[
            ProductImageSize(width=270, height=480),
        ]
    )
    thumbnail_image_size: ProductImageSize = Field(
        examples=[
```

```
                    ProductImageSize(width=68, height=120),
            ]
        )
```

With those changes in place, the assembly of the entire data set needed to create a new ProductImage object and save it to the database is nothing more than assembling those, creating the new object, and calling its save method, after which the results to be returned are generated in a manner similar to previous examples:

```
        request_params = {
            'oid': new_image_oid,
            'product_oid': product_oid,
            'caption':body.get('caption'),
            'alt_text':body['alt_text'],
        }
        image_params = {
            'original_image_size': {
                'width': image.width,
                'height': image.height,
            },
            'detail_image_size': {
                'width': detail_image.width,
                'height': detail_image.height,
            },
            'thumbnail_image_size': {
                'width': thumbnail_image.width,
                'height': thumbnail_image.height,
            },
        }
        new_product_image = ProductImage(
            **image_params | request_params
        )
        result = {
            'statusCode': 200,
            'body': new_product_image.model_dump_json()
        }
```

Python's dictionary union

The `**image_params | request_params` shown in the code just above is an example of Python's **dictionary union** capability — a feature introduced in version 3.9 that allows multiple dictionary objects to be combined using the **bitwise or operator** (`|`). This syntax is approximately equivalent to executing a `dict.update()` against the first `dict` object in the sequence with each subsequent `dict` object.

The error-handling needed follows a very similar pattern to previous endpoints, with the addition of specific handling for `AssertionError`, `TypeError`, and `ValueError` exceptions that can be raised by various sub-processes in the code, in addition to the handler for the new `VirusScanFailedError`, shown above.

```python
    except (AssertionError, TypeError, ValueError) as error:
        logger.exception(
            f'{error.__class__.__name__}: {error} '
            'occured in api_handler'
        )
        # Standard logging omitted for space
        result = {
            'statusCode': 400,
            'body': 'Bad Request: '
            f'({context.aws_request_id})'
        }
    except ProductNotFoundError as error:
        logger.exception(
            f'{error.__class__.__name__}: {error} '
            'occured in api_handler'
        )
        # Standard logging omitted for space
        result = {
            'statusCode': 404,
            'body': 'Not Found: '
            f'({context.aws_request_id})'
        }
```

At this point, the endpoint is nominally complete, at least for local development purposes. There will be further work needed once the system is deployed to the cloud, if only to execute the image save code for S3 bucket destinations, but the local service will accept the image upload and the related metadata that the artisan will supply, calculate the system-level metadata, save all of those elements appropriately, and return a result looking something like this (`BaseDataObject` fields omitted for space):

```
{
  "oid": "00000000-0000-0000-0000-00000000000a",
  "product_oid": "6a5d3431-8ba4-41d2-923a-b45336663c15",
  "is_primary_image": false,
  "caption": "Optional caption for the image",
  "alt_text": "Required alt-text for the image",
  "original_image_size": {
    "width": 94,
    "height": 94
  },
  "detail_image_size": {
    "width": 94,
    "height": 94
  },
  "thumbnail_image_size": {
    "width": 94,
    "height": 94
  }
}
```

This last endpoint completes all of the artisan and administrator endpoints that are needed to finalize the implementation of the user-facing endpoints: *List Products* and *View Product*. In the process of implementing these `ProductImage` changes, the previous endpoints that made use of the class to retrieve product image data were broken, because the addition of the new fields for the image variants had not been accounted for in the existing objects in the database. Handling those sorts of breaking changes will be discussed in the next chapter, as a deployment concern.

The Public List Products and Public View Product endpoints

These changes are tagged in the chapter repository as `Ch-17-public-list-products-endpoint` and `Ch-17-public-view-product-endpoint`, and their corresponding Bruno collections are at `bruno/hms-api-collection/Public List Products.bru` and `bruno/hms-api-collection/Public Get Product.bru`, respectively.

The *Public List Products* and *Public View Product* endpoints use cases are straightforward enough: getting the information needed to display a list of products to an end user in a front-end UI, and retrieving the details of a product for display in a product detail UI. The implementation of both the *Public List Products* and *Public View Product* endpoints did not require the use of any patterns not already established in previous endpoints' implementations:

- *Public List Products* used:

    - The calls to `Product.get` and `ProductImage.get` were both written to explicitly include `is_active=True` and `is_deleted=False` criteria, so that only approved, non-deleted items would be retrieved.

    - Filtering of response data fields using tuples of field names (`PRODUCT_FIELD_NAMES` and `PRODUCT_IMAGE_FIELD_NAMES`) to control which business object fields were returned in the response.

    - Pagination fields (`page_size` and `page_number`) and sorting control fields, using essentially the same implementation first presented in the *Admin List Artisans* endpoint.

    - Multiple business object get method calls, one for the actual `Product` objects, and another for `ProductImage` objects whose `product_oid` values were in the collection of `oid` members of the `Product` objects returned.

    - There was one noteworthy variation implemented in the *Public List Products* endpoint: It implemented an in-code determination of which `ProductImage` to return as the single `product_images` value for the response, prioritizing the images whose `is_primary_image` flag was `True`.

- With the exception of using the same explicit `is_active=True` and `is_deleted=False` criteria that were put in place in the *Public List Products* endpoint, to only allow approved, non-deleted items to be returned, the *Public Get Product* endpoint's implementation is essentially identical to the implementation of the *Admin Get Product* endpoint.

These fourteen endpoints, between them, show several factors that need to be considered and accounted for with respect to the **C**reate, **R**ead, and **U**pdate CRUD operations expected from a REST API. What has not been accounted for yet is any sort of actual **D**elete operation. Deletions *can* be simple operations too, but if there are relationships between an object to be deleted and other objects whose data would be left unlinked to anything after that deletion, there are several options available to prevent this sort of **orphaned data**.

Handling related objects in endpoints

> These changes are tagged in the chapter repository as `Ch-17-artisan-delete-product-endpoint`.

The *Artisan Delete Product* endpoint is as complex an example of a delete operation through the API as is likely to exist, so that will be used as the example for this discussion. The fundamental questions that need to be asked about deletions of data (or, in this system, business objects) boil down to:

- What needs to happen to child objects when a parent object is deleted?
- Where do those processes take place?
- In the case of the HMS system, this is complicated somewhat by the fact that not all objects are represented in the database — the images for a product are files living in a file system or something approximately equivalent. If we consider a relatively simple example structure, one `Artisan` with two related `Product` objects, and each of those with two `ProductImage` objects (each with their three associated files), the tree of relationships grows rather complex very quickly, as shown in *Figure 17.3*.

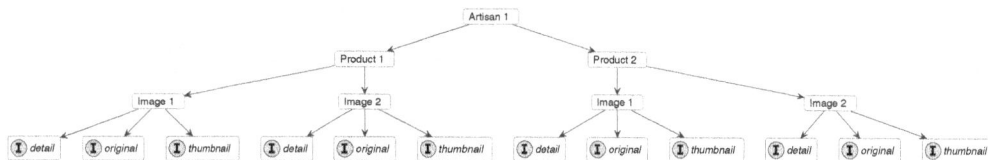

Figure 17.3: The relationships between a single Artisan, their two Product objects, those Products' two ProductImage objects, and the related three files for each ProductImage object

- From a basic data hygiene perspective, the idea that the deletion of any given business object in this tree should result in the deletion of all of that object's children seems fairly obvious. Once the parent object no longer exists, there is no good reason for the child objects to continue to exist, at least in the context of the HMS system. Given that basic rule, the answer to the *what needs to happen to child objects when a parent object is deleted?* question is straightforward: They should also be deleted.

- The question of where those deletions take place — in the code or in the database are both options for business objects' records — is less straightforward in this system. The main consideration in the HMS system's context is that the image files are not stored in the database, and there is no built-in way for a record deletion to trigger the deletion of the corresponding files.

> **Triggering file deletions from an AWS-resident database is an option**
>
> Both the serverless and EC2-based RDS database options provided by AWS provide built-in function additions to standard database capabilities to trigger a Lambda Function when certain database events occur. It is possible to leverage this functionality, writing a Lambda Function that accepts the database event, figures out which files need to be deleted, and deletes them. That capability does not carry across to local implementations well, however.

If the deletion of files was not a consideration, whether because there were no files to be deleted, or perhaps if those files were also stored in the database, there is a database mechanism that can handle child record/object deletions automatically: the ON DELETE CASCADE statement. When applied to the relationships between tables, like the Artisan, Products, and ProductImage tables in this system, a deletion of a parent business object record will trigger the deletion of any related child business object records in their respective tables. In the object tree shown in *Figure 17.3* (ignoring the files), that translates as the deletion of any object in the tree will trigger the deletion of any related objects that are connected to that object in the direction of the arrows in the diagram. That is:

- Deleting *Artisan 1* would delete everything in the entire tree
- Deleting *Product 1* would delete the connected *Image 1* and *Image 2* nodes, but leave *Product 2* and its child *Image* nodes alone

ON DELETE CASCADE varies across database engines

Although ON DELETE CASCADE is available in all of the database engines examined
for this project, the specifics of where the statement is applied vary a bit across those
database engines. Consult your database's documentation for the specifics of where
and how it should be applied.

An in-code process is better suited for the Artisan Delete Product endpoint's implementation, if
only because of the file deletion process that has to be incorporated. Much of its implementation
follows established patterns from previous endpoints: checking for an Artisan-owned Product
object and retrieving the related ProductImage objects based on the oid of the Product specified
follow previous implementations' patterns, for example. The main differences are in the business
object class method calls executed, delete vs. the previously used get. Once the Product and its
related ProductImage children are identified, a new helper function to delete the files created by
the *Artisan Create Product Image* endpoint for each *ProductImage* is called. The final output returned
is a complete collection of the entire Product/ProductImage data set that relates.

Summary

At this point, there is at least the start of a complete CRUD operation set for the API, though there
are some implementation details that still need to be worked out. The most significant of those is
the Authentication and Authorization (AuthN/Z) process, but even that has at least been started,
by creating and integrating placeholder functions in the endpoints whose access is expected to
be restricted. As the details of how AuthN/Z is expected to work start solidifying, those functions' implementations can be started and refined until they are complete. In much the same
way, pending a decision about how to handle the expected virus-scanning of uploaded product
image files, a placeholder for that functionality has been integrated that can also be fleshed out.

The next major step, and the topic for the next chapter, is how to build processes that actually
deploy the code and database changes to a cloud environment, accounting for some of the breaking changes that were discovered in finalizing these endpoints, and formulating processes and
strategies for handling breaking changes on an ongoing basis.

18

The Final API, Deployed to AWS

In this, the final chapter, we'll be putting all of the pieces from the previous chapters together and deploying a functionally complete API into an AWS account. The code written and tested locally will be packaged and made available in an Amazon S3 bucket, the database will be created as a serverless Aurora **Relational Database Service (RDS)** instance, compatible with MySQL/MariaDB standards, and an API Gateway resource will be created to provide access to the database through a REST API whose compute functionality will be provide by the Lambda functions that were tested with a local wrapper API. The entire process breaks out into two major pieces, with some follow-up items described that should be considered, if not implemented, before calling the API production-ready. This chapter will discuss:

- Deployment practices and options
- Defining and deploying the database resources
- Defining and deploying the API resources
- Making the system production-ready

> **Some constraints in this chapter's implementations**
>
> Because of the way that the chapter repository was set up, and the intricacies and complexity involved in starting up an AWS account with all the configuration needed for a fully automated CI/CD process, it was not practical to implement that full CI/CD process. The goal of this chapter is to provide as much information about how such a process could be implemented, and usable alternatives that illustrate what would actually be happening, while also providing a usable API when all is said and done. As a result, there is a mixture of manual processes and local tool scripts to get to that usable deliverable API.

Technical requirements

The bulk of the code presented in the text of this chapter is for illustrative purposes only. The code in the repository is expected to be executable, was written for Python 3.11, and assumes that it is available on the reader's machine. Download and installation instructions are available online at `https://www.python.org/downloads/` for Windows, Linux/Unix, macOS, and other systems. The package requirements for the chapter's code are captured in the `Pipfile` or `requirements. txt` files, and can be installed as described earlier in this book.

The various AWS command-line tools mentioned are not used, but information for them can be found online:

- The aws command-line tool (`https://docs.aws.amazon.com/cli/latest/userguide/ getting-started-install.html`)
- The AWS sam command-line tool (`https://docs.aws.amazon.com/serverless- application-model/latest/developerguide/install-sam-cli.html`)

This chapter focuses heavily on being able to make and view the results of requests to an API instance, initially without any concerns for a front-end UI. To that end, there are several tools available, including Bruno (`https://www.usebruno.com/`) and Postman (`https://www.postman. com/`), both of which provide a developer-friendly UI for making HTTP requests and seeing the responses to those requests.

The code for this chapter is provided in the book's repository at `https://github.com/ PacktPublishing/Hands-On-Software-Engineering-with-Python-Second-Edition/tree/ main/CH18-code`.

Deployment practices and options

Given the decision by HMS to deploy its API as AWS services, there are two primary options for handling that deployment, both of which are **Infrastructure as Code (IaC)** mechanisms. IaC allows the management and provisioning of IT infrastructure — servers, databases, storage, networking, and so on — using code and automation tools, removing or at least reducing the need for manual processes and configuration. In an AWS context, the IaC options worth considering are AWS CloudFormation (and derivatives of it), and Hashicorp's Terraform.

CloudFormation and its derivatives

CloudFormation, along with its derivatives, **Serverless Application Model (SAM)** and **Cloud Development Kit (CDK)**, which can be thought of as wrappers around core CloudFormation functionality, is the most mature of these technologies. At a high level, CloudFormation accepts a collection of resource definitions, a **template** written in JSON or YAML, and creates and configures the resources in that definition in the context of a given cloud account. CloudFormation is **declarative**, meaning that the resource definitions provided are the intended final state desired for the resources described, rather than the steps needed to create and configure those resources. When CloudFormation processes a template, the processes in the service work out any dependencies (what resources need to be created before others), figure out the specific sequence of events needed to create and configure those resources, and then execute against that sequence until everything required in the template exists in the desired state. Because the template is just code, it can be re-run for any of several different contexts, allowing consistent creation of resources for different environments (development vs. test vs. production) or across different AWS accounts.

The CloudFormation back-end keeps track of the finished state of the resources created in some fashion and will not recreate or change existing resources unless something in the definition has changed. Those changes can also include the deletion of existing resources; if a resource definition is removed from a template, the corresponding resource will be removed when the template is executed again. That ability to keep track of the state of a **stack** — a collection of service resources — contributes to several CloudFormation features:

- Automatic **rollback** of failed deployments, which keeps the current stack operational even if a deployment goes catastrophically wrong
- **Drift detection**, identifying when deployed resources have deviated from their last-known desired state
- **Change sets**, collections of proposed changes that can be reviewed before being deployed

Using CloudFormation to manage AWS service resources provides additional advantages. It is native to and well-integrated with AWS, which means that it generally has support for new AWS services, resources, and features the soonest after those new items are available — often as soon as those *are* available. That integration in AWS also provides good summary-level visibility into the resource members of any given stack, with cross-linking to the actual resources in many cases. It is also very cost-effective: CloudFormation itself is free to use, the resources created by a stack still cost what they normally would, but getting them provisioned and configured costs nothing but time.

The trade-offs when using CloudFormation include:

- **Vendor lock-in**: CloudFormation is exclusively offered by AWS, so it is not a good option if there are concerns about or desires for more portable IaC capabilities.

- **A substantial learning curve**: As this chapter was being written, CloudFormation's list of supported services alone came to 258 services, with several resource types available for each (the *CloudFormation Resource and Property Reference* documentation at `https://docs.aws.amazon.com/AWSCloudFormation/latest/UserGuide/aws-template-resource-type-ref.html` keeps track of those).

- **Verbose templates**: A complex system may require templating that is very long, and though subdivision into nested stacks, each represented by its own template, and referred to from a parent template is supported, those can still grow out of hand.

- **Limitations of the templates themselves**: CloudFormation may not support every configuration or capability of every resource for every service AWS offers.

SAM alleviates *some* of those concerns by providing simplified templating for a much smaller collection of resource types commonly used in serverless architectures. There are, as of late 2025, only nine such resources (see the AWS SAM resources and properties page at `https://docs.aws.amazon.com/serverless-application-model/latest/developerguide/sam-specification-resources-and-properties.html` for the current offerings), but those are sufficient for many applications, and standard CloudFormation resources can be mixed in with those as needed to provide additional resources. SAM templates are still JSON or YAML documents and are still run through the CloudFormation service, where SAM-specific resource definitions are transformed to more detailed CloudFormation equivalents, which are then processed by CloudFormation. The end result is no different than if the full CloudFormation that results from the SAM transformation were written as pure CloudFormation and deployed.

SAM still has the same vendor lock-in as regular CloudFormation, and has, in many respects, even more limitations in what the templates are allowed to describe, though the focus on common serverless components has made access to the commonly needed properties of those resources significantly simpler. That has also reduced the learning curve substantially for those resources, within the context of common use cases for those resources. The trade-off in that case is that not all properties and configurations for those resources are available without resorting to full Cloud-Formation definitions. Templates can still become verbose, but the simplification of templating for those common serverless resources reduces that potential significantly, provided that only serverless resources are actually needed.

AWS's CDK, like SAM, can be thought of as a wrapper around standard CloudFormation processes. That, though, is where the similarity ends. CDK provides native language components — Python classes and functions, for example — that allow a stack's components and resources to be defined using the same language that the application itself is written in. That also tends to allow more capability for reuse of component types within or even across stacks. The deployment of the stack relies on a CDK command-line tool being available that provides tools to create the CloudFormation required (the `cdk synth` command) and to deploy it (with `cdk deploy`). The trade-offs for CDK include:

- It still has the potential for a significant learning curve, though it may be less difficult to manage since the constructs needed are available as Python classes and functions.
- Template verbosity may be significantly reduced, possibly even eliminated as a potential concern, since the engineers writing the application code don't need to write *any* Cloud-Formation template definitions under most circumstances.
- CDK constructs *may* allow more or better access to properties and configuration than raw CloudFormation or SAM, though that is speculation on the author's part.
- AWS accounts cannot use CDK when they are first created — there are a number of permissions and required resources that have to be put in place first to bootstrap the account. The CDK command-line tool provides a specific command to deal with that initial setup, though: `cdk bootstrap`.

While the vendor lock-in may still be present when using CDK — it does, after all, create Cloud-Formation definitions, and uses CloudFormation to manage deployment of resources — there are third-party tools that *also* support CDK resource definition, but that do not require the use of CloudFormation. One such is the other main player in the IaC space for AWS: Terraform.

Terraform in an AWS context

Like CloudFormation and its derivatives, Terraform is an Infrastructure as Code (IaC) tool. It is also declarative, like CloudFormation, but relies on vendor-specific APIs to interact with the cloud accounts where resources are being provisioned and deployed. In a Python context, Terraform uses something equivalent, the boto3 package (https://pypi.org/project/boto3/), to read, analyze, and create or alter AWS resources. As a result, Terraform can perform more detailed analyses of existing resources when a change to an existing application is being executed, which in turn allows it to have finer-grained visibility into resource state and make correspondingly finer-grained changes to existing resources when necessary.

Terraform's detailed access is a double-edged sword; be cautious!

Terraform can create resources, detect changes in them, and update them in cases where that may not be desirable. A recent example the author encountered was the creation of an AWS Secrets Manager Secret resource, populated with placeholder values that were updated manually. In later deployments of the same application, Terraform detected that the placeholder values in those secrets had changed, and overwrote the desired values with the original placeholders until the configuration for those resources was changed to ignore changes in them if they already existed.

Terraform also provides multi-cloud support: it can manage resources in all of the major cloud providers (AWS, Azure, and Google Cloud Platform at a minimum). If vendor lock-in is a concern at all, Terraform is definitely worth looking at as a resource management tool for that reason alone. Whether moving an application from one cloud provider to another is simple or not will depend significantly on what resources need to be moved, and what the differences in their definitions are across the relevant cloud providers, at a minimum. It was noted earlier that AWS's CDK could be used with Terraform — that is, provided by **CDK for Terraform** (**CDKTF**, https://developer. hashicorp.com/terraform/cdktf), an add-on that can be installed for Terraform that allows CDK definitions to be read and processed by Terraform's main functionality. As of this writing, CDK for Terraform has not yet reached a 1.0 version release (release history can be found online at https://github.com/hashicorp/terraform-cdk/releases), and it is noted that "*CDKTF may still have breaking changes before our 1.0 release.*"

Even if CDKTF is not viable in and of itself, Terraform is a popular IaC solution, with a large community and ecosystem of resources, documentation, pre-built modules, and support resources. The trade-offs for Terraform include:

- **A potentially significant learning curve**: Terraform's **HashiCorp Configuration Language (HCL)** is mostly straightforward, but will take some time to get used to, especially for users who are not familiar with IaC concepts.

- **Learning to moderate state management**: The detailed resource inspection capabilities noted earlier mean that Terraform users have to be more aware of potential conflicts within and across resources in order to reconcile those if they should arise.

- **Lack of automatic reconciliation**: Terraform requires specific commands to be executed to apply changes, and does not automatically reconcile drift in all deployed resources, though it will make an effort to update resources that do not meet the desired state in their definition.

- **Lag behind available features and functionality**: Newer services and resources may not be supported immediately, requiring workarounds or waiting for Terraform to update as those become available.

None of these factors is significantly worse than the trade-offs that occur with any of the Cloud-Formation-based options. They are *different* in their specifics, to be sure, but the fact of the matter is that any tool or process that is going to meet the same set of needs for creating and managing resources in a cloud-based context will have to solve the same problems. Inevitably, that leads to similar degrees of complexity and similar sets of trade-offs: solving the same problems encounters the same challenges, and after that, the main differences stem from *how* those challenges were addressed. Armed with that knowledge, making the decision on how to implement becomes a matter of weighing all of the pros and cons of a given approach and picking the one that best meets the needs and requirements.

Making the IaC tooling decision

The HMS engineers, after reviewing all of these options, decided to move forward with SAM. While the potential learning curve for resources that are not part of the SAM resource set is somewhat complex, their review of the documentation available for SAM and CloudFormation resource definitions led them to feel that it was manageable, given the limited set of services and resources that are needed. Initially, all of the expected resources needed for the API to be operational are in the SAM set, except for the database. There will be additional resources that are needed, many of which will be automatically created, but may need to be explicitly defined later on to address any gaps that the default resources do not account for. The first stack that will be built out will be the one that defines and manages the database.

Defining and deploying the database resources

The changes for this section have been tagged in the chapter repository with `Ch-18-initial-serverless-database-setup`.

Note: the creation of the database, even in the serverless structure defined here, will start costing roughly 30¢ per day, before any databases or tables are even created. That cost is *just to have the relevant infrastructure active*.

The database definition is the first stack to be dealt with for several reasons. The main one is that the database is an **absolute dependency** for the entire API: Without the database, the API cannot perform the data creation and manipulation that it was designed to accomplish. The required resources for the database itself, along with some prerequisite resources that those resources require, are:

- A database cluster, a CloudFormation resource definition, documented at `https://docs.aws.amazon.com/AWSCloudFormation/latest/TemplateReference/aws-resource-rds-dbcluster.html`

- A database instance, also a CloudFormation definition, documented at `https://docs.aws.amazon.com/AWSCloudFormation/latest/TemplateReference/aws-resource-rds-dbinstance.html`

- A Secrets Manager Secret that contains the master username and password to apply to the database cluster when it's created

- Network access controls, generally set up as part of a **Virtual Private Cloud** (**VPC**)

Before the database resources can be created, the secret and VPC prerequisites need to exist, so examining those and deciding how to create and manage them is worth looking at first.

The prerequisites

The database cluster must have a master user defined that is allowed complete control over the database instances. This user is equivalent to the local master user that was set up for local development databases in *Chapter 13*, and serves the same purposes: to allow the administration (creation and management) of databases, tables, and other entities within those databases, non-administrative user accounts, and the permissions that those accounts need to be able to interact with the database as needed. The credentials for the master user need to be defined as an **AWS Secrets Manager Secret** resource: While using a **Systems Manager Parameter Store** (**SSM:PS**) resource would be less expensive, the CloudFormation requirements for specifying where those credentials are stored do not support anything other than a *Secret*.

> **Naming conventions for Secrets and SSM:PS items**
>
> In organizations where multiple teams need to unambiguously identify Secrets and SSM:PS items, it is common for a naming convention to be defined. A common variation would look something like this:
>
> `/{environment}/{team}/{service}/{resource}/{name}`
>
> Here, environment is a standard environment name abbreviation (dev, test, stage, prod); team is a team name or identifier, service is a service name or identifier, resource is an identifier for a resource in the context of the service, and name is the name of the resource. It is not uncommon for SSM:PS resources to extend that string with additional segments indicating things like environment variable names. SSM:PS calls can retrieve multiple items based on a common path, allowing application code to retrieve collections of values with a single SSM:PS call.

Since the *Secret* being stored **is** a secret, or more properly a collection of secret values, those values should not be stored in source control. Although the odds are good that any given source control system will not be compromised, those odds are still a non-zero value, and if the SCM is compromised, the potential for leaking credentials that protect application data or cloud infrastructure is also non-zero.

Taking all of that into consideration, the safest way to create and manage secrets is to do so *manually*. There is then **zero possibility** that those secret values will *ever* appear in SCM, and if future efforts are made to alter those secrets with resources defined in a stack, those efforts will fail, since the resource already exists.

Figure 18.1 shows the two relevant steps for manually creating a database-ready master user secret, with both username and password values defined. It also shows the end results of the process, both in the main Secrets Manager list view and the identifiers and metadata for the secret after it has been created successfully. The process is not difficult, nor does it take more than a few minutes, even under the worst of circumstances. It would also be feasible to create the Secret in a separate stack, perhaps one that sets up various resources for use across an entire environment. If that stack is used infrequently, and no actual secret values are ever supplied, the initial Cloud-Formation run would create it, it could be manually populated, and subsequent runs that do not make changes to the Secret's value would be stable as well. The main consideration behind all of these is that the secret must *exist* and have username and password values before the database stack is run, or that stack will fail.

Database username and password secrets have constraints

Database master user names for RDS databases must start with a letter, may be followed by letters, numbers, or underscore characters (_), and be no more than 127 characters in length. The regular expression pattern that they must conform to is ^[a-zA-Z][a-zA-Z0-9_]{0,127}$. Master passwords can contain any printable characters, be a minimum of eight characters long, and no more than 41 characters. Those constraints vary from one database engine to another: PostgreSQL and Oracle databases have different password length constraints.

Choose secret type

Secret type info

○ Credentials for Amazon RDS database   ○ Credentials for Amazon DocumentDB database   ○ Credentials for Amazon Redshift data warehouse

○ Credentials for other database   ● Other type of secret
                                      API key, OAuth token, other.

Key/value pairs info

Key/value   Plaintext

| username | dev.hms_ai_mysql_dba | Remove |
| password | dev.hms_ai_mysql_dba.password | Remove |

(+ Add row)

Configure secret

Secret name and description info

Secret name
A descriptive name that helps you find your secret later.

/dev/hms-backend/hms-api/database/master-secret

Secret name must contain only alphanumeric characters and the characters /_+=.@-

Description - optional

The username and password of the master user for the dev environment's MySQL database.

Maximum 250 characters.

≡ AWS Secrets Manager > Secrets   ⓘ   ⊙

Secrets   (C)   Store a new secret

🔍 Filter secrets by name, description, tag key, tag value, owning service or primary Region   ‹ 1 ›   ⚙

Secret name	Description
/dev/hms-backend/hms-api/database/master-secret	The username and password of the master user for the dev environment's MySQL database

≡ AWS Secrets Manager > Secrets > /dev/hms-backend/hms-api/database/master-secret   ⓘ   ⊙

/dev/hms-backend/hms-api/database/master-secret

Secret details   (C) (Actions ▼)

Encryption key   Secret description
🗗 aws/secretsmanager   🗗 The username and password of the master user for the dev environment's MySQL database

Secret name
🗗 /dev/hms-backend/hms-api/database/master-secret

Secret ARN
🗗 arn:aws:secretsmanager:us-east-2:485658242588:secret:/dev/hms-backend/hms-api/database/master-
secret-VRav6C

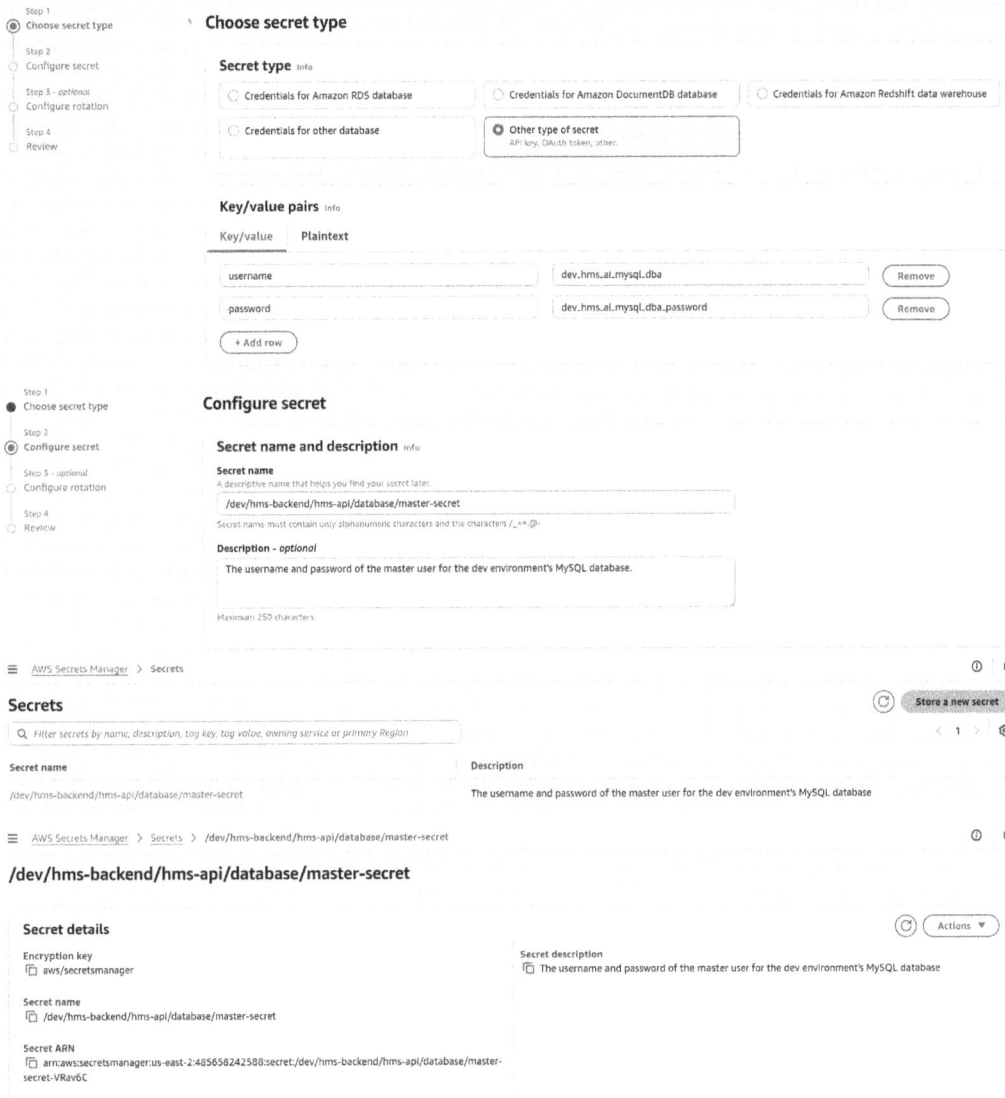

Figure 18.1: The steps involved in creating the database master user secret, and what the
final secret looks like in the AWS console

(This image is for visualization purpose only. Check the graphic bundle for a high resolution
version.)

AWS accounts, when they are first created, have a VPC created by default as long as the account was created in or after 2014. Those default VPCs have enough networking set up that they should be able to allow connection to the database across the internal AWS network, though it may be necessary to create custom Security Groups specifically to allow access to the database instance from the API resources.

The creation of the database behind the API can be broken out into four distinct operations:

- Creating the AWS resources to house the database
- Creating the database itself, where elements like users and tables will reside, within those resources
- Creating those elements
- Populating them, if needed

Each of these maps to a similar activity that was described in the chapter that discussed the set-up and population of the local development database. In some cases, where code was written to perform a given activity, that code is expected to be usable to perform the same activity, though some additional configuration or minor changes to that code may be necessary.

Differences because of cloud context

While the processes involved in establishing the cloud-resident database are essentially identical at a functional level, the mechanisms for *executing* them will differ. Ideally, they would be kicked off as part of an automated process that detects changes to code in a project's repository, but the book's repository, while hosted under a service that broadly supports that automation, is not configured for those processes. With that constraint in mind, the discussion here will focus on what processes need to be launched and when, showing those processes and outlining how they would be attached to a project's repository.

All of the CloudFormation/SAM templates used in this chapter can be found in the chapter repository, in the `Ch18-code/aws/infrastructure` directory therein.

The creation of the database resources

Provisioning the database resources — creating the infrastructure resources for the database, including its serverless cluster, the database engine, the networking required, and the minimum configuration needed for it to be accessible to other cloud resources — can be managed using AWS' CloudFormation/SAM IaC tools.

Since the creation of the database itself is only expected to be needed once per account or environment, the template written for it is separate from the templating for the API and its related resources.

The database template also contains a simple Lambda Function, intended to be used to verify connectivity to the database from within the VPC it is deployed into. Since the deployed database is intended to be used by resources defined in other templates, efforts have been made to make various properties of the deployed database accessible to other CloudFormation/SAM efforts, using exported Outputs values for values like the host name and port of the database, and various networking-related values that Lambda functions in the API implementation will need. Each collection of resources created and managed by a given template is commonly referred to as a **stack**, though the AWS console's verbiage refers to them as an **application**.

CloudFormation template structure is documented online at `https://docs.aws.amazon.com/AWSCloudFormation/latest/UserGuide/template-anatomy.html`, but here is a quick summary of the elements used in this template:

- **Description (optional)**: A human-friendly description of the stack
- **Parameters (optional, but commonly used)**: Key/value pairs that provide values for use in a stack's resources and their configuration, commonly used in those definitions with `Ref` and/or `Fn::Sub` (`!Sub`) intrinsic functions
- **Resources**: The logical names and definitions of the resources that the template deploys and manages
- **Outputs**: A collection of key/value pairs that identify and export those data points for use in other stacks in the account

> **CloudFormation's intrinsic functions**
>
> CloudFormation (and SAM) templating also supports several **intrinsic functions** (documented at `https://docs.aws.amazon.com/AWSCloudFormation/latest/TemplateReference/intrinsic-function-reference.html`) for various purposes. `Ref` and `Fn::Sub` (`!Sub`) are the most commonly used, typically providing access to names or identifiers of resources in the template. This template also makes use of `Fn::GetAtt` (`!GetAtt`) to retrieve specific attributes of specific resources.

The definition and creation of the database infrastructure is the primary goal of this first template.

Creating the database

The changes for this section are tagged as `Ch-18-initial-serverless-db-setup` in the chapter repository.

CloudFormation's templating supports a lot of AWS services and their related resources. As of late in 2025, the *AWS resource and property types reference* documentation at `https://docs.aws.amazon.com/AWSCloudFormation/latest/TemplateReference/aws-template-resource-type-ref.html` listed over 250 service-level entries, and a random sampling of the resources available under those would justify an estimate of five to eight resource types per service. That estimate would come to perhaps two thousand distinct resource types available. SAM, as a wrapper for specific serverless resource types, does not add to that estimate, but still adds several more distinct resource definitions to the overall mix, even if they are just serverless syntax variants of normal CloudFormation structures.

Finding resource types' documentation online

The links for CloudFormation and SAM resource documentation pages are typically very long, and there are a lot of them in use in this first template, so in the interests of keeping the text cleaner and easier to read, they will be referred to by their `Type` designations. For example, the database instance is a `Type` of `AWS::RDS::DBInstance`. Searching for these types, whether in the main CloudFormation resource and property reference (`https://docs.aws.amazon.com/AWSCloudFormation/latest/TemplateReference/aws-template-resource-type-ref.html`) or with your preferred search engine, should get you to the relevant pages quickly.

The database set up starts with the definition of a database cluster (`AWS::RDS::DBCluster`) resource, where the database instance will eventually live. Among its `Properties` values are the following:

- An `Engine` specification, set to `aurora-mysql`, that indicates that the cluster will be *serverless* and use a *MySQL-compatible* database engine.
- An `EngineVersion` that allows the specific MySQL version compatibility to be specified. This specification is provided by the `DatabaseEngineVersion` property defined in the template.

- An EngineMode that specifies that the database uses provisioned (serverless) processes.

- MasterUsername and MasterUserPassword properties that resolve the username and password from the Secrets Manager secret shown earlier. These are the *database administrator credentials* for databases in the cluster, **not** the credentials for general use of the databases within the cluster.

- A collection of security groups in the VPC (VpcSecurityGroupIds) that provide baseline networking permissions for the cluster.

The database cluster definition also requires a database subnet group to be defined and attached to the cluster's DBSubnetGroupName property. That subnet group is a separate resource (AWS::RDS::DBSubnetGroup) that requires at least two subnet identifiers (SubnetIds) to be provided, primary and backup/secondary network connections that access to the database can use. Those subnet identifiers are, in this case, provided by properties for the stack, SubnetID1 and SubnetID2, whose values were retrieved from the default VPC information for the account, and set up with those values as defaults.

With the cluster defined, the only resource remaining for the database to be complete is the actual database instance (AWS::RDS::DBInstance). It uses the following properties:

- A DBClusterIdentifier property that points to the cluster described above

- A DBInstanceClass, set to db.serverless, that specifies that the database instance is serverless

- Engine, EngineVersion, and DBSubnetGroupName specifications that duplicate their counterparts in the cluster definition

The collection of properties required for the database instance and all of its related resources is:

- DatabaseEngineVersion (defaults to 8.0.mysql_aurora.3.08.2).

- SubnetID1 and SubnetID2.

- There is also a VPCID parameter defined, though it is not used at this point. The intention here is twofold: First, right now, to record the VPC that the stack should deploy to, so that its identifier is available in the stack for later look-up. Second, for later, there will be Lambda function definitions that will need to know this value in order to connect to the database.

- Because the stack template is intended to allow deployment of resources across multiple environments and/or accounts, there are a few convenience properties set up to facilitate that:

  - Environment (defaulting to dev, and allowing dev, test, stage, and production values), defining an *environment name* that is used to define resource names and identifiers

  - Application (defaulting to hms-api-db), a service or application name, also used to define resource names and identifiers

Many of the resources that are created by the stack at this point have properties that will be of use later, when the definition of the Lambda functions that provide the functionality for API endpoints is created. To make those available to other stacks in the same account, this template leverages CloudFormation's Output functionality, exporting those values to names that can be accessed by other CloudFormation stacks later on. Those include:

- The **Amazon Resource Name (ARN)** for the DB cluster, exported as {Environment}-hms-api-db-cluster-arn.

- The connection endpoint for the DB cluster, a URL that may be used as the hostname for database connections, exported as {Environment}-hms-api-db-cluster-endpoint-address.

- The port number that will accept connections on the DB cluster, exported as {Environment}-hms-api-db-cluster-endpoint-port.

- The ARN for the DB instance, exported as {Environment}-hms-api-db-instance-arn. This is not expected to be needed, and could be removed from the exports later, but it is convenient to have for troubleshooting, even if it is not exported for use elsewhere.

- The connection endpoint for the DB instance, the URL that should generally be used to connect to the actual database, exported as {Environment}-hms-api-db-instance-endpoint-address.

- The port number that will accept connections on the DB instance, exported as {Environment}-hms-api-db-instance-endpoint-port.

- The name of the Secrets Manager secret that tracks the master user username and password values for the database cluster, exported as {Environment}-hms-api-db-master-user-secret.

- The subnets that the database can be accessed through, exported as {Environment}-hms-api-db-subnet1 and {Environment}-hms-api-db-subnet2.

At this point, the current CloudFormation template can be successfully deployed through the AWS console. As a long-term solution, that may be acceptable, since the creation of the database, as noted earlier, is likely to be a one-time effort. The current structure does not have any Python code resources, though, so there's no way to verify that the database can be reached. The idea of setting up a Lambda function that could eventually be used as a health-check process, verifying that the database is accessible and responsive, is not a bad idea, so that will be the next step.

A rudimentary Lambda function

The stack thus far does not include any resources that require Python code; at this point, it is entirely resource definitions for serverless equivalents to a database installation. The introduction of code, in this case a Lambda function, requires some additional setup and processing. It is technically possible to define all of the code for a single Lambda function's module inline in both CloudFormation and SAM templates, but there are inherent limitations to that: The most significant is that the Lambda function being created can only have the code specified in the template, which means that code that requires additional packages is going to be problematic at best, and likely not possible at all. As a corollary to that, the entire body of source code needed for a given Lambda function would have to be maintained in the body of the template. This is impractical at best, since the original code would have to be copied, then indented in the template text, with significant potential for errors to be introduced.

Lambda functions written in Python can be packaged into ZIP archives and uploaded to the function during and after its creation. To illustrate what that process would look like, the next iteration of the database stack will implement these changes in the initial template:

- Change the template from CloudFormation to SAM, in order to keep the definition for Lambda functions simpler.

- Add an AWS::EC2::SecurityGroup resource (LambdaSecurityGroup) for Lambda functions to use that provides network access to the database cluster/instance, tied to the existing SecurityGroup already in place.

- Add an AWS::EC2::SecurityGroup resource (SecretsEndpointSecurityGroup) that allows the newly-created LambdaSecurityGroup to interact with the AWS Secrets Manager service in the context of the VPC the stack lives in.

- Add an AWS::EC2::VPCEndpoint resource (SecretsManagerVPCEndpoint) that allows the subnets used by the stack to use Secrets Manager calls.

- Add an AWS::EC2::SecurityGroupIngress resource (DBAccessFromLambda) that allows the LambdaSecurityGroup to send requests to and receive responses from the database.

- Add a placeholder AWS::Serverless::Function resource (DBClusterTestFunction, note that this is defined using SAM syntax instead of CloudFormation) with the following properties:

  - Runtime: python3.11
  - Handler: db_cluster_test.lambda_handler
  - InlineCode with the code shown below
  - VpcConfig, SecurityGroupIds, and SubnetIds that point to the newly-created LambdaSecurityGroup, and use the existing SubnetID1 and SubnetID2 values already in the template.
  - Environment.Variables key/value pairs that will provide DB_SECRET_NAME (the database secret created earlier), and DB_ENDPOINT and DB_PORT variable values derived from the database cluster already in the stack.
  - An inline permissions policy that allows the Lambda to get the value of the database secret: the master username and password values created earlier.

The InlineCode in the placeholder function is *very* simple, looking like this:

```python
def lambda_handler(event, context):
    return {"status": "ok", "message": "hello world"}
```

When run from the AWS console, this stack still deploys as expected, and the new Lambda function exists, but since it only contains the code specified in the InlineCode, it is not actually *useful* at this point. The next step is coming up with a way to package the code for each Lambda function in the project, make it available to CloudFormation when the stack is deployed, and integrate those packages so that they are actually written to the Lambdas when the stack is deployed. AWS provides at least one command-line tool that handles all of the requirements needed for the processing of any given Lambda function: the sam **command-line interface** (**CLI**). When sam build is executed, it performs the following activities:

- The SAM template is read, and any Lambda functions (AWS::Serverless::Function resources) are identified.
- The CodeUri property of each is checked, and if it exists and evaluates to a directory on the local filesystem:
  - All of the files in that directory are added to a temporary local directory.
  - The requirements.txt file in that directory is used to install the package dependencies to the same local directory.

- The temporary directory is compressed into a `.zip` file with a filename that is unique to the current version of the collected code therein (an MD5 hash, by all appearances).

- The package file is uploaded to an S3 bucket, whether automatically named or user-specified.

- The S3 locations for the function packages are used to replace the `CodeUri` value in a copy of the SAM template, so that execution of `sam deploy` can simply read those package files during the deploy process.

The process for setting up and configuring an AWS account for SAM CLI access is outlined in AWS's online documentation (`https://docs.aws.amazon.com/serverless-application-model/latest/developerguide/prerequisites.html`), but that documentation may not include all of the permissions and role settings needed to successfully build and deploy a SAM-based application. Additionally, SAM, while it is a good, solid tool for deploying code to an AWS account, is, as noted earlier, hardly the *only* one. Any deployment tool will have to solve the same problems — packaging the code and making it available for deployment, whether that happens through a CloudFormation invocation or some other process that is built into the chosen deployment tool. With that in mind, we will walk through implementing all of the pieces of the code-packaging process in a portable enough manner that it could be used in any build context, including building locally, building as part of some source control automation (GitHub/GitLab Actions, Bitbucket Pipelines, etc.), or as part of an AWS CodeBuild resource.

Implementing a code-packaging process

> The changes for this section are tagged as `Ch-18-lambda-function-packaging` in the chapter repository.

The packaging process being implemented to build Lambda function packages that can be used as part of the SAM templates discussed in this chapter performs most of the same functions described earlier by the `sam` CLI. There are some variations here and there, but the net result and goal are essentially identical: To have all the code for each Lambda function in the project packaged into a ZIP archive, with all of their package dependencies, ready to be used in a SAM/CloudFormation template, or some other deployment process. Since the process performs a fair bit of file creation and manipulation that would not be otherwise visible, it will generate status report items for its various activities for each target being packaged.

The initial target is a new Lambda function, with a Pipenv category and source (src) directory name of db_cluster_test. All this function does, initially, is to make a database connection using the DBA-level master credentials stored earlier in Secrets Manager to query for the names of all available databases, and return those in a structure consistent with a Lambda Proxy Integration for an API Gateway. The final output desired is a packaged copy of the code, at a predictable location in an S3 bucket that can be used as a CodeUri value for the Lambda function definition in the database's SAM template. Although the initial target function does not make use of any of the code in the project's common directory, the packaging process will eventually need to support use of that common code: The Lambda functions that provide endpoint functionality for the final API will need the hms code tree and all of its dependencies to be included in their respective packages.

The code itself is, for the most part, quite straightforward, though it uses the built-in argparse package (https://docs.python.org/3.11/library/argparse.html), which has not been discussed previously, to support its command-line arguments and inline help. It is also incorporated into the project's tools using Pipenv's [scripts] support, and adds a [developer-tools] category to the Pipfile with a package needed by the process:

```
[developer-tools]
toml = "<1"
[scripts]
"packaging" = "python developer-tools/package-lambdas.py"
```

Taken together, these allow an engineer working with the project to build Lambda packages locally with variations of the command:

```
pipenv run packaging lambda
```

The use of argparse constructs also provides command-line help:

```
$ pipenv run packaging lambdas --help
usage: packaging lambdas [-h]
                              [--targets [TARGETS …]]
                              [--s3-bucket S3_BUCKET]
                              [--include-common]
options:
  -h, --help            show this help message and exit
  --targets [TARGETS ...], -t [TARGETS ...]
                        The Lambda Function directories to
                        package. Directories MUST have a
```

```
                                matching category entry in the
                                project's Pipfile! If not
                                specified, ALL directory/category
                                items will be processed.
    --s3-bucket S3_BUCKET, -b S3_BUCKET
                                The name of the AWS S3 bucket to
                                upload packages to.
    --include-common, -i  Whether to include the code in the
                                "common" directory in the
                                package(s). If not set, that code
                                will NOT be included.
```

Internally, the script is not much more than a loop over the targets specified, calling a half dozen helper functions. If no targets are specified, the default behavior is to use all available directory/ category combinations as the target set, essentially packaging every Lambda directory's code. For each target, the process is the same, after printing some common process information:

1. Create a temporary package directory in the project's packaged directory where all of the temporary files will live for the target.

2. Copy the source code from the relevant target directory under the project's src directory to the package target directory using the _copy_source_code helper function, which returns the Pipenv categories that will be needed for package-dependency installations in the next step. If the packaging run needs to include common code elements, they are also copied at this time.

3. Install the package dependencies for the target into the package directory. This involves generating a requirements.txt file in the packaging directory using pipenv require-ments, then using a targeted pip install process to ensure that the dependencies are adjacent to the copied source, and is handled by the _generate_requirements_file and _install_target_requirements helper functions.

4. Package all the files and directories under the temporary package directory into a ZIP archive file in the project's packaged directory. The name for that ZIP file is the same as the base target name; that is, for the initial Lambda whose code resides in src/db_ cluster_test, the package file is named db_cluster_test.zip. This process is handled by the _package_code_into_zip helper function.

5. Remove the packaging directory — it is no longer needed.

6. Make a copy of the package ZIP archive that includes the current date and time as part of the filename.

7. If a destination S3 bucket was specified, upload both of the ZIP archive files to that bucket, handled by the `_upload_packages_to_s3` helper function.

> **Change to the pymsql package from mysql-connector-python**
>
> As this script was being built and its resulting package being tested, it was discovered that the `mysql-connector-python` package was not going to include the appropriate compiled runtime if the Lambdas were packaged outside an AWS Linux context. A quick search for an alternative yielded the `pymysql` package, a pure Python implementation that could act as a drop-in replacement, and that change was made across the entire code base later.

After a couple of successful local executions, twice for the `db_cluster_test` Lambda function and once for the `public_create_artisan` Lambda function, there are five package files in both the local packaged directory and the target S3 bucket, as shown in *Figure 18.2*.

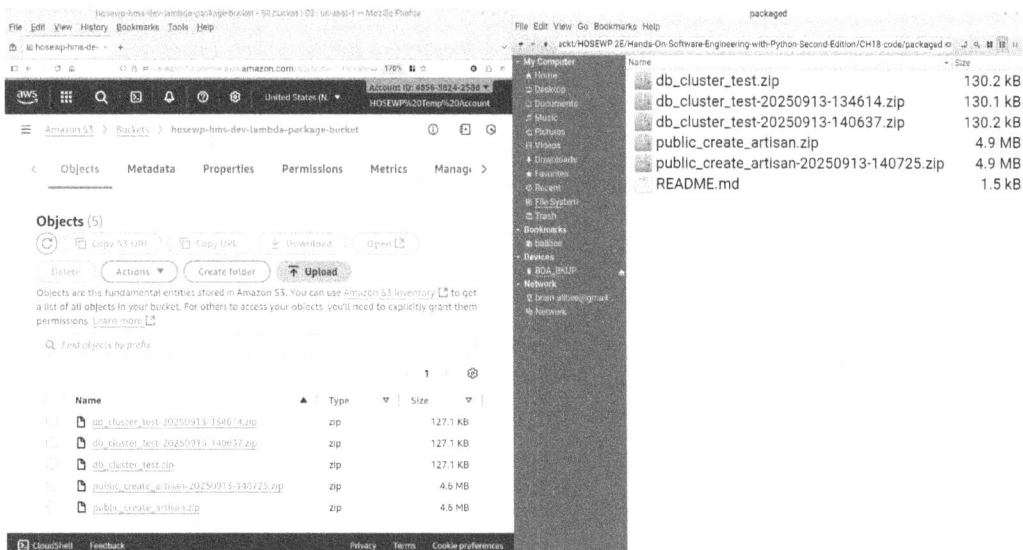

Figure 18.2: The bucket and local package files after successful executions of the packaging script

This approach is approximately equivalent to the `sam build` process mentioned earlier, but there is at least one important piece of functionality that provides that is not accounted for: altering the names of the package files, and their representations in the SAM template, as build processes generate new versions of those packages. This is an important consideration for deployment processes that rely on CloudFormation, because CloudFormation (and thus SAM) *may not be able to tell* that there is a difference between the most recently uploaded package file for a given Lambda and the package file that was last deployed. Without being able to make that package-version distinction, CloudFormation may simply *not update* an application Lambda function, leaving it in its previous version/state.

It would not be terribly difficult to write additional pre-processing code for a SAM or CloudFormation template that uses a master copy of the template, replacing some placeholder name for any given Lambda package with the most recent versioned package filename before sending that template on to the normal CloudFormation deployment process(es). If SAM is the preferred mechanism for handling deployments and defining infrastructure as code, though, that is a lower-effort solution: the code is already written, and not something that requires ongoing maintenance by an engineering team.

On the other hand, for deployment processes that do not rely on CloudFormation to detect changes in packages — Terraform falls into this category — this may be a *better* approach. Another advantage of this approach, if it is applicable to the requirements for a deployment process, is that the package files have *human-meaningful* names. This allows even fairly casual observers to be able to identify which package file is current, and which package file(s) are potential fallbacks if the current version is broken in some manner. The destination bucket would contain as complete a history of every Lambda function package version as desired, with readily identifiable snapshots of every packaged version of every Lambda to fall back on if needed.

With all of this in place, a simple modification to the current API database SAM template, removing the `InlineCode` that it started with and adding a `CodeUri` that points to the current `db_cluster.zip` file in the bucket, allows that stack to be deployed with the `hms-db-cluster-test-function` Lambda for that environment. It can be tested in the AWS console, and returns the expected results, for now — a `statusCode` indicating success, and a `databases` field with a string dump of the names of the databases available to the cluster (spacing altered for ease of reading):

```
{
    "statusCode": 200,
    "databases": "(('mysql',), ('information_schema',), "
        "('performance_schema',), ('sys',))"
}
```

That shows that the database exists and can be reached by the Lambdas that will be deployed later, provided that they share the networking configuration that was established for this Lambda. It also shows that the API database still needs to be created, as well as the database users that were discussed earlier.

Creating the database elements

> These changes are tagged as `Ch-18-example-ci-cd-and-related` in the chapter repository.

The definitions for tables and users were established in *Chapters 12* and *13*, and an initial script, at `database/HMS/implementation/apply-sql.py`, was created to handle the processes involved with implementing those definitions against a local database. The SQL statements and commands required to perform the same activities against the newly-created cloud-resident database instance are no different: the database engine is MySQL/MariaDB-compatible, and is expected to perform identically.

Under normal CI/CD process circumstances, with a build and/or deploy process that has access to the current source code of the project, those same SQL statements and commands would be available and could be executed in essentially the same manner. The main differences between the local and cloud context executions are in the processes for making a backup of the database prior to executing the collection of SQL; in how it acquires the information, including the master user credentials, needed to connect to the database instance in order to execute them; and how the processes involved are actually executed.

The backup process, in an AWS cloud context, can rely on the snapshot capabilities of the Relational Database Service (RDS). Rather than executing a `mysqldump` command, which is how the local backup process was implemented, the script that will run in the cloud uses the `create_db_snapshot` function provided by boto3 (`https://boto3.amazonaws.com/v1/documentation/api/latest/reference/services/rds/client/create_db_snapshot.html`) to initiate a database snapshot, and a waiter (`https://boto3.amazonaws.com/v1/documentation/api/latest/reference/services/rds/client/get_waiter.html`) to wait for that snapshot to complete before continuing. Once the snapshot is complete, the process of reading all of the SQL files and executing them is essentially the same, though some of the individual files were changed to allow the use of environment variables in their SQL statements, for reasons that will be explained shortly.

The actual process that *executes* the cloud-compatible database update process script (apply-sql-cloud.py, in the same directory as the original apply-sql.py script) is best implemented as an AWS CodeBuild (https://aws.amazon.com/codebuild/) resource. **CodeBuild** is a fully managed service that allows users to define ephemeral build servers, and the processes that the build server executes are defined in a separate YAML buildspec (https://docs.aws.amazon.com/codebuild/latest/userguide/build-spec-ref.html) file. A buildspec is simply a YAML-formatted series of commands that a CodeBuild instance will execute when it is triggered, typically by a **CodePipeline** build-orchestration resource (https://aws.amazon.com/codepipeline/). The relevant buildspec, included in the chapter repository at aws/buildspec-examples/database-population-buildspec.yaml, is quite straightforward, but it is worth adding some comments and showing it here:

```yaml
version: 0.2
phases:
  # The phase responsible for installing any build
  # requirements/prerequisites
  install:
    on-failure: ABORT
    runtime-versions:
      python: 3.11
    commands:
      # Install pipenv so that package dependencies
      # can be installed in a deterministic manner.
      # Be sure to use the same version that's in play
      # in the local dev-environments!
      - pip install pipenv==2023.12.1
      # Then install those dependencies, dev and common
      - pipenv sync -dev
      - pipenv sync --categories "common"
  # The phase responsible for executing actual "build"
  # activities - though this example just runs the script
  build:
    on-failure: ABORT
    commands:
      # Run the database-update script
      - >
        pipenv run python
        database/HMS/implementation/apply-sql-cloud.py
```

A *partial* resource definition for a CodeBuild resource is also provided in the updated `hms-api-database.yaml` SAM template. Though it is incomplete, it includes the setup needed to pass various environment variables to the database-update script, as well as a reference to the location of the buildspec file. This arrangement will work nicely in cases where the build process has access to a copy of the project source code, which would include the buildspec file. It would also require the creation of a service role that can be attached to the CodeBuild resource, allowing it access to the other varied AWS resources that it will need to execute successfully. The environment variables are highlighted in this stub of the resource definition:

```yaml
DBUpdaterProject:
  Type: AWS::CodeBuild::Project
  Properties:
    # ...
    Environment:
      EnvironmentVariables:
        - Name: MYSQL_MASTER_USER
          Value: >
            !Sub /${Environment}/hms-backend/
            ${Application}/database/master-secret:username
          Type: SECRETS_MANAGER
        - Name: MYSQL_MASTER_PASS
          Value: >
            !Sub /${Environment}/hms-backend/
            ${Application}/database/master-secret:password
          Type: SECRETS_MANAGER
        - Name: MYSQL_HOST
          Value: !Ref APIMySQLDatabase
        - Name: MYSQL_PORT
          Value: !GetAtt APIMySQLDatabase.Endpoint.Port
        - Name: MYSQL_DB
          Value: !Sub ${Environment}_api_database
        - Name: MYSQL_SERVICE_USER
          Value: >
            !Sub /${Environment}/hms-backend/
```

```
            ${Application}/database/service-user
        Type: PARAMETER_STORE
      - Name: MYSQL_SERVICE_PASS
        Value: >
          !Sub /${Environment}/hms-backend/
          ${Application}/database/service-pass
        Type: PARAMETER_STORE
  Source:
    Type: NO_SOURCE
    BuildSpec: >
      aws/buildspec-examples/
      database-population-buildspec.yaml
```

Doing all of this manually

Because of the constraints imposed by the book's repository, these automated processes were not fully implemented, with only examples of the important parts shown.
The actual execution of the SQL for the SQL files in the set-up and implementation
directories was executed manually against the database instance, after enabling its
RDS Data API, using the RDS Query Editor tools in the RDS console.

These steps and resources cover the processes for finishing the definition of the API database,
defining the tables and users that the Lambda functions providing the processing for the API's
endpoints will use. The next logical step is to define the API itself, along with all of its endpoints
and their backing Lambda functions, leveraging the outputs from the database stack to provide
common parameter values that are exported from that stack to streamline their definitions.

Defining and deploying the API resources

The changes made for this section have been tagged with Ch-18-api-deployment
in the chapter repository, and a Bruno collection similar to the one presented earlier
for local API testing has been provided in the bruno/aws-hms-api-collection
directory.

AWS's SAM, as noted earlier, provides a much simplified IaC structure for defining APIs and associating the backing Lambda function resources for each endpoint that the API provides. In the simplest approach, one that is *only* concerned with tying API requests to a backing Lambda, the actual API resource itself does not need to be specified — the IaC processes executed by the definitions for the Lambdas can handle construction of a single, common API Gateway resource automatically. Using the public read products endpoint as an example, the YAML that defines that endpoint function may be as simple as this:

```
Resources:
  ...

  PublicReadProductsEndpoint:
    Type: AWS::Serverless::Function
    Properties:
      CodeUri: # A path to the code to be used
      Handler: public_read_products.api_handler
      Description: The public API's products-list endpoint.
      Events:
        APIGetEvent:
          Type: Api
          Properties:
            Method: get
            Path: /api/v1/products
```

The various properties control specific aspects of the build and deployment processes, and how the results of the built and deployed code integrate with the automatically-created API Gateway REST API resource. Using the code-packaging process described earlier, and setting the CodeUri property to point to the public_read_products.zip file in the package bucket, this structure deploys a single endpoint that provides the public read products functionality, as shown in *Figure 18.3*. That includes an automatically-generated Lambda Proxy Integration that connects the endpoint to the relevant Lambda function.

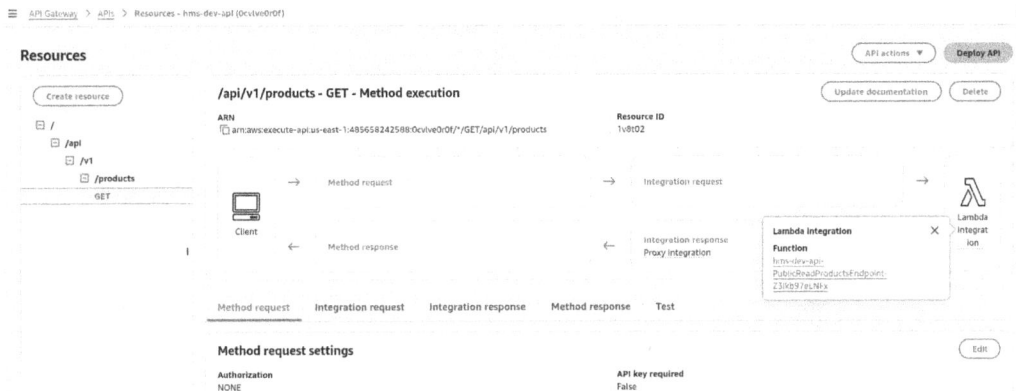

Figure 18.3: A successful minimal API deployment

Knowing that there is at least the potential for future endpoints to be linked to an S3 bucket (for product image uploads and retrieval), it is a good idea to explicitly define the main API resource, though, and reference it in the individual Lambdas. That resource is simple enough, at least to start:

```
Resources:
...

  MainAPI:
    Type: AWS::Serverless::Api
    Properties:
      Name: !Sub ${Environment}-${Application}
      StageName: Prod
```

... and the reference to it is a single additional line in the existing Lambda:

```
    PublicReadProductsEndpoint:
      Type: AWS::Serverless::Function
      Properties:
        # ...
        Events:
          APIGetEvent:
            Type: Api
            Properties:
              Method: get
              Path: /api/v1/products
              RestApiId: !Ref MainAPI
```

Following the same basic pattern for all of the Lambda functions and redeploying the stack yields all of the endpoints that have actual implementations in their Lambda code (*Figure 18.4*).

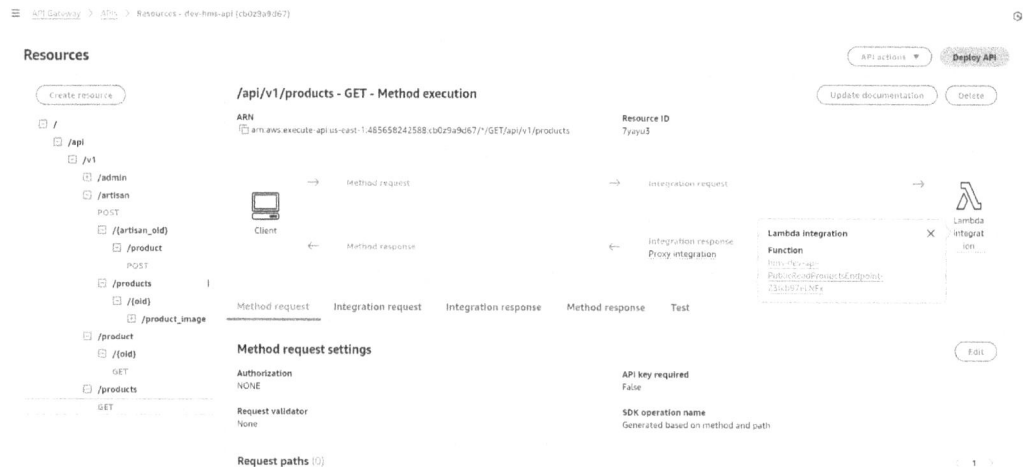

Figure 18.4: The fully deployed API

While these endpoints exist, they are not yet complete: They are not connected to the VPC that the database lives in, and do not have any of the various environment variables needed to connect to the database. Since all of the Lambdas in the API stack need that, it is easiest to define them all as a collection of Globals in the SAM template:

```
Globals:
  Function:
    Runtime: python3.11
    Timeout: 6
    VpcConfig:
      SecurityGroupIds:
        - !ImportValue dev-hms-api-db-lambda-access-sg
      SubnetIds:
        - !ImportValue dev-hms-api-db-subnet1
        - !ImportValue dev-hms-api-db-subnet2
    Environment:
      Variables:
        DB_SECRET_NAME: /.../database/master-secret
        MYSQL_HOST: !ImportValue dev-hms-api-db-cluster-endpoint-address
        MYSQL_PORT: !ImportValue dev-hms-api-db-cluster-endpoint-port
        MYSQL_DB: !ImportValue dev-hms-api-db-database-name
```

The various `!ImportValue` items here retrieve values from the *exports* from the database stack, allowing that stack to define those values in a single, common way and make them available to other stacks in the same AWS account. If a future update to that stack tries to change or remove any of those exported values that are in use, *that update will fail*, protecting the integrity of those values across however many stacks are relevant. That *also* prevents the database stack from being deleted, and breaking any other stacks that rely on it through those exports.

Handling database credentials

Two of the required parameters to establish a connection to the API database from inside a Lambda function have not been accounted for yet: `username` and `password`. There are two basic variations for handling values like these, which are considered *secrets*. The first is to simply include them in the environment variables in some fashion. An example of this approach might look something like this in the SAM template:

```
Globals:
  Function:
    ...
    Environment:
      Variables:
        ...
        MYSQL_USER: "hms_api_db_service_user"
        MYSQL_PASS: "hms-api-db-service-password:Fl0bn4R!"
```

This approach is functional (and was used in the example service code for convenience), but it is **not** a recommended approach. The argument against this approach basically boils down to the risk of secrets being exposed to bad actors, whether because the Lambda function console access gets compromised, or some other exposure vectors are in play. It also tends to leave credentials sitting in source code repositories, which is another potential vector for their exposure.

A much more secure approach is to use the Secrets Manager service, creating a resource that the Lambdas read during their execution. Secrets Manager is, presumably, the most secure option that AWS offers: secrets are encrypted, and processes can be set up to rotate secrets' values, using either *managed* or *Lambda-based* approaches (see `https://docs.aws.amazon.com/secretsmanager/latest/userguide/rotating-secrets.html` for details). The trade-off here is that Secrets Manager is *relatively* expensive: Each secret stored costs 40¢ per month just to store them, and 5¢ for every 10,000 API calls to retrieve any secret. If the HMS API saw a million calls to the Secrets Manager API per month, that's only $5 in traffic costs, so that is, perhaps, not a concern.

Another option is to use an AWS **Systems Manager Parameter Store (SSM:PS)**. Standard type SSM:PS items cost nothing to store or to use, but still provide the ability to encrypt values, and can be leveraged in several ways to make retrieval of those values, encrypted or not, within a Lambda function. Both Secrets Manager and SSM:PS would use much the same structure in a SAM template, defining an environment variable that stores the path name of the secret/parameter in the service, looking something like this:

```
Globals:
  Function:
    ...
    Environment:
      Variables:
        SERVICE_PARAMS_PATH: /path/to/resource/name[s]/
```

Retrieving and using the values stored would have to be implemented in the code. An example, using a collection of SSM:PS values with a common path prefix (/dev/hms-backend/hms-api-db/database/), is provided in the common/hms/environment.py module in the chapter repository, and will retrieve any specified names under that path prefix from SSM:PS.

Both of these options, given the VPC environment that the database and all of the Lambda functions live in, require the creation of a service endpoint that will allow resources inside the VPC to access the relevant service. One such, the SecretsManagerVPCEndpoint resource, was created in the database stack and could be adapted or used as a starting point for a VPC endpoint that allows access to SSM:PS resources.

> **The example in this book uses the convenient option**
>
> Because this book is more concerned with the Python implementation and code behind the API than the details of securing an AWS account (or its resources), the least secure option was used for convenience. Do **not** take this as a recommendation!

Deploying and testing the entire API

At this point, with the credentials accounted for, deploying and testing the final API in an AWS account is possible. It is functionally complete, apart from the processes around uploading and retrieving product images (more on that in a bit). Starting with a brand new AWS account, logged in with the account's root credentials (also not recommended, but chosen, again, for convenience):

1. Retrieve the CH18-code directory from the book's repository.

2. Navigate to the S3 console (AWS provides a **Search** field at the upper left of their console pages), and create a bucket to hold the packaged code.

3. From the project root, in a terminal/shell, run

```
pipenv run packaging lambdas --include-common \
--s3-bucket {bucket name}
```

and wait for the process to complete.

4. While that is running, navigate to the Secrets Manager console and create the master database secret. Keeping track of those for later use will be helpful.

5. Navigate to the CloudFormation console.

6. Deploy the database stack first:

   1. In the upper-right corner of the console page, click on **Create stack**, then **With new resources (standard)**.

   2. Under **Specify template**, select the **Upload a template** option, then **Choose file** and upload the aws/infrastructure/hms-api-database.yaml template file.

   3. Click **Next**, and set any parameters needed.

   4. Click **Next**, and accept the items under the **Transforms might require access capabilities** block at the bottom of the page.

   5. Click **Next**.

   6. Click **Submit**.

   7. Wait for the stack deployment to complete. This will take as long as ten minutes; provisioning the database takes a while.

   8. Navigate to the Aurora and RDS console, select the newly created database cluster, and enable the RDS Data API (bottom of the page).

   9. Click **Query editor**, connect to the database with the master credentials, and run the database/HMS/set-up SQL files, in the order from 001... to 003..., to set up the actual database, copying their code and pasting it into the editor text field. Note that you will need to change the placeholder values in those files (MYSQL_DB, MYSQL_SERVICE_USER, and MYSQL_SERVICE_PASS) in the query editor, and those should also be tracked for later use.

   10. Execute the SQL files in the database/HMS/implementation directory, also in order.

7. Deploy the API stack:

    1. Create a stack with new resources (standard), as before.

    2. Specify the template, upload a template, as before, but select the `aws/infrastructure/hms-api-resources.yaml` template file.

    3. Continue with the needed **Next, Transforms might require access capabilities**, and **Submit** items as they are presented.

Once the API stack has completed, a new API Gateway resource will be available in the API Gateway console pages. Clicking on the name of the newly deployed API will show a detail view, looking much like the fully deployed API shown in *Figure 18.4*. Near the top of that page, there will be a bread-crumbs list that ends with **Resources - your-api-name (10-char-api-id)**. That 10-character ID can be copied and pasted into the `hms-api-collection-aws` collection's settings (see *Figure 18.5*), and the collection's endpoints can be tested against your newly created API.

Figure 18.5: Bruno collection settings with an example api_id value

Be sure to delete the stacks when you're done with them!

These stacks do not cost a lot to keep active on a daily basis, but the charges related to them will accumulate over time, even if the database is not actively being used. If you want to keep the database available for a while, but not active, there is an option under **Actions** for a selected database (top right of the console page) called **Stop temporarily** that will disable the database for up to a week.

Remember, also, that the API stack has dependencies on the database stack, so it must be deleted first.

This state is, barring the image-related endpoints noted earlier, all that is really needed for the API implementation to be *functionally* complete. Although it *is* functionally complete at this point, in that it has all of the endpoint implementations available and usable, there are a number of other considerations that should be given some thought before it could be considered production-ready. The details behind those are well outside the scope of this book, but should be noted and given thought because they are *important*.

Making the system production-ready

Many of the remaining items to be considered before this API could be considered production-ready depend heavily on how and where it integrates with the main website that it was designed to provide data for. The story of this API's development has included mention of a front-end team, which implies similar design and implementation processes, with more website/UI focus, to the efforts that the API development has gone through. There are several implementation variations available for integrating that front-end work with this API, and each of those has some potential impact on various factors.

If the front-end implementation is also based on an API Gateway instance — it can serve nicely as a proxy, allowing a single API instance to map *other* API instances, or other services that follow standard HTTP methods and mechanisms — then it should be possible to consolidate all of those services' implementations under a single root URL. If that is not possible, or not desired, the API discussed here would also need to implement **Cross-Origin Resource Sharing** (**CORS**) standards. CORS is a mechanism that allows a web service to define what *other* websites are allowed to make requests for data that would normally be disallowed as violations of the **Same-Origin Policy** (**SOP**). SOP is a standard that only allows an HTTP client to make requests from within the same domain. For example, if the main HMS website were at `www.hand-made-stuff.com`, and this API was hosted at `api.hand-made-stuff.com`, pages served by the main website would not be allowed to interact with the API web service unless that service explicitly allowed it. If, on the other hand, the website implementation behind the `www.hand-made-stuff.com` site somehow mapped one or more of the `/api/` paths to the root of the API that was developed over the course of this book, CORS would *not* be needed: requests from a page at `www.hand-made-stuff.com/some-path` to `www.hand-made-stuff.com/api/some-path` are in the same top-level domain (`www.hand-made-stuff.com`), and would be allowed.

CORS and API Gateway

AWS's documentation for CORS as it relates to API Gateway services is available at
`https://docs.aws.amazon.com/apigateway/latest/developerguide/how-to-cors.html`

The ability of API Gateway to map endpoints to other AWS resources, or even to external URLs, leads to an architecture/ownership question for the product image uploads. Ideally, since those are just static image files, they should reside in some sort of static data store. An S3 bucket is ideal for this sort of use case: once an image file is stored there, it will change rarely, if ever, and simply mapping an endpoint to the appropriate bucket location would allow the uploaded images to simply be returned on demand, with no Lambda function or other compute involved. A product image upload is something that the front-end team will need to be heavily involved in if they don't own the process and its related resources outright. The retrieval of an uploaded and processed product image is also firmly in their bailiwick — there's no real back-end functionality needed for that, just retrieval of the image from wherever it lives, and transmission of that data. The back-end API, when it comes right down to it, is really only concerned with retrieving and working with what might be considered metadata *about* those images, and could probably be redefined as *administrative* metadata, if it came right down to it. All of those, put together, throw the idea of the back-end team owning the images themselves, or the processes to upload or download them, into doubt.

All that said, there are some interesting and potentially useful additional considerations around the image upload/download processes:

- API Gateway invocations have a maximum time limit of 30 seconds. While that should be sufficient for any reasonable single-image upload, the potential for images that are too large or being uploaded over too slow a connection is real. Amazon S3 services include the ability to generate presigned URLs (see `https://docs.aws.amazon.com/AmazonS3/latest/userguide/PresignedUrlUploadObject.html` and `https://docs.aws.amazon.com/AmazonS3/latest/userguide/using-presigned-url.html`) that can be used to upload directly to an S3 bucket.

- If a presigned URL was used to upload the actual image(s) as one part of a front-end form, and the metadata (administrative or otherwise) was a separate POST or PATCH operation, that would allow the front-end and back-end teams to keep a very clean separation of responsibilities in play with respect to which team was responsible for which aspects of the process.

- Any image-processing or checking — cropping or resizing, virus scans, or whatever else might be desired — could be implemented as a separate Lambda function triggered by an S3 event like the creation or replacement of an image file. That process could also then call the back-end API if needed to update any administrative metadata, if that was even needed.

While API Gateway itself is not a specific integration type, an entire category of integrations using direct and configurable HTTP calls is available, which opens the door for other API Gateway instances, along with applications and services that could run in *any* compute type (containers, Elastic Beanstalk, etc.). The list of other AWS services that API Gateway *can* integrate directly with is surprisingly large: As of when this chapter was written, there were 104 supported integration types that appeared in the console. Those included not only services that might be expected for compute (EC2 and the various container-related services, Step Functions for workflows) or data (DynamoDB, RDS, AppSync) purposes, but also queues (SQS), notifications (SNS), CI/CD services like CodeStar and CodePipeline, Machine Learning services, and more. There are even direct integration options for AWS Cognito, an identity management service, which segues nicely into the next point for consideration: Authentication and Authorization.

Protecting access to an API is a critical concern if there are any endpoints whose data should not be publicly accessible. It is still a concern, if less of one, if the API in question is intended for public consumption. At a minimum, denying access from referrers other than any related websites should be considered, if only to prevent unwanted exploration of an API by potential bad actors. While simply checking the incoming referrer headers may not be one hundred percent reliable, it is a good starting point. For endpoints like the admin and artisan path endpoints in this API, a more robust system is called for. Options for that include, but are not limited to:

- Using a standard **JSON Web Token (JWT)**, possibly managed by a Cognito service instance and user pool, validating the token on every request, and using its claims data to check for access permissions.

- Using federated identification processes with third-party providers, typically with an OAuth2 provider like Microsoft, Google, or a third-party provider like Auth0. Like the JWT approach, the resulting identity token is validated, and some set of data points from the token can be used to identify who the request is being made by/for, and it can be allowed or declined based on that determination.

- Some sort of active session management. In this scenario, a user logs in somehow, and is issued a session token that is transmitted with every request they make to the site from that point on until the token is canceled (a log-out) or it expires. On the back end, that session token identifies a user, and that user's data is used to determine whether they are allowed access to the requested resource.

All of these processes can be wrapped in a Lambda authorizer — a Lambda function that is attached to an API, or to any or all of its endpoints, and executed by the API Gateway before the request is sent to the backing resource. AWS's online documentation for Lambda authorizers starts at `https://docs.aws.amazon.com/apigateway/latest/developerguide/apigateway-use-lambda-authorizer.html`.

AWS also offers a **Web Application Firewall** service (**WAF**, see `https://aws.amazon.com/waf/`), designed to protect web applications and services from common exploits. The addition of a WAF should be considered for any public-facing API or web application, if only because it eases the need for in-house expertise on current and newly discovered exploits.

Final notes

The final assembly of the system that this chapter describes feels... kind of anticlimactic to me, looking back on it. I think, however, that is how it should be. This final piece of the API puzzle, manual work notwithstanding for the example, is really not much more than assembling the pieces that were built in earlier chapters. With a full CI/CD process in place, there are additional pieces that would be nice and useful add-ons, providing checks and guardrails to decrease the probability of bugs making their way into a production system. The operations built out in the Bruno collections could easily be made into a scripted end-to-end test for the process of an artisan signing up, creating a product, and it being made available in a public-facing product list. The individual API endpoints' Lambda functions could also be explicitly integration tested against either a local development database or a cloud-resident equivalent, and those assembled into a suite of tests that could stop a buggy build/deployment from being promoted as well.

In the end, though, even without the resources needed to implement a fully automated build/ deploy pipeline, the scripted and manual processes are not unreasonable. They are not ideal, to be sure, but they would be workable for a while, until full automation of them could be set up. Looking back on the steps that got us to this point, the one thing I would change would be to work through a provable, deployable database change-management process earlier. That strikes me as the most significant risk point in the service architecture, since it currently has no auto- mation, making it more error-prone, and is the source of truth for the system's data, making it much more sensitive to errors.

Still, I hope that the illustrations and walk-throughs of the (approximately) equivalent processes shed enough light on what needs to happen that they'll lend themselves well to understanding how a more complete deployment process works, and what items need to be accounted for in that. I also hope that the breakdown of all of the moving parts prior to this point is logical to the reader, and helpful in showing the kinds of thought and design processes that I feel are essential to the discipline of software engineering.

Happy coding!

Brian Allbee

Get This Book's PDF Version and Exclusive Extras

UNLOCK NOW

Scan the QR code (or go to `packtpub.com/unlock`). Search for this book by name, confirm the edition, and then follow the steps on the page.

Note: Keep your invoice handy. Purchases made directly from Packt don't require an invoice.

19

Unlock Your Exclusive Benefits

Your copy of this book includes the following exclusive benefits:

- ⟲ Next-gen Packt Reader
- 📄 DRM-free PDF/ePub downloads

Follow the guide below to unlock them. The process takes only a few minutes and needs to be completed once.

Unlock this Book's Free Benefits in 3 Easy Steps

Step 1

Keep your purchase invoice ready for *Step 3*. If you have a physical copy, scan it using your phone and save it as a PDF, JPG, or PNG.

For more help on finding your invoice, visit https://www.packtpub.com/unlock-benefits/help.

> **Note:** If you bought this book directly from Packt, no invoice is required. After *Step 2*, you can access your exclusive content right away.

Step 2

Scan the QR code or go to `packtpub.com/unlock`.

On the page that opens (similar to *Figure 19.1* on desktop), search for this book by name and select the correct edition.

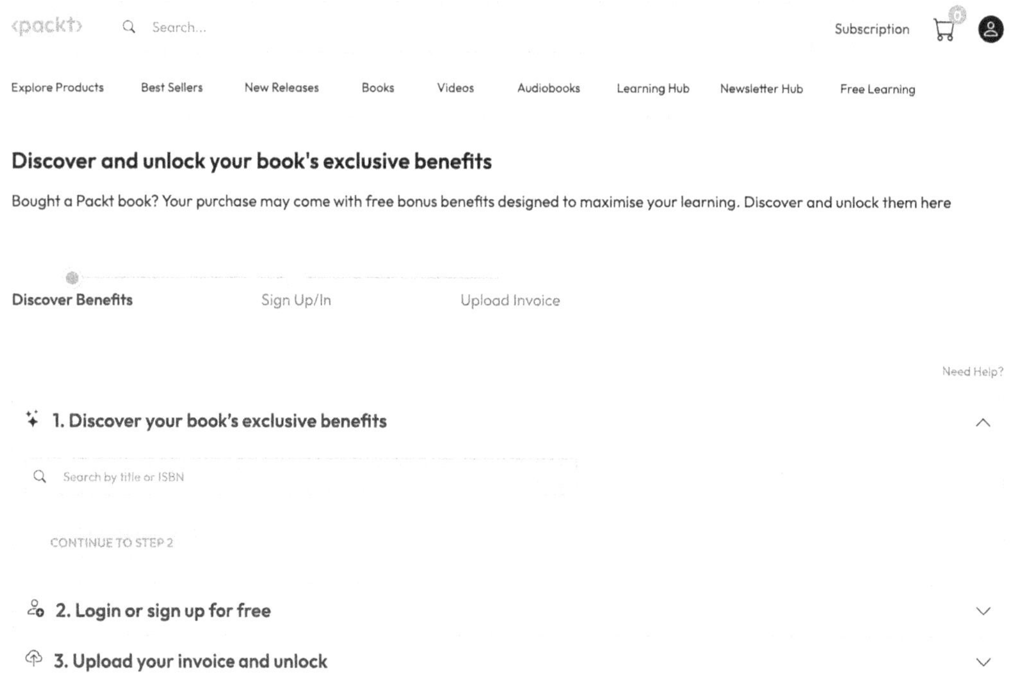

Figure 19.1: Packt unlock landing page on desktop

Step 3

After selecting your book, sign in to your Packt account or create one for free. Then upload your invoice (PDF, PNG, or JPG, up to 10 MB). Follow the on-screen instructions to finish the process.

Need help?

If you get stuck and need help, visit `https://www.packtpub.com/unlock-benefits/help` for a detailed FAQ on how to find your invoices and more. This QR code will take you to the help page.

Note: If you are still facing issues, reach out to `customercare@packt.com`.

‹packt›

packtpub.com

Subscribe to our online digital library for full access to over 7,000 books and videos, as well as industry leading tools to help you plan your personal development and advance your career. For more information, please visit our website.

Why subscribe?

- Spend less time learning and more time coding with practical eBooks and Videos from over 4,000 industry professionals
- Improve your learning with Skill Plans built especially for you
- Get a free eBook or video every month
- Fully searchable for easy access to vital information
- Copy and paste, print, and bookmark content

At www.packtpub.com, you can also read a collection of free technical articles, sign up for a range of free newsletters, and receive exclusive discounts and offers on Packt books and eBooks.

Other Books You May Enjoy

If you enjoyed this book, you may be interested in these other books by Packt:

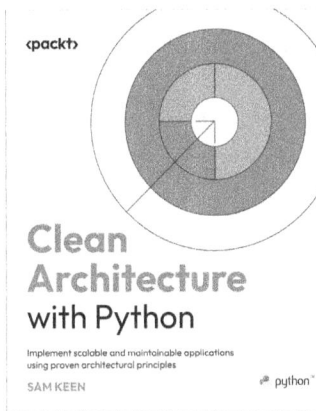

Clean Architecture with Python

Sam Keen

ISBN: 978-1-83664-289-3

- Apply Clean Architecture principles idiomatically in Python
- Implement domain-driven design to isolate core business logic
- Apply SOLID principles in a Pythonic context to improve code quality
- Structure projects for maintainability and ease of modification
- Develop testing techniques for cleanly architected Python applications
- Refactor legacy Python code to adhere to Clean Architecture principles
- Design scalable APIs and web applications using Clean Architecture

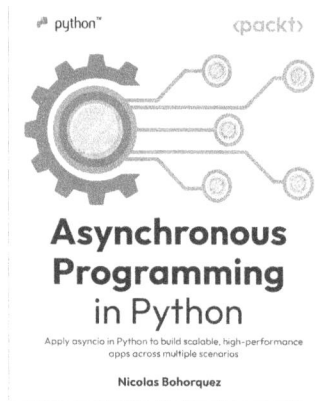

Asynchronous Programming in Python

Nicolas Bohorquez

ISBN: 978-1-83664-661-7

- Use generators, coroutines and async/await to build scalable Python functions
- Explore event loops to manage concurrency and orchestrate async flow
- Compare concurrency models to choose the right async strategy
- Optimize I/O-intensive programs to improve system throughput and efficiency
- Build async services using real-world APIs and popular Python libraries
- Apply structured concurrency and design patterns for cleaner async design
- Test and debug async Python code to ensure reliability and stability

Packt is searching for authors like you

If you're interested in becoming an author for Packt, please visit authors.packt.com and apply today. We have worked with thousands of developers and tech professionals, just like you, to help them share their insight with the global tech community. You can make a general application, apply for a specific hot topic that we are recruiting an author for, or submit your own idea.

Share your thoughts

Now you've finished *Hands-On Software Engineering with Python*, we'd love to hear your thoughts! Scan the QR code below to go straight to the Amazon review page for this book and share your feedback or leave a review on the site that you purchased it from.

https://packt.link/r-1835888011

Your review is important to us and the tech community and will help us make sure we're delivering excellent quality content.

Subscribe to Deep Engineering

Join thousands of developers and architects who want to understand how software is changing, deepen their expertise, and build systems that last.

Deep Engineering is a weekly expert-led newsletter for experienced practitioners, featuring original analysis, technical interviews, and curated insights on architecture, system design, and modern programming practice.

Scan the QR or visit the link to subscribe for free.

https://packt.link/deep-engineering-newsletter

Index

www.ingramcontent.com/pod-product-compliance
Lightning Source LLC
Chambersburg PA
CBHW081211220326
41598CB00037B/6750